Origami ^{6} I. Mathematics

Origami ^{6} I. Mathematics

Proceedings of the Sixth International
Meeting on Origami Science, Mathematics, and Education

Koryo Miura

Toshikazu Kawasaki

Tomohiro Tachi

Ryuhei Uehara

Robert J. Lang

Patsy Wang-Iverson

Editors

 AMERICAN MATHEMATICAL SOCIETY

2010 *Mathematics Subject Classification.* Primary 00-XX, 01-XX, 51-XX, 52-XX, 53-XX, 68-XX, 70-XX, 74-XX, 92-XX, 97-XX, 00A99.

Library of Congress Cataloging-in-Publication Data

International Meeting of Origami Science, Mathematics, and Education (6th : 2014 : Tokyo, Japan) Origami^6 / Koryo Miura [and five others], editors.

    volumes cm

    "International Conference on Origami Science and Technology ... Tokyo, Japan ... 2014"—Introduction.

    Includes bibliographical references and index.

    Contents: Part 1. Mathematics of origami—Part 2. Origami in technology, science, art, design, history, and education.

    ISBN 978-1-4704-1875-5 (alk. paper : v. 1)—ISBN 978-1-4704-1876-2 (alk. paper : v. 2)

    1.   Origami—Mathematics—Congresses. 2. Origami in education—Congresses. I. Miura, Koryo, 1930– editor. II. Title.

QA491.I55   2014

736′.982–dc23

                            2015027499

Origami^6 is dedicated to the memory of Klaus Peters (1937–2014), founder with Alice Peters of A K Peters, Ltd., publisher of *Origami^3*, *Origami^4*, and *Origami^5*, among many other genre-crossing books. His vision informed and explored the relationships between mathematics and many other fields, not least of which is the mathemagical world of origami.

Contents

Part 1: Mathematics of Origami

I. Mathematics of Origami: Coloring

II. Mathematics of Origami: Constructibility

III. Mathematics of Origami: Rigid Foldability

IV. Mathematics of Origami: Design Algorithms

Part 2: Origami in Technology, Science, Art, Design, History, and Education

V. Origami in Technology and Science

VI. Origami in Art, Design, and History

VII. Origami in Education

Acknowledgments

There are many people and organizations to thank for making it possible to present you, the reader, with this two-volume set of $Origami^6$. The publication of $Origami^6$ is made possible through their efforts over several years. First came the creation of committees to plan for and raise funds for the 6th International Meeting on Origami Science, Mathematics, and Education (6OSME), which took place August 11–13, 2014, in Tokyo, Japan. The *Organizing Committee* managed the details—from small to large—of making the meeting a reality: Ichiro Hagiwara, Yuko Adachi, Yan Chen, Koshiro Hatori, Takashi Hojyo, Sachiko Ishida, Kaori Kuribayashi-Shigetomi, Hideo Komatsu, Jason Ku, Jun Maekawa, Yuji Matsumoto, Jun Mitani, Seiji Nishikawa, Yoshio Tsuda, and Makoto Yamaguchi. The *Program Committee* members (including the $Origami^6$ editors) helped to shape the vision for the meeting: Roger Alperin, Hideaki Azuma, Erik D. Demaine, Martin L. Demaine, Emma Frigerio, Tomoko Fuse, Koshiro Hatori, Thomas C. Hull, Yves Klett, Kaori Kuribayashi-Shigetomi, Jun Maekawa(who edited the book of program and abstracts), Yoshinobu Miyamoto, Kazuya Saito, Koichi Tateishi, Arnold Tubis, and Zhong You. *Supporting organizations* provided time and financial support to help defray the cost of the meeting and to ensure participants took away memorable and positive experiences from the event: Tokyo-Shiki Co., Origami House, Miura-ori lab, Gabriella & Paul Rosenbaum Foundation, Toyo Corporation, Takeo Co., Kawakami Sangyo Co., Heiwa Paper Co., Maeda Corporation, Noiz Architects, Asahi Press, and Issey Miyake. *Special thanks* go to Gabriella & Paul Rosenbaum Foundation for providing scholarships to students and to Japan Origami Academic Society and Origami House (Makoto Yamaguchi, Eiko Matsuura, and Satoshi Kamiya) for their extraordinary efforts to ensure that the meeting proceeded smoothly.

The executive managers for 6OSME were Seiji Nishikawa and Tomohiro Tachi, who oversaw the event's smooth operation. Robert J. Lang and Patsy Wang-Iverson served as the international driving forces. Kiyoko Yoshizawa and Koji Miyazaki managed the origami exhibitions, old and new. Koshiro Hatori, Jason Ku, and Anne Lavin oversaw hospitality, including planning field trips for meeting participants. Masami Isoda and Masahiko Sakamoto offered participants an opportunity to observe a ninth grade public lesson in mathematics at the Junior High School attached to Tsukuba University in Otsuka, Japan.

Reviewers played a crucial role in ensuring the meeting offered high-quality experiences. They reviewed the abstracts submitted for consideration for presentation, and then they reviewed the manuscripts submitted for publication in $Origami^6$, offering detailed suggestions for improvement and then re-reviewing many manuscripts. A large number of individuals offered their services as reviewers, and we thank them for their time and commitment to the work: Hugo Akitaya,

Roger Alperin, Byoungkwon An, Richard Askey, Martin Barej, Alex Bateman, Alessandro Beber, sarah-marie belcastro, Mark Bolitho, Landen Bowen, Suryansh Chandra, Yan Chen, Herng Yi Cheng, Rostislav Chudoba, Keenan Crane, Erik D. Demaine, Martin L. Demaine, Peter Engel, Evgueni Filipov, Robin Flatland, Haruaki Fukuda, Matthew Gardiner, Ilan Garibi, Robert Geretschläger, Koshiro Hatori, Barry Hayes, Susanne Hoffmann, Takashi Horiyama, Larry Howell, Thomas C. Hull, Ushio Ikegami, Sachiko Ishida, Miyuki Kawamura, Martin Kilian, Yves Klett, Goran Konjevod, Jason Ku, Kaori Kuribayashi-Shigetomi, Anna Lubiw, Jun Maekawa, Spencer Magleby, Rupert Maleczek, Yoshinobu Miyamoto, Koji Miyazaki, Jeannine Mosely, Jun-Hee Na, Chris Palmer, Marian Palumbo, Rachel Philpott, Helmut Pottmann, Katherine Riley, Kazuya Saito, Saadya Sternberg, Cynthia Sung, Motoi Tachibana, Koichi Tateishi, Minoru Taya, Naoya Tsuruta, Emiko Tsutsumi, Arnold Tubis, Naohiko Watanabe, Michael Winckler, and Zhong You.

We thank the American Mathematical Society (AMS) for their unstinting support and publishing of *Origami*[6], in particular Sergei Gelfand for keeping us focused and on track, Teresa Levy for her beautiful artwork, Peter Sykes and Denise Wood for their marketing prowess, and Michael Haggett for pulling it all together. Lastly, we are indebted to Charlotte Byrnes for agreeing to undertake the chore of improving the books you hold in your hands.

Koryo Miura
Toshikazu Kawasaki
Tomohiro Tachi
Ryuhei Uehara
Robert J. Lang
Patsy Wang-Iverson

Introduction

The apparently disparate fields of origami (the Japanese art of paper-folding), mathematics, science, technology, design, and education have made tenuous connections with each other throughout recorded history, but they became firmly linked in 1989, with the First International Conference on Origami Science and Technology, organized by Humiaki Huzita and held in Ferrara, Italy. The outcome of that meeting was a book [Huzita 91]. That first conference, which brought together practitioners in origami, mathematicians, scientists, technologists, engineers, and educators, set the course for a series of meetings and subsequent proceedings books, in Otsu, Japan in 1994 [Miura 97]; Asilomar, California, USA in 2001 [Hull 02]; Pasadena, California, USA in 2006 [Lang 09]; Singapore in 2010 [Wang-Iverson et al. 11]; and, most recently, in Tokyo, Japan in 2014. Over a hundred papers were presented by speakers from 30 countries at that conference, spanning topics ranging from the mathematical fundamentals of origami to algorithms for origami design, applications in architecture, deployable structures, microfabrication, and the use of folding in teaching and pedagogy. With each year, the breadth, diversity, and depth of work in the field have grown. It has resulted in collaborations between scientists and artists, engineers and teachers, in numerous structures, mechanisms, devices, and artworks, and, most tangibly, in the collection of papers in the book you are holding right now.

Each Origami in Science, Mathematics, and Education (OSME) conference has grown in size and breadth, reflecting the many connections between the world of folding and diverse other fields. Traditionally, the art of origami has been one of great restriction: a single sheet of paper (usually), formed by folding only, with no cuts (again, usually). Yet, this restrictive rule set not only gave rise to vast variety in artistic forms, but the techniques that artists discovered to create their forms have turned out to have applications across technology. In addition, as the power of folding came to the attention of scientists, mathematicians, and technologists, they, in turn, brought powerful tools—abstraction, analysis, optimization, computation—to the world of folding, giving rise not just to new artworks but to new engineering applications that better the human condition. With the combination of geometric precision and physical tangibility that folding provides, it continues to serve as an educational tool, with ripple effects that extend far beyond the narrow province of paper alone.

As with previous volumes in this series, this book presents a cross section of the latest developments in the marriage between origami and scientific and technological fields. Those developments grow and expand, and there is no greater evidence of that growth than the fact that this work is now in two printed volumes.

Part 1 focuses on some of the deepest connections between origami and other fields: the mathematics of origami, whose roots go back well beyond the OSME phenomenon with developments on solving algebraic equations using origami back in the mid-twentieth century, and still older explorations of the mathematical properties of folded surfaces. Modern investigations form a rich and vibrant field; new results presented here include work on constructability, connections to graph theory and coloring, and a host of design algorithms that bring in concepts from two- and three-dimensional geometry. The mathematical underpinnings of folding and their implications remain a source of active exploration, as you will see in the many papers in this work.

Part 2 focuses on the connections between origami and more applied areas of science: engineering, physics, architecture, industrial design, and even other artistic fields that go well beyond the usual folded paper. When origami enters other fields, the medium changes: applications of origami use polymers, metals, textiles, and more as the folding medium, and they call for new developments in algorithms, manufacturing techniques, computational tools, and process development. In addition, the applications of origami are often informed and influenced by the deep roots of historical folding, and you will find history, design, and art among the rich mélange of interdisciplinary work explored in this volume. While origami can call upon highly abstruse mathematical concepts, it also can play a powerful role as a classroom tool at all educational levels, even the elementary grades. A number of papers explore and demonstrate the utility of origami as a pedagogical tool in mathematical education.

As is often the case in the academic milieu, the most exciting and novel developments take place at the edges of existing fields, where disparate and unexpected bodies of knowledge mix and interact—illustrated elegantly here by the interdisciplinary applications of origami.

Origami[6] contains a unique collection of papers accessible to a wide audience, including those interested in art, design, history, and education and researchers interested in the connections between origami and science, technology, engineering, and mathematics. We hope you will enjoy the works in these two volumes, both for their own interest and as harbingers (and perhaps triggers) of more exciting developments to come.

The Editors of *Origami*[6]:

Koryo Miura
Toshikazu Kawasaki
Tomohiro Tachi
Ryuhei Uehara
Robert J. Lang
Patsy Wang-Iverson

Bibliography

[Huzita 91] Humiaki Huzita (editor). *Proceedings of the First International Meeting of Origami Science and Technology*. Padova, Italy: Dipartimento di Fisica dell'Università di Padova, 1991.

[Miura 97] Koryo Miura (editor). *Origami Science and Art: Proceedings of the Second International Meeting of Origami Science and Scientific Origami*. Shiga, Japan: Seian University of Art and Design, 1997.

[Hull 02] Thomas Hull (editor). *Origami³: Proceedings of the Third International Meeting of Origami Science, Mathematics, and Education*. Natick, MA: A K Peters, 2002. MR1955754 (2003h:00017)

[Lang 09] Robert J. Lang (editor). In *Origami⁴: Fourth International Meeting of Origami Science, Mathematics, and Education*. Natick, MA: A K Peters, 2009. MR2590567 (2010h:00025)

[Wang-Iverson et al. 11] Patsy Wang-Iverson, Robert J. Lang, and Mark Yim (editors). *Origami⁵: Fifth International Meeting of Origami Science, Mathematics, and Education*. Boca Raton, FL: A K Peters/CRC Press, 2011. MR2866909 (2012h:00044)

I. Mathematics of Origami: Coloring

Coloring Connections with Counting Mountain-Valley Assignments

Thomas C. Hull

1. Introduction

In the history of origami-mathematics, studying the combinatorics of flat folds has been consistently difficult. The stamp-folding problem, where we aim to count the number of different ways to fold a grid of postage stamps, might be the oldest such problem that is still unsolved [Uehara 11] Determining the number of ways a given crease pattern can fold flat has also been found to have applications in science, such as in enumerating the energy states of a crumpled polymer sheet or in determining the mechanics of self-folding materials.

Many such problems amount to counting the number of valid mountain-valley (MV) assignments that will fold a given crease pattern into a flat state. Here, *valid* means that it will allow the crease pattern to fold flat without the paper self-intersecting or ripping. A recent advancement in this area is to convert such MV-assignment enumeration problems to graph-coloring problems and then use the vast field of graph colorings to help solve the problem.

Note that this general approach is not new; physicists have been converting folding problems from the science of polymer materials to coloring problems for over a decade [Francesco 00] In such work, however, the folding problems are typically counting the number of foldings whose crease patterns are a subset of a larger grid of creases, not focusing on a specific crease pattern and counting MV-assignments. In this paper we briefly survey recent approaches in linking the enumeration of valid MV-assignments to graph-coloring problems.

2. Preliminaries

To begin, we briefly review a few basic results from the combinatorics of flat origami. (See [Hull 02]or a more detailed treatment.)

Consider a crease pattern C to be a planar graph $C = (V, E)$ drawn on a piece of paper. We partition the vertices into two classes, $V = V_B \cup V_I$, where V_B are the vertices on the boundary of the paper and V_I are the vertices in the paper's interior. The edges in E are the crease lines of our origami model, and in this paper we will only consider crease patterns C that *fold flat*, or are *flat-foldable*, which means that all the creases can be folded to transform (in a piecewise isometric manner) the paper into a flat object such that the paper does not self-intersect.

We define an *MV-assignment* for a crease pattern $C = (V, E)$ to be a function $\mu : E \to \{-1, 1\}$. Here, -1 indicates that the crease is a valley, and 1 indicates a mountain crease. An MV-assignment μ is called *valid* if the crease pattern can fold flat (without self-intersecting) using the mountains and valleys as specified by μ.

Many results on flat-foldable crease patterns are *local* in that they pertain only to the foldability or MV-assignment at a single interior vertex. One of the most fundamental such results is Maekawa's Theorem.

THEOREM 2.1 (Maekawa's Theorem). *The difference between the number of mountain and valley creases meeting at a vertex in a flat-foldable crease pattern is two. That is, for the creases c_i adjacent to the vertex, we must have $\sum \mu(c_i) = \pm 2$.*

See [Hull 94] [Hull 02] or [Hull 13]or a proof. This means that at a degree-4 vertex in a flat-foldable crease pattern, we must have 3 mountain and 1 valley creases or vice versa. Note that Maekawa's Theorem is only a necessary condition for a vertex to fold flat.

Sometimes specifying the angles between the creases meeting at a vertex is needed. If the creases meeting at a vertex in a crease pattern are denoted l_i for $i = 1, ..., n$, then we let α_i denote the angles, in order, between these creases, where α_i is between creases l_i and l_{i+1}. The angles α_i are called the *angle sequence* for the vertex.

Another fundamental consideration is the fact that local conditions in flat-foldability do not typically translate to global conditions. The biggest such obstacle is the fact that if a crease pattern C with an MV-assignment μ satisfies the condition that every vertex locally folds flat under μ, then it is not guaranteed to globally fold flat. Examples of crease patterns that are locally but not globally flat-foldable can be found in [Hull 94, Hull 02, Hull 13] The best attempt in print at trying to create conditions for global flat-foldability can be found in [Justin 97] In 1996 Bern and Hayes proved that deciding whether or not a given crease pattern can globally fold flat is NP-hard, even if the MV-assignment is given as well [Bern and Hayes 96]

For this reason, when counting valid MV-assignments, we usually only count those that locally fold flat. Adding the global constraint makes such problems much more difficult, and there are currently no general techniques for addressing the global flat-foldability problem in MV-assignment enumeration.

3. Two-Colorable Crease Patterns

The simplest cases of MV-assignments in flat-foldable crease patterns are those that are equivalent to properly two-vertex coloring a graph. These are crease patterns where the mountains and valleys can be determined using simple rules. One of the most basic such rules in the world of flat-foldability is the following (see [Demaine and O'Rourke 07]:

LEMMA 3.1 (Big-Little-Big Lemma). *Let v be a flat vertex fold with angle sequence α_i and a valid MV assignment μ. If $\alpha_{i-1} > \alpha_i < \alpha_{i+1}$ for some i, then $\mu(l_i) \neq \mu(l_{i+1})$.*

The proof of this lemma is simple: If $\mu(l_i) = \mu(l_{i+1})$, then the sector of paper made by angle α_i will be covered on the same side of the paper by the two bigger adjacent angle sectors, forcing the paper to self-intersect or to create additional creases.

The Big-Little-Big Lemma allows us to examine crease patterns and quickly determine if some creases are forced to be the same or different. It can't be applied to all flat-foldable crease patterns, but it can be a great aid in certain families of crease patterns. In fact, we can make the influence of the Big-Little-Big Lemma and Maekawa's Theorem more precise by thinking of an MV-assignment μ as a two-coloring of the edges (with colors -1 and $+1$). Our goal, then, is to convert our MV-assignment into a proper two-vertex coloring of a graph.

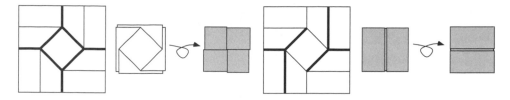

FIGURE 1. Two different MV-assignments of the square twist. Bold lines are mountain creases, and non-bold creases are valleys.

Before we do this, recall that in graph theory P_2 denotes a *path of length 2*, which has three vertices a, b, and c and edges $\{a, b\}$ and $\{b, c\}$. The vertices a and c are called the *ends of* P_2 and must get the same color when we two-color the vertices of P_2. In fact, the end vertices must always get the same color when two-coloring the vertices of any even-length path P_{2n}.

DEFINITION 3.2. Given a flat-foldable crease pattern $C = (V, E)$, we define the *origami line graph* $C_L = (V_L, E_L)$ to be a graph produced as follows: Start with an initial set of vertices V_L to be the creases $\{c_1, ..., c_n\}$ in E. Then, perform the following steps:

(1) For all pairs of creases $c_i, c_j \in E$, if the creases are forced to have different MV parity, then let $\{c_i, c_j\} \in E_L$.
(2) For all pairs of creases $c_i, c_j \in E$, if the creases are forced to have the same MV parity and c_i and c_j are not already the ends of a path of even length from performing Step (1), then add a new vertex $v_{i,j}$ to V_L and let $\{c_i, v_{i,j}\}, \{v_{i,j}, c_j\} \in E_L$.

This definition is an extension of one found in [Hull 94] The point of the origami line graph is the following:

THEOREM 3.3. *Given a crease pattern C, if the origami line graph C_L is not properly two-vertex colorable, then C is not flat-foldable.*

For the purposes of counting, if a crease pattern has the property that all of the ways in which mountains and valleys can influence each other is captured by the origami line graph, then counting the number of valid MV-assignments is just a matter of counting the number of proper two-colorings of the origami line graph. We say that in a flat-foldable crease pattern C, the MV-assignments are *determined by* C_L if every MV-assignment μ corresponds to a unique two-vertex coloring of C_L and vice versa. There are only two ways to properly two-color the vertices of a connected, two-colorable graph, and therefore we have the following:

THEOREM 3.4. *Let C be a flat-foldable crease pattern whose MV-assignments are determined be C_L, and let n be the number of connected components of C_L. Then, the number of valid MV-assignments of C (that locally fold flat) is 2^n.*

3.1. Example: Square twist tessellations. A *square twist* is an origami maneuver that literally twists a square in the paper $90°$, creating four perpendicular pleats radiating from the square as it does so. Examples are shown in Figure 1, where one can see that different MV-assignments for the square twist are possible. See [Hull 13]or a more detailed exposition on the number of ways to flat-fold a square twist.

Square twists are interesting because they easily tessellate. That is, we can arrange square twists in a grid on a single sheet of paper, making the pleats of the twists line up

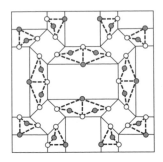

FIGURE 2. A 2×2 tessellation of square twists (solid lines) with the origami line graph superimposed (round dots and dashed lines).

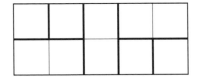

FIGURE 3. A 2×5 stamp-folding MV-assignment that is impossible to fold.

and taking mirror images of the square twist as needed. Then, the whole tessellated crease pattern should be able to fold flat (if done with care). This is an example of an *origami tessellation*, a genre of origami that has become quite popular. See [Gjerde 08]or more examples.

We let $S(m, n)$ denote the crease pattern of an $m \times n$ square-twist tessellation grid. The $S(2, 2)$ case is shown in Figure 2, along with its origami line graph $S(2, 2)_L$. Notice how, at each vertex of this crease pattern, we may employ the Big-Little-Big Lemma at the $45°$ angle. Also, by Maekawa's Theorem, the creases surrounding the $135°$ angle at each vertex must have the same MV parity. This explains the structure of $S(2, 2)_L$ shown in Figure 2.

The general square twist origami line graph $S(m, n)_L$ will have four components at each square twist. The $2(m+n)$ components on the border of the paper will only be touching one square twist; the others will be touching two. This gives $(4mn - 2(m+n))/2 + 2(m+n) = 2mn + m + n$ connected components of $S(m, n)_L$.

THEOREM 3.5. *The number of valid MV-assignments of $S(m, n)$ that locally fold flat is* $2^{2mn+m+n}$.

We conjecture that all of these MV-assignments of $S(m, n)$ are globally flat-foldable as well, but Theorem 3.5 should be viewed as an upper bound for global flat-foldability. In fact, it is quite possible for a crease pattern to be flat-foldable at every vertex and to have no mountain-valley contradictions that the origami line graph would detect, yet still be unfoldable. Figure 3 shows an example of this; see [Justin 97]r [Ginepro and Hull 14]or details on why it fails to globally fold flat.

4. The Miura-Ori

There are many interesting crease patterns for which Theorem 3.4 is not applicable. Any crease pattern whose origami line graph, as defined above, is inadequate for capturing the MV relationships between the creases will fall into this category. A simple example can be seen in a single, degree-4 flat-foldable vertex with two congruent acute angles that

FIGURE 4. A flat-foldable vertex (left) whose MV restrictions (right) are not captured by the origami line graph of Definition 3.2.

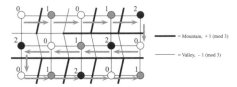

FIGURE 5. How we go from a locally flat-foldable Miura-ori MV-assignment to a proper three-vertex coloring of a grid graph, and vice versa.

are adjacent, as shown in Figure 4 (left). Note that by Maekawa's Theorem we need three mountains and one valley (or vice versa), and the crease labeled e_4 cannot be the sole valley (or the sole mountain). Otherwise, the two acute angles α would have to wrap around and contain the two obtuse angles $180° - \alpha$, which is impossible without the paper ripping or forming new creases. Thus, the only valid MV-assignments for such a vertex are those shown in Figure 4 (right). Notice that the creases labeled e_1, e_2, and e_3 switch in pairs from having the same to having different MV-assignments, which means the there would be no edges between these creases in the origami line graph. Nonetheless, there are MV restrictions between e_1, e_2, and e_3, and thus the origami line graph will not capture these restrictions. Other means must be used to count the number of valid MV-assignments for such vertices.

The vertex shown in Figure 4 is exactly the vertex that is tessellated in the classic Miura-ori crease pattern, also known as the Miura map fold [Miura 91] The Miura-ori has attracted considerable attention over the past 30 years for its applications in engineering and nature [Mahadevan and Rica 05, Wei et al. 13]

Recently, Ginepro and the author performed an analysis of MV-assignments for Miura-ori crease patterns that consist of an $m \times n$ grid of parallelograms. This led to a bijection between the number of locally flat-foldable $m \times n$ Miura-ori MV-assignments and the number of ways to properly three-vertex color an $m \times n$ grid graph with one vertex precolored. We summarize this bijection here and refer the reader to [Ginepro and Hull 14]or details of the proof.

The idea of the bijection is illustrated in Figure 5. Imagine overlying the $m \times n$ grid graph (with m rows and n columns of vertices) on top of the $m \times n$ Miura-ori so that each grid graph vertex is in the center of a parallelogram. (In graph theory terms, the grid graph is the planar dual to the Miura-ori crease pattern, ignoring the outside face.) The Miura-ori crease pattern should be oriented so that the top row of vertices are all "pointing left," i.e., so that the crease e_4 in Figure 4 is to the left of the upper-left Miura-ori vertex. We also use as our grid graph vertex colors the integers modulo three (that is, the elements of the group $\mathbb{Z}_3$), and we assume that the upper-left vertex in the grid graph gets color 0.

We then follow a zig-zag path on the $m \times n$ grid graph from the upper-left vertex, across the top row to the upper-right vertex, then down one vertex, then across the second row to the left, then down one vertex, then across to the right again, and so on. This path is illustrated by the gray arrows in Figure 5.

We use this path to establish our bijection, which we will now describe. Let the vertices of the $m \times n$ grid graph be denoted $v_1, v_2, \ldots, v_{mn}$ in the order that they are encountered on the zig-zag path. Let c_i denote the Miura-ori crease line between vertices v_{i-1} and v_i in the superimposed grid graph. The MV-assignment for the Miura-ori crease pattern $C = (V_C, E_C)$ will be $\mu : E_C \to \{-1, 1\}$, and the three-coloring of the grid graph $G = (V_G, E_G)$ will be $c : V_G \to \mathbb{Z}_3$.

- *To convert from μ to c:* Let $c(v_1) = 0$ and then recursively define
$$c(v_i) = c(v_{i-1}) + \mu(c_i) \quad \text{(where addition is mod 3)}.$$

- *To convert from c to μ:* For creases c_i between vertices v_{i-1} and v_i in the grid graph, define
$$\mu(c_i) = \begin{cases} 1 & \text{if } c(v_i) - c(v_{i-1}) \equiv 1 \ (\text{mod } 3), \\ -1 & \text{if } c(v_i) - c(v_{i-1}) \equiv 2 \ (\text{mod } 3). \end{cases}$$

  For the other creases, let $d_i \in E_C$ be the crease directly below vertex v_i and above v_j in the superimposed grid graph. Then, define
$$\mu(d_i) = \begin{cases} 1 & \text{if } c(v_i) - c(v_j) \equiv 1 \ (\text{mod } 3), \\ -1 & \text{if } c(v_i) - c(v_j) \equiv 2 \ (\text{mod } 3). \end{cases}$$

It should not be immediately obvious to the reader that these work. That is, converting from μ to c will create a proper coloring along the zig-zag path, but a proof is required to guarantee that the coloring will be proper along G's edges not in the zig-zag path. It turns out, however, that the MV restrictions of the Miura-ori crease pattern are exactly what is needed to ensure that c will be a proper coloring across these other edges. Similarly, when constructing μ from c as defined above, one needs to prove that the resulting MV-assignment is locally flat-foldable. In other words, every vertex in the Miura-ori C needs to look like one of the six possibilities in Figure 4 under μ. Proofs of these details are omitted here for space considerations and can be found in [Ginepro and Hull 14] An interesting application of this bijection to a further study of the Miura-ori can be found in [Ballinger et al. 15]

One interesting consequence of this bijection between MV-assignments of the Miura-ori and grid-graph three-vertex colorings is that one can then use results from graph theory to gain insight into the corresponding MV-assignment counting problem. Counting three-colorings of grid graphs is not a completely solved problem, although the numbers generated by counting such colorings is sequence A078099 in the On-Line Encyclopedia of Integer Sequences.[1] Under this sequence's encyclopedia entry, there is information on the transfer matrix for generating these numbers, which can thus be used to count the locally flat-foldable MV-assignments of an $m \times n$ Miura-ori.

Furthermore, in 1967 Lieb proved that this same grid-graph coloring problem is equivalent to enumerating the number of states in an antiferroelectric model for two-dimensional ice lattices, otherwise known as the *square ice model* [Lieb 67] Lieb further showed that in a grid graph with N vertices for N very large (say, on the order of 10^{23}, which corresponds to the number of atoms one might have in a piece of ice), we will have

$$(4/3)^{3N/2}$$

---

[1] http://oeis.org/A078099

ways to properly three-vertex color the grid graph with one vertex precolored. Because of our bijection, this means that the number of ways to locally fold flat a Miura-ori crease pattern with N parallelograms will be approximately $(4/3)^{3N/2}$ for N very large. Perhaps more importantly, this establishes a relationship between counting valid MV-assignments of origami crease patterns and Ising spin models in physics.

5. Conclusion

Counting the number of ways in which a crease pattern can be folded has been a challenging area of origami-mathematics. Counting valid MV-assignments in particular has seen little progress aside from the single-vertex case [Hull 03] Developing a more general way to convert such counting problems to graph coloring would be a major breakthrough in the area. The Ginepro-Hull bijection with Miura-ori crease patterns is very promising in this regard.

However, the bijection techniques used in the Miura-ori are very specific to that crease pattern. It is not clear how one would generalize this to other crease patterns, especially those with vertices of degree larger than four. There is plenty of further work to be done.

It is interesting to note how one could argue that the crease patterns that fall under the hypotheses of Theorem 3.4 (that is, where the origami line graph tells us everything we need to know) are much more common than other crease patterns. The idea is that in the configuration space of a flat-foldable vertex, the only components with nonzero volume are those that are *generic* in that the sequence of angles do not contain any consecutive equal angles or any other exploitable symmetries (see [Hull 09]or more details). Such vertices would have instances of the Big-Little-Big Lemma present and could thus have all of their MV restrictions captured by the origami line graph. It stands to reason that if we were to take a "generic" flat-foldable crease pattern (all of whose vertices are generic), then its MV restrictions might be completely described by the origami line graph. In other words, if we were to use these ideas to define a *random flat-foldable crease pattern*, then it could be true that almost every flat-foldable crease pattern could have its MV-assignments enumerated by the origami line graph and Theorem 3.4.

Nonetheless, it is also true that most of the crease patterns that we find interesting, like the Miura-ori, possess some amount of symmetry and thus would not be generic. Such crease pattern MV-assignments will remain more challenging to enumerate.

Acknowledgments

The author would like to thank Crystal Wang for useful discussions leading up to the preparation of this paper. This research was supported by the National Science Foundation grant EFRI-ODISSEI-1240441 "Mechanical Meta-Materials from Self-Folding Polymer Sheets."

References

[Ballinger et al. 15] Brad Ballinger, Mirela Damian, David Eppstein, Robin Flatland, Jessica Ginepro, and Thomas Hull. "Minimum Forcing Sets for Miura Folding Patterns." In *Proceedings of the Twenty-Sixth Annual ACM-SIAM Symposium on Discrete Algorithms*, edited by Piotr Indyk, pp. 136–147. Philadelphia: SIAM, 2015. Available online (http://epubs.siam.org/doi/abs/10.1137/1.9781611973730.11).

[Bern and Hayes 96] Marshall Bern and Barry Hayes. "The Complexity of Flat Origami." In *Proceedings of the Seventh Annual ACM-SIAM Symposium on Discrete Algorithms*, pp. 175–183. Philadelphia: SIAM, 1996. MR1381938 (97c:52016)

[Demaine and O'Rourke 07] E. D. Demaine and J. O'Rourke. *Geometric Folding Algorithms: Linkages, Origami, Polyhedra*. Cambridge, UK: Cambridge University Press, 2007. MR2354878 (2008g:52001)

[Francesco 00] Philippe Di Francesco. "Folding and Coloring Problems in Mathematics and Physics." *Bull. Amer. Math. Soc. (N.S.)* 37 (2000), 251–307. MR1754642 (2001g:82004)

[Ginepro and Hull 14] Jessica Ginepro and Thomas C. Hull. "Counting Miura-Ori Foldings." *Journal of Integer Sequences* 17 (2014), Article 14.10.8. Available online (https://cs.uwaterloo.ca/journals/JIS/VOL17/Hull/hull.html). MR3275876

[Gjerde 08] Eric Gjerde. *Origami Tessellations: Awe-Inspiring Geometric Designs*. Wellesley, MA: A K Peters, 2008. MR2474884 (2009m:52001)

[Hull 94] Thomas C. Hull. "On the Mathematics of Flat Origamis." *Congressus Numerantium* 100 (1994), 215–224. MR1382321 (96k:05196)

[Hull 02] Thomas C. Hull. "The Combinatorics of Flat Folds: A Survey." In *Origami³: Proceedings of the Third International Meeting of Origami Science, Mathematics, and Education*, edited by Thomas Hull, pp. 29–38. Natick, MA: A K Peters, 2002. MR1955757 (2004c:52030)

[Hull 03] Thomas C. Hull. "Counting Mountain-Valley Assignments for Flat Folds." *Ars Combinatoria* 67 (2003), 175–188. MR1973236 (2004c:05011)

[Hull 09] Thomas C. Hull. "Configuration Spaces for Flat Vertex Folds." In *Origami⁴: Fourth International Meeting of Origami Science, Mathematics, and Education*, edited by Robert J. Lang, pp. 361–370. Wellesley, MA: A K Peters, 2009. MR2590567 (2010h:00025)

[Hull 13] Thomas Hull. *Project Origami: Activities for Exploring Mathematics*, Second Edition. Boca Raton, FL: A K Peters/CRC Press, 2013. MR2987362

[Justin 97] Jacques Justin. "Toward a Mathematical Theory of Origami." In *Origami Science and Art: Proceedings of the Second International Meeting of Origami Science and Scientific Origami*, edited by K. Miura, pp. 15–29. Shiga, Japan: Seian University of Art and Design, 1997.

[Lieb 67] Elliot H. Lieb. "Residual Entropy of Square Ice." *Physical Review* 162 (1967), 162–172.

[Mahadevan and Rica 05] Lakshminarayanan Mahadevan and Sergio Rica. "Self-Organized Origami." *Science* 307 (2005), 1740.

[Miura 91] Koryo Miura. "A Note on Intrinsic Geometry of Origami." In *Proceedings of the First International Meeting of Origami Science and Technology*, edited by H. Huzita, pp. 239–249. Padova, Italy: Dipartimento di Fisica dell'Università di Padova, 1991.

[Uehara 11] Ryuhei Uehara. "Stamp Foldings with a Given Mountain-Valley Assignment." In *Origami⁵: Fifth International Meeting of Origami Science, Mathematics, and Education*, edited by Patsy Wang-Iverson, Robert J. Lang, and Mark Yim, pp. 585–597. Boca Raton, FL: A K Peters/CRC Press, 2011. MR2866906 (2012m:05015)

[Wei et al. 13] Z. Y. Wei, Z. V. Guo, L. Dudte, H. Y. Liang, and L. Mahadevan. "Geometric Mechanics of Periodic Pleated Origami." *Physical Review Letters* 110 (2013), 215501–215505.

DEPARTMENT OF MATHEMATICS, WESTERN NEW ENGLAND UNIVERSITY, SPRINGFIELD, MASSACHUSETTS
E-mail address: thull@wne.edu

Color Symmetry Approach to the Construction of Crystallographic Flat Origami

Ma. Louise Antonette N. De las Peñas, Eduard C. Taganap,
and Teofina A. Rapanut

1. Introduction

Flat origami is a type of origami in which the folded paper can be pressed in a book without crumpling. Flat origami that is invariant under a crystallographic group is called *crystallographic flat origami* [Kawasaki and Yoshida 88]

To arrive at flat origami, we consider a crease pattern. A *crease pattern* indicates where the folds are to be made and how the paper will be folded. It consists of segments called *crease lines* that can be assigned either a mountain fold or a valley fold but not both. Mountain folds are denoted by solid lines, and the valley folds are denoted by dashed lines. When the paper is folded, a mountain fold points upward while a valley fold points downward. How mountain (M) and valley (V) folds are assigned to the crease lines is called an *MV-assignment* of the crease pattern.

Crystallographic origami can be traced back from the works of Shuzo Fujimoto [Fujimoto 82]nd Yoshihide Momotani [Momotani 84] Among the key people working on crystallographic flat origami are Chris Palmer [Palmer 97] Paulo Barreto [Barreto 97] and Alex Bateman [Bateman 02] Their works deal with the construction and classification of crystallographic flat origami. Helena Verrill also presented methods of constructing crystallographic flat origami and discussed the relationships between these methods [Verrill 98] The work of Toshikazu Kawasaki and Masaaki Yoshida in [Kawasaki and Yoshida 88] which provides an algebraic treatment of crystallographic flat origami, formed the basis for the work of Sales and Felix in [Sales 00] Sales and Felix introduced the use of color symmetry theory in providing a solution to the problem, posed by Bern and Hayes [Bern and Hayes 96]f how many different flat origami models can have the same crease pattern. They focused on crease patterns where one or two colors can be used to represent MV-assignments. Here, we continue their work by considering locally flat-foldable crease patterns where the MV-assignments are represented by more than two colors. With this approach, we can systematically construct a wider variety of crystallographic flat origami, and we can determine inequivalent crystallographic flat origami whose associated colored crease patterns possess certain color symmetrical properties. In this study, we apply the process for crease patterns arising from Archimedean tilings through the hinged

M. De las Peñas would like to thank the Ateneo de Manila University for support under the Loyola Schools Scholarly Work grant.

E. Taganap would like to thank the Gabriella & Paul Rosenbaum Foundation for financial support.

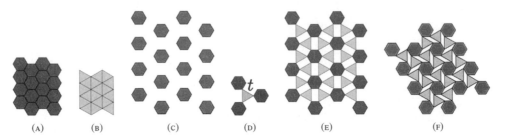

FIGURE 1. Steps in constructing the crease pattern CP 6^3 from the 6^3 tiling.

tiling method. We consider flat origami that is invariant under a plane crystallographic group.

We begin the discussion by presenting the method employed to obtain the crease patterns used in this work.

2. Constructing a Crease Pattern

We use the *hinged tiling method* [Verrill 98] developed by Palmer, Barreto, and Bateman, to construct the crease pattern of a crystallographic flat origami from an Archimedean tiling. The method is as follows:

(1) Consider an Archimedean tiling and its dual tiling.
(2) Space out the tiles in the Archimedean tiling.
(3) Insert the dual tiling between the tiles.
(4) Rotate the tiles relative to the dual tiling.
(5) Scale the dual relative to the Archimedean tiling as desired.

To illustrate this process, consider the Archimedean 6^3 tiling consisting of regular hexagons and its dual tiling, the 3^6 tiling by equilateral triangles, given in Figures 1(a) and (b) respectively. Performing Step (2) will obtain Figure 1(c). The 3^6 tiling is inserted into the 6^3 tiling as follows. Consider a tile t from the dual 3^6 tiling. Each of its three vertices is made to coincide with a vertex of three hexagonal tiles that meet in the 6^3 tiling (Figure 1(d)). We apply the process to each of the tiles in the 3^6 tiling to get the tiling in Figure 1(e). Applying Steps (4) and (5) to this tiling will yield the crease pattern CP 6^3 shown in Figure 1(f). Such a crease pattern, without MV-assignment, is called an *unassigned* creased pattern.

Let us now consider a generating unit of the unassigned crease pattern. A set s of faces of the crease pattern is a *generating unit* if the orbit of s under the action of a plane crystallographic group G, given by $G(s) = \{gs : g \in G\}$, is the entire crease pattern. We refer to gs, the image of s under g, as a *unit* of the crease pattern.

A proper MV-assignment will be given to the edges of the generating unit s to ensure that the crease pattern is locally flat-foldable. We refer to these assignments as *flat-foldability types* of the generating unit. If every unit is assigned a flat-foldability type of the generating unit, then a locally flat-foldable crease pattern arises. This means that each small disk around each vertex folds flat; that is, if $\theta_1, \theta_2, \ldots, \theta_{2n}$ are consecutive angles around a vertex, then $\theta_1 - \theta_2 + \theta_3 - \cdots - \theta_{2n} = 0$ (Kawasaki's Theorem) [Hull 02] In this work, we ignore global flat-foldability [Demaine and O'Rourke 07] To show that a crease pattern with multiple vertices is globally flat-foldable is an NP-hard problem [Bern and Hayes 96]

If a locally flat-foldable crease pattern obtained by the hinged tiling method is invariant under a plane crystallographic group $H \leq G$, $H \neq \{e\}$, then we obtain a crystallographic flat origami. Note that the fundamental region u of the locally flat-foldable crease pattern (the smallest region that generates the crease pattern under the action of its translation group) will correspond to a fundamental region $\bar{u}$ of the associated folded pattern. Thus, if the crease pattern with resulting MV-assignment is invariant under a plane crystallographic group, the resulting flat origami is also invariant under a plane crystallographic group.

In the case of the crease pattern CP 6^3, its generating unit s is composed of two parallelograms (Figure 2(b)) whose orbit under the plane crystallographic group $G = \langle a, x, y \rangle \cong p6$ (in IUCr notation [Schattschneider 78] is CP 6^3. The generators of G are the 60° counterclockwise rotation a about the center of a hexagon, translations x and y with vectors separated by a 60° angle, and the vector of x along the horizontal axis passing through the center of a. A parallelogram can be given one of two possible mountain and valley assignments that will give rise to a locally flat-foldable crease pattern [Kawasaki 05] Thus, we obtain four flat-foldability types of s (Figure 2(c)). An assignment of these flat-foldability types to the elements of $G(s)$ results in the crease pattern with MV-assignment shown in Figure 2(d). This gives rise to the crystallographic origami shown in Figure 2(e). The group consisting of symmetries in G that sends the crease pattern to itself is $H = \langle x, y \rangle \cong p1$. In this case, the crease pattern is invariant under H. The resulting folded pattern is invariant under a plane crystallographic group, also of type $p1$.

In the next section, we discuss a systematic way to arrive at a locally flat-foldable crease pattern that would give rise to a crystallographic origami.

3. Arriving at a Crystallographic Flat Origami

Consider a crease pattern that is obtained by the action of a plane crystallographic group G on a generating unit s of the pattern. Let C denote the set consisting of possible flat-foldability types that will be assigned to the units or elements of $G(s)$ so that the corresponding pattern will be locally flat-foldable. We let each flat-foldability type in C be represented by a distinct color.

Let s correspond to e, the identity element of G. Consequently, a unit, or an element of the G-orbit of s, $G(s) = \{gs : g \in G\}$, corresponds to an element of G. We have the one-to-one correspondence given by $gs \leftrightarrow g$, $g \in G$, so we label every unit with an element coming from G. An assignment of mountains and valleys that results in a flat origami corresponds to a coloring of the units of the crease pattern using the colors from C.

The coloring corresponds to a partition $P = \{P_i : i = 1, \ldots, r\}$ of G where each P_i is a set that contains the elements of G assigned the same color from C.

Now, given a coloring of the crease pattern, we can adopt ideas from color symmetry theory to aid us in determining whether the pattern folds into a crystallographic flat origami.

We use the following result from [De las Peñas et al. 99] which facilitates determining partitions of G that are invariant under a plane crystallographic subgroup H of G. This theorem gives a complete description of all partitions of a group G that are invariant under premultiplication by elements of H.

THEOREM 3.1. *Let G be a group and $H \leq G$. If P is an H-invariant partition of G, then P corresponds to a decomposition of G in the form $G = \cup_{i \in I} \cup_{h \in H} h J_i Y_i$ where $\cup_{i \in I} Y_i = Y$ is a complete set of right coset representatives of H in G and $J_i \leq H$ for every $i \in I$. If $K \leq H$ and K fixes the elements of P, then $K \leq J_i$ for each $i \in I$.*

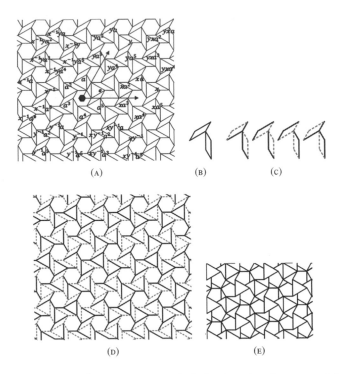

FIGURE 2. (a) CP 6^3 with its units labeled using the elements of G; the center of a and vectors of x and y are shown. (b) A generating unit of CP 6^3. (c) Flat-foldability types of (b). (d) An assignment of the flat-foldability types to the units of CP 6^3. (e) Crystallographic flat origami that arises from folding (d).

In the decomposition of G, $HY_i = \cup_{h \in H} hJ_iY_i$ corresponds to one orbit of colors under H and hJ_iY_i is one color in the given coloring.

To illustrate the process of arriving at a locally flat-foldable crease pattern invariant under a crystallographic group, consider CP 6^3. We start by identifying the generating unit s of the crease pattern and labeling it by e, the identity element of $G = \langle a, x, y \rangle \cong p6$. Any other unit is the image gs of s under $g \in G$. The image gs will be labeled by g. Then, the units in CP 6^3 can be labeled with elements from G as shown in Figure 2(a). To obtain an H-invariant coloring of CP 6^3, consider a subgroup $H = \langle x, y \rangle$ of G. H is an index-6 subgroup of G, so we select the set $Y = \{e, a, a^2, a^3, a^4, a^5\}$ to be a complete set of right coset representatives of H in G. Also consider a particular partition of G, say $G = H\{e, a\} \cup H\{a^2\} \cup H\{a^3, a^4\} \cup H\{a^5\}$. Referring to Theorem 3.1, we have $Y_1 = \{e, a\}$, $Y_2 = \{a^2\}$, $Y_3 = \{a^3, a^4\}$, $Y_4 = \{a^5\}$, and $J_i = H$ for $i = 1, 2, 3, 4$. Each unit of the crease pattern corresponding to elements of $H\{e, a\}$ will be given a color, say black. Similarly, units in the crease pattern corresponding to elements of $H\{a^2\}$, $H\{a^3, a^4\}$, and $H\{a^5\}$ will be colored in gray, stripes, and dots, respectively. We now arrive at a coloring of CP 6^3 shown in Figure 3(a). If each color in CP 6^3 is assigned a flat-foldability type of its generating unit as in Figure 3(d) then we get the locally flat-foldable crease pattern given in Figure 2(d). The pattern with this assignment will fold into a crystallographic flat origami as shown earlier in Figure 2(e).

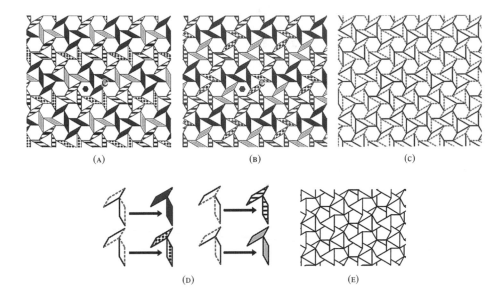

FIGURE 3. (a,b) Colorings of CP 6^3. The generating unit s, which corresponds to e, and the center of a 60° counterclockwise rotation a are shown. (c) Crease pattern with MV-assignment associated with the coloring in (b). (d) A correspondence of flat-foldability types and colors. (e) Crystallographic flat origami that arises by folding (c).

In the construction of a crystallographic flat origami, in particular, when arriving at an MV-assignment, a unit of the crease pattern may be assigned one of 1, 2, 3, 4, or r possible flat-foldability types.

In this section, we consider the situation where units are altogether assigned four flat-foldability types of the generating unit s. This assignment corresponds to a partition of the group G into the sets P_1, P_2, P_3, and P_4 as explained in the next result.

THEOREM 3.2. *Consider a crease pattern for a crystallographic flat origami with generating unit s. Let G be the plane crystallographic group whose action on s generates the entire crease pattern. Consider an MV-assignment of the crease pattern that results in a crystallographic flat origami. Then, this assignment—in which there are four flat-foldability types of s—corresponds to a partition $P = \{P_1, P_2, P_3, P_4\}$ of G. If P is invariant under left multiplication by a plane crystallographic group $H \leq G$, then one of the following must be true:*

    (i) *$P_1 = HY_1$, $P_2 = HY_2$, $P_3 = HY_3$, and $P_4 = HY_4$, where $Y = \cup_{i=1}^{4} Y_i$ is a complete set of right coset representatives of H in G.*

    (ii) *$P_1 = HY_1$, $P_2 = HY_2$, $P_3 = JY_3$, and $P_4 = hJY_3$, where J is an index-2 subgroup of H, $h \in H - J$, and $Y = \cup_{i=1}^{3} Y_i$ is a complete set of right coset representatives of H in G.*

    (iii) *$P_1 = HY_1$, $P_2 = JY_2$, $P_3 = hJY_2$, and $P_4 = h^2JY_2$, where J is an index-3 subgroup of H, $H \leq N_G(J)$, $h \in H - J$, and $Y = Y_1 \cup Y_2$ is a complete set of right coset representatives of H in G.*

> (iv) $P_1 = J_1Y_1$, $P_2 = h_1J_1Y_1$, $P_3 = J_2Y_2$, and $P_4 = h_2J_2Y_2$, where J_1 and J_2 are both index-2 subgroups of H, $h_1 \in H - J_1$, $h_2 \in H - J_2$, and $Y = Y_1 \cup Y_2$ is a complete set of right coset representative of H in G.
>
> (v) $P_1 = JY$, $P_2 = hJY$, $P_3 = h^2JY$, and $P_4 = h^3JY$, where J is an index-4 subgroup of H, $H \leq N_G(J)$, $h \in H - J$, and Y is a complete set of right coset representatives of H in G.

PROOF. Since there are altogether four flat-foldability types that are assigned to the units of the crease pattern, then a coloring using four colors is obtained. This corresponds to a partition $P = \{P_1, P_2, P_3, P_4\}$ of G where the units corresponding to P_i, $i = 1, 2, 3, 4$, are assigned one flat-foldability type (color).

To ensure that the partition results in a crystallographic flat origami, the partition must be invariant under a subgroup H of G. Consider the orbits formed by the action of H on P, which is H-invariant under left multiplication. There are four colors, so the following possibilities arise for the number of colors in an orbit:

(i) There are four orbits of colors $\{P_1\}$, $\{P_2\}$, $\{P_3\}$ and $\{P_4\}$. By Theorem 3.1, the ith color orbit is the set $HY_i = \{hJ_iY_i : h \in H\}$. Thus, $P_i = HY_i$, where Y_i is a set consisting of one representative for each right coset of H contained in P_i. In this case, $J_i = H$ and the stabilizer of each colors is H. Hence, $G = P_1 \cup P_2 \cup P_3 \cup P_4 = HY_1 \cup HY_2 \cup HY_3 \cup HY_4$, where $\cup_{i=1}^4 Y_i$ is a complete set of right coset representatives of H in G.

(ii) There are three orbits of colors $\{P_1\}$, $\{P_2\}$, and $\{P_3, P_4\}$. Following the same argument in (i), $P_i = HY_i$, $i = 1, 2$. Now, for $\{P_3, P_4\}$, consider the stabilizer J in H of P_3. We have $JP_3 = P_3$. There are only two colors in the orbit $\{P_3, P_4\}$, so $JP_4 = P_4$. Now, there is an element $h \in H$ that interchanges the colors: $hP_3 = P_4$ and $hP_4 = P_3$. Then, $h \in H - J$. By the orbit stabilizer theorem, $[H : J] = 2$ and $H = J \cup hJ$. Now, the third orbit of colors is HY_3. This can be written as $HY_3 = (J \cup hJ)Y_3 = JY_3 \cup hJY_3$, where Y_3 is a set consisting of one coset representative for each right coset of H contained in P_3. Thus, the partition of G is of the form $\{HY_1, HY_2, JY_3, hJY_3\}$, where $Y = \cup_{i=1}^3 Y_i$ is a complete set of right coset representatives of H in G.

(iii) There are two orbits of colors $\{P_1\}$ and $\{P_2, P_3, P_4\}$. Following the same argument in (i), $P_1 = HY_1$. With regards to $\{P_2, P_3, P_4\}$, let J be the stabilizer in H of P_2 such that $JP_2 = P_2$. This implies that $JP_3 = P_3$ and $JP_4 = P_4$. Suppose it is the case that $JP_3 = P_4$ and $JP_4 = P_3$. Consider $h \in H$ where $H \leq N_G(J)$. Because H permutes the colors, $hP_2 = P_3$ or $hP_2 = P_4$. If $hP_2 = P_3$, then $j(hP_2) = h'(j'P_2) = h'P_2 = P_3$, where $j, j' \in J, h' \in H$. But, $JP_3 = P_4$ and thus $j(hP_2) = jP_3 = P_4$. This implies that there is an element $jh \in H$ that sends P_2 to P_3 and P_4. This is a contradiction to the fact that $\{P_2, P_3, P_4\}$ is H-invariant. Thus, $JP_3 = P_3$. A similar argument will show that $JP_4 = P_4$.

    Now consider an element $h \in H$ that permutes the colors. Take, for instance, $hP_2 = P_3$, $hP_3 = P_4$, and $hP_4 = P_2$. It follows that $h^2P_2 = hP_3 = P_4$ and $h^3P_2 = P_2$. Then, $h, h^2 \in H - J$. By the orbit stabilizer theorem, $[H : J] = 3$ and $H = J \cup hJ \cup h^2J$. Now, the second orbit of colors is HY_2. This can be written as $HY_2 = (J \cup hJ \cup h^2J)Y_2 = JY_2 \cup hJY_2 \cup h^2JY_2$, where Y_2 is a set consisting of one coset representative for each right coset of H contained in P_2. Thus, the partition of G is of the form $\{HY_1, JY_2, hJY_2, h^2JY_2\}$, where $Y = Y_1 \cup Y_2$ is a complete set of right coset representatives of H in G.

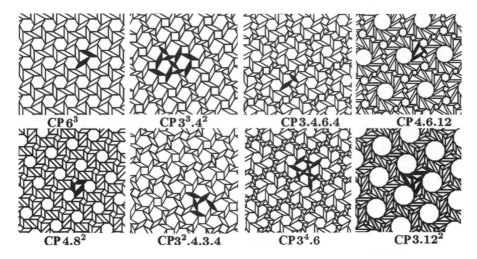

FIGURE 4. Crease patterns, derived from the Archimedean tilings via the hinged tiling method, with at least four flat-foldability types of its generating unit. The parallelograms colored black form a generating unit for each crease pattern. Each crease pattern is named after the Archimedean tiling from which it is derived.

(iv) There are two orbits of colors $\{P_1, P_2\}$ and $\{P_3, P_4\}$. This means that H permutes P_1 and P_2, as well as P_3 and P_4. Following the arguments used in (ii), $P_1 = J_1 Y_1$ and $P_2 = h_1 J_1 Y_1$, where J_1 is the stabilizer of P_1 in H, $[H : J_1] = 2$, and $h_1 \in H - J_1$. Similarly, we have $P_3 = J_2 Y_2$ and $P_4 = h_2 J_2 Y_2$, where J_2 is the stabilizer of P_3 in H, $[H : J_2] = 2$, and $h_2 \in H - J_2$ gives the partition of G of the form $\{J_1 Y_1, h_1 J_1 Y_1, J_2 Y_2, h_2 J_2 Y_2\}$ where $Y = Y_1 \cup Y_2$ is a complete set of right coset representatives of H in G.

(v) There is only one orbit of colors $\{P_1, P_2, P_3, P_4\}$. Similar arguments used in (iii) will show that the partition is of the form $\{JY, hJY, h^2 JY, h^3 JY\}$, where J is an index-4 subgroup of H, $H \leq N_G(J)$, $h \in H - J$, and Y is a complete set of right coset representatives of H in G.

$\square$

The coloring of CP 6^3 shown in Figure 3(a), given by $P = \{P_1 = H\{e, a\}, P_2 = H\{a^2\}, P_3 = H\{a^3, a^4\}, P_4 = H\{a^5\}\}$ is described by case (i) of Theorem 3.2 when there are altogether four H-orbits of colors.

A different decomposition of G satisfying case (i), such as that given by $\{H\{a, a^2\}, H\{a^3\}, H\{a^4, a^5\}, H\{e\}\}$, will lead to another crystallographic flat origami. Respectively assigning the colors black, grey, stripes, and dots to $H\{a, a^2\}$, $H\{a^3\}$, $H\{a^4, a^5\}$, and $H\{e\}$ leads to a coloring of the crease pattern given in Figure 3(b). Consequently, we obtain the crease pattern with MV-assignment shown in Figure 3(c) and the resulting crystallographic flat origami in Figure 3(e).

Note that, in arriving at the various MV-assignments of the crease pattern from the colorings that arise, we assume each time the same correspondence of a flat-foldability type to a particular color.

We remark that Theorem 3.2 provides us all the possible H-invariant partitions of G with four colors. Because most crease patterns from the Archimedean tilings (Figure 4)

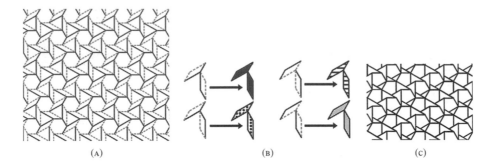

FIGURE 5. (a) Crease pattern with MV-assignment associated with the coloring in Figure 3(a). (b) A correspondence of flat-foldability types and colors different than the correspondence in Figure 3(d). (c) Crystallographic origami that arises from folding (b).

have at least four flat-foldability types, we could systematically construct a wide variety of crystallographic flat origami using Theorem 3.2. If a subgroup H of G is given, then we can list all crystallographic flat origami where their associated coloring of the crease pattern is invariant under H. Theorem 3.2 can be extended to obtain the various H-orbits for the case where there are r flat-foldability types.

4. Equivalent and Inequivalent Crystallographic Origami

Two colorings of a crease pattern are *equivalent* if their corresponding partitions P and P^* are such that $gP = P^*$ for some $g \in G$. If the correspondence of flat-foldability types to the colors is fixed, then the two equivalent colorings lead to two crease patterns with MV-assignments such that one can be obtained from the other by g. The MV-assignments to the crease pattern characterize the flat origami; consequently the resulting crystallographic flat origami arising from these colorings are *equivalent*.

Consider the two colorings of CP 6^3 shown in Figure 3(a) and 3(b). The first coloring corresponds to the partition $\{H\{e, a\}, H\{a^2\}, H\{a^3, a^4\}, H\{a^5\}\}$ and the second to $\{H\{a, a^2\}, H\{a^3\}, H\{a^4, a^5\}, H\{e\}\}$, where $H = \langle x, y \rangle$. Note that for $a \in G$,

$$a\{H\{e, a\}, H\{a^2\}, H\{a^3, a^4\}, H\{a^5\}\} = \{aH\{e, a\}, aH\{a^2\}, aH\{a^3, a^4\}, aH\{a^5\}\}$$

$$= \{Ha\{e, a\}, Ha\{a^2\}, Ha\{a^3, a^4\}, Ha\{a^5\}\}$$

$$= \{H\{a, a^2\}, H\{a^3\}, H\{a^4, a^5\}, H\{e\}\}.$$

These two colorings are equivalent, giving rise to the equivalent crystallographic flat origami shown in Figures 2(e) and 3(e). It can be observed that the flat origami in Figure 3(e) can be obtained from Figure 2(e) under a 60° counterclockwise rotation.

The same decompositions of G may result in inequivalent crystallographic flat origami if we vary the correspondence of flat-foldability types to colors. For example, if we consider the decomposition $\{H\{e, a\}, H\{a^2\}, H\{a^3, a^4\}, H\{a^5\}\}$ of G and use the correspondence of colors and flat-foldability types given in Figure 5(b), then this assignment leads to the MV-assignment shown in Figure 5(a), which folds to the crystallographic flat origami in Figure 5(c). This flat origami is inequivalent to the flat origami in Figure 2(e), obtained using the same decomposition.

5. Conclusion and Outlook

In this work, we considered an unassigned crease pattern that is the orbit of its generating unit s under a plane crystallographic group G. We construct its MV-assignment that results in a crystallographic flat origami, where there are altogether four flat-foldability types of s assigned to the units of the crease pattern. To arrive at such an MV-assignment, we determine an H-invariant partition (coloring) of G that consists of four elements (colors), where H is a plane crystallographic subgroup of G. We then arrive at different cases of constructing the partition of G using four colors, which are given in Theorem 3.2. These cases provide a systematic way of constructing crystallographic flat origami with four flat-foldability types of the generating unit. The crystallographic flat origami we obtain is invariant under a plane crystallographic group.

We use the partitions associated to two crease patterns to determine whether the resulting crystallographic flat origami are equivalent or inequivalent. The results given here can be extended to the general construction of crystallographic flat origami that has r flat-foldability types of the generating unit in the crease pattern.

As a next step in the research, one can also explore the color symmetry approach in constructing crystallographic flat origami from various crease patterns that can be derived from certain algorithms such as the weave and the star method in [Verrill 98] It will also be interesting to look at three-dimensional origami in the context of crystallographic groups and color symmetry theory. Moreover, one can also study the notion of iso-area crystallographic flat origami [Maekawa 02] It would also be worthwhile studying a method of constructing flat origami that results in a nonperiodic folded pattern.

References

[Barreto 97] Paulo Barreto. "Lines Meeting on a Surface: The 'Mars' Paperfolding." In *Origami Science and Art: Proceedings of the Second International Meeting of Origami Science and Scientific Origami*, edited by Koryo Miura, pp. 343–359. Shiga, Japan: Seian University of Art and Design, 1997.

[Bateman 02] Alex Bateman. "Computer Tools and Algorithms for Origami Tessellation Design." In *Origami^3: Proceedings of the Third International Meeting of Origami Science, Mathematics, and Education*, edited by Thomas Hull, pp. 121–127. Natick, MA: A K Peters, Ltd., 2002. MR1955754 (2003h:00017)

[Bern and Hayes 96] Marshall Bern and Barry Hayes. "The Complexity of Flat Origami." In *Proceedings of the Seventh Annual ACM-SIAM Symposium on Discrete Algorithms*, pp. 175–183. New York: ACM Press, 1996. MR1381938 (97c:52016)

[De las Peñas et al. 99] Ma. Louise Antonette De las Peñas, Rene Felix, and Maria Veronica Quilinguin. "Analysis of Colored Symmetrical Patterns." *RIMS Kokyuroku* 1109 (1999), 152–162. MR1754421

[Demaine and O'Rourke 07] Erik Demaine and Joseph O'Rourke. *Geometric Folding Algorithms: Linkages, Origami, Polyhedra*. Cambridge, UK: Cambridge University Press, 2007. MR2354878 (2008g:52001)

[Fujimoto 82] Shuzo Fujimoto. *Seizo Soru Origami Asobi no Shotai (Creative Invitation to Paper Play)*. Tokyo: Asahi Culture Center, 1982.

[Hull 02] Thomas Hull. "The Combinatorics of Flat Folds: A Survey." In *Origami^3: Proceedings of the Third International Meeting of Origami Science, Mathematics, and Education*, edited by Thomas Hull, pp. 29–38. Natick, MA: A K Peters, Ltd., 2002. MR1955757 (2004c:52030)

[Kawasaki 05] Toshikazu Kawasaki. *Roses, Origami & Math*. Tokyo: Japan Publications Trading Co., 2005.

[Kawasaki and Yoshida 88] Toshikazu Kawasaki and Masaaki Yoshida. "Crystallographic Flat Origamis." *Memoirs of the Faculty of Science, Kyushu University, Series A, Mathematics* 42:2 (1988), 153–157. MR963204 (89h:51020)

[Maekawa 02] Jun Maekawa. "The Definition of Iso-Area Folding." In *Origami^3: Proceedings of the Third International Meeting of Origami Science, Mathematics, and Education*, edited by Thomas Hull, pp. 53–59. Natick, MA: A K Peters, Ltd., 2002. MR1955759 (2004a:52011)

[Momotani 84] Yoshihide Momotani. "Wall." In *BOS Convention 1984 Autumn*. London: British Origami Society, 1984.

[Palmer 97] Chris Palmer. "Extruding and Tessellating Polygons from a Plane." In *Origami Science and Art: Proceedings of the Second International Meeting of Origami Science and Scientific Origami*, edited by Koryo Miura, pp. 323–331. Shiga, Japan: Seian University of Art and Design, 1997.

[Sales 00] Reamar Eileen Sales. "On Crystallographic Flat Origami." PhD dissertation, University of the Philippines Diliman, 2000.

[Schattschneider 78] Doris Schattschneider. "The Plane Symmetry Groups: Their Recognition and Notation." *American Mathematical Monthly* 85:6 (1978), 439–450. MR0477980 (57:17476)

[Verrill 98] Helena Verrill. "Origami Tessellations." In *Bridges: Mathematical Connections in Art, Music, and Science*, edited by Reza Sarhangi, pp. 55–68. Winfield, KS: Bridges Organization, 1998.

DEPARTMENT OF MATHEMATICS, ATENEO DE MANILA UNIVERSITY, QUEZON CITY, PHILIPPINES AND DEPARTMENT OF INFORMATION AND COMMUNICATION SCIENCES, SOPHIA UNIVERSITY, TOKYO, JAPAN
    E-mail address: mdelaspenas@ateneo.edu

DEPARTMENT OF MATHEMATICS AND PHYSICS, CENTRAL LUZON STATE UNIVERSITY, NUEVA ECIJA, PHILIPPINES
    E-mail address: eduardtaganap@gmail.com

DEPARTMENT OF MATHEMATICS AND COMPUTER SCIENCE, UNIVERSITY OF THE PHILIPPINES, BAGUIO CITY, PHILIPPINES
    E-mail address: tarapanut@yahoo.com

Symmetric Colorings of Polypolyhedra

sarah-marie belcastro and Thomas C. Hull

1. Introduction

Most origami practitioners are familiar with Hull's Five Intersecting Tetrahedra model [Hull 13] but fewer are familiar with Lang's 54 models that generalize this work [Lang 02] Lang terms these *polypolyhedra* because they are compounds of 1-skeleta (so there are many, or poly-, of them) that have polyhedral symmetries. Polypolyhedra are usually depicted with each component in a single color. Alternate colorings of polypolyhedra can highlight various, sometimes hidden, structures and symmetries related to the underlying polyhedral rotational symmetry group. Hull created a symmetric coloring of the Five Intersecting Tetrahedra that used six colors, each of which appeared on each of the five tetrahedra, and asked how many such colorings there are of the compound model. We answered this question (which turns out to be of primarily mathematical interest because the different colorings look quite similar to each other); then, belcastro wondered whether our analysis might extend to producing and counting symmetric colorings of Lang's polypolyhedra. The present work represents our findings.

2. Summary of Lang's Work

What exactly are the objects that we are coloring? They are nontrivial compounds of 1-skeleta, with the following properties [Lang 02]

- Each vertex has degree at least two. This excludes objects that are secretly piles of sticks.
- No two edges intersect except at vertices. This excludes objects such as the stella octangula (compound of two tetrahedra) and ensures that each edge may be made from a separate unit of paper.
- The compound is edge transitive; there exists a rotational symmetry of the compound mapping any given edge to any other given edge. Alternatively, there is only a single orbit of edges under the symmetry group action.
- Only tetrahedral (order 12), cuboctahedral (order 24), and icosidodecahedral (order 60) rotational symmetry groups are allowed.

It follows from edge-transitivity that there are at most two vertex orbits under the symmetry group action. Consider a sequence of group elements $g_1, \ldots, g_n$ acting on edge e to produce

2010 *Mathematics Subject Classification.* Primary 52B10; Secondary 52B15, 05A15.

Key words and phrases. polyhedra, coloring, modular origami.

The authors would like to thank Robert Lang for sharing the polypolyhedra Mathematica code that allowed us to produce the illustrations in this paper.

Name/Description	Symmetry Group	Vertex Transitivity	Variants
Five Intersecting Tetrahedra	icosidodecahedral	vertex transitive	n/a
five intersecting nonconvex hexahedra	icosidodecahedral	not vertex transitive	n/a
four intersecting bi-3-pyramids (no base edges)	cuboctahedral	not vertex transitive	2
five intersecting edge-dented tetrahedra	icosidodecahedral	not vertex transitive	2
ten intersecting bi-3-pyramids (no base edges)	icosidodecahedral	not vertex transitive	3
six intersecting bi-5-pyramids (no base edges)	icosidodecahedral	not vertex transitive	4
four interlaced triangles	cuboctahedral	vertex transitive	n/a
six interlaced pentagons	icosidodecahedral	vertex transitive	n/a
ten interlaced triangles	icosidodecahedral	vertex transitive	n/a
three interlaced squares	tetrahedral	not vertex transitive	n/a
four interlaced hexagons	cuboctahedral	not vertex transitive	n/a
six interlaced decagons	icosidodecahedral	not vertex transitive	n/a
ten interlaced hexagons	icosidodecahedral	not vertex transitive	n/a
four interlaced triangles	tetrahedral	vertex transitive	n/a
six interlaced squares	cuboctahedral	vertex transitive	2
eight interlaced triangles	cuboctahedral	vertex transitive	3
twelve interlaced pentagons	icosidodecahedral	vertex transitive	5
twenty interlaced triangles	icosidodecahedral	vertex transitive	23

TABLE 1. Lang's polypolyhedra; top part lists those with non-polygon components.

all n edges $g_1(e) = e_1, \ldots, g_n(e) = e_n$. Examine the orbits of the vertices v_1, v_2 of e under this sequence of actions; there are at most two distinct orbits generated.

Conspicuously missing from the list of properties is that the 1-skeleta are of two- or three-dimensional polytopes. This is because several of the 1-skeleta are nonconvex and many are not the skeleta of polytopes because it is not possible to induce 2-faces from the 1-skeleta. (These have skew polygon cycles bounding the areas that would visually indicate 2-faces.)

Lang used a comprehensive computer search to determine all possible types of polypolyhedra. Some types appear in several variants. Here is a straightforward way to think of the variants on a polypolyhedron type: View each component as a linkage, with hinges at the vertices and rods for edges. Now take the (radially) outermost vertices and push them toward the center. At some point, edges of different components will intersect; after passing through each other, the configuration has a different interlacing, and the set of these interlacings comprises the set of variants.

We list Lang's polypolyhedra in Table 1 with various symmetry properties noted, and we list first those that have non-polygon components.

3. Counting Symmetric Colorings of Polypolyhedra

We are interested in edge colorings of polypolyhedra that respect their underlying symmetry groups.

 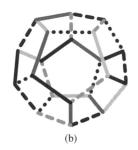 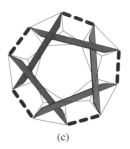

(a) (b) (c)

FIGURE 1. (a) The FIT inscribed in a dodecahedron, (b) the dodecahedron decomposed into matchings, and (c) a matching with corresponding bands highlighted (right).

DEFINITION 3.1. We call an edge coloring c of a polypolyhedron P a *symmetric coloring* if the action of any element of the underlying symmetry group either leaves all edges of a given color the same color or takes all edges of a given color to the set of edges of another color. That is, for the edges e_i in a fixed color class and g any element of the symmetry group, we have either $c(g(e_i)) = c(e_i)$ for all i or $c(g(e_i)) = c(g(e_j))$ exactly when $c(e_i) = c(e_j)$.

Because any action of the symmetry group takes one component of a polypolyhedron to another component, every component must use the same number of colors; thus, the number of colors must divide the number of edges in a component.

There always exists the symmetric coloring in which all edges of a component are the same color, and there is exactly one such coloring. At the other end of the spectrum, *rainbow colorings* have each edge of a component a different color.

We now carefully describe a particular type of symmetric coloring of the Five Intersecting Tetrahedra, and we note that this subsection serves as a model for how arguments will proceed in the remainder of this section.

3.1. Five Intersecting Tetrahedra (FIT). The FIT has icosidodecahedral rotational symmetry (group A_5) and thus may be inscribed in a dodecahedron, as shown in Figure 1(a). Every element of A_5 has order 1, 2, 3, or 5, corresponding to the identity and 2-fold, 3-fold, and 5-fold rotations around axes passing through antipodal dodecahedral edges, vertices, and faces, respectively. We may decompose the dodecahedron's edges into six non-perfect matchings; see Figure 1(b). The dodecahedron is trivially a polypolyhedron, and one can see by inspection that the edge-coloring given by the matching decomposition is a symmetric coloring.

DEFINITION 3.2. Given an edge e_i of the FIT considered as a vector in $\mathbb{R}^3$, find the 5-fold rotational axis a such that $e_i \cdot a$ is minimal. Consider any element $r_a \in A_5$ corresponding to a. The *band* generated by e_i is the orbit of e_i under r_a.

In Figure 1(c), we see that the edges that form a band in the FIT correspond to one of the six exhibited non-perfect matchings of the dodecahedron. Indeed, these non-perfect matchings can be defined in exactly the same way as bands, with corresponding matchings and bands sharing the same 5-fold rotational axis. We therefore refer to the matching corresponding to a band B as $M(B)$.

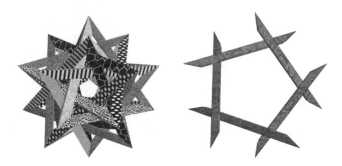

FIGURE 2. A symmetrically colored FIT (left) with an individual band forming a pentagonal circuit (right).

We may color the edges of the FIT in bands by repeatedly adding a color to an uncolored edge and generating the band corresponding to this edge. We refer to this FIT coloring as a *band coloring*. Because the bands are in correspondence with the dodecahedral matchings, and these matchings form a symmetric coloring, a band coloring is also a symmetric coloring.

Note that an individual tetrahedron has no 5-fold rotational symmetries, and so no two edges of a tetrahedron can belong to the same band; thus, a band coloring necessarily induces a rainbow coloring on each tetrahedron of an FIT. A band coloring is shown in Figure 2. Origami artist Denver Lawson also discovered band colorings of the FIT and displayed such a coloring at the 2012 Fall Convention of the British Origami Society.

3.1.1. *Counting band colorings of the FIT.* First, note that there are 60 different colorings for a rainbow edge-colored tetrahedron. Here is why: Fix the color of edge e_1, and note that there is one edge e_2 that is independent of e_1. There are then 5 color choices for e_2 and 4! color choices for the remaining 4 edges. However, this total of 120 overcounts by a factor of two because of the 2-fold rotational symmetry that fixes e_1 and e_2.

Second, note that while the FIT has symmetry group A_5, a single tetrahedron has symmetry group A_4.

THEOREM 3.3. *There are exactly 12 different band colorings of the FIT.*

PROOF 1 (TETRAHEDRAL). Edge-color one of the five tetrahedra, T, with one of the 60 possible rainbow edge-colorings. Consider an edge e_1 of T; it is part of a band $\{r_a^k(e_1)\}$, which determines an edge on each of the other four tetrahedra. Now consider a second edge e_2 of T with corresponding band $\{r_b^k(e_2)\}$. There is exactly one element $g \in A_4$ (and thus in A_5) such that $g(e_1) = e_2$, and thus $g(\{r_a^k(e_1)\}) = \{r_b^k(e_2)\}$ because the symmetries permute the bands. That is, the position of the e_2 band is determined and by the same reasoning so are the other bands. This produces 60 band colorings of the FIT, but we could have used any of the five tetrahedra as T. Thus, there are $60/5 = 12$ different FIT band colorings. □

PROOF 2 (BAND). Fix a band, $B_1 = \{r_a^k(e_1)\}$, and assign it a color. Fix a second band $B_2 = \{r_b^k(e_2)\}$; there are 5 colors that can be assigned to this band, but we could have chosen any of the 5 remaining bands to be B_2, so this does not affect the total number of

FIGURE 3. The cube (left) and tetrahedron (right) with matchings highlighted.

colorings. There are 4! ways to color the remaining 4 bands. However, $M(B_1)$ contains a dodecahedron edge opposite to an edge of $M(B_2)$ (see Figure 1(b)). Therefore, there exists $g \in A_5$ of order 2 such that B_1, B_2 are both invariant under action of g. Thus, there are $4!/2 = 12$ different ways to color the remaining bands and 12 different band colorings of the FIT.   □

PROOF 3 (BURNSIDE). Burnside's Lemma states that if G acts on S, then the number of orbits of the action is $\frac{1}{|G|} \sum_{g \in G} |\{s \in S \mid g(s) = s\}|$. Here, $G = A_5$ and S is the set of $6! = 720$ possible band colorings. No element of A_5 fixes any element of S, except for the identity $e \in A_5$ that fixes all $s \in S$. Thus, there are $720/60 = 12$ orbits of A_5 on S. Each orbit contains colorings that are equivalent under some symmetry in A_5, and thus there are 12 distinct FIT band colorings.   □

3.2. Generalizations from the FIT. The FIT is a remarkably symmetric polypoly-hedron, even among polypolyhedra. Each band has two properties: (a) it corresponds to a matching in the dodecahedron graph, and (b) the edge units in the band sequentially touch each other and form a visual cycle around the model. As we will see, these two proper-ties do not coincide for sets of edge units in other polypolyhedra. Thus, we investigate two types of symmetric polypolyhedra edge colorings: *matching* edge colorings and *visual band* edge colorings.

3.2.1. *Matching colorings.* A matching coloring descends directly from the under-lying symmetry group, so matching colorings always exist and counting such colorings will proceed analogously to the proofs given for the FIT in Section 3.1.1. In this way, we only need to make a one-to-one correspondence between polyhedral matchings and sets of polypolyhedral edges in order to quickly know the number of matching edge colorings.

Analogous to our matching decomposition of the dodecahedron, there is a decompo-sition of the cube (rotational symmetry group S_4) into four non-perfect matchings, each with three edges; see Figure 3 (left). Coloring this configuration properly requires four colors. We will compute the number of different colorings as Proof 2 (bands) above. Fix a matching M_1 and assign it a color. Choose a second matching M_2; assignment of color to M_2 does not affect the total number of colorings. There are 2! ways to color the other two matchings. Because M_1 contains an edge opposite to an edge of M_2, there exists $g \in S_4$ of order 2 such that M_1 and M_2 are both invariant under action of g. Thus, there is only $2!/2 = 1$ way to color these matchings of the cube. Alternatively, we could use Burnside's Lemma. Only the identity in S_4 leaves all $4! = 24$ colorings of the matchings invariant. Thus, there is only $24/24 = 1$ way to color such matchings.

The self-dual tetrahedron *only* decomposes into three perfect matchings, each with two edges; see Figure 3 (right). There are $3! = 6$ possible ways to color these matchings. All of these colorings remain fixed under the identity transformation and the three 2-fold

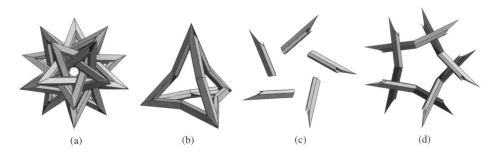

(a)   (b)   (c)   (d)

FIGURE 4. (a) FIET variant A, with (b) a single component, (c) a single matching, and (d) a pair of matchings.

symmetries of the tetrahedron. The tetrahedral rotational symmetry group A_4 has order 12, and thus there are $(6 + 3 \cdot 6)/12 = 2$ different ways to color these matchings.

3.2.2. *Visual band colorings.* A visual band must have struts touching sequentially, so existence of a visual band coloring depends on the incidence relations between the poly-polyhedron struts. Thus, identifying and counting visual band colorings is somewhat idiosyncratic. In particular, the existence of visual band colorings varies depending on which variant of a polypolyhedron we consider. Moreover, we will often encounter non-proper visual band colorings. Consider, for example, a polypolyhedron with polygon components. Any visual band will be composed of edges from a single component, and this induces the unique monochromatic-component coloring.

3.3. Five Intersecting Edge-dented Tetrahedra (FIET). On each component of the FIET, the vertices form 3-pyramids (without base edges), so there are four "faces," each of which has six edges. The FIET has icosidodecahedral symmetry, and there are two polypolyhedral variants. (It is denoted 5-4-6 in Lang's nomenclature.) The two polypoly-hedral variants are substantially different: the components in one (A, see Figure 4) look like indented tetrahedra, while the components in the other (B, see Figure 5) correspond to severely edge-out-dented tetrahedra.

Variant A has a matching coloring but not a visual band coloring. Taking one edge from each component, we form a dodecahedral matching M. However, there is a second matching M' of the FIET corresponding to this same dodecahedral matching (see Figure 4(d)) and a total of 12 matchings. Given a coloring of the six dodecahedron matchings (one of the 12 that exist), there are $\binom{12}{6}$ ways to assign 6 (of 12) colors to the six matchings $M_1, ..., M_6$. Then, there are 6! ways to assign the remaining colors to the matchings $M'_1, ..., M'_6$. Thus, there are $12 \cdot \binom{12}{6} \cdot 6!$ colorings of this configuration of polypolyhedral matchings.

For variant B, a visual band B looks like a five-pointed star (see Figure 5(c)), with one peak (two edges) from each component. It corresponds to a dodecahedral matching $M(B)$, so a visual band coloring uses 6 colors per component, and there are 12 such colorings. The matching colorings of variant B are the same as in A.

3.4. Five Intersecting Nonconvex Hexahedra (FINH). Each component of the FINH has skew 4-sided faces (see Figure 6(b)). The FINH has icosidodecahedral symmetry. (It is denoted 5-6-4 in Lang's nomenclature.) The matchings are identical to those of FIET variant A, and so are the combinatorics. There are no visual bands.

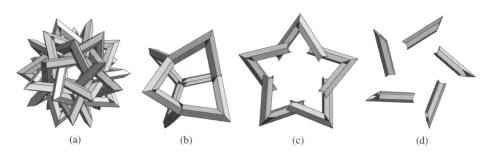

(a)   (b)   (c)   (d)

FIGURE 5. (a) The FIET variant B, with (b) a single component, (c) a visual band, and (d) a matching.

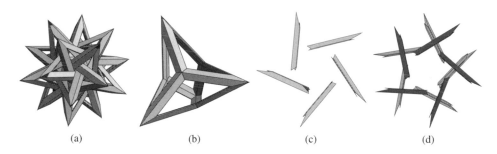

(a)   (b)   (c)   (d)

FIGURE 6. (a) The FINH, with (b) a single component, (c) a single matching, and (d) a pair of matchings.

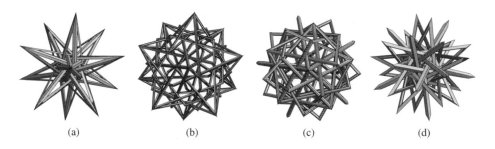

(a)   (b)   (c)   (d)

FIGURE 7. The SIB5P (a) variant A1, (b) variant A2, (c) variant B1, and (d) variant B2.

3.5. Six Intersecting Bi-5-pyramids without base edges (SIB5P). Each component of the SIB5P has five 4-sided "faces." The SIB5P has icosidodecahedral symmetry, and there are four polypolyhedral variants (denoted 6-5-4 in Lang's nomenclature). The four polypolyhedral variants form two pairs that are substantially different: the components in one pair (A1 and A2, see Figure 7 (a, b)) have 5-valent vertices visually prominent, while the components in the other (B1 and B2, see Figure 7(c, d)) have 2-valent vertices that are visually prominent. However, the combinatorics of coloring the four variants are all the same.

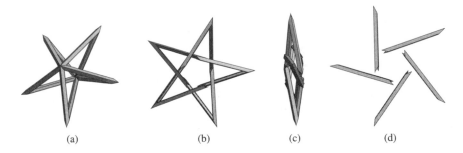

FIGURE 8. (a) The SIB5P component, (b) false visual band in variant B2,
(c) falseness of visual band in variant B2, and (d) a single matching.

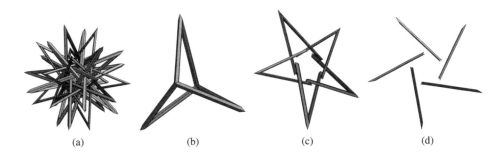

FIGURE 9. (a) The TIB3P variant A, with (b) a single component, (c) a
visual band, and (d) a single matching.

There is no visual band coloring of an A1 or A2 variant; a visual band would need
to use two of the five edges at a vertex, and as 2 does not divide 5, this would not extend
to a symmetric coloring. Consider instead variants B1 and B2. While there is a visual
five-pointed star formed by pairs of edges incident to 2-valent vertices, the pairs are not
incident and thus do not form a visual band (see Figure 8).

However, there is a matching coloring. The matchings (shown in Figure 8) are identical to those of FIET variant A, and so are the combinatorics.

3.6. Ten Intersecting Bi-3-pyramids without base edges (TIB3P). Each component of the TIB3P has three 4-sided "faces." The TIB3P has icosidodecahedral symmetry,
and there are three polypolyhedral variants. (It is denoted 10-3-4 in Lang's nomenclature.)

The three polypolyhedral variants are substantially different: the components in two
(A and B, see Figures 9 and 10) look like glued-together **Y**s, while the components in the
third (C, see Figure 11) look like sparse whisks.

Variants A and C have visual band colorings (see Figures 9 and 11), but variant B does
not. The visual bands have the same combinatorics as the FIET's visual band colorings. Of
course, all three variants have matching colorings. In this case, the components each use
six colors on six edges and have the same combinatorics as the FIT band colorings; thus,
there are 12 matching colorings.

3.7. Four Intersecting Bi-3-pyramids without base edges (FIB3P). Each component of the FIB3P has three 4-sided "faces." The FIB3P has cuboctahedral symmetry, and

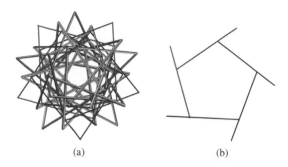

FIGURE 10. (a) The TIB3P variant B, with (b) a single matching.

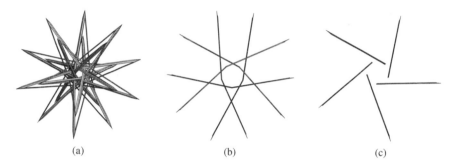

FIGURE 11. (a) The TIB3P variant A, with (b) a visual band and (c) a single matching.

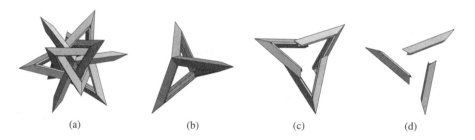

FIGURE 12. (a) The FIB3P variant A, with (b) a single component, (c) a band, and (d) a single matching.

there are two polypolyhedral variants. (It is denoted 4-3-4 in Lang's nomenclature.) The two polypolyhedral variants are substantially different: the components in one (A, see Figure 12) look like glued-together **Y**s, while the components in the other (B, see Figure 13) look like sparse whisks.

Variant A has visual bands as well as matchings (see Figure 12). The visual bands B are composed of two consecutive struts from each of three components and so correspond to a 3-edge matching $M(B)$ in the symmetry cube. Thus, there is only one visual band coloring (see Section 3.2.1). The matchings come in pairs to form the visual bands.

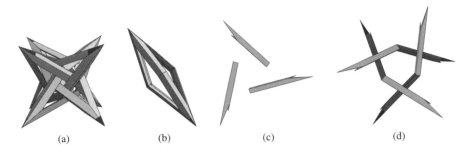

(a)   (b)   (c)   (d)

FIGURE 13. (a) The FIB3PT variant B, with (b) a single component, (c) a single matching, and (d) a pair of matchings.

Following the FIET argument, we have eight matchings, $\binom{8}{4}$ ways of assigning four colors to one matching in each pair, and 4! ways of assigning the remaining colors; so, there are $\binom{8}{4} \cdot 4!$ matching colorings in total.

In variant B, the whisk apices point to the vertices of a bounding cube. It has a matching coloring (see Figure 13) but no visual band coloring, as a visual band coloring would require using two struts of the same color at each 3-valent vertex. Even though there are no visual bands, the matchings come in pairs (see Figure 13(d)) so the combinatorics are the same as for variant A.

3.8. Colorings of the polypolyhedra with polygon components. When the components of a polypolyhedron are polygons, we easily obtain a visual band coloring where each component is monochromatic (see Section 3.2.2). There are other symmetric matching colorings where each component is rainbow colored. We will not go into the details, but the combinatorics of such examples is exactly the same as other examples already described.

4. Conclusions and Further Work

There are more symmetric colorings of polypolyhedra than described in this paper:

(1) There is a symmetric rainbow coloring of the components of the SIB5P that requires 10 colors.
(2) In the FIT there is a non-band set of edges, with *maximal* dot product to a 5-fold symmetry axis, that corresponds to the same dodecahedral matching as a band; this extends to a symmetric coloring of the FIT.
(3) The FIT also has a symmetric coloring that corresponds to a decomposition of the dodecahedron into 10 matchings that each have 3-fold symmetry.

Similar analysis as performed above can be done on these symmetric colorings. Other interesting questions abound. Are there other numbers of colors/matchings that can lead to symmetric colorings of polypolyhedra? What do the 23 variations of the 20 interlaced triangles have to offer?

There are also relationships between symmetric polypolyhedral colorings. Looking closely at the symmetric colorings of polypolyhedra with polygon components leads to the discovery of a *duality* between polyhedron-component polypolyhedra and polygon-component polypolyhedra. This will be described in a future paper (stay tuned!).

References

[Hull 13] Thomas Hull. *Project Origami: Activities for Exploring Mathematics*, Second Edition. Boca Raton, FL: A K Peters/CRC Press, 2013. MR2987362

[Lang 02] Robert J. Lang. "Polypolyhedra in Origami." In *Origami³: Proceedings of the Third International Meeting of Origami Science, Mathematics, and Education*, edited by Thomas Hull, pp. 153–167. Natick, MA: A K Peters, 2002.

MATHILY AND SMITH COLLEGE, NORTHAMPTON, MASSACHUSETTS
E-mail address: smbelcas@toroidalsnark.net

DEPARTMENT OF MATHEMATICS, WESTERN NEW ENGLAND UNIVERSITY, SPRINGFIELD, MASSACHUSETTS
E-mail address: thull@wne.edu

II. Mathematics of Origami: Constructibility

Geometric and Arithmetic Relations Concerning Origami

Jordi Guàrdia and Eulàlia Tramuns

1. Introduction

The determination of constructible numbers with origami is a problem with an interesting development, which was completely solved only after the axiomatization proposed by Huzita and Justin [Huzita 91, Brill 84]).

The work by Alperin and Lang [Alperin and Lang 09] proved that the list of possible one-fold axioms was complete and settled a new scenario, where the role of new axioms was still emphasized. The axiomatic viewpoint seems a natural perspective for the study of other geometrical instruments and may lead to solving theoretical problems, as in [Uehara 10].

In this work we present a general-purpose formal language for the axiomatization of geometrical instruments. Our formalization takes into account both the geometric and arithmetic properties of the instruments: the concept of *tool* formalizes an instrument as a set of axioms, while the concept of *map* formalizes the constructible points and curves of the instrument. Our formalization provides a natural frame to express well-known results, but it also leads to new relations between instruments.

The key concepts of our language are introduced in Section 2. In Section 3, we define *geometric equivalence* and *virtual equivalence of tools* and prove relations between the tools described in this work. In Section 4, we present an equivalence relation between maps and define an *arithmetical equivalence of tools*. We conclude with an arithmetic classification of the tools described.

A more extended version of this work can be found in [Tramuns 12] as an evolution of a previous work [Tramuns 11].

2. Definitions

2.1. Axioms.

DEFINITION 2.1. A *construction axiom* **C** is an elementary geometric process that generates a finite ordered set of curves from a nonempty, finite, and ordered set of points and curves.

An *intersection axiom* **I** is a an elementary geometric process that generates a finite ordered set of points from a nonempty, finite and ordered set of curves and points.

The first author is partially supported by MTM2012-34611 from Spanish MEC..
The second author is partially supported by MTM2011-28800-C02-01 from Spanish MEC.

The notation we will use for axioms is $O_1, O_2, \ldots, O_r = \textbf{AxiomName}(I_1, I_2, \ldots, I_s)$, where the I_j are the given curves and points and the O_i are the elements generated by the axiom.

We collect in the appendix (Section 6) a list of basic axioms that formalize the common tasks performed by the geometric instruments that will be considered in this work (mainly ruler, compass, and origami). A more comprehensive list of axioms can be found in [Tramuns 12].

We will assume that the input objects appearing in an axiom are in a generic position that guarantees the existence of the output objects. Since we are only concerned with feasible geometric constructions, this is a natural assumption.

2.2. Tools. We formalize geometric instruments in terms of their capabilities, i.e., by means of the axioms they can perform.

DEFINITION 2.2. A *tool* T is a couple $\langle C, I \rangle$, where C is a nonempty finite set of construction axioms and I is a nonempty finite set of intersection axioms.

Here are some basic examples of tools:

- *Ruler:*
$$\mathcal{R} := \langle \{\textbf{Line}\}, \{\textbf{LineIntersect}\} \rangle,$$

- *Compass:*
$$C := \langle \{\textbf{Circle}, \textbf{RadiusCircle}\}, \{\textbf{CircleIntersect}\} \rangle,$$

- *Ruler and compass:*
$$\mathcal{RC} := \langle \{\textbf{Line}, \textbf{Circle}, \textbf{RadiusCircle}\},$$
$$\{\textbf{LineIntersect}, \textbf{CircleIntersect}, \textbf{LineCircleIntersect}\} \rangle,$$

- *Euclidean compass:*
$$\mathcal{EC} := \langle \{\textbf{Circle}\}, \{\textbf{CircleIntersect}\} \rangle,$$

- *Ruler and Euclidean compass:*
$$\mathcal{REC} := \langle \{\textbf{Line}, \textbf{Circle}\},$$
$$\{\textbf{LineIntersect}, \textbf{CircleIntersect}, \textbf{LineCircleIntersect}\} \rangle,$$

- *Origami:*
$$O := \langle \{\textbf{Line}, \textbf{PerpendicularBisector}, \textbf{Bisector}, \textbf{Perpendicular}, \textbf{Tangent},$$
$$\textbf{CommonTangent}, \textbf{PerpendicularTangent}\}, \{\textbf{LineIntersect}\} \rangle,$$

- *Thalian origami* [Alperin 00]*:*
$$\mathcal{TO} := \langle \{\textbf{Line}, \textbf{PerpendicularBisector}\}, \{\textbf{LineIntersect}\} \rangle,$$

- *Pythagorean origami* [Alperin 00]*:*
$$\mathcal{PO} := \langle \{\textbf{Line}, \textbf{PerpendicularBisector}, \textbf{Bisector}\}, \{\textbf{LineIntersect}\} \rangle,$$

- *Conics* [Videla 97]*:*
$$CO := \langle \{\textbf{Line}, \textbf{Circle}, \textbf{RadiusCircle}, \textbf{Conic}\}, \{\textbf{LineIntersect},$$
$$\textbf{CircleIntersect}, \textbf{LineCircleIntersect}, \textbf{ConicLineIntersect},$$
$$\textbf{ConicCircleIntersect}, \textbf{ConicIntersect}\} \rangle.$$

2.3. Constructions.

DEFINITION 2.3. A *construction* of a set of points and lines V from U_0 is a finite sequence

$$C(U_0; V) = \{O_1 = A_1(U_1), ..., O_n = A_n(U_n)\},$$

where

- U_0 is an initial ordered nonempty set of points and curves;
- $A_1, \ldots, A_n$ are axioms;
- every U_k is a subset of $U_0 \cup \cdots \cup U_{k-1} \cup O_1 \cup \cdots \cup O_{k-1}$;
- $V \subset O_1 \cup \cdots \cup O_n$, but $V \not\subset O_1 \cup \cdots \cup O_{n-1}$.

We say that $C(U_0; V)$ is a construction with the tool $\mathcal{E} = \langle C, I \rangle$ if $A_1, \ldots, A_k \in C \cup I$, and we write $C(U_0; V) \in \mathcal{E}$ in this case.

REMARK 2.4. Any construction can be interpreted as a sequence of simple steps $O_k = A_k(U_k)$. In every step, a set of output objects is generated from a subset U_k of the set of previously generated object.

NOTATION. To simplify the notation, we enumerate the elements of the sets U_0, V in a single list, using a semicolon to separate the last element of U_0 and the first of V.

EXAMPLE 2.5. Given a line ℓ and a point P not on ℓ, the construction **Parallel** generates a line ℓ_2 parallel to the line ℓ passing through the point P:

$$\textbf{Parallel}(P, \ell; \ell_2) = \{\, \ell_1 = \textbf{Perpendicular}(\ell, P),$$
$$\ell_2 = \textbf{Perpendicular}(\ell_1, P)\,\}.$$

Clearly **Parallel**$(P, \ell; \ell_2) \in O$.

A wide catalog of constructions is given in [Tramuns 12].

2.4. Maps.

DEFINITION 2.6. A *map* is a pair $\mathbf{M} = (\mathcal{E}, \mathcal{U}_0)$ composed by a tool $\mathcal{E}$ and a nonempty finite *initial set* $\mathcal{U}_0$ of points and curves.

NOTATION. Given a set U of points and curves, we will write $U = [C, P]$ to specify its subset C of curves and its subset P of points.

DEFINITION 2.7. Let $\mathbf{M} = (\mathcal{E}, \mathcal{U}_0)$ be a map with $\mathcal{E} = \langle C, I \rangle$. The *sequence of layers* $\mathcal{U}_n = \{[\mathfrak{C}_n, \mathfrak{P}_n]\}_{n \in \mathbb{N}}$ is the sequence defined by

(1) $\mathcal{U}_0 = [\mathfrak{C}_0, \mathfrak{P}_0]$;

(2) $\mathfrak{C}_n$, which is the union of $\mathfrak{C}_{n-1}$ with the set of curves obtained by applying all construction axioms from C in all possible ways to the elements of $\mathcal{U}_{n-1}$;

(3) $\mathfrak{P}_n$, which is the union of $\mathfrak{P}_{n-1}$ with the set of points that is obtained applying all intersection axioms from I in all possible ways to the elements of $[\mathfrak{C}_n, \mathfrak{P}_{n-1}]$.

We write $\mathcal{U}^{\mathbf{M}} = [\mathfrak{C}^{\mathbf{M}}, \mathfrak{P}^{\mathbf{M}}] := \cup_{n=0}^{\infty} \mathcal{U}_n$ to denote the *set of constructible points and curves with* $\mathbf{M}$. A map is *infinite* if $\mathcal{U}^{\mathbf{M}}$ is infinite.

Table 1 describes the set of constructible points of the tools introduced in the previous section. As usual, $\mathbb{P}$ denotes the Pythagorean closure of $\mathbb{Q}$ (i.e., the smallest extension of $\mathbb{Q}$ where every sum of two squares is a square); the field of Euclidean numbers (i.e., the smallest subfield of $\overline{\mathbb{Q}}$ closed under square roots) is denoted by $\mathscr{C}$; and $\mathscr{O}$ is the field of origami numbers (i.e., the smallest subfield of $\overline{\mathbb{Q}}$ that is closed under the operations of taking square roots, cubic roots, and complex conjugation).

Map	Initial set	$\mathfrak{P}^M$	References
Ruler	$\{1, 2, i, 2i\}$	$\mathbb{Q}(i)$	[Martin 98, page 79]
Compass	$\{0, 1\}$	$\mathscr{C}$	[Martin 98, Chapter 3]
Ruler and compass	$\{0, 1\}$	$\mathscr{C}$	[Cox 04, page 261]
Euclidean compass	$\{0, 1\}$	$\mathscr{C}$	[Martin 98, page 7]
Ruler and Euclidean compass	$\{0, 1\}$	$\mathscr{C}$	[Martin 98, page 7]
Origami	$\{0, 1\}$	$\mathscr{O}$	[Alperin 00]
Pythagorean Origami	$\{0, 1\}$	$\mathbb{P}(i)$	[Alperin 00, Theorem 3.3]
Conics	$\{0, 1\}$	$\mathscr{O}$	[Videla 97]

TABLE 1. Sets $\mathfrak{P}^M$ for different maps

For a description of the set of constructible points of the Thalian origami map, see [Alperin 00, Theorem 3.3].

3. Geometric Relations between Tools

Since we have defined tools in terms of their capabilities, it is natural to classify them according to this philosophy. We will consider the arithmetic capabilities in the next section, and we concentrate now on the geometric capabilities. It seems reasonable to say that two tools are equivalent if they can solve the same problems, but this has to be carefully defined. For instance, the second problem of Euclid is normally formulated as follows: Given three points A, B, C in general position, one has to determine a point D such that the segments AD and BC are congruent. Clearly, the point D is not uniquely determined, and indeed, there exist several different constructions generating different solution points. This kind of situation leads to the introduction of the following definition.

DEFINITION 3.1. We say that the constructions $C(U_0; V)$ and $C'(U_0; V')$ are *equivalent*, $C(U_0; V) \sim C'(U_0'; V')$, if V and V' have the same geometric links with U_0.

A *problem* $P(U_0; V)$ is an equivalence class of constructions under this relation.

A *solution* of the problem $P(U_0; V)$ is any representant of this equivalence class, that is, any construction $C(U_0; V)$ of V from U_0.

A problem can be solved with $\mathcal{E}$ if it has a solution $C(U_0; V) \in \mathcal{E}$.

DEFINITION 3.2. The tool $\mathcal{E}$ generates the tool $\mathcal{E}'$, $\mathcal{E} \multimap \mathcal{E}'$, if any problem that can be solved with $\mathcal{E}'$ can also be solved with $\mathcal{E}$. Two tools $\mathcal{E}$ and $\mathcal{E}'$ are *geometrically equivalent*, $\mathcal{E} \multimap\!\!\circ \mathcal{E}'$, if they solve the same problems.

Obviously, if the set of axioms of a tool $\mathcal{E}'$ is a subset of the axioms of the tool $\mathcal{E}$, then $\mathcal{E} \multimap \mathcal{E}'$. Hence, we have the following relations:

$$CO \multimap \mathcal{RC} \multimap \mathcal{REC} \multimap \mathcal{R};$$

$$O \multimap \mathcal{PO} \multimap \mathcal{TO} \multimap \mathcal{R}.$$

PROPOSITION 3.3. *The tool $\mathcal{TO}$ does not generate the tools $\mathcal{PO}$ or O.*

PROOF. It is enough to see that $\mathcal{TO}$ does not generate $\mathcal{PO}$. Let us suppose we have two perpendicular lines and their point of intersection constructed. With the tool $\mathcal{PO}$ and the use of axiom **Bisector**, we can construct the bisectors of these couple of lines. However, with the tool $\mathcal{TO}$, we can construct neither a new line nor a new point. □

While it is evident that the compass C does not generate the ruler and compass $\mathcal{RC}$ because it cannot construct lines, both tools generate the same points from the initial set $\{0, 1\}$. To describe this situation in a more general setting, we introduce the following definitions.

DEFINITION 3.4. A *construction of points with points* (CPP) is a construction $CPP(U_0; V)$ where U_0 and V contain only points.

DEFINITION 3.5. The tool $\mathcal{E}$ *generates virtually* the tool $\mathcal{E}'$, $\mathcal{E} :- \mathcal{E}'$, if any CPP with $\mathcal{E}'$ is equivalent to a construction with $\mathcal{E}$. The tools $\mathcal{E}$ and $\mathcal{E}'$ are *virtually equivalents*, $\mathcal{E} :-: \mathcal{E}'$, if $\mathcal{E} :- \mathcal{E}'$ and $\mathcal{E}' :- \mathcal{E}$.

As mentioned before, the compass C does not generate the ruler and compass $\mathcal{RC}$ but does generate virtually it.

THEOREM 3.6. *The origami tool O generates virtually the ruler and Euclidean compass tool $\mathcal{REC}$.*

PROOF. It is enough to describe constructions of the intersection of a line with a circle and of the intersection of two circles with O. We can find them in [Geretschlager 95]. □

As a more advanced example of construction, we describe the intersection of a circle and a line in our formal language. The construction **LineCircleIntersectOrigami** $(A, B, C, D; E, F)$ generates the intersection points of the line through the points A and B with the circle with center C passing through D.

This construction requires the point C to be exterior to the parabola with focus D and the directrix to be the line through A and B. Thus,

$$\mathbf{LineCircleIntersectOrigami}(A, B, C, D; E, F) = \{\ell_1 = \mathbf{Line}(A, B),$$
$$\ell_2, \ell_3 = \mathbf{Tangent}(\ell_1, D, C),$$
$$\ell_4 = \mathbf{Perpendicular}(\ell_2, D),$$
$$\ell_5 = \mathbf{Perpendicular}(\ell_3, D),$$
$$E = \mathbf{LineIntersect}(\ell_1, \ell_4),$$
$$F = \mathbf{LineIntersect}(\ell_1, \ell_5)\}.$$

Figure 1 summarizes the main relations between tools.

4. Arithmetic Relations between Maps and Tools

DEFINITION 4.1. The maps **M** and **M'** are *equivalent* if $\mathfrak{P}^{\mathbf{M}} = \mathfrak{P}^{\mathbf{M'}}$.

Figure 2 shows the relations between sets of points of maps of Table 1.

DEFINITION 4.2. Two tools $\mathcal{E}, \mathcal{E}'$ are *arithmetically equivalent*, $\mathcal{E} \overset{\text{ar}}{\longleftrightarrow} \mathcal{E}'$, if there exist finite sets of points $\mathcal{U}_0, \mathcal{U}_0'$ such that
   (1) The maps $\mathbf{M} = (\mathcal{E}, \mathcal{U}_0)$ and $\mathbf{M}' = (\mathcal{E}', \mathcal{U}_0')$ are infinite and equivalent.
   (2) The construction of the set $\mathcal{U}^{\mathbf{M}}$ (respectively, $\mathcal{U}^{\mathbf{M'}}$) needs the application of all the axioms of $\mathcal{E}$ (respectively, $\mathcal{E}'$).

In order to determine whether two given tools are arithmetically equivalent, two different approaches can be taken: One can consider the geometric properties of the tools, or one can associate particular maps to the tools and relate them. The following results illustrate these ideas.

THEOREM 4.3 (Mohr-Mascheroni). *The tools C and $\mathcal{RC}$ are arithmetically equivalent.*

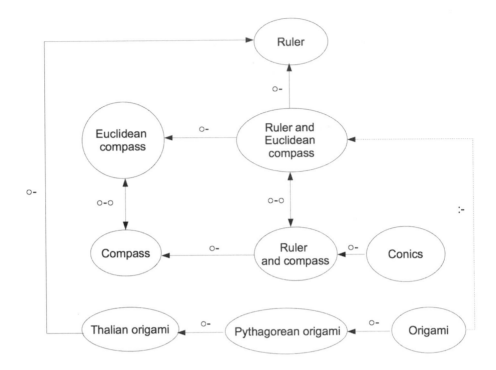

FIGURE 1. Geometric relations between tools.

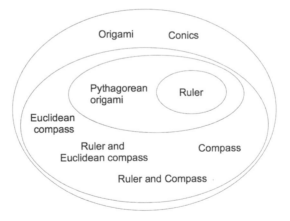

FIGURE 2. Equivalence relations between maps.

PROOF. The first step consists in proving that we obtain the same points with $\mathcal{RC}$ as with doing inversions of points respect to circles. Then, we have to prove that any point obtained from an inversion respect to a circle can be constructed with C in a finite, arbitrarily high, number of steps. The details can be found in [Tramuns 12]. □

THEOREM 4.4 (Poncelet-Steiner). *The maps* **RC** *and*

RP $:= (\langle\{\textbf{Line}\}, \{\textbf{LineIntersect}, \textbf{LineUnitCircleIntersect}\}\rangle, \mathcal{U}_0 = \{0, 2, 2i, X^2 + Y^2 = 1\}).$

are equivalent.

PROOF. Of course, a totally geometric proof can be given [Hartshorne 00, page 192], but we present here an arithmetic proof in our language, following [Martin 98, page 98]. It is clear that $1, i \in \mathfrak{P}^{RP}$, and thus $\mathbb{Q}(i) = \mathfrak{P}^R \subset \mathfrak{P}^{RP} \subset \mathfrak{P}^{RC} = \mathscr{C}$. Because $\mathscr{C}$ is the smallest extension of $\mathbb{Q}$ closed under square roots, it is sufficient to see that $\mathfrak{P}^{RP}$ is closed under square roots. The construction of the square roots of a complex number reduces to the construction of the bisector of two lines through the origin and the construction of the square root of a positive real number.

Given two points $A, B \in \mathfrak{P}^{RP}$ on the unit circle, let C be the second point of intersection of the diameter through A with the unit circle. Then, the angle AOB is twice the angle OCB. The equality

$$\sqrt{r} = \left(\frac{r+1}{2}\right) \sqrt{1 - \left(\frac{r-1}{r+1}\right)^2}$$

shows that we only need the construction of the square root of numbers of the form $1 - c^2$ with $c \in (-1, 1)$, and this consists of constructing a point on the circle having $1 - c^2$ as a x-coordinate. This can be done constructing the perpendicular to the x-axis through point $1 - c^2$. An example of the construction of this perpendicular is described in [Martin 98, pages 79–80]. $\square$

Finally, using the sets of constructible points of maps in Table 1, we can deduce the following relations.

THEOREM 4.5 (Arithmetical Classification of Tools).

(1) $C \xleftrightarrow{\text{ar}} \mathcal{RC} \xleftrightarrow{\text{ar}} \mathcal{EC} \xleftrightarrow{\text{ar}} \mathcal{REC}.$

(2) $O \xleftrightarrow{\text{ar}} CO.$

5. Conclusions

We have introduced a new formal language and illustrated it with the most common geometric instruments, even though a more extended study can be found in [Tramuns 12]. Some of the instruments presented there, such as the marked ruler or the marked ruler and compass, require a precise description of the *neusis* process and lead to interesting axioms, involving curves such as the conchoid of Nicomedes or the Limaçon of Pascal.

The language proposed here has the advantage that it is open, in the sense that other instruments different than those we have considered can be studied and formalized in this way: It suffices to analyze the axioms they can perform and define them using curves and points. After that, the geometric and arithmetic relations between this instrument and other existing instruments can be studied.

Finally, another significant advantage of this language is the possibility of introducing virtual tools, that is, tools not necessarily attached to any physical instrument: we can choose some existing axioms and combine them to create a virtual tool. These kinds of tools can be both interesting on their own and useful as auxiliary resources for studying known instruments.

6. Appendix

Here is a list of axioms and their descriptions:

ℓ =**Line**(A, B): Line through points A, B.

c =**Circle**(A, B): Circle with center A through B.

c =**RadiusCircle**(A, B, C): Circle with center A and radius the distance BC.

ℓ_1, ℓ_2 =**Bisector**(ℓ, ℓ'): Bisectors of the angle formed by the lines ℓ and ℓ'.

ℓ =**PerpendicularBisector**(A, B): Perpendicular bisector of the segment AB.

ℓ' =**Perpendicular**(ℓ, P): Line perpendicular to line ℓ passing through point P.

ℓ =**PointPerpendicular**(A, B, C): Line perpendicular to the segment AB through C.

ℓ_1, ℓ_2 =**Tangent**(ℓ, F, A): Tangents through A to the parabola with directrix ℓ and focus F.

ℓ_1, ℓ_2, ℓ_3 =**CommonTangent**(ℓ, F, ℓ', F'): Common tangents to the parabola with directrix ℓ and focus F and the parabola with directrix ℓ' and focus F'.

ℓ =**PerpendicularTangent**(ℓ_1, F, ℓ_2): The tangent line to the parabola with directrix ℓ_1 and focus F that is perpendicular to the line ℓ_2.

c =**Conic**(ℓ, F, A, B): Conic with directrix ℓ, focus F and excentricity the distance between A and B.

P =**LineIntersect**(ℓ, ℓ'): Intersection point of lines ℓ and ℓ'.

P_1, P_2 =**CircleIntersect**(c, c'): Intersection points of circles c and c'.

P_1, P_2 =**LineCircleIntersect**(ℓ, c): Intersection points of line ℓ with circle c.

$P_1, ..., P_4$ =**ConicIntersect**(c, c'): Intersection points of conics c and c'.

P_1, P_2 =**LineConicIntersect**(ℓ, c): Intersection points of line ℓ with conic c.

$P_1, ..., P_4$ =**CircleConicIntersect**(c, c'): Intersection points of circle c with conic c'.

For the axioms generating several objects, one has to specify an ordering to properly identify each of them. When there is no natural ordering, we use a *radial sweep*, a common technique in computational geometry. It consists in sweeping counterclockwise the plane with a given half-line; the points are ordered in the order they are met. For the axioms described here, we propose the following ordering:

- **Bisector**: Line ℓ_1 bisects the oriented angle $\widehat{\ell\ell'}$ and line ℓ_2 bisects $\widehat{\ell'\ell}$.
- **Tangent**: The lines ℓ_1 and ℓ_2 are ordered following a radial sweep with center A and half-line AF.
- **CommonTangent**: The lines ℓ_1, ℓ_2, and ℓ_3 are ordered according to the order of their contact points with the first parabola in a radial sweep with center F and half-line FF'.
- **CircleIntersect**: Let C and C' be the centers of circles c and c', respectively. The order of points P_1 and P_2 is given by a radial sweep with center C and half-line CC'. We use the same criterion to order the output of axioms **ConicIntersect** and **CircleConicIntersect**, taking as the center of a conic the midpoint of the segment defined by the focus.
- **LineCircleIntersect**: If ℓ is not a diameter of circle c, we order P_1 and P_2 to assure that the angle $P_2 C P_1$ is positive. If the line is a diameter, we order points P_1 and P_2 as points on the line ℓ, using a radial sweep with center C and half-line CO. We use the same criterion to order the output of the axiom **LineConicIntersect**.

References

[Alperin 00] R. C. Alperin. "A Mathematical Theory of Origami Constructions and Numbers." *New York Journal of Mathematics* 6 (2000), 119–133. MR1772561 (2001g:51017)

[Alperin and Lang 09] R. C. Alperin and R. Lang. "One-, Two-, and Multi-Fold Origami Axioms." In *Origami⁴: Fourth International Meeting of Origami Science, Mathematics, and Education*, edited by Robert J. Lang, pp. 371–393. Wellesley, MA: A K Peters, 2009. MR2590565 (2011b:51030)

[Baragar 02] A. Baragar. "Constructions Using a Compass and Twice-Notched Straightedge." *The American Mathematical Monthly* 109 (2002), 151–164. MR1903152 (2003d:51015)

[Brill 84] D. Brill. "Asides: Justin's Angle Trisection." *British Origami* 107 (1984), 14–15.

[Cox 04] D. A. Cox. *Galois Theory*. Hoboken, NJ: Wiley, 2004. MR2119052 (2006a:12001)

[Geretschlager 95] R. Geretschlager. "Euclidean Constructions and the Geometry of Origami." *Mathematics Magazine* 68 (1995), 357–371. MR1365647 (96m:51024)

[Hartshorne 00] R. Hartshorne. *Geometry: Euclid and Beyond*. New York: Springer-Verlag, 2000. MR1761093 (2001h:51001)

[Huzita 91] H. Huzita. "Axiomatic Development of Origami Geometry." In *Proceedings of the First International Meeting of Origami Science and Technology*, edited by H. Huzita, pp. 143–158. Padova, Italy: Dipartimento di Fisica dell'Università di Padova, 1991.

[Martin 98] George E. Martin. *Geometric Constructions*. New York: Springer-Verlag, 1998. MR1483895 (98j:51032)

[Tramuns 11] E. Tramuns. "The Speed of Origami versus Other Construction Tools." In *Origami⁵: Fifth International Meeting of Origami Science, Mathematics, and Education*, edited by Patsy Wang-Iverson, Robert J. Lang, and Mark Yim, pp. 531–542. Boca Raton, FL: A K Peters/CRC Press, 2011. MR2866902

[Tramuns 12] E. Tramuns. "A Formalization of Geometric Constructions." PhD dissertation, Universitat Politècnica de Catalunya, 2012.

[Uehara 10] R. Uehara. "The Undecidability of Origami." Technical Report, IPSJ SIG, 2010-AL-131-11, 1–3, 2010.

[Videla 97] C. Videla. "On Points Constructible from Conics." *The Mathematical Intelligencer* 19 (1997), 53–57. MR1457448 (98h:01003)

DEPARTAMENT DE MATEMÀTICA, UNIVERSITAT POLITÈCNICA DE CATALUNYA, SPAIN
E-mail address: guardia@ma4.upc.edu

DEPARTAMENT DE MATEMÀTICA, UNIVERSITAT POLITÈCNICA DE CATALUNYA, SPAIN
E-mail address: etramuns@ma4.upc.edu

Abelian and Non-Abelian Numbers via 3D Origami

José Ignacio Royo Prieto and Eulàlia Tramuns

1. Introduction

1.1. The scope of origami folding axioms. A classical result of number theory (see, for example, [Cox 04, Corollary 10.1.7]) establishes that the set C of points constructed using compass and straightedge (CS for short) with initial set $\{0, 1\}$ is the smallest subfield of the complex plane $\mathbb{C}$ that is closed under the operation of taking square roots. Thus, constructions that involve solving cubic equations, such as the trisection of an arbitrary angle or finding the side length of a cube whose volume is the double of another given cube, are not possible in general using CS. More than two thousand years before those constructions were proven to be impossible by Pierre Wantzel, Archimedes found a verging construction (i.e., *neusis* construction) with a marked ruler that made it possible to trisect any given angle. So, the usage of new tools (formally, new axioms) allowed mathematicians to go beyond C.

It is well known that the description of the origami folding operations described by the Huzita–Justin axioms (HJAs for short, see Section 2) leads to the set of points constructible with origami, which is the smallest subfield O of $\mathbb{C}$ that is closed under the operations of taking square roots, cubic roots, and complex conjugation (see [Alperin 00, Theorem 5.2]). The elements of O are called *origami numbers*. Thus, we have $C \subset O$ and both as fields. Notice that this inclusion is a strict one: origami numbers like $\cos(\pi/9)$, $\sqrt[3]{2}$, and the seventh root of unity $\zeta_7 = e^{2\pi i/7}$ do not belong to C (and thus, the trisection of an angle of 60 degrees, the duplication of a cube of volume 1, and the construction of a regular heptagon are not possible with CS). Moreover, using the HJAs, one can solve any cubic equation (see Lemma 2.2), thus allowing all the geometric constructions described above. Nevertheless, there are algebraic numbers like the 11th root of unity $\zeta_{11} = e^{2\pi i/11}$ that are not constructible using origami, as modeled by the HJAs.

We are interested in extending the scope of the referred origami axioms, that is, in adding new axioms to the HJAs in order to get fields larger than O, and studying the arithmetic properties of those new numbers.

1.2. Beyond the Huzita–Justin axioms: n-fold axioms. The description of the folding moves given by the HJAs just covers a small part of the maneuvers usually performed by origamists, and it is natural to consider extending the set of folding axioms. In [Alperin and Lang 09] it is proved that the HJAs form a *complete set of 1-fold axioms*

The first author is partially supported by the UPV/EHU grants EHU12/05 and EHU12/34.
The second author is partially supported by MTM2011-28800-C02-01 from Spanish MEC.

in the sense that they describe all possible combinations of alignments (among points and lines) that may be achieved by one single fold. As a consequence, no more folding axioms are to be found, if we stick to axioms where just one fold is performed. In the same article new axioms requiring the performance of n simultaneous folds are introduced, considering alignments that involve the new lines determined by the creases of those n folds. For example, one of the 2-fold axioms consists in trisecting a given angle (notice that the alignments required involve the input lines defining the angle and the output ones that trisect it). The payoff from considering those moves as axioms is enormous from the arithmetic point of view: using Lill's method to evaluate polynomials (see [Lill 67]), it is shown how to find the real roots of any polynomial of degree n and coefficients in $\mathbb{Z}$ using $(n-2)$-fold axioms. In turn, every real algebraic number can be reached.

1.3. New 3D folding axioms. In this work we propose new folding axioms that, added to the HJAs, allow us to construct new numbers. The new ingredient we propose consists in incorporating three-dimensional (3D) origami moves, that is, folds that do not leave the paper flat after being executed. We want the folding procedures behind our axioms to satisfy the following properties:

(1) The folds involved should be fully referenced.
(2) The maneuvers should represent relatively easy and common folding.
(3) The alignment skills needed to perform the moves should be similar to those needed in the HJAs.

The third condition rules out the n-fold axioms of Section 1.2 for $n \geq 2$. Thus, we shall stick to moves easier to perform. Our first additional axioms are based on the fact that, starting with a regular polygon of $n + 1$ sides, an easy folding sequence using 3D moves (see Figure 1) yields a regular polygon of n sides. We call those new axioms the *Regular Polygon Axioms* (RPAs for short). Using the RPAs and the HJAs and starting with $\{0, 1\}$, we can get regular polygons with any number of sides (in particular, we can construct a regular 11-gon, which was not possible with the HJAs). As we show in Section 4, this leads us to all the algebraic numbers whose Galois group is Abelian. Our second axioms generalize the RPAs by starting with a cyclic polygon (i.e., a polygon inscribed in a circle). We call them the *Cyclic Polygon Axioms* (CPAs for short), and they take us further on, so that we can get numbers whose Galois group is non-solvable (in particular, those numbers cannot be expressed using radicals).

This article is organized as follows: In Section 2 we briefly recall the HJAs and the characterization of the origami numbers. In Section 3 we describe the origami moves that lead us to the new axioms and discuss their axiomatization. In Section 4 we introduce the RPAs and describe the number fields we get using them. In Section 5 we establish the geometric validity of our constructions and deal with the CPAs. Finally, in Section 6 we discuss the arithmetic limits of polyhedral constructions and pose some open questions for further research.

2. Origami Numbers

In this section we briefly recall the Huzita–Justin axioms (HJAs) and their arithmetic scope. We refer to the introduction of [Alperin and Lang 09] for a good account of their discovery, history, and references. Those axioms are the following:

O1: We can fold the line connecting two given points.
O2: We can fold the mediatrix of two given points.

O3: We can fold the bisector of the angle defined by two given lines, or the mid-parallel of two given parallel lines.

O4: We can fold, through a given point, a perpendicular to a given line.

O5: We can fold a line passing through a given point that places another given point onto a given line.

O6: We can fold a line that places simultaneously two given points onto two given lines, respectively.

O7: We can fold a line perpendicular to a given line that places a given point onto another given line.

In the literature of constructions, the phrases "we can fold" and "given" stand for "we can construct" and "constructible." For technical reasons, we shall also consider the following intersection axiom:

Line Intersection (LI): The intersection point of two given non-parallel lines is constructible.

In the literature, sometimes this axiom is only implicitly assumed, but notice that it is needed in order to get points. As a convention, here we shall consider the HJAs as the set of axioms O1–O7 along with LI.

DEFINITION 2.1. We say that $\alpha \in \mathbb{C}$ is an *origami number* if there is a finite sequence of the HJAs that starts with $\{0, 1\}$ and ends in α. We denote the set of all origami numbers as O.

Given 0 and 1, axioms O1 and O6 easily construct anything the others do. The latter yields the simultaneous tangents to the parabolas given by the points and lines of the input and involves solving of a cubic equation. In fact, we have the following result, the proof of which we reproduce, essentially, following [Alperin 00, Section 5.1]:

LEMMA 2.2. *Consider a number field K as initial set. Then, the application of the HJAs yields all the solutions of any cubic equation with coefficients in K.*

PROOF. Field operations allow us to perform a change of variable and reduce ourselves to the case $x^3 + ax + b = 0$. Consider the parabolas $(y - a/2)^2 = 2bx$ and $y = x^2/2$, whose directrices and foci are constructible using field operations involving a, b. Axiom O6 constructs a line that is tangent to both. A straightforward computation (see [Alperin 00, Section 5.1]) shows that the slope m of that line satisfies $m^3 + am + b = 0$. Notice that, given an oblique line ℓ, its slope is realized as the vertical side of a straight triangle with horizontal side of length 1 and hypotenuse parallel to ℓ. So, using the HJAs, we can construct a real root m of the cubic. Using m and just field operations, we can factor the cubic (e.g., using the Ruffini-Horner scheme), reducing ourselves to finding the roots of a quadratic equation, which is solvable using CS and, thus, with the HJAs.   □

The following result summarizes some characterizations of O (see [Cox 04, 10.3] for a proof of part (3)—just adding O6 to the usual axioms of CS constructions):

THEOREM 2.3. *The set $O \subseteq \mathbb{C}$ of origami numbers is the smallest subfield of $\mathbb{C}$ that is closed under the operations of taking square and cubic roots and complex conjugation* [Alperin 00]. *Moreover, $\alpha \in O$ is equivalent to each of the following:*

   (1) α is constructible by a marked ruler [Martin 98]*,*
   (2) α is constructible by intersecting conics [Alperin 00]*,*
   (3) α lies in a 2-3 tower $\mathbb{Q} = F_0 \subset \cdots \subset F_n$; that is, $2 \leq [F_{i+1} : F_i] \leq 3$ for $i = 0, \ldots, n - 1$ [Videla 97]*.*

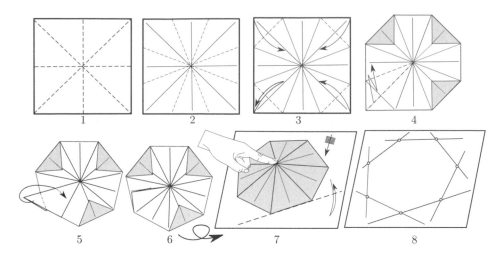

FIGURE 1. Using three dimensions to crease the sides of a regular heptagon.

REMARK 2.4. As a consequence of (3), every origami number belongs to a solvable extension of $\mathbb{Q}$. Not all origami numbers have Abelian Galois group. Namely, the only real root m of $x^3 - 2x - 2$, which is irreducible over $\mathbb{Q}$ by Eisenstein's rule, is an origami number due to (3). By the following standard exercise in Galois Theory [Cox 04, p.139], its Galois group is the non-Abelian symmetric group S_3.

LEMMA 2.5. *Let $f \in \mathbb{Z}[x]$ be irreducible over $\mathbb{Q}$ with $\deg(f) = p$ prime and exactly $p - 2$ real roots. Then, its Galois group over $\mathbb{Q}$ is the symmetric group S_p.*

3. Origami Folds behind the New 3D Axioms

In this section we present some easy 3D origami constructions that motivate the introduction of our new axioms.

Consider the folding sequence of Figure 1. Steps 1–3 use the HJAs. In Steps 4–6, no new line is constructed, but a pleat prevents the model from remaining flat. We get a flexible triangulated surface whose dihedral angles are not fixed. Now, if we put our finger at the apex and push gently against a flat surface (Step 7), we get a right regular pyramid, which yields a physical origami realization of a regular heptagon in the plane, say, a paper underneath. Folding that paper upward along the sides of the pyramid, we retrieve the result as a set of creases (Step 8). In Figure 2 we have a more artistic folding sequence rendering the same flexible surface, based on a traditional octagonal tato we learned about thanks to the initial folds of [Palmer 05].

It is remarkable that, in both models, the side faces of the pyramid remain flat despite all the extra creases. This is a consequence of the classic Rigidity Theorem:

THEOREM 3.1 (Legendre–Cauchy). *Any two convex polyhedra with the same graph and congruent corresponding faces are congruent.*

Notice that, for the sake of clarity, we have used two separate pieces of paper to show the construction; however, it is not hard to get everything with just one sheet of paper (e.g., [Royo Prieto 14], or the pyramidal eyes of [Engel 89, Step 65]).

The axiomatization of this construction can be done in many ways. One could be to develop a theory of constructible points in the three-dimensional space, describing every

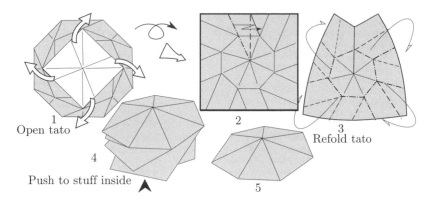

1
Open tato

2

3
Refold tato

4

Push to stuff inside ▲

5

FIGURE 2. Alternative folding sequence using an octagonal tato.

possible move with some axiom. Instead, as our interest is focused on the arithmetic aspects of the construction, we have chosen to keep working in the plane and to define the axioms using an abstract input–output scheme. In this case, the input of the axiom is the set of vertices of a regular $(n + 1)$-gon, and its output is the set of lines defining the sides of a regular n-gon (see Figure 3).

In the second axiom (see Figure 5), we drop regularity, just asking the starting polygon to be *cyclic*: its vertices belong to a circle. Given a cyclic polygon with sides of lengths $a_1, \ldots, a_{n+k}$, Steps 4–8 of Figure 1 retrieve a cyclic polygon of side lengths $a_1, \ldots, a_n$, where $k = 1, 2$ is the number of sides sacrificed by the pleat in Step 4 (it is easy to pleat and lock two triangles).

We will prove the geometric validity of these constructions in Proposition 5.1.

4. Regular Polygon Axioms

Here, for the sake of brevity, we shall adopt the following convention:

Convention: Unless otherwise explicitly stated, we shall suppose that the vertices and side lengths of a polygon are listed in counterclockwise order.

Based on the first construction of Section 3, we present our first 3D axioms, the *Regular Polygon Axioms* (RPAs). For $n \geq 3$, we have the following:

RPA$_n$: Given the vertices $A_1, \ldots, A_{n+1}$ of a regular $(n + 1)$-gon, we can fold the line containing any side of the regular n-gon of vertices $B_1, \ldots, B_n$, determined by $B_1 = A_1$ and $B_2 = A_2$.

Now we describe the arithmetic consequences of the application of the RPAs.

LEMMA 4.1. *Assume the notation in the definition of Axiom RPA$_n$, and let K be a number field containing $A_1, \ldots, A_{n+1}$. Then, we have*

$$K(B_1, \ldots, B_n) = K(\zeta_n).$$

PROOF. Let C be the circumcenter of the resulting polygon. We have

$$(4.1) \qquad B_i - C = (\zeta_n)^{i-1}(B_1 - C), \quad \forall i = 2, \ldots, n,$$

which gives $K(B_1, \ldots, B_n) \subset K(B_1, B_2, \zeta_n, C) = K(\zeta_n)$, because $B_i = A_i \in K$ for $i = 1, 2$ and $C = (A_2 - A_1\zeta_n)/(1 - \zeta_n)$. For the converse, as $C = (B_1 + \cdots + B_n)/n$, we have $C \in K(B_1, \ldots, B_n)$. Now, $\zeta_n = (B_2 - C)/(B_1 - C)$ yields $K(\zeta_n) = K(\zeta_n, C) \subset K(B_1, \ldots, B_n)$, and we are done. $\qquad \square$

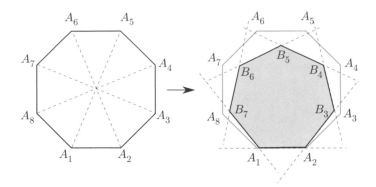

FIGURE 3. Input and output of RPA_7.

REMARK 4.2. In the conditions of Lemma 4.1, the coefficients and slope m of the Cartesian equation of the lines containing the sides of P are easily constructed from $K(\zeta_n)$, as described in the proof of Lemma 2.2. Thus, they belong to some 2-extension of $K(\zeta_n)$.

DEFINITION 4.3. We say that $\alpha \in \mathbb{C}$ is a *regular origami number* if there is a finite sequence of the HJAs and the RPAs that starts with $\{0, 1\}$ and ends in α. We denote the set of all regular origami numbers as O_{RP}.

LEMMA 4.4. *The field O_{RP} contains ζ_n, for every $n \in \mathbb{N}$.*

PROOF. Fix $n \geq 3$, and take $k > \log_2(n + 1)$. Divide the square into 2^{k+1} equal angles from the center using bisections, like in Step 2 of Figure 1. Folding perpendiculars, we obtain a regular polygon of 2^k sides whose vertices belong to the final field F of a 2-3 tower, by Theorem 2.3(3). We get a new regular polygon of $m = 2^k - 1 > n$ sides from RPA_m. Its vertices belong to $F(\zeta_m)$ by lemma 4.1. Applying the RPAs successively, we get regular polygons of $m, m - 1, \ldots, n$ sides, thus proving that $F(\zeta_n) \subset O_{RP}$.   □

Denote by $\mathbb{Q}_{Ab}$ the maximal Abelian extension of $\mathbb{Q}$. Now, we recall the following theorem:

THEOREM 4.5 (Kronecker-Weber). *Every finite Abelian extension $K \subset \mathbb{C}$ of $\mathbb{Q}$ is a subfield of a cyclotomic field (i.e., $K \subset \mathbb{Q}(\zeta_k)$, for some $k \in \mathbb{N}$).*

As a consequence of the celebrated Theorem 4.5, $\mathbb{Q}_{Ab}$ is the smaller extension of $\mathbb{Q}$ that contains all the roots of unity. So, by Lemma 4.4, we have that O_{RP} is an extension of $\mathbb{Q}_{Ab}$. Now we present the main result of this section:

THEOREM 4.6. *O_{RP} is the smallest subfield of $\mathbb{C}$ that contains $\mathbb{Q}_{Ab}$ and that is closed under the operations of taking square roots, cubic roots, and complex conjugation. Moreover, $\alpha \in O_{RP}$ if and only if there exists a tower*

$$(4.2) \qquad\qquad \mathbb{Q} = F_0 \subset \cdots \subset F_n$$

such that $\alpha \in F_n$ and, for $i = 0, \ldots, n - 1$, either $2 \leq [F_{i+1} : F_i] \leq 3$ or $F_{i+1} = F_i(\zeta_k)$ for some $k \in \mathbb{N}$ (we call such a tower a 2-3-c tower, with c for cyclotomic).

PROOF. For the first part of the statement, we adapt the argument of [Alperin 00, Theorem 4.2]. By Lemmas 2.2 and 4.4, the minimal subfield satisfying the conditions of the statement must be a subfield of O_{RP}. The converse follows from the fact that the application of the HJAs just involves field operations or solving quadratic or cubic equations, and from Lemma 4.1.

For the second part of the statement, we proceed as in [Cox 04, Theorem 10.3.4]. If $\alpha \in F_n$ belongs to the tower in Equation (4.2), then Lemma 2.2 permits us to solve each cubic or quadratic equation involved, and the RPAs allow us to adjoin any needed root of unity. Conversely, given a number $\alpha \in O_{RP}$, we can proceed by induction on the number of axioms applied to construct α. Notice that in order to apply the proof of [Cox 04, Theorem 10.3.4], we just need to show that the coefficients and slopes of the lines involved in the application of the last used axiom belong to a 2-3-c tower; this follows from Remark 4.2 in the case of the RPAs and from the arguments given in [Cox 04, Theorem 10.3.4] in the case of the other axioms. By juxtaposition with the 2-3-c tower given by the induction argument, we get a 2-3-c tower. □

COROLLARY 4.7. *Every regular origami number has solvable Galois group.*

PROOF. Every $\alpha \in O_{RP}$ belongs to a 2-3-c tower as in Equation (4.2). As every extension $F(\zeta_k)/F$ is radical (thus, solvable) and the juxtaposition of solvable extensions is solvable, we have the result. □

5. Cyclic Polygon Axioms

In this section, we generalize the RPAs by starting with a cyclic polygon, not necessarily regular. We first recall some known facts about cyclic polygons.

5.1. Cyclic polygons. Recall that a *cyclic* polygon is a polygon whose vertices belong to a circle. Let's see that for positive numbers $a_1, \ldots, a_n$ satisfying

$$(5.1) \qquad \max_{1 \le i \le n} a_i \le \frac{a_1 + \cdots + a_n}{2},$$

there exists a unique convex cyclic polygon with sides in that order. Following [Pak 05, Section 1], take a circle with large enough radius r, so that placing vertices on it at distances $a_1, \ldots, a_n$ in that order, we get an open polygonal. Shrinking r until the polygonal is closed, we get a convex polygon due to Condition (5.1). The radius of the circumscribed circle is called the *circumradius* of the cyclic polygon.

The circumradius, the area, and the lengths of the diagonals of cyclic polygons have been the objects of active research in the last two decades (see [Pak 05] for a survey). They, or their squares, are roots of polynomials with coefficients in $\mathbb{Q}(a_1^2, \ldots, a_n^2)$. Those polynomials are difficult to compute, but explicit formulas can be found for cyclic pentagons, hexagons, and heptagons of degrees 7, 14, and 38, respectively (see [Robbins 94], [Sabitov 02], [Varfolomeev 03], and [Moritsugu 12]). General formulas are, nowadays, computationally intractable as the degree and the number of summands quickly become gargantuan.

5.2. Validity of the origami constructions. In this subsection, we prove the geometric legitimacy of the origami constructions of Section 3.

PROPOSITION 5.1. *Consider a flexible polyhedral surface S imbedded in $\mathbb{R}^3$, formed by a closed circuit of isosceles triangles, glued along their equal sides around some point O. Assume that the sum of the angles at O is less than 2π. Then, there exists only one polygon that, glued to S by the boundary, forms a pyramid.*

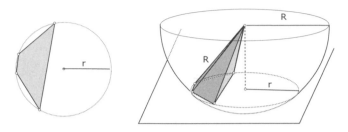

FIGURE 4. Construction of a cyclic non-central polygon with a pyramid.

PROOF. Denote the triangles by $T_1, \ldots, T_n$ in counterclockwise order. Denote by R the length of the equal sides of T_i, and for $i = 1, \ldots, n$, denote by a_i the remaining side and θ_i its opposite angle. Note that $\sin(\theta_i/2) = a_i/(2R)$. Without loss of generality, we suppose that $a_1 = \max\{a_1, \ldots, a_n\}$. We claim that Condition (5.1) holds. By *reductio ad absurdum*, suppose $a_1 > a_2 + \cdots + a_n$. Then,

$$(5.2) \qquad \sin\frac{\theta_1}{2} = \frac{a_1}{2R} > \frac{a_2 + \cdots + a_n}{2R} = \sin\frac{\theta_2}{2} + \cdots + \sin\frac{\theta_n}{2} \geq \sin\frac{\theta_2 + \ldots \theta_n}{2},$$

where we have repeatedly used $\sin\alpha_1 + \sin\alpha_2 \geq \sin(\alpha_1 + \alpha_2)$, which follows immediately from the sum of sines formula. By the hypothesis, both $\theta_1/2$ and $(\theta_2 + \cdots + \theta_n)/2$ belong to $(0, \pi)$. So, by Equation (5.2), it follows that $\theta_1 > \theta_2 + \cdots + \theta_n$, a contradiction.

So, $a_1, \ldots, a_n$ are the side lengths of a cyclic convex polygon P. Denote by r its circumradius. Notice that $r < R$ by construction. Consider in $\mathbb{R}^3$ the sphere of radius R centered at $A = (0, 0, \sqrt{R^2 - r^2})$, whose intersection with the plane $z = 0$ is a circle of radius r. Placing P in that circle and joining its vertices with A, we get a pyramid that satisfies the statement (see Figure 4). To prove the uniqueness of P, consider any other such pyramid. Then, the vertices of its base belong to the intersection of its plane with the sphere of radius R centered at its apex. Hence, the base is a cyclic convex polygon and, thus, is unique. $\square$

5.3. Cyclic origami numbers.
We denote by $Cy(a_1, \ldots, a_n; A_1, A_2)$ the cyclic polygon of side lengths $a_1, \ldots, a_n$ such that A_1 and A_2 are the vertices of the first side. We shall say that a cyclic polygon is *central* if its circumcenter belongs to its interior (this is needed to apply the folding sequence described in Section 3). We present the *Cyclic Polygon Axioms* (CPAs) for $n \geq 3$ and $k = 1, 2$:

CPA$_{n,k}$: Given the vertices $A_1, \ldots, A_{n+k}$ of the central cyclic polygon
$P_1 = Cy(a_1, \ldots, a_{n+k}; A_1, A_2)$, we can fold the line containing any side of
$P_2 = Cy(a_1, \ldots, a_n; A_1, A_2)$, provided (1) the circumradius of P_1 is greater than
that of P_2; and (2) $a_1, \ldots, a_n$ satisfy Condition (5.1).

REMARK 5.2. Condition (1) is needed for the origami construction (see the proof of Proposition 5.1). Condition (2) is needed for P_2 to exist; P_2 may not be central.

Now, we show that the CPAs and the HJAs can construct any cyclic polygon.

LEMMA 5.3. *Given two points $A_1, A_2 \in \mathbb{C}$ and lengths $a_1 = |A_2 - A_1|, a_2, \ldots, a_n$ satisfying Condition (5.1), the vertices of $P = Cy(a_1, \ldots, a_n; A_1, A_2)$ can be constructed using the HJAs and the CPAs.*

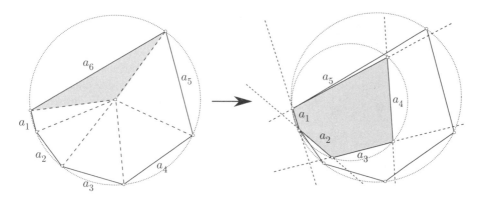

FIGURE 5. Input and output of CPA$_{5,1}$. The used lengths are $(a_1, a_2, a_3, a_4, a_5) = (1, 2, 3, 4, 5)$, as in the proof of Theorem 5.6.

PROOF. Take $R \in \mathbb{Q}$ greater than the circumradius of P. Consider the circle C of radius R passing through A_1, A_2. Name O its center, and add vertices A_j in C satisfying $|A_{j+1} - A_j| = a_j$ for $j = 2, \ldots, n$. If the angle $A_1\widehat{OA}_{n+1}$ is greater than π, then $Cy(a_1, \ldots, a_n, |A_n - A_{n+1}|; A_1, A_2)$ is central, and CPA$_{n,1}$ gives P. If $A_1\widehat{OA}_{n+1} \leq \pi$, let A'_2 be the antipodal point of A_2. Then, we have that $Cy(a_1, \ldots, a_n, |A'_2 - A_{n+1}|, |A_1 - A'_2|; A_1, A_2)$ is central and CPA$_{n,2}$ gives P. □

REMARK 5.4. Let P be a cyclic polygon of vertices $A_1, \ldots, A_n$, circumcenter O, and circumradius r satisfying $A_1\widehat{OA}_n > \pi/2$. Then, it is easy to check that we can take R slightly greater than r, so that CPA$_{n,1}$ gives P with the method of Lemma 5.3. Thus, CPA$_{n,2}$ is only strictly needed when $A_1\widehat{OA}_n \leq \pi/2$.

DEFINITION 5.5. We say that $\alpha \in \mathbb{C}$ is a *cyclic origami number* if there is a finite sequence of the HJAs and the CPAs that starts with $\{0, 1\}$ and ends in α. We denote the set of all cyclic origami numbers as O_{CP}.

Our last result shows that using the CPAs we can go beyond O_{RP}.

THEOREM 5.6. *The inclusion $O_{RP} \subset O_{CP}$ is a strict one.*

PROOF. The inclusion is clear because both RPA$_n$ and CPA$_{n,1}$ yield the same result when applied to a regular n-gon. We now show that the inclusion is a strict one. Consider $Cy(1, 2, 3, 4, 5; 0, 1)$, and write $d = |A_3 - A_1|$. Notice that $d \in O_{CP}$. Using [Varfolomeev 04, Formula (1)], we obtain the minimal polynomial of d:

$$P_d(x) = 4x^7 + 51x^6 + 160x^5 - 246x^4 - 1836x^3 - 1785x^2 + 1800x + 2160.$$

Computer algebra (e.g., Mathematica) shows that P_d is irreducible over $\mathbb{Q}$. As P_d has exactly five real roots, by Lemma 2.5 its Galois group over $\mathbb{Q}$ is isomorphic to S_7, which is not solvable. By Corollary 4.7, we have $d \notin O_{RP}$. □

REMARK 5.7. In fact, in [Varfolomeev 04, Theorem 1] it is shown that the Galois group of P_d for any cyclic pentagon over the field generated by its side lengths is S_7.

6. Conclusions and Further Questions

In this work we have introduced new folding axioms involving easy 3D maneuvers with the aim to push forward the arithmetic limits of the Huzita–Justin axioms. Using those folding moves, we have shown that we can construct all Abelian numbers and numbers whose Galois group is not solvable.

Our new axioms just describe a very small part of what can be determined in a plane using 3D origami. On the one hand, the constructions behind our axioms can be generalized by starting with any convex polygon $A_1, \ldots, A_{n+1}$ and a chosen center O inside it, so that $|A_1 - O| = |A_{n+1} - O|$. If we sacrifice $\widehat{A_1 O A_{n+1}}$ as in Step 4 of Figure 1, we get a new n-gon. On the other hand, we could consider more than one node inside the starting polygon. Instead of a pyramid, we would get a different polyhedron.

It follows from [Sabitov 02, Theorem 1] that all the diagonals of a polyhedron P are roots of a polynomial whose coefficients are rational numerical functions of the side lengths and of the diagonals of the faces of P. This implies that lengths obtained by constructing polyhedra with side lengths in some number field K will be algebraic over K. So, we cannot expect any *polyhedral origami number* to be transcendental. It is left as a challenge to find a full characterization of O_{CP} in terms of field towers. It would also be nice to find explicit elegant folding sequences (not using a compass) leading to the construction of cyclic polyhedra of given lengths.

References

[Alperin 00] R. C. Alperin. " Mathematical Theory of Origami Constructions and Numbers." *New York Journal of Mathematics* 6 (2000), 119–133. MR1772561 (2001g:51017)

[Alperin and Lang 09] R. C. Alperin and R. J. Lang. "One-, Two-, and Multi-Fold Origami Axioms." In *Origami⁴: Fourth International Meeting of Origami Science, Mathematics, and Education*, edited by Robert J. Lang, pp. 371–393. Wellesley, MA: A K Peters, 2009. MR2590565 (2011b:51030)

[Cox 04] D. A. Cox. *Galois Theory*. Hoboken, NJ: Wiley-Interscience, 2004. MR2119052 (2006a:12001)

[Engel 89] P. Engel. "Butterfly." In *Origami from Angelfish to Zen*, pp. 226–237. New York: Dover 1989.

[Lill 67] M. E. Lill. "Résolution graphique des équations numériques de tous degrés à une seule inconnue, et description d'un instrument inventé dans ce but." *Nouvelles Annales de Mathématiques* 2:6 (1867), 359–362.

[Martin 98] G. E. Martin. *Geometric Constructions*. Berlin: Springer-Verlag, 1998. MR1483895 (98j:51032)

[Moritsugu 12] H. Moritsugu. "Computing Explicit Formulae for the Radius of Cyclic Hexagons and Heptagons." *Bulletin of JSSAC* 18 (2011), 3–9.

[Pak 05] I. Pak. "The Area of Cyclic Polygons: Recent Progress on Robbins' Conjectures." *Advances in Applied Mathematics* 34 (2005), 690–696. MR2128993 (2006b:51017)

[Palmer 05] C. K. Palmer. "12-Fold Flower Tower." In *Folding Australia 2005*, p. 56. Melbourne: Australian Association of Origami, 2005. (Video tutorial by the author available at https://www.youtube.com/watch?v=0FVH157LdME.)

[Robbins 94] D. P. Robbins. "Areas of Polygons Inscribed in a Circle." *Discrete and Computational Geometry* 12 (1994), 223–236. MR1283889 (95g:51027)

[Royo Prieto 14] J. I. Royo Prieto. "Orthodox Folding Sequences for Cyclic Polygons." Available at http://www.ehu.eus/joseroyo/pdf/cyclic.pdf, 2014.

[Sabitov 02] I. K. Sabitov. "Algorithmic Solution of the Problem of Isometric Realization for Two-Dimensional Polyhedral Metrics." *Izvestiya: Mathematics* 66 (2002), 159–172. MR1918847 (2003b:52005)

[Varfolomeev 03] V. V. Varfolomeev. "Inscribed Polygons and Heron Polynomials." *Sbornik: Mathematics* 194 (2003), 311–331. MR1992154 (2004d:51014)

[Varfolomeev 04] V. V. Varfolomeev. "Galois Groups of Heron-Sabitov Polynomials for Inscribed Pentagons." *Sbornik: Mathematics* 195 (2004), 310–216. MR2068949 (2005b:12010)

[Videla 97] C. R. Videla. "On Points Constructible from Conics." *Math. Intelligencer* 19 (1997), 53–57. MR1457448 (98h:01003)

DEPARTMENT OF APPLIED MATHEMATICS, UNIVERSITY OF THE BASQUE COUNTRY UPV/EHU, BILBAO, SPAIN
E-mail address: joseignacio.royo@ehu.eus

DEPARTAMENT DE MATEMÀTICA APLICADA IV, UNIVERSITAT POLITÈCNICA DE CATALUNYA, BARCELONA TECH., BARCELONA, SPAIN
E-mail address: etramuns@ma4.upc.edu

Interactive Construction and Automated Proof in Eos System with Application to Knot Fold of Regular Polygons

Fadoua Ghourabi, Tetsuo Ida, and Kazuko Takahashi

1. Introduction

In origami geometry, the construction and the verification should go hand in hand. When we present a new origami by a new fold method, we will show certain geometric properties that enable us to claim its novelty by formal argument, i.e., by proof. It is desirable to have some kind of automation by a computer toward computer-assisted origami. Several systems have been implemented to simulate and treat complex origami constructions, whereas proving in origami geometry remains in the hands of the constructor or someone well versed in geometric theorem proving.

We have been developing a computational origami system with computational theorem proving capabilities, called Eos. A description of an earlier version of Eos system was given in *Origami*[4] [Ida et al. 09]. Since then, Eos underwent several improvements. Its usability has been extended to solve and prove construction problems beyond Huzita's folds. In particular, the knot fold construction is an interesting example that exhibits some of the new features in Eos. The use of knot folds to make regular polygons has been studied by a few researchers (e.g., [Brunton 61, Sakaguchi 82, Maekawa 11]). Making regular polygons by knot fold is a construction problem that can be fully tackled with the Eos system, i.e., construction and proof of correctness. In this chapter, we explain how knot folding is translated to a constraint solving problem for Eos. We show that Eos can express, solve, and reason about the constraints. We show this with the examples of regular pentagons and heptagons.

The rest of the work is organized as follows. In Section 2, we present the Eos system. In Section 3, we discuss the constraints of pentagonal knots. In Section 4, we present another method of defining knot folds. We illustrate it with the construction of a regular heptagon. In Section 5, we show how we prove the correctness of knot fold constructions using Eos. In Section 6, we summarize our results and point out directions of further research.

2. Eos System

2.1. Brief overview. The engine of Eos consists of a solver, a graphical visualizer, and a prover. The main functionality of the solver is to find a fold line by solving algebraic

This work was supported by JSPS KAKENHI Grant Number 25330007. The first author was supported by the postdoctoral fellowship at Kwansei Gakuin University when the research was done.

constraints. The properties that the fold line(s) should satisfy are described by a formula in a many-sorted first-order language. The solver generates the algebraic interpretation of the formula that corresponds to a system of multivariate polynomial equations, then it solves the system of equations to determine suitable fold line(s) [Ghourabi et al. 07]. The graphical visualizer interacts with the solver and produces a graphical output that applies the fold along the line obtained by the solver. The visualizer uses a graph model of origami structure.   The fold along a line is reduced to a graph rewriting problem [Ida and Takahashi 10]. After the completion of the construction, the user invokes the prover to prove the correctness of the construction—in other words, to prove geometric properties of the origami object obtained at the end of the construction [Ida et al. 11].

Eos is implemented on top of Mathematica and follows its syntactical conventions.[1] Due to space limitation, we only explain the elements of syntax that are used here. For the clarity of this work, we will use the common notation for function call $f(x_1, \ldots, x_n)$ instead of Mathematica's $f[x_1, \ldots, x_n]$. In Eos, the set notation is extended to the incidence relation between points and lines. Expression $X \in m$ means that point X is incident to line m, and $\{X_1, \ldots, X_k\} \subset m$ means that all the points $X_1, \ldots, X_k$ are incident to line m. The reflection of point X across a line t is denoted by X^t in Eos. To refer to a line passing through points X and Y, we use $\overline{XY}$, or XY if the denotation is clear from the context.

2.2. Fold operation. The main operation in geometric origami is folding paper along line(s). In Eos, a fold operation is specified by a logical formula of the following form:

$$(2.1) \qquad \exists_{x_1:\tau_1} \ldots \exists_{x_i:\tau_i} \, \phi_1(t_{1,1}, \ldots, t_{1,k_1}) \wedge \ldots \wedge \phi_s(t_{s,1}, \ldots, t_{s,k_s}).$$

The existentially quantified variables $x_1, \ldots, x_i$ are of sorts $\tau_1, \ldots \tau_i \in \{\text{Line, Point, Num}\}$. The variables of sort Line denote the fold lines along which the folds are to be preformed. The variables of sort Point denote the points of intersections of fold lines and existing lines. The variables of sort Num denotes numbers.

Note that $\phi_1(t_{1,1}, \ldots, t_{1,k_1}), \ldots, \phi_s(t_{s,1}, \ldots, t_{s,k_s})$ are literals over the geometric objects $t_{1,1}, \ldots, t_{s,k_s}$. When we apply a fold operation, we first find instances for $x_1, \ldots, x_i$ such that $\phi_1(t_{1,1}, \ldots, t_{1,k_1}) \wedge \ldots \wedge \phi_s(t_{s,1}, \ldots, t_{s,k_s})$ holds, and then we fold the origami along the lines $x_1, \ldots, x_i$. Huzita's six fold operations O1–O6 [Huzita 91] can be written in the form of formula (2.1):[2]

$$(2.2) \qquad \exists_{x:\text{Line}} \, x = Oi(t_{i,1}, \ldots, t_{i,k_i}), \quad \text{for } i = 1, 2, 4$$

$$(2.3) \qquad \exists_{x:\text{Line}} \, Oi(t_{i,1}, \ldots, t_{i,k_i-1}, x), \quad \text{for } i = 3, 5, 6$$

Given the geometric objects $t_{i,1}, \ldots, t_{i,k_i}$, the function $Oi(t_{i,1}, \ldots, t_{i,k_i})$ in (2.2) computes the fold line that satisfies operation Oi, where $i = 1, 2, 4$. The equality "=" is polymorphic and can be instantiated to be the equality between Lines, Points, and Nums, as well. In (2.3), O3, O5, and O6 are predicates and not functions that return a fold line x, because x may not be unique. For instance, $O5(P, m, Q, x)$ states that there is a fold line x passing through point Q and superposes point P and line m. There may be one or two fold lines, if any exist.

---

[1]The most recent version of Eos requires an installation of Mathematica 9 or 10, and it can be downloaded from http://www.i-eos.org:8080/ieos/tutorial.
[2]Here, we treat the six Huzita basic fold operations that he proposed in 1989, although one more presented later by Justin can be included for the exhaustive enumeration of basic fold operations that rely on incidence relations of points and lines.

Function HO (which stands for *Huzita Ori*) allows the origamist to interact with Eos and perform a fold operation specified by formula (2.1). Huzita's fold operations O1–O6 are implemented in Eos by translating them to formulas (2.2) and (2.3). The call HO(P, m, Q), for instance, asks Eos to internally treat the formula $\exists_{x:\text{Line}}$ O5(P, m, Q, x) and solve for x that satisfies O5(P, m, Q, x). The implementation of the fold operation in Eos is extensible. The origamist may ask the system to perform a fold operation that cannot be performed by Huzita's fold operations alone. The origamist can pass formula (2.1) to Eos as an argument of function HO:

$$HO((\exists_{x_1:\tau_1} \ldots \exists_{x_i:\tau_i} \; \phi_1(t_{1,1}, \ldots, t_{1,k_1}) \wedge \ldots \wedge \phi_s(t_{s,1}, \ldots, t_{s,k_s})),$$

$$\langle\text{keyword arguments}\rangle)$$

Furthermore, the origamist may need to do more than solve for $x_1, \ldots, x_i$. He or she can specify the names of the newly solved points or tell Eos the direction of the fold along the line(s) $x_1, \ldots, x_i$, i.e., mountain or valley, and so on. Such information is given as optional arguments in the HO call of the form "keyword → value". Otherwise, Eos undertakes these tasks using their default values.

3. Knot Fold of Regular Pentagon

The construction of the simplest knot can be decomposed into the four steps shown in Figure 1. We start with rectangular paper or *origami tape* depicted in Figure 1(a). First, we perform two folds as shown in Figure 1(b). Next, we take the end of the upper face and mountain-fold it while inserting it immediately above the bottom face. The result is shown in Figure 1(c). Finally, we pull the two ends of the folded tape to secure the knot and obtain a final shape of the regular pentagon in Fig 1(d).

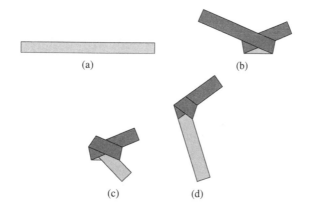

(a) (b)

(c) (d)

FIGURE 1. The steps of constructing a simple origami knot.

The three folds in Figure 1(b) and 1(c) and the act of pulling the tape are obviously beyond Huzita's fold operations. The involved folds are mutually dependent and can be regarded as a variant of the Alperin–Lang multi-fold operation [Alperin and Lang 09]. The multi-fold required for the knot fold can be given by a formula of the form (2.1). We first analyze the geometric properties of the knot. To this end, we mark the key points of the knot, unfold it, and examine the fold lines and the points that have been constructed during the knotting, as shown in Figure 2.

The following shows the Eos program to construct the regular pentagon EHGKF in Figure 2(a) by knot folding.

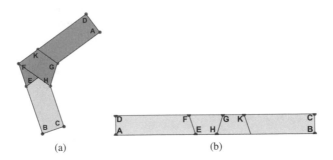

(a)   (b)

FIGURE 2. Unfolding knot fold of regular pentagon.

PROGRAM 3.1 (Construction of a Pentagonal Knot).

1. BeginOrigami(Pentagonal-knot, {100, 10})
2. NewPoint({E → {40, 0}})
3. HO($\exists_{m:\text{Line}} \exists_{n:\text{Line}} \exists_{l:\text{Line}} \exists_{f:\text{Point}} \exists_{g:\text{Point}} \exists_{h:\text{Point}} \exists_{k:\text{Point}}$
   ($h \in \text{AB} \land \{f, g, k\} \subset \text{CD} \land f \in m \land h \in n \land k^n \in l \land$
   $\text{O5}(g, \text{EA}, \text{E}, m) \land \text{O5}(f, \text{EB}, g, n) \land \text{O5}(h, \overline{C^n g}, f, l) \land$
   $k^n \in \overline{D^m f} \land \text{E} \in \overline{f}\ (\text{B}^n)^l),$
   Case → 4, MarkPointAt → {F, G, H, K}, Handles → {A, B, B},
   Direction → {Valley, Valley, Mountain}, InsertFace → {0, 0, *Bottom*})

Steps 1–3 are the calls of Eos functions, i.e., the calls of BeginOrigami, NewPoint, and one HO. Steps 1 and 2 are preparatory steps. At Step 1, we start a new session of an origami construction that we name "Pentagonal-knot" with an initial paper ABCD of size 100×10. Eos defines a Cartesian coordinate system whose x-axis and y-axis are along lines AB and AD, respectively. Initial points A, B, C, and D are located at $(0, 0)$, $(100, 0)$, $(100, 10)$, and $(0, 10)$, respectively. Eos uses this coordinate system to represent points as pairs of real numbers (Cartesian coordinates) and lines and curves as polynomial equations. In particular, a line m is represented by the equation $ax + by + c = 0$. At Step 2, let E be an arbitrary points on the line AB. For the sake of the well-formed construction, we put the point E at $(40, 0)$. At Step 3, Eos, internally, computes the algebraic forms of the argument formula of HO, solves them, and returns three fold lines bound to variables m, n, and l and four points bound to f, g, h, and k. Note that points F, G, H, and K in Figure 2(a) are solutions for variables f, g, h, and k.

We now explain the argument formula of HO. Referring to Figure 2(b), we establish the incidence relations between points and lines involved in the knot fold, i.e., $h \in \text{AB} \land \{f, g, k\} \subset \text{CD} \land f \in m \land h \in n \land k^n \in l$. Note that variable k corresponds to the location of point K before knotting, i.e., point K in Figure 2(b), whereas point k^n in $k^n \in l$ corresponds to the location of point K after knotting, i.e., Figure 2(a).

As indicated by $\text{O5}(g, \text{EA}, \text{E}, m) \land \text{O5}(f, \text{EB}, g, n) \land \text{O5}(h, \overline{C^n g}, f, l)$, we perform three O5 operations. Regarding the third O5, we first explain how to read Eos's notation $\overline{C^n g}$ in $\text{O5}(h, \overline{C^n g}, f, l)$. Recall that C^n denotes the reflection of point C across the line n. Then, the expression $\overline{C^n g}$ is the line passing through points C^n and g. The fold along line l passing through f superposes point h and line $\overline{C^n g}$. The "overbar" in line $\overline{C^n g}$ is used here to correctly parse the line.

FIGURE 3. The knot fold before pulling the tape.

For any point f on CD, we can perform the three O5 operations; hence, there are infinite solutions for the above properties. We see that the shape in Figure 3 results from the three O5 operations. To make it a rigid knot, we need to pull the paper until all the points are moved to their "proper" locations in Figure 2(a). The difference immediately noticed in the shape of Figure 2(a) versus the one in Figure 3 is that points K and E are incident to lines FD and FB, respectively. We therefore add the following incidence constraint: $k^n \in \overline{D^m f} \wedge E \in \overline{f(B^n)^l}$. By solving the constraint, Eos returns three fold lines and four points. However, there are four distinct solutions. The argument "Case → 4" is added to HO to choose the solution that leads to a regular pentagon. The solutions for variables f, g, h, and k are given the names F, G, H, and K. This is specified by argument "MarkPointAt → {F, G, H, K}". Thus, the points bound to the existential variables become available in the later steps of the construction. The keyword argument "Handles → {A, B, B}" determines which side of the fold lines are to be moved. In this case, the face that is to the left to the fold line m, i.e., the face containing point A, is moved by the fold. The face to the right of fold line n is moved. The face that is to the left of the fold line l is moved. "Direction → {Valley, Valley, Mountain}" asks Eos to perform valley folds along lines m and n and a mountain fold along line l. "InsertFace → {0, 0, Bottom}" ask the program to insert the moving faces above (below in the case of the valley fold) the face in the list. The argument may be a list of faces for the same reason as for Direction. The outputs of the above HO call are shown in Figure 4.

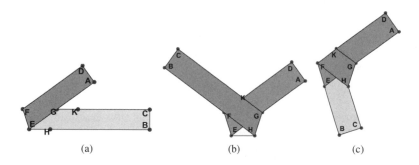

(a)　　　　　　　　　(b)　　　　　　　　　(c)

FIGURE 4. Construction of regular pentagon EFKGH.

4. Knot Fold of Regular Heptagon

We now examine the knot fold from an algebraic point of view. Through the example of the regular heptagon, we show another alternative formulation to define the constraints on the knot fold using polynomial equations relating point locations. Starting from an initial tape ABCD and a point E on the line AB, we will construct the regular heptagon ELHGJKF shown in Figure 5(a). The algebraic constraints specified on points F, H, G, J, K, and L are written as a formula of form (2.1) as follows:

$$\exists_{m:\text{Line}} \exists_{n:\text{Line}}$$

$$\exists_{f:\text{Point}} \exists_{h:\text{Point}} \exists_{g:\text{Point}} \exists_{j:\text{Point}} \exists_{k:\text{Point}} \exists_{l:\text{Point}}$$

$$\exists_{ht:\text{Num}} \exists_{p:\text{Num}} \exists_{q:\text{Num}} \exists_{r:\text{Num}}$$

(4.1) $(\{f, g, j, k\} \subset \text{CD} \wedge \{h, l\} \subset \text{AB} \wedge \{\text{E}, f\} \subset m \wedge \{h, g\} \subset n \wedge$

(4.2) $f - \text{E} = \text{Point}(-ht \times p, ht) \wedge g - h = \text{Point}(ht \times p, ht) \wedge$

(4.3) $h - \text{E} = \text{Point}(2ht \times r \times q, 0) \wedge k - g = \text{Point}(2ht \times r \times q, 0) \wedge$

(4.4) $j - f = \text{Point}(2ht \times r \times q) \wedge \text{E} - l = g - j \wedge$

(4.5) $p^2 + 1 = q^2 \wedge p = (4r^3 - 3r)q \wedge 8r^3 - 4r^2 - 4r + 1 = 0)$

The existentially quantified variables m and n of sort Line; f, g, h, j, k, and l of sort Point; and ht, p, and q of sort Num satisfy the constraints (4.1)–(4.5). Relations (4.1) show the relations of incidences between points f, g, j, k, and l and lines m, n, AB, and CD. Equations (4.2)–(4.4) state the following properties about the locations of points f, g, h, j, k, and l with respect to the location of point E:

- The interior angles of the regular heptagon ELHGJKF are equal to $\frac{5\pi}{7}$, in particular $\angle\text{LEF} = \frac{5\pi}{7}$. Let $\theta = \frac{\pi}{7}$. We deduce that $\angle\text{AEF} = 3\theta$ and $\angle\text{HEL} = \theta$ as depicted in Figure 5(b). The slope of fold line EF is, therefore, equal to $-\tan(3\theta)$. Furthermore, let p, q, and r be three variables satisfying $\frac{p}{q} = \cos(3\theta)$ and $r = \cos(\theta)$. We construct the perpendicular FX to line AB passing through F and whose foot is point X on AB. Let ht be the height of the tape, i.e., $ht = |\text{AD}|$, where $|\text{AD}|$ denotes the distance between points A and D. We infer that $|\text{FX}|$, $|\text{XE}|$, and $|\text{EF}|$ are equal to ht, $ht \times p$, and $ht \times q$, respectively. Similarly, we can infer that $|\text{GY}|$, $|\text{HY}|$, and $|\text{HG}|$ are equal to ht, $ht \times p$, and $ht \times q$, respectively, where line HY is perpendicular to line CD and whose foot is point Y on CD. The operators minus and plus are extended to points. The expression $X - Y$ for points X and Y is a coordinate-wise subtraction yielding a new point. Namely, $\text{Point}(x_1, y_1) - \text{Point}(x_2, y_2)$ is $\text{Point}(x_1 - x_2, y_1 - y_2)$. Thus, in expression (4.2), we have $f - \text{E} = \text{Point}(-ht \times p, ht)$ and $g - h = \text{Point}(ht \times p, ht)$.
- In order to determine the location of point H, we consider the isosceles triangle $\triangle\text{LHE}$ in Figure 5(b). It is straightforward to see that the slope of line EL is equal to $-\tan(\theta)$. Let LZ be the perpendicular to line AB whose foot is point Z on AB. We have that $|\text{EZ}| = |\text{EF}| \times r$, and we deduce that $|\text{EH}| = 2ht \times q \times r$ (see Figure 5(b)). The same property holds for the isosceles triangles $\triangle\text{JGK}$ and $\triangle\text{KFJ}$ in Figure 5(a), and hence we deduce the equalities in (4.3) and (4.4).

Regarding the polynomial equalities in (4.5), recall that $p = q \times \cos(3\theta)$. By the use of trigonometric laws, we have $p = q(4r^3 - 3r)$ and $p^2 + 1 = q^2$. The number r (i.e., $\cos(\theta)$) is a solution of the cubic equation $8r^3 - 4r^2 - 4r + 1 = 0$. Hence, p, q, and r satisfy the equations $\{p^2 + 1 = q^2,\ p = (4r^3 - 3r)q,\ 8r^3 - 4r^2 - 4r + 1 = 0\}$ (i.e., equation (4.5)).

Function HO solves the algebraic constraints and yields six distinct sets of solutions. Each solution set includes the coefficients of lines m and n; the coordinates of points F, G, H, J, K, and L (when the knot is unfolded); and the values of numbers p, q, and r. Only for explanation purposes, we compute and draw the final coordinates of points F, G, H,

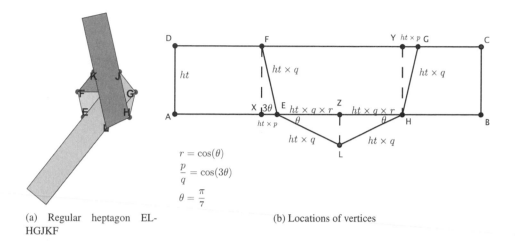

(a) Regular heptagon EL-HGJKF

(b) Locations of vertices

FIGURE 5. The knot fold of a regular heptagon.

J, K, and L as well as the edges of the desired regular heptagon. We obtain the six cases depicted in Figure 6. Equation $8r^3 - 4r^2 - 4r + 1 = 0$ has three distinct solutions of the form $\cos(n\theta)$, where $n = 1, 3, 5$. The regular heptagon in Figures 6(a) and 6(f) corresponds to the solution $\cos(\theta)$, the star polygons in Figures 6(b) and 6(c) to the solution $\cos(3\theta)$, and the star polygons in Figures 6(d) and 6(e) to the solution $\cos(5\theta)$. Since point H is on line AB, it can be either on the half-line EA or on the half-line EB, which explains the symmetry of the solutions. The choice of the sixth case that corresponds to Figure 6(f) leads to the regular heptagon ELHGJKF in Figure 5(a).

After solving and choosing the locations of points L, H, G, J, K and F, the rest of the construction is a sequence of HO calls for operation O1. The folds along the lines passing through the edges of the regular heptagon (i.e., EF, HG, GJ, KF and HL) are performed to obtain the knot fold in Figure 5(a).

5. Correctness of Knot Fold

After an origami construction is completed, we prove its correctness. From the provers' point of view, the Eos system is in the category of systems that employ automated proving methods based on algebraic algorithms, i.e., Gröbner basis computation [Buchberger 98] and the cylindrical algebraic decomposition [Collins 96].

5.1. Proof of correctness in Eos. Proving in Eos means showing that a relevant geometric property, called *conclusion* or *goal*, follows from a collection of geometric hypotheses, called *premise*. In Eos, the premise is the conjunction of the predicates specified in HO calls that we denote by $\mathcal{P}$. The formula $\mathcal{P}$ is internally recorded during the construction. The conclusion is a certain geometric property that we claim holds for the constructed shape, e.g., the regularity of the constructed shape in the case of the polygonal knot fold. The conclusion is specified by the origamist. We use C to denote the conclusion formula.

Depending on the algebraic forms of $\mathcal{P}$ and C, Eos first decides which method to employ. In the case that only equalities (and disequalities) are involved in the algebraic forms, Eos uses Gröbner basis computation. If inequalities are involved, Eos uses the cylindrical

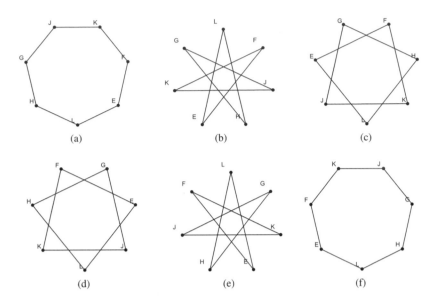

(a)   (b)   (c)

(d)   (e)   (f)

FIGURE 6. All the cases generated by function HO.

algebraic decomposition. In both cases, Eos uses Mathematica's built-in functions for performing Gröbner basis computation and cylindrical algebraic decomposition. When the computation terminates, Eos generates a ProofDoc that describes the details of the construction and the proof [Ghourabi et al. 11].

Because only polynomial equalities are involved in the knot fold constructions described in Sections 3 and 4, the proof employed by Eos is Gröbner basis computation. Let $\mathcal{P}$ be $\forall \underline{x}\mathcal{P}'$ and C be $\forall \underline{x}\forall \underline{y}C'$, where $\mathcal{P}'$ and C' are conjunctions of quantifier-free equalities and the sequences of variables $\underline{x}$ and $\underline{y}$ are distinct. What we want to prove then is

(5.1) $\forall \underline{x}\forall \underline{y}(\mathcal{P}' \Rightarrow C').$

We prove proposition (5.1) by contradiction, i.e., we show that proposition (5.1) holds by showing the negative formula $\exists \underline{x}\exists \underline{y}(\mathcal{P}' \wedge \neg C')$ does not hold. Algebraically, it is reduced to finding the Gröbner basis of the set of polynomials generated from $\exists \underline{x}\exists \underline{y}(\mathcal{P}' \wedge \neg C')$. If the reduced Gröbner basis is $\{1\}$, proposition (5.1) is true.

In the next two sections, we explain the proof of the correctness of the knot fold of the regular pentagon and the regular heptagon.

5.2. Proof of knot fold of regular pentagon. We prove the correctness of the knot fold of the regular pentagon by showing that EFKGH in Figure 4(c) is regular. Let O be the center of EFKGH and $\theta = \angle$EOF. We use vectors to prove the equalities of the edges and of the incidence angles simultaneously. Namely, we prove that the vectors $\overrightarrow{FK}$, $\overrightarrow{KG}$, $\overrightarrow{GH}$, and $\overrightarrow{HE}$ are the rotations of $\overrightarrow{EF}$, $\overrightarrow{FK}$, $\overrightarrow{KG}$, and $\overrightarrow{GH}$, respectively, by angle θ around origin O and, furthermore, that θ is equal to $\frac{\pi}{5}$. We use function Goal of Eos to specify these geometric properties:

$$\text{Goal}(\forall_{\alpha:\mathbb{C}} \ (\alpha \ \text{ToZ}(\overrightarrow{EF}) - \text{ToZ}(\overrightarrow{FK}) = 0 \Rightarrow$$

$$\alpha \ \text{ToZ}(\overrightarrow{FK}) - \text{ToZ}(\overrightarrow{KG}) = 0 \ \wedge \ \alpha \ \text{ToZ}(\overrightarrow{KG}) - \text{ToZ}(\overrightarrow{GH}) = 0 \ \wedge$$

$$\alpha \ \text{ToZ}(\overrightarrow{GH}) - \text{ToZ}(\overrightarrow{HE}) = 0 \ \wedge \ \alpha^5 - 1 = 0))$$

Note that $\forall \underline{x}$ of proposition (5.1) is not specified because it can be generated by Eos automatically. Function $\text{ToZ}(\overrightarrow{XY})$ computes the complex number $(v - u) + \iota \ (w - s)$ from points $X = \text{Point}(u, s)$ and $Y = \text{Point}(v, w)$. Hence, $\alpha \ \text{ToZ}(\overrightarrow{XY})$ is the rotation of vector $\overrightarrow{XY}$ by an angle θ, where $\alpha = \cos(\theta) + \iota \ \sin(\theta)$.

We call function Prove to ask Eos to prove the correctness:

Prove("Regular knot pentagon",
    Mapping $\rightarrow$ {A $\rightarrow$ $\{-w, 0\}$, B $\rightarrow$ $\{w, 0\}$, C $\rightarrow$ $\{w, 1\}$, D $\rightarrow$ $\{-w, 1\}$, E $\rightarrow$ $\{0, 0\}\}$
    Tactics $\rightarrow$ {Split,
        Subgoal $\rightarrow$ {"Lemma Trapezoid",
            SquaredDistance(E, F)=SquaredDistance(H, G)}})

The first parameter of the function call of Prove is the label naming the proposition to be proved, and the second parameter is a list of the initial point mapping. Without loss of generality, we let the height of the initial rectangle to be 1. The mapping assigns to points E, A, B, C, and D the coordinates $(0, 0)$, $(-w, 0)$, $(w, 0)$, $(w, 1)$, and $(-w, 1)$, respectively. Variable w is arbitrary and treated by Eos as an independent variable. This mapping is used to prove $\mathcal{P} \Rightarrow C$ in the general case, i.e., for any edge AB of length $2w$.

The keyword argument "Tactics" introduces a set of proof tactics. In the above call of Prove, we ask Eos to use an extra subgoal. Eos first proves a useful lemma about the following equality. Folds in Figure 1(b) are about making two congruent isosceles triangles $\triangle$GFE and $\triangle$FHG. Therefore, polygon EFGH in Figure 1(b) is an isosceles trapezoid with |EF| = |HG| [Sakaguchi 82]. This equality of the segment lengths is expressed by the formula SquaredDistance(E, F) = SquaredDistance(H, G). When introducing a subgoal $\mathcal{E}$ written as $\forall \underline{x} \forall \underline{z} \mathcal{E}'$, Eos shows the two formulas $\forall \underline{x} \forall \underline{z} (\mathcal{P}' \Rightarrow \mathcal{E}')$ and $\forall \underline{x} \forall \underline{z} \forall y (\mathcal{P}' \wedge \mathcal{E}' \Rightarrow C')$. Note that in this particular case, the sequence $\underline{z}$ is empty. The introduction of the subgoal $\mathcal{E}$ is not necessary but has the advantage of considerably speeding up the computation of the Gröbner basis.

The proofs of the above two formulas are successful. The CPU times used for computing the Gröbner basis of the polynomials generated by the two formulas on Mac OSX (Intel Core i7 8GB 2.9GHz) are 42 seconds and 380 seconds, respectively.

5.3. Proof of knot fold of regular heptagon.
Similarly to the proof of the knot fold of a regular pentagon, we specify a logical formula for the conclusion and pass it to Eos:

$$\text{Goal}(\forall_{\alpha:\mathbb{C}} \ (\alpha \ \text{ToZ}(\overrightarrow{EF}) - \text{Toz}(\overrightarrow{FK}) = 0 \Rightarrow$$

$$\alpha \ \text{ToZ}(\overrightarrow{FK}) - \text{ToZ}(\overrightarrow{KJ}) = 0 \ \wedge \ \alpha \ \text{ToZ}(\overrightarrow{KJ}) - \text{ToZ}(\overrightarrow{JG}) = 0 \ \wedge$$

$$\alpha \ \text{ToZ}(\overrightarrow{JG}) - \text{ToZ}(\overrightarrow{GH}) = 0 \ \wedge \ \alpha \ \text{ToZ}(\overrightarrow{GH}) - \text{ToZ}(\overrightarrow{HL}) = 0 \ \wedge$$

$$\alpha \ \text{ToZ}(\overrightarrow{HL}) - \text{ToZ}(\overrightarrow{LE}) = 0 \ \wedge \ \alpha^7 - 1 = 0)$$

We call function Prove to prove that the polygon EFKJGHL in Figure 5(a) is a regular heptagon for arbitrary point E on edge AB:

Prove("Regular knot heptagon",

   Mapping $\rightarrow \{A \rightarrow \{-w, 0\}, B \rightarrow \{w, 0\}, C \rightarrow \{w, 1\}, D \rightarrow \{-w, 1\}, E \rightarrow \{0, 0\}\}$,

   Tactics $\rightarrow \{\text{Split}\}$)

Note that conclusion $\forall_{\alpha:\mathbb{C}} C'$ is of the form

(5.2) $\forall_{\alpha:\mathbb{C}}(C_1' \Rightarrow C_2' \wedge \ldots \wedge C_7')$.

By writing "Tactics $\rightarrow \{\text{Split}\}$", we ask Eos to split expression (5.2) into separate formulas: $\forall_{\alpha:\mathbb{C}}\mathcal{P}' \Rightarrow (C_1' \Rightarrow C_i')$, where $2 \leq i \leq 7$. Eos proves the six propositions independently. The proof is successful. The total time for computing the Gröbner basis is 151 seconds on the same machine as the one used for the proof in Section 5.2.

6. Conclusion

We presented the construction of the knot folds of a regular pentagon and a regular heptagon by specifying logically the geometric properties of the knots. The final knotted origami is obtained by solving algebraic constraints generated from the logical specification. We further showed the proof of the correctness of the construction. The examples presented here are available at http://www.i-eos.org:8800/ieos/tutorial.

As the number of the edges of the knotted polygons increases, the degree of the algebraic equations as well as the number of equations and variables increases. This requires further computation time of the Gröbner basis, and reduction of the computation time remains a challenging task. Toward proving the knot fold of regular $(2(n \geq 4)+1)$-gons in a reasonable computation time, we need to investigate strategies for optimization, e.g., orderings of the variables.

References

[Alperin and Lang 09] R. C. Alperin and R. J. Lang. "One-, Two, and Multi-fold Origami Axioms." In *Origami⁴: Fourth International Meeting of Origami Science, Mathematics, and Education*, edited by Robert J. Lang, pp. 371–393. Wellesley, MA: A K Peters, 2009. MR2590565 (2011b:51030)

[Brunton 61] J. K. Brunton. "Polygonal Knots." *The Mathematical Gazette* 45:354 (1961), 299–301.

[Buchberger 98] B. Buchberger. "Introduction to Gröbner Bases." In *Gröbner Bases and Applications*, pp. 3–31. Cambridge, UK: Cambridge University Press, 1998. MR1699811 (2000e:13003)

[Collins 96] George E. Collins. "Quantifier Elimination by Cylindrical Algebraic Decomposition." In *Automata Theory and Formal Languages*, Lecture Notes in Computer Science 33, pp. 134–183. Berlin: Springer, 1996.

[Ghourabi et al. 07] F. Ghourabi, T. Ida, H. Takahashi, M. Marin, and A. Kasem. "Logical and Algebraic View of Huzita's Origami Axioms with Applications to Computational Origami." In *Proceedings of the 22nd ACM Symposium on Applied Computing (SAC'07)*, pp. 767–772. New York: ACM, 2007.

[Ghourabi et al. 11] F. Ghourabi, T. Ida, and A. Kasem. "Proof Documents for Automated Origami Theorem Proving." In *Automated Deduction in Geometry*, Lecture Notes in Computer Science 6877, pp. 78–97. New York: Springer, 2011. MR2874685 (2012m:68376)

[Huzita 91] H. Huzita. "Axiomatic Development of Origami Geometry." In *Proceedings of the First International Meeting of Origami Science and Technology*, edited by H. Huzita, pp. 143–158. Padova, Italy: Dipartimento di Fisica dell'Università di Padova, 1991.

[Ida and Takahashi 10] T. Ida and H. Takahashi. "Origami Fold as Algebraic Graph Rewriting." *Journal of Symbolic Computation* 45 (2010), 393–413. MR2599819 (2011d:05170)

[Ida et al. 09] T. Ida, H. Takahashi, M. Marin, A. Kasem, and F. Ghourabi. "Computational Origami System Eos." In *Origami⁴: Fourth International Meeting of Origami Science, Mathematics, and Education*, edited by Robert J. Lang, pp. 285–293. Wellesley, MA: A K Peters, 2009.

[Ida et al. 11] T. Ida, A. Kasem, F. Ghourabi, and H. Takahashi. "Morley's Theorem Revisited: Origami Construction and Automated Proof." *Journal of Symbolic Computation* 46:5 (2011), 571–583. MR2781939 (2012b:51021)

[Maekawa 11] J. Maekawa. "Introduction of the Study of Knot Tape." In *Origami⁵: Fifth International Meeting of Origami Science, Mathematics, and Education*, edited by Patsy Wang-Iverson, Robert J. Lang, and Mark Yim, pp. 395–403. Boca Raton, FL: A K Peters/CRC Press, 2011. MR2866909 (2012h:00044)

[Sakaguchi 82] K. Sakaguchi. "On Polygons Made by Knotting Slips of Paper." *Technical Report of Research Institute of Education, Nara University of Education* 18 (1982), 55–58.

OCHANOMIZU UNIVERSITY, JAPAN
E-mail address: ghourabi.fadoua@ocha.ac.jp

UNIVERSITY OF TSUKUBA, JAPAN
E-mail address: ida@cs.tsukuba.ac.jp

KWANSEI GAKUIN UNIVERSITY, JAPAN
E-mail address: ktaka@kwansei.ac.jp

Equal Division on Any Polygon Side by Folding

Sy Chen

1. Introduction

In origami, Haga's theorem [Takahama and Kasahara 87, Kasahara 88], crossing-diagonals method [Lang 10], Fujimoto's method [Fujimoto and Nishiwaki 82], and many other methods exist for dividing the side of a square into N equal parts without using a ruler. All these techniques are useful when the folder begins with a square. But what if the beginning shape is not a square? After the first few folds, most models are no longer squares. The needed division may be on one of the non-square flaps. In order to divide non-square shapes, the author has devised a systematic approach, the median binary method, to fold any polygon side into equal divisions.

This generalized method can be proven using similar triangles. The procedure starts with a few binary folds on a chosen median line adjacent to the target side of the triangle (the side to be divided). An extension line connects the apex opposite the target side to the newly created division along the median line. This extension line divides the target side into one of the desired N divisions (Figure 1). This method can be easily applied to any polygon, since a polygon is composed of multiple triangles (Figure 2).

With practice, the median binary method can be easily memorized and used without diagrams or other references in the beginning or middle of the folding process.

2. Procedure and Analysis

Any polygon is composed of multiple connected triangles (Figure 2). Because we can divide any triangle side into N equal parts, the method can be applied to any polygon. Binary division is the most commonly used folding step in origami. The *median binary*

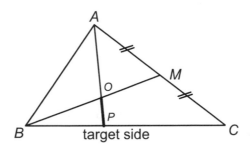

FIGURE 1. Connecting the opposite apex to a point on the median.

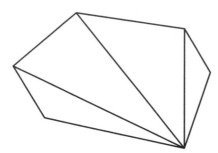

FIGURE 2. Polygon composed of multiple triangles.

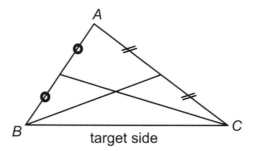

FIGURE 3. Two medians attached to one of the triangle sides.

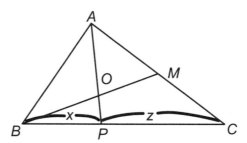

FIGURE 4. Extension line connecting opposite apex to a point on the median.

method starts with a binary division on a median line that is attached to the end of the target side.

For any triangle ABC, if the target side is BC, one can find two medians attached to either end of the target side, BC (Figure 3). The median binary method can be applied on either of the median lines. Let's pick line BM at this time (Figure 4). For any point O along the median, one can construct a line segment extending AO to the edge of the target side, BC.

The extension line divides the target side into BP of length x and PC of length z. In order to find the relationship of the target side division length (x or z) in terms of the median division length (w), a congruent triangle, ACD is added that shares the edge AC to help to solve the problem, as shown in Figure 5.

The two combined triangles make a parallelogram. The original median extension will be the diagonal, BD, of the new parallelogram (Figure 6).

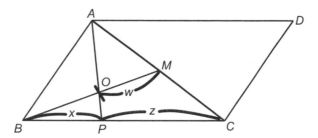

FIGURE 5. Added congruent triangle ACD to form a parallelogram.

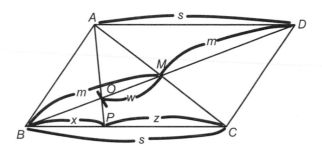

FIGURE 6. The original median extension is the diagonal of the new parallelogram, $ABCD$.

Triangle ADO is similar to triangle PBO. All the corresponding sides have lengths in the same ratio:

$$(2.1) \qquad \frac{BP}{AD} = \frac{BO}{DO}.$$

Define s as the length of the triangle target side, BC; m as the length of midline, BM; x as the length of the divided segment BP on the target side; and z as length of the segment PC. Equation (2.1) becomes

$$(2.2) \qquad \frac{x}{s} = \frac{m-w}{m+w}.$$

The fraction of the other segment, PC, becomes

$$(2.3) \qquad \frac{z}{s} = \frac{s-x}{s} = \frac{2w}{m+w}.$$

Using binary divisions, we can divide the median line BC into Q equal parts, where Q is the largest power of 2 less than or equal to N, i.e.,

$$(2.4) \qquad Q = 2^q \le N,$$

where q is the largest integer for given N. Define each division length as d, and the median line length becomes

$$m = Qd.$$

Define point O as the kth division on the median line from midpoint M. Then, the length of OM, w, becomes

$$(2.5) \qquad w = kd.$$

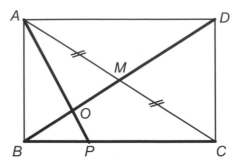

FIGURE 7. The crossing diagonal method is a special case of the median binary method on a rectangle.

Using $m = Qd$ and $w = kd$, Equations (2.2) and (2.3) become

$$\frac{x}{s} = \frac{m-w}{m+w} = \frac{Qd-kd}{Qd+kd} = \frac{Q-k}{Q+k},$$

$$\frac{z}{s} = \frac{2w}{m+w} = \frac{2kd}{Qd+kd} = \frac{2k}{Q+k}.$$

To divide side BC into N equal parts, we can obtain one of the Nth divisions using N as a denominator of the fraction, i.e.,

$$N = Q + k \quad \text{or} \quad k = N - Q.$$

The divided fractions $\frac{x}{s}$ and $\frac{z}{s}$ become

(2.6)
$$\frac{x}{s} = \frac{2Q-N}{N},$$

$$\frac{z}{s} = \frac{2(N-Q)}{N}.$$

Point P divides target side BC into one of the N divisions with fractions $\frac{x}{s}$ and $\frac{z}{s}$. It is also the first target division point found by the median binary method; $\frac{x}{s}$ and $\frac{z}{s}$ are the first target fractions.

Consider the special case of a 90-degree parallelogram, i.e., a rectangle; then, the median binary method is an extension of the crossing-diagonals method. The median line, BM, in the lower triangle is half of the diagonal in the rectangle $ABCD$ (Figure 7).

3. Application on Triangle Side

To divide any side of any triangle into N equal parts, we construct a median line attached to one end of the target side. On the median line, apply binary divisions to divide the line into Q equal parts (see Equation (2.4)). Locate point O as the kth division point (see Equation (2.5)) counted from the midpoint M. Extend line AO to touch the target side. The intersection point, P, divides the target side into the two fractions defined in Equation (2.6).

4. Application on Non-triangular Shape

To divide any side of any polygon, we can make a triangle by connecting both ends of the target side to any of the polygon's other vertices. Figure 8 shows the median binary

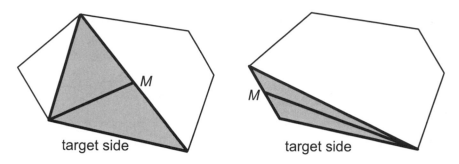

FIGURE 8. Median binary method on a polygon's side using different triangles.

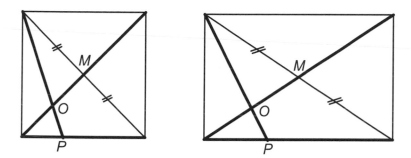

FIGURE 9. Median binary method on the side of a square (left) and rectangle (right).

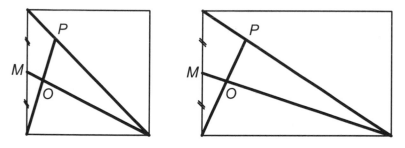

FIGURE 10. Median binary method on the diagonal of a square (left) and rectangle (right).

application on a triangle within a polygon. The median binary method is used to divide the specified triangle side, which is also the desired polygon side.

For a chosen polygon side, there are multiple triangle options. Using the adjacent side to construct the triangle results in fewer folding steps.

Two of the special shapes for a polygon are a square and a rectangle. The median binary method can be applied on the side (Figure 9) or on the diagonal (Figure 10).

When the division point, P, is very close to the corner that is connected to the median (Figure 11), precise folding becomes difficult (for example, with division fraction $1/15$ or $1/31$). Applying the median binary method on the median connected to the other end of the target side can be useful and practical.

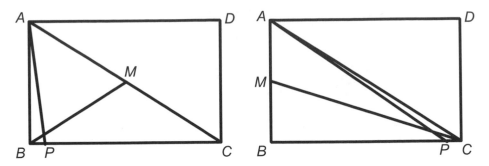

FIGURE 11. Median binary alternative to avoid narrow angle folding.

FIGURE 12. Application of the method on different polygons.

This application of the median binary method can be used on any polygon side (Figure 12).

5. Application Demonstration: Step-by-Step Folding Guide for a Few Odd Divisions

The three median binary examples illustrated here are seven divisions on a square side (Figure 13), thirteen divisions on a square side (Figure 14), and five divisions on a pentagon side (Figure 15). In each diagram, the final step is getting the first target division point. The rest of the division points can be found by binary folding between newly found reference points and one of the end points.

6. Rank Comparison among Different Equal Division Methods

The number of creases needed to fold a given proportion is called the *rank* of the sequence [Lang 10]. For the same N divisions, each method has some advantage on certain fractions in terms of folding ranks [Lang 10]. In practice, one would prefer to obtain the fraction of the denominator, N, with the lowest rank (the first target fraction). The rest of the fractions can be easily obtained by applying binary divisions on the newly found division points.

Because all the other methods divide a square side, the square is used here to obtain the ranking comparison. The rank for the first target fraction can be calculated as $2 + q + 1$, or $3 + q$, where q is the exponent of power of 2 in Equation (2.4). A few comparisons of ranks among the median binary, crossing-diagonals [Lang 10], Fujimoto's, and Haga's methods are listed in Table 1.

Regardless of the first target fraction difference among methods, all of them except the median binary method have the same ranks for the same N divisions. The rank from the

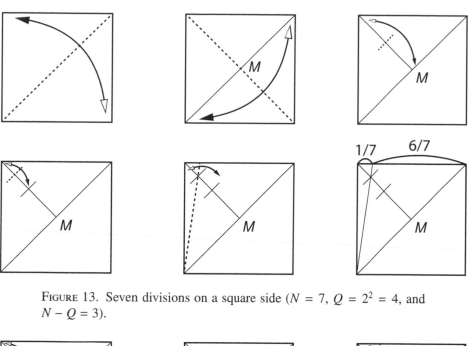

FIGURE 13. Seven divisions on a square side ($N = 7$, $Q = 2^2 = 4$, and $N - Q = 3$).

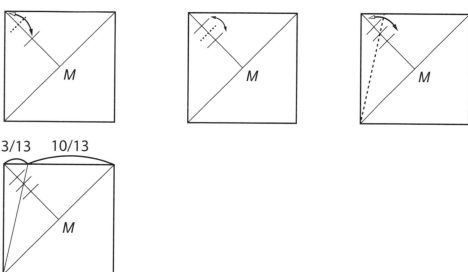

FIGURE 14. Thirteen divisions on a square side ($N = 13$, $Q = 2^3 = 8$, and $N - Q = 5$).

median binary method is exactly one rank higher than the other methods. The main reason that the median binary method has one number higher rank is that it starts from a triangle shape instead of a square.

7. Conclusion

The median binary method is an extension of the crossing-diagonals method. There is no advantage using this method when the starting shape is a square. The best part of

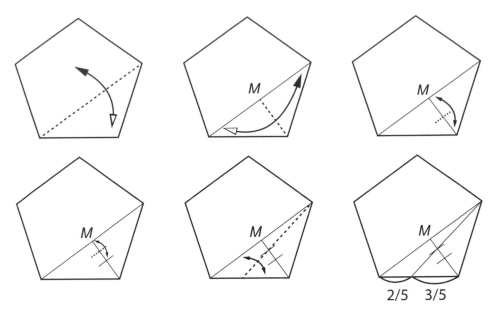

2/5   3/5

FIGURE 15. Five divisions on a pentagon side ($N = 5$, $Q = 2^2 = 4$, and $N - Q = 1$).

Division (N)	Power of 2 < N (Q = 2q)	Median Binary		Rank (first target fraction)		
		First Target Fraction (2Q − N)/N	Rank* 2 + q + 1	Crossing Diagonals	Fujimoto's Method	Haga's Method
3	$2^1 = 2$	1/3	2 + 1 + 1 = 4	3 (1/3)	3 (2/3)	3 (2/3)
5	$2^2 = 4$	3/5	2 + 2 + 1 = 5	4 (1/5)	4 (4/5)	4 (4/5)
7	$2^2 = 4$	1/7	2 + 2 + 1 = 5	4 (3/7)	4 (4/7)	4 (4/7)
9	$2^3 = 8$	7/9	2 + 3 + 1 = 6	5 (1/9)	5 (8/9)	5 (8/9)
11	$2^3 = 8$	5/11	2 + 3 + 1 = 6	5 (3/11)	5 (8/11)	5 (8/11)
13	$2^3 = 8$	3/13	2 + 3 + 1 = 6	5 (5/13)	5 (8/13)	5 (8/13)
15	$2^3 = 8$	1/15	2 + 3 + 1 = 6	5 (7/15)	5 (8/15)	5 (8/15)

* Including two diagonal creases.

TABLE 1. Median binary folding ranks and other methods

this method is the application scope, which can be extended to any polygon shape or any existing three points within a polygon. The folding procedures can be easily derived and memorized with practice.

References

[Fujimoto and Nishiwaki 82] S. Fujimoto and M. Nishiwaki. *Sozo Suru Origami Asobi Eno Shotai (Invitation to Creative Origami Playing)*. Tokyo: Asahi Culture Centre, 1982.

[Kasahara 88] K. Kasahara. *Origami Omnibus*. Tokyo: Japan Publications, 1988.

[Lang 10] R. J. Lang. "Origami and Geometric Constructions." http://www.langorigami.com/science/math/hja/origami_constructions.pdf, 2010.

[Takahama and Kasahara 87] T. Takahama and K. Kasahara. *Origami for the Connoisseur*. Tokyo: Japan Publications, 1987.

ORIGAMI ARTIST
E-mail address: shiyew@gmail.com

A Survey and Recent Results about Common Developments of Two or More Boxes

Ryuhei Uehara

1. Introduction

Polygons that can fold into a convex polyhedron have been investigated since Lubiw and O'Rourke posed the problem in 1996 [Lubiw and O'Rourke 96]. Demaine and O'Rourke published a great book about geometric folding algorithms that includes many results about the topic [Demaine and O'Rourke 07, Chapter 25]. In this context, there are few general results for the relationship between polygons and polyhedra folded from those polygons. Almost the only nice result is the following characterization of the polygons that fold into a tetramonohedron,[1] in terms of tiling (a simple example is given in Figure 1; see [Akiyama 07, Akiyama and Nara 07] for the details): A polygon P is a development of a tetramonohedron if and only if (1) P has a p2 tiling, (2) four of the rotation centers exist in the triangular lattice formed by the triangular faces of the tetramonohedron, (3) the four rotation centers are the lattice points, and (4) no two of the four rotation centers belong to the same equivalence class of the tiling.

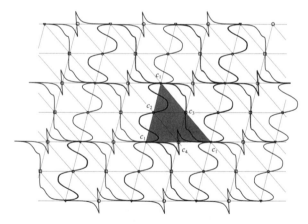

FIGURE 1. A simple example of a p2 tiling. Briefly, the tiling pattern is 180° rotational symmetry, the rotation centers c_1, c_2, c_3, c_4 form the triangular lattice, and these rotation centers of a tile also form the vertices of the tetramonohedron when the tile is folded.

---

[1] A *tetramonohedron* is a tetrahedron that consists of four congruent triangular faces.

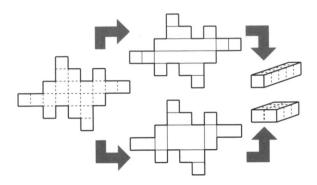

FIGURE 2. A polygon that folds into two boxes of sizes $1 \times 1 \times 5$ and $1 \times 2 \times 3$.

In this article, we concentrate on polygons that consist of unit squares and orthogonal convex polyhedra, i.e., *boxes*, folded from them. Biedl et al. first found two polygons that fold into two incongruent orthogonal boxes [Biedl et al. 99] (see also [Demaine and O'Rourke 07, Figure 25.53]). The first one folds into two boxes of sizes $1 \times 1 \times 5$ and $1 \times 2 \times 3$, and the second one folds into two boxes of sizes $1 \times 1 \times 8$ and $1 \times 2 \times 5$. The author showed that these two polygons are not exceptional. You can see a third example in Figure 2.

We survey the series of our research on this topic. Especially, we give an affirmative answer to the natural question that asks whether there exists a polygon that folds into three different boxes: Yes, there exist infinitely many polygons that fold into three different boxes. So far, it is still open whether there exists a polygon that folds into four or more distinct boxes.

2. Preliminaries

We concentrate on orthogonal polygons that consist of unit squares. A convex orthogonal polyhedron of six rectangular faces is called a *box*. For a positive integer S, we denote by $P(S)$ the set of three integers a, b, c with $0 < a \leq b \leq c$ and $ab + bc + ca = S$, i.e., $P(S) = \{(a, b, c) \mid ab + bc + ca = S\}$. Intuitively, $2S = 2(ab + bc + ca)$ indicates the surface area of the box of size $a \times b \times c$. Therefore, it is necessary to satisfy $|P(S)| \geq k$ to have a polygon of size $2S$ that can fold into k incongruent orthogonal boxes. For example, the two known polygons in [Biedl et al. 99] correspond to $P(11) = \{(1, 1, 5), (1, 2, 3)\}$ and $P(17) = \{(1, 1, 8), (1, 2, 5)\}$. Using a simple algorithm that computes $ab + bc + ca$ for all possible combinations of a, b, c with $1 \leq a \leq b \leq c \leq 50$, we have a list of sets of 3-tuples (a, b, c) with $|P(S)| > 1$:

$$P(11) = \{(1, 1, 5), (1, 2, 3)\}, P(15) = \{(1, 1, 7), (1, 3, 3)\},$$
$$P(17) = \{(1, 1, 8), (1, 2, 5)\}, P(19) = \{(1, 1, 9), (1, 3, 4)\},$$
$$P(23) = \{(1, 1, 11), (1, 2, 7), (1, 3, 5)\}, P(27) = \{(1, 1, 13), (1, 3, 6), (3, 3, 3)\},$$
$$P(29) = \{(1, 1, 14), (1, 2, 9), (1, 4, 5)\}, P(31) = \{(1, 1, 15), (1, 3, 7), (2, 3, 5)\},$$

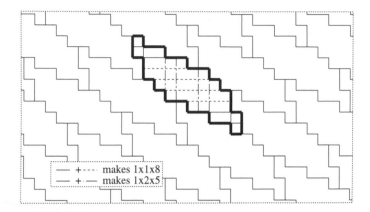

FIGURE 3. Polygon that folds into two boxes of sizes $1 \times 1 \times 8$ and $1 \times 2 \times 5$ and that tiles the plane.

$P(32) = \{(1, 2, 10), (2, 2, 7), (2, 4, 4)\}$, $P(35) = \{(1, 1, 17), (1, 2, 11), (1, 3, 8), (1, 5, 5)\}$,

$P(44) = \{(1, 2, 14), (1, 4, 8), (2, 2, 10), (2, 4, 6)\}$, $P(45) = \{(1, 1, 22), (2, 5, 5), (3, 3, 6)\}$,

$P(47) = \{(1, 1, 23), (1, 2, 15), (1, 3, 11), (1, 5, 7), (3, 4, 5)\}$,

$P(56) = \{(1, 2, 18), (2, 2, 13), (2, 3, 10), (2, 4, 8), (4, 4, 5)\}$,

$P(59) = \{(1, 1, 29), (1, 2, 19), (1, 3, 14), (1, 4, 11), (1, 5, 9), (2, 5, 7)\}$,

$P(68) = \{(1, 2, 22), (2, 2, 16), (2, 4, 10), (2, 6, 7), (3, 4, 8)\}$,

$P(75) = \{(1, 1, 37), (1, 3, 18), (3, 3, 11), (3, 4, 9), (5, 5, 5)\}$,

and so on. That is, there is no polygon that folds into two different boxes if its surface area is less than $22 = 2 \times 11$ because $|P(i)| < 2$ for all $0 < i < 11$. On the other hand, if we try to find a polygon that folds into three different boxes, its surface should be at least $2 \times 23 = 46$, and in this case, the three possible combinations of height, width, and depth are $1 \times 1 \times 11$, $1 \times 2 \times 7$, and $1 \times 3 \times 5$.

3. Polygons Folding into Two Boxes

Even for small surface areas, it is not easy to check all common developments of boxes since they are too numerous. In 2008, we first developed some randomized algorithms that check a portion of the common developments [Mitani and Uehara 08]. By compu-tational experimentation, we obtained more than 25,000 common developments of two different boxes (including the one in Figure 2, which is my most favorite one). Thousands of them can be found at http://www.jaist.ac.jp/~uehara/etc/origami/nets/index-e.html. We show here some interesting ones among them.

Tiling pattern. The discovered polygonal patterns reminded us of *tiling*. Indeed, there exists a simple polygon that can fold into two boxes and forms a tiling. The polygon in Figure 3 can fold into two boxes of sizes $1 \times 1 \times 8$ and $1 \times 2 \times 5$, and it tiles the plane.

A polygon is called a *double packable solid* if it tiles the plane and a polyhedron folded from the polygon fills the space [Kano et al. 07, Section 3.5.2]. It is easy to see that every orthogonal box fills the space. Therefore, the polygon in Figure 3 forms two double packable solids.

As shown in Section 1, any development of a tetramonohedron is characterized by the notion of p2 tiling [Akiyama 07, Akiyama and Nara 07]. We have not yet checked if the developments of two boxes can fold into a tetramonohedron.

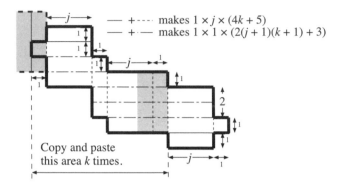

FIGURE 4. Polygon folding into two boxes of sizes $1 \times 1 \times (2(j + 1)(k + 1) + 3)$ and $1 \times j \times (4k + 5)$.

Infinitely many polygons. A natural question is whether or not there are infinitely many distinct[2] polygons that can fold into two boxes. The answer is yes. Some polygons in our catalogue can be generalized. From one of them, we find a polygon that can fold into two boxes of sizes $1 \times 1 \times (2(j + 1)(k + 1) + 3)$ and $1 \times j \times (4k + 5)$ for any positive integers j and k (Figure 4).

The first parameter j just stretches each rectangle in Figure 4 by the same amount, which has no effect on the construction of the two distinct boxes; the two ways of folding are similar to those of the polygon in Figure 3. For the second parameter k, we copy the left side of the polygon in Figure 4 and glue it to the leftmost square (with overlapping at gray areas) and repeat this k times. Then, the way to fold a box of size $1 \times 1 \times (2(j+1)(k+1)+3)$ is essentially the same for every k; we just roll up four unit squares vertically. The way to fold a box of size $1 \times j \times (4k + 5)$ depends on k. We spiral up the polygon k times and obtain vertically long rectangles. By folding in these ways, we construct two distinct boxes of different sizes from a polygon. Therefore, there exists an infinite number of distinct polygons that can fold into two boxes.

4. Polygons Folding into Three Boxes

In 2011, we succeeded in enumerating all common developments of surface area 22, which is the smallest one admitting two boxes of sizes $1 \times 1 \times 5$ and $1 \times 2 \times 3$. By an exhaustive search, we found that the number of common developments of two boxes of sizes $1 \times 1 \times 5$ and $1 \times 2 \times 3$ is 2263 [Abel et al. 11]. Among resulting common developments, there is only one exceptional development that folds into not only two boxes of sizes $1 \times 1 \times 5$ and $1 \times 2 \times 3$, but also one of size $0 \times 1 \times 11$ (Figure 5; it is also a tiling pattern). Each column of the development has height 2 except both endpoints, which allows the folding of a third box of volume 0. But this is kind of cheating: if you allow volume 0, a long ribbon can wrap doubly covered rectangles in many ways (see [Abel et al. 11] for further details).

In 2013, we finally found a development that folds into three different boxes of sizes $2 \times 13 \times 58$, $7 \times 14 \times 38$, and $7 \times 8 \times 56$ (Figure 6). The basic idea is simple; first, we start

---

[2]Precisely, *distinct* means $gcd(a, b, c, a', b', c') = 1$ for two boxes of sizes $a \times b \times c$ and $a' \times b' \times c'$.

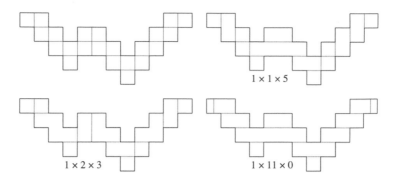

FIGURE 5. Polygon that folds into two boxes of sizes $1 \times 1 \times 5$ and $1 \times 2 \times 3$ and a "box" of size $0 \times 1 \times 11$.

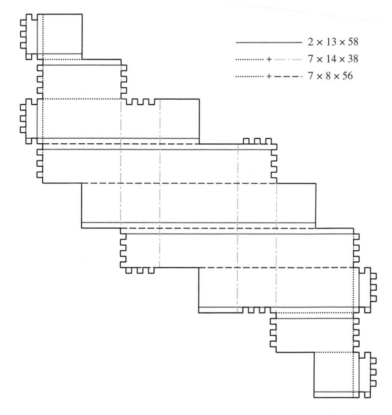

—————— $2 \times 13 \times 58$

·········· + — · — $7 \times 14 \times 38$

·········· + — — — · $7 \times 8 \times 56$

FIGURE 6. Polygon that folds into three boxes of sizes $2 \times 13 \times 58$, $7 \times 14 \times 38$, and $7 \times 8 \times 56$.

with a common development of sizes $1 \times 1 \times 8$ and $1 \times 2 \times 5$. The third box is obtained by "squashing" the box of size $1 \times 1 \times 8$ to half its height, roughly to size $\frac{1}{2} \times 2 \times 8$. But, this intuitive idea does not work in a straightforward way; a square of size 1×1 has perimeter 4, which is not equal to the perimeter 5 of the rectangle of size $\frac{1}{2} \times 2$. So, we use a trick to move some area from two lid squares of size 1×1 to four side rectangles of size 1×8 in a nontrivial way (Figure 7). Intuitively, the zig-zag pattern can be generalized as shown in

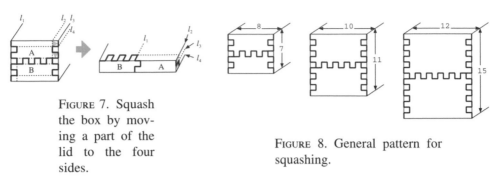

FIGURE 7. Squash the box by moving a part of the lid to the four sides.

FIGURE 8. General pattern for squashing.

Figure 8, and we finally obtain infinitely many polygons that fold into three different boxes of positive volumes. See [Shirakawa and Uehara 13] for further details.

In 2012, Toshihiro Shirakawa found two polygons that can fold into two boxes of sizes $1 \times 1 \times 7$ and $\sqrt{5} \times \sqrt{5} \times \sqrt{5}$. These polygons have surface area 30, which might allow a folding into another box of size $1 \times 3 \times 3$. We enumerated all common developments of two boxes of sizes $1 \times 1 \times 5$ and $1 \times 2 \times 3$, whose surface area is 22, but it took 10 hours in 2011, and 5 hours in 2014. Therefore, in order to investigate the area 30, we used a supercomputer (Cray XC30) for three months using nontrivial hybrid searches combining both breadth-first and depth-first search techniques (see [Xu 14] for further details). As a result, we succeeded in enumerating all common developments of two boxes of sizes $1 \times 1 \times 7$ and $1 \times 3 \times 3$, and the number is 1080. (Later, we used a completely diffrent algorithm based on zero-suppressed binary decision diagrams (ZDDs), and it computed in 10.2 days on a usual desktop computer [Xu et al. 15].) For these common developments, we designed a new algorithm that checked if an orthogonal polygon of area 30 can fold into a box of size $\sqrt{5} \times \sqrt{5} \times \sqrt{5}$. The details of the algorithm can be found in [Xu et al. 15]. Among the 1080 common developments of two boxes of sizes $1 \times 1 \times 7$ and $1 \times 3 \times 3$, there are nine polygons that can also fold into the other box of size $\sqrt{5} \times \sqrt{5} \times \sqrt{5}$. Surprisingly, among these nine developments, one polygon can fold into the box of size $\sqrt{5} \times \sqrt{5} \times \sqrt{5}$ in two different ways. This amazing polygon is shown in Figure 9.

5. Concluding Remarks

So far, the smallest polygon that folds into three boxes based on the same idea in Figure 6 requires more than 500 unit squares. On the other hand, we have enumerated all common developments of surface area 30 that can fold into two boxes of sizes $1 \times 1 \times 7$ and $1 \times 3 \times 3$. Therefore, enumeration of all common developments of the smallest surface area 46 that may fold into three different boxes of sizes $1 \times 1 \times 11$, $1 \times 2 \times 7$, and $1 \times 3 \times 5$ is the next challenging problem.

The main motivation of this research is to investigate the relationship between a polygon and a polyhedra that can be folded from that polygon and vice versa. From this viewpoint, the extensions to nonorthogonal and/or nonconvex polygons are also interesting for future work. For example, Araki, Horiyama, and Uehara have investigated the set of polygons obtained from Johnson–Zalgaller solids by edge cutting [Araki et al. 15]. From that set, they extract all polygons that can fold into regular tetrahedra. However, general characterization of the relationship between a polygon and a polyhedra folded from it is still wide open.

FIGURE 9. Polygon that folds into three boxes of sizes $1 \times 1 \times 7$, $1 \times 3 \times 3$, and $\sqrt{5} \times \sqrt{5} \times \sqrt{5}$. The last box of size $\sqrt{5} \times \sqrt{5} \times \sqrt{5}$ can be folded in two different ways.

References

[Abel et al. 11] Z. Abel, E. Demaine, M. Demaine, H. Matsui, G. Rote, and R. Uehara. "Common Development of Several Different Orthogonal Boxes." In *Proceedings of the 23rd Annual Canadian Conference on Computational Geometry (CCCG)*, pp. 77–82. Toronto: Fields Institute, 2011.

[Akiyama 07] J. Akiyama. "Tile-Makers and Semi-Tile-Makers." *American Mathematical Monthly* 114 (2007), 602–609. MR2341323 (2008j:52032)

[Akiyama and Nara 07] J. Akiyama and C. Nara. "Developments of Polyhedra Using Oblique Coordinates." *J. Indonesia. Math. Soc.* 13:1 (2007), 99–114. MR2321849 (2008a:52013)

[Araki et al. 15] Yoshiaki Araki, Takashi Horiyama, and Ryuhei Uehara. "Common Unfolding of Regular Tetrahedron and Johnson-Zalgaller Solid." In *WALCOM: Algorithms and Computation—9th International Workshop, WALCOM 2015, Dhaka, Bangladesh, February 26–28, 2015, Proceedings*, Lecture Notes in Computer Science 8973, pp. 294–305. Berlin: Springer-Verlag, 2015.

[Biedl et al. 99] T. Biedl, T. Chan, E. Demaine, M. Demaine, A. Lubiw, J. I. Munro, and J. Shallit. "Algorithmic Problem Session." Notes, University of Waterloo, Waterloo, Canada, September 8, 1999.

[Demaine and O'Rourke 07] E. D. Demaine and J. O'Rourke. *Geometric Folding Algorithms: Linkages, Origami, Polyhedra.* Cambridge, UK: Cambridge University Press, 2007. MR2354878 (2008g:52001)

[Kano et al. 07] M. Kano, Mari-Jo P. Ruiz, and Jorge Urrutia. "Jin Akiyama: A Friend and His Mathematics." *Graphs and Combinatorics* 23[Suppl] (2007), 1–39. MR2320617

[Lubiw and O'Rourke 96] A. Lubiw and J. O'Rourke. "When Can a Polygon Fold to a Polytope?" Technical Report 048, Department of Computer Science, Smith College, Northampton, MA, 1996.

[Mitani and Uehara 08] J. Mitani and R. Uehara. "Polygons Folding to Plural Incongruent Orthogonal Boxes." In *Proceedings of the 20th Canadian Conference on Computational Geometry (CCCG 2008)*, pp. 39–42. Montreal: McGill University, 2008.

[Shirakawa and Uehara 13] Toshihiro Shirakawa and Ryuhei Uehara. "Common Developments of Three Incongruent Orthogonal Boxes." *International Journal of Computational Geometry and Applications* 23:1 (2013), 65–71. MR3108779

[Xu 14] Dawei Xu. "Research on the Common Developments of Plural Cuboids." Master's thesis, Japan Advanced Institue of Science and Technology, Nomi, Japan, 2014.

[Xu et al. 15] Dawei Xu, Takashi Horiyama, Toshihiro Shirakawa, and Ryuhei Uehara. "Common Developments of Three Incongruent Boxes of Area 30." In *Theory and Applications of Models of Computation: 12th Annual Conference, TAMC 2015, Singapore, May 18–20, 2015, Proceedings*, Lecture Notes in Computer Science 9076, pp. 236–247. Berlin: Springer-Verlag, 2015.

SCHOOL OF INFORMATION SCIENCE, JAPAN ADVANCED INSTITUTE OF SCIENCE AND TECHNOLOGY, ISHIKAWA, JAPAN
E-mail address: uehara@jaist.ac.jp

Unfolding Simple Folds from Crease Patterns

Hugo A. Akitaya, Jun Mitani, Yoshihiro Kanamori, and Yukio Fukui

1. Introduction

Traditionally, the folding process of origami was transmitted orally and visually by directly showing the folded paper. However, throughout history, attempts have been made to register instructions of particular origami models. Among all types of "written origami," only two are frequently used by contemporary origami artists. They are commonly referenced as *origami diagrams* and *crease patterns*. Origami diagramming was initially devised by Akira Yoshizawa in the 1950s and 1960s [Robinson 04]. It uses lines and arrows indicating the position of the folds and the movement of the paper, as shown in Figure 3 (top). Each step shows the current state of the paper and some indications on how to obtain the state shown in the next step. Usually, the diagrams show the unfolded paper in the first step and the final model in the last step. In this paper, we will show the paper with one side white and the other gray. Dot-dot-dash lines mark the locations of mountain folds, and dashed lines mark the locations of valley folds.

On the other hand, crease patterns show only one picture, which is the unfolded paper containing the creases left by the folds that define the origami model. An example of a crease pattern can be seen in Figure 1. In this paper, we will show the crease pattern white face up with solid lines marking valley folds and dashed lines marking mountain folds. The importance of the crease pattern grew with the rise of mathematical origami and the new design techniques that allowed origami to reach an incredible level of complexity. The fact that the crease pattern only shows the developed/opened state of the paper makes it difficult for nonexperts to grasp any important information regarding the model. However, it indeed can be more illuminating about the origami structure than the image of the folded shape or even diagrams [Lang 04a]. For this reason, many techniques for origami design give a crease pattern as the output. Usually, when the designer produces a technical design, he or she ends up with a crease pattern but has no clue of how to actually fold the model. In fact, it is very hard to fold a model based on a crease pattern. Besides the fact that there is no apparent folding sequence expressed in it, some crease patterns might not even have a folding sequence at all [Lang 11].

Origami diagrams are composed of steps showing subsequent states of the paper. In general, what differs from one state to another is the execution of a fold. In this work, we consider a *fold* to be the bending of one or more layers of the paper localized in a finite number of straight line segments resulting in a dihedral angle of π or $-\pi$. Let us consider that a fold can be categorized as a *simple fold* or a *complex fold*. A simple fold is a fold along a single line that does not end in any internal point of the paper. A complex fold is

©2015 American Mathematical Society

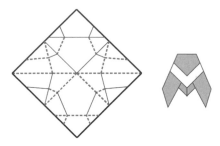

FIGURE 1. Crease pattern (left) and folded form (right) of the traditional cicada origami. Mountain and valley creases are respectively shown as dashed and solid lines.

a combination of folds and unfolds along lines that intersect at internal points. If a crease pattern can be folded with the exclusive use of simple folds, it is called *simply-foldable*.

The paper [Arkin et al. 04] also addressed simple folds. In the authors' models, the paper is only allowed to bend at the creases, and a simple fold causes a rigid movement of the paper around the folding line. The fold is only successful if the movement can be done without unfolding any (already performed) fold and without causing the paper to self-intersect. The authors work with three different models of simple folds: *one-layer*, *some-layers*, and *all-layers*. The one-layer model requires that only one layer is folded at a time. The all-layers model requires that all the layers that are crossed by the folding line are folded simultaneously. The some-layers model supports any number of layers for a given fold. Our model is close to the some-layers model with respect to the number of folded layers, but it is different regarding the general concept of a simple fold. We allow the paper to bend at any place during the fold, making our model closer to what is called *pureland origami* [Smith 80].

Origami designs are usually published in books in the form of origami diagrams. After obtaining a sequence, which is done usually by trial and error, individual drawings that show the folded state of each step have to be drawn. Consequently, diagramming an origami piece is very time consuming. Having this as the motivation, this work aims to produce semi-automatic generated diagrams having a crease pattern as the input. This algorithm was roughly described in [Akitaya et al. 13]. Here, we focus on the theoretical description of simple folds in terms of the crease pattern. Our main contribution is the definition of the minimal set of creases that can be created by a simple fold in a single-vertex origami, which makes possible the identification and the unfolding of any simple fold. With our results, we can determine if a crease pattern of a flat origami is simply-foldable and obtain a folding sequence for it.

2. Background and Related Work

A crease pattern is called *flat-foldable* if it can be flattened in its folded form. Many researchers have investigated the properties of flat origami [Hull 94, Bern and Hayes 96]. We can split the problem of flat-foldability of a crease pattern into local and global. In *local flat-foldability*, we investigate whether the area in the vicinity of a vertex of the crease pattern can be folded flat. *Global flat-foldability* addresses if the origami as a whole can be folded flat, which in general is an NP-hard problem [Bern and Hayes 96].

When checking for local flat-foldability, we consider that each vertex is in the center of a disk of paper and that the paper contains only this vertex. Such a configuration is

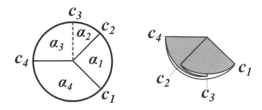

FIGURE 2. Single-vertex origami crease pattern with enumerated creases and angles.

referred to as *single-vertex origami*. A vertex that is located on one of the edges of the paper is called a *border vertex*. All the other vertices are called *internal vertices*. There are three conditions that an internal vertex must obey to be flat-foldable.

Let us consider the single-vertex origami with four creases (c_1, c_2, c_3, c_4) ordered in counterclockwise direction shown in Figure 2. The sequence $(\alpha_1, \alpha_2, \alpha_3, \alpha_4)$ represents the angles around the vertex such that α_i is the angle between c_i and c_{i+1}. The first condition is called *Maekawa's theorem* and states that the number of mountain creases that emanate from the vertex minus the number of valley creases must be either $+2$ or -2. The second condition is called *Kawasaki's theorem* and enunciates that the alternate angles in such a sequence must sum to π. In the example in Figure 2, $\alpha_1 + \alpha_3 = \pi$ and $\alpha_2 + \alpha_4 = \pi$. A consequence of this condition is that the alternating sum of the angles around a vertex must be equal to zero, i.e., $\alpha_1 - \alpha_2 + \alpha_3 - \alpha_4 = 0$. For proofs of both theorems, see [Hull 94].

The third condition was stated by Kawasaki [Kawasaki 91] and enunciates that if $\alpha_i < \alpha_{i-1}$ and $\alpha_i < \alpha_{i+1}$, then, c_i and c_{i+1} must have different mountain/valley assignments. In the example, α_2 is a strict minimum relative to its neighbors and c_2 has opposite assignment to c_3. The proof for this theorem can be found in [Bern and Hayes 96].

The above mentioned conditions are necessary for flat-foldability, but not sufficient. Sufficiency is obtained by a recursive reduction of the crease pattern and application of the third condition, as described in [Demaine and O'Rourke 07]. The third condition must also be followed by the border vertices.

Some origami simulators and diagramming tools have been created. One example is ORIPA, developed by Jun Mitani [Mitani 05]. In addition to the x-ray vision of the folded form, it also obtains the layer ordering. With this information, a rendered image of the folded form is produced. Some simulators try to mimic the interaction between paper and artist in the digital environment. Some examples of this type of approach are the Origami Simulator by Tung Lam [Lam 09] and the Origami Simulation by Robert Lang [Lang 04b]. However, to produce origami diagrams, the user has to already know the folding sequence in advance. Another study investigates simply-foldability in crease patterns containing exclusively orthogonal creases [Arkin et al. 04].

3. Simple Folds

Simple folds, as suggested by the name, are the simplest way to fold a flat configuration of the paper into another flat state. A simple fold always divides the faces where it is applied. Consequently, it will add as many creases to the crease pattern as faces are divided. We assume that simple folds do not unfold any of the pre-existing folds but can only divide them in two, leaving their position and mountain/valley assignment unchanged. Figure 3 shows simple folds applied to one and three layers of paper.

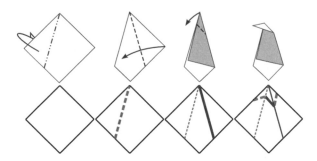

FIGURE 3. How simple folds affect the crease pattern. The corresponding crease pattern of the folded form is shown below each step. Thick lines represents recently added creases.

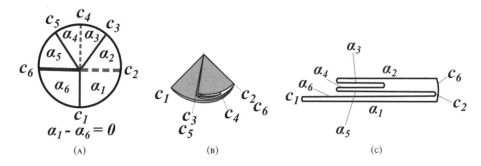

FIGURE 4. (a) Example of reflection creases in a flat-foldable single-vertex origami: c_2 and c_6 are a pair of reflection creases and are shown with thick lines. (b) Folded origami: Creases c_2 and c_6 lie in the same position, as do creases c_3 and c_5. (c) Bottom view of the model with exaggerated thickness.

3.1. Reflection creases.
Let us consider a simple fold in a single-vertex origami.

POSTULATE 3.1. *A single-vertex origami must, after the execution of a simple fold, follow the conditions of local flat-foldability.*

A direct consequence of Postulate 3.1 is that, by removing the creases that were added by a simple fold from a flat-foldable single-vertex crease pattern, one would get a flat-foldable crease pattern.

Let us consider two creases c_2 and c_6 shown in Figure 4. The sequence of angles from c_2 to c_6 in counterclockwise direction is $\alpha_2, \alpha_3, \alpha_4, \alpha_5$. Although these creases were created by the same simple fold, the crease pattern shown in Figure 4 is not simply-foldable.

Two creases are folded into the same position if the alternating sum of angles between them is zero. This comes from the fact that a fold bends the paper in the crease region about π or $-\pi$ and can be visualized in Figure 4(c).

DEFINITION 3.2. A pair of creases are called reflection creases of each other, or simply reflection creases, if they have different mountain/valley assignment and the alternating sum of the angles between them add up to zero.

In Figure 4, creases c_2 and c_6 are reflection creases because they have different crease assignments and $\alpha_2 - \alpha_3 + \alpha_4 - \alpha_5 = 0$ and, therefore, $\alpha_1 - \alpha_6 = 0$. The creases of a reflection pair map to folds that coincide when the model is folded. We can observe that if the single-vertex origami is flat-foldable, both clockwise and counterclockwise circling between reflection creases will generate alternate sums that add up to zero. This is a consequence of Kawasaki's theorem. The alternate sum of the whole circumference around the vertex must be zero. Consequently, if the alternate sum from the clockwise direction is zero, the one from the counterclockwise direction will also be zero.

PROPOSITION 3.3. *The removal of a pair of reflection creases from a flat-foldable single-vertex crease pattern generates a new crease pattern that obeys Maekawa's and Kawasaki's theorems.*

PROOF. Since the starting index of the enumeration of creases is arbitrary, to facilitate the notation, let us say that the reflection creases to be removed are c_1 and c_k. Because the creases in the reflection pair have different mountain/valley assignments, if they are removed, the condition of Maekawa's theorem will still be followed. Let the alternate sum of angles around the vertex be $A = (\alpha_1 - \alpha_2 + \alpha_3 - \ldots)$. A can be divided into two terms $(A = A_1 + A_2)$ such that A_1 contains the angles from c_1 to c_k and A_1 contains the angles from c_k to c_1 in counterclockwise direction. From the definition of reflection creases, $A_1 = A_2 = 0$. The removal of the pair will cause the fusion of the first/last angle of A_1 with the last/first angle of A_2. The alternate sum for the new vertex (without the creases) will be $A_1 - A_2$, which is also zero. In the example shown in Figure 4, this sum is $(\alpha_1 + \alpha_2) - \alpha_3 + \alpha_4 - (\alpha_5 + \alpha_6) = (\alpha_2 - \alpha_3 + \alpha_4 - \alpha_5) - (\alpha_6 - \alpha_1) = 0$. □

From the proof of Proposition 3.3, we can also conclude that if the removal of a pair of creases produces a crease pattern that obeys the two first conditions of flat-foldability (Maekawa's and Kawasaki's theorems), those creases are a pair of reflection creases.

LEMMA 3.4. *Every simple fold that is performed in a nonempty single-vertex origami adds only pairs (at least one pair) of reflection creases.*

PROOF. A simple fold is performed through a line on the folded model. Every crease that is added by a simple fold must lie in the same position when the pattern is completely folded. Consequently, the alternate sum of angles between the added creases is zero, as previously stated. Considering Postulate 3.1 and Maekawa's theorem, the number of added creases must be even. Each pair of added creases with different assignments is a reflection pair. □

The inverse affirmation, though, is not true; there are reflection pairs that, when removed, produce crease patterns that are not flat-foldable. This is due to the third condition of local flat-foldability described in Section 2.

Lemma 3.4 says that a reflection pair is the minimal unit of creases that can be created by a simple fold in a single-vertex origami.

3.2. Reflection paths. Now that simple folds have been analyzed in a single-vertex origami, this subsection will describe their behavior in multi-vertex origami.

Let a multi-vertex crease pattern be the undirected graph $CP = (V, C)$, where V is the set of vertices and C is the set of creases. Let R_v be the binary relation defined in $C \times C$ such that $c_1 R_v c_2$ is true if c_1 and c_2 are a reflection pair based on the internal vertex $v \in V$.

DEFINITION 3.5. A *reflection path* is a simple walk in CP as $(v_1, c_1, v_2, c_2, \ldots, v_n)$ or a closed walk in which $v_1 = v_n$ such that $c_i R_{v_i} c_{i+1}$ with $i \in [1, n)$. We call this reflection path *maximal* if it is a closed walk or if $\nexists c'$ such that $c' R_{v_1} c_1$ or $c_{n-1} R_{v_n} c'$.

In each crease pattern shown in Figure 3, the highlighted creases form a maximal reflection path.

LEMMA 3.6. *The removal of a reflection path affects only its beginning and ending vertices regarding Maekawa's and Kawasaki's theorems.*

PROOF. Every internal vertex will have a pair of reflection creases removed when the reflection path is removed. By Lemma 3.3, the conditions of Maekawa's and Kawasaki's theorems will remain unchanged by such vertices. However, at the beginning and ending vertices, only one crease will be removed and the conditions will be altered, in the case of a simple walk.   □

From Lemma 3.6 we can also conclude that a reflection path that forms a closed walk produces, if removed, a crease pattern that obeys the first two conditions of flat-foldability. We call a reflection path *complete* if it is a closed walk or if it begins and ends with border vertices.

THEOREM 3.7. *The execution of a simple fold can only produce creases that form complete reflection paths.*

PROOF. Because border vertices do not have to obey the conditions of Maekawa's and Kawasaki's theorems, the addition or removal of reflection paths that begin and end with border vertices does not affect the first two conditions for flat-foldability at any vertex. If a simple fold adds at least one pair of reflection creases to the vertices it passes through (Lemma 3.4), the combination of these creases will compose reflection paths that have to end/begin at border vertices or form a closed walk.   □

A simple fold can add one or more complete reflection paths. Analogous to the single-vertex case, a complete reflection path is the minimal unit of creases that can be created by a simple fold. Consequently, the unfold of a simple fold can be modeled as the removal of the corresponding complete reflection path. However, there may be reflection paths that, when removed, lead to crease patterns that are not flat-foldable due to of self-intersections because the third condition and global flat-foldability are not guaranteed.

4. Results

An implementation of the unfolding method described in this work was made using ORIPA to calculate the folded forms at each step. Notice that the theory described in Section 3 allows us to simplify crease patterns only and not unfold a folded form of the origami. ORIPA also checks the flat-foldability of the model, using a brute-force approach to find valid layer orderings. If a result is not flat-foldable, it can simply be discarded. If more than one folded states are possible (when multiple layer orderings are valid), the user can use an interface similar to ORIPA to choose one of them for the diagrams. The input is a crease pattern in ORIPA file format.

The system checks if there are complete reflection paths. If by removing the path the crease pattern is still flat-foldable, we can unfold a simple fold. If there are more then one complete reflection paths that can be unfolded, there are more than one folding sequences capable of producing the input crease pattern. Figure 5 shows a graph that contains all possible unfolds of an input crease pattern, called a *step sequence graph*.

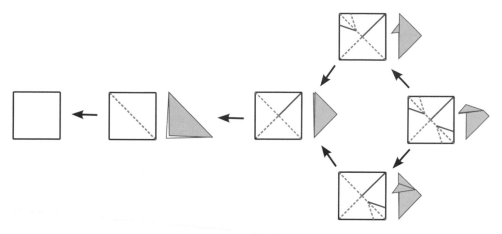

FIGURE 5. A step sequence graph that contains the possible unfoldings of a model.

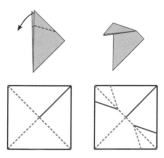

FIGURE 6. A simple fold that folds through many layers of paper and adds more than one complete reflection path to the crease pattern.

Some simple folds can be applied to many layers of paper, as in Figure 6, generating multiple complete reflection paths. Although our method does not produce an unfolding of all the layers at once, the folding sequence shown in Figure 6 is contained in one of the possible generated sequences. Theorem 3.7 assures that our method can unfold any simple fold, by removing the corresponding complete reflection paths.

The user can choose the path in this graph by selecting the desired unfolding and then gradually unfolding the origami until it reaches a square of paper completely developed. The path chosen in this unfolding graph represents an unfolding sequence. By reversing this sequence, we can get a folding sequence. Each crease pattern generates a folded form, using the ORIPA method, and each folded form can be used as a step in an origami diagram. Figure 7 shows diagrams generated by our system. The symbols such as arrows and fold lines were produced automatically by comparing two subsequent steps.

5. Conclusion

In this chapter, a method for the semi-automatic generation of origami diagrams containing simple folds was presented. The proposed method is capable of simplifying gradually the input and generating origami diagrams based on the simplification sequence. The proposed method is capable of generating locally valid flat intermediate states between

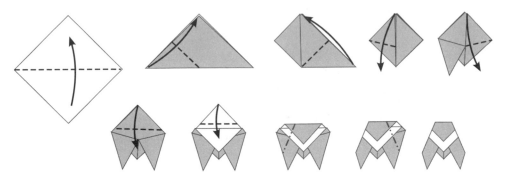

FIGURE 7. Diagrams for the traditional origami cicada model. The folding sequence was generated using our method.

the final model and the unfolded paper. The results can be used to automatically generate diagrams.

Each unfolding is checked for flat-foldability using ORIPA. From Theorem 3.7, we can conclude that all possible simple folds can be unfolded by removing one or more complete reflection paths; therefore, simply-foldability can also be checked using our method. Also, for a simply-foldable origami, all possible folding sequences using simple folds are found.

This method only focuses on flat states of the origami, not worrying about the three-dimensional intermediary states. Therefore, there is no guarantee that the simple folds can be performed without collisions, as in the rigid origami model. In other words, some folds might require some bending of the paper.

The method described here is also the basis for unfolding complex folds. We investigated the use of graph rewriting to unfold four common complex folds in order to generate folding sequences [Akitaya et al. 13].

References

[Akitaya et al. 13] Hugo A. Akitaya, Jun Mitani, Yoshihiro Kanamori, and Yukio Fukui. "Generating Folding Sequences from Crease Patterns of Flat-Foldable Origami." In *ACM SIGGRAPH 2013 Posters, SIGGRAPH '13*, pp. 20:1–20:1. New York: ACM, 2013.

[Arkin et al. 04] Esther M. Arkin, Michael A. Bender, Erik D. Demaine, Martin L. Demaine, Joseph S. B. Mitchell, Saurabh Sethia, and Steven S. Skiena. "When Can You Fold a Map?" *Computational Geometry* 29:1 (2004), 23–46. MR2080063 (2005c:52009)

[Bern and Hayes 96] Marshall Bern and Barry Hayes. "The Complexity of Flat Origami." In *Proceedings of the Seventh Annual ACM-SIAM Symposium on Discrete Algorithms*, pp. 175–183. Philadelphia: Society for Industrial and Applied Mathematics, 1996.

[Demaine and O'Rourke 07] Erik D. Demaine and Joseph O'Rourke. *Geometric Folding Algorithms: Linkages, Origami, Polyhedra*. Cambridge, UK: Cambridge University Press, 2007. MR2354878 (2008g:52001)

[Hull 94] Thomas Hull. "On the Mathematics of Flat Origamis." *Congressus Numerantium* 94 (1994), 215–224. MR1382321 (96k:05196)

[Kawasaki 91] Toshikazu Kawasaki. "On the Relation between Mountain-Creases and Valley-Creases of a Flat Origami." In *Proceedings of the First International Meeting of Origami Science and Technology*, edited by H. Huzita, pp. 229–237. Padova, Italy: Dipartimento di Fisica dell'Università di Padova, 1991.

[Lam 09] Tung Ken Lam. "Computer Origami Simulation and the Production of Origami Instructions." In *Origami⁴: Fourth International Meeting of Origami Science, Mathematics, and Education*, edited by Robert J. Lang, pp. 237–250. Wellesley, MA: A K Peters, 2009. MR2590567 (2010h:00025)

[Lang 04a] Robert J. Lang. "Crease Patterns for Folders." http://www.langorigami.com/art/creasepatterns/creasepatterns_folders.php, 2004.

[Lang 04b] Robert J .Lang. "Origami Simulation." http://www.langorigami.com/science/computational/origamisim/origamisim.php, 2004.

[Lang 11] Robert J. Lang. *Origami Design Secrets: Mathematical Methods for an Ancient Art*, Second Edition. Boca Raton, FL: A K Peters/CRC Press, 2011. MR2841394

[Mitani 05] Jun Mitani. "ORIPA: Origami Pattern Editor." http://mitani.cs.tsukuba.ac.jp/oripa/, 2005.

[Robinson 04] Nick Robinson. *The Origami Bible: A Practical Guide to the Art of Paper Folding.* London: Collins & Brown, 2004.

[Smith 80] John Smith. *Pureland Origami*, Booklet 14. London: British Origami Society, 1980.

DEPARTMENT OF COMPUTER SCIENCE, UNIVERSITY OF TSUKUBA, JAPAN
E-mail address: hugoakitaya@gmail.com

DEPARTMENT OF COMPUTER SCIENCE, UNIVERSITY OF TSUKUBA, JAPAN
E-mail address: mitani@cs.tsukuba.ac.jp

DEPARTMENT OF COMPUTER SCIENCE, UNIVERSITY OF TSUKUBA, JAPAN
E-mail address: kanamori@cs.tsukuba.ac.jp

DEPARTMENT OF COMPUTER SCIENCE, UNIVERSITY OF TSUKUBA, JAPAN
E-mail address: fukui@cs.tsukuba.ac.jp

III. Mathematics of Origami: Rigid Foldability

Rigid Folding of Periodic Origami Tessellations

Tomohiro Tachi

1. Introduction

Repetitive origami tessellations, such as Miura, Yoshimura, Resch, and Waterbomb tessellations, are attracting the attention of engineers and designers; their applications include reconfigurable mechanisms in both small and large scales [Resch and Christiansen 70, Kuribayashi et al. 06, Tachi et al. 12], as well as light-weight material such as the folded core of a sandwich panel [Miura 72]. In such applications, we use hard materials such as thick panels and metal sheets instead of soft paper; the folding motion of such materials can be modeled as that of rigid origami, in which only folding along the creases is allowed and the bending of material or continuous traveling of creases is forbidden. In order to materialize designs using origami tessellations, it is important to study the continuous rigid folding of a planar pattern into the three-dimensional tessellated form. For example, a smaller portion of the tessellation can be naturally folded into a double curved synclastic surface, with a less folded part in the center and a more folded part around the boundary (Figure 1, left). However, if we increase the number of repeating modules, we can observe that the heterogeneity of the folding will block the rigid folding process, as can be seen in Figure 1 (right). This poses a question: Is rigid folding of the entire tessellation a universal behavior, scalable to different industrial purposes, or just a boundary effect that is limited by the size of the pattern?

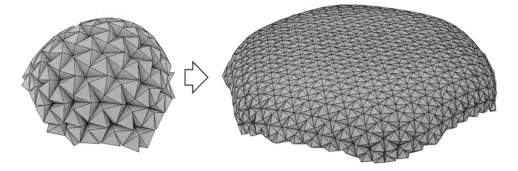

FIGURE 1. Small portion of Resch's triangular pattern forming a synclastic surface (left). Larger portion of the pattern (right). The folding motion is obstructed when the center part remains almost unfolded.

Supported by the JST Presto program.

In this work, we investigate the continuous rigid folding motion of triangulated ori-gami tessellations when their crease patterns are periodically tessellating an infinite plane. Presently, we also assume the repeating symmetry of the folding angles, so that we can avoid the heterogeneity of the folding angles because the heterogeneity potentially blocks the continuous folding paths from a flat state to the completely folded state. An initial and naive approach toward understanding the flexibility of a rigid origami system is to compare the number of variables and constraints; the variable fold angles are constrained by the identity of rotation around interior vertices [Kawasaki 97, belcastro and Hull 02]. Therefore, an origami pattern is estimated to be rigid-foldable if $E - 3V > 0$, where E and V denote the numbers of fold lines and interior vertices, respectively, and every periodic triangular patten follows $E = 3V$. This suggests the non–rigid-foldability of a generic tri-angular pattern. However, in a numeric simulation, it is observed that a generic triangular tessellation forms a mechanism with two degrees of freedom (DOF). We will identify the degeneracy of the constraints originating in the periodic symmetry of the tessellations, and we will demonstrate different behaviors for different patterns. In addition, we show that the folded form of repetitive tessellations are normally constrained to cylindrical surfaces, as opposed to the behavior of a finite portion of the tessellation, which can be folded into a double curved surface.

2. Rigid Origami Basics

Because each panel is planar in rigid origami, we assume that creases are straight. In addition, we allow the surfaces to globally intersect, as most of the patterns intersect themselves if the surface is expanded to infinity.

DEFINITION 2.1. A *crease pattern C* on a planar region P is a planar straight-line graph embedding that partitions P. P denotes a piece of paper.

DEFINITION 2.2. A *rigid folding* $f : \mathbb{R}^2 \to \mathbb{R}^3$ (allowing a collision) by crease pattern C is an intrinsically isometric transformation of a piece of paper P in three dimensions such that each planar region partitioned by C is congruently mapped, i.e., kept planar. The *folded form* of C is the image $f(P)$. This forms an orientable polyhedral 2-manifold, where its set of non-differentiable points lie on the image $f(C)$; for each segment e of C, termed a *crease*, we can assign the *fold angles* ρ_e in $(-\pi, \pi)$ by measuring the exterior dihedral angle at the folded form of the crease. Here, it is possible that the crease is mapped onto a planar region, in which case the fold angle is 0. We call the edges *mountains* or *valleys* when their fold angles are negative or positive, respectively.

We use the fold-angle–based representation of rigid origami.

DEFINITION 2.3. A *single crease fold* $\mathbf{R}_e$, by crease e, in direction $\mathbf{t}$ (not parallel to e) is the rotation about an axis along e orienting to the right side of $\mathbf{t}$ by a folding angle ρ_e of e. For a given oriented curve γ on a plane, not passing though vertices and not tangent to creases, a *relative rigid folding* $\mathbf{F}(\gamma)$ by a crease pattern C along γ is the rigid transformation formed by the product of single crease folds by intersecting creases of C, in tangent directions of γ at the intersections, where the product is calculated in order along γ. The flipped path of γ is denoted by $\overleftarrow{\gamma}$, and $\mathbf{F}(\overleftarrow{\gamma}) = \mathbf{F}^{-1}(\gamma)$.

A relative rigid folding $\mathbf{F}(\gamma)$ can be represented by a homogeneous matrix, using single crease folds $\mathbf{R}_i$ of the ith edge along γ:

$$(2.1) \qquad\qquad\qquad \mathbf{F}(\gamma) = \mathbf{R}_1 \mathbf{R}_2 \cdots \mathbf{R}_n,$$

where $\mathbf{R}_i$ can be decomposed as

$$\mathbf{R}_i = \mathbf{Y}_i \mathbf{P}_i \mathbf{Y}_i^{-1}$$

$$= \begin{bmatrix} c_i & -s_i & 0 & -rs_i \\ s_i & c_i & 0 & rc_i \\ 0 & 0 & 1 & 0 \\ 0 & 0 & 0 & 1 \end{bmatrix} \begin{bmatrix} 1 & 0 & 0 & 0 \\ 0 & \cos\rho_i & -\sin\rho_i & 0 \\ 0 & \sin\rho_i & \cos\rho_i & 0 \\ 0 & 0 & 0 & 1 \end{bmatrix} \begin{bmatrix} c_i & s_i & 0 & 0 \\ -s_i & c_i & 0 & -r \\ 0 & 0 & 1 & 0 \\ 0 & 0 & 0 & 1 \end{bmatrix},$$

where the rotation axis passing along crease i is represented by its normalized orientation vector $\mathbf{l}_i = (c_i, s_i) = (\cos\theta_i, \sin\theta_i)$ and its shortest distance from the origin r. The sign of θ is determined such that $\mathbf{l}_i$ orients to the right side with respect to the tangent vector of γ at the intersection point. Subsequently, rigid-foldability, allowing intersection, is given as follows.

THEOREM 2.4. *A rigid folding (allowing intersection) of a planar region by a crease pattern with given fold angles exists if and only if for any simple closed curve on a plane, not passing though vertices and not tangent to creases, the relative folding along the curve is the identity.*

This can be written as

(2.2) $$\mathbf{F}(\gamma) = \mathbf{R}_0 \mathbf{R}_1 \cdots \mathbf{R}_{n-1} = \mathbf{I}.$$

This is implied in the works of [Kawasaki 97] and [belcastro and Hull 02], but we give a separate proof.

PROOF. The necessity is obvious, i.e., the existence of a rigid folding yields Equation (2.2) for any loop because, otherwise, it is not a valid mapping. In addition, the existence of a rigid folding is equivalent to the existence of rigid folding whose fold angles match the set of fold angles satisfying Equation (2.2).

Sufficiency is shown as follows. Construct a mapping f by spanning a tree structure starting from a root facet R, so that connecting edges have fold angles satisfying Equation (2.2). Then, construct a path γ for each facet F, such that it starts from the center of R, ends at the center of F, and crosses the creases in the sequence of the tree construction. Because each facet is isometrically mapped, this mapping is a valid rigid folding if there is no gap between adjacent facets. Consider a crease e shared by facets F_a and F_b, whose paths from R are γ_a and γ_b, respectively (Figure 2). Consider a path γ_c connecting the endpoints of γ_a and γ_b and crossing only crease e. The closed loop consisting of γ_a, γ_c, and $\overleftarrow{\gamma}_b$ gives a constraint $\mathbf{F}(\gamma_a)\mathbf{F}(\gamma_c)\mathbf{F}(\gamma_b)^{-1} = \mathbf{I}$. Consider an arbitrary point $\mathbf{x}$ on e and points $\mathbf{x}_a$ on F_a and $\mathbf{x}_b$ on F_b, both approaching $\mathbf{x}$ from opposite sides. Then,

$$\lim_{\mathbf{x}_a \to \mathbf{x}} f(\mathbf{x}_a) = \mathbf{F}(\gamma_a)\mathbf{F}(\gamma_c)\mathbf{x} = \mathbf{F}(\gamma_b)\mathbf{x} = \lim_{\mathbf{x}_b \to \mathbf{x}} f(\mathbf{x}_b).$$

We can well define $f(\mathbf{x}) = \lim_{\mathbf{x}_a \to \mathbf{x}} f(\mathbf{x}_a)$, and thus f is continuous at $\mathbf{x}$. Similarly, the mapping is continuous at vertices, and thus the entire mapping is a valid folding. $\square$

Theorem 2.4 can be reduced in the case where the paper is homeomorphic to a disk, as follows.

DEFINITION 2.5. The *single-vertex compatibility* of an interior vertex is the property that the relative rigid folding along a small circle centered at the vertex is equal to the identity, where small means that the circle intersects only with creases that are incident to the vertex.

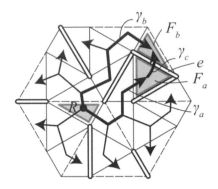

FIGURE 2. Compatibility at edge e.

THEOREM 2.6. *A rigid folding (allowing intersection) of a planar disk region by a crease pattern with given fold angles exists if and only if single-vertex compatibility is satisfied for every interior vertex.*

PROOF. The necessity follows from Theorem 2.4. In order to show sufficiency, we consider any simple closed loop γ and show that it satisfies $\mathbf{F}(\gamma) = \mathbf{I}$, from the conditions around each vertex. Consider a continuous contraction of γ to a point and its corresponding events, i.e., the change in the sequence of creases $e_0, e_1, \ldots, e_{n-1}$. There are two possible types of such events: (1) the curve sweeps across a crease, and (2) the curve sweeps across an interior vertex (Figure 3). In case (1), for curves γ and γ' before and after the event, $\mathbf{F}(\gamma)$ and $\mathbf{F}(\gamma')$ are equal, because

$$\mathbf{F}(\gamma) = \mathbf{R}_A \left(\mathbf{R}_i \mathbf{R}_i^{-1} \right) \mathbf{R}_B,$$
$$\mathbf{F}(\gamma') = \mathbf{R}_A \mathbf{R}_B,$$

where $\mathbf{R}_A$ and $\mathbf{R}_B$ represent the product of the rotations that are shared by both curves. Similarly, in case (2),

$$\mathbf{F}(\gamma) = \mathbf{R}_A \left(\mathbf{R}_i \mathbf{R}_{i+1} \cdots \mathbf{R}_{i+j} \right) \mathbf{R}_B,$$
$$\mathbf{F}(\gamma') = \mathbf{R}_A \left(\mathbf{R}_{i-1}^{-1} \mathbf{R}_{i-2}^{-1} \cdots \mathbf{R}_{i-(N-j-1)}^{-1} \right) \mathbf{R}_B.$$

Here, the single-vertex compatibility of the interior vertex swept by γ gives $\mathbf{R}_{i-1}^{-1} \mathbf{R}_{i-2}^{-1} \cdots$ $\mathbf{R}_{i-(N-j-1)}^{-1} = \mathbf{R}_i \mathbf{R}_{i+1} \cdots \mathbf{R}_{i+j}$. Therefore, $\mathbf{F}(\gamma) = \mathbf{F}(\gamma')$. Since γ is contracted to a point, $\mathbf{F}(\gamma) = \mathbf{I}$.   □

In the case of a disk with a hole, a necessary and sufficient condition is as follows.

THEOREM 2.7. *A rigid folding (allowing intersection) of a planar disk with a hole (the two boundaries do not share a point) by a crease pattern with given fold angles exists if and only if single-vertex compatibility is satisfied for every interior vertex and there exists a closed curve around the hole such that the relative folding along the curve is the identity.*

PROOF. The necessity follows from Theorem 2.4. In order to show sufficiency, consider the contraction process as in the case of a disk. A closed loop that can be contracted to a point is the same as in the case of a disk. If a closed loop cannot be contracted to a point, then it is a loop around a hole. Any such loops can be continuously transformed to

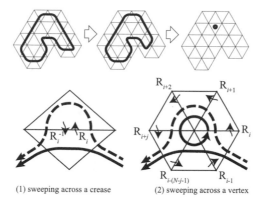

(1) sweeping across a crease   (2) sweeping across a vertex

FIGURE 3. Contraction of a curve.

each other through the sequence of events (1) and (2) in the previous proof, and thus the relative folding is equal to the identity. □

Note that in the case of the disk, even though it is written as a 4×4 matrix equation, the single-vertex compatibility of each interior vertex essentially yields three equality constraints, as the creases pass through a common vertex and the translation term disappears. These constraints form a system of variables of fold angles $\rho_1, \ldots, \rho_E$, with V rotational constraints, i.e., $3V$ equations, imposed on them, where E and V are the numbers of interior edges and interior vertices, respectively. Therefore, rigid-foldability and the number of DOF can first be estimated through $M := E - 3V$. If there is no singularity in the system, $M > 0$ represents rigid-foldability and the number of DOF is M.

2.1. Infinitesimal folding. How does the rigid origami transform? One way to look at it (and to simulate rigid origami) is to consider the *infinitesimal folding motion*. It is known that infinitesimal folding motion of a single vertex can be represented using the sum of vectors around the vertex [Watanabe and Kawaguchi 09, Tachi 09]. Here, we give a similar relation for a generalized loop. Consider a loop passing through creases 0, 1, ..., i, ..., $n - 1$ in this order, and consider the folding of the crease pattern such that the facet before crease 0 does not move. In such a folded state, let $\mathbf{L}_i = \left(L_i^x, L_i^y, L_i^z \right)^\mathsf{T}$ denote the orientation of crease i, and let $\mathbf{O}_i$ denote a (any) point on the crease. Then, differentiating Equation (2.1) gives

$$\sum_i \frac{\partial \mathbf{F}(\gamma)}{\partial \rho_i} d\rho_i = \mathbf{0},$$

where

$$\frac{\partial \mathbf{F}(\gamma)}{\partial \rho_i} = \mathbf{R}_0 \mathbf{R}_1 \cdots \frac{\partial \mathbf{R}_i}{\partial \rho_i} \cdots \mathbf{R}_{n-1}$$

$$= \left[\begin{array}{ccc|c} 0 & -L_i^z & L_i^y & \\ L_i^z & 0 & -L_i^x & \mathbf{L}_i \times \mathbf{O}_i \\ -L_i^y & L_i^x & 0 & \\ \hline 0 & 0 & 0 & 0 \end{array} \right].$$

This is equivalent to

$$(2.3) \qquad \begin{cases} \sum_i \mathbf{L}_i d\rho_i & = \mathbf{0}, \\ \sum_i \mathbf{L}_i d\rho_i \times \mathbf{O}_i & = \mathbf{0}. \end{cases}$$

This means that the infinitesimal motion of rigid origami with a single vertex or multiple vertices can be described as the equilibrium of a point or a rigid body, respectively, when we substitute axial force for angular velocity.[1] As rigid-foldability implies infinitesimal rigid-foldability, the dimension of the solution space of the linear system in Equation (2.3) is greater than or equal to the number of DOF in the actual rigid-folding system.

3. Periodic Origami Tessellations

In the following, we will detail the property of the folded form of periodic origami tessellations (if it exists) as well as the proof of its actual existence and the number of DOF of the mechanism.

DEFINITION 3.1. A *periodic crease pattern C* is a crease pattern on a full plane that partitions the plane into periodic polygonal tiles, such that the symmetry group G is wallpaper group $p1$.

DEFINITION 3.2. A *symmetric rigid folding* by a periodic crease pattern C is a rigid folding by C such that any pair of creases e and f of C that map onto each other by transformation in G share the same fold angle $\rho_e = \rho_f$.

DEFINITION 3.3. A *fundamental region D* of a periodic crease pattern C is a planar disk region that tessellates a plane by the symmetry group G of C, such that its boundary does not pass through any vertex of C. A *fundamental crease pattern C_D* of D is a subset of C within D.

DEFINITION 3.4. For a periodic crease pattern C and its generating translations $\mathbf{T}_1$ and $\mathbf{T}_2$, define two curves γ_1 and γ_2 sharing the starting point $\mathbf{x}$ and ending at $\mathbf{T}_1\mathbf{x}$ and $\mathbf{T}_2\mathbf{x}$, respectively. We call γ_1 and γ_2 *generating paths* if a joined path $\gamma_1, \mathbf{T}_1\gamma_2, \mathbf{T}_2\overleftarrow{\gamma}_1, \overleftarrow{\gamma}_2$ forms the boundary of a fundamental region.

3.1. Cylindrical surface. If there exists a periodic rigid folding, then in a generic case, the folded form approximately follow a cylindrical surface.

LEMMA 3.5. *Consider a pair of generating paths γ_1 and γ_2, the relative foldings $\mathbf{F}(\gamma_1)$ and $\mathbf{F}(\gamma_2)$ along the paths, and their corresponding translations $\mathbf{T}_1$ and $\mathbf{T}_2$, respectively. Then, the relative folding along the boundary of the corresponding fundamental figure is equal to the identity if and only if $\mathbf{F}(\gamma_1)\mathbf{T}_1$ and $\mathbf{F}(\gamma_2)\mathbf{T}_2$ are commutative.*

PROOF. Consider the four corner facets of the fundamental figure A, $\mathbf{T}_1A$, $\mathbf{T}_1\mathbf{T}_2A$, and $\mathbf{T}_2A$. Without loss of generality, the folding f is assumed not to transform facet A, i.e., $A = f(A)$. Since $\mathbf{T}_2$ translates the set of creases intersecting γ_1 onto the creases intersecting $\mathbf{T}_2\gamma_1$,

$$\mathbf{F}(\mathbf{T}_2\gamma_1) = \mathbf{T}_2\mathbf{F}(\gamma_1)\mathbf{T}_2^{-1}.$$

In a similar way,

$$\mathbf{F}(\mathbf{T}_1\gamma_2) = \mathbf{T}_1\mathbf{F}(\gamma_2)\mathbf{T}_1^{-1}.$$

Then,

$$\begin{aligned}
\mathbf{F}(\gamma_1, \mathbf{T}_1\gamma_2, \mathbf{T}_2\overleftarrow{\gamma}_1, \overleftarrow{\gamma}_2) &= \mathbf{F}(\gamma_1)\mathbf{F}(\mathbf{T}_1\gamma_2)\mathbf{F}(\mathbf{T}_2\gamma_1)^{-1}\mathbf{F}(\gamma_2)^{-1} \\
&= \mathbf{F}(\gamma_1)(\mathbf{T}_1\mathbf{F}(\gamma_2)\mathbf{T}_1^{-1})\left(\mathbf{T}_2\mathbf{F}(\gamma_1)\mathbf{T}_2^{-1}\right)^{-1}\mathbf{F}(\gamma_2)^{-1} \\
&= (\mathbf{F}(\gamma_1)\mathbf{T}_1)(\mathbf{F}(\gamma_2)\mathbf{T}_2)(\mathbf{F}(\gamma_1)\mathbf{T}_1)^{-1}(\mathbf{F}(\gamma_2)\mathbf{T}_2)^{-1}.
\end{aligned}$$

---

[1]This interesting duality is also straightforwardly described in terms of screw theory in kinematics.

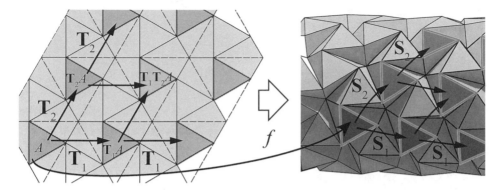

FIGURE 4. Symmetric rigid folding of a periodic crease pattern forms a periodic folded form.

Here, we used the commutativity of translations, $\mathbf{T}_1^{-1}\mathbf{T}_2 = \mathbf{T}_2\mathbf{T}_1^{-1}$. Therefore, the left-hand side is equal to the identity if and only if $\mathbf{F}(\gamma_1)\mathbf{T}_1$ and $\mathbf{F}(\gamma_2)\mathbf{T}_2$ are commutative. □

THEOREM 3.6. *The folded form of a symmetric rigid folding by a periodic crease pattern is periodic, and its symmetry group is generated by two commutative rigid body displacements.*

PROOF. Consider a periodic crease pattern C, whose symmetry group G is generated by two linearly independent translations $\mathbf{T}_1$ and $\mathbf{T}_2$. For an arbitrary facet A and its translated copy $\mathbf{T}_1A$, we consider their folded forms $f(A)$ and $f(\mathbf{T}_1A)$ by rigid folding f (Figure 4). Define congruent transformations $\mathbf{S}_1$ and $\mathbf{S}_2$ as $f(\mathbf{T}_1A) = \mathbf{S}_1 f(A)$ and $f(\mathbf{T}_2A) = \mathbf{S}_2 f(A)$. Without loss of generality, we assume that $f = f(A)$. Then, $\mathbf{S}_1 = \mathbf{F}(\gamma_1)\mathbf{T}_1$ and $\mathbf{S}_2 = \mathbf{F}(\gamma_2)\mathbf{T}_2$, where we follow the notations in Lemma 3.5. From Lemma 3.5, $\mathbf{S}_1$ and $\mathbf{S}_2$ are commutative. Because of the periodic crease pattern, the configuration of the creases and fold angles around A and $\mathbf{T}_1A$ are the same. As a result of this property, any disk portion of the folded form around $f(A)$ is congruently mapped to that of around $f(\mathbf{T}_1A)$ by $\mathbf{S}_1$. Therefore, for any facet B, $f(\mathbf{T}_1B) = \mathbf{S}_1 f(B)$ is satisfied, and thus $f(\mathbf{T}_1^nB) = \mathbf{S}_1 f(\mathbf{T}_1^{n-1}B) = \mathbf{S}_1^n f(B)$. In a similar way, $f(\mathbf{T}_2^nB) = \mathbf{S}_2^n f(B)$. For any copy $B_{m,n} = \mathbf{T}_1^m\mathbf{T}_2^nB$ $(n, m \in \mathbb{Z})$, we can obtain $f(B_{m,n}) = \mathbf{S}_1^m\mathbf{S}_2^n f(B)$. Therefore, the folded form is periodic, and its symmetry group is generated by two commutative rigid transformations $\mathbf{S}_1$ and $\mathbf{S}_2$. □

A rigid transformation is represented as a screw motion, including singular cases of rotation, translation, and identity. A *screw motion* is represented by six parameters, i.e., axis orientation (2DOF) and positions (2DOF), rotation angle (1DOF), and translation along the axis (1DOF). Two rigid transformations are commutative in the following cases:

(1) two screws/rotations sharing a common axis,
(2) a screw/rotation and a translation parallel to the axis of the other,
(3) two translations,
(4) an arbitrary motion and an identity transformation,
(5) two 180° rotations whose axes cross perpendicularly.

The unfolded state follows case (3), while a generic case follows either case (1) or (2), resulting in an approximately cylindrical surface whose axis is located on the shared axis (Figure 5). An interesting example of case (4) is given by a torus origami, as shown in Figure 6. Case (5) cannot actually happen for origami because the developability is violated. Consider a Gauss map along a closed loop corresponding to sequence $\mathbf{S}_1, \mathbf{S}_2, \mathbf{S}_1^{-1}, \mathbf{S}_2^{-1}$.

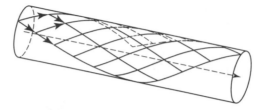

FIGURE 5. Two motions sharing a common screw axis approximately form a cylindrical surface.

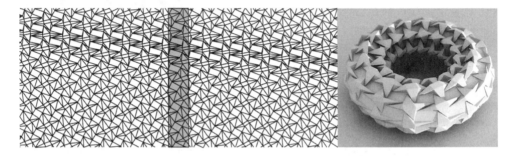

FIGURE 6. A torus origami. The fundamental crease pattern shown covers 1/16 of the entire crease pattern. The repeated module in the vertical direction folds to an identical or 360° rotated position. This pattern does not rigidly fold.

Then, the path turns by 90° at each corner in the same orientation, leading to integral curvature of 360° ≠ 0.

3.2. Rigid foldability. Does a periodic origami tessellation actually rigidly fold? Here, we assume that every panel is triangulated to maximize the flexibility. Let us count the number of variables and constraints. Because of the translational symmetry in two directions, the Euler characteristic of the fundamental crease pattern is equal to that of a torus, i.e., $V - E + F = 0$, where F is the number of facets. Because facets are triangulated, we have that $F = \frac{2}{3}E$, which leads to $M = E - 3V = 0$. Therefore, we might initially estimate that generic periodic crease patterns are not rigid-foldable even if they are triangulated. However, this is not true. Through numerical simulation of different rigid origami structures, we can observe that triangulated periodic crease patterns are generically rigid-foldable, forming a 2DOF structure, with some special cases forming a 1DOF mechanism (Section 4).

This mechanical flexibility originates in degeneracy caused by the periodic symmetry of the pattern. Note that Lemma 3.5 converts one identity of rigid body motions along a loop, represented by six equations, into commutativity of two rigid motions. Because the commutativity can be achieved by making the motions share a screw axis, six equations are reduced to four equations. More formally, we can consider a fundamental crease pattern with a triangular hole whose rigid-foldability is same as the rigid-foldability of the original mesh (Figure 7). Subsequently, rigid-foldability is the intersection of (1) single-vertex compatibility for each interior vertex and (2) the identity of the relative folding along a curve around the hole, which is converted to the commutativity of two rigid motions, yielding (generically) two degrees of freedom.

FIGURE 7. Triangular pattern with a hole.

4. Numerical Calculation

In this section, we discuss the behaviors of different patterns through numerical kinematics. First, we extract the fundamental crease pattern, so that the boundary does not pass the vertex. The continuous rigid folding motion is simulated by using either a hinge-based model or a truss model as the base kinematic simulation and by adding the symmetry constraints that make the corresponding fold angles equal. A *hinge-based model* is the system where the configuration is represented by fold angles that are constrained around each vertex, an example of which is the *rigid origami simulator* [Tachi 09]. In this system, we get a global folding motion by iteratively integrating a valid infinitesimal motion obtained from Equation (2.3). We employ the *truss model*, where vertex coordinates are constrained to make the length of the edges constant. We implemented such a system based on the rigid origami simulation mode of freeform origami [Tachi 10], while adding the equal angle constraints $\rho_e - \rho_f = 0$ for each symmetric pair e and f. In the case of the truss model, the system forms a system with $n + 6$ variables and n constraints (where $n = 3V = E$). Because six DOF correspond to the rigid body motion of the whole model, they can be eliminated by orienting and fixing one of the facets. In this system, the Jacobian matrix for each infinitesimal step is an $(n + 6) \times (n + 6)$ square matrix. If there is a continuous rigid folding motion, the matrix is singular with rank m ($< n + 6$). We obtain a folding motion as a path on an m-dimensional manifold solution space in $(n + 6)$-dimensional configuration space.

4.1. Generic patterns. Here, we show examples of periodic origami tessellations that exhibit a 2DOF mechanism. One of the two degrees of freedom in the mechanism represents a "folding–unfolding" motion, and the other represents a "twisting" motion, i.e., a change in the orientation of the axis of cylinder.

4.1.1. *Resch's triangulated pattern.* The fundamental figure of Resch's triangulated pattern has 4 distinct vertices and 12 distinct edges. The degeneracy described by Theorem 3.5 gives a continuous folding motion, with two degrees of freedom (Figure 8). Although the crease pattern itself has threefold rotational symmetry, the periodic folding does not. As seen in Figure 1, a smaller finite portion is rigid-foldable with rotational symmetry, but this is blocked when the model becomes large. If we break the rotational symmetry and chose one cylindrical axis, we can continuously fold a tessellation of any size to and from two extreme states, i.e., the unfolded and completely folded states (which are rotationally symmetric).

4.1.2. *Waterbomb tessellations.* Figure 9 shows the behavior of waterbomb tessellations, similarly exhibiting a 2DOF configuration space.

4.1.3. *Yoshimura pattern.* The Yoshimura pattern or a diamond buckling pattern has only three distinctive creases and one distinctive vertex, and this pattern also exhibits 2DOF motion (Figure 10).

4.1.4. *Cylindrical Miura-ori.* The pattern shown in Figure 11 is a variation of the regular Miura-ori that folds into a cylindrical surface. If each quadrangular panel is planar,

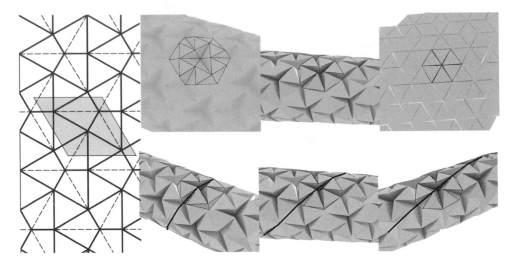

FIGURE 8. Symmetric rigid folding of Ron Resch's triangular tessellation with symmetry constraints. It forms a 2DOF mechanism; one of the two degrees corresponds to a folding–unfolding motion and the other to a twisting motion.

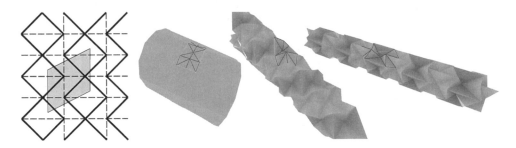

FIGURE 9. Twisting motion in the waterbomb tessellation.

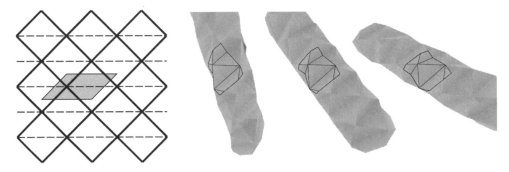

FIGURE 10. Twisting motion in the Yoshimura pattern.

this forms a 1DOF rigid-foldable mechanism. If we split each of the quadrangles into two triangles, we obtain a generic 2DOF mechanism, allowing for a twist motion that utilizes the twist of each triangulated quadrangular panel.

FIGURE 11. Twisting motion of the cylindrical Miura-ori.

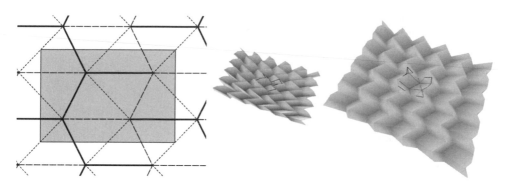

FIGURE 12. The regular Miura-ori cannot be twisted.

4.2. Degenerate case: Miura-ori. The pattern shown in Figure 12 is a regular version of Miura-ori, which forms approximately a planar surface with a 1DOF rigid-foldable mechanism if each panel is planar. Unlike the cylindrical version, the regular version only has one DOF, even if triangulated. The pattern can be rigidly folded without folding diagonal creases, but this does not allow the possibility of being twisted to utilize the diagonal fold lines. Such a folded form is in a singular configuration. The singularity can be examined by using the infinitesimal folding mode obtained from Equation (2.3), which can be expressed as a 12×12 matrix. Interestingly, the rank of the matrix is 9, instead of 10, and there exist three DOF infinitesimal folding modes; however, two of them do not represent a valid finite folding.

5. Conclusion

We have demonstrated that a generic periodic triangulated origami rigidly folds to a cylindrical form. The resulting structure has two DOF; this flexibility can be explained in terms of the periodic symmetry of the pattern. Some exceptions exist; the folded state of an origami torus has no rigid folding motion, and a triangulated regular Miura-ori has only one DOF and thus cannot twist. Rigid-foldability supports the manufacturability of these tessellations using different sheet materials. Potential applications include the roll forming of fold core structures, used for sandwich panels. In this work, we focused only on the wallpaper group $p1$ because it is a subgroup of any other wallpaper group. Further investigation into rigid origami with other symmetry groups would be an interesting direction for future work.

References

[belcastro and Hull 02] sarah-marie belcastro and Thomas Hull. "A Mathematical Model for Non-flat Origami." In *Origami³: Proceedings of the Third International Meeting of Origami Science, Mathematics, and Education*, edited by Thomas Hull, pp. 39–51. Natick, MA: A K Peters, 2002. MR1955758 (2004a:52008)

[Kawasaki 97] Toshikazu Kawasaki. "$R(\gamma) = \mathbf{I}$." In *Origami Science and Art: Proceedings of the Second International Meeting of Origami Science and Scientific Origami*, edited by K. Miura, pp. 31–40. Shiga, Japan: Seian University of Art and Design, 1997.

[Kuribayashi et al. 06] Kaori Kuribayashi, K. Tsuchiya, Zhong You, D. Tomus, M. Umemoto, T. Ito, and M. Sasaki. "Self-Ceployable Origami Stent Grafts as a Biomedical Application of Ni-rich TiNi Shape Memory Alloy Foil." *Materials Science and Engineering A* 419 (2006), 131–137.

[Miura 72] Koryo Miura. "Zeta-Core Sandwich: Its Concept and Realization." *ISAS Report* 37:6 (1972), 137–164.

[Resch and Christiansen 70] Ronald D. Resch and Henry N. Christiansen "Design and Analysis of Kinematic Folded Plate Systems", in Proceedings of International Shell Association, Vienna, Austria, September 1970.

[Tachi et al. 12] Tomohiro Tachi, Motoi Masubuchi, and Masaaki Iwamoto. "Rigid Origami Structures with Vacuumatics: Geometric Considerations." Paper presented at IASS-APCS 2012, Seoul, Korea, May 21–24, 2012. (Available at http://www.tsg.ne.jp/TT/cg/VacuumaticOrigamiIASS2012.pdf.)

[Tachi 09] Tomohiro Tachi. "Simulation of Rigid Origami." In *Origami⁴: Fourth International Meeting of Origami Science, Mathematics, and Education*, edited by Robert J. Lang, pp. 175–187. Wellesley, MA: A K Peters, 2009. MR2590567 (2010h:00025)

[Tachi 10] Tomohiro Tachi. "Freeform Variations of Origami." *Journal for Geometry and Graphics* 14:2 (2010), 203–215. MR2799369

[Watanabe and Kawaguchi 09] Naohiko Watanabe and Ken-ichi Kawaguchi. "The Method for Judging Rigid Foldability." In *Origami⁴: Fourth International Meeting of Origami Science, Mathematics, and Education*, edited by Robert J. Lang, pp. 165–174. Wellesley, MA: A K Peters, 2009.

DEPARTMENT OF GENERAL SYSTEMS STUDIES, THE UNIVERSITY OF TOKYO, JAPAN
E-mail address: tachi@idea.c.u-tokyo.ac.jp

Rigid Flattening of Polyhedra with Slits

Zachary Abel, Robert Connelly, Erik D. Demaine, Martin L. Demaine,
Thomas C. Hull, Anna Lubiw, and Tomohiro Tachi

1. Introduction

In many real-life situations we want polyhedra or polyhedral surfaces to flatten—think of paper bags, cardboard boxes, and foldable furniture. Although paper is flexible and can bend and curve, materials such as cardboard, metal, and plastic are not. The appropriate model for such non-flexible surfaces is *rigid origami*, where the polyhedral faces are rigid and folding occurs only along predefined creases. In rigid origami, flattening is not always possible, and in fact, often no movement is possible at all. In particular, Cauchy's theorem of 1813 says that if a convex polyhedron is made with rigid faces hinged at the edges then no movement is possible (see [Demaine and O'Rourke 07]). Connelly [Connelly 80] showed that this is true even if finitely many extra creases are added.

However, cutting the surface of the polyhedron destroys rigidity and may even allow the polyhedron to be flattened. For example, a paper bag is a box whose top face has been removed, so the aforementioned rigidity results do not apply. Everyone knows the "standard" folds for flattening a paper bag. Surprisingly, these folds do not allow flattening with rigid faces unless the bag is short [Balkcom et al. 06]. Taller bags can indeed be flattened with rigid faces, but a different crease pattern is required [Wu and You 11]. Many of the clever ways of flattening cardboard boxes involve not only removal of the top face but also extra slits and interlocking flaps in the bottom face.

In this paper we initiate the study of *rigid flattening* of a polyhedron: continuous flattening with rigid faces after the addition of finitely many cuts and creases. We require that the final flat folding be a flat folding of the original polyhedron, i.e., that every cut closes up at the end of the flattening process.

We can use previous results to show that every convex polyhedron has a rigid flattening. Without the requirement about cuts closing up, we could just cut every edge of the polyhedron and move the faces to the plane. Alternatively, we could keep the surface connected and use the *continuous blooming* of the source unfolding of a convex polyhedron [Demaine et al. 11].

With our requirement that cuts close up, the final state is a flat folding of the original polyhedron, so we first need to know that every convex polyhedron has a flat-folded state. There are three proofs of this result: [Bern and Hayes 11], using a disk-packing method that applies to any polyhedral surface; [Itoh et al. 12] via a continuous motion; and [Abel et al. 14] via an easily computable continuous motion resulting in a flat folding

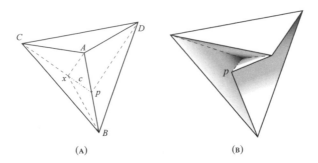

FIGURE 1. Flat folding of a regular tetrahedron: (a) the creases and (b) part way toward the flat folding (shown schematically because the faces will not really be flat in this configuration).

that respects the straight-skeleton gluing. Using these results, we can obtain a rigid flattening by just cutting every fold in the flat-folded state. Note that the surface becomes disconnected.

It is an open question whether every convex polyhedron has a rigid flattening using cuts that do not disconnect the surface. More generally, we might ask to minimize the lengths of the cuts. Another interesting question is whether there is a rigid flattening with only one degree of freedom.

In this paper we begin exploring these ideas by studying the regular tetrahedron. We show that a surprisingly small cut allows rigid flattening. Specifically, if the tetrahedron has side length 1, a cut of length .046 suffices. We explicitly specify the few extra creases that are needed. There is one degree of freedom during the flattening. We use Mathematica to model the motion and verify that no self-intersections occur.

We argue that our particular slit cannot be reduced in length, but it is possible that a smaller slit in a different position works. In fact, it is even possible that the slit length can approach 0 while the number of creases grows. We discuss these and other open questions in the final section of the paper.

2. Flattening a Regular Tetrahedron

In this section we show that a regular tetrahedron with side length 1 can be rigidly flattened with a cut of length .046. We specify the cut and the extra creases, and we verify in Mathematica that the result folds flat rigidly without self-intersections.

In order to describe the cut and the extra creases, we first explore a rigid flattening using a longer cut. The most natural flattening of a regular tetrahedron with vertices A, B, C, D uses creases as shown in Figure 1: faces ACD and BDC are intact; face ADB has one crease bisecting the angle at D and arriving at point p of the opposite edge AB; and the final face ABC has four creases to its centroid x—three from the vertices and the fourth crease, c, from p to x. We call c the *centroid normal*. All the creases are valley folds except c, which is a mountain fold.

This flat folding yields a rigid flattening if we cut the centroid normal c and add two mountain creases that go from the vertices A and B to the cut c and bisect the angles $\angle xAp$ and $\angle xBp$, respectively. See Figure 2. (In fact, mountain creases from A and B to the midpoint of c would also work.) This rigid flattening was first shown by Connelly [Connelly 80].

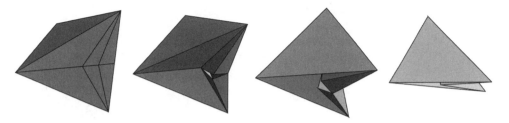

FIGURE 2. Rigid flattening of a tetrahedron after cutting the centroid normal c.

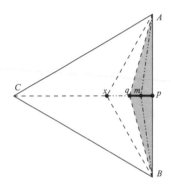

FIGURE 3. The plan of the creases to allow rigid flattening of a tetrahedron after cutting segment pq. (Other faces remain the same.) The flaps Apq and Bpq are shaded.

We argue that this flattening has only one degree of freedom (DOF). Suppose that face BCD is fixed in 3-space. Faces ACD and BCD are rigid and the one degree of freedom is the angle between them. Given a value for that angle, the positions of x and p are fixed in 3-space. (The fact that Cx and Dp are valley folds rules out the other possible position for each). This in turn fixes the positions of the final two mountain creases.

Our rigid flattening with a small slit is based on the one shown in Figure 2 but uses a shorter cut along the centroid normal. The cut goes from p, the midpoint of edge AB, to a point q on the centroid normal. See Figure 3. The final length of pq will be .046, although we will discuss other possibilities. The triangles Apq and Bpq are called the *flaps*. Creases Ax, Bx, and Cx remain valleys. Crease xq is a mountain. Creases Aq and Bq will alternate between mountain and valley folds during the rigid flattening. Point m is placed on the centroid normal segment px and on the angle bisector of $\angle qAp$. We would like to add mountain creases Am and Bm, but this plan needs some refinement.

There are two limitations on the length of the cut pq. The first one can be remedied, but the second one is more fundamental and makes it impossible to shorten the cut below .046. The second limitation is described in Section 2.1. Here we address the first limitation.

The first limitation is that as the slit becomes smaller the flaps can interfere with each other during the folding process. In particular, the two copies of m will collide in the rigid unfolding. This can be remedied by adding pleat folds to the flaps so that the two sides of the cut fold out of the way. In order to achieve the cut length of .046, we place pleat folds as shown in Figure 4. The pleat creases emanate from points p and q, with the the largest pleat crease at p forming angle $\angle qpr = 45°$. The smaller pleat angles at p, going counterclockwise in order, are 15°, 15°, 5°, 10° and then repeat in reverse order. This choice of

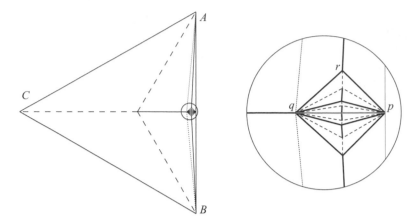

FIGURE 4. Crease pattern for rigid flattening of a regular tetrahedron after cutting a slit of length .046. Crease pattern on face ABC (left) and closeup of the circled slit region (right); solid lines are mountain folds, dashed lines are valleys, and the dotted creases switch between the two.

angles is made so as to avoid collisions between the pleats across the slit when folding; merely quadrisecting the 45° angles at p causes collisions near the flat-folded state. Such pleats are effective in addressing the first limitation because they break the line Am (in Figure 3) so that instead of being a long mountain crease, it is now a shorter mountain and then short valley-mountain-valley-mountain creases as we approach the slit. This makes Am contract into a zig-zag near the slit, which keeps the two copies of m away from each other during the folding process.

Note that the unfolded creases from the point r to the center of the slit in Figure 4 (which are the same as the creases from x_3 to x_7 in Figure 5(a) below) form a slight zig-zag instead of a straight line. This is needed to ensure that the vertices of the pleats (x_3-x_7 in Figure 5(a)) will be flat-foldable. That is, the angles around these vertices must satisfy Kawasaki's Theorem, which states that the opposite pairs of angles at each vertex must sum to 180° in order to fold flat (see [Hull 02]).

This completes the description of the cut and the extra folds to enable rigid flattening of a regular tetrahedron with a slit length of .046. There is still one degree of freedom because the folding of the degree-4 vertices of the pleats will be determined by the neighboring creases adjacent to vertices A and B. Figure 6 shows four frames of the rigid flattening. Note in particular that Frame 3 shows how the flaps have folded out of the way and avoided colliding. With careful observation, one can see that the fold Aq is a mountain in Frame 3 and a valley in Frame 4.

2.1. A limitation on the cut length. In this section we show that the cut length cannot be shorter than 0.046 if we place the cut and the creases as shown in Figure 3 and allow extra folds only in the flaps. Note that this is a very limited result. It is quite possible that there is a rigid flattening using a shorter cut in a different position, or even in the same position but with extra folds outside the flaps.

Consider the creases in Figure 3. We will ignore the flaps—just cut them out of the surface. The remaining surface consists of eight rigid triangles: four on face ABC of the tetrahedron, two on face ABD, and the two intact faces. There is only one degree of

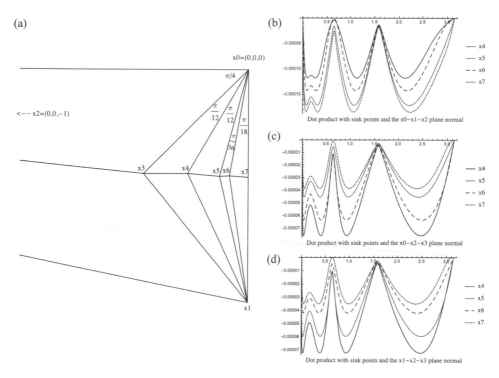

FIGURE 5. (a) Schematic of the pleat "sink" points. (b)–(d) Graphs of the dot product between the sink point vectors and the normals to the sides of the cone from x_2 to the triangle made by x_0, x_1, and x_3.

freedom during the rigid flattening. Points C, D, x, p, q remain on the same plane. A cross section in that plane is shown in Figure 7.

During the flattening process, the distance between points p and q changes. Our main observation is that the cut pq must be long enough to accommodate this. In particular, if the flaps are included, they prevent p and q from being farther apart than the length of the cut. This is true even if the flaps are completely flexible.

We wrote a Mathematica program to compute the distance between points p and q in the plane of C, D, x during the rigid flattening of the eight rigid triangles described above. As can be seen in Figure 8, if the cut length is less than 0.0461201, then at some point during the rigid flattening, points p and q will be further apart than the cut length. Thus, the minimum possible cut is approximately 0.0461201.

2.2. Checking potential collisions. We have verified the rigid flattening of this model in Mathematica using a kinematics model for the regions between the creases. Figure 5(a) shows a detail of the pleats near the slit in the crease pattern, which we could also refer to as a *sink* to borrow origami terminology. The points x_0, x_1, and x_2 correspond to the points p, q, and A from Figure 4, respectively, except that we imagine them to be in the xz-plane. To argue that the sink points x_4–x_7 do not collide with other parts of the model, we examine the polygonal cone made by x_2 (the cone point) and the triangle $x_0 x_1 x_3$. If the sink points remain inside this cone throughout the folding process, then they will not collide with other sides of the folding tetrahedron. To this end, we graph the dot products of the outward-pointing vectors normal to the sides of this cone and the sink point vectors;

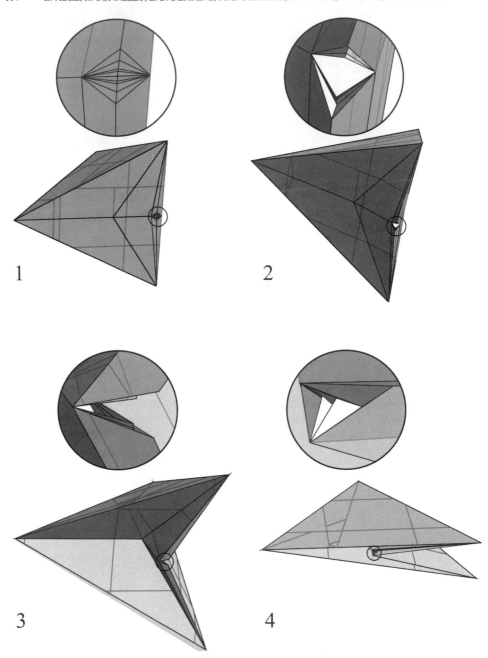

FIGURE 6. Rigid flattening of a regular tetrahedron after cutting a slit of length .046, showing four frames of the flattening, each with the detail of the slit region shown in the circular closeup.

as long as these dot products are nonpositive, the sink points will not penetrate the planes made by the cone sides and thus will remain inside the cone. Graphs of these dot products are shown in Figure 5(b)–(d), where the horizontal axis is the folding angle $0 \leq t \leq \pi$ and the length of the slit is taken to be approximately 0.046. Note that the dot products

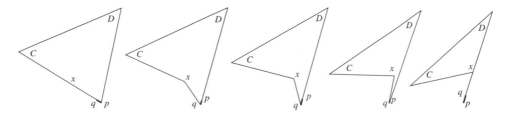

FIGURE 7. Cross sections in the plane of C, D, x showing how points p and q change distance during the rigid flattening process.

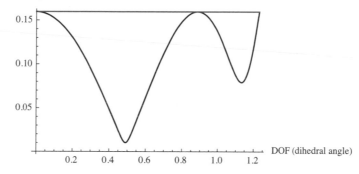

FIGURE 8. A graph of the distance between points p and q (y-axis) during the rigid flattening (x-axis) of the crease pattern in Figure 3 when the cut length is 0.0461201. Observe that the graph has a local maximum at an intermediate point of the flattening and this local maximum reaches the original cut length of 0.0461201 (indicated by the horizontal line). If we decrease the cut length, the new graph has a local maximum that exceeds the cut length.

all remain negative with the slight exception of the point x_7 in graph (d) at the end of the folding process ($t \approx \pi$). This is because when the cone is nearly flat, the sink pleat made by x_7 is inclined upward and escapes the cone. However, examining this case shows that x_7 quickly folds flat and remains clear of any collisions as $t \to \pi$.

We also must show that none of the sink points collide with their mirror-image counterparts on the other side of the sink. As mentioned previously, if the angles of the sink pleats are not chosen with care, then such collisions will occur and obstruct the rigid folding of the model. One way to check this with our current model is to see if during the folding the sink points pass through the plane through $p = x_0$, C, and the perpendicular to AB in Figure 4. In our Mathematica model, this plane is the xy-plane throughout the folding, so all we need to do is plot the z-coordinates of the sink points x_4–x_7. This is shown in Figure 9(a), where the slit length is taken to be 0.046. Since the z-coordinates remain negative, the sink points will not collide with their counterparts on the other side of the slit. Note, however, that x_7 does touch its mirror-image at the folding angle $t \approx 0.62$, where the slit closes up before opening again, as seen in Figure 9(b).

Therefore, with the pleats in Figure 4 included, the two sides of the cut will not intersect throughout the folding process. Interested readers can download and examine the Mathematica code for this model at http://mars.wne.edu/~thull/rigidtet/tet.html.

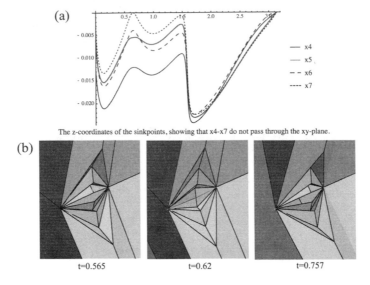

FIGURE 9. (a) Plots of the z-coordinate of the sink points in our Mathematica model for slit length 0.046. (b) Closeups of the slit opening and closing near $t = 0.62$.

3. Discussion and Open Problems

Our investigation of rigid flattening of a regular tetrahedron leaves many open questions:

(1) Does every convex polyhedron have a rigid flattening using cuts that leave the surface connected? Connelly [Connelly 80] shows that cuts in the interiors of faces will not suffice.

(2) Is there such a rigid flattening with one degree of freedom?

(3) Does a regular tetrahedron with unit side lengths have a rigid flattening using a cut of length less than .046? Can the cut length approach 0 (as the number of extra creases grows)?

(4) Does every box have a rigid flattening using one straight cut? We suppose the answer is yes if you cut almost all the way around one equator and apply the rigid flattening for shallow paper bags [Balkcom et al. 06], but will a shorter cut suffice?

Regarding the main open question (1), it may be easier to start from the flat-folded state and ask what slits (plus extra creases) allow the flat-folded state to unfold. Based on the example in Figure 2, where the regular tetrahedron is slit from the centroid of one face to an edge normal, we conjecture that it suffices to slice all the mountain folds in the flat folding. This is not true for polyhedral surfaces in general (the square twist is a counterexample), but it might be true for convex polyhedra—or at least for straight skeleton flat foldings of convex polyhedra [Abel et al. 14]. As a starting point, what happens if we cut the mountain folds *and* the edges of the polyhedron?

Acknowledgments

This work was begun at the 2013 Bellairs Workshop on Computational Geometry, co-organized by Erik Demaine and Godfried Toussaint. We thank the other participants of the workshop for stimulating discussions.

This research could not have been accomplished without the Rigid Origami Simulator written by Tomohiro Tachi, which allowed us to test rigid foldability of convex polyhedra with various cuts and creases.

Research of E. Demaine and M. Demaine is supported in part by NSF grant EFRI-ODISSEI-1240383 and NSF Expedition grant CCF-1138967. Research of T. Hull is supported by NSF grant EFRI-ODISSEI-1240441 "Mechanical Meta-Materials from Self-Folding Polymer Sheets." Research of A. Lubiw is supported by the Natural Sciences and Engineering Research Council of Canada. Research of T. Tachi is supported by the Japan Science and Technology Agency Presto program.

References

[Abel et al. 14] Zachary Abel, Erik D Demaine, Martin L Demaine, Jin-ichi Itoh, Anna Lubiw, Chie Nara, and Joseph O'Rourke. "Continuously Flattening Polyhedra Using Straight Skeletons." In *Proceedings of the 30th Annual Symposium on Computational Geometry (SoCG)*, pp. 396–405. New York: ACM, 2014.

[Balkcom et al. 06] Devin J. Balkcom, Erik D. Demaine, Martin L. Demaine, John A. Ochsendorf, and Zhong You. "Folding Paper Shopping Bags." In *Origami⁴: Fourth International Meeting of Origami Science, Mathematics, and Education*, edited by Robert J. Lang, pp. 315–334. Wellesley, MA: A K Peters, 2006. MR2590567 (2010h:00025)

[Bern and Hayes 11] Marshall Bern and Barry Hayes. "Origami Embedding of Piecewise-Linear Two-Manifolds." *Algorithmica* 59:1 (2011), 3–15. MR2754978 (2012a:52039)

[Connelly 80] Robert Connelly. "The Rigidity of Certain Cabled Frameworks and the Second-Order Rigidity of Arbitrarily Triangulated Convex Surfaces." *Advances in Mathematics* 37:3 (1980), 272–299. MR591730 (82a:53059)

[Demaine and O'Rourke 07] Erik D. Demaine and Joseph O'Rourke. *Geometric Folding Algorithms: Linkages, Origami, Polyhedra.* CAmbridge, UK: Cambridge University Press, 2007. MR2354878 (2008g:52001)

[Demaine et al. 11] Erik D. Demaine, Martin L. Demaine, Vi Hart, John Iacono, Stefan Langerman, and Joseph O'Rourke. "Continuous Blooming of Convex Polyhedra." *Graphs and Combinatorics* 27:3 (2011), 363–376. MR2787423 (2012d:52023)

[Hull 02] Thomas C. Hull. "The Combinatorics of Flat Folds: A Survey." In *Origami³: Proceedings of the Third International Meeting of Origami Science, Mathematics, and Education*, edited by Thomas Hull, pp. 29–38. Natick, MA: A K Peters, 2002. MR1955757 (2004c:52030)

[Itoh et al. 12] Jin-ichi Itoh, Chie Nara, and Costin Vîlcu. "Continuous Flattening of Convex Polyhedra." In *Computational Geometry*, Lecture Notes in Computer Science 7579, pp. 85–97. New York: Springer, 2012.

[Wu and You 11] Weina Wu and Zhong You. "A Solution for Folding Rigid Tall Shopping Bags." *Proceedings of the Royal Society A: Mathematical, Physical and Engineering Science* 467:2133 (2011), 2561–2574. MR2824062 (2012e:52068)

DEPARTMENT OF MATHEMATICS, MASSACHUSETTS INSTITUTE OF TECHNOLOGY, CAMBRIDGE, MA
E-mail address: zabel@mit.edu

DEPARTMENT OF MATHEMATICS, CORNELL UNIVERSITY, ITHACA, NY
E-mail address: rc46@cornell.edu

MIT COMPUTER SCIENCE AND ARTIFICIAL INTELLIGENCE LAB., CAMBRIDGE, MA
E-mail address: edemaine@mit.edu

MIT COMPUTER SCIENCE AND ARTIFICIAL INTELLIGENCE LAB., CAMBRIDGE, MA
E-mail address: mdemaine@mit.edu

DEPARTMENT OF MATHEMATICS, WESTERN NEW ENGLAND UNIVERSITY, SPRINGFIELD, MA
E-mail address: thull@wne.edu

SCHOOL OF COMPUTER SCIENCE, UNIVERSITY OF WATERLOO, WATERLOO, ON, CANADA
E-mail address: alubiw@uwaterloo.ca

DEPARTMENT OF GENERAL SYSTEMS STUDIES, THE UNIVERSITY OF TOKYO, JAPAN
E-mail address: tachi@idea.c.u-tokyo.acjp

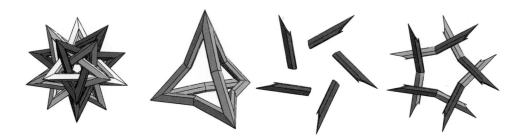

FIGURE 4. (a) FIET variant A, with (b) a single component, (c) a single matching, and (d) a pair of matchings. (Page 26)

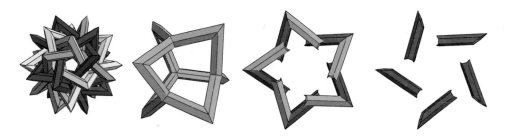

FIGURE 5. (a) The FIET variant B, with (b) a single component, (c) a visual band, and (d) a matching. (Page 27)

FIGURE 7. The SIB5P (a) variant A1, (b) variant A2, (c) variant B1, and (d) variant B2. (Page 27)

Rigid Folding of Periodic Origami Tesselations,
Tomohiro Tachi

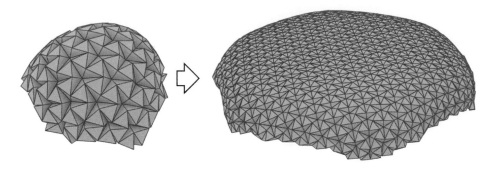

FIGURE 1. Small portion of Resch's triangular pattern forming a synclastic surface (left). Larger portion of the pattern (right). The folding motion is obstructed when the center part remains almost unfolded. (Page 97)

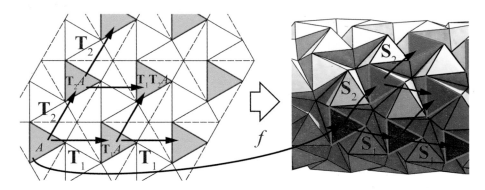

FIGURE 4. Symmetric rigid folding of a periodic crease pattern forms a periodic folded form. (Page 103)

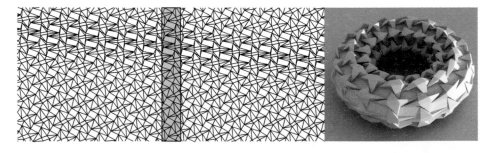

FIGURE 6. A torus origami. The fundamental crease pattern shown covers 1/16 of the entire crease pattern. The repeated module in the vertical direction folds to an identical or 360° rotated position. This pattern does not rigidly fold. (Page 104)

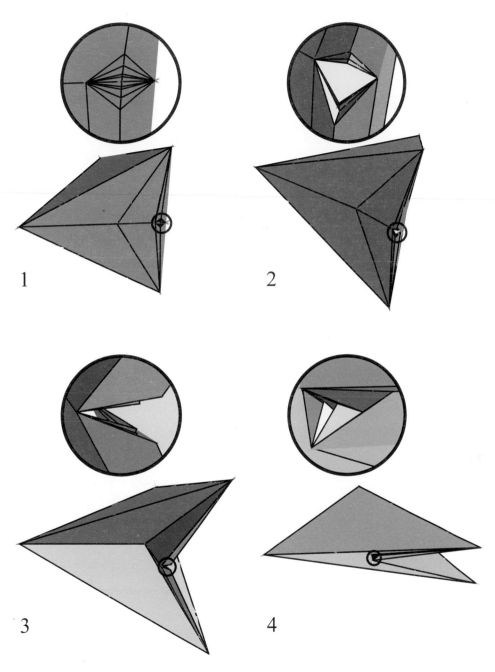

FIGURE 6. Rigid flattening of a regular tetrahedron after cutting a slit of length .046, showing four frames of the flattening, each with the detail of the slit region shown in the circular closeup. (Page 114)

Locked Rigid Origami with Multiple Degrees of Freedom,
Zachary Abel, Thomas C. Hull, and Tomohiro Tachi

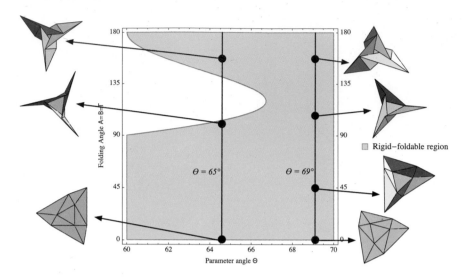

FIGURE 6. A parameter space plot where we let $\alpha = \beta = \gamma$ be the vertical axis and θ be the horizontal axis. (Page 136)

Scaling Any Surface Down to Any Fraction,
Erik D. Demaine, Martin L. Demaine, Kayhan F. Qaiser

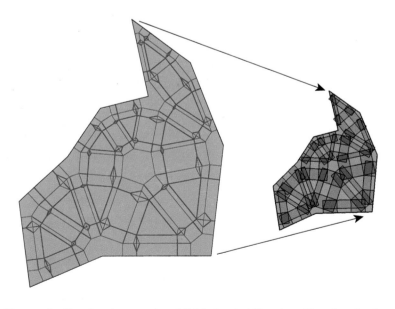

FIGURE 1. Dog head creased and folded to half its size. (Rendered using Tomohiro Tachi's Freeform Origami software, http://www.tsg.ne.jp/TT/software/.) (Page 202)

Curve-Folding Polyhedra Skeletons through Smoothing,
Suryansh Chandra, Shajay Bhooshan, and Mustafa El-Sayed

FIGURE 1. *Curved Folded Polyhedra Skeleton*, made of aluminium, at the
AA Visiting School Bangalore, 2012. (Page 231)

Design Methods of Origami Tessellations for Triangular Spiral Multiple Tilings,
Takamichi Sushida, Akio Hizume, and Yoshikazu Yamagishi

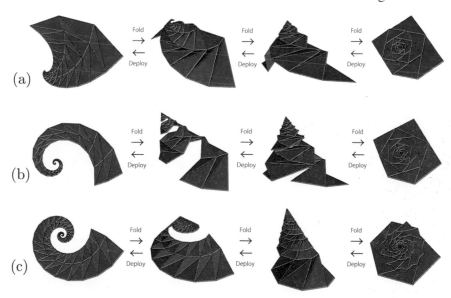

FIGURE 6. Three examples of the one-DOF folding motion of Design Method 5.
(a) An origami sheet of Figure 5(a). In this case, there are no intersections of
facets. (b) An origami sheet for a triangular spiral tiling of Figure 2(c). In
this case, there are no intersections of facets. (c) An origami sheet of a spiral
multiple tiling by right triangles with the angles 30°, 60°, and 90°. In this case,
we can observe intersections of facets. (Page 250)

A New Scheme to Describe Twist-Fold Tessellations,
Thomas R. Crain

FIGURE 3. Basket-weave patterns, original. (Page 258)

On Pleat Rearrangements in Pureland Tessellations,
Goran Konjevod

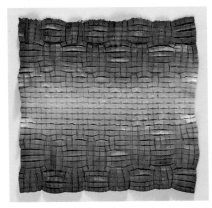

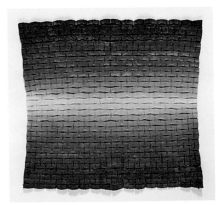

(a) Change study no. 5.　　　　　　　　　　(b) Change study no. 6.

FIGURE 7. Two from a series of pieces I folded on the theme of change. Change studies no. 5 and no. 6 were commissioned by Alameda County and are on display at the Highland Hospital in Oakland, California. (Page 298)

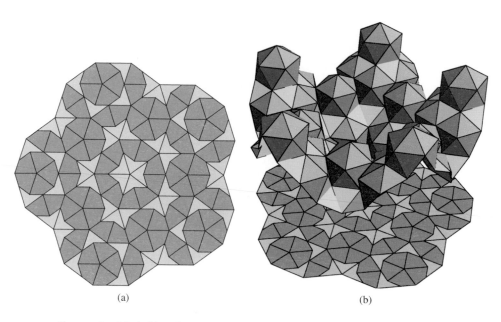

(a)   (b)

FIGURE 1. (a) A kite-dart Penrose tiling. (b) An image of a portion of
Pentasia, superimposed over its corresponding Penrose kite-dart tiling.
(Page 330)

FIGURE 9. The folded single-sheet Pentasia: top side (left) and underside
(right), showing the curved flanges. (Page 337)

Two Calculations for Geodesic Modular Works, Miyuki Kawamura

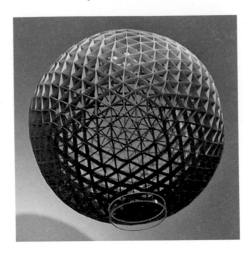

FIGURE 1. Cosmosphere (left). (Page 357)

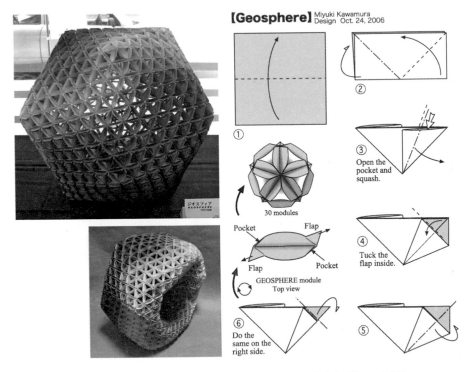

【Geosphere】 Miyuki Kawamura Design Oct. 24, 2006

①

②

③ Open the pocket and squash.

④ Tuck the flap inside.

⑤

⑥ Do the same on the right side.

30 modules

Pocket   Flap

Flap   Pocket

GEOSPHERE module Top view

FIGURE 3. Geosphere (left) and its diagrams (right). (Page 360)

Rigidly Foldable Origami Twists

Thomas A. Evans, Robert J. Lang, Spencer P. Magleby, and Larry L. Howell

1. Introduction

Rigid foldability is an important characteristic of origami structures that becomes significant with non-paper materials. A rigidly foldable origami tessellation is one where the sectors remain rigid and all deflection occurs at the crease lines. Many rigidly foldable patterns have only one degree of freedom, making them potentially useful for deployable structures. Methods have been developed to construct rigidly foldable origami tessellations using materials with finite thickness based on zero-thickness rigidly foldable patterns [Tachi 11].

Origami methods have been considered for application in deployable structures such as solar panels [Miura 85, Zirbel et al. 13] and sterile shrouds [Francis et al. 13]. Other recent developments have included self-deployable origami stent grafts [Kuribayashi et al. 06], self-folding membranes [Pickett 07], and sandwich panel cores [Lebee and Sab 10]. A better understanding of how to create rigidly foldable tessellations can lead to previously unexplored applications.

This paper develops a method for evaluating the rigid foldability of origami tessellations by examining relationships between the dihedral angles in the pattern. The method is then used to determine what configurations allow origami twists, in particular, to be rigidly foldable. Rigidly foldable twists may be arrayed in a tessellation, providing a foundation for deployable origami-based structures to be constructed out of rigid materials.

2. Rigidly Foldable Origami

We will focus on patterns composed of degree-4 vertices, where a typical vertex is illustrated in Figure 1. Four creases meet at each vertex; the paper between adjacent creases is a *sector*, and the angle between adjacent creases is a *sector angle*, designated α. The angle of the fold itself is the *dihedral angle*, denoted by γ, which is the angle between the surface normals of the two incident sectors. A crease may be a *mountain fold* ($\gamma < 0$) or a *valley fold* ($\gamma > 0$) or may be *unfolded* ($\gamma = 0$). We will indicate valley folds by dashed lines and mountain folds by solid lines in our figures. We index the sector angles α_i and dihedral angles γ_i so that sector α_i lies between folds γ_i and γ_{i+1}, as illustrated in Figure 1.

2.1. Flat-foldability in degree-4 vertices. A *flat-foldable* vertex can be folded so that all dihedral angles are equal to $\pm\pi$. Likewise, an origami pattern is considered *flat-foldable* if there exists a configuration where all dihedral angles in the pattern are equal

©2015 American Mathematical Society

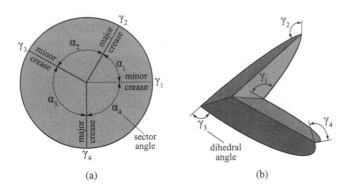

FIGURE 1. A Degree-4 origami vertex is its (a) unfolded and (b) partially folded states.

to $\pm\pi$. The conditions for flat-foldability are well known (see, e.g., [Hull 03]); for degree-4 vertices, they can be summarized as follows:

- Opposite sector angles must sum to π.
- There exist three folds of one parity and one fold of the other.
- The smallest-angled sector, if unique, is incident to folds of opposite parity (*anto*).
- The largest-angled sector, if unique, is incident to folds of the same parity (*iso*).

If there exist two equal smallest-angled sectors, at least one of these sectors must be anto and its opposite sector must be iso. We call the two opposite creases with equal parity the *major* creases and the other two the *minor* creases.

These conditions imply a relationship between the sector angles:

$$(2.1) \qquad \alpha_1 + \alpha_3 = \alpha_2 + \alpha_4 = \pi.$$

These are necessary conditions, not sufficient; an origami pattern composed entirely from flat-foldable vertices may still not be flat-foldable due to self-intersection. However, any origami tessellation containing one or more non-flat-foldable vertices cannot be flat-foldable.

2.2. Fold-angle multipliers. We now introduce relationships between dihedral angles in a flat-foldable degree-4 vertex. Huffman [Huffman 76], Lang [Hull 03], and Tachi [Tachi 10] derived several relationships (which were equivalent under trigonometric transformation). We present equivalent, but new, and somewhat simpler expressions here.

For the degree-4 vertex of Figure 1 where γ_2, γ_4 are the major creases and γ_1, γ_3 are the minor creases, in all configurations between the unfolded and fully folded states, the following relationships apply:

$$(2.2) \qquad \gamma_3 = -\gamma_1, \quad \gamma_2 = \gamma_4 = 2\arctan\left(\frac{\sin\left(\frac{1}{2}(\alpha_1 + \alpha_2)\right)}{\sin\left(\frac{1}{2}(\alpha_1 - \alpha_2)\right)} \tan\left(\frac{1}{2}\gamma_1\right)\right)$$

or, equivalently,

$$(2.3) \qquad \frac{\tan\left(\frac{1}{2}\gamma_2\right)}{\tan\left(\frac{1}{2}\gamma_1\right)} = \frac{\tan\left(\frac{1}{2}\gamma_4\right)}{\tan\left(\frac{1}{2}\gamma_1\right)} = \frac{\sin\left(\frac{1}{2}(\alpha_1 + \alpha_2)\right)}{\sin\left(\frac{1}{2}(\alpha_1 - \alpha_2)\right)}.$$

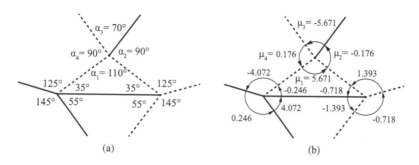

FIGURE 2. Rigidly foldable triangle: (a) sector angles and (b) fold-angle multipliers for each consecutive pair of creases.

The ratio between the half-angle tangents of any two dihedral angles in a flat-foldable degree-4 vertex is a constant that depends solely on the (fixed) values of the sector angles. We call this ratio the *fold-angle multiplier*, μ:

$$(2.4) \qquad \mu \equiv \frac{\sin\left(\frac{1}{2}(\alpha_1 + \alpha_2)\right)}{\sin\left(\frac{1}{2}(\alpha_1 - \alpha_2)\right)} = \frac{\tan\left(\frac{1}{2}\gamma_2\right)}{\tan\left(\frac{1}{2}\gamma_1\right)} = \frac{\tan\left(\frac{1}{2}\gamma_4\right)}{\tan\left(\frac{1}{2}\gamma_1\right)}.$$

We further define μ_i to be the ratio between the half-angle tangents of the dihedral angles adjacent to the ith sector, i.e., $\mu_i \equiv \tan(\frac{1}{2}\gamma_{i+1})/\tan(\frac{1}{2}\gamma_i)$. Then,

$$(2.5) \qquad \mu_1 = -\mu_3 = \mu, \quad \mu_2 = -\mu_4 = -\frac{1}{\mu}.$$

There is a special case to note: When the major crease fold lines are collinear ($\alpha_2 + \alpha_3 = \pi$), zero and infinite fold-angle multipliers are obtained. This occurs because the major crease lines must be completely folded before the minor crease lines begin folding.

2.3. Rigidly foldable polygons. The fold-angle multipliers (μ_i) capture the relationship between consecutive folds around a vertex. They can therefore be used to evaluate the rigid foldability of arrays of vertices. For an origami tessellation to be rigidly foldable, each vertex and each closed polygon in the tessellation must be rigidly foldable. (Again, there are longer-range self-intersection issues that must be considered for global rigid foldability, which we are intentionally not addressing.) For an n-degree polygon with interior angles 1 through n, the fold-angle multipliers (μ_i) associated with the crease pairs at each vertex define a loop condition that enforces consistency around the polygon, namely

$$(2.6) \qquad \prod_{i=1}^{n} \mu_i = 1.$$

Figure 2 shows the sector angles and fold-angle multipliers for a rigidly foldable triangle. Each vertex is rigidly foldable in isolation; since the product of the fold-angle multipliers around the interior polygon is 1 ($-0.246 \times 5.671 \times -0.718 = 1$), the entire pattern is similarly rigidly foldable.

3. Rigid Foldability of Origami Twists

The origami twist is a building block of many origami patterns that have applications to deployable structures. It consists of a central polygon plus parallel pairs of creases extended from each side of the central polygon, as shown in Figure 3(a). The angle between

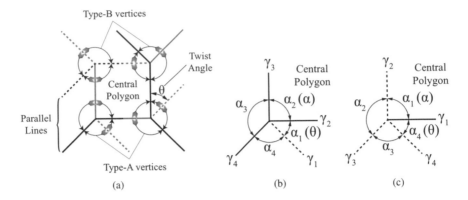

FIGURE 3. (a) A rigidly foldable square twist with twist angle θ. Arrows point from the minor to the major crease lines. (b) A Type-A vertex. (c) A Type-B vertex.

each parallel pair and its adjacent side is the *twist angle*; in a flat-foldable origami twist, all vertices have the same twist angle.

We will classify twist vertices as one of two types. If conventional numbering is used and the first sector lies counterclockwise from a minor crease, a vertex is of *Type-A* if the sector that includes the central polygon is evenly numbered (see Figure 3(b)). Conversely, if this sector is oddly numbered, the vertex is of *Type-B* (see Figure 3(c)). Another method of differentiating vertex types is shown in Figure 3(a). If an arrow is drawn from minor crease lines to major crease lines at each vertex, a Type-A vertex will have a clockwise arrow in the central polygon while a Type-B vertex will have a counterclockwise arrow. Subsequent plots show these directional arrows in the central polygon. A twist polygon can be characterized by the sequence of its vertices; the square twist of Figure 3(a) is AABB.

Note that zero and infinite multipliers can occur if the twist angle is equal to the interior angle of a Type-B vertex or if the twist angle is equal to the complement of the interior angle of a Type-A vertex.

For a Type-A vertex of a twist with interior angle $\alpha = \alpha_2$ and twist angle $\theta = \alpha_1$, we can evaluate the fold-angle multiplier (μ_A) for that vertex:

$$(3.1) \qquad \mu_A = -\frac{\sin\left(\frac{1}{2}(\theta - \alpha)\right)}{\sin\left(\frac{1}{2}(\theta + \alpha)\right)} = \frac{\sin\left(\frac{1}{2}(\alpha - \theta)\right)}{\sin\left(\frac{1}{2}(\alpha + \theta)\right)}.$$

For a Type-B vertex with interior angle $\alpha = \alpha_1$ and twist angle $\theta = \alpha_4$, we have

$$(3.2) \qquad \mu_B = \frac{\sin\left(\frac{1}{2}(\alpha + \pi - \theta)\right)}{\sin\left(\frac{1}{2}(\alpha - \pi + \theta)\right)} = -\frac{\cos\left(\frac{1}{2}(\alpha - \theta)\right)}{\cos\left(\frac{1}{2}(\alpha + \theta)\right)}.$$

With the constraints $0 < \alpha < 180°$ and $0 < \theta < 180°$, it follows that

$$(3.3) \qquad |\mu_A| < 1 < |\mu_B|.$$

This gives us the following result.

THEOREM 3.1 (No Rigidly Foldable Vertex-Uniform Twists). *No origami twist with degree-4 vertices having all Type-A or all Type-B vertices is rigidly foldable.*

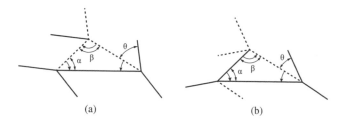

(a)   (b)

FIGURE 4. Two flat-foldable triangle twist configurations. (a) AAB: The α and β vertices are both Type-A while the third is Type-B. (b) ABB: The α vertex is Type-A while the other two are Type-B.

The proof follows directly from Equations (3.3) and (2.6).

4. Triangle Twists

We now consider triangular twists. In this section we will prove the following:

THEOREM 4.1 (No Rigidly Foldable Triangle Twists). *No origami triangle twist is rigidly foldable.*

To prove this theorem, we will consider the two basic configurations with potential to be rigidly foldable for a triangle twist. These two configurations are ABA and ABB (cyclic permutations are equivalent).

For the ABA configuration (see Figure 4(a)), substituting Equations (3.1) and (3.2) into Equation (2.6) results in the condition

(4.1)
$$\frac{\sin\left(\frac{\alpha-\theta}{2}\right)\sin\left(\frac{\beta-\theta}{2}\right)\cos\left(\frac{\alpha+\beta+\theta}{2}\right)}{\sin\left(\frac{\alpha+\theta}{2}\right)\sin\left(\frac{\beta+\theta}{2}\right)\cos\left(\frac{\alpha+\beta-\theta}{2}\right)} = 1.$$

This equation is satisfied only if $\theta = \pi$ or $\alpha + \beta = 2\pi$. In the first case the angle opposite of the twist angle becomes zero, and in the second case the triangle violates geometric compatibility. Therefore, there is no rigidly foldable ABA triangle twist.

For the ABB configuration (see Figure 4(b)), Equation (2.6) results in

(4.2)
$$\frac{\sin\left(\frac{\alpha-\theta}{2}\right)\cos\left(\frac{\theta-\beta}{2}\right)\cos\left(\frac{\alpha+\beta+\theta}{2}\right)}{\sin\left(\frac{\alpha+\theta}{2}\right)\cos\left(\frac{\beta+\theta}{2}\right)\cos\left(\frac{\alpha+\beta-\theta}{2}\right)} = 1.$$

This equation is satisfied only if $\theta = 0$ or $\alpha + \beta = \pi$. In the first case the twist angle becomes zero, and in the second case the third interior angle becomes zero. Therefore, there is no rigidly foldable ABB triangle twist. Because all other triangle twists with two Type-A and one Type-B or two Type-B and one Type-A vertices may be obtained by rotating the AAB or ABB twists, we conclude that no triangle twist is rigidly foldable. Because our definition of an origami twist requires parallel pleats, Theorem 4.1 does not eliminate the possibility of rigidly foldable triangles with nonparallel pleats.

5. Quadrilateral Twists

For simplification, quadrilateral twists have been divided into several standard types of quadrilaterals. These are discussed below.

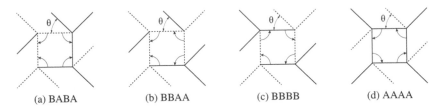

(a) BABA   (b) BBAA   (c) BBBB   (d) AAAA

FIGURE 5. Flat-foldable rectangular twists. Note that (a) and (b) are rigidly foldable while (c) and (d) are not. The vertex label for each twist starts at the lower-left vertex and runs counterclockwise.

5.1. Rectangle and square twists. Because side length does not factor into the fold-angle multipliers, square and rectangular twists have the same conditions for rigid foldability.

THEOREM 5.1 (Rectangle and Square Twists). *A square or rectangular twist is rigidly foldable if and only if it contains two Type-A and two Type-B vertices, with a twist angle not equal to 90°.*

The proof is as follows. For a rectangular twist, $\alpha = 90°$. Therefore, Equations (3.1) and (3.2) simplify to give the following result:

$$(5.1) \qquad \mu_A = \cot\left(\frac{\pi}{4} + \frac{\theta}{2}\right),$$

$$(5.2) \qquad \mu_B = -\tan\left(\frac{\pi}{4} + \frac{\theta}{2}\right).$$

As can be seen from Equations (5.1) and (5.2), the fold-angle multipliers for Type-A and Type-B vertices in such a twist are negative reciprocals of one another. Therefore, any rectangular twist with two Type-A and two Type-B vertices will satisfy Equation (2.6) and is rigidly foldable. The only exception is when $\theta = 90°$, where multipliers become infinite. Conversely, those with unequal numbers of Type-A and Type-B vertices cannot satisfy Equation (2.6) and are not rigidly foldable. Figure 5 shows all of the possibilities (to within cyclic permutation and/or global parity reversal).

5.2. Parallelogram, rhombus, and isosceles trapezoid twists. All three of these types of polygons contain two sets of supplementary interior angles, although the order in which these angles are arranged differs. Since this order does not affect rigid foldability, rhombus, parallelogram, and isosceles trapezoid twists have the same conditions for rigid foldability.

THEOREM 5.2 (Parallelogram, Rhombus, and Isosceles Trapezoid Twists). *A parallelogram, rhombus, or isosceles trapezoid twist is rigidly foldable if and only if it contains two Type-A and two Type-B vertices, with a twist angle not equal to the interior angle of a Type-A vertex.*

To prove this, we will define α as the value of one of the interior angles of the polygon. Of necessity, there are two interior angles with a value of α and two with a value of $\pi - \alpha$. The multipliers for the α-vertices may be calculated using Equations (3.1) and/or (3.2). The multipliers for the other two vertices are found by substituting into Equations (3.1)

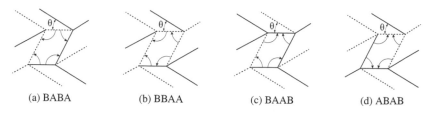

(a) BABA   (b) BBAA   (c) BAAB   (d) ABAB

FIGURE 6. Rigidly foldable parallelogram twist configurations for $\theta < \alpha_{\min}$.

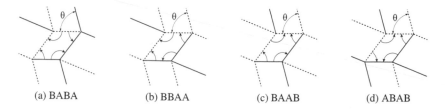

(a) BABA   (b) BBAA   (c) BAAB   (d) ABAB

FIGURE 7. Rigidly foldable parallelogram twist configurations for $\alpha_{\min} < \theta < 90°$.

and (3.2), resulting in

$$(5.3) \qquad \mu_A = \frac{\cos\left(\frac{1}{2}(\alpha + \theta)\right)}{\cos\left(\frac{1}{2}(\alpha - \theta)\right)}$$

$$(5.4) \qquad \mu_B = -\frac{\sin\left(\frac{1}{2}(\alpha + \theta)\right)}{\sin\left(\frac{1}{2}(\alpha - \theta)\right)}$$

The product of any two of these Type-A multipliers and two of these Type-B vertices is equal to one, satisfying Equation (2.6). Therefore, a parallelogram, rhombus, or isosceles trapezoid twist is rigidly foldable if it contains two Type-A and two Type-B vertices. The exception is where the twist angle is equal to the interior angle of a Type-A vertex, where infinite multipliers are obtained. Conversely, twists with unequal numbers of Type-A and Type-B vertices cannot satisfy Equation (2.6) and are not rigidly foldable.

Figure 6 shows the four rigidly foldable configurations for a parallelogram twist where the twist angle (θ) is smaller than any of the interior angles (again allowing for cyclic permutation and/or global parity reversal). Figure 7 shows the four rigidly foldable configurations for the case where one of the sets of interior angles is less than θ. Figure 8 shows the six rigidly foldable configurations for an isosceles trapezoid for the case where the twist angle is less than any of the interior angles. Figure 9 shows the six rigidly foldable configurations for the case where the twist angle is greater than one pair of interior angles.

5.3. Scalene trapezoid twists.

THEOREM 5.3 (Scalene Trapezoid Twists). *A scalene trapezoid twist is rigidly foldable if and only if the pairs of supplementary interior angles each include a Type-A and a Type-B vertex and the twist angle is not equal to the interior angle of a Type-A vertex.*

The proof is as follows. If α_1 and α_2 are two non-supplementary interior angles, then of necessity the other two interior angles must be the supplements to α_1 and α_2. As can

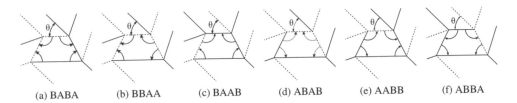

(a) BABA   (b) BBAA   (c) BAAB   (d) ABAB   (e) AABB   (f) ABBA

FIGURE 8. Rigidly foldable isosceles trapezoidal twist configurations for $\theta < \alpha_{min}$.

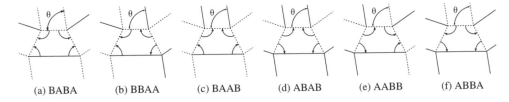

(a) BABA   (b) BBAA   (c) BAAB   (d) ABAB   (e) AABB   (f) ABBA

FIGURE 9. Rigidly foldable isosceles trapezoidal twist configurations for $\alpha_{min} < \theta < 90°$.

Case	Vertex 1	Vertex 2	Vertex 3	Vertex 4
1	B	A	B	A
2	B	A	A	B
3	A	B	B	A
4	A	B	A	B

TABLE 1. Rigidly foldable scalene trapezoid twist vertex types.

be seen from Equations (3.1), (3.2), (5.3), and (5.4), the product of the multipliers for two supplementary-angled vertices of opposite type is -1. Therefore, the product of two such sets is equal to 1, satisfying Equation (2.6). Therefore, a scalene trapezoidal twist is rigidly foldable if the two sets of supplementary interior angles each have a Type-A and a Type-B vertex. Table 1 shows the possible vertex configurations for a rigidly foldable scalene trapezoid twist where Vertex 1 and Vertex 2 contain supplementary interior angles, as do Vertex 3 and Vertex 4. The exception is if the twist angle is equal to the interior angle of a Type-A vertex, in which case infinite multipliers are obtained.

Theorem 3.1 rules out the possibility of a twist with all vertices of the same type. Any scalene trapezoid twist with three vertices of one type must include a set of supplementary vertices of opposite type. Since the product of the multipliers for such vertices is equal to -1, the product of the multipliers of the other two vertices must also be -1 for it to be rigidly foldable. This dismisses the possibility of a scalene trapezoid twist with three vertices of the same type. The only remaining possibility is that one set of supplementary vertices is of one type and the other set is of the opposite type. However, this configuration is only rigidly foldable if $\alpha_1 = \alpha_2$, resulting in an isosceles trapezoid or a parallelogram. Therefore, no conditions other than those stated in the previous paragraph result in a rigidly foldable scalene trapezoid twist.

5.4. Kite twists. The previous discussions apply for kites that are squares, rectangles, parallelograms, rhombuses, or trapezoids and the rigidly foldable configurations having two Type-A and two Type-B vertices. However, unlike the parallelogram, rectangle, or trapezoid twists, a kite twist can be rigidly foldable with three vertices of one type and one vertex of the other type.

We will call α and β the two unique interior angles of a kite and θ the twist angle. For any combination of α and β where $\alpha \neq \beta$ and $\alpha + \beta \neq \pi$, there exists a unique θ that results in a rigidly foldable kite twist for each of the six configurations with three vertices of one type and one of the other. The type labeling in this section labels the α vertex first and the β vertex third, with the other two vertices second and fourth.

For the configurations with Type-A α and β vertices and one other vertex of each type (AAAB/ABAA), a kite twist is rigidly foldable if

$$(5.5) \qquad \cos(\theta) = \frac{\sin(\alpha + \beta)}{\sin(\alpha) + \sin(\beta)}.$$

For the configurations with Type-B α and β vertices and one other vertex of each type (BABB/BBBA), a kite twist is rigidly foldable if

$$(5.6) \qquad \cos(\theta) = -\frac{\sin(\alpha + \beta)}{\sin(\alpha) + \sin(\beta)}.$$

For the configuration with Type-A α vertex, Type-B β vertex, and two other Type-A vertices (AABA), a kite twist is rigidly foldable if

$$(5.7) \qquad \cos^2\left(\frac{\theta}{2}\right) = \frac{4\cos\left(\frac{\alpha}{2}\right)\sin\left(\frac{\beta}{2}\right)\sin^2\left(\frac{\alpha+\beta}{4}\right)}{\sin(\alpha) - \sin(\beta) + 2\sin\left(\frac{\alpha+\beta}{2}\right)}.$$

For the configuration with Type-A α vertex, Type-B β vertex, and two other Type-B vertices (ABBB), a kite twist is rigidly foldable if

$$(5.8) \qquad \cos^2\left(\frac{\theta}{2}\right) = \frac{4\cos\left(\frac{\alpha}{2}\right)\sin\left(\frac{\beta}{2}\right)\cos^2\left(\frac{\alpha+\beta}{4}\right)}{\sin(\beta) - \sin(\alpha) + 2\sin\left(\frac{\alpha+\beta}{2}\right)}.$$

For the configuration with Type-B α vertex, Type-A β vertex, and two other Type-A vertices (BAAA), a kite twist is rigidly foldable if

$$(5.9) \qquad \cos^2\left(\frac{\theta}{2}\right) = \frac{4\sin\left(\frac{\alpha}{2}\right)\cos\left(\frac{\beta}{2}\right)\sin^2\left(\frac{\alpha+\beta}{4}\right)}{\sin(\beta) - \sin(\alpha) + 2\sin\left(\frac{\alpha+\beta}{2}\right)}.$$

For the configuration with Type-B α vertex, Type-A β vertex, and two other Type-B vertices (BBAB), a kite twist is rigidly foldable if

$$(5.10) \qquad \cos^2\left(\frac{\theta}{2}\right) = \frac{4\sin\left(\frac{\alpha}{2}\right)\cos\left(\frac{\beta}{2}\right)\cos^2\left(\frac{\alpha+\beta}{4}\right)}{\sin(\alpha) - \sin(\beta) + 2\sin\left(\frac{\alpha+\beta}{2}\right)}.$$

Figure 10 shows the twists that result from the integer angle solutions to Equations (5.5) to (5.10).

6. Regular Polygon Twists

For an n-sided regular polygon, we define the interior angle at each vertex as α, where

$$(6.1) \qquad \alpha = \pi - \frac{2\pi}{n}.$$

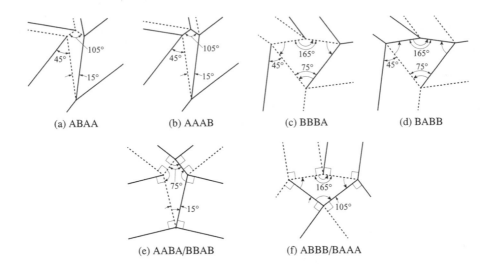

(a) ABAA   (b) AAAB   (c) BBBA   (d) BABB

(e) AABA/BBAB   (f) ABBB/BAAA

FIGURE 10. Rigidly foldable kite twists with integer angles: The α vertex is shown at the bottom in these figures ($\alpha = 15°$ in (a)) and the β vertex is shown at the top ($\beta = 105°$ in (a)). The alphabetical labeling lists the α vertex first and then moves clockwise around the central polygon. Note that cases (e) and (f) may be rotated and/or mirrored to obtain any of the four configurations listed.

If an n-degree regular polygon twist has a Type-A vertices and b Type-B vertices, then from Equation (2.6)

$$(6.2) \qquad \mu_A^a \times \mu_B^b = 1,$$

where of necessity

$$(6.3) \qquad a + b = n.$$

Substituting Equations (3.1) and (3.2) into Equation (6.2) and simplifying gives

$$(6.4) \qquad \left(\frac{\sin\left(\frac{1}{2}(\alpha - \theta)\right)}{\sin\left(\frac{1}{2}(\alpha + \theta)\right)} \right)^a \left(\frac{-\cos\left(\frac{1}{2}(\alpha - \theta)\right)}{\cos\left(\frac{1}{2}(\alpha + \theta)\right)} \right)^b = 1.$$

Substituting Equation (6.1) into Equation (6.4) yields

$$(6.5) \qquad \left(\frac{\cos\left(\frac{\pi}{n} + \frac{\theta}{2}\right)}{\cos\left(\frac{\pi}{n} - \frac{\theta}{2}\right)} \right)^a \left(-\frac{\sin\left(\frac{\pi}{n} + \frac{\theta}{2}\right)}{\sin\left(\frac{\pi}{n} - \frac{\theta}{2}\right)} \right)^b = 1.$$

This results in the following theorem:

THEOREM 6.1 (Rigidly Foldable Regular Polygon Twists). *A regular, n-degree polygon twist with a Type-A vertices, b Type-B vertices, and twist angle θ is rigidly foldable if and only if Equation (6.5) is satisfied.*

From Equations (3.3) and (6.2), it can be seen that there exist no rigidly foldable regular polygon twists where all vertices are of the same type. However, for each unique a, b, and n, with $0 < a < n$ and $n > 4$, there exists one unique twist angle which satisfies Equation (6.5). This gives us the following result for regular polygon twists:

Degree n	Type-A a	Type-B b	Twist Angle $\theta\ (°)$	Inner Angle $\beta\ (°)$
4	2	2	$\neq 90.0$	90.0
5	1	4	107.1	108.0
5	2	3	96.8	108.0
5	3	2	83.2	108.0
5	4	1	72.9	108.0
6	1	5	117.4	120.0
6	2	4	104.5	120.0
6	3	3	90.0	120.0
6	4	2	75.5	120.0
6	5	1	62.6	120.0
7	1	6	124.1	128.6
7	2	5	110.7	128.6
7	3	4	96.8	128.6
7	4	3	83.2	128.6
7	5	2	69.3	128.6
7	6	1	55.9	128.6
8	1	7	129.6	135.0
8	2	6	115.9	135.0
8	3	5	102.7	135.0
8	4	4	90.0	135.0
8	5	3	77.3	135.0
8	6	2	64.1	135.0
8	7	1	50.4	135.0

TABLE 2. Twist angles for rigidly foldable regular polygon twists.

THEOREM 6.2 (Rigidly Foldable Regular Polygon Twist Angles). *For an n-degree regular polygon twist with n > 4, there exist n − 1 unique twist angles which result in a rigidly foldable twist.*

Table 2 shows the twist angles that result in a rigidly foldable twist for regular pentagon, hexagon, heptagon, and octagon twists. For any even polygon twist, a 90° twist angle is rigidly foldable with $a = n/2$ and $b = n/2$. It can be seen that the twist angles larger than 90° are complementary to the twist angles for the opposite configuration. For $n > 4$ rigidly foldable regular polygon twists, all interior folds must have the same parity because the interior angle is the largest angle at each vertex. For a square twist with $a = b = 2$, Equation (6.5) is true for any value of θ other than 90°, where it becomes undefined.

7. Conclusion

We described a method for evaluating the rigid foldability of origami tessellations. We then applied this method to origami twists to discover what parameters allow an origami twist to be rigidly foldable. It was shown that there is no possible configuration for a rigidly foldable triangle twist. It was also shown that many possible rigidly foldable quadrilateral twists exist. Finally, a method for determining twist angles for a rigidly foldable regular polygon twist was presented. This method was used to calculate all possible twist angles for rigidly foldable regular polygons of degree eight or less.

Acknowledgments

This paper is based on work supported by the National Science Foundation and the Air Force Office of Scientific Research through NSF Grant No. EFRI-ODISSEI-1240417.

References

[Francis et al. 13] K. C. Francis, J. E. Blanch, S. P. Magleby, and L. L. Howell. "Origami-Like Creases in Sheet Materials for Compliant Mechanism Design." *Mechanical Sciences* 4 (2013), 371–380.

[Huffman 76] David A. Huffman. "Curvature and Creases: A Primer on Paper." *IEEE Transactions on Computers* C-25 (1976), 1010–1019.

[Hull 03] Thomas Hull. "Counting Mountain-Valley Assignments for Flat Folds." *Ars Combinatoria* 67 (2003), 175–188. MR1973236 (2004c:05011)

[Kuribayashi et al. 06] Kaori Kuribayashi, Koichi Tsuchiya, Zhong You, Dacian Tomus, Minoru Umemoto, Kahiro Ito, and Masahiro Sasaki. "Self-Deployable Origami Stent Grafts as a Biomedical Application of Ni-Rich TiNi Shape Memory Alloy Foil." *Materials Science and Engineering* A 419 (2006), 131–137.

[Lebee and Sab 10] A. Lebee and K. Sab. "Transverse Shear Stiffness of a Chevron Folded Core Used in Sandwich Construction." *International Journal of Solids and Structures* 47 (2010), 2620–2629.

[Miura 85] Koryo Miura. "Method of Packaging and Deployment of Large Membranes in Space." *Intstitute of Space and Asronautical Science* 618 (1985), 1–9.

[Pickett 07] G. T. Pickett. "Self-Folding Origami Membranes." *EPL* 78 (2007), 48003.

[Tachi 10] Tomohiro Tachi. "Freeform Rigid-Foldable Structure using Bidirectional Flat-Foldable planar Quadrilateral Mesh." In *Advances in Architectural Geometry 2010*, edited by C. Ceccato, L. Hesselgren, M. Pauly, H. Pottmann, and J. Wallner, pp. 87–102. Vienna: Springer, 2010.

[Tachi 11] Tomohiro Tachi. "Rigid-Foldable Thick Origami." In *Origami⁵: Fifth International Meeting of Origami Science, Mathematics, and Education*, edited by Patsy Wang-Iverson, Robert J. Lang, and Mark Yim, pp. 253–263. Boca Raton, FL: A K Peters/CRC Press, 2011. MR2866909 (2012h:00044)

[Zirbel et al. 13] Shannon A. Zirbel, Robert J. Lang, Mark W. Thomson, Deborah A. Sigel, Phillip E. Walkemeyer, Brian P. Trease, Spencer P. Magleby, and Larry L. Howell. "Accommodating Thickness in Origami-Based Deployable Arrays." *Journal of Mechanical Design* 135 (2013), 111005–111005-11.

DEPARTMENT OF MECHANICAL ENGINEERING, BRIGHAM YOUNG UNIVERSITY, PROVO, UTAH
E-mail address: tevans11@byu.edu

LANG ORIGAMI, ALAMO, CALIFORNIA
E-mail address: robert@langorigami.com

DEPARTMENT OF MECHANICAL ENGINEERING, BRIGHAM YOUNG UNIVERSITY, PROVO, UTAH
E-mail address: magleby@byu.edu

DEPARTMENT OF MECHANICAL ENGINEERING, BRIGHAM YOUNG UNIVERSITY, PROVO, UTAH
E-mail address: lhowell@byu.edu

Locked Rigid Origami with Multiple Degrees of Freedom

Zachary Abel, Thomas C. Hull, and Tomohiro Tachi

1. Introduction

Many practical applications of origami involve folding hard or thick material such as metal and cardboard sheets. Such situations are well modeled as rigid origami, i.e., a model based on rigid panels and hinges that forbids both the material bending and traveling creases. The continuous foldability of rigid origami from a flat unfolded state to the folded state is essential for enabling folding-based manufacturing processes to make various three-dimensional forms and tessellations.

Many origami models are not rigidly foldable from the unfolded state because they contain a "locked" state that cannot be unfolded without bending the material. We tend to explain such a lock as being attributed to the collision of facets or the lack of degrees of freedom. In fact, many locked rigid origami models can be continuously unfolded in kinematic simulations if the crease pattern, which is a polygonal mesh, is triangulated to have multiple degrees of freedom. This observation leads to a hypothesis that any triangulated mesh origami can be continuously folded from an unfolded state. However, in this paper we show that a triangulated crease pattern is not enough to make it rigid-foldable by constructing a locked rigid origami model from a triangulated crease pattern. The proposed rigid origami model is a developable triangular mesh with six boundary edges (thus with three degrees of freedom) and yet has a folded state that cannot be continuously unfolded to a flat sheet of paper even if faces are allowed to penetrate each other (as explained at the end of Section 3).

We investigate the full three-dimensional configuration space of the proposed model and prove that the configuration space is comprised of two disconnected domains. We further parameterize the pattern by a sector angle θ and explore its family to find out the critical patterns at which the configuration space changes its topology.

2. Description of the Model

The crease pattern of the origami model can be seen in Figure 1 (left), where the bold lines are mountain creases and the dashed lines are valleys. There is a small valley-folded equilateral triangle in the center and a larger mountain-folded equilateral triangle surrounding it. The vertices of the valley triangle meet the edges of the mountain triangle at the 2/3 point along the mountain edges.

This crease pattern is based on the triangle twist (see [Fujmoto and Nishiwaki 82] or [Gjerde 08]); if we take $\theta = 60°$ and the short, mountain creases that are perpendicular to the valley equilateral triangle (like OA) are removed, then this is exactly a triangle twist.

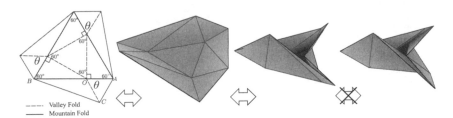

FIGURE 1. The crease pattern (left), continuous folding (middle two), and locked folded states (right) of the proposed pattern. Bold and dashed lines indicate mountain and valley creases, respectively; θ is the parameter that changes the connectivity of the configuration space (in this figure θ is set to 62°).

Triangle twists with this mountain-valley assignment do not fold rigidly (the reasoning is the same as for square twists with similar mountain-valley assignments; see [Hull 13]). With the addition of the short mountain creases OA and its symmetric counterparts, however, the crease pattern will fold rigidly into a three-dimensional shape, as seen in the middle two images of Figure 1.

We claim that for $60° < \theta < 66.715°$ this origami model will have a *locked state*, by which we mean a folded state where the three degrees of freedom cannot be continuously changed to rigidly unfold the model to the flat, unfolded state. Here, a continuous rigid folding/unfolding motion in our model allows for self-penetration but not for *facet flipping*. A facet flip occurs when a fold angle of a crease becomes $\pm\pi$ and jumps to $\mp\pi$. We avoid such a motion so that the continuous transformation is a discrete (piecewise isometric) version of a homotopy of two states. The rightmost image in Figure 1 is meant to illustrate a locked state for the model where $\theta = 62°$.

3. Proof of the Locked State

To prove that this model has a locked rigidly-folded state, we need to analyze the rigid motions of the faces. Figure 2 shows the two nested triangles in the crease pattern and how we situate it in the xy-plane. Think of this as embedded in $\mathbb{R}^3$ so that we can fold it into a three-dimensional shape. The point O is the origin.

Our aim is to find equations that govern how the folding angles (which equal π − the dihedral angles) labeled α, β, and γ interact as we fold the model rigidly. Because the crease with folding angle α lies on the positive y-axis, the point A will swing along a circle as α increases (from an unfolded angle of 0° up to possibly a flat-folded angle of 180°). Thus, the position of A as this model is folded will be

$$\overrightarrow{OA} = (\cos\alpha, 0, \sin\alpha).$$

The motion of point B will be similar, except governed by folding angle β and in a different position. We can find its position by rotating the vector $\overrightarrow{OA}$ by −120° and

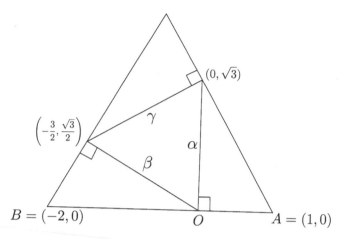

FIGURE 2. Setting the crease pattern in the xy-plane; O is the origin, and the z-axis is perpendicular to the page.

translating by $(-3/2,\ \sqrt{3}/2, 0)$. Thus

$$\overrightarrow{OB} = \begin{pmatrix} -\frac{1}{2} & \frac{\sqrt{3}}{2} & 0 \\ -\frac{\sqrt{3}}{2} & -\frac{1}{2} & 0 \\ 0 & 0 & 1 \end{pmatrix} \begin{pmatrix} \cos\beta \\ 0 \\ \sin\beta \end{pmatrix} + \begin{pmatrix} -\frac{3}{2} \\ \frac{\sqrt{3}}{2} \\ 0 \end{pmatrix}$$

$$= \left(-\frac{1}{2}\cos\beta - \frac{3}{2}, -\frac{\sqrt{3}}{2}\cos\beta + \frac{\sqrt{3}}{2}, \sin\beta \right).$$

Now, referring to the crease pattern in Figure 1 again, we can see that as the inner triangle of valley creases folds, whether or not $\triangle OAC$ and $\triangle OBC$ intersect can be determined by the angle between the vectors $\overrightarrow{OA}$ and $\overrightarrow{OB}$ as they fold. Now, $\angle AOC = \theta$ and $\angle COB = 180° - \theta$. The triangles in question will lie in the same plane if and only if the angle between $\overrightarrow{OA}$ and $\overrightarrow{OB}$ in a folded state is $180° - 2\theta$. This angle cannot be less that $180° - 2\theta$; it represents the smallest angle that can be between $\overrightarrow{OA}$ and $\overrightarrow{OB}$ or else the paper would have to rip, say, along OC. A good way to check this is to use the dot product of $\overrightarrow{OA}$ and $\overrightarrow{OB}$, which will equal $2\cos\rho$ where ρ is the angle between the vectors. (Note from Figure 2 that $|OA| = 1$ and $|OB| = 2$.)

Thus, we obtain

(3.1) $$-\frac{1}{2}\cos\alpha\cos\beta - \frac{3}{2}\cos\alpha + \sin\alpha\sin\beta = 2\cos\rho \le 2\cos(180° - 2\theta).$$

The reason for the direction of the inequality is because vectors $\overrightarrow{OA}$ and $\overrightarrow{OB}$ start at $180°$ from each other in the unfolded state, so the dot product will be -2. As the model folds, this dot product will increase until the angle reached between these two vectors is $180° - 2\theta$, after which the angle cannot get any smaller. So, keeping the dot product $\le 2\cos(180° - 2\theta)$ is desired.

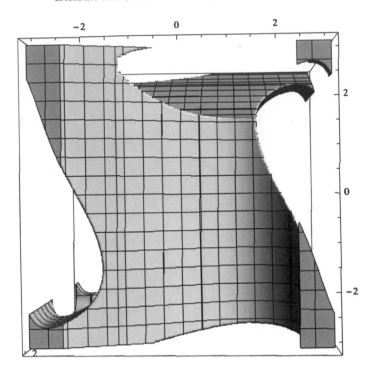

FIGURE 3. The configuration space of points (α, β, γ) that satisfy the dot product inequalities, where $\theta = 62°$.

Of course, we can do this with all pairs of the folding angles about the valley-folded inner triangle:

$$(3.2) \qquad -\frac{1}{2}\cos\beta\cos\gamma - \frac{3}{2}\cos\beta + \sin\beta\sin\gamma \leq 2\cos(180° - 2\theta),$$

$$(3.3) \qquad -\frac{1}{2}\cos\gamma\cos\alpha - \frac{3}{2}\cos\gamma + \sin\gamma\sin\alpha \leq 2\cos(180° - 2\theta).$$

Plotting the region of triples (α, β, γ) that satisfy all these equations gives the diagram in Figure 3, where $-\pi \leq \alpha, \beta, \gamma \leq \pi$ and we take $\theta = 62°$. Notice that the space appears disconnected. The isolated corner where the folding angles α, β, and γ are all close to π (and thus the inner valley triangle is close to being folded flat) will be a locked state of our folded crease pattern, with no way to rigidly unfold to the flat paper state.

We need to prove, however, that this configuration space (in the range $[-\pi, \pi]$ and with $\theta = 62°$) is disconnected. To do this, fix one of the folding angles, say γ, to be $2\pi/3$, and let the other two angles have values $2\pi/3 \leq \alpha$ and $\beta \leq \pi$. If we graph the left-hand side of one of the inequalities (either the α, γ one or the β, γ one) along with the constant function $y = 2\cos 56°$ (since $180° - 2 \cdot 62° = 56°$), then we can see that the expression is clearly greater than $2\cos 56°$ (see Figure 4). Thus, the α, γ inequalities will not hold when $\gamma = 2\pi/3$ and $2\pi/3 \leq \alpha \leq \pi$. Because the equations are exactly the same, we also get that the inequalities will not hold when $\gamma = 2\pi/3$ and $2\pi/3 \leq \beta \leq \pi$. This means that the square $2\pi/3 \leq \alpha, \beta \leq \pi$ when $\gamma = 2\pi/3$ is a region in $\mathbb{R}^3$ where the inequalities do not hold.

Similarly, the squares $2\pi/3 \leq \beta, \gamma \leq \pi$ when $\alpha = 2\pi/3$ and $2\pi/3 \leq \alpha, \gamma \leq \pi$ when $\beta = 2\pi/3$ are regions where the inequalities do not hold. These three squares in $\mathbb{R}^3$ isolate

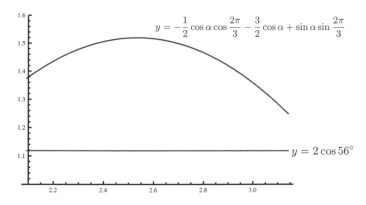

FIGURE 4. Comparing the left-hand side of an inequality with $y = 2\cos 56°$ when $\gamma = 2\pi/3$.

the corner of the configuration space seen in Figure 3 around the point (π, π, π), proving that this section is disconnected from the main part of the configuration space. In other words, we cannot rigidly unfold from this corner near (π, π, π) to the unfolded state, which is the point $(0, 0, 0)$.

The dot product we use in this model also describes what is going wrong with the folded paper to make the configuration space disconnected. Because inequality (3.1) amounts to

$$\overrightarrow{OA} \cdot \overrightarrow{OB} = 2\cos\rho \leq \cos(180° - 2\theta),$$

where ρ is the angle between the vectors $\overrightarrow{OA}$ and $\overrightarrow{OB}$ and $180° - 2\theta$ is the smallest ρ can be, we have that *the folded paper fails to be rigid because $\overrightarrow{OA}$ and $\overrightarrow{OB}$ are too close together*, not necessarily because the paper is penetrating itself, for instance. This is quite counterintuitive; examining a physical model and simulations like that shown in Figure 1 make it seem that the paper is trying to self-intersect. The failure of our inequalities (3.1), (3.2), and (3.3) is not caused by self-intersection of the paper.

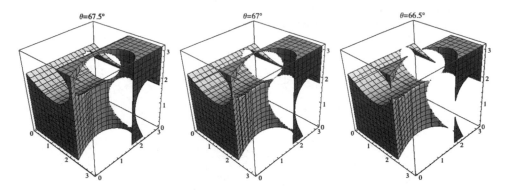

FIGURE 5. Details of the configuration space for three values of θ showing how the disconnection emerges.

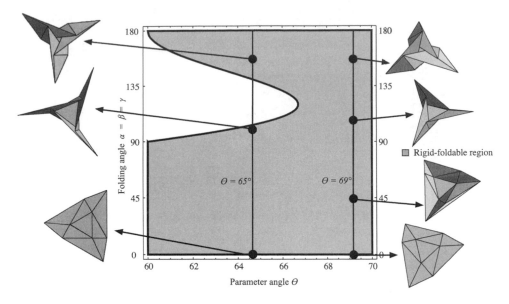

FIGURE 6. A parameter space plot where we let $\alpha = \beta = \gamma$ be the vertical axis and θ be the horizontal axis.

4. The Critical Value of θ

Examination of the configuration space for different values of θ reveals the existence of a critical value of θ where the space becomes disconnected along the line $\alpha = \beta = \gamma$. This is shown in Figure 5, where this critical value seems to be in the range $66.5° < \theta < 67°$. Note that in the $\theta = 67°$ image in Figure 5, there are "bridges" when one of the folding angles equals π connecting the main configuration space to the soon-to-be-disconnected portion where one of the angles α, β, or γ equals π. However, these bridges do not exist, as such a motion requires a facet flip where the fold angle of the crease OA passes $\pm\pi$. This cannot happen not only in reality because of self-collision, but also in our model allowing for self-intersection. We conclude that the bridges are merely artifacts of the dot product inequalities (3.1)–(3.3) and are not actually part of the configuration space. (See Section 5 for more evidence of this.)

The critical value for θ along this diagonal of the configuration space can be computed by letting $\alpha = \beta = \gamma$ in our dot product inequality and noticing that the left-hand side becomes a quadratic in $\cos \alpha$:

$$(4.1) \qquad -\frac{3}{2}\left(\cos \alpha + \frac{1}{2}\right)^2 + \frac{11}{8} \leq 2\cos(180° - 2\theta).$$

The left side of (4.1) reaches its maximum of $11/8$ at $\alpha = 120°$, and the right-hand side will equal this when

$$\theta = \frac{1}{2}\arccos\left(-\frac{11}{16}\right) \approx 66.7163°.$$

Another way to see the critical value emergence is to plot values of θ with the dot product inequality with $\alpha = \beta = \gamma$. The inequality will define a region where rigid folding is allowed, and each vertical line in this plot will illustrate if the folding angles can be made from 0 to 180 degrees with the our inequalities remaining valid. This is shown in

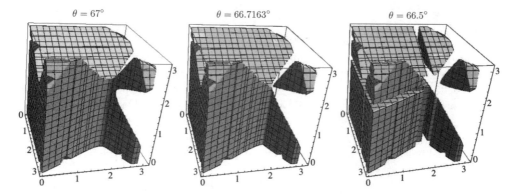

$\theta = 67°$ $\theta = 66.7163°$ $\theta = 66.5°$

FIGURE 7. The configuration space for self-intersections where the axes are the folding angles α, β, and γ, taken at three values of θ near the critical value $\theta = 66.7163°$.

Figure 6. This plot verifies that the range of θ where a locked state exists in the model is from $\theta = 60°$ to approximately $\theta = 66.716°$. Also notice that the boundary between the locked state region and the rigidly foldable region approximates a quadratic curve near the critical value.

5. Configuration Space for Self-Intersections

Since the dot product model captured in the inequalities (3.1)–(3.3) only addresses one type of rigidity failure (where certain crease lines move too close together), it is natural to seek a way to capture the failure of rigidity by way of the paper intersecting itself. This can be done by making a kinematic model of the folding paper, which is based on rotations in $\mathbb{R}^3$ done in sequence to model the multiple creases folding simultaneously. (See [Balkcom and Mason 08] for details.) This model was implemented in Mathematica; the code can be downloaded at this web page: http://mars.wne.edu/~thull/trimesh/mesh. html

Once we have this kinematic model, we can detect facet flips as follows: During the folding, consider the vector $\overrightarrow{OA}$ (see Figure 1) and the vector $\overrightarrow{n} = \overrightarrow{OB} \times \overrightarrow{OC}$ that is normal to the OBC plane. When the paper first folds from a flat state, $\overrightarrow{OA}$ and $\overrightarrow{n}$ will form an acute angle to one another, making their dot product nonnegative. If $\overrightarrow{OA} \cdot \overrightarrow{n} < 0$ then $\overrightarrow{OA}$ will have passed through the OBC plane and caused a facet flip. Checking this condition with the similar creases at the other two vertices gives us the configuration spaces shown in Figure 7, where we have taken different values of θ near the critical value $\theta = 66.7163°$.

We notice a few things: (1) Facet flipping seems to be happening around the same critical value for θ as for the creases OA and OC getting too close together. This makes sense because these creases seem to get too close to each other only after OA folds onto the OBC plane. (2) The "bridges" from the configuration spaces in Figures 3 and 5 are absent from the non-facet flipping configuration space, confirming our previous claim that those bridges are not actually foldable configurations.

6. Conclusion

We have created a triangular crease pattern (mesh) that can be put into a three-dimensional locked state, where attempts to unfold from such a state would cause rigidity of the triangles in the mesh to fail. This proves that it is possible to have a triangulated crease pattern that does not allow full rigid folding in the model's configuration space. In other words, triangulating a non-rigidly-foldable crease pattern is not always enough to attain a rigid folding. By changing one angle parameter, we can control the gap between two separate configuration spaces. In real elastic material, such a gap yields a snap-through effect, possibly leading to engineering applications with multi-stable structures. (For example, see [Silverberg et al. 15].)

Of course, this is only one example, and other such triangle meshes with locked, rigid states must exist. Nonetheless, our example has a number of parameters one could adjust to meet design constraints (like the shape of the boundary or modifying the other angles in the crease pattern). Also, it would be very interesting to find a way to tessellate this crease pattern, which might be possible since the triangle twist, on which our example is based, tessellates easily (see [Gjerde 08]). However, our changing of the angle θ to be greater than $60°$, so as to make a truly three-dimensional locked model, prohibits the obvious method of tessellating that one would try, and we have not yet found an alternate solution.

Acknowledgments

This work began at the 2013 Bellairs Workshop on Computational Geometry, co-organized by Erik Demaine and Godfried Toussaint. We thank the other participants of the workshop for helpful discussions.

Research by Z. Abel is supported by NSF Graduate Fellowship, NSF ODISSEI grant EFRI-1240383, and NSF Expedition grant CCF-1138967. Research of T. Hull is supported by NSF grant EFRI-ODISSEI-1240441 "Mechanical Meta-Materials from Self-Folding Polymer Sheets." Research of T. Tachi is supported by the Japan Science and Technology Agency Presto program.

References

[Balkcom and Mason 08] Devin J. Balkcom and Matthew T. Mason. "Robotic Origami Folding." *International Journal of Robotics Research* 27:5 (2008), 613–627.

[Fujmoto and Nishiwaki 82] Shuzo Fujmoto and Masami Nishiwaki. *Sozo suru origami asobi e no shotai (Invitation to Playing with Creative Origami, Japanese)*. Tokyo: Asahi Culture Center, 1982.

[Gjerde 08] Eric Gjerde. *Origami Tessellations: Awe-Inspiring Geometric Designs*. Wellesley, MA: A K Peters, 2008. MR2474884 (2009m:52001)

[Hull 13] Thomas Hull. *Project Origami: Activities for Exploring Mathematics*, Second Edition. Boca Raton, FL: A K Peters/CRC Press, 2013. MR2987362

[Silverberg et al. 15] Jessie L. Silverberg, Jun-Hee Na, Arthur A. Evans, Bin Liu, Thomas C. Hull, Christian D. Santangelo, Robert J. Lang, Ryan C. Hayward, and Itai Cohen. "Origami Structures with a Critical Transition to Bistability Arising from Hidden Degrees of Freedom." *Nature Materials*, to appear, 2015. (3/09/15 advance online publication.)

MIT Computer Science and Artificial Intelligence Lab., Cambridge, MA
E-mail address: zabel@mit.edu

Department of Mathematics, Western New England University, Springfield, MA
E-mail address: thull@wne.edu

Department of General Systems Studies, The University of Tokyo, Japan
E-mail address: tachi@idea.c.u-tokyo.acjp

Screw Algebra Based Kinematic and Static Modeling of Origami-Inspired Mechanisms

Ketao Zhang, Chen Qiu, and Jian S. Dai

1. Introduction

Geometry of origami [Lang 88, McArthur and Lang 13, Miura 91], [Demaine and O'Rourke 07] and kirigami [Temko and Takahama 78, Zhang and Dai 14] presents a new way for mechanism innovation and engineering design. This cross-disciplinary way of associating artistic origami to engineering kinematic structures was coined *artmimetics* [Rodriguez Leal and Dai 07, Wei and Dai 14], [Zhang et al. 10] as a philosophy that converts artistic origami to engineering products. With and in parallel to this philosophy, origami has inspired many researchers to innovative work in compliant mechanisms [Greenberg et al. 11], emergent mechanisms [Wilding et al. 12], foldable structures [Ahmed et al. 13, Felton et al. 14], stent grafts [Kuribayashi et al. 06], inchworm robots [Koh and Cho 09], micro-robotic systems [Paik et al. 11, Salerno et al. 14], [Dollar et al. 15], manufacturing processes [Carroll et al. 05], and architectural design [Tachi and Epps 11].

With this philosophical thought, the equivalent-mechanism approach [Dai and Jones 99, Dai and Jones 02] was proposed in 1998 to map an origami fold into a kinematic structure by taking creases as kinematic pairs and panels as links. A complete set of equivalent kinematic pairs [Winder et al. 09] was generated in 2009 based on origami folding.

In contrast to a conventional mechanism, a mechanism created by this approach as an origami-inspired mechanism has distinct foldability [Dai and Jones 99] and versatility, initiating a step change in the development of reconfigurable mechanisms and robots. Following this, various new mechanisms [Dollar et al. 15, Salerno et al. 14] were created. On the other hand, the equivalent-mechanism approach creates a way of analyzing origami folds by initiating a variety of mathematical tools including graph theory for the topological representation, screw theory for the motion representation, and Lie groups for the trajectory investigation. This use of mathematical tools to study [belcastro and Hull 02, Lang 11, Mentrasti et al. 13, Wu and You 10] origami folds results in creativity in mechanism development [Bowen et al. 13, Zhang et al 13] and conversely contributes to the investigation of fascinating artistic artifacts [Lang 88] full of mathematical intrigue [Zhang and Dai 14].

In use of the equivalent-mechanism approach, the stiffness element that exists in creases [Dai and Cannella 08, Qiu et al. 13, McGough et al. 14] is to be considered when mapping into a kinematic pair. The stiffness is naturally related to reaction forces due to the crease property. The goal of the current work is to investigate this reaction force due

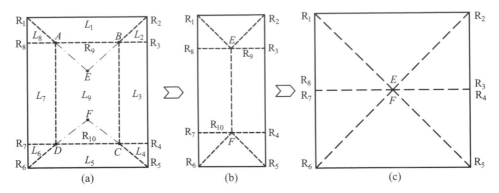

FIGURE 1. Three typical origami bases: (a) Huffman's base, (b) the rectangular tile, and (c) the waterbomb base.

to crease stiffness using screw algebra. By examining the geometrical variation from Huffman's base to a rectangular tile then to a waterbomb, we present kinematic equivalents of
these origami folds and investigate their motion using screw algebra
[Davidson and Hunt 04, Dai 12, Dai 14]. With the waterbomb as a kinematic chain following the principal of kinematic equivalence, an origami parallel mechanism is created
by using three waterbombs as kinematic chains. Based on this, static analysis is carried out
to investigate the reaction force of the origami mechanism, presenting a way of developing
origami-inspired mechanisms.

2. Geometry Variation of Origami Bases from Huffman's Design to Waterbomb

The diagram in Figure 1(a) presents an origami base of Huffman's design. This origami base in a rectangular shape is divided into nine panels denoted by L_i ($i = 1, 2, \ldots, 9$).
The central panel is defined by vertices A, B, C, and D. Panels L_1 and L_5 are isosceles
trapezoids and panels L_2, L_4, L_6, and L_8 are isosceles triangles, which are also right-
angled triangles. Panels L_3, L_7, and L_9 are rectangles. All creases are denoted by R_j
($j = 1, 2, \ldots, 10$); creases R_1 and R_5 are perpendicular to creases R_2 and R_6. Huffman's
design can be obtained by connecting a set of duplications of this base.

The evolution from Huffman's base to a rectangular tile can be made by shrinking
the width of Huffman's base to make point B coincident to point A, and simultaneously to
make point C coincident to point D. In this way, the central rectangular panel shrinks to a
line, as illustrated in Figure 1(b). Further transformation can be made by shrinking the line
between points E and F; this evolves the rectangular tile into the waterbomb base, shown
in Figure 1(c).

The geometry variation from the above evolution illustrates that the waterbomb base
can be derived by changing the form of the central panel of Huffman's base.

3. Kinematic Analysis with the Equivalent-Mechanism Approach

Taking panels as links and creases as hinges, an origami base can be modeled as an
equivalent mechanism with compliant joints. In such a way, origami bases are regarded
as a typical class of closed-loop mechanisms that use purely compliant rotary hinges. An
origami tessellation consisting of multiple bases can be taken as a hyper-redundant mechanism with integrated closed-loop modules.

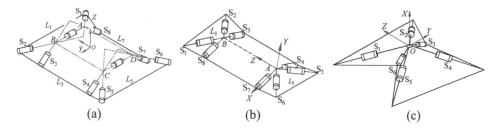

FIGURE 2. Kinematic equivalents of the origami bases: (a) one degree-of-freedom (1DOF) multi-loop linkage, (b) 3DOF 8R linkage, and (c) 3DOF 6R linkage.

3.1. Kinematic equivalent of Huffman's base. With such an approach, creases R_1, R_8, R_9, and AD in the upper-left corner of Figure 1(a) form a spherical 4R linkage. With four such equivalent linkages in four corners, a mechanism of four spherical 4R linkages with bilateral symmetry is extracted, as in Figure 2(a). Following the symmetric structure, the origin of the global coordinate frame O-XYZ is attached to point O with the X- and Y-axes parallel to creases AD and AB, respectively. The Z-axis is perpendicular to the central rectangular panel and completes the coordinate frame following the right-hand rule.

Take L_1 as a fixed link and L_5 as an output link of the equivalent mechanism; then, the output link is connected to the fixed link by three kinematic chains. Kinematic chain 1 consists of four joints represented by screws S_2, S_3, S_4, and S_5. Motion screws for this chain expressed in the global frame O-XYZ are given by

$$\mathbb{S}_1 = \begin{cases} S_2 = [x_e - x_b & -y_b & z_e & y_b z_e & -x_b z_e & -y_b z_e]^T, \\ S_3 = [0 & -y_b & z_p & y_b z_p & -x_b z_p & -x_b y_b]^T, \\ S_4 = [0 & -y_b & z_p & y_b z_p & x_b z_p & x_b y_b]^T, \\ S_5 = [x_b - x_e & -y_b & z_e & y_b z_e & x_b z_e & y_b z_e]^T, \end{cases}$$

where (x_b, y_b, z_b), $(x_e, 0, z_e)$, and $(x_b, 0, z_p)$ are the coordinates of points B, E, and P, respectively, in the global frame.

Kinematic chain 2 consists of four joints presented by screws S_1, S_6, S_7, and S_8 as

$$\mathbb{S}_2 = \begin{cases} S_1 = [x_e - x_b & y_b & z_e & -y_b z_e & -x_b z_e & y_b z_e]^T, \\ S_6 = [x_b - x_e & y_b & z_e & -y_b z_e & x_b z_e & -y_b z_e]^T, \\ S_7 = [0 & y_b & z_e & -y_b z_p & x_b z_p & -x_b y_b]^T, \\ S_8 = [0 & y_b & z_p & -y_b z_p & -x_b z_p & x_b y_b]^T. \end{cases}$$

Kinematic chain 3 consists of only two successively connected revolute joints whose axes align to creases AB and CD, respectively. Motion screws of this chain are expressed in the global frame as

$$\mathbb{S}_3 = \begin{cases} S_9 = [0 & 1 & 0 & 0 & 0 & x_b]^T, \\ S_{10} = [0 & 1 & 0 & 0 & 0 & -x_b]^T. \end{cases}$$

Hence, constraints applied to output link L_5 by these three kinematic chains span a fifth-order constraint-screw system, and the possible motion of link L_5 can be derived from this constraint-screw system by deriving its reciprocal screws. The screw algebra based analysis reveals that the mechanism has only one degree-of-freedom (DOF) and that output link L_5 implements a general screw motion with respect to fixed link L_1.

3.2. Kinematic equivalent of the rectangular tile. In a similar way, the kinematic equivalent of the rectangular tile, shown in Figure 2(b), can be extracted from Figure 1(b). This gives a single-loop 8R linkage with two spherical linkages.

The origin of the global coordinate frame O-XYZ is located at the common point A in Figure 2(a). The X-axis is collinear with the axis of screw $\mathbf{S}_7$, the Y-axis is perpendicular to the axis of screw $\mathbf{S}_7$, and both axes are located in the plane formed by $\mathbf{S}_7$ and $\mathbf{S}_4$. The Z-axis aligns with the common line passing through spherical centers A and B to form a right-handed coordinate frame.

Motion screws of kinematic chain 1 in Figure 2(b) expressed in the global frame O-XYZ are given by

$$(3.1) \qquad \mathbb{S}_1 = \begin{cases} \mathbf{S}_1 = [l_1 \quad m_1 \quad n_1 \quad -cm_1 \quad cl_1 \quad 0]^{\mathrm{T}}, \\ \mathbf{S}_6 = [l_2 \quad m_2 \quad n_2 \quad 0 \quad 0 \quad 0]^{\mathrm{T}}, \\ \mathbf{S}_7 = [1 \quad 0 \quad 0 \quad 0 \quad 0 \quad 0]^{\mathrm{T}}, \\ \mathbf{S}_8 = [1 \quad 0 \quad 0 \quad 0 \quad c \quad 0]^{\mathrm{T}}, \end{cases}$$

where (l_1, m_1, n_1) and (l_2, m_2, n_2) are unit vectors pointing in the direction of screws $\mathbf{S}_1$ and $\mathbf{S}_6$, respectively, and $(0, 0, c)$ is the position vector of point B in the global frame.

Motion screws of the kinematic chain 2 in the global frame are expressed as

$$(3.2) \qquad \mathbb{S}_2 = \begin{cases} \mathbf{S}_2 = [l_3 \quad m_3 \quad n_3 \quad -cm_3 \quad cl_3 \quad 0]^{\mathrm{T}}, \\ \mathbf{S}_3 = [l_4 \quad m_4 \quad 0 \quad -cm_4 \quad cl_4 \quad 0]^{\mathrm{T}}, \\ \mathbf{S}_4 = [l_4 \quad m_4 \quad 0 \quad 0 \quad 0 \quad 0]^{\mathrm{T}}, \\ \mathbf{S}_5 = [l_3 \quad m_5 \quad n_5 \quad 0 \quad 0 \quad 0]^{\mathrm{T}}, \end{cases}$$

where (l_3, m_3, n_3), $(l_4, m_4, 0)$, and (l_5, m_5, n_5) are unit vectors pointing in the direction of screws $\mathbf{S}_2$, $\mathbf{S}_4$, and $\mathbf{S}_5$, respectively.

Motion screws of output link L_5 are the reciprocals of the constraint screws in Equations (3.1) and (3.2) and can be calculated as

$$(3.3) \qquad \mathbb{S}_f = \begin{cases} \mathbf{S}_1 = [1 \quad 0 \quad 0 \quad 0 \quad -p_2/m_4 \quad 0]^{\mathrm{T}}, \\ \mathbf{S}_2 = [0 \quad 1 \quad 0 \quad -p_1 \quad (l_4 p_1 - q_2)/m_4 \quad 0]^{\mathrm{T}}, \\ \mathbf{S}_3 = [0 \quad 0 \quad 1 \quad -r_1 \quad (l_4 r_1 - r_2)/m_4 \quad 0]^{\mathrm{T}}, \end{cases}$$

where

$$p_2 = -cm_4 \frac{l_5 m_4 n_3 - l_4 m_5 n_3}{l_5 m_4 n_3 + l_4 m_3 n_5 - l_3 m_4 n_5 - l_4 m_5 n_3},$$

$$q_1 = \frac{cm_2 n_1}{m_2 n_1 - m_1 n_2},$$

$$q_2 = cl_4 n_3 \frac{l_5 m_4 - l_4 m_5}{l_5 m_4 n_3 + l_4 m_3 n_5 - l_3 m_4 n_5 - l_4 m_5 n_3},$$

$$r_1 = \frac{cm_1 m_2}{m_1 n_2 - m_2 n_1},$$

$$r_2 = \frac{c(l_3 m_4 - l_4 m_3)(l_5 m_4 - l_4 m_5)}{l_5 m_4 n_3 + l_4 m_3 n_5 - l_3 m_4 n_5 - l_4 m_5 n_3}.$$

The motion screws in Equation (3.3) indicate that link L_5 implements two rotations and one screw motion. Thus, motion analysis of the kinematic equivalent reveals that the rectangular tile in Figure 1(b) has three degrees of freedom.

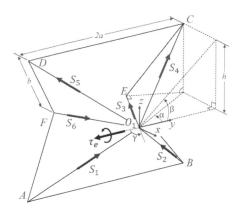

FIGURE 3. Equivalent mechanism of the waterbomb base with motion screws.

3.3. Kinematic equivalent of the waterbomb base. The kinematic equivalent of the waterbomb base in Figure 1(c) is a spherical 6R linkage, shown in Figure 2(c), with a symmetric structure. Motion screws expressed in coordinate frame O_1-xyz, shown in Figure 3, are

$$(3.4) \quad \mathbb{S} = \begin{cases} \mathbf{S}_1 = [\sin\alpha \quad \cos\alpha\cos\beta \quad \cos\alpha\sin\beta \quad 0 \quad 0 \quad 0]^T, \\ \mathbf{S}_2 = [\sin\alpha \quad -\cos\alpha\cos\beta \quad \cos\alpha\sin\beta \quad 0 \quad 0 \quad 0]^T, \\ \mathbf{S}_3 = [-\sin\gamma \quad \cos\gamma \quad 0 \quad 0 \quad 0 \quad 0]^T, \\ \mathbf{S}_4 = [-\sin\alpha \quad \cos\alpha\cos\beta \quad \cos\alpha\sin\beta \quad 0 \quad 0 \quad 0]^T, \\ \mathbf{S}_5 = [-\sin\alpha \quad -\cos\alpha\cos\beta \quad \cos\alpha\sin\beta \quad 0 \quad 0 \quad 0]^T, \\ \mathbf{S}_6 = [\sin\gamma \quad \cos\gamma \quad 0 \quad 0 \quad 0 \quad 0]^T, \end{cases}$$

where α, β, and γ are the angles used to describe screws. Their relationship is given by

$$(3.5) \quad \tan\alpha = \frac{b\sin\theta_2}{a}, \quad \tan\beta = b\cos\theta_2, \quad \gamma = 2\alpha, \quad \theta_2 \in [0, \pi/2].$$

The motion screws in Equation (3.4) span a three-system, and all links in this mechanism implement a spherical motion at the spherical center O.

4. Statics Analysis of Integrated Waterbomb Parallel Mechanism

4.1. Torque equilibrium of kinematic equivalent joint of a waterbomb linkage. Assuming that a single waterbomb linkage is configuration symmetric with respect to a plane determined by the axes of screws $\mathbf{S}_3$ and $\mathbf{S}_6$, the linkage in Figure 3 can be simplified to a virtual revolute joint. Further, previous work [Qiu et al. 13] revealed that the resistant torque of an origami crease can be simplified as a function of both material and geometrical properties of creases. Thus, the torque of the virtual revolute joint equals the resistant torques generated by all six creases. The origin of coordinate frame O-xyz is at the spherical center O, the x- and y-axis are located in the symmetric plane, and z-axis is perpendicular to that plane. Thus, the torque equilibrium of the waterbomb base in the configuration in Figure 3 can be written as

$$(4.1) \quad \tau_\mathbf{e} = \mathbf{J}_\tau \tau,$$

where $\tau_\mathbf{e} = [0 \quad 0 \quad 0 \quad 0 \quad -\tau_e \quad 0]^T$ is expressed in Plücker ray coordinates, $\mathbf{J}_\tau$ is the Jacobian matrix in which each column vector is in the ray coordinates of the screws in

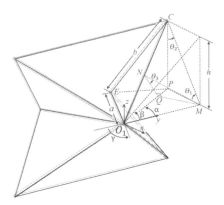

FIGURE 4. Geometric properties of creases within the waterbomb base.

Equation (3.4), and τ is the resistant-torque vector of six creases, which has the form

(4.2) $\tau = [\tau_1 \quad -\tau_2 \quad -\tau_3 \quad \tau_4 \quad -\tau_5 \quad -\tau_6]$.

Due to the symmetric structure of this waterbomb base, values of each torque are given by

(4.3) $\begin{cases} \tau_1 = \tau_2 = \tau_4 = \tau_5 = \tau_l, \\ \tau_3 = \tau_6 = \tau_s. \end{cases}$

Substituting Equations (3.4), (3.5), (4.2), and (4.3) into Equation (4.1), a simplified result of the equivalent torque is derived as

(4.4) $\tau_e = 4\tau_l \cos \alpha \cos \beta - 2\tau_s \cos \gamma$.

Equation (4.4) indicates that the resulting torque τ_e of all six creases can be calculated from the resistant torques τ_l and τ_s, and it presents the geometric relationship between the creases. The problem of determining τ_e is hence converted to finding the resistant torques τ_l and τ_s.

During the folding motion, rotation angles θ_l and θ_s of creases $\mathbf{S}_3$ and $\mathbf{S}_4$ are the main parameters characterizing the geometric properties of the origami base. The other four creases have the same rotation angles as the selected creases. The rotation angle of the equivalent revolute joint is defined as θ_e. According to the symmetric configuration in Figure 4, it can be derived that $\theta_e = 2\theta_3$ and $\theta_s = \theta_e = 2\theta_2$. The relationship between them can be established through α and is given by

$$\sin \theta_3 = \sqrt{a^2 + b^2} \frac{\sin \alpha}{b}.$$

4.2. Force equilibrium of integrated waterbomb parallel mechanism. Duplicating the waterbomb base in Figure 1(c) to generate three identical folds and using them as kinematic chains to connect two triangular panels, an origami parallel mechanism can be constructed, as shown in Figure 5. Each of these kinematic chains is a spherical 6R linkage [Zhang et al. 10]. Under a vertical external force, the kinematic equivalent of each chain of the parallel mechanism can be simplified to a 3R serial chain with parallel axes.

Having the relationship between the resulting torque τ_e and resistant torque of all six creases in the equivalent revolute joint, the relationship between external force $\mathbf{W}_e$ and resistant torque τ_j^i ($i = 1, 2, 3$; $j = 1, 2, 3$) of all three kinematic chains in the parallel

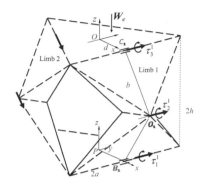

FIGURE 5. Diagram of torque equilibrium of the integrated waterbomb parallel mechanism.

mechanism in Figure 5 can be modeled. Taking kinematic chain 1, for example, torques τ_j^1 generated by the upper and lower creases can be obtained directly according to their material and geometric properties; torque τ_2^1 is equal to τ_e, which is obtained as in Section 4.1. Because all three kinematic chains of the waterbomb parallel mechanism are symmetrically assembled, without loss of generality, kinematic chain 1 is selected to derive the force equilibrium and to be used in determining the external force.

For kinematic chain 1, the Jacobian matrix in the coordinate frame B_1-xyz can be written as

$$(4.5) \quad \mathbf{J}_{b1} = \begin{bmatrix} r_1^1 \times s_1^1 & r_2^1 \times s_2^1 & r_3^1 \times s_3^1 \\ s_1^1 & s_2^1 & s_3^1 \end{bmatrix} = \begin{bmatrix} 0 & 0 & 0 & 0 & -1 & 0 \\ b\sin\theta_1 & 0 & -b\cos\theta_1 & 0 & -1 & 0 \\ 2b\sin\theta_1 & 0 & 0 & 0 & -1 & 0 \end{bmatrix}^{\mathrm{T}}.$$

Assuming that a reaction force, $\mathbf{W}_{b1}$, is applied to the output link of chain 1 and that the force is balanced with resistant torque τ_j^1 in each revolute joint R_j ($j = 1, 2, 3$), the relationship between $\mathbf{W}_{b1}$ and τ_j^1 can be derived as

$$\tau_1 = \mathbf{J}_{b1}^{\mathrm{T}} \mathbf{W}_{b1},$$

where $\tau^1 = [\tau_1^1 \;\; \tau_2^1 \;\; \tau_3^1]$ is the torque vector of all three revolute joints in kinematic chain 1. Conversely, the resulting force can be calculated as

$$(4.6) \qquad\qquad \mathbf{W}_{b1} = (\mathbf{J}_{b1}^{\mathrm{T}})^{-1} \tau_1.$$

According to Equation (4.5), the inverse of $\mathbf{J}_{b1}^{\mathrm{T}}$ calculated with pseudo-inverse can be obtained:

$$(\mathbf{J}_{b1}^{\mathrm{T}})^{+} = \mathbf{J}_{b1}(\mathbf{J}_{b1}^{\mathrm{T}} \mathbf{J}_{b1})^{-1} = \begin{bmatrix} -\frac{1}{2b\sin\theta} & 0 & \frac{1}{2b\cos\theta} & 0 & -1 & 0 \\ 0 & 0 & -\frac{1}{b\cos\theta} & 0 & 0 & 0 \\ \frac{1}{2b\sin\theta} & 0 & \frac{1}{2b\cos\theta} & 0 & 0 & 0 \end{bmatrix}^{\mathrm{T}}.$$

Thus, $\mathbf{W}_{b1}$ can be calculated according to Equation (4.6) as

$$(4.7) \qquad\qquad \mathbf{W}_{b1} = \begin{bmatrix} -\frac{\tau_3^1-\tau_1^1}{2b\sin\theta_1} & 0 & \frac{\tau_3^1+\tau_1^1-2\tau_2^1}{2b\cos\theta_1} & 0 & -1 & 0 \\ 0 & 0 & -\frac{1}{2b\cos\theta_1} & 0 & -\tau_1^1 & 0 \end{bmatrix}^{\mathrm{T}}.$$

Following the aforementioned force equilibrium, the reaction force $\mathbf{W}_{bi}$ of kinematic chains 2 and 3 can be obtained in a similar way. Subsequently, the force equilibrium of the moving platform of the parallel mechanism can be established in the platform coordinate frame O-xyz as

$$(4.8) \qquad \sum_{i=1}^{3} Ad_{bi} \mathbf{W}_{bi} + \mathbf{W}_e = 0,$$

where Ad_{bi} is the adjoint transformation matrix between coordinate frame O_i-xyz and coordinate frame O-xyz and has the form

$$(4.9) \qquad Ad_{bi} = \begin{bmatrix} \mathbf{R}_{bi} & \mathbf{0} \\ \hat{\mathbf{p}}_{bi}\mathbf{R}_{bi} & \mathbf{R}_{bi} \end{bmatrix},$$

in which $\mathbf{R}_{bi}$ is a 3×3 rotation matrix and $\hat{\mathbf{p}}_{bi}$ is the skew-symmetric matrix representing the coordinate translation vector $\mathbf{p}_{bi}$. For kinematic chain i, the rotation matrix and translation vector are

$$(4.10) \qquad \begin{cases} \mathbf{R}_{bi} = \mathbf{R}_z(2\pi(i-1)/3), & i = 1, 2, 3; \\ \mathbf{p}_{bi} = [d \quad 0 \quad -2b\sin\theta_1]^{\mathrm{T}}. \end{cases}$$

Substituting Equations (4.7), (4.9), and (4.10) into Equation (4.8), the external force can be obtained as

$$\mathbf{W}_e = \begin{bmatrix} 0 & 0 & \dfrac{3(2\tau_2^1 - \tau_1^1 - \tau_3^1)}{2b\cos\theta_1} & 0 & 0 & 0 \end{bmatrix}.$$

5. Conclusions

This work presented an evolution between origami bases through geometrical variation and investigated the kinematic equivalents of these bases. The mathematical models of the kinematics and statics of the kinematic equivalents associated with various geometries and topologies are developed in terms of screw algebra by aggregating folding characteristics of single creases. In particular, motions of the panels and creases of these kinematic equivalents are revealed, and analytical models for predicting internal properties with different configurations are presented.

The chapter further presented an integrated waterbomb parallel mechanism as an origami-inspired mechanism and investigated its statics. The overall compliance of the parallel mechanism is based on the stiffness of individual creases/joints.

The analytical models developed here are capable of predicting the resistant force with respect to an external force in an articulated origami mechanism with compliant hinges, given the static behavior of an origami-inspired mechanism with compliant hinges. This approach for modeling origami mechanisms with kinematic principles of mechanisms provides a fundamental base for the development of novel mechanisms and robots.

Acknowledgments

The authors acknowledge the European Commission for support in the human-robot interaction project SQUIRREL under Grant No. 610532 and the support of the National Natural Science Foundation of China under Grant No. 51205016.

References

[Ahmed et al. 13] Saad Ahmed, Kevin McGough, Zoubeida Ounaies, and Mary Frecker. "Origami-Inspired Folding and Unfolding of Structures: Fundamental Investigations of Dielectric Elastomer-Based Active Materials." In *ASME 2013 Conference on Smart Materials, Adaptive Structures and Intelligent Systems*, pp. V001T01A029. New York: American Society of Mechanical Engineers, 2013.

[belcastro and Hull 02] sarah-marie belcastro and Thomas C. Hull. "Modelling the Folding of Paper into Three Dimensions Using Affine Transformations." *Linear Algebra and Its Applications* 348:1 (2002), 273–282. MR1902132 (2003b:15003)

[Bowen et al. 13] L. A. Bowen, C. L. Grames, S. P. Magleby, R. J. Lang, L. L. Howell. "An Approach for Understanding Action Origami as Kinematic Mechanisms." *Journal of Mechanical Design* 135 (2013), 111008, DOI: 10.1115/1.4025379.

[Carroll et al. 05] Daniel W. Carroll, Spencer P. Magleby, Larry L. Howell, Robert H. Todd, and Craig P. Lusk. "Simplified Manufacturing through a Metamorphic Process for Compliant Ortho-planar Mechanisms." *Am. Soc. Mech. Eng., Des. Eng. Div.(Publication) DE A* 118 (2005), 389–399.

[Dai 12] Jian S. Dai. "Finite displacement screw operators with embedded Chasles' motion." *Journal of Mechanisms and Robotics, Trans. ASME* 4:4 (2012), 041002.

[Dai 14] Jian S. Dai. *Geometrical Foundations and Screw Algebra for Mechanisms and Robotics.* Chinese translations, Higher Education Press, Beijing (2014), ISBN: 9787040334838 (translated from Dai, J. S., *Screw Algebra and Kinematic Approaches for Mechanisms and Robotics,* to be published by Springer, London).

[Dai and Cannella 08] Jian S. Dai and Ferdinando Cannella. "Stiffness Characteristics of Carton Folds for Packaging." *Journal of Mechanical Design* 130:2 (2008), 022305.

[Dai and Jones 99] Jian S. Dai and J. Rees Jones. "Mobility in Metamorphic Mechanisms of Foldable/Erectable Kinds." *Journal of Mechanical Design* 121:3 (1999), 375–382.

[Dai and Jones 02] J. S. Dai and J. Rees Jones. "Kinematics and Mobility Analysis of Carton Folds in Packing Manipulation Based on the Mechanism Equivalent." *Proceedings of the Institution of Mechanical Engineers, Part C: Journal of Mechanical Engineering Science* 216:10 (2002), 959–970.

[Davidson and Hunt 04] J. K. Davidson and K. Hunt. *Robots and Screw Theory: Applications of Kinematics and Statics to Robotics.* Oxford University Press, New York, 2014.

[Demaine and O'Rourke 07] Erik D. Demaine and Joseph O'Rourke. *Geometric Folding Algorithms: Linkages, Origami, Polyhedra.* Cambridge, UK: Cambridge University Press, 2007. MR2354878 (2008g:52001)

[Dollar et al. 15] Aaron M. Dollar, Kyu-Jin Cho, Ronald S. Fearing, and Yong-Lae Park. "Special Issue: Fabrication of Fully Integrated Robotic Mechanisms." *Journal of Mechanisms and Robotics* 7:2 (2015), 020201.

[Felton et al. 14] S. Felton, M. Tolley, E. Demaine, D. Rus, and R. Wood. "A Method for Building Self-Folding Machines." *Science* 345:6197 (2014), 644–646.

[Greenberg et al. 11] H. C. Greenberg, M. L. Gong, S. P. Magleby, and L. L. Howell. "Identifying Links between Origami and Compliant Mechanisms." *Mech. Sci* 2:2 (2011), 217–225.

[Koh and Cho 09] Je-Sung Koh and Kyu-Jin Cho. "Omegabot: Biomimetic Inchworm Robot Using SMA Coil Actuator and Smart Composite Microstructures (SCM)." In *Proceedings of the 2009 IEEE International Conference on Robotics and Biomimetics (ROBIO)*, pp. 1154–1159. Washington, DC: IEEE, 2009.

[Kuribayashi et al. 06] Kaori Kuribayashi, Koichi Tsuchiya, Zhong You, Dacian Tomus, Minoru Umemoto, Takahiro Ito, and Masahiro Sasaki. "Self-Deployable Origami Stent Grafts as a Biomedical Application of Ni-Rich TiNi Shape Memory Alloy Foil." *Materials Science and Engineering: A* 419:1 (2006), 131–137.

[Lang 88] Robert J. Lang. *The Complete Book of Origami: Step-by-Step Instructions in Over 1000 Diagrams.* New York: Dover Publications, 1988.

[Lang 11] Robert J. Lang. *Origami Design Secrets: Mathematical Methods for an Ancient Art*, Second Edition. Boca Raton, FL: A K Peters/CRC Press, 2011. MR2841394

[McArthur and Lang 13] Meher McArthur and Robert J. Lang. *Folding Paper: The Infinite Possibilities of Origami.* Singapore: Tuttle Publishing, 2013.

[McGough et al. 14] Kevin McGough, Saad Ahmed, Mary Frecker, and Zoubeida Ounaies. "Finite Element Analysis and Validation of Dielectric Elastomer Actuators Used for Active Origami." *Smart Materials and Structures* 23:9 (2014), 094002.

[Mentrasti et al. 13] Lando Mentrasti, Ferdinando Cannella, Mirko Pupilli, and Jian S. Dai. "Large Bending Behavior of Creased Paperboard. I. Experimental Investigations." *International Journal of Solids and Structures* 50:20 (2013), 3089–3096.

[Miura 91] Koryo Miura. "A Note on Intrinsic Geometry of Origami." In *Proceedings of the First International Meeting of Origami Science and Technology*, edited by H. Huzita, pp. 239–249. Padova, Italy: Dipartimento di Fisica dell'Università di Padova, 1991.

[Paik et al. 11] J. Paik, Byoungkwon An, Daniela Rus, and Robert J. Wood. "Robotic Origamis: Self-Morphing Modular Robots." Paper presented at the 2nd International Conference on Morphological Computation, September 12–14, 2011.

[Qiu et al. 13] C. Qiu, Vahid Aminzadeh, and Jian S. Dai. "Kinematic Analysis and Stiffness Validation of Origami Cartons." *Journal of Mechanical Design* 135:11 (2013), 111004.

[Rodriguez Leal and Dai 07] Ernesto Rodriguez Leal and Jian S. Dai. "From Origami to a New Class of Central-ized 3-DOF Parallel Mechanisms." In *ASME 2007 International Design Engineering Technical Conferences and Computers and Information in Engineering Conference*, pp. 1183–1193. New York: American Society of Mechanical Engineers, 2007.

[Salerno et al. 14] M. Salerno, K. Zhang, A. Menciassi, and J. S. Dai. "A Novel 4-DOFs Origami Enabled, SMA Actuated, Robotic End-Effector for Minimally Invasive Surgery." In *Proceedings of the 2014 IEEE International Conference on Robotics and Automation (ICRA)*, pp. 2844–2849. Washington, DC: IEEE, 2014.

[Tachi and Epps 11] Tomohiro Tachi and Gregory Epps. "Designing One-DOF Mechanisms for Architecture by Rationalizing Curved Folding." Paper presented at International Symposium on Algorithmic Design for Architecture and Urban Design (ALGODE-AIJ), Tokyo, Japan, March 14–16, 2011.

[Temko and Takahama 78] Florence Temko and Toshie Takahama. *The Magic of Kirigami: Happenings with Paper and Scissors by Florance Temko and Toshie Takahama.* Tokyo: Japan Publications, 1978.

[Wilding et al. 12] Samuel E. Wilding, Larry L. Howell, and Spencer P. Magleby. "Spherical Lamina Emergent Mechanisms." *Mechanism and Machine Theory* 49 (2012), 187–197.

[Winder et al. 09] Brian G. Winder, Spencer P. Magleby, and Larry L. Howell. "Kinematic Representations of Pop-up Paper Mechanisms." *Journal of Mechanisms and Robotics* 1:2 (2009), 021009.

[Wei and Dai 14] G. Wei and J. S. Dai. "Origami-inspired integrated planar-spherical overconstrained mecha-nisms." *Journal of Mechanical Design, Trans. ASME* 136:5 (2014), 051003.

[Wu and You 10] Weina Wu and Zhong You. "Modelling Rigid Origami with Quaternions and Dual Quater-nions." *Proceedings of the Royal Society A: Mathematical, Physical and Engineering Science* 466:2119 (2010), 2155–2174. MR2652739 (2011j:70006)

[Zhang and Dai 14] K. Zhang and J. S. Dai. "A Kirigami-Inspired 8R Linkage and Its Evolved Overconstrained 6R Linkages with the Rotational Symmetry of Order Two." *Journal of Mechanisms and Robotics, Trans. ASME* 6:2 (2014), 021008.

[Zhang et al 13] K. Zhang, J. S. Dai, and Y. Fang. "Geometric Constraint and Mobility Variation of Two 3SvPSv Metamorphic Parallel Mechanisms." *Journal of Mechanical Design, Trans. ASME* 135:1 (2013), 11001.

[Zhang et al. 10] Ketao Zhang, Yuefa Fang, Hairong Fang, and Jian S. Dai. "Geometry and Constraint Analysis of the 3-Spherical Kinematic Chain Based Parallel Mechanism." *Journal of Mechanisms and Robotics* 2:3 (2010), 031014.

KING'S COLLEGE LONDON, UNITED KINGDOM
E-mail address: chen.qiu@kcl.ac.uk

KING'S COLLEGE LONDON, UNITED KINGDOM
E-mail address: chen.qiu@kcl.ac.uk

SCHOOL OF NATURAL AND MATHEMATICAL SCIENCES, KING'S COLLEGE LONDON, UNITED KINGDOM
E-mail address: jian.dai@kcl.ac.uk

Thick Rigidly Foldable Structures Realized by an Offset Panel Technique

Bryce J. Edmondson, Robert J. Lang, Michael R. Morgan, Spencer P. Magleby, and Larry L. Howell

1. Introduction

Rigid-panel origami is often mathematically modeled with idealized zero-thickness panels. When paper is used to realize an origami design, the zero-thickness models are a good approximation. However, many origami-inspired designs require the use of thicker materials that likely will not behave as the zero-thickness kinematic models predict.

The offset panel technique defined previously by the authors [Edmondson et al. 14] maintains the kinematics of a zero-thickness origami source model over its full range of motion. The offset panel technique accommodates uniform and varying panel thickness as well as offset panels or gaps between panels. The preserved kinematic behavior allows designers to select an origami model based on desired motion and instantiate it in thick materials.

In this work, we review the offset panel technique and illustrate its capabilities and limitations through several example hardware demonstrations. The examples in the paper are based on the rigidly foldable M3V twist[1] shown in Figure 1. This twist tessellation was developed using the method of fold-angle multipliers [Evans et al. 15].

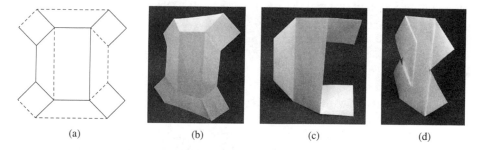

FIGURE 1. This origami model is a unit from an M3V twist tessellation: (a) Crease pattern, (b) open position, (c) midway position, and (d) closed position.

This work was funded by the National Science Foundation and Air Force Office of Scientific Research under Grant #1240417.

[1]M3V (or M^3V) refers to the crease assignment around the central polygon of the structure: three mountain folds and one valley fold.

2. Background

2.1. Action origami. Action origami is a subset of origami of special interest because its mechanisms can be applied to engineering problems. In action origami, some models require deformation of their panels to enable action, one example being the traditional flapping bird [Shafer 01, Shafer 10, Lang 11, Lang 97]. Others achieve their motion purely through rotation about the folds without the bending of panels. Such models are called *rigidly foldable origami* or *kinematic origami* [Bowen et al. 13].

2.2. Modeling and kinematics. Kinematic origami may be modeled as a network of spherical mechanisms where panels are links and folds are joints [Greenberg et al. 11] and can be analyzed using spherical kinematics theory. Each vertex within the structure is modeled as a spherical kinematic mechanism. Spherical kinematics is a subset of three-dimensional kinematics where any given point on the mechanism is constrained to move on a spherical surface and all joint axes, whether fixed or instantaneous, intersect at the spherical center. Spherical kinematic motion is the behavior of the rotational axes about the spherical center [Chiang 00, Bowen et al. 14]. The spherical kinematics of a model can be preserved as long as the rotational axes' locations and behaviors remain constant even if link size, shape, or both are altered.

2.3. Deployable structures. One potential area of application for origami-inspired design is deployable structures. Deployable structures often use a repeating pattern of coupled mechanisms [Gan and Pellegrino 03], such as the Bricard linkage [Chen et al. 05] or the Bennett linkage [Chen and You 05], to create large single-degree-of-freedom (DOF) mechanisms. Deployable structures are often classified as highly over-constrained mechanisms because the Kutzbach criterion would calculate zero (or negative) DOF, yet they have one DOF due to their highly coupled construction [Mavroidis and Roth 95a], [Mavroidis and Roth 95b].

2.4. Thickness accommodation. In engineering applications of origami-inspired design, accommodation of material thickness is frequently necessary to achieve the design's objective. Existing methods for thickness accommodation can be grouped into two categories: methods that preserve range of motion, and methods that preserve kinematics. Figure 2 shows a side-by-side illustration of some of the methods described below using a simple four-panel accordion fold.

The axis-shift method [Tachi 11] maintains the range of motion of an origami source model. This method allows the panels to fold by shifting all joints' rotational axes from the center plane to the panel edges (see Figure 2(b)). Interior degree-4 vertices fold such that there are two inside and two outside panels. The inside panels fit within the outside panels in thin materials but not in thick materials. A drawback is that in many origami patterns of interest, the vertical offsets break the kinematic motion of the individual vertices.

The offset joint method [Hoberman 10] is related to the axis shift method in that each hinge is positioned at the edge of the material (see Figure 2(b)). The panels are not restricted to be planar, coplanar, or uniform thickness. By extending the hinges away from the panels, gaps are created to allow interior vertices full range of motion, tucking the inside panel into the gap created by the offset. Fully compact cubic bundles were created using this method that can fold and unfold sequentially rather than with preserved kinematics. By utilizing symmetric single-parameter vertices, single-DOF mechanisms can be created in thick material using this method.

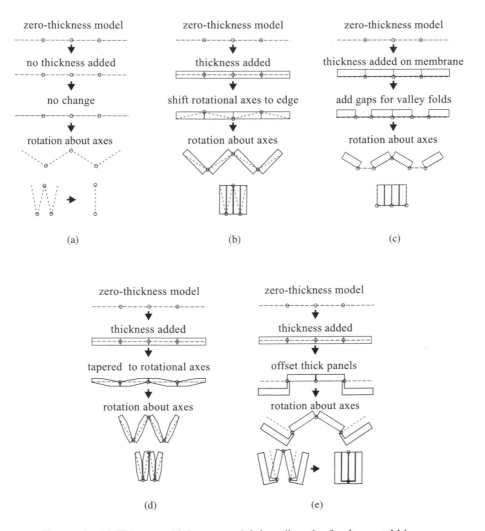

FIGURE 2. (a) The zero-thickness model describes the fundamental kinematic behavior. (b) The axis-shift alters the kinematics but can be folded
fully compact [Tachi 11]. The offset joint method results in an identical structure due to the simplicity of this example. (c) The membrane
folds method alters the kinematics but can be folded fully compact. (d)
The tapered panels method with limited range of motion [Tachi 11]. (e)
The offset panel technique has the same kinematics as the zero-thickness
model and has full range of motion.

In the membrane folds method [Zirbel et al. 13], all rigid panels are attached to one
side of a flexible membrane as shown in Figure 2(c). By controlling the spacing between
adjacent panels, full range of motion folding is enabled. Zero gap between panels only
allows a mountain fold, whereas a larger gap is necessary for a valley fold with gap width
set by panel thicknesses and desired maximum rotational angle. This gap also provides

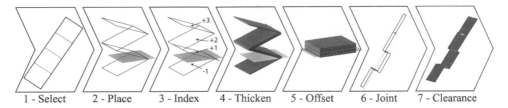

| 1 - Select | 2 - Place | 3 - Index | 4 - Thicken | 5 - Offset | 6 - Joint | 7 - Clearance |

FIGURE 3. There are seven steps to design a thick origami model that preserves the kinematics and allows full range of motion using the offset panel technique. Design protocol is followed from the closed position. Partially folded views are used here to distinguish between panels for concept visualization.

extra DOFs with small additional motions that can allow a theoretically non-rigidly foldable structure to fold up in practice; however, it can permit undesirable (and unpredictable) additional motions in the deployment.

The tapered panel method [Tachi 11] is designed to preserve origami source model kinematics. The panels are trimmed until the panel edges are coincident with the plane defined by the zero-thickness model (see Figure 2(d)). Because the rotational axes are unchanged, the thick panels' kinematics are equivalent to that of the zero-thickness model. The tapered panel technique, however, yields models that may not be foldable to a fully compact state and typically do not achieve the full range of motion of the zero-thickness model.

The offset panel technique [Edmondson et al. 14] can preserve the kinematics and full range of motion of the origami source mechanism, thus enabling origami-inspired designs to more closely mimic properties identified in zero-thickness models (see Figure 2(e)).

3. Offset Panel Technique

In rigid origami, panels (facets) can be treated as links and folds as joints [Wang and Chen 11, Balkcom and Mason 08, Schenk and Guest 11]. Origami mechanisms can be treated as zero-thickness spherical mechanisms, which are mechanisms whose links and joints all lie in a plane in at least one position and whose links are idealized with zero thickness. In the offset panel technique, the source model's panels are shaped and thickened while maintaining the zero-thickness spherical mechanisms' joint relationships.

The key concept of the technique is that in the fully folded state, all joints lie in a common plane *even if one or both panels incident to any joint are spatially offset from that plane*, which we refer to as the *joint plane*. This requirement allows the thick origami mechanism's behavior to be kinematically equivalent to the zero-thickness origami source model, aside from considerations of self-intersections, which must be addressed separately. We accomplish this requirement by creating extensions that connect each panel, whatever its position, with the joint in the joint plane.

Instructions for implementing this technique are reviewed below and include step-by-step examples based on the rigidly foldable M3V twist mechanism. A design-based representation of the steps is provided in Figure 3.

Step 1. Model Selection: Select an origami source model that gives the desired motion and/or form. The source model must be rigid/flat-foldable. When panels are constrained to be parallel to one another in the folded state, the layer ordering

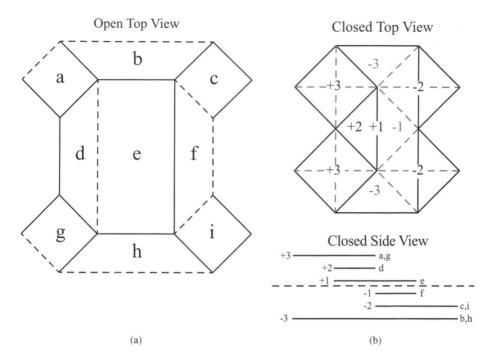

FIGURE 4. (a) Each panel is labeled with a unique letter on the crease pattern. (b) Step 2 (Place Joint Plane) and Step 3 (Index Panels). Side view is shown to illustrate index sequence. Figure 5(a) further clarifies the panel letter/sequence relationship. Solid lines represent panels and dashed lines represent the joint plane in the side view.

graph on the facets of the source model (a directed graph indicating relative facet order) must be sortable.

Example: We chose the M3V twist shown in Figure 1.

Step 2. Place Joint Plane: Choose the location of the joint plane, the plane within which all of the joints will lie. Although it is not a requirement, the design is often simplified by assigning the joint plane to be parallel to the panels or even coplanar with the face of one of the panels.

Example: We chose the joint plane to be the center of the closed panels (see Figure 4(a)). This minimizes the offset distances, which will reduce the potential for self-intersection during the folding motion.

Step 3. Index Panels: Assign each panel an index according to its position relative to the joint plane in the closed state. The joint plane is designated as "0," the panel directly above it as "+1," the panel below it as "−1," and so on.

Example: Figure 4(b) shows the joint plane in the center of the indexed layers.

Step 4. Thicken Panels: Assign thickness to each panel based on the application.

Example: We assigned a uniform thickness of 3 mm.

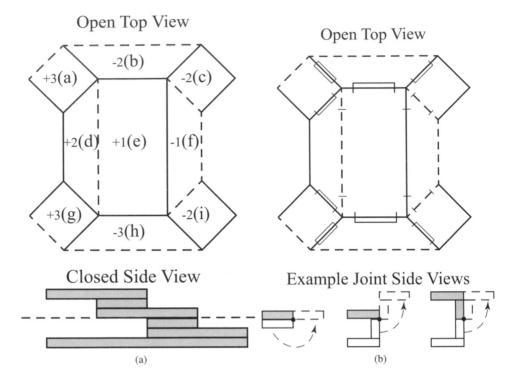

FIGURE 5. (a) An open top view with index labels is shown for reference (compare to Figure 4): Step 4 (Thicken Panels) and Step 5 (Offset Panels). Shaded rectangles represent thickened panels. (b) Step 6 (Determine Joints) is shown. The example joint side views show a noncomprehensive sample of isolated individual joints and their adjacent panels.

Step 5. Offset Panels: Arrange the panels into the closed state according to the indices assigned in Step 3. They can be stacked panel to panel or spaced with gaps between panels.

    Example: Figure 5(a) shows the thickened panels stacked in indexed layers.

Step 6. Determine Joints: Extend each joint from the offset position of each panel to the joint plane using rigid extensions so that the axis of rotation lies in the joint plane even if both panels are offset from it [Edmondson et al. 14]. This ensures that the rotational axes remain unchanged from those of the zero-thickness model throughout the folding motion.

    Example: Figure 5(b) illustrates the joint alignment on the crease pattern and sample joint extension configurations. The extensions are rigidly attached to panels with length equal to the panel offset such that the rotational axis remains in the joint plane even if one or both panels are offset.

Step 7. Address Self-Intersection: To prevent panel-joint interference, create clearance holes in panels that lie between another panel's joint and the joint plane. These holes guarantee that the mechanism can be assembled in the fully closed position. These clearance holes are necessary, but not sufficient, to guarantee that the mechanism is able to move throughout the entirety of its range of motion. To

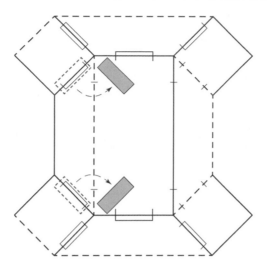

FIGURE 6. An illustration of Step 7 (Address Self-Intersection). Shaded areas indicate clearance holes located by reflecting a clearance boundary around joints to interfering panels.

guarantee full range of motion with no self-intersection, the entire mechanism volume needs to be mapped through the full motion, removing any intersecting material from one or both interfering surfaces. In many cases the clearance holes in the fully closed configuration will be sufficient to avoid self-intersection through the full range of motion.

Example: Clearance holes are located by drawing clearance boundaries around joints and reflecting them about fold lines to their positions on the interfering panels as shown by shaded areas in Figure 6. This process was performed manually in these simple cases but more complex cases could be calculated numerically.

4. General Examples

We present several configurations of the offset panel technique that are kinematically equivalent to the zero-thickness structure. The following configurations are not an exhaustive list, but they illustrate some of the capabilities and limitations of the offset panel technique.

The models were created using 3 mm acrylic sheet stock and approximated joints using adhesive fabric tape to create hinges with minimal play. Each configuration is a version that is kinematically equivalent to the zero-thickness approximation paper model shown in Figure 1.

4.1. Uniform thickness panels. The simplest configuration demonstrates uniform panel thickness. Figure 7 shows the M3V twist of Figure 1 in 3 mm thick panels. By placing the joint plane at the center of the model and offsetting panels to either side, the sum of the distances from panels to the joint plane is minimized, which, in turn, minimizes the number and size of the required clearance holes. Each panel offset is determined by the sum of thicknesses of the panels that lie between that panel and the joint plane.

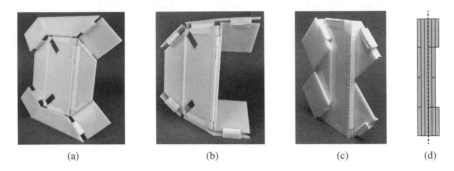

FIGURE 7. Uniform thickness model shows the M3V twist in (a) open, (b) midway, and (c) closed positions. (d) A side view with the joint plane at the dashed line.

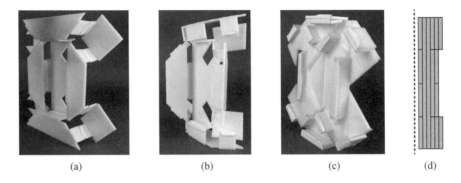

FIGURE 8. Far offset model is made with all panels offset to one side of the joint plane in the closed position. This results in the panels spaced far apart in the open position and requires more clearance holes due to more interfering panels. (a) Open, (b) midway, and (c) closed positions. (d) A side view with the joint plane at the dashed line.

4.2. Offset joint plane. It may be desirable to have relatively large distances between panels in the open state. This can be achieved by offsetting all of the panels to one side of the joint plane. The location of the joint plane will affect the positioning of the panels as well as the volume swept by panels in motion. The joint plane is not restricted to a panel's face. Figure 8 shows a model with all panels on one side of the joint plane. Each panel offset is equal to the sum of thicknesses of the panels between that panel and the joint plane plus the offset distance.

4.3. Gaps between panels. The previous models had no spacing between panels in the closed state. However, gaps between panels could be beneficial, for example, in a folded wiring board to provide clearance for surface-mounted devices that extend above/below the panels. By offsetting the panels such that spaces exist between them, a model with gaps is created (Figure 9). The offset distances are now determined by the same sum of panel thicknesses plus the sum of the gaps between the panel and the joint plane.

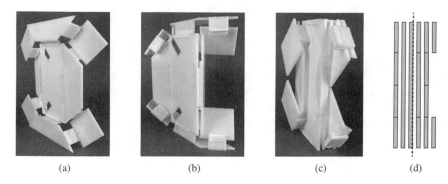

FIGURE 9. This model is designed with panels that are spaced apart in the closed position. This has similar open position as the fully compact model but with greater offset distances between panels. (a) Open, (b) midway, and (c) closed positions. (d) A side view with the joint plane at the dashed line.

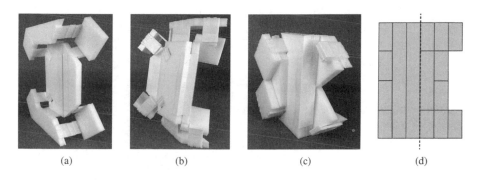

FIGURE 10. This model is four times as thick as the initial thick model. The thickness accommodation capability is clearly shown by this very thick model. (a) Open, (b) midway, and (c) closed positions. (d) A side view with the joint plane at the dashed line.

4.4. Arbitrary uniform thickness panels. The offset panel technique accommodates any thickness. Figure 10 shows the same model as Figure 7 with panel thickness four times the previous model's thickness. The farther the panels are offset from the joint plane due to joint plane location or thickness of interior panels, the larger the volume that is swept by the panel and joint, which generally requires increased self-intersection clearance.

4.5. Variable thickness panels. Different panels can have different thicknesses, and not all applications require that all mechanical system panels be equal thickness. Figure 11 shows the example model with panel thicknesses ranging from 3 mm to 12 mm.

4.6. Morphing volumes. Panels do not have to be sheet-like. As long as the relative joint positions remain fixed within the model, any panel can take on any three-dimensional shape, as long as self-intersections are avoided during deployment. This allows the creation

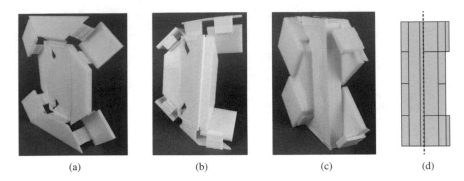

(a)   (b)   (c)   (d)

FIGURE 11. This model is made from panels all with different thicknesses. (a) Open, (b) midway, and (c) closed positions. (d) A side view with the joint plane at the dashed line.

of a structure with one unique shape when closed that morphs into a different shape when opened.

In Figure 12 we show one such example. We begin with a split-diagonal MVMV twist (adding a fold across the diagonal of the square twist to create a rigidly foldable structure), using the crease pattern shown in Figure 12(a). We cut away the four corners of the crease pattern, erect eight cubes on distinct facets of the pattern, and thicken the panels according to the offset panel technique. The result is a structure that, in the folded state, forms a larger cube but, in the unfolded state, takes on a dramatically different shape, with each cube rotating through a unique path throughout the folding motion.

5. Conclusions

5.1. Limitations. Though the offset panel technique does preserve the origami source model's kinematics and full range of motion, it does have some implementation challenges in particular situations. The key issue is related to the stacking of panels and the large offsets that can be required by some patterns. Large offsets can also complicate self-intersection clearance challenges to preserve full folding motion. For example, the offset panel technique does not work well with the Miura-ori pattern because it is highly overlapped in the closed position. This requires the total thickness of the panels to accumulate by the order of the number of panels. The offset joint method by Hoberman or the tapered panels method by Tachi, however, can handle this pattern within certain design parameters.

The offset panel technique often requires clearance holes that do not allow thick panel mechanisms with one continuous surface. Many applications can handle this limitation, but those requiring a watertight surface would disqualify this technique from use.

Considerations of implementation issues can help designers determine whether or not the offset panel technique is appropriate for developing a thick-panel mechanism using a particular origami model.

5.2. Advantages. Using the offset panel technique, one can design a deployable structure using finite-thickness panels while preserving the full range of motion of a zero-thickness idealized origami mechanism. The offset preserves the source model's kinematics so long as the joint rotational axes are unchanged from the zero-thickness model. Preserving these joint relationships guarantees that the kinematics are equivalent, so the

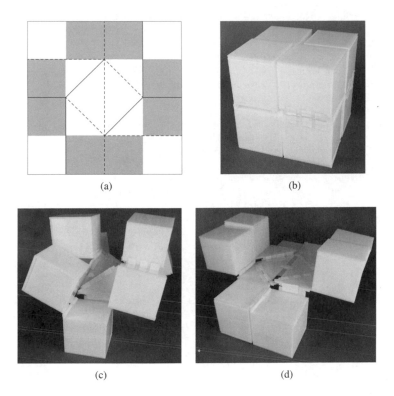

FIGURE 12. (a) The MVMV square twist crease pattern for a morphing cube. The shaded regions show where the small cubes were added. (b) Closed, (c) midway, and (d) open configurations.

link/panel size and shape can change freely. However, self-intersections must be avoided to ensure the full range of motion, generally, by adding clearance holes. Suitable choice of the location of the joint plane and the joints themselves can minimize the need for clearance holes and in some cases eliminate them entirely.

5.3. Future work. Possible small-scale applications that could be built on the concepts presented here include packaging, display stands/cases, foldable circuit boards, and solar panels. On a larger scale, the offset panel technique could prove beneficial in morphing architecture, deployable structures, temporary shelters, and deployable solar arrays.

The work in this chapter highlights valuable areas of future research that build on the basic technique. These include the development of systematic methods for determining clearances required to avoid self-intersection, modifying motion paths of panels by offsetting the joint plane, and changing the shapes of the panels beyond just adjusting the thickness.

References

[Balkcom and Mason 08] D. Balkcom and M. Mason. "Robotic Origami Folding." *The International Journal of Robotics Research* 27 (2008), 613–627.

[Bowen et al. 13] Landen A. Bowen, Clayton L. Grames, Spencer P. Magleby, Larry L. Howell, and Robert J. Lang. "A Classification of Action Origami as Systems of Spherical Mechanisms." *Journal of Mechanical Design* 135:11 (2013), 111008.

[Bowen et al. 14] Landen A. Bowen, Weston Baxter, Spencer P. Magleby, and Larry L. Howell. "A Position Analysis of Coupled Spherical Mechanisms Found in Action Origami." *Mechanism and Machine Theory* 77 (2014), 13–44.

[Chen and You 05] Yan Chen and Zhong You. "Deployable Structure." US Patent 6941704 B2, 2005.

[Chen et al. 05] Yan Chen, Zhong You, and Tibor Tarnai. "Threefold-Symmetric Bricard Linkages for Deployable Structures." *International Journal of Solids and Structures* 42:8 (2005), 2287–2301.

[Chiang 00] C. H. Chiang. *Kinematics of Spherical Mechanisms*, Second Edition. Malabar, FL: Krieger Publishing Co., 2000.

[Edmondson et al. 14] Bryce J. Edmondson, Robert J. Lang, Spencer P. Magleby, and Larry L. Howell. "An Offset Panel Technique for Rigidly Foldable Origami." In *ASME 2014 International Design Engineering Technical Conferences and Computers and Information in Engineering Conference*, Paper No. DETC2014-35606. New York: ASME, 2014.

[Evans et al. 15] Thomas A. Evans, Robert J. Lang, Spencer P. Magleby, and Larry L. Howell. "Rigidly Foldable Origami Twists." In *Origami^6: Sixth International Meeting of Origami Science, Mathematics, and Education*, edited by Koryo Miura, Toshikazu Kawasaki, Tomohiro Tachi, Ryuhei Uehara, Robert J. Lang, and Patsy Wang-Iverson, Providence: American Mathematical Society, 2016.

[Gan and Pellegrino 03] W. W. Gan and Sergio Pellegrino. "Closed-Loop Deployable Structures." In *Proceedings of 44th AIAA/ASME/ASCE/AHS/ASC Structures, Structural Dynamics, and Materials Conference*, pp. 7–10. Reston, VA: AIAA, 2003.

[Greenberg et al. 11] H. Greenberg, M. Gong, S. Magleby, and L. Howell. "Indentifying Links between Origami and Compliant Mechanisms." *Mechanical Sciences* 2 (2011), 217–225.

[Hoberman 10] Charles Hoberman. "Folding Structures Made of Thick Hinged Panels." US Patent 7794019, 2010.

[Lang 97] R. Lang. *Origami in Action: Paper Toys That Fly, Flap, Gobble, and Inflate*. London: St. Martin's Griffin, 1997.

[Lang 11] Robert J. Lang. *Origami Design Secrets: Mathematical Methods for an Ancient Art*, Second Edition. Boca Raton, FL: A K Peters/CRC Press, 2011. MR2841394

[Mavroidis and Roth 95a] C. Mavroidis and B. Roth. "Analysis of Overconstrained Mechanisms." *Journal of Mechanical Design* 117 (1995), 69–74.

[Mavroidis and Roth 95b] C. Mavroidis and B. Roth. "New and Revised Overconstrained Mechanisms." *Journal of Mechanical Design* 117 (1995), 75–82.

[Schenk and Guest 11] M. Schenk and S. Guest. "Origami Folding: A Structural Engineering Approach." In *Origami^5: Fifth International Meeting of Origami Science, Mathematics, and Education*, edited by Patsy Wang-Iverson, Robert J. Lang, and Mark Yim, pp. 291–304. Boca Raton, FL: A K Peters/CRC Press, 2011. MR2866909 (2012h:00044)

[Shafer 01] J. Shafer. *Origami to Astonish and Amuse*. London: St. Martin's Griffin, 2001.

[Shafer 10] J. Shafer. *Origami Ooh La La! Action Origami for Performance and Play*. CreateSpace Independent Publishing Platform, 2010.

[Tachi 11] T. Tachi. "Rigid-Foldable Thick Origami." In *Origami^5: Fifth International Meeting of Origami Science, Mathematics, and Education*, edited by Patsy Wang-Iverson, Robert J. Lang, and Mark Yim, pp. 253–264. Boca Raton, FL: A K Peters/CRC Press, 2011. MR2866909 (2012h:00044)

[Wang and Chen 11] K. Wang and Y. Chen. "Folding a Patterned Cylinder by Rigid Origami." In *Origami^5: Fifth International Meeting of Origami Science, Mathematics, and Education*, edited by Patsy Wang-Iverson, Robert J. Lang, and Mark Yim, pp. 265–276. Boca Raton, FL: A K Peters/CRC Press, 2011. MR2866909 (2012h:00044)

[Zirbel et al. 13] Shannon A. Zirbel, Robert J. Lang, Mark W. Thomson, Deborah A. Sigel, Phillip E. Walkemeyer, Brian P. Trease, Spencer P. Magleby, and Larry L. Howell. "Accommodating Thickness in Origami-Based Deployable Arrays 1." *Journal of Mechanical Design* 135:11 (2013), 111005.

DEPARTMENT OF MECHANICAL ENGINEERING, BRIGHAM YOUNG UNIVERSITY, PROVO, UTAH
E-mail address: edmondbr@byu.edu

LANG ORIGAMI, ALAMO, CALIFORNIA
E-mail address: robert@langorigami.com

DEPARTMENT OF MECHANICAL ENGINEERING, BRIGHAM YOUNG UNIVERSITY, PROVO, UTAH
E-mail address: morgan44@byu.edu

DEPARTMENT OF MECHANICAL ENGINEERING, BRIGHAM YOUNG UNIVERSITY, PROVO, UTAH
E-mail address: magleby@byu.edu

DEPARTMENT OF MECHANICAL ENGINEERING, BRIGHAM YOUNG UNIVERSITY, PROVO, UTAH
E-mail address: lhowell@byu.edu

Configuration Transformation and Mathematical Description of Manipulation of Origami Cartons

Jian S. Dai

1. Introduction

Dexterity, complexity, and variety of packaging present a challenge to industrial automation. Examples of such packaging are commonly found in department stores ranging from food to the luxury end of the personal products including cosmetics and perfumery, involving a very wide range of sizes and variety of shapes and styles of origami cartons.

Current carton erectors/packers are normally designed to accept a range of carton sizes but few variations of style [Stewart 96] and do not have the ability to manipulate the entire range of cartons [Ekiguchi 88], particularly origami cartons that either exist or may materialize through innovation. Thus, manufacturers tend to meet difficulties by the provision of manual lines and rely on the flexibility of workers to adapt to different requirements of complex packaging.

To automate this type of small batch and short run productions [Dai 96], ways of describing configurations [O'Rourke 00] of cut and creased origami cartons in analytical terms have to be found and ways of identifying folding sequence and manipulation planning need to be created.

In this respect, interest has been raised in describing and modeling folding operations that could be intelligible to a machine. This is twofold. First, it requires an effective description of origami cartons. Second, it requires a description of the folding process. For the former, the research is carried out based on the assumption that all cartons used in packaging have flat-foldable crease patterns and some cartons take types of origami. In 1997, Dai and Rees Jones proposed a systematic way of converting cartons, particularly origami folds, to equivalent mechanisms [Dai and Rees Jones 97a] as an equivalent mechanism approach by presenting creases as revolute joints and panels as links that form a new class of mechanisms, coined as *metamorphic mechanisms* [Dai and Rees Jones 99]. In such equivalence, a mechanism analysis including a topological graph and an adjacency matrix was used for the first time to model [Dai and Rees Jones 97b] cartons and origami. In 2002, belcastro and Hull developed a model for non-flat origami based on the description of vertex movement and on a composite map from a creased paper to a complete fold [belcastro and Hull 02, Hull 02]. In 2002, Dai and Rees Jones proposed a way of describing origami cartons by using screws to describe creases that identify the continuous motion of origami [Dai and Rees Jones 02]. In 2013, Bowen et al [Bowen et al. 13a] published a way of using kinematic mechanisms to understand action origami, this led to a classification [Bowen et al 13b] of action origami as a system of spherical mechanisms.

A more difficult task is to describe the folding process. In 1999, Lu and Akella used the similarity between a carton motion sequence and a robot operation to develop automatic folding of a carton with fixtures [Lu and Akella 99]. In 2001, Song and Amato modeled a foldable object as a tree-link multilink object that could be applied with a motion-planning technique [Song and Amato 00]. The foldability was proposed as a spin-off and would be applied to a computational biology problem. In the same year, Dubey and Dai applied the equivalent-mechanism approach to simulate the folding of origami [Dubey and Dai 01]. Demaine investigated quantitatively the potential relation between paper folds and polyhedra [Demaine 01]. In 2002, Liu and Dai proposed the hereditary connectivity and presented the adjacency connectivity matrix that dictates the folding sequence of an origami carton or an origami fold [Liu and Dai 02]. In 2003, Liu and Dai used the hereditary connectivity to reveal the folding sequence with configuration control points [Liu and Dai 03]. Linkage folding problems have also been a center of interest [Kapovich and Millson 95, Lenhart and Whitesides 95, Sallee 73, Whitesides 92]. In 2003, a tree structure based on a graph, but in a way similar to three-dimensional sketches, was proposed by Shimanuki, Kato, and Watanabe for folding origami in drill books, with a way of converting a sequence of origami illustrations into a three-dimensional animation automatically [Shimanuki et al. 04]. In 2004, Demaine et al. investigated the foldability of paper and produced a quantitative description [Demaine et al. 04].

The studies are based on quantitative representation and present a relationship between topological configuration states with a study of origami that provides a good understanding of folding. The proposed equivalent-mechanism approach [Dai and Rees Jones 99] presents a way of relating origami carton models to industrial automation [Dai, Medland and Mullineux 09, Dai and Caldwell 10]. It is hence imperative to produce a framework that could produce a generic way of describing an arbitrary foldable carton qualitatively and its folding manipulation, leading to industrial automation of packaging various cartons.

Manipulating an origami carton using robotic fingers is a combined problem of the above studies and one of the most versatile uses of robotic fingers. In 2004, Balkcom and Mason introduced the concept of robotic origami folding by demonstrating that a SCARA robot arm with four degrees of freedom (DOF) could be used to operate a clamp for creating creases on a paper [Balkcom and Mason 04]. In 2006, Dubey and Dai presented a multifingered device for folding origami by using four robotic fingers in a reconfigurable platform [Dubey and Dai 06]. The origami-folding device was extended to fold complex origami cartons [Dubey and Dai 07]. In 2008, Yao and Dai investigated the dexterity in folding origami using four robotic fingers based on interactive configuration space [Yao and Dai 08]. In review of the past development, folding an origami carton needs to qualitatively present an origami carton. In using the equivalent-mechanism approach [Dai and Rees Jones 99], origami modeling and folding can be related to mechanism study. Therefore, the study of origami can fully utilize the methodology of mechanism study. In the relevant mechanism study, Han and Amato developed a kinematics-based probabilistic method for a closed chain system, on which the closed-loop chain was broken and a link was picked up to fix its position and orientation to construct a kinematics roadmap [Han and Amato 01]. Similarly, LaValle executed a randomized search to develop a probabilistic roadmap for a closed chain [LaValle 03], and Ascher and Lin used sequential regularization for closed loops by involving the Runge-Kutta algorithm [Ascher and Lin 00]. However, the motion represented by the equivalent mechanism of a carton is more complex. Contrary to a conventional mechanism that has a fixed topological configuration state, the equivalent mechanism has various configuration states [Qin et al. 14]. This presents a challenge to automatically folding cartons.

This chapter presents an integrated qualitative framework for origami cartons and their folding. It investigates the change of topological configuration states in folding an origami carton and for the first time relates distinct configuration states. This evolves into a folding process that can be used for industrial automation. The chapter further integrates a qualitative description from kinematics into a quantitative description in topology and presents the hereditary connectivity of folding. This is then translated into hereditary manipulation for robotic fingers.

2. Equivalent Mechanism Models of Origami Cartons

Cardboard is commonly used to produce origami cartons for holding consumer products. After printing, the board is cut and creased. The cuts may form the outer profile, cut-out-hole profiles, or line/curve incisions [BPCC Taylowe 93], and flat-foldable creases are prepared for bending.

The cut and creased board is received by the end packer in either one of two basic types: the *open type* in the form of origami or the *cuboidal type* [BPCC Taylowe 93] (sometimes described as a "skillet") with a glued side seam. The cuboidal type has a preglued seam that makes four main panels from a closed main body of a carton and is one of the most common types of cartons.

Both types require a formalism to describe the state of the topological configuration at each stage of carton folding manipulation and to potentially produce a new way of recording the folding process so that automatic manipulation can become feasible.

If cardboard carton panels are regarded as stiff and creases as equivalent to hinges, an origami carton can be regarded as equivalent to a mechanism. An origami carton blank can be regarded as a combination of several spherical linkages [McCarthy 00] with a number of serial chains. A cuboidal carton can be regarded as a closed-loop linkage [Dai and Kerr 91]. Origami cartons with complicated forms can be regarded as multiloop linkages that result from a mixture of several serial linkages. The resultant equivalent mechanism has revolute joints only, has characteristics that the adjacent joint axes are coplanar, and has such proportions that it can always be folded into flat configurations.

Seen as an equivalent mechanism, an origami carton can be readily mapped onto a topological graph using graph theory [O'Rourke 00], [Bondy and Murty 76] with crease lines being represented as edges of a topological graph and panels as nodes or vertices of the graph. Different configurations of an origami carton with different connectivity of panels and flaps in its various stages of packaging manipulation can be modeled with distinct topological graphs in an analytical way.

An example is illustrated by an origami carton that can be erected and folded entirely from a piece of blank cardboard with precut creases without resorting to using glue. A section of this carton is illustrated in Figure 1. In this section, the base panel numbered 1 is fixed. Panels 2, 3, 4, and 5 are movable. Taking creases as revolute joints and panels as links, the section provides an equivalent mechanism. The fact that all creases intersect at a point presents a five-bar spherical linkage as an equivalent mechanism in Figure 2. This five-bar spherical linkage is a guiding linkage in carton motion.

Thus, a topological graph can be produced by mapping links as nodes and joints as edges. The resultant graph is symmetrical. It is a simple graph and an edge graph. The process of presenting a carton as a topological graph is an essential step in modeling packaging manipulation and gives intrinsic characteristics in graph representation.

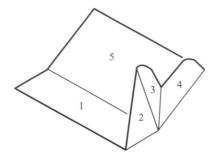

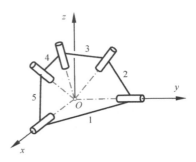

FIGURE 1. A corner
section of an origami
carton.

FIGURE 2. An equiva-
lent five-bar spherical
linkage.

In order to identify the connectivity of the structure of the five panels, an adjacency
matrix is produced as

$$\mathbf{A}_0 = \begin{bmatrix} 0 & 1 & 0 & 0 & 1 \\ 1 & 0 & 1 & 0 & 0 \\ 0 & 1 & 0 & 1 & 0 \\ 0 & 0 & 1 & 0 & 1 \\ 1 & 0 & 0 & 1 & 0 \end{bmatrix}.$$

An entry in the matrix indicates the state of the connectivity between two vertices in the
graph corresponding to two panels of the carton section. The adjacency matrix presents a
topological configuration state of the carton.

The dimension of the matrix is the number of nodes (vertices) in a graph, equivalent
to the number of panels, including flaps, of the carton. The sum of the entries in a row
corresponding to a vertex is the degree of that vertex, or vertex degree in short, indicating
the number of edges connecting to the vertex. This adds to the matrix's potential use in
searching for open flaps and in determining if work is complete at each stage of the carton
packaging manipulation.

3. Matrix Operation Model Equivalent to Manipulating Origami Cartons in a Packaging Process

A carton creates distinct topological configuration states in folding manipulation. To
relate these configuration states, a matrix operation model (EU-model
[Dai and Rees Jones 05]) was developed that converts a carton configuration state from
one to another. Thus, the manipulation process and operation sequence can be modeled by
a sequence of matrix operations starting from an adjacency matrix representing an initial
configuration state.

For the simplicity of our argument, a simpler example is presented to illustrate the
matrix operation model for changing the carton configuration states. The matrix operation
model equates to the carton manipulation in an industrial process.

A rectangular carton section is illustrated in Figure 3 with a closed loop of four panels,
1, 2, 3 and 4, attached with the flipping panel 5 and flap 6. Its equivalent mechanism is in
Figure 4.

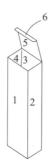

FIGURE 3. A section of a cuboidal carton.

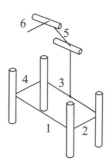

FIGURE 4. The equivalent mechanism.

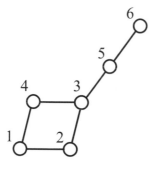

FIGURE 5. Topological graph of the equivalent mechanism.

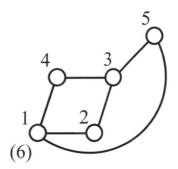

FIGURE 6. Graph of a folded carton section.

The carton section is in its open state and is shown with its topological graph in Figure 5. The corresponding adjacency matrix $\mathbf{A}$ is

$$\mathbf{A} = \begin{bmatrix} 0 & 1 & 0 & 1 & 0 & 0 \\ 1 & 0 & 1 & 0 & 0 & 0 \\ 0 & 1 & 0 & 1 & 1 & 0 \\ 1 & 0 & 1 & 0 & 0 & 0 \\ 0 & 0 & 1 & 0 & 0 & 1 \\ 0 & 0 & 0 & 0 & 1 & 0 \end{bmatrix}.$$

The folding manipulation of this carton section is to fold panel 5, to tuck flap 6, and then to link flap 6 to panel 1. This can be translated into hereditary manipulation [Liu and Dai 02] by integrating the adjoint transformation [Dai 12, Dai 15] between adjacent panels as a component in the adjacency matrix. An adjacency configuration matrix hence can be obtained to reflect the hereditary elements in the operation. This integrates a manifold into the topological model and presents a hereditary manipulation following the introduction of the adjoint transformation.

This process equates to the operation on the topological graph of making a union of nodes 6 and 1 and then removing node 6. The resulting topological graph after the manipulation is in Figure 6. The manipulation thus reduces the number of nodes in the graph and equivalently the number of degrees of freedom of the carton section.

This manipulation and its corresponding configuration changes in the topological graph can be represented by a matrix operation model, and consequently a final adjacency matrix for the manipulated carton that can be obtained. Similar to operation in the topological graph, the matrix operation model can be decomposed into modeling the above two steps in folding manipulation.

The first step of the manipulation is modeled in the form of matrix operation by using an elementary matrix that passes the connectivity from the link to be removed to the link to be made a union. This is implemented by introducing a U-elementary matrix, identified as $\mathbf{U}_{1,6}$ by

$$\mathbf{U}_{1,6} = \begin{bmatrix} 1 & 0 & 0 & 0 & 0 & 1 \\ 0 & 1 & 0 & 0 & 0 & 0 \\ 0 & 0 & 1 & 0 & 0 & 0 \\ 0 & 0 & 0 & 1 & 0 & 0 \\ 0 & 0 & 0 & 0 & 1 & 0 \\ 0 & 0 & 0 & 0 & 0 & 1 \end{bmatrix}.$$

The matrix is an identity matrix with extra 1 for passing the connectivity of node 6 to node 1. The subscript of the U-matrix denotes that row 6 of the initial adjacency matrix will be added to row 1 when premultiplying with it and that column 6 will be added to column 1 when postmultiplying with the transpose of it. The operation uses modulo-2 arithmetic, sometimes known as exclusive-or arithmetic [Gillie 65]. The connectivity shown in the original matrix $\mathbf{A}$ is thus updated after the U-matrix operation. This gives

$$\mathbf{A}'_f = \mathbf{U}_{1,6}\mathbf{A}\mathbf{U}_{1,6}^{\mathrm{T}} = \begin{bmatrix} 0 & 1 & 0 & 1 & 1 & \cdot \\ 1 & 0 & 1 & 0 & 0 & \cdot \\ 0 & 1 & 0 & 1 & 1 & \cdot \\ 1 & 0 & 1 & 0 & 0 & \cdot \\ 1 & 0 & 1 & 0 & 0 & \cdot \\ \cdot & \cdot & \cdot & \cdot & \cdot & \cdot \end{bmatrix}.$$

The obtained matrix $\mathbf{A}'_f$ is a 6×6 matrix of which the 5×5 submatrix gives the new configuration of the carton section after taking the union of nodes 6 and 1 in the corresponding graph. The entries in the last row and column become redundant when taking into account that nodes 1 and 6 are joined to be a single node, and therefore these entries are to be removed. Hence, notation "." is used to denote entries in the last row and column.

The second step of the manipulation is modeled by eliminating the last row and column of the intermediate matrix, $\mathbf{A}'_f$. This is done by introducing an E-elementary matrix:

$$\mathbf{E}_r = \begin{bmatrix} \mathbf{I}_5 & \mathbf{0} \end{bmatrix} = \begin{bmatrix} 1 & 0 & 0 & 0 & 0 & 0 \\ 0 & 1 & 0 & 0 & 0 & 0 \\ 0 & 0 & 1 & 0 & 0 & 0 \\ 0 & 0 & 0 & 1 & 0 & 0 \\ 0 & 0 & 0 & 0 & 1 & 0 \end{bmatrix}.$$

This new matrix will eliminate the last row of an adjacency matrix by premultiplying the matrix with it and will eliminate the last column of the adjacency matrix by postmultiplying the matrix with the transpose of it.

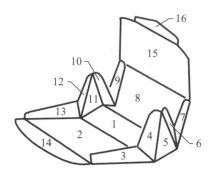

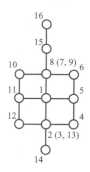

FIGURE 7. Half-erect origami carton.

FIGURE 8. A graph after two substeps of matrix operations.

Premultiplying matrix $\mathbf{A}'_f$ with $\mathbf{E}_r$ and postmultiplying the matrix with the transpose of $\mathbf{E}_r$ results in the following adjacency matrix:

$$\mathbf{A}_f = \mathbf{E}_r\mathbf{A}'_f\mathbf{E}_r^T = \begin{bmatrix} 0 & 1 & 0 & 1 & 1 \\ 1 & 0 & 1 & 0 & 0 \\ 0 & 1 & 0 & 1 & 1 \\ 1 & 0 & 1 & 0 & 0 \\ 1 & 0 & 1 & 0 & 0 \end{bmatrix}.$$

This agrees with the topological graph of the folded carton section in Figure 6.

Thus, the carton manipulation from one configuration state in matrix $\mathbf{A}$ to another configuration in matrix $\mathbf{A}_f$ can be modeled by a sequence of matrix operations as

$$\mathbf{A}_f = \mathbf{E}_r\mathbf{A}'_f\mathbf{E}_r^T = \mathbf{E}_r\mathbf{U}_{1,6}\mathbf{A}\mathbf{U}_{1,6}^T\mathbf{E}_r^T = (\mathbf{E}_r\mathbf{U}_{1,6})\,\mathbf{A}\,(\mathbf{E}_r\mathbf{U}_{1,6})^T.$$

In a general case, when a row to be eliminated is not the last in the matrix, an extra step is taken to interchange that row with the last row. This is achieved by an additional elementary matrix $\mathbf{U}_{l,c}$ for swapping the current row c with the last row l.

Hence, the change from one configuration state to another in carton folding manipulation can be presented by the matrix operation model and can be decomposed into several elementary operations.

The matrix operation model thus records the change of the carton configuration states during a folding process and plays an important role in the recognition phase of the folding process. This makes it possible to describe an industrial process of folding cartons in mathematical terms.

4. Configuration Transformation of Origami Cartons in Hereditary Manipulation

The matrix operation model discussed above can be implemented in an origami carton one section of which is illustrated in Figure 1. Its half-erect state is illustrated in Figure 7.

This generates a new configuration with the configuration transformation based on the following matrix operation:

$$\mathbf{A}_{g2} = (\mathbf{U}_{2,13}\mathbf{U}_{2,3})\,\mathbf{A}_{g1}\,(\mathbf{U}_{2,13}\mathbf{U}_{2,3})^T.$$

The further step is to make the union of node 8(7,9) with nodes 6 and 10, the union of node 2(3,13) with nodes 4 and 12, and then the union of node 8(7,9) with node 14. The matrix

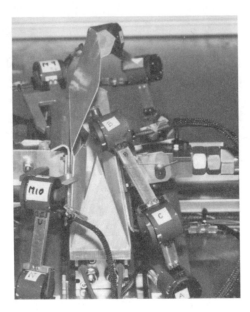

FIGURE 9. Holding the carton with two robotic fingers and tucking the panels with the other two fingers.

operation is

$$A_{g3} = (E_{r9}U_{2,12}U_{2,4}U_{8,10}U_{8,6}U_{2,13}U_{2,3}U_{8,9}U_{8,7}) A_{g0}$$
$$(E_{r9}U_{2,12}U_{2,4}U_{8,10}U_{8,6}U_{2,13}U_{2,3}U_{8,9}U_{8,7})^{T}.$$

The configuration transformation hence relates a configuration state to another and effectively describes the carton folding process by implementing the matrix operation model. Integrating the adjoint transformation in the connectivity matrix, a manipulation can be set up.

Further manipulation transforms the configuration to another by taking the union between node 2 and nodes 15 and 16 to tuck in flap 16 and to attach the flipping panel 15 to panel 2. The manipulation can be represented by the following matrix operation:

$$A_{gf} = (E_{r2}U_{2,15}U_{2,16}) A_{g3} (E_{r2}U_{2,15}U_{2,16})^{T}.$$

The corresponding adjacency matrix is thus obtained as

$$A_{gf} = \begin{bmatrix} 0 & 1 & 1 & 1 & 1 \\ 1 & 0 & 1 & 1 & 1 \\ 1 & 1 & 0 & 1 & 0 \\ 1 & 1 & 1 & 0 & 1 \\ 1 & 1 & 0 & 1 & 0 \end{bmatrix}.$$

The matrix operation is hence translated to moving two robotic fingers to the edges and the other two fingers to the top for folding the flap as in Figure 9.

For collision avoidance, volume-controlled manipulation is introduced. This volume-control manipulation is created from the final completed carton by dividing the complete carton into four spaces whose volumes could then be attached to four robotic fingers to give a minimum space gap between two fingers; geometrical restraints are introduced for obstacle avoidance. This is demonstrated in Figure 10.

FIGURE 10. Cooperative manipulation (left) and tucking a flap with two robotic fingers (right).

This completes the folding manipulation of an origami carton with matrix operations and transformations. The robotic folding operation hence corresponds to a set of matrix operations and leads to a quantitative description of the folding operation.

5. Conclusions

This chapter presented a matrix operation model that relates distinct topological configuration states during folding and manipulation of origami cartons and proposed an integrated topological representation of an origami carton with kinematics transformation. Configuration transformation is hence proposed to model the packaging manipulation in a distinct and programmable way.

The mathematical models and corresponding algorithms provide a useful tool for transferring one configuration to another and give an analytical form for developing automated packaging manipulation of origami cartons. The approach was used in a novel multifingered reconfigurable packaging device for automatically manipulating origami cartons, leading to a versatile and reconfigurable packaging process.

This work hence presented a framework that can be used for automating folding origami cartons with robotic fingers and creating a new way for packaging automation.

Acknowledgments

The authors wish to thank Prof. J. Rees Jones for early discussion of the work, Dr. K. Stamp of Unilever Research and Dr. V. N. Dubey of Burnemouth University for early experimentation, Prof. H. Liu of Portsmouth University for early work in folding origami, and Dr. F. Cannella of Italian Institute of Technology for reset of the experimental work. Thanks also go to Unilever Research, Port Sunlight, for the support of the early work and the Engineering and Physical Science Research Council (EPSRC) of the United Kingdom under grant number GR/R09725 for support of this research.

References

[Ascher and Lin 00] U. Ascher and P. Lin. "Sequential Regularization Methods for Simulating Mechanical Systems with Many Closed Loops." *SIAM Journal on Scientific Computing* 21:4 (2000), 1244–1262. MR1740394 (2001b:70003)

[Balkcom and Mason 04] D. J. Balkcom and M. T. Mason. "Introducing Robotic Origami Folding." In *Proceedings of the IEEE International Conference on Robotics and Automation 2004*, pp. 3245–3250. Los Alamitos, CA: IEEE, 2004.

[belcastro and Hull 02] s. m. belcastro and T. C. Hull. "A Mathematical Model for Non-flat Origami." In *Origami³: Proceedings of the Third International Meeting of Origami Science, Mathematics, and Education*, edited by Thomas Hull, pp. 39–51. Natick, MA: A K Peters, 2002. MR1955758 (2004a:52008)

[Bondy and Murty 76] J. A. Bondy and U. S. R. Murty. *Graph Theory with Applications*. London: Macmillan Press Ltd., 1976.

[Bowen et al. 13a] L. A. Bowen, C. L. Grames, S. P. Magleby, R. J. Lang, L. L. Howell. "An Approach for Understanding Action Origami as Kinematic Mechanisms". *Journal of Mechanical Design*, 135 (2013), 111008. DOI: 10.1115/1.4025379, 2013.

[Bowen et al 13b] L. A. Bowen, C. L. Grames, S. P. Magleby, L. L. Howell, R. J. Lang. "A Classification of Action Origami as Systems of Spherical Mechanisms", *Journal of Mechanical Design*, 135:11 (2013), 111008.

[BPCC Taylowe 93] BPCC Taylowe Ltd. *The Creation of a Carton*, Berkshire: BPCC Taylowe Ltd., 1993.

[Dai 96] J. S. Dai. "Survey and Business Case Study of the Dexterous Reconfigurable Assembly and Packaging System." Technical Report PS 960321, Unilever Research, 1996.

[Dai 12] J. S. Dai. "Finite Displacement Screw Operators with Embedded Chasles' Motion", *Journal of Mechanisms and Robotics, Trans. ASME*, 4:4 (2012), 041002.

[Dai 15] J. S. Dai. "Euler-Rodrigues Formula Variations, Quaternion Conjugation and Intrinsic Connections." *Mechanism and Machine Theory* 92 (2015), 144–152.

[Dai and Caldwell 10] J. S. Dai and D. G. Caldwell. "Origami-Based Robotic Paper-and-Board Packaging for Food Industry", Invited to submit to special issue of advances in food processing and packaging automation, *Trends in Food Science and Technology*, 21:3 (2010), 153–157.

[Dai, Medland and Mullineux 09] J. S. Dai, A. Medland, and G. Mullineux. "Carton Erection Using Reconfigurable Folder Mechanisms", *Packaging Technology and Science*, 22:7 (2009), 385–395.

[Dai and Rees Jones 97a] J. S. Dai and J. Rees Jones. "Structure and Mobility of Cartons in a Packaging Process." Technical Report PS 970067, Unilever Research, 1997.

[Dai and Rees Jones 97b] J. S. Dai and J. Rees Jones. "Theory on Kinematic Synthesis and Motion Analysis of Cartons." Technical Report PS 970184, Unilever Research, 1997.

[Dai and Rees Jones 99] J. S. Dai and J. Rees Jones. "Mobility in Metamorphic Mechanisms of Foldable/Erectable Kinds." *ASME J. Mech. Des.* 121:3 (1999), 375–382.

[Dai and Rees Jones 02] J. S. Dai and J. Rees Jones. "Kinematics and Mobility Analysis of Carton Folds in Packing Manipulation Based on the Mechanism Equivalent." *J. Mech. Eng. Sci., Proc. IMechE* 216:10 (2002), 959–970.

[Dai and Rees Jones 05] J. S. Dai and J. Rees Jones. "Matrix Representation of Topological Configuration Transformation of Metamorphic Mechanisms." *J. Mech. Design, Trans. ASME* 127:4 (2005), 837–840.

[Dai and Kerr 91] J. S. Dai and D. R. Kerr. "Geometric Analysis and Optimisation of Symmetrical Watt 6 Bar Mechanisms." *Journal of Mechanical Engineering Science, Proc. I., Mech.E, Part C* 205:C1 (1991), 275–280.

[Demaine 01] E. D. Demaine. "Folding and Unfolding Linkages, Paper, and Polyhedra." *Discrete and Computational Geometry* 2098 (2001), 113–124. MR2043642

[Demaine et al. 04] E. D. Demaine, S. L. Devadoss, J. S. B. Mitchell, and J. O'Rourke. "Continuous Foldability of Polygonal Paper." In *Proceedings of the 16th Canadian Conference on Computational Geometry (CCCG'04)*, pp. 64–67. Available at http://www.cccg.ca/proceedings/2004/, 2004.

[Dubey and Dai 01] V. N. Dubey and J. S. Dai. "Modelling and Kinematics Simulation of a Mechanism Extracted from a Cardboard Fold." *Int. Journal of Engineering Simulation* 2:3 (2001), 3–10.

[Dubey and Dai 06] V. N. Dubey and J. S. Dai. "A Packaging Robot for Complex Cartons." *Industrial Robot: An International Journal* 33:2 (2006), 82–87.

[Dubey and Dai 07] V. N. Dubey and J. S. Dai. "Complex Carton Packaging with Dexterous Robot Hands." In *Industrial Robotics: Programming, Simulation and Applications*, edited by L. K. Huat, pp. 583–594. Mammendorf, Germany: Pro Literatur Verlag Robert Mayer-Scholz/Advanced Robotics Systems International, 2007.

[Ekiguchi 88] K. Ekiguchi. *The Book of Boxes*. New York: Kodansha International, 1988.

[Gillie 65] A. C. Gillie. *Binary Arithmetic and Boolean Algebra*. New York: McGraw-Hill, 1965. MR0191754 (32:9156)

[Han and Amato 01] L. Han and N. M. Amato. "A Kinematics-Based Probabilistic Roadmap Method for Closed Chain Systems." In *Algorithmic and Computational Robotics: New Directions*, edited by B. Donald, k. Lynch, and D. Rus, pp. 233–245. Boston: A K Peters, 2001.

[Hull 02] T. C. Hull. "The Combinatorics of Flat Folds: A Survey." In *Origami³: Proceedings of the Third International Meeting of Origami Science, Mathematics, and Education*, edited by Thomas Hull, pp. 29–38. Natick, MA: A K Peters, 2002. MR1955757 (2004c:52030)

[Kapovich and Millson 95] M. Kapovich and J. Millson. "On the Moduli Space of Polygons in the Euclidean Plane." *Journal of Differential Geometry* 42:5 (1995), 133–164. MR1350697 (98b:52019)

[LaValle 03] S. M. LaValle. "From Dynamic Programming to RRTs: Algorithmic Design of Feasible Trajectories." In *Control Problems in Robotics: 2nd International Workshop on Control Problems in Robotics and Automation, Las Vegas, Dec. 14, 2002*, Springer Tracts in Advanced Robotics, edited by A. Bicchi, H. I. Christensen, and D. Prattichizzo, 19–37. Berlin: Springer-Verlag, 2003.

[Lenhart and Whitesides 95] W. J. Lenhart and S. H. Whitesides. "Reconfiguring Closed Polygonal Chains in Euclidean *d*-Space." *Discrete Comput. Geom.* 13 (1995), 123–140. MR1300512 (95g:52026)

[Liu and Dai 02] H. Liu and J. S. Dai. "Carton Manipulation Analysis Using Configuration Transformation." *Journal of Mechanical Engineering Science, Proc. IMechE* 216:5 (2002), 543–555.

[Liu and Dai 03] H. Liu and J. S. Dai. "An Approach to Carton-Folding Trajectory Planning Using Dual Robotic Fingers." *Robotics and Autonomous Systems* 42:1 (2003), 47–63.

[Lu and Akella 99] L. Lu and S. Akella. "Folding Cartons with Fixtures: A Motion Planning Approach." *IEEE Transactions on Robotics and Automation* 16:4 (1999), 1570–1576.

[McCarthy 00] J. M. McCarthy. *Geometric Design of Linkages*. New York: Springer, 2000.

[O'Rourke 00] J. O'Rourke. "Folding and Unfolding in Computational Geometry." In *Discrete and Computational Geometry: Japanese Conference, JCDCG'98 Tokyo, Japan, December 9–12, 1998, Revised Papers*, Lecture Notes in Computer Science 1763, pp. 258–266. Berlin: Springer-Verlag, 2000. MR1787532

[Qin et al. 14] Y. Qin, J. S. Dai, and G. Gogu. "Multi-furcation in a Derivative Queer-Square Mechanism." *Mechanisms and Machine Theory* 81:6 (2014), 36–53.

[Sallee 73] G. T. Sallee. "Stretching Chords of Space Curves." *Geom. Dedicata* 2 (1973), 311–315. MR0336560 (49:1334)

[Shimanuki et al. 04] H. Shimanuki, J. Kato, and T. Watanabe. "A Recognition System for Folding Process of Origami Drill Books." In *Graphics Recognition: Recent Advances and Perspectives*, Lecture Notes in Computer Science 3088, edited by L. Lladós and Y.-B. Kwon, pp. 244–255. Berlin: Springer-Verlag, 2004.

[Song and Amato 00] G. Song and N. M. Amato. "A Motion Planning Approach to Folding: From Paper Craft to Protein Folding." *IEEE Transactions on Robotics and Automation* 20:1 (2000), 60–71. MR1767253 (2001g:16019)

[Stewart 96] B. Stewart. *Packaging as Marketing Tool*. Philadelphia: Kogan Page, Ltd., 1996.

[Whitesides 92] S. Whitesides. "Algorithmic Issues in the Geometry of Planar Linkage Movement." *Australian Computer Journal* 24:2 (1992), 42–50.

[Yao and Dai 08] W. Yao and J. S. Dai. "Dexterous Manipulation of Origami Cartons with Robotic Fingers Based on the Interactive Configuration Space." *Journal of Mechanical Design, Trans. ASME* 130:2 (2008), 022303.

CENTRE FOR ROBOTICS RESEARCH, KING'S COLLEGE LONDON, UNITED KINGDOM
E-mail address: jian.dai@kcl.ac.uk

IV. Mathematics of Origami: Design Algorithms

Filling a Hole in a Crease Pattern: Isometric Mapping from Prescribed Boundary Folding

Erik D. Demaine and Jason S. Ku

1. Introduction

Many problems in origami require the folder to map the perimeter of a piece of paper to some specified folded configuration. In the tree method of origami design, circle packing breaks the paper up into polygonal molecules whose combined perimeter must be mapped to a specific tree. The fold-and-cut problem inputs a set of polygonal silhouettes whose perimeters must be mapped onto a common line. These two problems are well studied; one solution to the molecule folding problem is the universal molecule [Lang 96], while a solution to the fold-and-cut problem lies in the polygon's straight skeleton [Demaine et al. 98, Bern et al. 02]. Both of these problems can be considered as specific versions of a more general problem: the hole problem.

Given a crease pattern with a hole in it (an area of the paper with the creases missing), can we fill in the hole with suitable creases? More precisely, given a sheet of paper and a prescribed folding of its boundary, is there a way to fold the paper's interior without stretching so that the boundary lines up with the prescribed boundary folding? This hole problem was originally proposed by Barry Hayes at 3OSME in 2001 with the motivation of finding flat-foldable gadgets with common interfaces satisfying certain properties, such as not-all-equal clauses for an NP-hardness reduction [Bern and Hayes 96].

This problem formulation can be transformed to solve several existing problems, as well as some new applications (see Figure 1). If we map the boundary to a line, the polygon is now a molecule to be filled with creases or one half of a fold-and-cut problem cutline. The hole problem can also address problems where the boundary is not mapped to a line, i.e., mappings into the plane or into three dimensions, potentially leading to the algorithmic design of multi-axial bases, color changes, or complex three-dimensional tessellations or modulars. When trying to combine separately designed parts of an origami model, a solution to the hole problem could be used to design an interfacing crease pattern between them.

In this paper, we show that the hole problem always has a solution for polygonal input boundaries folded at finitely many points under the obvious necessary condition that the input folding is nonexpansive, and we present a polynomial-time algorithm to find one. We restrict ourselves to isometry and ignore self-intersection, leaving layer ordering (if

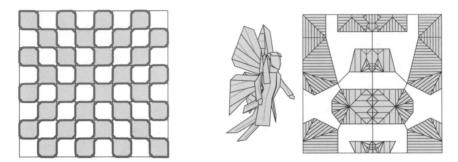

FIGURE 1. A boundary mapping that might be used to design a color-change checker board model (left). An unfinished crease pattern with parts of the crease pattern unknown (right).

possible) as an open problem. Section 2 introduces notation and defines the problem. Section 3 discusses the necessary condition that will turn out to be sufficient. Section 4 constructs vertex creases satisfying local isometry. Section 5 propagates the creases. Section 6 describes partitioning polygons. Section 7 describes the algorithm. Section 8 discusses application and implementation. Section 9 summarizes the results.

2. Notation and Definitions

First some notation and definitions. Let $\|\cdot\|$ denote Euclidean distance. Given a set of points $A \subseteq B \subset \mathbb{R}^c$, $c \in \mathbb{Z}^+$, and mapping $f : B \to \mathbb{R}^d$, $d \in \mathbb{Z}^+$, we say that A is *expansive* (respectively, *contractive*, *critical*) under f if $\|u - v\| <$ (respectively, $>, =$) $\|f(u) - f(v)\|$ for every $u, v \in A$, with *nonexpansive* (respectively, *noncontractive*, *noncritical*) referring to the negation. The definition of *critical* is the same as that of *isometric* under the Euclidean metric, but because we will use the term *isometry* to refer to isometric maps under the shortest-path metric [Demaine and O'Rourke 07], we use a different term for clarity. We say two line segments *cross* if their intersection is nonempty. We now prove two relations on crossing segments under certain conditions using the above terminology, including a generalization of Lemma 1 from [Connelly et al. 03].

LEMMA 2.1. *Consider distinct points $p, q, u, v \in \mathbb{R}^2$ with p, u, v not collinear, line segment (p, q) crossing line segment (u, v), and a mapping $f : \{p, q, u, v\} \to \mathbb{R}^d$.*

(a) *If $\{q, u, v\}$ is critical and $\{p, u, v\}$ is nonexpansive under f, then $\{p, q\}$ is nonexpansive under f.*

(b) *If $\{u, v\}$ is critical and $\{p, u, v\}, \{q, u, v\}$ are nonexpansive under f, then $\{p, q\}$ is nonexpansive under f; additionally, if $\{p, q\}$ is critical under f, then $\{p, q, u, v\}$ is also.*

PROOF. (a) Consider the following d-dimensional balls: S_0 centered at $f(q)$ with radius $\|p - q\|$, S_1 centered at $f(u)$ with radius $\|p - u\|$, and S_2 centered at $f(v)$ with radius $\|p - v\|$ (see Figure 2). The fact that $\{p, u, v\}$ is nonexpansive under f implies $f(p) \in S_1 \cap S_2$. Also, $\{q, u, v\}$ being critical and (p, q) crossing (u, v) implies $S_1 \cap S_2 \subset S_0$. Because $f(p) \in S_0$, $\{p, q\}$ is nonexpansive under f.

(b) Let $x = u + t(v - u)$ be the intersection of (p, q) and (u, v), and let $x_f = f(u) + t(f(v) - f(u))$. Repeated application of Lemma 2.1(a) yields $\|x - i\| \geq \|x_f - f(i)\|$ for $i \in \{p, q\}$.

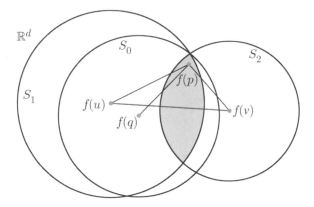

FIGURE 2. Points $f(u), f(v), f(q), f(p)$ with spheres S_0, S_1, S_2. The shaded area $S_1 \cap S_2 \subset S_0$ is the region in which $f(p)$ may exist if $\{p, u, v\}$ is nonexpansive under f.

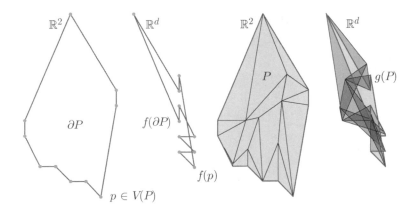

FIGURE 3. Input and output to the hole problem showing notation.

Combining with $\|x - p\| + \|x - q\| = \|p - q\|$ and the triangle inequality, $\left\|x_f - f(p)\right\| + \left\|x_f - f(q)\right\| \geq \|f(p) - f(q)\|$, yields that $\{p, q\}$ is nonexpansive under f. Further, if $\{p, q\}$ is critical under f, then so is $\{p, q, x_f\}$. Segments $(f(p), f(q))$ and $(f(u), f(v))$ are coplanar, crossing at x_f such that $\{u, p\}$ being expansive implies that $\{u, q\}$ is contractive under f. Because $\{p, q, u, v\}$ is nonexpansive, $\{p, q, u, v\}$ must be critical under f. □

We will consider a *polygon* P to be a bounded closed figure in $\mathbb{R}^2$ bounded by finitely many line segments connected in a simple cycle, with non-touching boundary. This definition restricts polygons to topological disks and allows adjacent edges to be collinear. Let $V(P)$ denote the vertices of P and ∂P denote the boundary of P, with $V(P) \subset \partial P \subset P$. An edge of P is a line segment in ∂P with endpoints at adjacent vertices. We say that a point $p \in P$ is *visible* from a vertex $v \in V(P)$ if the line segment from p to v is in P. With the terminology in place, we can now state the problem (see Figure 3).

PROBLEM 2.1 (Hole Problem). Given a polygon P in the plane with a boundary mapping $f : \partial P \to \mathbb{R}^d$, find an isometric mapping $g : P \to \mathbb{R}^d$ such that $g(\partial P) = f(\partial P)$.

We call g a *solution* to the hole problem, if one exists. Mapping P into $\mathbb{R}$ requires infinitely many folds, so we restrict the remainder to $d \geq 2$.

3. Necessary Condition

In this section, we define *valid* boundary mappings and give a necessary condition for the hole problem under the weak assumption that the polygon boundary is folded at finitely many points.

DEFINITION 3.1 (Valid Mapping). Given polygon P and boundary mapping $f : \partial P \to \mathbb{R}^d$, define f to be *valid* if ∂P is nonexpansive under f and adjacent vertices of P are critical under f.

LEMMA 3.2. *Consider an instance of the hole problem with input polygon P and boundary mapping $f : \partial P \to \mathbb{R}^d$ that is nonstraight at finitely many boundary points. If f is not valid then the instance has no solution.*

PROOF. Modify $V(P)$ to include boundary points nonstraight under f (vertices adjacent to collinear edges are allowed), so that f is straight for $\partial P \setminus V(P)$. Assume a solution g exists and f is not valid. Then, either two points $a, b \in \partial P$ are expansive under f, or two adjacent vertices $u, v \in V(P)$ are noncritical. If the former, then $\{a, b\}$ is also expansive under g, so g cannot be isometric. If the latter, then $f(p)$ is nonstraight for some p on the edge from u to v, a contradiction. □

To determine the validity of f, checking expansiveness between all pairs of points in ∂P is impractical. Instead, it suffices to show that the set of vertices is nonexpansive under f and that edges of P map to congruent line segments.

LEMMA 3.3. *Given polygon P and boundary mapping $f : \partial P \to \mathbb{R}^d$, f is valid if and only if $V(P)$ is nonexpansive and edges of P map to congruent line segments under f.*

PROOF. If f is valid, $V(P)$ is nonexpansive under f since $V(P) \subset \partial P$, and edges map to congruent line segments because adjacent vertices are critical and points interior to edges are nonexpansive with endpoints. To prove the other direction, if edges of P map to congruent line segments, adjacent vertices are critical and pairs of points on the same edge are nonexpansive (indeed critical) under f. To show that points from different edges are nonexpansive under f, consider vertex p and point q interior to the edge from vertex u to v. By Lemma 2.1(a), $\{q, p\}$ is nonexpansive under f for any vertex p. Now consider point $q' \in \partial P$ not on the edge from u to v. By the same argument as above, $\{q', u, v\}$ is nonexpansive under f, so by Lemma 2.1(a), $\{q, q'\}$ is also nonexpansive. □

4. Bend Lines

When the interior angle of the polygon boundary at a vertex decreases in magnitude under a valid boundary mapping, the local interior of the polygon will need to curve or bend to accommodate. For simplicity, we consider only single-fold solutions to satisfy such vertices, which will still be sufficient to construct a solution. We call these creases *bend lines* made up of *bend points*.

DEFINITION 4.1 (Bend Points and Lines). Given polygon P with valid boundary mapping $f : \partial P \to \mathbb{R}^d$ and vertex $v \in V(P)$ adjacent to two vertices $\{u, w\}$ contractive under f, define $p \in P$ to be a *bend point* of (P, f, v) if there exists some $q \in \mathbb{R}^d$ (called a *bend point image* of p) for which $\|p - i\| = \|q - f(i)\|$ for $i \in \{u, v, w\}$ and p is visible from v. Further, define a *bend line* of (P, f, v) to be a maximal line segment of bend points of (P, f, v), with

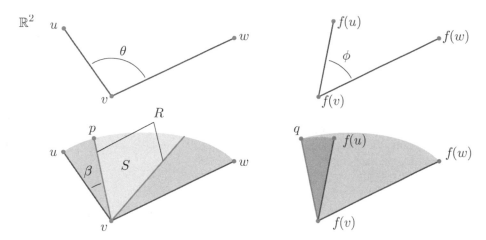

FIGURE 4. The bend points of (P, f, v) showing relavent angles $\{\theta, \phi, \beta\}$, points $\{u, v, w, p, f(u), f(v), f(w), q\}$, and sets $\{R, S\}$. The upper figures show only the boundary mapping, while the lower images show filled, locally satisfying mappings of the interior.

one endpoint at v and the other in ∂P; and let a *bend line image* be a set of bend point images of the bend points in a bend line, congruent to the bend line.

A bend point corresponds to a point in the polygon such that triangles $\triangle pvu$ and $\triangle pvw$ isometrically map to triangles $\triangle qf(v)f(u)$ and $\triangle qf(v)f(w)$, respectively. Bend lines correspond to single folds of P that locally satisfy isometry for the boundary from u to w through v. Lemma 4.2 represents bend points explicitly (see Figure 4).

LEMMA 4.2. *Consider polygon P with valid boundary mapping $f : \partial P \to \mathbb{R}^d$ and vertex v adjacent to two vertices $\{u, w\}$ contractive under f. Let $\theta = \angle uvw$ be the internal angle of P at v; let $\phi = \angle f(u)f(v)f(w)$; and let*

$$R = \left\{ p \in P \, \middle| \, \begin{matrix} \angle pvu \in \left\{ \frac{\theta-\phi}{2}, \frac{\theta+\phi}{2} \right\} \\ p \text{ visible from } v \end{matrix} \right\}, \quad S = \left\{ p \in P \, \middle| \, \begin{matrix} \angle pvu \in \left[\frac{\theta-\phi}{2}, \frac{\theta+\phi}{2} \right] \\ p \text{ visible from } v \end{matrix} \right\}.$$

Then, the set of bend points of (P, f, v) is R if $d = 2$, and S otherwise.

PROOF. A point $p \in P$ visible from v is a bend point of (P, f, v) only if triangles $\triangle pvu$ and $\triangle pvw$ are congruent to $\triangle qf(v)f(u)$ and $\triangle qf(v)f(w)$, respectively, for some bend point image q by definition. Let $\beta = \angle pvu$. If $d = 2$, $\triangle pvu$ and $\triangle pvw$ must be coplanar. Then, the internal angles of both triangles at v must sum to θ, and the magnitude of their difference $|(\theta - \beta) - \beta|$ must be ϕ. This condition is satisfied only when $\beta \in \left\{ \frac{\theta-\phi}{2}, \frac{\theta+\phi}{2} \right\}$. Thus, for $d = 2$, the set of bend points of (P, f, v) is R.

For $d > 2$, triangles $\triangle qf(v)f(u)$ and $\triangle qf(v)f(w)$ need not be coplanar. Because $\{u, w\}$ is contractive under f, $\phi \geq |\theta - 2\beta|$, so $\frac{\theta-\phi}{2} \leq \beta \leq \frac{\theta+\phi}{2}$, and points in $P \setminus S$ cannot be bend points. It remains to show that for each point $p \in S$ there exists a satisfying bend point image $q \in \mathbb{R}^d$. For a given p, q must lie on two hyper-cones each with apex v, one symmetric about the segment from $f(v)$ to $f(u)$ with internal half angle β and the other symmetric about the segment from $f(v)$ to $f(w)$ with internal half angle $\theta - \beta$. These hyper-cones have nonzero intersection H because $(\theta - \beta) + \beta > \phi$ and $\phi \geq \max(\theta - \beta, \beta) - \min(\theta - \beta, \beta)$. The intersection of two hyper-cones with common apex v is a set of rays emanating from v, so H intersects the $(d-1)$-sphere centered at $f(v)$ with radius $\|p-v\|$. Any point in this intersection satisfies all three constraints of a bend point image for any $p \in S$.   □

For every $d > 2$, the set of bend points of (P, f, v) is the same, but the set of bend point images increases with dimension. The set of bend point images is a ruled hypersurface of bend line images emanating from $f(v)$. In the case of $d = 2$ above, hyper-cones are simply two rays, leading to disjoint line segments of bend points. For $d = 3$, the set of bend points is a standard cone-like surface. Mapping generally to $\mathbb{R}^d$, the set is a ruled hypersurface of rays emanating from a point.

5. Split Points

Bend lines locally satisfy the boundary around a vertex with a single crease. We want to find the bend point on a bend line farthest from the vertex that remains nonexpansive with the rest of the boundary. We call such a point a *split point*.

DEFINITION 5.1 (Split Points). Given polygon P with valid boundary mapping $f : \partial P \to \mathbb{R}^d$ and vertex v contractive under f with every visible nonadjacent vertex and adjacent to two vertices $\{u, w\}$ contractive under f, define p to be a *split point* of (P, f, v), q to be its *split point image*, and x to be its *split end* if

(1) p is a bend point of (P, f, v), with q its bend point image;
(2) $\|p - i\| \geq \|q - f(i)\|$ for $i \in V(P)$;
(3) $\|p - x\| = \|q - f(x)\|$ for some $x \in V(P) \setminus \{u, v, w\}$;
(4) p is visible from x.

LEMMA 5.2. *Given polygon P with valid boundary mapping $f : \partial P \to \mathbb{R}^d$ and vertex v adjacent to two vertices $\{u, w\}$ contractive under f with v contractive under f with any visible nonadjacent vertex, there exists a split point, image, or end triple (p, q, x) for every bend line or image pair (L, L_f) of (P, f, v) with $p \in L$ and $q \in L_f$.*

PROOF. Given bend line/image pair (L, L_f), we construct (p, q, x). Parameterize L so that $p(t)$ is the unique point in L such that $\|p(t) - v\| = t$ for $t \in [0, \ell]$, where ℓ is the length of L; and let $q(t)$ be the corresponding bend point image of $p(t)$ in L_f. For any $t \in [0, \ell]$ and vertex x, let $d(t, x) = \|p(t) - x\| - \|q(t) - f(x)\|$. Let t^* be the maximum $t \in (0, \ell]$ for which $d(t, x) \geq 0$ for all $x \in V(P)$, and let X be the set of such vertices $x \in V(P) \setminus \{u, v, w\}$ for which $d(t^*, x) = 0$ and $d(t^* + \delta, i) < 0$ for all $\delta \in (0, \varepsilon]$ for some $\varepsilon > 0$. If we can prove that there exists some $x \in X$ from which $p(t^*)$ is visible, then $p = p(t^*)$ is a split point with $q = q(t^*)$ its split point image, satisfying the split point conditions by construction.

Suppose for contradiction that t^* does not exist so that for all $t \in (0, \ell]$, $d(t, x) < 0$ for some $x \in V(P)$. Because d is continuous and $d(0, x) \geq 0$ for all $x \in V(P)$, there exists a vertex $x' \in V(P) \setminus \{u, v, w\}$ not visible from and critical with v under f such that $d(\delta, x') < 0$ for all $\delta \in (0, \varepsilon]$ for some $\varepsilon > 0$. Either x' is in the infinite sector C induced by $\angle uvw$ or it is not. If the former, the line segment from v to x' must cross some edge (a, b) of P and $\{a, b, x', v\}$ is critical under f by Lemma 2.1(b). Since neither a nor b can be visible from v, then u and w must be in $\triangle abv$, and $\{u, v, w\}$ must be critical, contradicting that $\{u, w\}$ is contractive under f. Alternatively, x' is not in C, and for every $\delta \in (0, \varepsilon]$ for some $\varepsilon > 0$, the line segment from $p(\delta)$ to x' crosses either (v, u) or (v, w). By Lemma 2.1(b), $d(\delta, x') \geq 0$, a contridiction, so t^* exists.

We now prove that p is visible from some $x \in X$. Suppose for contradiction that p is not visible from any $x \in X$ so that for each x there exists point $c \in \partial P$, the boundary crossing closest to p on the segment from p to x. Note that c cannot be strictly interior to edge

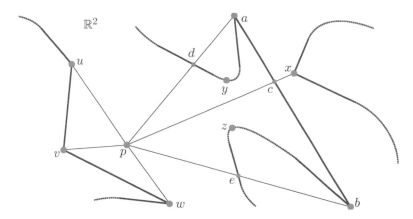

FIGURE 5. Visibility of p: If $x \in X$ is not visible from v, one of $\{a, b, y, z\} \in X$ will be.

(v, u) or (v, w) because Lemma 2.1(b) implies $\|p(t^* + \delta) - x\| = \|q(t^* + \delta) - f(x)\|$ for all $d \in (0, \varepsilon]$ for some ε, a contridiction. And, c cannot be v or else $\|p(t) - x\| = \|q(t) - f(x)\|$ for all $t \in [0, \ell]$. So, c crosses some other edge (a, b) (see Figure 5). Then, Lemma 2.1(b) implies $\|p - i\| = \|q - f(i)\|$ for $i \in \{a, b\}$, and the contrapositive of Lemma 2.1(a) implies for at least one vertex $i \in \{a, b\}$, $\|p(t^* + \delta) - i\| < \|q(t^* + \delta) - f(i)\|$ for all $\delta \in (0, \varepsilon]$ for some $\varepsilon > 0$. Without loss of generality, assume $i = a$. Because $a \in X$, p cannot be visible from a. Let $d \in \partial P$ be the boundary crossing closest to p on the segment from p to a. There must exist some vertex y in triangle $\triangle acp$ from which p is visible because the boundary of the polygon entering the triangle at d must return to a without crossing edge (c, p). By the same argument, at least one of $\{y, b\}$ is in X, and since p is visible from y, $b \in X$. Replacing (b, e, z) for (a, d, y) in the argument above, one of $\{y, z\}$ is in X. But p is visible from both, a contradiction. □

LEMMA 5.3. *Given polygon P with valid boundary mapping $f : \partial P \to \mathbb{R}^d$ and vertex v that is contractive under f with every visible nonadjacent vertex and adjacent to two vertices $\{u, w\}$ contractive under f, a split point/image/end triple of (P, f, v) exists and can be identified in $O(d|V(P)|)$ time.*

PROOF. This result follows directly by choosing any bend line/image pair of (P, f, v) according to Lemma 4.2, then constructing the split point/image/end triple specified by Lemma 5.2. Choosing a bend line/image pair can be done in $O(d)$ time. Constructing the split point/image/end triple requires a d-dimensional comparison at each vertex yielding total construction time $O(d|V(P)|)$. □

6. Partitions

To find an overall solution to the hole problem, we will repeatedly split a polygon in half, solve each piece recursively, and then join the pieces back together. Specifically, we want to find a *partition* consisting of two *partition polygons* together with respective boundary mappings such that

- the partition polygons exactly cover the original polygon;
- the partition polygons intersect, and only on their boundaries;
- each partition function maps the partition polygon boundaries into the same dimensional space as the original function;

- the original boundary mapping of the polygon boundary is preserved by the partition functions;
- the intersection of the partition polygons map to the same place under both partition functions;
- the partition functions are valid.

DEFINITION 6.1 (Valid Partition). Given polygon P and valid boundary mapping $f : \partial P \to \mathbb{R}^d$, define (P_1, P_2, f_1, f_2) to be a *valid partition* of (P, f) if the following properties hold:

(1) P_1, P_2 polygons with $P = P_1 \cup P_2$;   (2) $P_1 \cap P_2 = \partial P_1 \cap \partial P_2 = L \neq \emptyset$;

(3) $f_1 : \partial P_1 \to \mathbb{R}^d, f_2 : \partial P_2 \to \mathbb{R}^d$;   (4) $f(p) = \begin{cases} f_1(p) & p \in \partial P \cap \partial P_1, \\ f_2(p) & \text{otherwise}; \end{cases}$

(5) $f_1(p) = f_2(p)$ for $p \in L$;   (6) f_1, f_2 valid.

7. Algorithm

THEOREM 7.1. *Given polygon P and boundary mapping $f : \partial P \to \mathbb{R}^d, d \geq 2$, that is nonstraight at finitely many boundary points, an isometric mapping $g : P \to \mathbb{R}^d$ with $g(\partial P) = f(\partial P)$ exists if and only if f is valid. A solution can be computed in polynomial time.*

The theorem implies that the necessary condition in Lemma 3.2 is also sufficient. Our approach is to iteratively divide P into valid partitions and combine them back together. We partition non-triangular polygons into smaller ones differently depending on which of two properties (P, f) satisfies. First, we show that (P, f) satisfies at least one of these properties.

LEMMA 7.2. *For every polygon P with $|V(P)| > 3$ and valid boundary mapping $f : \partial P \to \mathbb{R}^d$, either (a) there exist two nonadjacent vertices $\{u, v\}$ critical under f and visible from each other, or (b) there exists a vertex $v \in V(P)$ adjacent to two vertices $\{u, w\}$ contractive under f, or (c) both exist.*

PROOF. Suppose for contradiction that there exists some (P, f) such that no two nonadjacent vertices critical under f are visible from each other and no vertex is adjacent to two vertices contractive under f. Consider any vertex v that, by the contrapositive of the latter condition, will be adjacent to two vertices $\{u, w\}$ critical under f. Since $|V(P)| > 3$, u and v are nonadjacent and cannot be visible from each other, so there must be at least one other distinct vertex x interior to $\triangle uvw$ visible from vertex v. But, since x is nonexpansive with $\{u, v, w\}$ under f, $\{x, u, v, w\}$ must be critical under f, a contradiction.   □

LEMMA 7.3. *Consider polygon P with valid boundary mapping $f : \partial P \to \mathbb{R}^d$ containing nonadjacent vertices $\{u, v\}$ critical under f with u visible from v. Construct polygon P_1 from the vertices of P from u to v, and construct P_2 from the vertices of P from v to u. Construct boundary mapping functions $f_1 : \partial P_1 \to \mathbb{R}^d$ and $f_2 : \partial P_2 \to \mathbb{R}^d$ so that $f_1(x) = f(x)$ for $x \in V(P_1)$ and $f_2(x) = f(x)$ for $x \in V(P_2)$, with f_1, f_2 mapping edges of P_1, P_2 to congruent line segments. Then, (P_1, P_2, f_1, f_2) is a valid partition.*

PROOF. Because P_1 and P_2 are constructed by splitting P along line segment $L \subset P$ from u to v, $P = P_1 \cup P_2$ and $L = P_1 \cap P_2 = \partial P_1 \cap \partial P_2$, satisfying properties (1) and (2) of a valid partition. Property (3) is satisfied by definition. Property (4) holds because f is valid, $\{u, v\}$ is critical, and points in L are nonexpansive with points in ∂P_1 and ∂P_2 by Lemma 2.1(a). Property (5) holds by construction. Lastly, Property (6) holds because f_1, f_2 satisfy the conditions in Lemma 3.3 by construction.   □

LEMMA 7.4. *Consider polygon P with valid boundary mapping $f : \partial P \to \mathbb{R}^d$ and vertex $v \in V(P)$ that is contractive under f with every visible nonadjacent vertex and adjacent to two vertices $\{u, w\}$ contractive under f. Let (p, q, x) be a split point/image/end triple of (P, f, v). Construct polygon P_1 from p and the vertices of P from v to x, and construct P_2 from p and the vertices of P from x to v. Construct boundary mapping functions $f_1 : \partial P_1 \to \mathbb{R}^d$ and $f_2 : \partial P_2 \to \mathbb{R}^d$ so that $f_1(x) = f(x)$ for $x \in V(P_1) \setminus p$, $f_2(x) = f(x)$ for $x \in V(P_2) \setminus p$, and $f_1(p) = f_2(p) = q$, with f_1, f_2 mapping edges of P_1, P_2 to congruent line segments. Then, (P_1, P_2, f_1, f_2) is a valid partition.*

PROOF. Because P_1 and P_2 are constructed by splitting P along two line segments fully contained in P, $P = P_1 \cup P_2$ and $P_1 \cap P_2 = \partial P_1 \cap \partial P_2$, satisfying properties (1) and (2) of a valid partition. Property (3) is satisfied by definition. Property (4) holds because (P, f) is valid, $V(P_1)$ and $V(P_2)$ are nonexpansive with adjacent vertices critical under f by definition of a split point/image, and points in the new line segments are nonexpansive with points in ∂P_1 and ∂P_2 by Lemma 2.1(a). Property (5) holds by construction. Lastly, Property (6) holds because f_1, f_2 satisfy the conditions in Lemma 3.3 by construction. □

Next, we establish the base case for our induction. Specifically, a triangle with a valid boundary mapping of its boundary has a unique isometric mapping of its interior consistent with the provided boundary condition.

LEMMA 7.5. *Given polygon P with $|V(P)| = 3$ and valid boundary mapping $f : \partial P \to \mathbb{R}^d$, there exists a unique isometric mapping $g : P \to \mathbb{R}^d$ such that $g(B) = f(B)$.*

PROOF. Because f is valid, the vertices of P are critical under f. The triangles ∂P and $f(\partial P)$ are congruent, so their convex hulls are isometric. Specifically, if P with vertices $\{u, v, w\}$ is parameterized by $P = \{p(a, b) = a(v - u) + b(w - u) + u \mid a, b \in [0, 1], a + b \leq 1\}$, then the affine map $g : P \to \mathbb{R}^d$ defined by

$$g(p(a, b) \in P) = a[f(v) - f(u)] + b[f(w) - f(u)] + f(u)$$

is a unique isometry for $g(B) = f(B)$. □

Lastly, we show that we can combine isometric mappings of valid partitions into larger isometric mappings.

LEMMA 7.6. *Consider polygon P with valid boundary mapping $f : \partial P \to \mathbb{R}^d$ and with valid partition (P_1, P_2, f_1, f_2). Given isometric mappings $g_1 : P_1 \to \mathbb{R}^d$ and $g_2 : P_2 \to \mathbb{R}^d$ with $g_1(\partial P_1) = f_1(\partial P_1)$ and $g_2(\partial P_2) = f_2(\partial P_2)$, the mapping $g : P \to \mathbb{R}^d$ defined below is also isometric, with $g(\partial P) = f(\partial P)$:*

$$g(p \in P) = \begin{cases} g_1(p) & p \in P_1, \\ g_2(p) & \text{otherwise.} \end{cases}$$

PROOF. First, $g(\partial P) = f(\partial P)$ because the partition is valid. Consider the shortest path K between points $p, q \in P$ composed from a finite set of line segments. Suppose for contradiction that $g(K)$ is not the same length as K. Every point in K either lies in P_1, P_2, or both by property (1) of a valid partition. Split K into a connected set of line segments, each segment fully contained in either P_1 or P_2 with endpoints in $P_1 \cap P_2$. Because g_1 and g_2 are isometric, these line segments remain the same length under g. Further, the endpoints of adjacent segments map to the same place under g_1 and g_2 by definition of a valid parition. The total length of $g(K)$ is the sum of the lengths of the intervals, the same length as K, a contradiction. □

Now we are ready to prove the theorem.

Proof of Theorem 7.1. Lemma 3.2 implies that f is valid if g exists. We show g exists for valid f by construction. Partition (P, f) with $|V(P)| > 3$ as follows. If (P, f) contains two nonadjacent vertices $\{u, v\}$ critical under f and visible from each other, divide using Routine 1: partition using the construction in Lemma 7.3. Otherwise divide using Routine 2: partition using the construction in Lemma 7.4, applying Routine 1 to each partitioned polygon immediately after. Note that both polygons generated by the construction from Lemma 7.4 are guaranteed to contain two nonadjacent vertices critical under f and visible from each other, namely $\{u, p\}$ and $\{w, p\}$, so each can be divided using Routine 1. Recursively fill each partitioned polygon with an isometric mapping of their interior and combine them into a mapping $g : P \to \mathbb{R}^d$ using the construction in Lemma 7.6. Since the partitions are valid, g is isometric with $g(\partial P) = f(\partial P)$. Construct isometries for triangular polygons, the base case of the recursion, according to Lemma 7.5.

To show the recursion terminates, consider state i where P is partitioned into a set of n_i polygons $\mathcal{P}_i = \{P_1, \ldots, P_{n_i}\}$. Define potential $\Phi_i = \sum_{P_j \in \mathcal{P}_i} (|V(P_j)| - 3)$ with $\Phi_0 = |V(P)| - 3$. Partitioning a polygon using Routine 1 yields state $i + 1$ with $\Phi_{i+1} = \Phi_i - 1$: Lemma 7.3 adds two vertices, the number of polygons increases by one, and $2 - 3 = -1$. Partitioning a polygon using Routine 2 also yields $\Phi_{i+1} = \Phi_i - 1$: Lemma 7.4 adds four vertices, Lemma 7.3 adds two vertices with each application, the number of polygons increases by three, and $4 + 2 \times 2 - 3 \times 3 = -1$. Lemma 7.2 ensures that one of the routines can always be applied to any non-triangular polygon. When $\Phi_i = 0$, all partitioned polygons are triangles and no polygon can be partitioned further. The iteration terminates after Φ_0 calls to either routine.

Let n be the number of vertices $|V(P)|$ in the input polygon. At the start of the algorithm, all critical vertex pairs can be identified naively in $O(dn^2)$ time. Application of either routine requires at most $O(dn)$ time, and both routines can update and maintain new critical vertex pairs in partition polygons at no additional cost. Each routine is called no more than $O(n)$ times. Only a linear number of triangles are produced and the construction of each g_i takes constant time. The running time of the entire construction is thus $O(dn^2)$, which is polynomial.   □

8. Applications

Much of the intuition for this algorithm was developed while working on the design of various three-dimensional tessellations, specifically while working on Maze Folding [Demaine et al. 11] and a private commission designing an origami chandelier for Moksa, a restaurant in Cambridge, MA (see Figure 6). A version of this algorithm was implemented for flat-folds ($d = 2$) in 2010 using MATLAB (see Figure 7). We leave an implementation of this algorithm in three dimensions for future work.

9. Conclusion

We have proposed an algorithm for finding isometric mappings consistent with prescribed boundary mappings that runs in polynomial time. This algorithm was inspired by the universal molecule construction; instead of insetting an input polygon perimeter at a constant rate from all edges at once, our algorithm insets each vertex serially as far as possible. Our construction cannot find all possible isometric solutions, though the algorithm provides a rich family of solutions given choice of bend line and image with each application of Routine 2: two choices when $d = 2$ and an infinite set of choices for $d > 2$. This

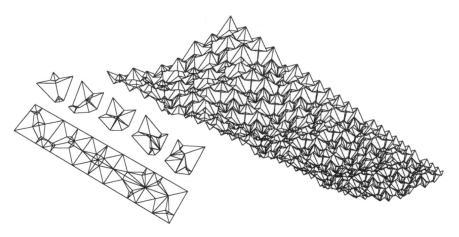

FIGURE 6. A three-dimensional abstract tessellation formed by tiling five different square units, each corner in either a binary low or a binary high state. Units were designed using our algorithm and having common boundaries, connected to form single-sheet tessellations.

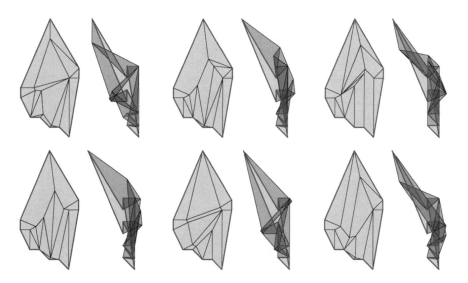

FIGURE 7. Various solutions for the same input polygon and boundary mapping found by our MATLAB implementation for $d = 2$.

algorithm can be generalized by not insetting vertices all the way to split points and by solving vertices locally with more than one crease at a vertex. We conjecture that adding such flexibility would allow construction of the entire space of isometric solutions following a similar procedure to our construction.

Recall that the proposed algorithm does not address self-intersection and cannot guarantee the existence of a valid layer ordering for the isometries found; however, because the space of solutions is large for a generic input, one might be able to construct non-self-intersecting solutions by directing the algorithm's decisions appropriately through the solution space. Additionally, the proposed algorithm only addresses instances for f folded at finitely many points. It is conceivable that a similar algorithm could be used to design curved foldings. We leave these as open problems.

Acknowledgments

The authors would like to thank Barry Hayes for introducing us to this problem and to thank Robert Lang and Tomohiro Tachi for helpful discussions. E. Demaine is supported in part by NSF ODISSEI grant EFRI-1240383 and NSF Expedition grant CCF-1138967.

References

[Bern and Hayes 96] Marshall Bern and Barry Hayes. "The Complexity of Flat Origami." In *Proceedings of the Seventh Annual ACM-SIAM Symposium on Discrete Algorithms*, pp. 175–183. Philadelphia: SIAM, 1996. MR1381938 (97c:52016)

[Bern et al. 02] Marshall Bern, Erik Demaine, David Eppstein, and Barry Hayes. "A Disk-Packing Algorithm for an Origami Magic Trick." In *Origami³: Proceedings of the Third International Meeting of Origami Science, Mathematics, and Education*, edited by Thomas Hull, pp. 17–28. Natick, MA: A K Peters, 2002. MR1955756 (2004b:52030)

[Connelly et al. 03] Robert Connelly, Erik D. Demaine, and Günter Rote. "Straightening Polygonal Arcs and Convexifying Polygonal Cycles." *Discrete & Computational Geometry* 30:2 (2003), 205–239. MR2007962 (2004h:52028)

[Demaine and O'Rourke 07] Erik D. Demaine and Joseph O'Rourke. *Geometric Folding Algorithms: Linkages, Origami, Polyhedra*. CAmbridge, UK: Cambridge University Press, 2007. MR2354878 (2008g:52001)

[Demaine et al. 98] Erik D. Demaine, Martin L. Demaine, and Anna Lubiw. "Folding and Cutting Paper." In *Discrete and Computational Geometry: Japanese Conference, JCDCG'98 Tokyo, Japan, December 9–12, 1998, Revised Papers*, Lecture Notes in Computer Science 1763, pp. 104–117. Berlin: Springer-Verlag, 1998. MR1787519

[Demaine et al. 11] Erik D. Demaine, Martin L. Demaine, and Jason Ku. "Folding Any Orthogonal Maze." In *Origami⁵: Fifth International Meeting of Origami Science, Mathematics, and Education*, edited by Patsy Wang-Iverson, Robert J. Lang, and Mark Yim, pp. 449–454. Boca Raton, FL: A K Peters/CRC Press, 2011. MR2866900 (2012k:00005)

[Lang 96] Robert J. Lang. "A Computational Algorithm for Origami Design." In *Proceedings of the Twelfth Annual Symposium on Computational Geometry*, pp. 98–105. New York: ACM, 1996.

MIT COMPUTER SCIENCE AND ARTIFICIAL INTELLIGENCE LAB., CAMBRIDGE, MASSACHUSETTS
E-mail address: edemaine@mit.edu

MIT FIELD INTELLIGENCE LABORATORY, CAMBRIDGE, MASSACHUSETTS
E-mail address: jasonku@mit.edu

Spiderwebs, Tilings, and Flagstone Tessellations

Robert J. Lang

1. Introduction

Origami tessellations are a branch of geometric origami in which an abstract tiling is physically embodied by folding a single uncut sheet of paper in such a way that the folded edges of the paper define a pattern related to the underlying tiling. Although numerous independent artists developed versions of the concept (see, e.g., [Resch 68, Huffman 76]), the field is generally considered to have received its key impetus from the developments of Shuzo Fujimoto in the 1970s and 1980s [Fujimoto 82]; Yoshihide Momotani was also active in this period and developed many patterns that we would call origami tessellations today [Momotani 84]. Kawasaki et al. [Kawasaki and Yoshida 88] gave a more formal definition of "crystallographic origamis" that we would now recognize as tessellations. In the West, the field was significantly developed by Paulo Taborda Barreto [Barreto 97] and Chris K. Palmer [Palmer 97] in the 1990s and then received another boost with the 2009 publication of Gjerde's landmark book [Gjerde 09]. Today, the field is one of the most vibrant genres of origami.

Much of current origami tessellation development is *grid based*, wherein the paper is initially creased into a regular grid pattern, usually either square or hexagonal-triangular, and then the folds of the tessellation pattern are geometrically constructed from the points and lines of the grid. However, there are many tessellations that cannot be realized by grid-based folding; rather, they must be computationally constructed, often developed from an underlying tiling. Computational tessellation techniques allow the realization of many beautiful patterns based on unusual, complex, aperiodic, or even totally irregular tilings.

One of the first general-tiling computational tessellation algorithms was the *shrink-rotate* algorithm, which was computationally described and realized by Bateman [Bateman 02, Bateman 10]. In this procedure, one begins with an underlying tiling expressed as a plane graph; each polygon is then shrunken and rotated about a point, using the same shrinkage and rotation factor for all polygons but a different point for each polygon as the center of shrinkage and rotation. Additional lines are added to this modified network to realize a crease pattern that is metrically flat-foldable, meaning that if one folds upon the crease lines and ignores the possibility of self-intersection, the resulting folded form will lie flat. Of course, with real paper, one cannot truly ignore self-intersection; however, in shrink-rotate tessellations it is always possible to find a rotation angle for which a crease assignment can be chosen so that the resulting crease pattern truly folds flat with no self-intersection.

The key to the shrink-rotate algorithm is the suitable choice of the centers of shrink-age/rotation for each polygon. Not all tilings possess such a suitable choice. In a previous work [Lang and Bateman 11], the author and Bateman showed that the shrink-rotate algorithm is only possible if the tiling possesses a non-crossing embedding of the dual graph in which each dual edge is orthogonal to its corresponding original tiling edge. Such a dual graph and its embedding were originally studied by James Clerk Maxwell [Kappraff 02, Maxwell 64], who called it a *reciprocal figure*. In Maxwell's analysis, the reciprocal figure encoded the field of compression and/or tension in a truss network defined by the original graph. The condition that the dual is non-crossing is equivalent to the condition that every member of the truss network is under tension; such a network is called a *spiderweb*. Thus, a tiling that has such a non-crossing reciprocal figure satisfies the *spiderweb condition*, and a tiling can be folded into a tessellation using the shrink-rotate algorithm if and only if it satisfies this condition. When it does, the vertices of the reciprocal figure provide the centers of shrinkage and rotation.

An origami tessellation constructed by shrink-rotate is an array of *simple flat twists*, a concept identified by Fujimoto [Fujimoto 82] and widely found throughout origami tessellations. An origami tessellation composed of simple flat twists consists of a series of mutually overlapping polygons. In such tessellations, some polygons are on top of all of their neighbors; others may be wholly or partially covered by all of their neighbors; but usually, most are somewhere in between, partially covering some of their neighbors and partially covered by others.

However, there is a class of origami tessellations in which every visible polygon lies entirely on top of all of its neighbors and no other polygon covers any visible polygon. In such tessellations, the visible polygons must necessarily butt-join (with no overlaps) at their folded edges. Such tessellations are called *flagstone tessellations*, because the pattern of polygons separated by recessed linear gaps resembles the flagstones of a walkway. Flagstone tessellations have a special appeal in the origami tessellation world, and there are many examples (see, e.g., Gjerde [Gjerde 09]). However, most examples to date have been grid-based tessellations.

We may define a flagstone tessellation as follows. We assume a crease pattern P is partitioned into vertices, creases, and facets, all of which have both position and layer ordering defined in the folded form.

DEFINITION 1.1 (Flagstone Tessellation). A *flagstone tessellation* is a flat-foldable origami crease pattern P containing a subset $\mathcal{F}$ of facets (the *flagstone facets*) that satisfies the following:

- *No gaps:* In the folded form, the closure of $\mathcal{F}$ is simply connected.
- *No overlaps:* In the folded form, no facet of P overlaps and covers any part of any facet in $\mathcal{F}$.

This definition is quite broad and supports many possible schemes for constructing flagstone tessellations. In this paper, I give a general construction algorithm for a family of flagstone tessellations that works for both grid-based and non–grid-based tilings. I show that, as with shrink-rotate tessellations, the tiling must satisfy the spiderweb condition. While shrink-rotate tessellations resemble their underlying plane graph imperfectly due to overlaps between adjacent polygons, in constructed flagstone tessellations, the resemblance is exact; the boundaries between adjacent flagstone polygons are a reduced version of the original tiling and its boundary. Not every spiderweb tiling gives rise to an injective (non–self-intersecting) folding pattern, however; I give conditions for when a solution exists and present examples, both computed and folded.

2. The Spiderweb Condition

Before getting into flagstone tessellations, let us revisit the more common simple flat twist tessellation. Figure 1 shows the crease pattern and folded form for a simple flat twist created from an irregular quadrilateral.

In the crease pattern (Figure 1(a)), I have drawn gray vectors that are perpendicular to the valley folds of the pleats and that connect a point on the mountain fold to the point that it maps to on the opposite side of the valley fold. These four *pleat vectors* are then connected by *wedge vectors* (solid black), head-to-tail, forming a closed loop. Since the head-to-tail vectors form a closed loop, the vector sum of all eight vectors must be zero.

Now, in the folded form (Figure 1(b)), the wedge vectors connect with each other to form a closed loop. So, they, too, must independently vectorially sum to zero.

If the sum of the pleat vectors and wedge vectors together is zero, and the sum of the wedge vectors alone is zero, then the sum of the pleat vectors must also be zero. This is illustrated in Figure 2, in which the four pleat vectors have been translated together to connect head-to-tail. Indeed, they do form a closed loop, as the figure shows.

Now, if we rotate all four vectors by 90°, they will be parallel to their respective pleats, but the rotation will not change the fact that they vectorially sum to zero. But, if we translate them so that their tails touch the common point, we can give a different interpretation to this diagram: the vectors are lines of force along their four corresponding lines, and because they sum to zero, we can say that these are the forces that would be experienced by a static network of four lines in tension at a common point. This condition is the mechanical spiderweb condition; thus, we can see that there is a direct correspondence between the forces on a spiderweb under static tension and the pleat widths (the lengths of the gray vectors) needed to realize a simple flat twist in origami. But this has a broader interpretation: if we somehow "remove" parallel strips of paper along the boundaries of a tiling to bring the edges of the tiling together, the widths of the removed strips must obey the spiderweb condition. So, we can use this property to create other types of tessellations.

3. The Flagstone Geometry

A simple flat twist tessellation removes parallel-edged strips of paper; in Figure 1, the gray pleats are completely hidden from view. But, a simple flat twist isn't compatible with the flagstone concept because the paper on one side of the removed region lies on top of the paper on the other side. We can imagine, though, that some other arrangement of folds and layers could hide the gray region and also give rise to the flagstone configuration, for example, a double pleat, as illustrated schematically in Figure 3. If the parallel-sided gray region were folded with two opposite-polarity pleats, as in Figure 3(b), rather than with a single pleat as in Figure 3(a), then the top surfaces would meet along their folded edges, realizing the flagstone condition.

In fact, if we were allowed to cut away regions of the paper, a very simple algorithm could be used to realize a flagstone tessellation. As with the simple flat twist tessellation, we construct the reciprocal figure and use those vertices as the centers of shrinkage of each polygon—but without rotation. This has the effect of inserting rectangles between the edges of formerly touching tiles; these rectangles are our parallel-edged strips. We cut away the polygon outlined by the rectangles, then we add two side-by-side pleats to these rectangles. The construction is illustrated in Figure 4, where we have created each pleat by dividing the rectangles evenly into fourths.

In the folded form, the white wedges of the crease pattern all come together at a point, which means that the vectors that define the pleat widths must form a closed loop, as they

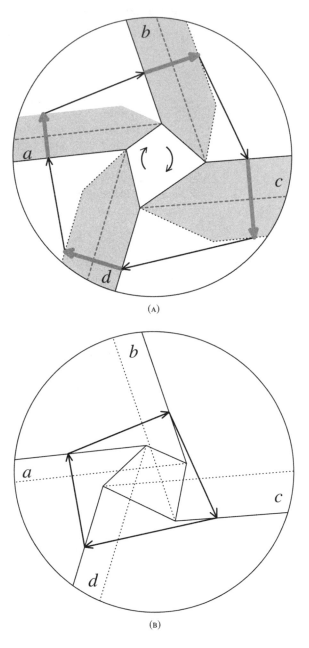

FIGURE 1. A simple flat twist. (a) Crease pattern: Mountain folds are solid, and valley folds are dashed. Light-gray regions are not visible in the folded form. (b) The folded form.

do on the crease pattern. So, we already know how wide the pleats must be. Their width vectors must sum to zero, and so the original tiling must satisfy the spiderweb condition, exactly the same way as a tiling must to create a simple flat twist tessellation.

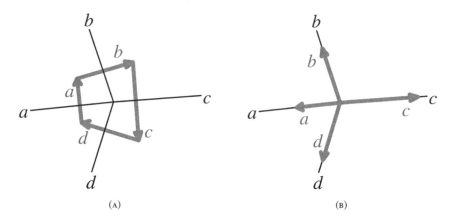

(A)   (B)

FIGURE 2. (a) Illustration that the pleat vectors independently must sum to zero. (b) Rotating each of the four vectors by 90° aligns each vector with its corresponding line.

(A)   (B)

FIGURE 3. Side view of (a) a single pleat, as in a simple flat twist, and (b) a double pleat, which can be used to realize flagstone tessellations.

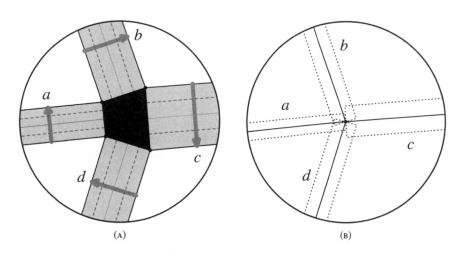

(A)   (B)

FIGURE 4. (a) Geometry for a flagstone construction. The black region is cut away. (b) The folded form. Dotted lines indicate hidden layers.

So, satisfaction of the spiderweb condition is a necessary condition for the realization of a flagstone tessellation. By solving for the edge lengths of the reciprocal figure, we can have pleat widths for all of the pleats of the flagstone tessellation (to within an arbitrary constant of proportionality). The problem is that we cannot simply cut away the polygons at the corners; we must find folds that cleanly continue the pleats between the tiles and interact in such a way that the corner structure lies flat and has no self-intersections.

There is also the question of how wide to make the pairs of pleats. In Figure 4, we divided each pleat region evenly, but that division is not required; we could have as easily devoted most of the paper to one side or the other of each pair.

There is, as it turns out, some freedom in choosing the folding pattern for the pleats and the junctions. We will now present one possible folding pattern that has some elegant symmetry properties with respect to the underlying tiling; we will then show that it is flat-foldable and gives the desired flagstone property.

4. The Flagstone Vertex Construction

In principle, one could choose the pleat pair widths quite arbitrarily, as long as each pair sums to the width indicated by the spiderweb condition. Recent work by Ku and Demaine [Demaine and Ku 16] has shown that given a polygon with specified flat-foldable creases on its boundary, one may construct a finite crease pattern that completes the creases and folds flat (although injectivity is not guaranteed). For our problem, one could choose the pleat widths (and thus crease positions) on the border of the black polygon and then apply the Ku–Demaine algorithm to determine the remaining creases within the polygon. However, the pattern thereby constructed could be quite irregular.

For many tiling patterns that satisfy the spiderweb condition, an embedding of the reciprocal figure may be found such that each vertex of the dual graph is enclosed by its corresponding primal polygon. Such graphs permit a particularly elegant choice of flag-stone pleat vertex construction that permits a purely geometric (as opposed to numerical) construction, allowing the entire construction to be carried out within a computer drawing program.[1] Once we have shrunken each polygon about its corresponding dual graph vertex, each edge of the primal graph lies parallel to and strictly between the corresponding edges of its shrunken polygon, and each vertex of the primal graph lies within the "cut-out" polygon, which is, in fact, a shrunken polygon of the dual graph. This situation is illustrated in Figure 5.

When the pleats are made that bring two polygon edges together, those pleats must bring the polygon edges onto a common line that lies somewhere in the interior region of the pleat rectangle. We make the choice that that line is the original line of the tiling. The valley folds of the pleats then each lie halfway between the mountain folds (the edges of the shrunken polygons) and the lines of the original tiling, as shown in Figure 5(b).

In the same way, when the pattern is folded, the corners of the shrunken polygons around a vertex must all come together at a point somewhere in the cut-out polygon; we choose that point to be the original vertex of the primal tiling.

With those two choices, the remaining creases are forced and can be constructed geometrically—in fact, they may be constructed using only reflection and translation, as follows and as illustrated in Figure 6 for the central polygon of Figure 5. These operations are typically built into standard computer drawing programs.

 (a) Begin with the central polygon and its incident mountain and valley folds.
 (b) Construct perpendicular bisectors of the (dotted) segments between each of the shrunken polygon corners and the original corner to outline a new polygon with valley folds, the *central polygon*.
 (c) Connect each vertex of the central polygon with the two adjacent shrunken-polygon corners, using mountain folds.

---

[1] Or, for those of a more traditional bent, using compass and straightedge.

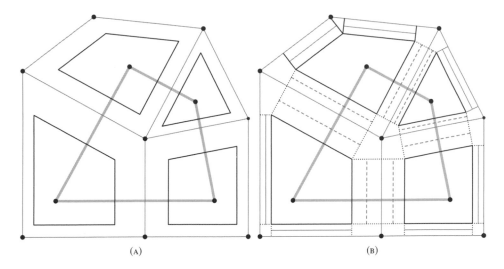

FIGURE 5. Geometry for a flagstone vertex construction. (a) The primal graph (fine black) is the original tiling. Its polygons are shrunken about the vertices of the reciprocal figure (thick gray). (b) Construction of valley folds. Dotted lines connect corresponding vertices in adjacent polygons.

(d) Translate copies of the central polygon by the vector from the original vertex to each of the shrunken vertices.

(e) For each pair of corresponding corners on copies that straddle each pleat, re-flect each corner across both the mountain and valley (in that order) folds of the adjacent pleat, resulting in one pair of coincident points for each pleat.

(f) Construct perpendicular bisectors of the segments between each of the new points and the corresponding corner of the central polygon using mountain folds, ex-tending each bisector to the valley folds within each pleat.

(g) Connect the new vertices with those of the central polygon and the surrounding shrunken polygons using valley folds.

(h) Remove the original tiling, leaving the completed crease pattern.

This completes the construction. Applying this construction to each vertex of the tiling gives a flagstone tessellation for the entire tiling. Note that the procedure applies even for vertices on the boundary of the original tiling. By construction, each of the added vertices satisfies Kawasaki's Theorem and Maekawa's Theorem, and thus the entire crease pattern is always isometrically flat-foldable.

We note that the choice of using the original tiling lines and vertex as the alignment features was an aesthetic choice, not driven by mathematical necessity. In fact, the lines along which the shrunken polygon edges align may be chosen arbitrarily between said edges, and the point where the shrunken polygon corners come together may be chosen arbitrarily in the vicinity of the tiling vertex. Figure 6(i) shows an example of an alter-nate construction, where I have divided each pleat evenly in fourths and have shifted the alignment point (black dot) from the original vertex tiling (gray dot). In all cases, the construction technique gives a pattern that is isometrically flat foldable, although in some

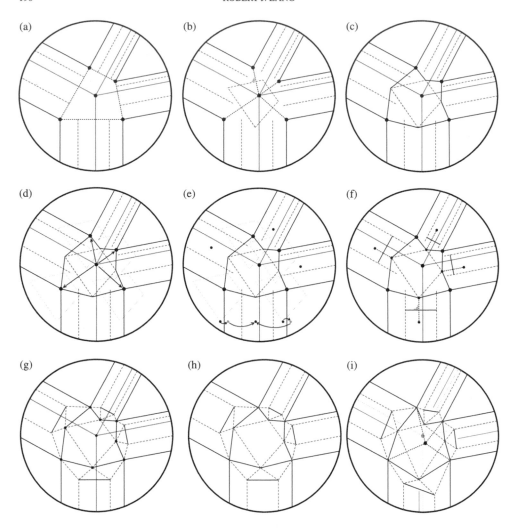

FIGURE 6. Construction sequence for a vertex of the flagstone tessellation.

cases the construction will be physically unfoldable because the central polygon ends up with crossing edges.

Whether the crease pattern satisfies injectivity—it is non–self-intersecting—is a separate issue, and in fact, it is not uncommon to arrive at a pattern that, without modification, results in violations of the Big-Little-Big (BLB) Angle Theorem [Hull 06] at one or more vertices of the shrunken polygons. The potential for this type of self-intersection can be seen in Figure 4; if the widths of the bases of the overlapping pleats exceed the angular span between them, a BLB violation occurs. However, if such a violation occurs, it is readily ameliorated in practice by simply pleating the overlapping flaps back and forth as needed to reduce their angular widths to acceptable amounts.

5. Discussion

I have implemented the algorithm above in a Mathematica package that can accept an arbitrary embedding of a plane graph and produces both the computed crease pattern

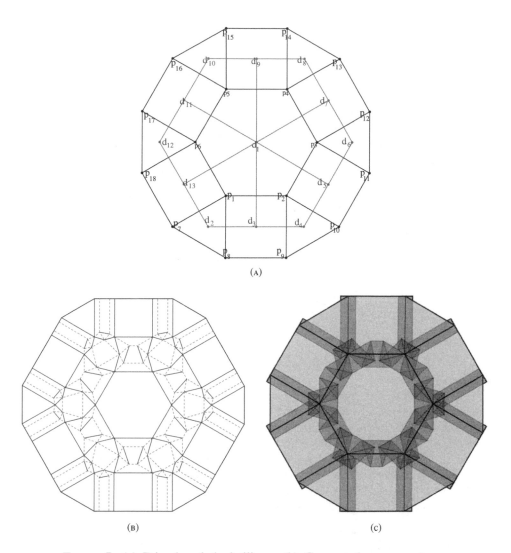

FIGURE 7. (a) Primal and dual tiling.   (b) Computed crease pattern.
(c) Computed folded form.

and a rendering of the folded form. An example of both is shown in Figure 7 (using the same portion of a 3.4.6.4 Archimedean tiling as the shrink-rotate tessellation example in [Lang and Bateman 11]). Photographs of a fully folded example are shown in Figure 8.

As noted already, this algorithm only works for a tiling (a) that satisfies the spiderweb condition and (b) for which each polygon encloses the corresponding vertex of its recipro-cal figure. This includes many tilings of aesthetic interest, including all tilings composed of regular polygons and/or arbitrary acute triangles. For such tilings, the dual graph vertices are simply the circumcenters of each polygon. The restriction to acute triangles is neces-sary to ensure that the circumcenter lies in the interior of every triangle. Since the dual graph may be translated relative to the primal graph, even if there are non-acute triangles, there may still be a flagstone tiling if the graph can be translated so that all dual vertices

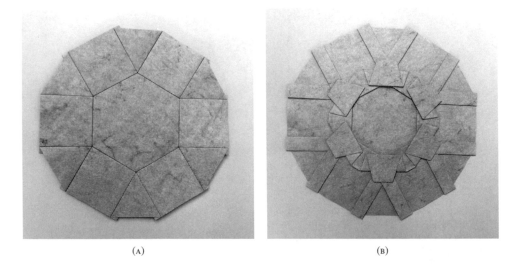

(A)   (B)

Figure 8. (a) The folded flagstone tessellation. (b) Back of the tessellation, showing the pleats.

lie within their corresponding polygons (and/or exceptions lie outside the boundary of the
polygon).

An interesting property of flagstone tessellations is that the completed tessellation is a
reduced-size copy of the original tiling. This is in contrast to ordinary shrink-rotate tilings,
for which the tiles are offset relative to one another. Because of these offsets, in shrink-
rotate tessellations the silhouette of the folded shape can differ significantly from that of
the original paper. In this form of flagstone tessellation, the silhouette of the tiles in the
folded form is an identical smaller copy of the original tiling.

These properties lead to a technique for reducing the size of any polygon by folding
while mapping the old boundary continuously to the boundary of the new polygon:

- Construct an acute triangulation of the polygon [Erten and Üngör 07].
- Construct the interior dual graph, choosing the dual graph vertices to be the circumcenters of the triangles.
- Split each boundary edge in half, adding a vertex to each edge. Add edges connecting these vertices to the dual graph vertices of their corresponding incident
  facets.
- Add edges connecting these vertices to the original vertices of the polygon.

The resulting plane graph is a partitioning of the original polygon into tiles whose
interior orthogonal dual graph consists of the edges of our acute triangulation. If we now
use this graph and its dual to construct a flagstone tessellation, the pleats hit the boundary
edges at right angles. The resulting tessellation has a silhouette that is a smaller copy of
the original polygon, with the boundary of the original polygon mapping to the boundary
of the reduced-size copy, as illustrated in Figure 9.

A similar self-scaling result may be found in [Demaine et al. 16], elsewhere in this
volume.

While our algorithm requires that the tiling satisfy the spiderweb condition, we note
that there are other forms of flagstone tessellation that may or may not require the same

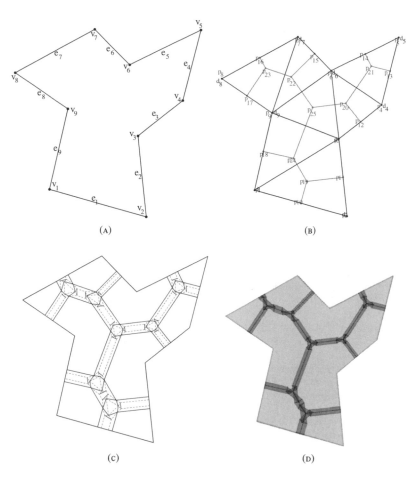

FIGURE 9. Size reduction of an arbitrary polygon. (a) The original polygon. (b) Acute triangulation and the dual graph. (c) Crease pattern of the flagstone tessellation. (d) Folded form.

condition. There is another distinct class of flagstone tessellation, an example of which may be found in Gjerde [Gjerde 09, p. 91]. Instead of constructing each pleat with the two mountain folds parallel to the two valleys, it is possible to angle each mountain/valley pair so that both pairs intersect at a shrunken polygon vertex, and the vertex structure takes a form similar to that of a flat twist. (The result is, in fact, a flattened version of a generalized Ron Resch tessellation [Resch 68].) We also note that the interior surface of a shape constructed via Tachi's *Origamizer* algorithm [Tachi 09] is also essentially a flagstone tessellation (in three dimensions, no less), albeit a non-flat one. There is a common concept to all of these algorithms: one creates a sparse tiling on the surface of the paper and then "hides" the paper between the tiles by folding. The result of such a design can be functional or aesthetic—or a combination of the two. It is clear, though, that there are many further algorithms in this family still to be explored and discovered.

References

[Barreto 97] Paulo Taborda Barreto. "Lines Meeting on a Surface: The 'Mars' Paperfolding." In *Origami Science and Art: Proceedings of the Second International Meeting of Origami Science and Scientific Origami*, edited by Koryo Miura, pp. 343–359. Shiga, Japan: Seian University of Art and Design, 1997.

[Bateman 02] Alex Bateman. "Computer Tools and Algorithms for Origami Tessellation Design." In *Origami³: Proceedings of the Third International Meeting of Origami Science, Mathematics, and Education*, edited by Thomas Hull, pp. 121–127. Natick, MA: A K Peters, 2002.

[Bateman 10] Alex Bateman. "Tess: Origami Tessellation Software." http://www.papermosaics.co.uk/software.html, retrieved June 6, 2010.

[Demaine et al. 16] Erik D. Demaine, Martin L. Demaine, and Kayhan F. Qaiser. "Scaling Any Surface Down to Any Fraction." In *Origami⁶: Sixth International Meeting of Origami Science, Mathematics, and Education*, edited by Koryo Miura, Toshikazu Kawasaki, Tomohiro Tachi, Ryuhei Uehara, Robert J. Lang, and Patsy Wang-Iverson, pp. 201–208. Providence: American Mathematical Society, 2016.

[Erten and Üngör 07] Hale Erten and Alper Üngör. "Computing Acute and Non-obtuse Triangulations." In *Proceedings of the 19th Annual Canadian Conference on Computational Geometry (CCCG)*, pp. 205–208. Ottawa, Canada: Carelton University, 2007.

[Fujimoto 82] Shuzo Fujimoto. *Seizo Soru Origami Asobi no Shotai (Creative Invitation to Paper Play)*. Tokyo: Asahi Culture Center, 1982.

[Gjerde 09] Eric Gjerde. *Origami Tessellations: Awe-Inspiring Geometric Designs*. Natick, MA: A K Peters, 2009. MR2474884 (2009m:52001)

[Huffman 76] David A. Huffman. "Curvature and Creases: A Primer on Paper." *IEEE Transactions on Computers* C-25:10 (1976), 1010–1019.

[Hull 06] Thomas Hull. *Project Origami: Activities for Exploring Mathematics*. Wellesley, MA: A K Peters, 2006. MR2330113 (2008d:00001)

[Kappraff 02] Jay Kappraff. *Connections: The Geometric Bridge between Art and Science*. Singapore: World Scientific Publishing Co., 2002. MR1868159 (2003e:00020)

[Kawasaki and Yoshida 88] Toshikazu Kawasaki and Masaaki Yoshida. "Crystallographic Flat Origamis." *Memoirs of the Faculty of Science, Kyushu University, Series A, Mathematics* XLII:2 (1988), 153–157. MR963204 (89h:51020)

[Demaine and Ku 16] Erik D. Demaine and Jason S. Ku. "Filling a Hole in a Crease Pattern: Isometric Mapping from Prescribed Boundary Folding." In *Origami⁶: Sixth International Meeting of Origami Science, Mathematics, and Education*, edited by Koryo Miura, Toshikazu Kawasaki, Tomohiro Tachi, Ryuhei Uehara, Robert J. Lang, and Patsy Wang-Iverson, pp. 177–188. Providence: American Mathematical Society, 2016.

[Lang and Bateman 11] Robert J. Lang and Alex Bateman. "Every Spiderweb Has a Simple Flat Twist Tessellation." In *Origami⁵: Fifth International Meeting of Origami Science, Mathematics, and Education*, edited by Patsy Wang-Iverson, Robert J. Lang, and Mark Yim, pp. 455–474. Boca Raton, FL: A K Peters/CRC Press, 2011. MR2866909 (2012h:00044)

[Maxwell 64] James Clerk Maxwell. "On Reciprocal Figures and Diagrams of Forces." *London, Edinburgh, and Dublin Philosophical Magazine and Journal of Science* 27:24 (1864), 514–525.

[Momotani 84] Yoshihide Momotani. "Wall." In *BOS Convention 1984 Autumn*. London: British Origami Society, 1984.

[Palmer 97] Chris K. Palmer. "Extruding and Tessellating Polygons from a Plane." In *Origami Science and Art: Proceedings of the Second International Meeting of Origami Science and Scientific Origami*, edited by Koryo Miura, pp. 323–331. Shiga, Japan: Seian University of Art and Design, 1997.

[Resch 68] Ronald D. Resch. "Self-Supporting Structural Unit Having a Series of Repetitions Geometric Modules." U.S. Patent 3,407,558, 1968.

[Tachi 09] Tomohiro Tachi. "3D Origami Design Based on Tucking Molecules." In *Origami⁴: Fourth International Meeting of Origami Science, Mathematics, and Education*, edited by Robert J. Lang, pp. 259–272. Wellesley, MA: A K Peters, 2009. MR2590567 (2010h:00025)

LANG ORIGAMI, ALAMO, CALIFORNIA
E-mail address: robert@langorigami.com

Scaling Any Surface Down to Any Fraction

Erik D. Demaine, Martin L. Demaine, and Kayhan F. Qaiser

1. Introduction

In recent years, origami has found a wealth of applications in engineering, science, and manufacturing. One of these application areas is the ability to transform an object into a smaller form, for storage or transportation and possibly later deployment in full scale (deployable structures). Examples include Miura-ori applied to solar cells and collapsible maps/atlases [Miura 09], Lang and LLNL's eyeglass telescope lens [Heller 03], airbag folding [Cromvik and Eriksson 09], and the origami stent graft [Kuribayashi et al. 06].

In this chapter, we explore a precise form of this general problem, where the goal is to fold a given polyhedral shape into a scaled-down copy of itself, instead of just any smaller shape. (See Figure 1.) Specifically, we show how to fold a given polyhedral surface into itself scaled down by a factor of $\lambda \in [\frac{1}{3}, 1]$ using a new kind of tessellation fold. By repeated application of the same folding, one could in theory fold an object down to any smaller scaling of itself.

This problem is part of a general family of problems that aim to find the most efficient folding for a particular family of constructions. Our approach follows in a similar vein to Maze Folding [Demaine et al. 11]. By breaking the problem into simplified subunits, we obtain a very general result. In our case, the subunits are acute triangles further divided into three quadrilaterals. We specify the folding for each quadrilateral unit separately and then merge the units together, showing there are no inconsistencies between units during merging.

The folding of each quadrilateral is a simple flat twist fold defined by Lang and Bateman in [Lang and Bateman 11] as "a construction composed of a polygon (usually, but not always, regular) with pleats radiating away from the polygon." The creasing results in a folded form of smaller surface area than the original and with the inner polygon rotated by some angle between 0 and 180°. The folding is usually accompanied by a hinging motion on the vertices of the inner polygon. Because our polygons are rotated by 180°, they can be thought of as a special case of the simple twist because they do not twist but rather perform two flips or reflections. We will thus refer to the maneuver as a *double flip*.

The construction provides a new way to create tessellations. It is worth noting that tessellations themselves are fairly old. Their original ancestors were likely pleated fabrics, which appeared in Europe in the 20th century (or earlier). Twist-folds were popularized in Japan by Shuzo Fujimoto, who self-published the first origami tessellation book *Twist Origami* in 1976. The twist-fold provided an alternative to folding representational objects

Supported in part by NSF ODISSEI grant EFRI-1240383 and NSF Expedition grant CCF-1138967.

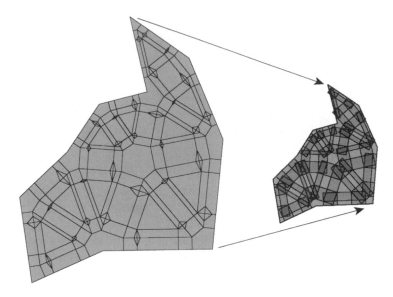

FIGURE 1. Dog head creased and folded to half its size. (Rendered using
Tomohiro Tachi's Freeform Origami software, http://www.tsg.ne.jp/TT/
software/.)

like animals, and the new folding technique opened up fascinating geometric possibilities
that naturally led to tessellations. Ron Resch had previously patented designs of three-
dimensional tessellations in 1966 [Resch 68]. He was followed by David Huffman who
pioneered work on curved crease sculptures [Huffman 76]. In more modern times, Chris
K. Palmer [Palmer 97] and Eric Gjerde [Gjerde 09] have explored the artistic potential of
the twist and tessellations. The field has academic, artistic, and practical avenues awaiting
exploration.

2. Algorithm

2.1. Overview. The high-level steps of the algorithm are outlined below:

(1) Divide the surface into acute triangles.
(2) Overlay each triangle's Voronoi diagram to further divide the polygon into
    quadrilaterals.
(3) Crease a double flip on each quad.
(4) Merge the quads into triangles and then those triangles into the original surface.
(5) Fold.

2.2. Acute triangulation. The starting point for our algorithm is an acutely triangulated surface. (See Figure 2, left and center.) While it is easy to triangulate a polygon
or polyhedral surface, creating an acute triangulation is a challenging problem popularized by Martin Gardner [Gardner 95, pp. 34, 39–42]. If the surface is a single polygon
with n sides, Maehara [Maehara 02] proved that $O(n)$ acute triangles suffice, and the constant was later improved by Yuan [Yuan 05]. For general polyhedral surfaces, existence
of acute triangulations was proved by Burago and Zalgaller [Burago and Zalgaller 60] and
later simplified by Saraf [Saraf 09]. Unfortunately, neither result gives a good bound on

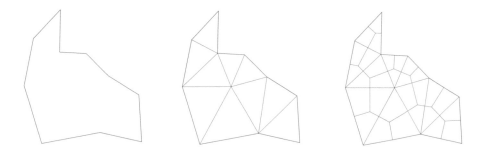

FIGURE 2. Original shape (left), triangulation (center), and Voronoi diagram (right).

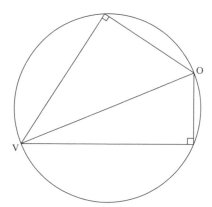

FIGURE 3. Space in which quads exist.

the number of required triangles. Furthermore, both results give only a *geodesic* triangulation, so the edges of the triangulation are shortest paths that may cross the edges of the polyhedron. Fortunately, such a geodesic triangulation suffices for our purposes, as we can conceptually fold each triangle separately to a scaled-down copy of itself, then bend it to match the three-dimensional geometry of the given polyhedron.

2.3. Voronoi diagram. We divide each triangle into three quadrilaterals by extending lines from the circumcenter to each side. This is equivalent to dividing the triangulation along its Voronoi diagram. (See Figure 2, right.) Because every triangle is acute, the circumcenter will lie inside it. That is why we need an acute triangulation of the surface.

The quadrilaterals created in the this step are the units we will fold. It is worth noting some properties of these quadrilaterals as shown in Figure 3. Each quad has an obtuse angle at O and an acute angle at V. The other two vertices are right angles. Each quad lies within the circle with diameter from O to V because the other two angles are right and due to Thales' Theorem. In addition, each quad also must have a circumcenter lying at the midpoint of OV because each quad is comprised of two right-angled triangles joined on their hypotenuses.

2.4. Double flip. We will now begin to outline the double flip construction and the constraints required to make it a valid folding. Before introducing the general double

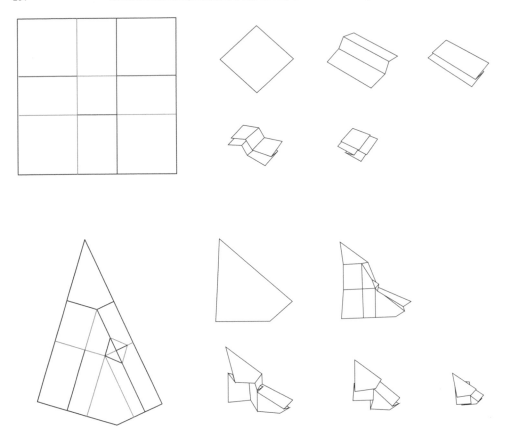

FIGURE 4. Square (top) and quad (bottom) double flip.

flip, let us consider the special case where the quadrilateral is a square. Although our algorithm would never produce this case, the generalized folding follows from it. As shown in Figure 4, the folding for the square is simply two pleats that are perpendicular to each other. The darker creases are mountains and the lighter creases are valleys. The foldings in Figure 4 are for scale factor $\lambda = 1/2$, where the lengths of the surface shrink by λ and the pleat lengths are $\lambda/2$. It is also important to note that the square and the quad are simply transformed versions of each other.

The generation procedure of the crease pattern is shown in Figure 5. We begin by copying the quad and scaling by $\lambda/2$ about its circumcenter. We then extend lines from each vertex of the inner quad perpendicular to the sides of the parent. We assign mountain and valley folds to each of these lines, creating pleats, where the folds on the acute vertex are mountains and the obtuse vertex are valleys. In every case, there are two ways to satisfy Maekawa's theorem. Currently the model should fold flat. However, there is a self-intersection that will occur. One further maneuver is required to guarantee a valid folding. To avoid collision between the two pleats at the obtuse vertex intersection, we perform a simple reverse fold so that the pleats can lie inside each other. We reflect line OV about line OV' and extend it until it intersects the long mountain fold CM. This line is then reflected three times around the cross-hair vertex C and assigned mountains and valleys to allow for a valid reverse fold. This reverse fold folds out of the quad, so it cannot intersect any of the flaps inside.

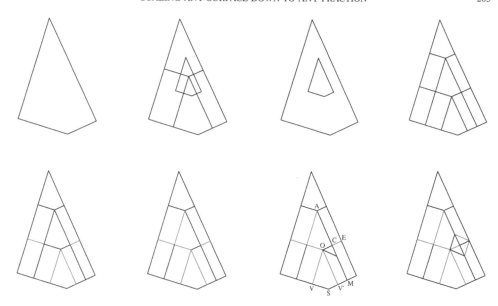

FIGURE 5. Quad creasing algorithm and reverse fold construction with $\lambda = 1/3$.

It is easy to show that the reverse fold created by the algorithm will be well formed for every possible quad, i.e., that the vertices of the reverse fold lie on the correct creases and that the reverse fold does not extend outside of the boundaries of the quad. Using a single pleat, the smallest we can scale a quad to is to a third of its size. We will use this worst-case scale factor $\lambda = 1/3$ and show that of the vertices of the reverse fold, two lie on OE and two lie on AM. The first vertex of the fold must be O by construction, and the other must be E because OC and OE are equal in length. We then observe that extending OV until it intersects AC gives us one of the creases of the reverse fold. When extended, OV must always intersects AC as AOV cannot be a line. This is evident because AOS is a line and S and V cannot be the same vertex. The last vertex must now always lie on CM as CM is the same length as AC.

The size of the reverse fold decreases as the quad's acute angle increases, and in the case of the square, it vanishes. The algorithm will so far fold flat any quad scaled by λ; however, the folded form may not be the correct shape since an internal layer may lie outside the boundaries of the shrunken quad. Such overhangs will occur in skinny or lopsided quads and are easily solved by one or more reverse folds. We state the enclosed sandwich lemma to help prove this.

LEMMA 2.1. *If there exists a surface folded flat along a crease, then it consists of a layer t on top and a layer b on the bottom. If a reverse fold is performed to create two new layers m and m′ in the middle of t and b such that they fall outside the boundaries of t or b, then a finite number of reverse folds can always be carried out on m and m′ so that no paper hangs out of the boundaries of t or b.*

Thus, if overhangs occur, they can be folded back into the model via a reverse fold or sometimes multiple reverse folds, without self-intersections because the new layers are in between the old ones. In practice there are rarely more than two reverse folds required. Figure 6 shows more examples of the algorithm being applied to quads.

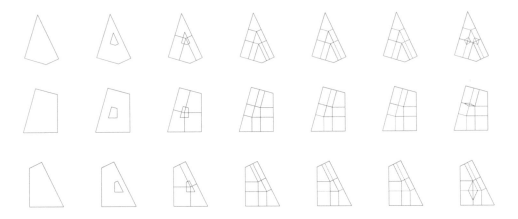

FIGURE 6. Quad creasing algorithm with $\lambda = 1/2$.

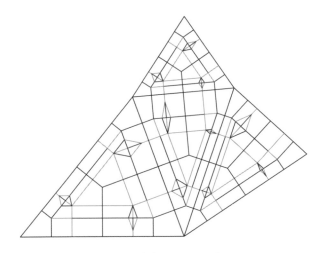

FIGURE 7. Merging quads into a complete crease pattern.

2.5. Merging. So far, it is evident that any quad can be scaled between a factor of $1/3$ and 1. However, it remains to be seen if this folding holds once the quads are merged. There are two conditions that must hold for a successful merging: The pleats of each quad must meet at the same points, and their fold directions must be the same. The former condition must hold by construction because any two quads from one triangle share one side and each inner quad was scaled about the quad's circumcenter. The parity condition must also hold because by construction, on the obtuse side of the quad, the two pleats had valley folds near the obtuse vertex and mountain folds away from it. Thus, valley folds are always near the center of the triangle and mountain folds surround them. Every acute triangle can be scaled down. (See Figure 7.)

A similar argument follows for merging all triangles. If any two triangles share a side, their creases must meet at the same points because the inner quads were scaled about the quad circumcenters. The parity is also correct as there are always two valley folds from the pleats near the middle of each side and two mountain folds surrounding them. In the case where the scale factor is exactly $1/3$, two reverse folds may interface with each other at a point on the side of a triangle. In these cases the models will also fold flat.

Thus, all acute triangles can be merged into the original surface. The entire surface can now be folded to scale down to a factor of its size between $1/3$ and 1. If a scale factor less than this is desired, the algorithm can simply be reapplied on the scaled surface to further scale it.

Acknowledgments

We would like to thank Byoungkwon An for his suggestions on how to fold the quads flat, Abigail Crawford McLellan for her queries on maximal pleats and subsequently the scale factors the algorithm applies to, and finally Ben Parker for his helpful advice on how tessellations fold. We would also like to acknowledge travel support provided by the Gabriella & Paul Rosenbaum Foundation. The authors were supported in part by NSF ODISSEI grant EFRI-1240383 and NSF Expedition grant CCF-1138967.

References

[Burago and Zalgaller 60] Ju. D. Burago and V. A. Zalgaller. "Polyhedral Embedding of a Net." *Vestnik Leningrad University: Mathematics* 15:7 (1960), 66–80. MR0116317 (22:7112)

[Cromvik and Eriksson 09] Christoffer Cromvik and Kenneth Eriksson. "Airbag Folding Based on Origami Mathematics." In *Origami⁴: Fourth International Meeting of Origami Science, Mathematics, and Education*, edited by Robert J. Lang, pp. 129–139. Wellesley, MA: A K Peters, 2009. MR2590567 (2010h:00025)

[Demaine et al. 11] Erik D. Demaine, Martin L. Demaine, and Jason Ku. "Folding Any Orthogonal Maze." In *Origami⁵: Fifth International Meeting of Origami Science, Mathematics, and Education*, edited by Patsy Wang-Iverson, Robert J. Lang, and Mark Yim, pp. 449–454. Boca Raton, FL: A K Peters/CRC Press, 2011. MR2866900 (2012k:00005)

[Gardner 95] Martin Gardner. *New Mathematical Diversions*. Washington, DC: Mathematical Association of America, 1995. MR1335231

[Gjerde 09] Eric Gjerde. *Origami Tessellations: Awe-Inspiring Geometric Designs*. Wellesley, MA: A K Peters, 2009. MR2474884 (2009m:52001)

[Heller 03] Arnie Heller. "A Giant Leap for Telescope Lenses." *Science & Technology Review* (March 2003), 12–18.

[Huffman 76] David A. Huffman. "Curvature and Creases: A Primer on Paper." *IEEE Trans. Computers* 25:10 (1976), 1010–1019.

[Kuribayashi et al. 06] Kaori Kuribayashi, Koichi Tsuchiya, Zhong You, Dacian Tomus, Minoru Umemoto, Takahiro Ito, and Masahiro Sasaki. "Self-Deployable *Origami* Stent Grafts as a Biomedical Application of Ni-Rich TiNi Shape Memory Alloy Foil." *Materials Science & Engineering A* 419 (2006), 131–137.

[Lang and Bateman 11] Robert J. Lang and Alex Bateman. "Every Spider Web Has a Simple Flat Twist Tessellation." In *Origami⁵: Fifth International Meeting of Origami Science, Mathematics, and Education*, edited by Patsy Wang-Iverson, Robert J. Lang, and Mark Yim, pp. 455–473. Boca Raton, FL: A K Peters/CRC Press, 2011. MR2866909 (2012h:00044)

[Maehara 02] H. Maehara. "Acute Triangulations of Polygons." *European Journal of Combinatorics* 23:1 (2002), 45–55. MR1878775 (2003a:52019)

[Miura 09] Koryo Miura. "The Science of *Miura-Ori*: A Review." In *Origami⁴: Fourth International Meeting of Origami Science, Mathematics, and Education*, edited by Robert J. Lang, pp. 87–99. Wellesley, MA: A K Peters, 2009.

[Palmer 97] Chris K Palmer. "Extruding and Tesselating Polygons from a Plane." In *Origami Science and Art: Proceedings of the Second International Meeting of Origami Science and Scientific Origami*, edited by K. Miura, pp. 323–331. Shiga, Japan: Seian University of Art and Design, 1997.

[Resch 68] Ronald D. Resch. "Self-Supporting Structural Unit Having a Series of Repetitious Geometrical Modules." US Patent 3,407,558, 1968.

[Saraf 09] Shubhangi Saraf. "Acute and Nonobtuse Triangulations of Polyhedral Surfaces." *European Journal of Combinatorics* 30:4 (2009), 833–840. MR2504642 (2010e:52028)

[Yuan 05] Liping Yuan. "Acute Triangulations of Polygons." *Discrete & Computational Geometry* 34:4 (2005), 697–706. MR2173934 (2006g:52032)

MIT COMPUTER SCIENCE AND ARTIFICIAL INTELLIGENCE LAB., CAMBRIDGE, MASSACHUSETTS
E-mail address: edemaine@mit.edu

MIT COMPUTER SCIENCE AND ARTIFICIAL INTELLIGENCE LAB., CAMBRIDGE, MASSACHUSETTS
E-mail address: mdemaine@mit.edu

MCGILL UNIVERSITY, MONTRÉAL, QUÉBEC, CANADA
E-mail address: kayhan.qaiser@mail.mcgill.ca

Characterization of Curved Creases and Rulings:
Design and Analysis of Lens Tessellations

Erik D. Demaine, Martin L. Demaine, David A. Huffman, Duks Koschitz,
and Tomohiro Tachi

1. Introduction

The past two decades have seen incredible advances in applying mathematics and computation to the analysis and design of origami made by straight creases. But, we lack many similar theorems and algorithms for origami made by curved creases.

In this chapter, we develop several basic tools (definitions and theorems) for curved-crease origami. These tools in particular characterize the relationship between the crease pattern and rule lines/segments, and they relate creases connected by rule segments. Some of these tools have been developed before in other contexts (e.g., [Fuchs and Tabachnikov 99, Fuchs and Tabachnikov 07, Huffman 76]) but have previously lacked a careful analysis of the levels of smoothness (C^1, C^2, etc.) and other assumptions required. Specific high-level properties we prove include the following:

(1) Regions between creases decompose into noncrossing rule segments, which connect from curved crease to curved crease, and planar patches (a result from [Demaine et al. 11]).

(2) The osculating plane of a crease bisects the two adjacent surface tangent planes (when they are unique).

(3) A curved crease with an incident cone ruling (a continuum of rule segments at a point) cannot fold smoothly: It must be kinked at the cone ruling.

(4) Rule segments on the convex side of a crease bend mountain/valley the same as the crease, and rule segments on the concave side of a crease bend mountain/valley opposite from the crease.

(5) If two creases are joined by a rule segment on their concave sides, or on their convex sides, then their mountain/valley assignments must be equal. If the rule segment is on the convex side of one crease and the concave side of the other crease, then the mountain/valley assignments must be opposite.

We apply these tools to analyze one family of designs called the *lens tessellation*. Figure 1 shows an example originally designed and folded by the third author in 1992, and

E. Demaine and M. Demaine supported in part by NSF ODISSEI grant EFRI-1240383 and NSF Expedition grant CCF-1138967.

D. Koschitz performed this research while at MIT.

T. Tachi supported by the JST Presto program.

(A) Huffman's original hand-drawn sketch of crease pattern of lens design (1992).

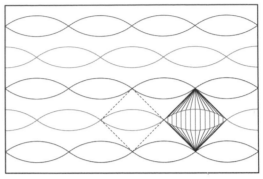

(B) Computer-drawn crease pattern of lens design.

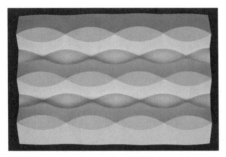

(C) Huffman's original hand-folded vinyl model (1992). Photo by Tony Grant.

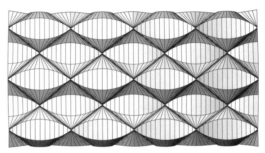

(D) Computer-simulated 3D model using Tachi's Freeform Origami software.

FIGURE 1. Lens tessellation: 1992 original (left) and digital reconstruction (right).

now modeled digitally. We prove that this curved crease pattern folds into three dimensions, with the indicated rule segments, when the "lens" is *any* smooth convex curve. We also show that the model is "rigidly foldable," meaning that it can be continuously folded without changing the ruling pattern.

The three-dimensional (3D) configuration of the curved folding is solved through identifying the correspondence between pairs of points connected by rule segments, using the qualitative properties described above. These properties separate the tessellation into independent kite-shaped tiles and force the rulings between the lenses to be particular cones with their apices coinciding with the vertices of the tiling. The ruling inside each lens is free (can twist) but, assuming no twist or global planarity/symmetry, is cylindrical (vertical rule segments). The tiling exists by rotation/reflection of the 3D model of each kite around its four straight boundary edges. From the tiling symmetry, each tile edge has a common tangent to its neighbors regardless of the type of curves, as long as it is a convex curve.

The rest of this paper is organized as follows. Section 2 introduces some basic notation for 2D and 3D curves. Section 3 defines creases, crease patterns, foldings, rule segments, cone ruling, orientation of the paper, and surface normals (and analyzes when they exist). Section 4 proves the powerful bisection property—that the osculating plane of a crease bisects the two adjacent surface tangent planes—and uses it to rule out some strange situations such as rule segments tangent to creases or zero-length rule segments. Section 5 characterizes smooth folding: A crease is folded C^1 if and only if it is folded C^2 if and only if there are no incident cone rulings. Section 6 defines mountains and valleys for both creases and the bending of rule segments, and relates the two. Finally, Section 7 uses all these tools to analyze lens tessellations, proving a necessary and sufficient condition on their foldability.

2. Curves

In this section, we define some standard parameterizations of curves in two and three dimensions, which we will use in particular for describing creases in the unfolded paper and folded state. Our notation introduces a helpful symmetry between 2D (unfolding) and 3D (folding): lowercase indicates 2D, while uppercase indicates the corresponding notion in 3D.

2.1. 2D curves. Consider an arclength-parameterized C^2 2D curve $\mathbf{x} : (0, \ell) \to \mathbb{R}^2$ (or in any metric 2-manifold). For $s \in (0, \ell)$, define the (unit) *tangent* at s by

$$\mathbf{t}(s) = \frac{d\mathbf{x}(s)}{ds}.$$

Define the *curvature*

$$k(s) = \left\| \frac{d\mathbf{t}(s)}{ds} \right\|.$$

In particular, call the curve *curved* at s if its curvature $k(s)$ is nonzero. In this case, define the (unit) *normal* at s by

$$\mathbf{n}(s) = \frac{d\mathbf{t}(s)}{ds} \bigg/ k(s).$$

The curve is *curved* (without qualification) if it is curved at all $s \in (0, \ell)$.

Define the *convex side* at s to consist of directions having negative dot product with $\mathbf{n}(s)$, and define the *concave side* at s to consist of directions having positive dot product with $\mathbf{n}(s)$.

2.2. 3D curves. For an arclength-parameterized C^2 space curve $\mathbf{X} : [0, \ell] \to \mathbb{R}^3$, and for a parameter $s \in [0, \ell]$ inducing a point $\mathbf{X}(s)$, define the (unit) *tangent*

$$\mathbf{T}(s) = \frac{d\mathbf{X}(s)}{ds}.$$

Define the *curvature*

$$K(s) = \left\| \frac{d\mathbf{T}(s)}{ds} \right\|.$$

In particular, call the curve *curved* at s if its curvature $K(s)$ is nonzero (and *curved* without qualification if it is curved at all $s \in (0, \ell)$). In this case, define the (unit) *normal* at s by

$$\mathbf{N}(s) = \frac{d\mathbf{T}(s)}{ds} \bigg/ K(s),$$

define the (unit) *binormal*

$$\mathbf{B}(s) = \mathbf{T}(s) \times \mathbf{N}(s),$$

and define the *torsion*

$$\tau(s) = -\frac{d\mathbf{B}(s)}{ds} \cdot \mathbf{N}(s).$$

Equivalently, these definitions follow from the Frenet–Serret formulas:

$$\begin{bmatrix} 0 & K(s) & 0 \\ -K(s) & 0 & \tau(s) \\ 0 & -\tau(s) & 0 \end{bmatrix} \cdot \begin{bmatrix} \mathbf{T}(s) \\ \mathbf{N}(s) \\ \mathbf{B}(s) \end{bmatrix} = \frac{d}{ds} \begin{bmatrix} \mathbf{T}(s) \\ \mathbf{N}(s) \\ \mathbf{B}(s) \end{bmatrix}.$$

LEMMA 2.1. *For any curved C^2 3D curve $\mathbf{X}(s)$, the Frenet frame $(\mathbf{T}(s), \mathbf{N}(s), \mathbf{B}(s))$ and curvature $K(s)$ exist and are continuous.*

PROOF. Because $\mathbf{X}(s)$ is differentiable, $\mathbf{T}(s)$ exists. Because $\mathbf{X}(s)$ is twice differentiable, $K(s)$ exists, and because $\mathbf{X}(s)$ is C^2, $K(s)$ is continuous. Because the curve is curved, $K(s) \neq 0$, so we do not divide by 0 in computing $\mathbf{N}(s)$. Thus, $\mathbf{N}(s)$ exists and is continuous. The cross product in $\mathbf{B}(s)$ exists and is continuous because $\mathbf{T}(s)$ and $\mathbf{N}(s)$ are guaranteed to be normalized (hence nonzero) and orthogonal to each other (hence not parallel). □

The same lemma specializes to 2D, by dropping the $\mathbf{B}(s)$ part:

COROLLARY 2.2. *For any curved C^2 2D curve $\mathbf{x}(s)$, the frame $(\mathbf{t}(s), \mathbf{n}(s))$ and curvature $k(s)$ exist and are continuous.*

3. Foldings

The following definitions draw from [Demaine et al. 11, Demaine and O'Rourke 07].

We start with 2D (unfolded) notions. A *piece of paper* is an open 2-manifold embedded in $\mathbb{R}^2$. A *crease* $\mathbf{x}$ is a C^2 2D curve that is contained in the piece of paper and is not self-intersecting (i.e., does not visit the same point twice). A *crease point* is a point $\mathbf{x}(s)$ on the relative interior of the crease (excluding endpoints). The endpoints of a crease are *vertices*. A *crease pattern* is a collection of creases that meet only at common vertices. Equivalently, a crease pattern is an embedded planar graph, where each edge is embedded as a crease. This definition effectively allows piecewise-C^2 curves, by subdividing the edge in the graph with additional vertices; "creases" are the resulting C^2 pieces. A *face* is a maximal open region of the piece of paper not intersecting any creases or vertices.

Now we proceed to 3D (folded) notions. A *(proper) folding* of a crease pattern is a piecewise-C^2 isometric embedding of the piece of paper into three dimensions that is C^1 on every face and not C^1 at every crease point and vertex. Here, *isometric* means that intrinsic path lengths are preserved by the mapping, and *piecewise-C^2* means that the folded image can be decomposed into a finite complex of C^2 open regions joined by points and C^2 curves. We use the terms *folded crease*, *folded vertex*, *folded face*, and *folded piece of paper* to refer to the image of a crease, vertex, face, and entire piece of paper under the folding map, respectively. Thus, each folded face subdivides into a finite complex of C^2 open regions joined by points called *folded semivertices* and C^2 curves called *folded semicreases*. Each folded crease $\mathbf{X}(s)$ can be subdivided into a finite sequence of C^2 curves joined by C^1 points called *semikinks* and not-C^1 points called *kinks*. (Here, C^1/not-C^1 is a property measured of the crease $\mathbf{X}(s)$; crease points are necessarily not C^1 on the folded piece of paper.) In fact, semivertices do not exist [Demaine et al. 11, Corollary 2] and neither do semikinks (Corollary 6.4 below).

LEMMA 3.1. *A curved crease $\mathbf{x}(s)$ folds into a 3D curve $\mathbf{X}(s)$ that contains no line segments (and thus is curved except at kinks and semikinks).*

PROOF. Suppose $X(s)$ is a 3D line segment for $s \in [s_1, s_2]$. Then, the distance between $\mathbf{X}(s_1)$ and $\mathbf{X}(s_2)$ as measured on the folded piece of paper is the length of this line segment, i.e., the arclength of $\mathbf{X}$ over $s \in [s_1, s_2]$, which, by isometry, equals the arclength of $\mathbf{x}$ over

$s \in [s_1, s_2]$. However, in the 2D piece of paper, there is a shorter path connecting $\mathbf{x}(s_1)$ and $\mathbf{x}(s_2)$ because the 2D crease is curved (and not on the paper boundary, because the paper is an open set), contradicting isometry. □

3.1. Developable surfaces.

A folded face is also known as an uncreased developable surface: it is *uncreased* in the sense that it is C^1, and it is *developable* in the sense that every point p has a neighborhood isometric to a region in the plane. The following theorem from [Demaine et al. 11] characterizes what uncreased developable surfaces look like:

THEOREM 3.2 (Corollaries 1–3 of [Demaine et al. 11]). *Every interior point p of an uncreased developable surface M not belonging to a planar neighborhood belongs to a unique rule segment C_p. The rule segment's endpoints are on the boundary of M. In particular, every semicrease is such a rule segment.*

COROLLARY 3.3. *Any folded face decomposes into planar regions and nonintersecting rule segments (including semicreases) whose endpoints lie on creases.*

For a folded piece of paper, we use the term *(3D) rule segment* for exactly these segments C_p computed for each folded face, for all points p that are not folded vertices, are not folded crease points, and do not belong to a planar neighborhood. In particular, we view the interior of planar regions as not containing any rule segments (as they would be ambiguous); however, the boundaries of planar regions are considered rule segments. As a consequence, all rule segments have a neighborhood that is nonplanar.

For each 3D rule segment in the folded piece of paper, we can define the corresponding 2D rule segment by the inverse mapping. By isometry, 2D rule segments are indeed line segments.

Define a *cone ruling* at a crease point $\mathbf{x}(s)$ to be a fan of 2D rule segments emanating from $\mathbf{x}(s)$ in a positive-length interval of directions $[\theta_1, \theta_2]$.

3.2. Orientation.

We orient the piece of paper in the xy-plane by a consistent normal $\mathbf{e}_z$ (in the $+z$ direction) called the *top side*. This orientation defines, for a 2D crease $\mathbf{x} = \mathbf{x}(s)$ in the crease pattern, a *left normal* $\hat{\mathbf{n}}(s) = \mathbf{e}_z \times \mathbf{t}(s)$. Where $\mathbf{x}(s)$ is curved and thus $\mathbf{n}(s)$ is defined, we have $\hat{\mathbf{n}}(s) = \pm \mathbf{n}(s)$ where the sign specifies whether the left or right side corresponds to the convex side of the curve. We can also characterize a 2D rule segment incident to $\mathbf{x}(s)$ as being *left* of $\mathbf{x}$ when the vector emanating from $\mathbf{x}(s)$ has positive dot product with $\hat{\mathbf{n}}(s)$ and *right* of $\mathbf{x}$ when it has negative dot product. (In Lemma 4.6 below, we prove that no rule segment is tangent to a crease, and thus every rule segment is either left or right of the crease.)

We can also define the *signed curvature* $\hat{k}(s)$ to flip sign where $\hat{\mathbf{n}}(s)$ does: $\hat{k}(s)\hat{\mathbf{n}}(s) = k(s)\mathbf{n}(s)$. Then, $\hat{k}(s)$ is positive where the curve turns left and negative where the curve turns right (relative to the top side).

3.3. Unique ruling.

Call a crease point $\mathbf{x}(s)$ *uniquely ruled on the left* if there is exactly one rule segment left of $\mathbf{x}(s)$; symmetrically define *uniquely ruled on the right*; and define *uniquely ruled* to mean uniquely ruled on both the left and right.

By Corollary 3.3, there are two possible causes for a crease point $\mathbf{x}(s)$ to be not uniquely ruled (say, on the left). First, there could be one or more cone rulings (on the left) at $\mathbf{x}(s)$. Second, there could be one or more planar 3D regions incident to $\mathbf{X}(s)$ (which, in 2D, lie on the left of $\mathbf{x}(s)$, meaning the points have positive dot product with $\hat{\mathbf{n}}(s)$).

One special case of unique ruling is when a rule segment is tangent to a curved crease. Ultimately, in Lemma 4.6, we will prove that this cannot happen, but for now we need that the surface normals remain well-defined in this case. There are two subcases depending on

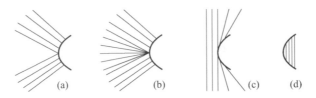

FIGURE 2. Possibilities for a crease to be not uniquely ruled.

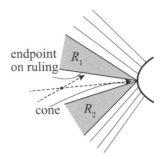

FIGURE 3. Two adjacent planar regions at a point.

whether the rule segment is on the convex or concave side of the crease, as in Figure 2(c) and (d). The rule segment's direction in 3D and surface normal vector remain well-defined in this case, by taking limits of nearby rule segments. In the concave subcase (d), we take the limit of rule segments on the same side of the curve. In the convex subcase (c), the rule segment splits the surface locally into two halves, and we take the limit of rule segments in the half not containing the crease. Because the surface normals are thus well-defined, we do not need to distinguish this case in our proofs below.

Call a crease point $\mathbf{x}(s)$ *cone free* if there are no cone rulings at $\mathbf{x}(s)$; similarly define *cone free on the left/right*. Such a point may still have a planar region, but only one.

LEMMA 3.4. *If a crease point $\mathbf{x}(s)$ is cone free, then it has at most one planar region on each side.*

PROOF. Refer to Figure 3. Suppose $\mathbf{x}(s)$ had at least two planar regions on, say, the left side. Order the regions clockwise around $\mathbf{x}(s)$, and pick two adjacent planar regions R_1 and R_2. By Corollary 3.3, the wedge with apex $\mathbf{x}(s)$ between R_1 and R_2 must be covered by rule segments. But, by Theorem 3.2, a rule segment cannot have its endpoints on the boundaries of R_1 and R_2, as it must extend all the way to creases. Thus, the only way to cover the wedge locally near $\mathbf{x}(s)$ is to have a cone ruling at $\mathbf{x}(s)$.   □

3.4. Surface normals. In 3D, the orientation defines a top-side normal vector at every C^1 point.[1] For a crease point $\mathbf{X}(s)$ that is cone free on the left, we can define a unique *left surface normal* $\mathbf{P}_L(s)$. First, if there is a planar region on the left of $\mathbf{X}(s)$, then by Lemma 3.4 there is only one such planar region, and we define $\mathbf{P}_L(s)$ to be the unique top-side normal vector of the planar region. Otherwise, $\mathbf{X}(s)$ is uniquely ruled on the left, and we define $P_L(s)$ to be the top-side surface normal vector that is constant along this unique rule segment. (As argued above, this definition makes sense even when the rule segment

---

[1] For example, take infinitesimally small triangles around the point, oriented counterclockwise in 2D, and compute their normals in 3D.

is a zero-length limit of rule segments.) Similarly, we can define the right surface normal $\mathbf{P}_R(s)$ when $\mathbf{X}(s)$ is cone free on the right.

4. Bisection Property

In this section, we prove that, at a cone-free folded curved crease, the binormal vector bisects the left and right surface normal vectors, which implies that the osculating plane of the crease bisects the two surface tangent planes. Proving this bisection property requires several steps along the way, and it has several useful consequences.

4.1. C^2 case. First, we prove the bisection property at C^2 crease points, using the following simple lemma:

LEMMA 4.1. *For a C^2 folded curved crease $\mathbf{X}(s)$ that is cone-free on the left,*

$$(K(s)\mathbf{N}(s)) \cdot (\mathbf{P}_L(s) \times \mathbf{T}(s)) = \hat{\mathbf{k}}(s).$$

For a C^2 folded curved crease $\mathbf{X}(s)$ that is cone-free on the right,

$$(K(s)\mathbf{N}(s)) \cdot (\mathbf{P}_R(s) \times \mathbf{T}(s)) = \hat{\mathbf{k}}(s).$$

PROOF. We prove the left case; the right case is symmetric. The left-hand side is known as the geodesic curvature at $\mathbf{X}(s)$ on surface S_L and is known to be invariant under isometry. In the unfolded 2D state, the geodesic curvature is

$$(k(s)\mathbf{n}(s)) \cdot (\mathbf{e}_z \times \mathbf{t}(s)) = (k(s)\mathbf{n}(s)) \cdot \hat{\mathbf{n}}(s) = \hat{\mathbf{k}}(s).$$

$\square$

LEMMA 4.2. *For a C^2 cone-free folded curved crease $\mathbf{X}(s)$, $\mathbf{B}(s)$ bisects $\mathbf{P}_L(s)$ and $\mathbf{P}_R(s)$. In particular, the tangent planes of the surfaces on both sides of $\mathbf{X}(s)$ form the same angle with the osculating plane.*

PROOF. A C^2 cone-free folded curved crease $\mathbf{X}(s)$ has unique left and right surface normals $\mathbf{P}_L(s)$ and $\mathbf{P}_R(s)$. By Lemma 4.1, the left and right geodesic curvatures match:

$$(K(s)\mathbf{N}(s)) \cdot (\mathbf{P}_L(s) \times \mathbf{T}(s)) = (K(s)\mathbf{N}(s)) \cdot (\mathbf{P}_R(s) \times \mathbf{T}(s)).$$

The $K(s)$ scalars cancel, leaving a triple product:

$$\mathbf{N}(s) \cdot (\mathbf{P}_L(s) \times \mathbf{T}(s)) = \mathbf{N}(s) \cdot (\mathbf{P}_R(s) \times \mathbf{T}(s)),$$

which is equivalent to

$$\mathbf{P}_L(s) \cdot (\mathbf{T}(s) \times \mathbf{N}(s)) = \mathbf{P}_R(s) \cdot (\mathbf{T}(s) \times \mathbf{N}(s)).$$

Therefore, $\mathbf{B}(s) = \mathbf{T}(s) \times \mathbf{N}(s)$ forms the same angle with $\mathbf{P}_L(s)$ and $\mathbf{P}_R$. Because $\mathbf{B}$, $\mathbf{P}_L$, and $\mathbf{P}_R$ lie in a common plane orthogonal to $\mathbf{T}$, $\mathbf{B}$ bisects $\mathbf{P}_L$ and $\mathbf{P}_R$. $\square$

4.2. Top-side Frenet frame. By Lemma 4.2, at C^2 cone-free points $\mathbf{X}(s)$, we can define the *top-side normal* of the osculating plane $\hat{\mathbf{B}} = \pm\mathbf{B} = \pm\mathbf{T} \times \mathbf{N}$ whose sign is defined such that $\hat{\mathbf{B}} \cdot \mathbf{P}_L = \hat{\mathbf{B}} \cdot \mathbf{P}_R > 0$. Thus, $\hat{\mathbf{B}}$ consistently points to the front side of the surface. By contrast, $\mathbf{B}$'s orientation depends on whether the 2D curve locally turns left or right (given by the sign of $k(s)$), flipping orientation at inflection points (where $k(s) = 0$).

More formally, we will use the *top-side Frenet frame* given by $(\mathbf{T}(s), \hat{\mathbf{N}}(s), \hat{\mathbf{B}}(s))$, where $\hat{\mathbf{N}}(s) = \hat{\mathbf{B}}(s) \times \mathbf{T}(s)$.

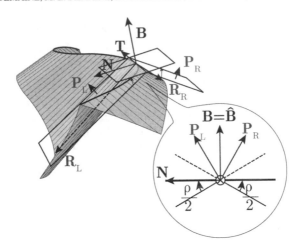

FIGURE 4. Binormal vector **B** bisects surface normals $\mathbf{P}_L$ and $\mathbf{P}_R$.

LEMMA 4.3. *Consider a folded curved crease* $\mathbf{X}(s)$ *that is cone-free at a semikink* $s = \tilde{s}$. *The top-side Frenet frames are identical in positive and negative limits:*

$$\lim_{s \to \tilde{s}^+} (\mathbf{T}(s), \hat{\mathbf{N}}(s), \hat{\mathbf{B}}(s)) = \lim_{s \to \tilde{s}^-} (\mathbf{T}(s), \hat{\mathbf{N}}(s), \hat{\mathbf{B}}(s)).$$

Thus, the top-side Frenet frame is continuous at $s = \tilde{s}$.

PROOF. First, $\mathbf{T}(\tilde{s})$ is continuous because $\mathbf{X}(s)$ is C^1 at a semikink $s = \tilde{s}$.

Second, by Lemma 4.2, in the positive and negative limits, $\mathbf{B}(s)$ bisects $\mathbf{P}_L(s)$ and $\mathbf{P}_R(s)$. Because there is no cone ruling at $s = \tilde{s}$, the left and right surface normals $\mathbf{P}_L(s)$ and $\mathbf{P}_R(s)$ have equal positive and negative limits at $\tilde{s}$, so $\mathbf{P}_L(\tilde{s})$ and $\mathbf{P}_R(\tilde{s})$ are continuous. Thus, $\mathbf{B}(\tilde{s}^+)$ and $\mathbf{B}(\tilde{s}^-)$ must lie on a common bisecting line of $\mathbf{P}_L(\tilde{s})$ and $\mathbf{P}_R(\tilde{s})$, and $\hat{\mathbf{B}}(\tilde{s})$ is uniquely defined by having positive dot product with $\mathbf{P}_1(\tilde{s})$ and $\mathbf{P}_2(\tilde{s})$. This gives us a unique definition of $\hat{\mathbf{B}}(s)$.

Third, $\hat{\mathbf{N}}(s)$ is continuous as $\hat{\mathbf{B}}(s) \times \mathbf{T}(s)$. Therefore, $(\mathbf{T}(s), \hat{\mathbf{N}}(s), \hat{\mathbf{B}}(s))$ is continuous at $s = \tilde{s}$.   □

At C^2 points $X(s)$, we can define the *signed curvature* $\hat{K}(s)$ to flip sign where $\hat{\mathbf{N}}(s)$ does: $\hat{K}(s)\hat{\mathbf{N}}(s) = K(s)\mathbf{N}(s)$. As in 2D, $\hat{K}(s)$ is positive where the curve turns left and negative where the curve turns right (relative to the top side).

4.3. General bisection property. By combining Lemmas 4.2 and 4.3, we obtain a stronger bisection lemma:

COROLLARY 4.4. *For a cone-free folded curved crease* $\mathbf{X}(s)$, $\hat{\mathbf{B}}(s)$ *bisects* $\mathbf{P}_L(s)$ *and* $\mathbf{P}_R(s)$. *In particular, the tangent planes of the surfaces on both sides of* $\mathbf{X}(s)$ *form the same angle with the osculating plane.*

4.4. Consequences. Using the bisector property, we can prove the nonexistence of a few strange situations.

LEMMA 4.5. *A crease* $\mathbf{X}$ *curved at* s *cannot have a positive-length interval* $s \in (s - \varepsilon, s + \varepsilon)$ *incident to a planar region.*

PROOF. If this situation were to happen, then the osculating plane of the curve must equal the plane of the planar region, which is, say, the left surface plane. By Corollary 4.4, the right surface plane must be the same plane. But then, the folded piece of paper is actually planar along the crease, contradicting that it is not C^1 along the crease. □

LEMMA 4.6. *A rule segment cannot be tangent to a cone-free curved crease point (at a relative interior point, in 2D or 3D).*

PROOF. Suppose by symmetry that a rule segment is tangent to a crease point on its left side. If a rule segment is tangent to the crease point $\mathbf{x}(s)$ in 2D, then it must also be tangent to $\mathbf{X}(s)$ in 3D. There are two cases: (1) The left surface is a tangent surface generated from the crease, and (2) the surface is trimmed by the crease and is only tangent at the point $\mathbf{X}(s)$.

In Case 1, there is a finite portion of the crease that is C^2 and tangent to the incident rule segment. Then, for that portion of the crease (including s), the tangent plane of the left surface is the osculating plane of the curve.

In Case 2, consider surface normal $\mathbf{P}_L(s)$ at $\mathbf{X}(s)$. By assumption, the tangent vector $\mathbf{T}$ is parallel to the rule segment incident to $\mathbf{X}(s)$. Suppose by symmetry that $\mathbf{T}$ is actually the direction of the rule segment from $\mathbf{X}(s)$. (Otherwise, we could invert the parameterization of $\mathbf{X}$.) Because the surface normal is constant along the rule segment, and thus in the rule-segment direction, we have

$$\frac{d\mathbf{P}_L}{ds^+} = \mathbf{0}.$$

Because $\mathbf{P}_L$ and $\mathbf{T}$ are perpendicular, $\frac{d}{ds^+}(\mathbf{P}_L \cdot \mathbf{T}) = 0$, which expands to

$$\frac{d\mathbf{P}_L}{ds^+} \cdot \mathbf{T} + \mathbf{P}_L \cdot \frac{d\mathbf{T}}{ds^+} = 0.$$

Thus, we obtain $\mathbf{P}_L \cdot \frac{d\mathbf{T}}{ds^+} = 0$. Because the folded crease is not straight (Lemma 3.1), $\mathbf{N}$ is perpendicular to $\mathbf{P}_L$. Therefore, the left tangent plane equals the osculating plane.

By Corollary 4.4, in either case, the right tangent plane must also equal the osculating plane, meaning that the folded piece of paper is actually planar along the crease, contradicting that it is not C^1 along the crease. □

When the crease is C^2, Lemma 4.6 also implicitly follows from the Fuchs–Tabachnikov relation between fold angle and rule-segment angle [Fuchs and Tabachnikov 99], [Fuchs and Tabachnikov 07].

COROLLARY 4.7. *For a crease $\mathbf{X}$ curved and cone-free at s, the point $\mathbf{X}(s)$ has an incident positive-length rule segment on the left side of $\mathbf{X}$ and an incident positive-length rule segment on the right side of $\mathbf{X}$.*

PROOF. First, by Lemma 4.5, $\mathbf{X}(s)$ is not locally surrounded by a flat region on either side, so by Corollary 3.3, $\mathbf{X}(s)$ must have a rule segment on its left and right sides. Furthermore, such a rule segment cannot be a zero-length limit of nearby rule segments, because such a rule segment would be tangent to the curve, contradicting Lemma 4.6. □

COROLLARY 4.8. *If a face's boundary is a C^1 curved closed curve, then the folded face's boundary is not C^1.*

PROOF. Consider the decomposition from Corollary 3.3 applied to the face, resulting in planar and ruled regions. By Lemma 4.5, the ruled regions' boundaries collectively cover the face boundary. The planar regions form a laminar (noncrossing) family in the face, so there must be a ruled region adjacent to only one planar region (or zero if the entire folded face is ruled). This ruled region is either the entire folded face or bounded by a portion of

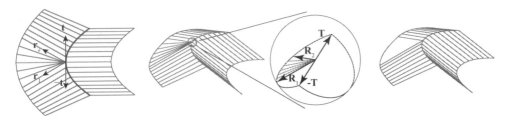

FIGURE 5. Cone rulings must fold into a kink in 3D.

the face boundary and by a single rule segment (bounding a planar region). For each rule segment in the ruled region, we can discard the side that (possibly) contains the boundary rule segment, effectively shrinking the rule region while preserving its boundary structure of partial face boundary and one rule segment. In the limit of this process, we obtain a rule segment that is tangent to the face boundary. By Lemma 4.6, this situation can happen only if the face is cone ruled at some point, which by Theorem 5.1 implies that the folded face boundary is not C^1.   □

5. Smooth Folding

A *smoothly folded crease* is a folded crease that is C^1, i.e., kink-free. In Corollary 6.4 below, we will show that a smoothly folded crease is furthermore C^2, i.e., it cannot have semikinks. A *smooth folding* of a crease pattern is a folding in which every crease is smoothly folded. In this section, we characterize smooth folding as cone-free.

THEOREM 5.1. *If a folded crease* $\mathbf{X}$ *has a cone ruling at a point* $\mathbf{X}(s)$, *then* $\mathbf{X}$ *is kinked at* s.

PROOF. Assume by symmetry that $\mathbf{X}(s)$ has a cone ruling on the left side, say clockwise from rule vector $\mathbf{R}_1$ to rule vector $\mathbf{R}_2$. Because the unfolded crease $\mathbf{x}$ is C^1, it has a tangent vector $\mathbf{t}$, so the left side of $\mathbf{x}(s)$ is, to the first order, the cone clockwise from $-\mathbf{t}$ to $\mathbf{t}$. Thus, we have $-\mathbf{t}, \mathbf{r}_1, \mathbf{r}_2$, and $\mathbf{t}$ appearing in clockwise order around $\mathbf{x}(s)$, giving us the angle following relation:

$$180° = \angle(-\mathbf{t}, \mathbf{t}) = \angle(-\mathbf{t}, \mathbf{r}_1) + \angle(\mathbf{r}_1, \mathbf{r}_2) + \angle(\mathbf{r}_2, \mathbf{t}).$$

Now assume for contradiction that $\mathbf{X}$ is C^1 at s, so we can define the tangent vector $\mathbf{T}(s)$. By triangle inequality on the sphere, we have

$$180° = \angle(-\mathbf{T}, \mathbf{T}) \leq \angle(-\mathbf{T}, \mathbf{R}_1) + \angle(\mathbf{R}_1, \mathbf{R}_2) + \angle(\mathbf{R}_2, \mathbf{T}).$$

The latter three 3D angles must be smaller than or equal to the corresponding angles in 2D, by isometry. Furthermore, $\angle(R_1, R_2) < \angle(\mathbf{r}_1, \mathbf{r}_2)$, because the surface must be bent along the entire cone ruling (otherwise it would have a flat patch). Therefore,

$$\angle(-\mathbf{T}, \mathbf{R}_1) + \angle(\mathbf{R}_1, \mathbf{R}_2) + \angle(\mathbf{R}_2, \mathbf{T}) < \angle(-\mathbf{t}, \mathbf{r}_1) + \angle(\mathbf{r}_1, \mathbf{r}_2) + \angle(\mathbf{r}_2, \mathbf{t}) = 180°,$$

a contradiction.   □

Now we get a characterization of smooth folding:

COROLLARY 5.2. *A folded curved crease* $\mathbf{X}$ *is kinked at* s *if and only if it has a cone ruling at* $\mathbf{X}(s)$.

PROOF. Theorem 5.1 proves the "if" implication.

To prove the converse, consider a cone-free crease point $\mathbf{X}(s)$. In 2D, we have a $180° = \angle(-\mathbf{t}, \mathbf{t})$ angle on either side of the crease. We claim that this $180°$ angle between the backward tangent and forward tangent is preserved by the folding, so the folded crease $\mathbf{X}$ has a continuous tangent and thus is C^1 at s.

First, suppose that there is no planar region incident to $\mathbf{X}(s)$ on, say, the left side. Then, the left side is locally a uniquely ruled C^2 surface, with no rule segments tangent to the curve by Lemma 4.6, and thus the surface can be extended slightly to include $\mathbf{X}(s)$ in its interior. In a C^1 surface, it is known that geodesic (2D) angles equal Euclidean (3D) angles, so folding preserves the $180°$ angle between the backward and forward tangents.

Now suppose that there is a planar region on the left side of $\mathbf{X}(s)$. By Lemma 3.4, there can be only one, and by Lemma 4.5, there must be two uniquely ruled surfaces separating such a planar region from the crease. These three surfaces meet smoothly with a common surface normal, as the surface is C^2 away from the crease, so the overall angle between the backward and forward tangents of the crease equals the sum of the three angles of the surfaces at $\mathbf{X}(s)$. The previous paragraph argues that the two uniquely ruled surfaces preserve their angles, and the planar region clearly preserves its angle (it is not folded). Hence, again, folding preserves the $180°$ angle between the backward and forward tangents. □

6. Mountains and Valleys

6.1. Crease. Refer to Figure 4. For a smoothly folded (cone-free) crease $\mathbf{X}$, the *fold angle* $\rho \in (-180°, 180°)$ at $\mathbf{X}(s)$ is defined by $\cos\rho = \mathbf{P}_L \cdot \mathbf{P}_R$ and $\sin\rho = [(\mathbf{P}_L \times \mathbf{P}_R) \cdot \mathbf{T}]$. The crease is *valley* at s if the fold angle is negative, i.e., $(\mathbf{P}_L \times \mathbf{P}_R) \cdot \mathbf{T} < 0$. The crease is *mountain* at s if the fold angle is positive, i.e., $(\mathbf{P}_L \times \mathbf{P}_R) \cdot \mathbf{T} > 0$.

LEMMA 6.1. *A smoothly folded curved crease $\mathbf{X}$ has a continuous fold angle $\rho \neq 0$.*

PROOF. By Corollary 5.2, the crease is cone-free, so the surface normals $\mathbf{P}_L(s)$ and $\mathbf{P}_R(s)$ are continuous. If the resulting fold angle $\rho(s)$ were zero, then we would have $\mathbf{P}_L(s) = \mathbf{P}_R(s)$, contradicting that the folded piece of paper is not C^1 at crease point $\mathbf{X}(s)$. □

COROLLARY 6.2. *A smoothly folded curved crease $\mathbf{X}$ is mountain or valley throughout.*

PROOF. By Lemma 6.1, $\rho(s)$ is continuous and nonzero. By the intermediate value theorem, $\rho(s)$ cannot change sign. □

LEMMA 6.3. *For a smoothly folded curved crease $\mathbf{X}(s)$,*

$$\hat{K}(s)\cos\frac{1}{2}\rho(s) = \hat{k}(s).$$

In particular, folding increases curvature: $|\hat{k}(s)| < |\hat{K}(s)|$, *i.e.,* $k(s) < K(s)$.

PROOF. Referring to Figure 4, we have

$$\cos\frac{1}{2}\rho(s) = \mathbf{P}_L(s) \cdot \hat{\mathbf{B}}(s).$$

By definition of $\hat{\mathbf{B}}(s)$, this dot product is the triple product

$$\mathbf{P}_L(s) \cdot (\mathbf{T}(s) \times \hat{\mathbf{N}}(s)) = \hat{\mathbf{N}}(s) \cdot (\mathbf{P}_L(s) \times \mathbf{T}(s))$$

(similar to the proof of Lemma 4.2). Multiplying by $\hat{K}(s)$, we obtain

$$(\hat{K}(s)\hat{N}(s)) \cdot (\mathbf{P}_L(s) \times \mathbf{T}(s)) = (K(s)N(s)) \cdot (\mathbf{P}_L(s) \times \mathbf{T}(s)).$$

By Lemma 4.1, this geodesic curvature is $\hat{k}(s)$.   □

COROLLARY 6.4. *A folded crease cannot have a semikink, and thus a smoothly folded crease* $\mathbf{X}$ *is* C^2.

PROOF. Suppose $\mathbf{X}(s)$ had a semikink at $s = \tilde{s}$. Applying Lemma 6.3 with positive and negative limits, we obtain that

$$\lim_{s \to \tilde{s}^+} \hat{K}(s) = \frac{\hat{k}(s)}{\cos \frac{1}{2}\rho} = \lim_{s \to \tilde{s}^-} \hat{K}(s),$$

and thus the signed curvature $\hat{K}(s)$ is continuous at $s = \tilde{s}$. By Lemma 4.3, $\hat{N}(s)$ is continuous at $s = \tilde{s}$. Therefore, $\frac{d^2\mathbf{X}(s)}{ds^2} = \hat{K}(s)\hat{N}(s)$ is continuous at $s = \tilde{s}$, so $\mathbf{X}(\tilde{s})$ is not actually a semikink.   □

LEMMA 6.5. *A smoothly folded crease* $\mathbf{X}$ *is valley if and only if* $(\mathbf{P}_L \times \hat{\mathbf{B}}) \cdot \mathbf{T} < 0$, *and mountain if and only if* $(\mathbf{P}_L \times \hat{\mathbf{B}}) \cdot \mathbf{T} > 0$.

PROOF. Refer to Figure 4. Vectors $\mathbf{P}_L$, $\mathbf{P}_R$, and $\hat{\mathbf{B}}$ are all perpendicular to $\mathbf{T}$ and thus live in a common oriented plane with normal $\mathbf{T}$. By the choice of $\hat{\mathbf{B}}$ to have positive dot products with $\mathbf{P}_L$ and $\mathbf{P}_R$, the three vectors in fact live in a common half-plane. In this plane, we can see the fold angle $\rho = \angle(\mathbf{P}_L, \mathbf{P}_R)$, where $\angle$ measures the convex angle between the vectors, signed positive when the angle is convex in the counterclockwise orientation within the oriented plane with normal $\mathbf{T}$ and signed negative when clockwise.

By Corollary 4.4, $\mathbf{P}_L \cdot \mathbf{B} = \mathbf{P}_R \cdot \mathbf{B}$, so $\mathbf{P}_L \cdot \hat{\mathbf{B}} = \mathbf{P}_R \cdot \hat{\mathbf{B}}$. Thus, $\cos \angle(\mathbf{P}_L, \hat{\mathbf{B}}) = \cos \angle(\mathbf{P}_R, \hat{\mathbf{B}})$, i.e., $|\angle(\mathbf{P}_L, \hat{\mathbf{B}})| = |\angle(\mathbf{P}_R, \hat{\mathbf{B}})|$.

If $\angle(\mathbf{P}_L, \hat{\mathbf{B}}) = \angle(\mathbf{P}_R, \hat{\mathbf{B}})$, then $\mathbf{P}_L = \mathbf{P}_R$, contradicting that $\mathbf{X}$ is a crease. Therefore, $\angle(\mathbf{P}_L, \hat{\mathbf{B}}) = \angle(\hat{\mathbf{B}}, \mathbf{P}_R) = \pm\frac{1}{2}\angle(\mathbf{P}_L, \mathbf{P}_R)$. Because $|\angle(\mathbf{P}_L, \hat{\mathbf{B}})| < 90°$, we must in fact have $\angle(\mathbf{P}_L, \hat{\mathbf{B}}) = \angle(\hat{\mathbf{B}}, \mathbf{P}_R) = \frac{1}{2}\angle(\mathbf{P}_L, \mathbf{P}_R)$, i.e., $\hat{\mathbf{B}}$ bisects the convex angle $\angle(\mathbf{P}_L, \mathbf{P}_R)$. Hence, $\hat{\mathbf{B}}$ lies in between $\mathbf{P}_L$ and $\mathbf{P}_R$ within the half-plane. Therefore, the cross products $\mathbf{P}_L \times \mathbf{P}_R$, $\mathbf{P}_L \times \hat{\mathbf{B}}$, and $\hat{\mathbf{B}} \times \mathbf{P}_R$ are all parallel, so their dot products with $\mathbf{T}$ have the same sign.   □

6.2. Rule segment. We can also define whether a rule segment bends the paper mountain or valley; refer to Figure 6. Consider a relative interior point $\mathbf{Y}$ of a rule segment with direction vector $\mathbf{R}$, with top-side surface normal $\mathbf{P}$. Then, we can construct a local Frenet frame at $\mathbf{Y}$ with tangent vector $\mathbf{Q} = \mathbf{R} \times \mathbf{P}$, normal vector $\mathbf{P}$, and binormal vector $\mathbf{R}$. These frames define a 3D curve $\mathbf{Y}(t)$, where $\mathbf{Y}(0) = \mathbf{Y}$, which follows the principle curvature of the surface. Parameterize this curve by arclength.

First, consider the case when the surface is C^2 at $Y(t)$. The surface *bends valley* at $\mathbf{Y}(t)$ if the curvature vector $\frac{d^2\mathbf{Y}(t)}{dt^2} = \frac{d\mathbf{Q}(t)}{dt}$ is on the top side, i.e., has positive dot product with $\mathbf{P}(t)$; and it *bends mountain* if $\frac{d\mathbf{Q}(t)}{dt} \cdot \mathbf{P}(t) < 0$. In particular, at $t = 0$, we determine whether the original rule segment bends mountain or valley at $\mathbf{Y}$.

If the surface is not C^2 at $Y(t)$, then the rule segment is a semicrease, which connects two C^2 surfaces sharing a surface normal at the crease; refer to Figure 7. In this case, the surface bends valley at $\mathbf{Y}(t)$ when the two surfaces bend valley or when one of the surfaces is planar and the other bends valley. Similarly, the surface bends mountain at $\mathbf{Y}(t)$ when the two surfaces bend mountain or one of the surfaces is planar and the other bends mountain. At an inflection point, there is no mountain/valley assignment.

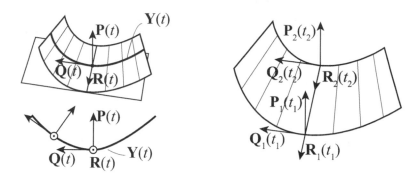

FIGURE 6. Defining a frame around an interior point to define mountain versus valley bending.

FIGURE 7. Definition of mountain and valley for a semicrease.

LEMMA 6.6. *A developable uncreased surface bends the same direction (mountain or valley) at every relative interior point of a rule segment.*

PROOF. First, consider the case when the surface is C^2. Consider two points $\mathbf{Y}_1$ and $\mathbf{Y}_2$ on the rule segment, with principle curvature frames $(\mathbf{Q}_i(t_i), \mathbf{R}_i(t_i), \mathbf{P}_i(t_i))$. Choose t_2 as a function of t_1 such that $\mathbf{Y}_1(t_1)$ and $\mathbf{Y}_2(t_2)$ lie on a common rule segment. Then, the frames are in fact identical: $\mathbf{R}_1(t_1) = \mathbf{R}_2(t_2)$ is the common rule direction, $\mathbf{P}_1(t_1) = \mathbf{P}_2(t_2)$ is the common top-side surface normal, and $\mathbf{Q}_1(t_1) = \mathbf{Q}_2(t_2)$ is their cross product. Because the surface is locally C^2 around the ruled segment $\mathbf{Y}_1$ and $\mathbf{Y}_2$, we have $\frac{dt_2}{dt_1} > 0$, so

$$\frac{d\mathbf{Q}_2(t_2)}{dt_2} \cdot \mathbf{P} = \frac{d\mathbf{Q}_1(t_1)}{dt_2} \cdot \mathbf{P} = \frac{dt_2}{dt_1} \frac{d\mathbf{Q}_1(t_1)}{dt_1} \cdot \mathbf{P}.$$

Therefore, the surface bends the same direction.

Next, consider the case when the surface is not C^2, i.e., the rule segment is a semicrease between C^2 surfaces S^+ and S^-. By the above argument, in a C^2 patch, the inflection occurs along the rule segment where $\frac{d\mathbf{Q}(t)}{dt} \cdot \mathbf{P} = 0$ is satisfied. Also, if the surface is not C^2, then it is on a rule segment. Therefore, if the S^- surface is bent in a different direction at $\lim_{t \to t_1^-} \mathbf{Y}_1(t)$ and $\lim_{t \to t_2^-} \mathbf{Y}_2(t_2)$, then a path from $\mathbf{Y}_1$ to $\mathbf{Y}_2$ must cross a rule segment. Because rule segments do not intersect, S^+ and S^- keep their own bending orientations. Therefore, the assignment for the semicrease is unchanged along the segment. $\square$

By Lemma 6.6, we can define the bending direction of a rule segment: A developable uncreased surface bends mountain or valley at a rule segment if a relative interior point of the rule segment bends mountain or valley, respectively. Furthermore, because the frames are identical, we can define the principle curvature frame $(\mathbf{Q}, \mathbf{R}, \mathbf{P})$ of a rule segment by the principle curvature frame at any relative interior point on the rule segment.

6.3. Crease versus rule segment. Next we consider the mountain-valley relation between a rule segment and a crease.

First, consider a smoothly folded crease $\mathbf{X}$ with left and right surface *ruling vectors* $\mathbf{R}_L$ and $\mathbf{R}_R$, defined as unit vectors that lie along the rule segments on surfaces S_L and S_R incident to $\mathbf{X}$. (If there is a planar region incident to $\mathbf{X}$, these ruling vectors will not be unique.) A left-side ruling vector $\mathbf{R}_L$ lives in the plane perpendicular to $\mathbf{P}_L$. Therefore, the vector can be represented by

$$\mathbf{R}_L = (\cos \theta_L)\mathbf{T} + (\sin \theta_L)(\mathbf{P}_L \times \mathbf{T}),$$

where we call θ_L the *left-side ruling angle* of the ruling, which is nonzero by Lemma 4.6. Because the ruling angle is intrinsic, the ruling vector in 2D is represented by $\mathbf{r}_L = (\cos \theta_L)\mathbf{t} + (\sin \theta_L)\hat{\mathbf{b}}$. The orientation of the left-side ruling vector is chosen to orient to the left, i.e., $\mathbf{r}_L \cdot \hat{\mathbf{b}} > 0$, so θ_L is positive. Similarly, ruling vector $\mathbf{R}_R$ on the right surface is represented by $\mathbf{R}_R = (\cos \theta_R)\mathbf{T} - (\sin \theta_R)(\mathbf{P}_R \times \mathbf{T})$, using *right-side ruling angle* θ_R. The orientation is chosen to be on the right side, so $\theta_R > 0$.

LEMMA 6.7. *Consider a uniquely ruled smoothly folded crease $\mathbf{X}$ with locally C^2 surfaces on both sides (no semicreases). Then, the rule segment on the left side of $\mathbf{X}$ bends valley if and only if $\mathbf{N} \cdot \mathbf{P}_L > 0$. Symmetrically, the surface bends valley on the right side if and only if $\mathbf{N} \cdot \mathbf{P}_R > 0$.*

PROOF. Build the principle curvature frame $(\mathbf{Q}(t), \mathbf{R}(t), \mathbf{P}(t))$ of rule segment parameterized by the arclength t in the principle curvature direction. Consider corresponding point $\mathbf{X}(s)$ and the arclength parameter $s = s(t)$ along the crease at the rule segment parameterized by t. Because the surface is locally C^2 around the rule segment, $\frac{ds}{dt} > 0$. Because we consider the left side of the surface, $\mathbf{P}_L(s) = \mathbf{P}(t)$. Let θ be the angle between $\mathbf{R}(t)$ and $\mathbf{T}(s)$, i.e., $\mathbf{T}(s) = \sin \theta \mathbf{Q}(t) + \cos \theta \mathbf{R}(t)$. By Lemma 4.6, $0 < \theta < \pi$, and we get

(6.1) $$\mathbf{Q} = (\csc \theta)\mathbf{T} - (\cot \theta)\mathbf{R}.$$

Assume that the surface bends valley at the rule segment, i.e.,

(6.2) $$V(t) = \frac{d\mathbf{Q}(t)}{dt} \cdot \mathbf{P}(t) > 0.$$

Using orthogonality of vectors $\mathbf{Q}$ and $\mathbf{P}$, i.e., $\mathbf{Q}(t) \cdot \mathbf{P}(t) = 0$, and taking derivatives, we obtain

$$\frac{d\mathbf{Q}}{dt} \cdot \mathbf{P} + \mathbf{Q} \cdot \frac{d\mathbf{P}}{dt} = 0.$$

Then,

$$V(t) = -\mathbf{Q} \cdot \frac{d\mathbf{P}}{dt}$$
$$= -\left((\csc \theta)\mathbf{T} - (\cot \theta)\mathbf{R}\right) \cdot \frac{d\mathbf{P}}{dt}$$
$$= -(\csc \theta)\mathbf{T} \cdot \frac{d\mathbf{P}}{dt}.$$

Here, we used Equation (6.1). By the orthogonality of vectors $\mathbf{T}$ and $\mathbf{P}$, we get

$$\mathbf{T} \cdot \frac{d\mathbf{P}}{dt} = \frac{d\mathbf{T}}{dt} \cdot \mathbf{P}.$$

Then,

$$V(t) = (\csc \theta) \frac{d\mathbf{T}(s)}{dt} \cdot \mathbf{P}(t)$$

$$= (\csc \theta) \frac{ds}{dt} \frac{d\mathbf{T}(s)}{ds} \cdot \mathbf{P}(t)$$

$$= (\csc \theta) \frac{ds}{dt} K(s)\mathbf{N}(s) \cdot \mathbf{P}_L(s).$$

Because $\csc \theta > 0$, $\frac{ds}{dt} > 0$, and $K(s) > 0$, Equation (6.2) is equivalent to $\mathbf{N}(s) \cdot \mathbf{P}_L(s) > 0$. $\square$

Now we make a stronger statement, allowing the ruling vectors to be not unique and the surfaces to be not C^2.

COROLLARY 6.8. *Consider a smoothly folded crease* $\mathbf{X}$. *Then, a rule segment on the left side of* $\mathbf{X}$ *bends valley if and only if* $\mathbf{N} \cdot \mathbf{P}_L > 0$. *Symmetrically, the surface bends valley on the right side if and only if* $\mathbf{N} \cdot \mathbf{P}_R > 0$.

PROOF. Consider rule segments at $\mathbf{X}(\tilde{s})$. By Theorem 5.1, the crease is cone free, so a rule segment is either (1) between two C^2 ruled surfaces or (2) between a plane and a C^2 ruled surfaces.

Consider Case 1, and let S^- and S^+ be the two surfaces. Because there are no cone rulings, S^- and S^+ are locally formed by unique rulings emanating from $\mathbf{X}(s)$ at $s < \tilde{s}$ and $s > \tilde{s}$, respectively. Then,

$$\lim_{s \to \tilde{s}^-} \mathbf{N}(s) \cdot \mathbf{P}_L(s) = \lim_{s \to \tilde{s}^+} \mathbf{N}(s) \cdot \mathbf{P}_L(s) = \mathbf{N}(s) \cdot \mathbf{P}_L(s).$$

So, both surfaces S^- and S^+ bend valley if and only if $\mathbf{N}(s) \cdot \mathbf{P}_L(s) > 0$.

Next, consider Case 2. By symmetry, assume that S^- is planar and S^+ is a C^2 ruled surface. Then, S^+ is locally formed by unique rule segments emanating from $\mathbf{X}(s)$ at $s > \tilde{s}$. Hence, S^+, and thus the rule segment, bends valley if and only if $\mathbf{N}(s) \cdot \mathbf{P}_L(s) > 0$. $\square$

THEOREM 6.9. *Consider a smoothly folded curved crease* $\mathbf{X}$. *A rule segment incident to* $\mathbf{X}(\tilde{s})$ *on the convex side of* $\mathbf{X}(\tilde{s})$ *has the same mountain/valley assignment as the crease, while a rule segment incident to* $\mathbf{X}(\tilde{s})$ *on the concave side of* $\mathbf{X}(\tilde{s})$ *has the opposite mountain/valley assignment as the crease.*

PROOF. Assume by symmetry that the left side of the paper is the convex side ($\hat{k}(s) < 0$). Also, assume that the crease is a valley, i.e., $(\hat{\mathbf{B}} \times \mathbf{P}_L) \cdot \mathbf{T} = (\mathbf{P}_L \times \mathbf{B}) \cdot \mathbf{T} > 0$. Then, the top-side normal of the osculating plane is $\hat{\mathbf{B}} = -\mathbf{B}$, and thus $\hat{\mathbf{N}} = -\mathbf{N}$.

Now

$$(\mathbf{P}_L \times \mathbf{B}) \cdot \mathbf{T} = (\mathbf{P}_L \times (\mathbf{T} \times \mathbf{N})) \cdot \mathbf{T}$$

$$= (\mathbf{T}(\mathbf{P}_L \cdot \mathbf{N}) - \mathbf{N}(\mathbf{P}_L \cdot \mathbf{T})) \cdot \mathbf{T} > 0.$$

The second term disappears because $\mathbf{P}_L \cdot \mathbf{T} = 0$. Therefore, $\mathbf{P}_L \cdot \mathbf{N} > 0$, so the left side is valley. $\square$

6.4. Creases connected by a rule segment. Now consider two creases connected by a rule segment. By Lemma 6.9, we get the following:

COROLLARY 6.10. *Consider two smoothly folded creases connected by a rule segment. If the rule segment is on the concave sides of both creases, or on the convex sides of both creases, then the creases must have the same direction (mountain or valley). If a rule*

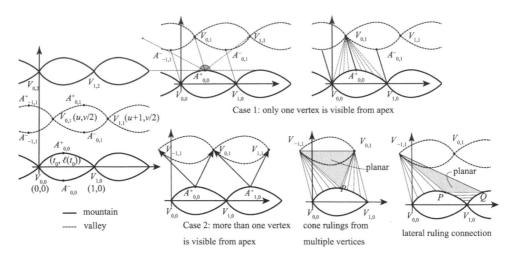

Case 1: only one vertex is visible from apex

— mountain
---- valley

Case 2: more than one vertex
is visible from apex

cone rulings from
multiple vertices

lateral ruling connection

FIGURE 8. Ruling conditions for a lens tessellation.

segment is on the convex side of one crease and the concave side of the other crease, then the creases must have the opposite direction (one mountain and one valley).

7. Lens Tessellation

In this section, we use the qualitative properties of rulings obtained in previous sections to reconstruct rule segments from a crease pattern of the generalized version of lens tessellation.

First, as illustrated in Figure 8, we define the *lens tessellation* parameterized by a convex C^2 function $\ell : [0, 1] \to [0, \infty)$ with $\ell(0) = \ell(1) = 0$, horizontal offset $u \in [0, 1)$, and vertical offset $v \in (0, \infty)$, to consist of

(1) mountain creases $\gamma_{i,2j}^{\pm} = \{(t + i, \pm\ell(t) + jv) \mid t \in [0, 1]\}$ for $i, j \in \mathbb{Z}$;

(2) valley creases $\gamma_{i,2j+1}^{\pm} = \{(1 - t + i + u, \pm\ell(1 - t) + (j + \frac{1}{2})v)\} \mid t \in [0, 1]\}$ for $i, j \in \mathbb{Z}$.

Define the *vertices* to be points of the form $V_{i,2j} = (i, jv)$ and $V_{i,2j+1} = (i + u, (j + \frac{1}{2})v)$. Four creases meet at each vertex.

Because $\ell(t)$ is convex, it has a unique maximum $\ell(t^*)$ at some $t = t^*$. Define the *apex* $A_{i,k}$ of crease $\gamma_{i,k}^{\pm}$ to be the point of the crease at $t = t^*$, i.e., $A_{i,2j}^{\pm} = (t^* + i, \pm\ell(t^*) + jv)$ and $A_{i,2j+1}^{\pm} = (1 - t^* + i + u, \pm\ell(1 - t^*) + (j + \frac{1}{2})v)$.

7.1. Necessary conditions. Consider a crease point $\mathbf{x}(s)$. A point $\mathbf{y}$ on the crease pattern (a vertex or crease point) is *visible* from $\mathbf{x}(s)$ on the left (right) side of $\mathbf{x}$ at $\mathbf{x}(s)$ if the oriented open line segment $\overrightarrow{\mathbf{x}(s)\mathbf{y}}$ is on the left (right) side of $\mathbf{x}(s)$ and does not share a point with the crease pattern. If $\mathbf{x}(s)$ and $\mathbf{y}$ are the endpoints of a rule segment, then certainly they must be visible from each other.

THEOREM 7.1. *A lens tessellation can smoothly fold only if there is a vertex $V_{i,1}$ visible from every point on crease $\gamma_{0,0}^+$ on the convex side.*

PROOF. Refer to Figure 8. By Corollary 4.7, there must be a rule segment emanating from $A_{0,0}^+$ on the convex side of $\gamma_{0,0}^+$. The other endpoint B of that rule segment must be visible from $A_{0,0}^+$ on the convex side of $\gamma_{0,0}^+$. Because the tangent line of $\gamma_{0,0}^+$ at $A_{0,0}^+$ is horizontal, any such visible point B must lie on the union of creases $\gamma_{i,1}^-$ and vertices $V_{i,1}$

for $i \in \mathbb{Z}$. By Theorem 6.10, B cannot be on the relative interior of one of the valley creases $\gamma_{i,1}^-$ because then the rule segment would be on the concave sides of creases of opposite direction. Thus, B must be among the vertices $V_{i,1}$ for $i \in \mathbb{Z}$.·

First, consider the case that only one vertex $V_{n,1}$ is visible from $A_{0,0}^+$ on the convex side of $\gamma_{0,0}^+$. Then, $A_{0,0}^+ V_{n,1}$ must be a rule segment. By symmetry, $V_{1,0} A_{n,1}^-$ is also a rule segment. Consider a point on $\gamma_{0,0}^+$ between $A_{0,0}^+$ and $V_{0,1}$, which by Corollary 4.7 has a rule segment on the positive side of $\gamma_{0,0}^+$. This rule segment cannot cross the existing rule segments $A_{0,0}^+ V_{n,1}$ and $V_{1,0} A_{n,1}^-$, so its other endpoint must be $V_{n,1}$, $A_{n,1}^-$, or between $V_{n,1}$ and $A_{n,1}^-$ on curve $\gamma_{n,1}^-$. By Theorem 6.10, the only possible ruling is to have a cone apex at $V_{n,1}$. Similarly, rule segments from points between $V_{0,0}$ and $A_{0,0}^+$ on $\gamma_{0,0}^+$ must end at $V_{n,1}$. Therefore, $V_{n,1}$ is visible from every point on crease $\gamma_{0,0}^+$ on the convex side.

Second, consider the case in which more than one vertex $V_{i,1}$ is visible from apex $A_{0,0}^+$ on the convex side of $\gamma_{0,0}^+$. Suppose for contradiction that there is no common vertex visible from the entire curve $\gamma_{0,0}^+$. Similar to the previous case, there must be a rule segment from apex $A_{0,0}^+$ to one of the vertices $V_{n,1}$. But, we assumed that some other point of $\gamma_{0,0}^+$ cannot see $V_{n,1}$. By symmetry, suppose that point is to the right of $A_{0,0}^+$. There is a transition point P on the relative interior of $\gamma_{0,0}^+$ when the endpoints of rulings change from $V_{n,1}$ to either (a) another vertex $V_{m,1}$ with $m > n$ or (b) a point on $\gamma_{1,0}^+$. (See Figure 8.) At such a point P, we have two rule segments. By Theorem 5.1, P cannot be a cone apex. Hence, there must be a planar region between the two rule segments. Specifically, in case (a), the triangle $P V_{n,1} V_{m,1}$ is planar, which contains all of $\gamma_{n,1}^-$, contradicting that the folded piece of paper is not C^1 on $\gamma_{n,1}^-$. In case (b), let Q be the point on $\gamma_{1,0}^+$. The triangle $P Q V_{n,1}$ is planar. This triangle cannot intersect $\gamma_{n,1}^-$, because the folded piece of paper is not C^1 on $\gamma_{n,1}^-$. In particular, the curve $\gamma_{n,1}^-$ cannot intersect the segment $V_{n,1} V_{0,1}$ (which begins in the triangle). Because $\gamma_{1,0}^+$ is a $180°$ rotation of $\gamma_{n,1}^-$ mapping $V_{n,1}$ to $V_{0,1}$, we symmetrically have that the curve $\gamma_{1,0}^+$ cannot intersect the same segment $V_{n,1} V_{0,1}$. Thus, this segment is a visibility segment, as is $V_{n,1} V_{0,0}$. By convexity of the lens, $V_{n,1}$ can see the entire curve $\gamma_{1,0}^+$. Therefore, there is in fact a common vertex visible from the curve $\gamma_{0,0}^+$. □

7.2. Existence and sufficiency. Finally we prove that the condition from Theorem 7.1 is also sufficient:

THEOREM 7.2. *A lens tessellation can fold smoothly if there is a vertex $V_{i,1}$ visible from every point on crease $\gamma_{0,0}^+$ on the convex side.*

PROOF. First, we construct the folding of one "gadget," $(i, j) = 0$; refer to Figure 9. We can add an integer to u to assume that $V_{0,1}$ is the visible vertex from apex $A_{0,0}^+$. In 2D, this gadget is bounded by a quadrangle of rule segments with vertex coordinates $V_{0,0} = (0,0)$, $V_{0,-1} = (u, -\frac{1}{2}v)$, $V_{1,0} = (1,0)$, and $V_{0,1} = (u, \frac{1}{2}v)$. This kite module is decomposed by its creases into an upper wing part U, middle lens part M, and lower wing part L. We assume that M is ruled parallel to the y-axis: The rule segments of M are of the form $(t, \ell(t))$ and $(t, -\ell(t))$ parameterized by t. (We can make this assumption because we are constructing a folded state.) We also assume that U consists of cone rulings between $V_{0,1}$ and $(t, \ell(t))$ while L consists of cone rulings between $V_{0,-1}$ and $(t, -\ell(t))$ using the same parameter t.

The folding $f(M)$ is a cylindrical surface with parallel rulings. We orient the folded form such that this ruling direction is parallel to the y-axis and $\overrightarrow{f(V_{0,0})f(V_{1,0})}$ is parallel to the positive direction of the x-axis. Then, the orthogonal projection of $f(M)$ to the xz-plane is a curve γ, and a ruling at t on M corresponds to a point on $\gamma(t)$ while t is the arclength parameter.

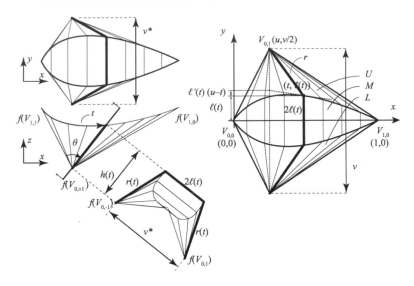

FIGURE 9. A modular kite structure.

We further assume that the folded state is symmetric with respect to reflection through a plane passing through $\overrightarrow{f(V_{0,0})f(V_{1,0})}$ and parallel to the xz-plane. Let the distance between $f(V_{0,-1})$ and $f(V_{0,1})$ be denoted by v^*, where $0 < v^* < v$. We will show that there is a valid folded state for arbitrary v^* if it is sufficiently close to v.

Consider the set of rule segments of U, M, and L at parameter t and its folding. Then, by our symmetry assumption, these segments form a planar polyline that, together with segments $f(V_{0,-1})$ and $f(V_{0,1})$, forms an isosceles trapezoid with base length v^* and top length $2\ell(t)$. The legs are the length of the rule segments, which can be calculated from the crease pattern as $r(t) = \sqrt{(u - t)^2 + (v/2 - \ell(t))^2}$. Such a trapezoid exists because $0 < v^* < v \leq 2\ell(t) + 2r(t)$. The height of the trapezoid $h(t)$ is given by

$$h(t) = \sqrt{(v - v^*)\left(\frac{v + v^*}{4} - \ell(t)\right) + (t - u)^2}.$$

Now consider the projection of this trapezoid in the xz-plane. This projection is a line segment between two points, namely the projections of $V_{0,1}$ and $\gamma(t)$, and it must have length of $h(t)$. We use the following lemma to solve for γ:

LEMMA 7.3. *If an arclength-parameterized crease $\mathbf{x}(s)$ has unique rule segments on one side incident to cone apex $\mathbf{a}$, then an embedding $\mathbf{f}$ is a proper folding if and only if folded curve $\mathbf{X} = \mathbf{f} \circ \mathbf{x}$ is also arclength parameterized, and rule segments from $\mathbf{a}$ to $\mathbf{x}(s)$ map isometrically to rule segments from $\mathbf{A}$ to $\mathbf{X}(s)$, where $\mathbf{A} = \mathbf{f} \circ \mathbf{a}$.*

PROOF. Necessity ("only if" part) is obvious, so we prove sufficiency ("if" part). The folded curve is arclength parameterized by s as $\frac{d\mathbf{X}(s)}{ds} = \frac{d\mathbf{x}(s)}{ds} = 1$, and the length of ruling segment $L(s)$ must equal $L(s) = \|\mathbf{x}(s) - \mathbf{a}\| = \|\mathbf{X}(s) - \mathbf{A}\|$. Let $\mathbf{r}(s)$ denote the unit ruling vectors from the apex toward the curve in 2D, i.e., $\mathbf{r}(s) = (\mathbf{x}(s) - \mathbf{a})/L(s)$. Similarly denote the unit ruling vector in 3D by $\mathbf{R}(s) = (\mathbf{X}(s) - \mathbf{A})/L(s)$. Consider a coordinate system using arclength s and radius ℓ. The conical portion of the face formed by the crease and a point is uniquely ruled at any point, so (s, ℓ) uniquely represent a point on the portion. A point (s, ℓ) in 2D corresponds to $\mathbf{a} + \ell\mathbf{r}(s)$, which is mapped to 3D to $\mathbf{A} + \ell\mathbf{R}(s)$. Consider a 2D

C^1 curve $\mathbf{y}(t)$ represented by $(s(t), \ell(t))$, where t is the arclength parameterization. Then, the total derivative of $\mathbf{y}(t) = \mathbf{a} + \ell(t)\mathbf{r}(s(t))$ is

$$\frac{d\mathbf{y}}{dt} = \frac{\partial \mathbf{y}}{\partial s}\frac{ds}{dt} + \frac{\partial \mathbf{y}}{\partial \ell}\frac{d\ell}{dt} = \ell\frac{d\mathbf{r}}{ds}\frac{ds}{dt} + \mathbf{r}\frac{d\ell}{dt}.$$

Then, by taking the dot product with itself,

$$\left\|\frac{d\mathbf{y}}{dt}\right\|^2 = \qquad \ell^2\left\|\frac{d\mathbf{r}}{ds}\right\|^2\left(\frac{ds}{dt}\right)^2 + 2\ell\frac{d\mathbf{r}}{ds}\cdot\mathbf{r}\left(\frac{ds}{dt}\right)\left(\frac{d\ell}{dt}\right) + \|\mathbf{r}\|^2\left(\frac{d\ell}{dt}\right)^2$$

$$= \qquad\qquad \ell^2\left\|\frac{d\mathbf{r}}{ds}\right\|^2\left(\frac{ds}{dt}\right)^2 + \left(\frac{d\ell}{dt}\right)^2,$$

where we used $\mathbf{r}\cdot\mathbf{r} = 1$ and $2\frac{d\mathbf{r}}{ds}\cdot\mathbf{r} = \frac{d}{ds}(\mathbf{r}\cdot\mathbf{r}) = 0$. Because $L(s)\mathbf{r}(s) = \mathbf{x}(s) - \mathbf{a}$, taking derivatives yields

$$L\frac{d\mathbf{r}}{ds} + \frac{dL}{ds}\mathbf{r} = \frac{d\mathbf{x}}{ds}.$$

By taking the dot product,

$$L^2\left\|\frac{d\mathbf{r}}{ds}\right\|^2 + \left(\frac{dL}{ds}\right)^2 = \left\|\frac{d\mathbf{x}}{ds}\right\|^2 = 1,$$

again using $\frac{d\mathbf{r}}{ds}\cdot\mathbf{r} = 0$ and $\mathbf{r}\cdot\mathbf{r} = 1$. Thus,

$$\left\|\frac{d\mathbf{y}}{dt}\right\|^2 = \frac{\ell^2}{L^2}\left(1 - \left(\frac{dL}{ds}\right)^2\right)\left(\frac{ds}{dt}\right)^2 + \left(\frac{d\ell}{dt}\right)^2.$$

The mapped crease $\mathbf{Y}(t)$ in 3D is defined by $\mathbf{Y}(t) = \mathbf{A} + \ell(t)\mathbf{R}(s(t))$. Then,

$$\left\|\frac{d\mathbf{Y}}{dt}\right\|^2 = \frac{\ell^2}{L^2}\left(1 - \left(\frac{dL}{ds}\right)^2\right)\left(\frac{ds}{dt}\right)^2 + \left(\frac{d\ell}{dt}\right)^2,$$

similarly using $\mathbf{R}\cdot\mathbf{R} = 1$, $\frac{d\mathbf{R}}{ds}\cdot\mathbf{R} = 0$, and $\left\|\frac{d\mathbf{X}}{ds}\right\|^2 = 1$. Therefore, $\left\|\frac{d\mathbf{y}}{dt}\right\|^2 = \left\|\frac{d\mathbf{Y}}{dt}\right\|^2 = 1$ and the mapping is isometric. $\square$

A similar argument works for cylindrical surfaces.

LEMMA 7.4. *If an arclength-parameterized crease $\mathbf{x}(s)$ has unique rule segments on one side parallel to $\mathbf{r}$, such that $\mathbf{r}$ is perpendicular to segment c, then an embedding $\mathbf{f}$ is a proper folding if and only if folded curve $\mathbf{X} = \mathbf{f}\circ\mathbf{x}$ is also arclength parameterized, and the perpendicular rule segments from $\mathbf{x}(s)$ to c map isometrically to rule segments from $\mathbf{X}(s)$ perpendicularly to a planar curve C, where $C = \mathbf{f}\circ c$.*

PROOF. Necessity ("only if" part) is obvious, so we prove sufficiency ("if" part). The folded curve is arclength parameterized by s as $\frac{d\mathbf{X}(s)}{ds} = \frac{d\mathbf{x}(s)}{ds} = 1$, and the length of ruling segment $L(s)$ must equal $L(s) = \|\mathbf{x}(s) - \mathbf{c}(s)\| = \|\mathbf{X}(s) - \mathbf{C}(s)\|$. Let $\mathbf{r}$ denote the unit ruling vectors from the apex toward the curve in 2D, i.e., $\mathbf{x}(s) = \mathbf{c}(s) + L(s)\mathbf{r}$. Similarly denote the unit ruling vector in 3D by $\mathbf{X}(s) = \mathbf{C}(s) + L(s)\mathbf{R}$. Consider a coordinate system using arclength s and length along the ruled segments ℓ. The face is uniquely ruled between the crease and the curve at any point, so (s, ℓ) uniquely represent a point on the portion. A point (s, ℓ) in 2D corresponds to $\mathbf{c}(s) + \ell\mathbf{r}$, which is mapped to 3D to $\mathbf{C}(s) + \ell\mathbf{R}$. Consider a 2D C^1 curve $\mathbf{y}(t)$ represented by $(s(t), \ell(t))$, where t is the arclength parameterization. Then, the total derivative of $\mathbf{y}(t) = \mathbf{c}(s) + \ell(t)\mathbf{r}$ is

$$\frac{d\mathbf{y}}{dt} = \frac{\partial \mathbf{y}}{\partial s}\frac{ds}{dt} + \frac{\partial \mathbf{y}}{\partial \ell}\frac{d\ell}{dt} = \frac{d\mathbf{c}}{ds}\frac{ds}{dt} + \mathbf{r}\frac{d\ell}{dt}.$$

Then,

$$\left\|\frac{d\mathbf{y}}{dt}\right\|^2 = \left\|\frac{d\mathbf{c}}{ds}\right\|^2 \left(\frac{ds}{dt}\right)^2 + 2\frac{d\mathbf{c}}{ds}\cdot\mathbf{r}\left(\frac{ds}{dt}\right)\left(\frac{d\ell}{dt}\right) + \|\mathbf{r}\|^2\left(\frac{d\ell}{dt}\right)^2$$

$$= \left\|\frac{d\mathbf{c}}{ds}\right\|^2 \left(\frac{ds}{dt}\right)^2 + \left(\frac{d\ell}{dt}\right)^2,$$

where we used $\mathbf{r}\cdot\mathbf{r} = 1$ and $\frac{d\mathbf{c}(s)}{ds}\cdot\mathbf{r} = 0$. Now differentiate $L(s)\mathbf{r} + \mathbf{c}(s) = \mathbf{x}(s)$ to obtain

$$\frac{d\mathbf{c}}{ds} + \frac{dL}{ds}\mathbf{r} = \frac{d\mathbf{x}}{ds}.$$

By taking the dot product,

$$\left\|\frac{d\mathbf{c}}{ds}\right\|^2 + \left(\frac{dL}{ds}\right)^2 = \left\|\frac{d\mathbf{x}}{ds}\right\|^2 = 1,$$

again using $\frac{d\mathbf{c}}{ds}\cdot\mathbf{r} = 0$ and $\mathbf{r}\cdot\mathbf{r} = 1$. Thus,

$$\left\|\frac{d\mathbf{y}}{dt}\right\|^2 = \left(1 - \left(\frac{dL}{ds}\right)^2\right)\left(\frac{ds}{dt}\right)^2 + \left(\frac{d\ell}{dt}\right)^2.$$

The mapped crease $\mathbf{Y}(t)$ in 3D is defined by $\mathbf{Y}(t) = \mathbf{C}(s) + \ell(t)\mathbf{R}$. Then,

$$\left\|\frac{d\mathbf{Y}}{dt}\right\|^2 = \left(1 - \left(\frac{dL}{ds}\right)^2\right)\left(\frac{ds}{dt}\right)^2 + \left(\frac{d\ell}{dt}\right)^2,$$

similarly using $\mathbf{R}\cdot\mathbf{R} = 1$, $\frac{d\mathbf{C}}{ds}\cdot\mathbf{R} = 0$, and $\left\|\frac{d\mathbf{X}}{ds}\right\|^2 = 1$. Therefore, $\left\|\frac{d\mathbf{y}}{dt}\right\|^2 = \left\|\frac{d\mathbf{Y}}{dt}\right\|^2 = 1$ and the mapping is isometric.   □

By Lemmas 7.3 and 7.4, the existence of the folded form is ensured by constructing the folded crease $f(\gamma)$ such that, in the folded state, the distance between $V_{0,1}$ and $f(\gamma(t))$ is always $r(t)$ and the distance from the xz-plane is always $\ell(t)$. If we view the projection of the curve, this is equivalent to constructing a curve represented by polar coordinate $(\theta(t), h(t))$ $(\theta \in \mathbb{R})$ such that (i) the curve has arclength t and (ii) $\theta(t)$ is a monotonic function (in order to avoid self-intersection). Condition (i) yields a differential equation:

$$1 = h^2\left(\frac{d\theta(t)}{dt}\right)^2 + h'(t)^2.$$

Condition (ii) gives us $0 < \frac{d\theta(t)}{dt}$ and $h(t) > 0$, so the differential equation becomes

$$\frac{d\theta(t)}{dt} = \frac{1}{h(t)}\sqrt{1 - \left(\frac{dh(t)}{dt}\right)^2},$$

which has solution

$$\theta(t) = \int_0^t \frac{1}{h(t)}\sqrt{1 - \left(\frac{dh(t)}{dt}\right)^2}\, dt$$

if and only if $(\frac{dh(t)}{dt})^2 \le 1$ for $t \in (0, 1)$. Combined with condition (ii), $(\frac{dh(t)}{dt})^2 < 1$, and

$$\left(\frac{dh(t)}{dt}\right)^2 = \frac{\left[(t - u) - \frac{1}{2}(v - v^*)\ell'(t)\right]^2}{(t - u)^2 + (v - v^*)\left[\frac{1}{4}(v + v^*) - \ell(t)\right]} < 1,$$

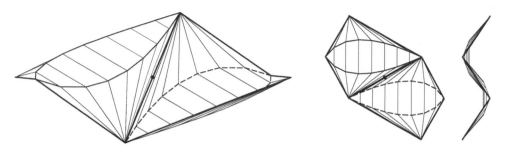

FIGURE 10. The connection of kite structures.

which is equivalent to

$$-\frac{1}{4}(v - v^*)\left[1 + \left(\frac{d\ell(t)}{dt}\right)^2\right] + \left[\frac{1}{2}v - \left(\ell(t) + \frac{d\ell(t)}{dt}(u - t)\right)\right] > 0.$$

Because $\ell(t) + \frac{d\ell(t)}{dt}(u-t)$ represents the y-coordinate of the intersection between the tangent line to $\gamma_{0,0}^+$ at t and a vertical line passing through $V_{0,1}$, $\frac{v}{2} - (\ell(t) + \frac{d\ell(t)}{dt}(u - t))$ is always positive. Also, $1 + (\frac{d\ell(t)}{dt})^2$ is positive, so the condition is given by

$$v - v^* < \frac{4\left[\frac{v}{2} - \left(\ell(t) + \frac{d\ell(t)}{dt}(u - t)\right)\right]}{1 + \left(\frac{d\ell(t)}{dt}\right)^2}.$$

If we define $v_{lim}^* < v$ as

$$v - v_{lim}^* = 4\left[\frac{v}{2} - \left(\ell(t) + \frac{d\ell(t)}{dt}(u - t)\right)\right]\bigg/\left[1 + \left(\frac{d\ell(t)}{dt}\right)^2\right],$$

then there exists a continuous solution for v^* in (v_{lim}^*, v).

Now that we have folded an individual gadget, we can tile the gadget to get a proper folding of the overall crease pattern. Here, we use the fact that the oriented folded module, for a sufficiently small fold angle, projects to a kite in the xy-plane.

Consider inversions of the oriented folded module through the midpoints of its boundary edges, followed by negating all normals to swap the top and bottom sides of the paper (Figure 10). If we consider the xy-projection, the operation corresponds to $180°$ rotation around the midpoint of the kite, resulting in a tessellation. Thus, in particular, there are no collisions between the copies of the folded module. Because each connecting edge is mapped onto itself in 3D, this tessellation has no gaps in 3D. Also, because the boundary is on a ruled segment, the surface normal vector is constant along each edge. The surface normal is flipped by the inversion and then negated back to its original vector, so the surface normals at corresponding points match. Thus, the shared boundaries remain uncreased in the tessellated folding. To show that this tessellated folding comes from one sheet of paper, we can apply the same tiling transformation to the crease-pattern module, which is also a kite, so it tiles the plane with the same topology and intrinsic geometry. Therefore, the plane can fold into the infinitely tiled folding. □

8. Conclusion

We still have a long way to go to obtain a general theory of curved creases. Nonetheless, we hope that the tools built in this work will enable the design and analysis of more curved-crease origami models and will serve as a useful foundation to build up the underlying mathematics.

Acknowledgments

We thank the Huffman family for access to the third author's work and permission to continue in his name.

References

[Demaine and O'Rourke 07] Erik D. Demaine and Joseph O'Rourke. *Geometric Folding Algorithms: Linkages, Origami, Polyhedra.* Cambridge, UK: Cambridge University Press, 2007. MR2354878 (2008g:52001)

[Demaine et al. 11] Erik D. Demaine, Martin L. Demaine, Vi Hart, Gregory N. Price, and Tomohiro Tachi. "(Non)existence of Pleated Folds: How Paper Folds between Creases." *Graphs and Combinatorics* 27:3 (2011), 377–397. MR2787424 (2012i:52030)

[Fuchs and Tabachnikov 99] Dmitry Fuchs and Serge Tabachnikov. "More on Paperfolding." *The American Mathematical Monthly* 106:1 (1999), 27–35. MR1674137 (99m:53009)

[Fuchs and Tabachnikov 07] Dmitry Fuchs and Serge Tabachnikov. "Developable Surfaces." In *Mathematical Omnibus: Thirty Lectures on Classic Mathematics*, Chapter 4. Providence: American Mathematical Society, 2007. MR2350979 (2008h:00002)

[Huffman 76] David A. Huffman. "Curvature and Creases: A Primer on Paper." *IEEE Transactions on Computers* C-25:10 (1976), 1010–1019.

MIT COMPUTER SCIENCE AND ARTIFICIAL INTELLIGENCE LAB., CAMBRIDGE, MASSACHUSETTS
E-mail address: edemaine@mit.edu

MIT COMPUTER SCIENCE AND ARTIFICIAL INTELLIGENCE LAB., CAMBRIDGE, MASSACHUSETTS
E-mail address: mdemaine@mit.edu

DEPARTMENT OF COMPUTER SCIENCE, UNIVERSITY OF CALIFORNIA, SANTA CRUZ, CALIFORNIA

SCHOOL OF ARCHITECTURE, PRATT INSTITUTE, BROOKLYN, NEW YORK
E-mail address: duks@pratt.edu

DEPARTMENT OF GENERAL SYSTEMS STUDIES, THE UNIVERSITY OF TOKYO, JAPAN
E-mail address: tachi@idea.c.u-tokyo.ac.jp

Curve-Folding Polyhedra Skeletons through Smoothing

Suryansh Chandra, Shajay Bhooshan, and Mustafa El-Sayed

1. Introduction

The research and prototypes documented in the chapter operate in the context of the exciting potential of curved-crease folding in manufacturing curved surfaces from flat sheet material. This paper describes a designer-friendly computational method to design and fabricate a class of curved folded geometries—our proposed method generates developable surfaces that are curved-foldable, skeletal representations of a given user-defined, convex mesh. (See, for example, Figure 1.)

FIGURE 1. *Curved Folded Polyhedra Skeleton*, made of aluminium, at the AA Visiting School Bangalore, 2012.

The work draws inspiration both from the precedent works of Richard Sweeney, Ron Resch, and others and from the observed ease of physical exploration, in paper, of such geometries by students in our workshops (Figure 2). Further, we aim to address the current difficulties in recreating that ease in digital explorations. These difficulties stem from both the lack of appropriate geometric descriptions and constructive tools in ubiquitous CAD software; this points toward the need for exploration-friendly digital methods to find and describe such geometries [Bhooshan et al. 14]. Thus, the key contributions of the chapter

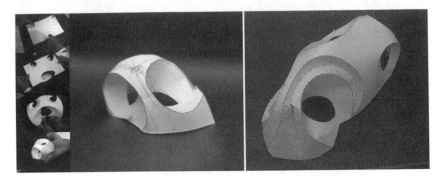

FIGURE 2. Student work in our workshop.

stem from addressing these issues: an extensible, exploration-friendly digital method and the description of procedural methods to produce manufacturing data from digitally produced geometry. It concludes with potential avenues of architectural-scale application of the method.

1.1. Exploratory methods for digital geometry. Most of the precedent projects and available literature on design methods highlight the difficulty in developing an intuitive, exploratory digital-design method to generate feasible three-dimensional geometries. Our initial survey of methods included both the iterative optimization-based method [Kilian et al. 08] and the simple constructive method—the method of reflection [Mitani and Igarashi 11]. Most methods, including the two above, presented difficulties toward incorporation within an intuitive, real-time, edit-and-observe exploratory method. Further, most of the methods aim at applicability toward a wider range of feasible geometries, whereas our interest was a specific class of geometries. Lastly, they are also iterative methods that minimize one or more "energies" with the aim to capture the physical behavior of sheet material. For an extensive overview on the precedents and computational methods related to curve-crease folding, we refer the reader to a survey [Demaine et al. 11].

Our key point of departure was to geometrically construct feasible geometry like Mitani and Igarashi as opposed to a physically based, iterative, construct-and-correct solution. As such, the method benefits speedy computation and thus an edit-and-observe exploratory strategy to design. Critically, however, it is applicable to a specific class of geometries, i.e., convex polyhedra. It is worth mentioning that we do implement an iterative solution to produce planarized polyhedra from nonplanar meshes [Poranne et al. 13], to aid less restrictive modeling operations for the designer.

1.2. Discrete representation for curve-crease folded mesh. There are several discrete representations—*exact* and *inexact*—of curve-crease folded geometries. We chose to use a representation based on planar-quad (PQ) meshes that additionally incorporate *developability* constraints [Kilian et al. 08] (Figure 3). For a comprehensive list of representations, we refer the reader to [Solomon et al. 12]. Given the representation, we used various mesh operations to derive a predominantly quad-faced mesh from the form-found mesh.

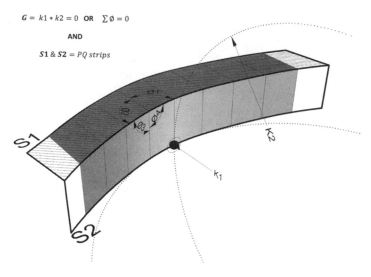

FIGURE 3. Essential requirements of a discrete representation.

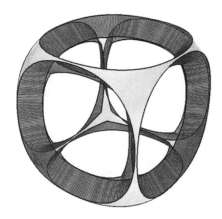

FIGURE 4. Designed surface in white, and derived surface in dark gray.

2. Method

Our proposed method takes a convex, user-defined, input mesh (*base mesh*) and forces its faces toward planarity to produce a polyhedron (Section 2.1). This polyhedron is subsequently used to generate developable surfaces that are its curved-foldable, skeletal representation. This process has two procedural steps—the *designed surface* (Section 2.2), and the *derived surface* (Section 2.3). Lastly, the resultant geometry is used to produce manufacturing information such as cut patterns and their assemblies (Section 2.4).

The designed surface (white surfaces in Figure 4) forms the base structure of the curved folded polyhedron (CFP) and is shaped through parameters external to the method, thereby allowing elaborate interactive control further to the shape of the base mesh itself. The derived surface forms the inward extrusions from the designed surface (dark gray surfaces in Figure 4) and is computed through an adaptation of the reflection method

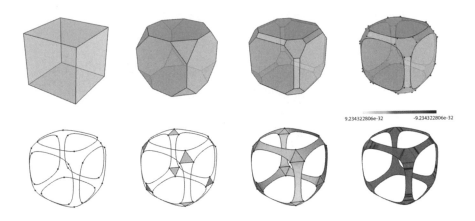

9.234322806e-32   -9.234322806e-32

FIGURE 5. Geometric operations to extract designed surface from a polyhedron.

[Mitani and Igarashi 11] that is capable of generating zero-Gaussian-curvature surfaces. It is worth noting that by generating the derived surface in this manner, there is no explicit computing of rulings, which benefits computing time.

2.1. Planarization of base polyhedron. Curve-folded geometry is still a very challenging domain, and it is well acknowledged that planar curved folds are significantly simpler to solve [Mitani and Igarashi 11]. Further, several iterations of paper models of CFPs demonstrated that the creases remained nearly planar unless they were forced out of the plane by external forces. Therefore, we run an iterative planarization routine similar to the one proposed in [Poranne et al. 13] on the faces of the base mesh, as all curved creases in our proposed method lie on the faces of the polyhedron.

2.2. Designed surface and parametric variations. Our method generates the design surface by applying the following series of operations on a convex polyhedron (Figure 5):

(1) Chamfer Conway operator [Hart 98] is applied to all vertices.
(2) Bevel Conway operator [Hart 98] is applied to all edges.
(3) Cubic Bezier curves are extracted from the faces of the polyhedron.
(4) Planar polygonal surfaces are generated at each vertex.
(5) Translational surfaces are generated at each edge.

In the above sequence, operations 1–3 permit a significant range of design variations and define the curves that form the edges of the designed surface. Operations 4 and 5 are surfacing operations, replacing each vertex of the original polyhedron with a planar polygonal surface and each edge with a translational surface. These translation surfaces have no Gaussian curvature by virtue of the planar faces of the initial polyhedron.

2.3. Derived surface. Our early attempts to compute the derived surface involved using the method of reflection [Mitani and Igarashi 11], but we had limited success with it because the reflected surfaces tended to intersect each other (Figure 6). Subsequently, we used an energy minimization method iteratively converging toward zero-Gaussian-curvature geometries that we describe in [Bhooshan et al. 14]. Eventually, we found a noniterative, closed-form method specific to the geometry of CFPs that is significantly

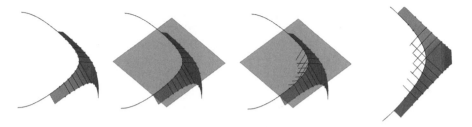

FIGURE 6. The method of reflection produces intersecting surfaces.

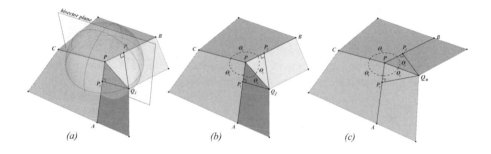

FIGURE 7. Calculating the derived surface.

faster to compute over the energy minimization method. This is the method described here.

Our proposed method operates on a discretized mesh representation of the designed surface and computes an extrusion vector at each vertex such that the angles projected by the existing faces and the new faces sums up to 360 degrees. In Figure 7, consider P, A, and B to be border vertices and the line PC to be an interior edge on the designed surface. A solution set $\{Q\}$ exists such that for every vertex Q_i

$$\angle APC + \angle BPC + \angle APQ + \angle BPQ = 2\pi$$

or

$$\theta_1 + \theta_2 + \theta_x + \theta_y = 2\pi.$$

Because $\{Q\}$ contains an infinite number of solutions, we constraint our solution space to the bisector plane of angle $\angle APB$ (Figure 7(a)) and its intersection with a unit sphere centered at P, which limits the number of solutions to two: the folded-state with vertex Q_f (Figure 7(b)), and a the unfolded-state with vertex Q_u (Figure 7(c)). We could also make this assumption about other linear and polynomial relations between θ_x and θ_y, which will result in higher-order roots for Q_i. If no assumption is made regarding the relation between the two angles, the solution space $\{Q\}$ would be the intersection of a quartic surface and the unit sphere centered at P. The formulation noted in [Kilian et al. 08] would imply a similar result.

If P_1 and P_2 are points on edges PA and PB, respectively, nearest to Q_i, and if d_1 and d_2 are the distances from P to P_1 and P_2, respectively, we can state that

$$d_1 = d_2 = \sqrt{(\cos(2\pi - \theta_1 - \theta_2) + 1)0.5}.$$

Thus, the solution can be understood as the intersection of a unit sphere centered at P, with a line connecting Q_u and Q_f. Further, this line is the intersection of two planes, one

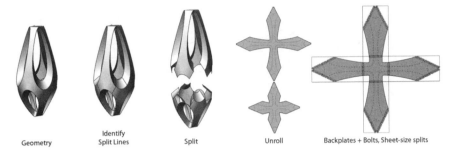

Geometry | Identify Split Lines | Split | Unroll | Backplates + Bolts, Sheet-size splits

FIGURE 8. Process of CAD/CAM data generation.

centered at P_1 with PA as its normal and the other centered at P_2 and PB as its normal. This results in a system with quadratic roots. This makes the length of the extrusion vector the only designer-controllable parameter in the derived surface:

$$\mathbf{Q}_u = \mathbf{P}_0 + \lambda_u \mathbf{V} \quad \text{and} \quad \mathbf{Q}_f = \mathbf{P}_0 + \lambda_f \mathbf{V},$$

where

$$\lambda_u = \frac{-b - \sqrt{b^2 - 4ac}}{2a}, \qquad \lambda_f = \frac{-b + \sqrt{b^2 - 4ac}}{2a},$$

$$\mathbf{V} = \mathbf{PA} \times \mathbf{PB},$$

$$a = \mathbf{V} \cdot \mathbf{V},$$

$$b = 2(\mathbf{V} \cdot \mathbf{P}),$$

$$c = (\mathbf{P}_0 \cdot \mathbf{P}_0 - 1),$$

$$\mathbf{P}_0 = \langle x_0, y_0, 0 \rangle, \qquad x_0 = \frac{d_1 y_2 - y_1 d_2}{x_1 y_2 - y_1 x_2}, \qquad y_0 = \frac{x_1 d_2 - d_1 x_2}{x_1 y_2 - y_1 x_2},$$

$$d_1 = d_2 = \sqrt{(\cos(2\pi - \theta_1 - \theta_2) + 1)0.5}.$$

In the equations above, bold face indicates vectors, $\times$ is the cross product, and $\cdot$ is the dot product of two vectors.

2.4. Manufacturing Information. The resultant geometry is used to generate manufacturing information, in the form of unfolded CAD/CAM data. (See Figure 8.)

3. Results and Discussion

The resulting geometry is a zero-Gaussian-curvature mesh. The method currently does not solve the mesh faces for planarity. For the purpose of architectural installations in paper and sheet aluminium, we have found the resulting geometry to be within acceptable tolerance for fabrication, as further illustrated by the reasonably precise edge alignment in a cluster of the 1 m tall polyhedra in Figure 9 made from 1.5 mm cardstock paper.

Unfolding a resultant quad mesh produces an unfold error due to the nonplanarity of mesh faces. However, since we were working with a discrete representation of a curve-foldable mesh that relied on a PQ mesh with a developability constraint, we addressed the planarity issue in the two-dimensional unfolded pattern. This means that the physical object will not match the digital three-dimensional model. However, because the sculpture is a free-standing object and due to constraints of time, this issue was not addressed. In order to quantify the error in the geometry, we digitally unfolded different mesh resolution

FIGURE 9. Precise edge alignment in clusters of CFPs.

	Discretization Level 1	Discretization Level 2	Discretization Level 3	Discretization Level 4
Average Edge Length	15.0	11.6	8.8	6.8
Minimum Error	0.076	0.093	0.124	0.129
Maximum Error	0.137	0.164	1.05	1.54

TABLE 1. Key results from unfold error measurements.

variants of the same base polyhedron (Table 1). We observed that lower mesh resolution computed to significantly higher accuracy.

4. Conclusion

Here we have described a method of generating a class of curved folded geometry—a smoothed skeleton of a convex polyhedron—as also producing the necessary fabrication information from the generated geometries. Further, we also noted the intuitive nature of using polyhedral meshes and their manipulation using ubiquitous mesh modeling tools.

FIGURE 10. Parametric variations of the designed and derived surface computed from the same base polyhedron.

This then enables speedy exploration of variations and the edit-and-observe strategies of designers (Figure 10).

Apart from the obvious benefit of using sheet material to produce curved surfaces, we also noted the fabrication benefits of such geometry in general. They ease the on-site description of geometry and assembly of parts due to their capacity to be formed with minimal effort. In our workshops, we have been able to build 2 m tall CFPs from sheet aluminium with teams of 10–15 students within a matter of 6–8 hours (Figure 11).

Based on the prototypes and research thus far, we can envision the use of the method in the production of architectural-scale assembly of skeletal geometries. Such folded geometries, especially from smooth sheet material such as aluminium or plastic, could also be beneficial in their use as false-work or lost form-work to cast concrete and other hardening structural materials [Larsen et al. 13].

5. Future Work

A significant aspect of curved folded geometries in general is that, barring a few exceptions [Rohim et al. 13], not much is known in regard to their structural behavior. Some of difficulties of using conventional FEM methods on such geometries stems from complexities in computationally describing features such as removal of material along crease lines, tendencies of spring-back in the folded shape, etc. Thus, an exciting and critical aspect of future work that we envision is the development of discrete (i.e., bar-and-node) form-finding methods that also incorporate structural parameters alongside the exploratory design and fabrication parameters that we currently investigate.

Acknowledgments

We would like to thank Zaha Hadid Architects and the AA School of Architecture for providing platforms to conduct this research. Further, we would like to thank AA Visiting School Bangalore teams from 2012 and 2013 and the Fragile Beasts 2014 workshop team

FIGURE 11. Some 2 m long aluminium CFPs folded and assembled in 6 hours by a group of 15 students.

from Lodz University of Technology for helping with the design and execution of the installations.

References

[Bhooshan et al. 14] Shajay Bhooshan, Mustafa El-Sayed, and Suryansh Chandra. "Design-Friendly Strategies for Computational Form-Finding of Curved-Folded Geometries: A Case Study." In *Proceedings of the Symposium on Simulation for Architecture & Urban Design* (SimAUD 2014), edited by Dr. David Gerber and Rhys Goldstein, pp. 117–124. San Diego, CA: Society for Computer Simulation International, 2014.

[Demaine et al. 11] Eric Demaine, Martin Demaine, Duks Koschitz, and Tomohiro Tachi. "Curved Crease Folding: A Review on Art, Design and Mathematics." In *Proceedings of the IABSE-IASS Symposium: Taller, Longer, Lighter (IABSE-IASS2011)*, pp. 20–23. London: IABSE/IASS, 2011.

[Hart 98] George W. Hart. "Conway Notation for Polyhedra." http://www.georgehart.com/virtual-polyhedra/conway_notation.html, 1998.

[Kilian et al. 08] Martin Kilian, Simon Flöry, Zhonggui Chen, Niloy J. Mitra, Alla Sheffer, and Helmut Pottmann. "Curved Folding." In *ACM SIGGRAPH 2008 Papers*, pp. 75–83. New York: ACM, 2008.

[Larsen et al. 13] Niels Martin Larsen, Ole Egholm Pedersen, and David Pigram. "Realisation of Complex Precast Concrete Structures through the Integration of Algorithmic Design and Novel Fabrication Techniques." In *Advances in Architectural Geometry 2012*, edited by Lars Hesselgren at al., pp. 161–174. Vienna: Springer-Verlag, 2013.

[Mitani and Igarashi 11] Jun Mitani and Takeo Igarashi. "Interactive Design of Planar Curved Folding by Reflection." In *Proceedings of the Pacific Conference on Computer Graphics and Applications*, edited by Bing-Yu Chen, Jan Kautz, Tong-Yee Lee, and Ming C. Lin, pp. 77–81. Kaohsiung, Taiwan: The Eurographics Association, 2011.

[Poranne et al. 13] Roi Poranne, Elena Ovreiu, and Craig Gotsman. "Interactive Planarization and Optimization of 3D Meshes." *Computer Graphics Forum* 32:1 (2013), 152–163.

[Rohim et al. 13] Rohamezan Rohim, Kok Keong Choong, and Thavaraj Jeevaratnam. "Structural Behaviour of Origami Inspired Folded Shell Surface." *World Applied Sciences Journal* 24:4 (2013), 497–502.

[Solomon et al. 12] Justin Solomon, Etienne Vouga, Max Wardetzky, and Eitan Grinspun. "Flexible Developable Surfaces." *Computer Graphics Forum* 31:5 (2012), 1567–1576.

Zaha Hadid Architects, London, United Kingdom
E-mail address: s@getautomata.com

Zaha Hadid Architects, London, United Kingdom
E-mail address: shajay.bhooshan@zaha-hadid.com

Zaha Hadid Architects, London, United Kingdom
E-mail address: m@getautomata.com

Design Methods of Origami Tessellations for Triangular Spiral Multiple Tilings

Takamichi Sushida, Akio Hizume, and Yoshikazu Yamagishi

1. Introduction

Origami tessellation is an origami technique that represents geometric tiling patterns by using one sheet of paper. Recently, several *origami sheets* (diagrams of crease lines, also know as *crease patterns*) for origami tessellations have been devised by many artists and scientists. In particular, there is a mathematical design method of origami sheets for origami tessellations described by Lang and Bateman [Lang and Bateman 11]. Also, as a recent development, computational design methods have enabled the generation of origami tessellations for complicated geometric patterns [Tachi 13].

On one hand, a history of origami tessellations for triangular spiral multiple tilings starts from origami towers with rotational symmetry devised by Fuse [Fuse 02]. The towers are origami models called *whirlpool spirals*, and their origami sheets allow flat-foldability. In particular, when they are folded flatly, their top-down views are polygonal tilings with rotational symmetry. Thus, the whirlpool spirals are origami tessellations. Figure 1 shows an example of a whirlpool spiral with fivefold rotational symmetry. (See [Fuse 12] for more such origami artwork.)

On the other hand, Hizume focused on beautiful phyllotactic patterns of sunflower seeds [Azukawa 85] and devised a family of phyllotactic triangular spiral tilings called *Fibonacci tornados* [Hizume 05] (see Figure 2(c)), where *phyllotaxis* is a term referring to arrangements of leaves and other organs of plants, and it is well known that the golden ratio $\tau = (1 + \sqrt{5})/2$ and Fibonacci numbers play vital roles in such arrangements. Moreover, he designed origami sheets for origami tessellations of Fibonacci tornados by applying the design method of the whirlpool spirals. (See [Hizume 06] for examples of his artwork.)

After that, Hizume and Yamagishi expanded a theory of triangular spiral tilings by applying the continued fraction theory [Hizume 08, Hizume and Yamagishi 09]. Recently, we described a topological and geometrical study of triangular spiral tilings comprehensively in [Sushida et al. 12]. In this study, we constructed a generalized framework of spiral multiple tilings that admit multiple coverings of the plane. Throughout this study, we obtained several examples of spiral multiple tilings by typical triangles such as the equilateral triangle and origami sheets of their origami tessellations. An origami sheet of a spiral multiple tiling by right triangles with the angles 30°, 60°, and 90° and its composition were selected for the cover of *Journal of Physics A: Mathematical and Theoretical*, Volume 45, Number 23, 2012.

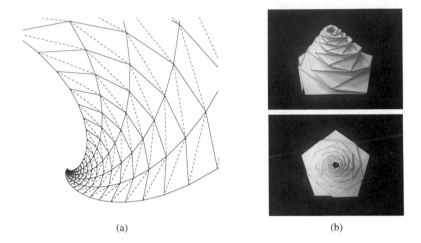

(a)   (b)

FIGURE 1. (a) An origami sheet for a whirlpool spiral with fivefold rotational symmetry. Solid lines are mountain folds and dashed lines are
valley folds. (b) Side view before being squashed (top) and top-down
view after being squashed (bottom). This origami sheet represents an
origami tessellation for a tiling by triangles with angles 30°, 45°, and
105°. See [Fuse 02].

In this work, we present a design method of origami sheets for origami tessellations
of triangular spiral multiple tilings. Moreover, we show that these origami sheets allow at
least one-degree-of-freedom (DOF) folding motion, by representing a folding motion as
a one-parameter family of discrete surfaces, where we admit intersections of facets. This
folding motion implies that all folding angles are parameterized by one parameter. Unfortunately, we do not know whether the origami sheets allow two-DOF, or more, folding
motions.

First, in Section 2, we review three design methods of triangular spiral multiple tilings,
which appear in [Sushida et al. 12]. In the beginning of Section 3, we show a design
method of origami sheets of origami tessellations that represent triangular spiral multiple
tilings with opposed parastichy pairs. Later in Section 3, we show a design method having one-DOF folding motion of these origami sheets. Finally, in Section 4, we present a
conclusion and future work.

At the Sixth International Meeting on Origami Science, Mathematics and Education
(6OSME), we presented examples of origami sheets for triangular spiral tilings. Readers can download these origami sheets from the following webpage: http://www.math.
ryukoku.ac.jp/~www-yg/sushida/sushida_en.html. Moreover, by applying the design methods described here, readers can make new examples of triangular spiral multiple tilings and
corresponding origami sheets and observe the one-DOF folding motion as a computational
simulation.

2. Triangular Spiral Multiple Tilings

In tiling theory [Grünbaum and Shephard 87], a *tiling* of a two-dimensional manifold
is defined as a family of topological disks that cover the manifold without gaps or overlaps.
Each topological disk is called a *tile*.

In this section, we review three design methods for triangular spiral multiple tilings as a fundamental preparation of this work. See [Sushida et al. 12] for mathematical descriptions of triangular spiral multiple tilings.

2.1. A fundamental design method of triangular spiral multiple tilings. A *triangular spiral multiple tiling* is a triangular tiling of the punctured plane $\mathbb{C}^* := \mathbb{C}\backslash\{0\}$ that admits a transitive action of a similarity transformation group $S = \{z^j : j \in \mathbb{Z}\}$ generated by a single element $z = re^{\sqrt{-1}\theta}$, where $0 < r < 1$ and $\theta/2\pi \in \mathbb{R}\backslash\mathbb{Z}$.

DESIGN METHOD 1. The following steps give a fundamental design method of triangular spiral multiple tilings:

(1) Fix the parameters r and θ.
(2) Take relatively prime integers $m, n > 0$.
(3) Connect z^j with z^{j+m} and z^j with z^{j+n} by line segments, respectively.
(4) Adjust the parameters r and θ such that $T_0 := \square(1, z^m, z^{m+n}, z^n)$ is a quadrilateral in this order of vertices. Then, the family of quadrilaterals

(2.1) $$\mathcal{T} = \{T_j : j \in \mathbb{Z}\}, \quad T_j := \square(z^j, z^{j+m}, z^{j+m+n}, z^{j+n}),$$

gives a quadrilateral spiral multiple tiling with multiplicity $|v|$, where

(2.2) $$v = \frac{n\mathrm{Arg}(z^m) - m\mathrm{Arg}(z^n)}{2\pi}.$$

Note that $-\pi < \mathrm{Arg}(z) \leq \pi$ denotes the principal argument of $z \neq 0$.

(5) Adjust the parameters r and θ such that three vertices of the quadrilateral T_0 lie on a same line. Then, the quadrilateral spiral multiple tiling in Equation (2.1) with multiplicity $|v|$ becomes a triangular spiral multiple tiling.

In the quadrilateral or triangular spiral multiple tilings $\mathcal{T}$, the pair (m, n) is called the *parastichy pair* in phyllotaxis theory [Jean 94]. If $\mathrm{Arg}(z^m)\mathrm{Arg}(z^n) < 0$, (m, n) is called an *opposed parastichy pair*. Otherwise, if $\mathrm{Arg}(z^m)\mathrm{Arg}(z^n) > 0$, it is called a *non-opposed parastichy pair*.

Next, we review two design methods for triangular spiral multiple tilings with opposed parastichy pairs. When a complex number z produce a triangular spiral multiple tiling with an opposed parastichy pair (m, n), the three vertices z^m, z^{m+n}, and z^n lie on a same line in this order of vertices. Thus, we obtain the following equation:

(2.3) $$r^m \sin n\theta - r^n \sin m\theta + \sin(m - n)\theta = 0.$$

Equation (2.3) plays a vital role in the later two design methods. Figure 2 shows an example obtained by applying Design Method 1.

2.2. A design method of triangular spiral multiple tilings with opposed parastichy pairs using continued fractions. First, we recall continued fractions. For $x \in \mathbb{R}$, let

$$x = a_0 + \cfrac{1}{a_1 + \cfrac{1}{a_2 + \cdots}}, \quad a_0 \in \mathbb{Z}, \ a_i \in \mathbb{N}, \ i \in \mathbb{N},$$

be a *continued fraction expansion* of x.

Second, we recall convergents of $x \in \mathbb{R}$. We define the sequences $\{p_i : i \geq -1\}$ and $\{q_i : i \geq -1\}$ with $p_{-1} = 1$, $p_0 = a_0$, $p_1 = a_0a_1 + 1$, $p_i = a_ip_{i-1} + p_{i-2}$ $(i \geq 2)$; and $q_{-1} = 0$, $q_0 = 1$, $q_1 = a_1$, $q_i = a_iq_{i-1} + q_{i-2}$ $(i \geq 2)$, respectively. Then, the finite continued fraction $p_i/q_i = [a_0, a_1, a_2, \cdots, a_i]$ is called a *principal convergent* of x. Next, we define the sequences $\{p_{i,k} : i \geq -1, 0 < k < a_{i+1}\}$ and $\{q_{i,k} : i \geq -1, 0 < k < a_{i+1}\}$

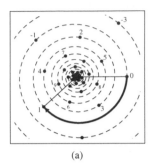 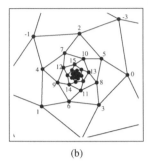 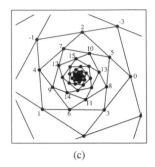

(a)   (b)   (c)

FIGURE 2. (a) The complex sequence S determined by $r = 0.9$ and $\theta = 2\pi(\tau - 2)$. Each number $j \in \mathbb{Z}$ indicates a position of the complex coordinate $z^j \in S$. A marked curve indicates the angle $\theta = 2\pi(\tau - 2) \simeq -137.5°$. (b) A quadrilateral spiral tiling with the sequence S of (a). The opposed parastichy pair is $(m, n) = (5, 3)$. (c) A triangular spiral tiling obtained by adjusting the parameter r, where an adjusted parameter is $r = 0.9328\ldots$ determined as a unique root of Equation (2.3) for $m = 5$, $n = 3$, and $\theta = 2\pi(\tau - 2)$.

with $p_{i,k} = a_i p_i + p_{i-1}$ and $q_{i,k} = a_i q_i + q_{i-1}$. Then, the finite continued fraction $p_{i,k}/q_{i,k} = [a_0, a_1, a_2, \cdots, a_i, k]$, $0 < k < a_{i+1}$, is called an *intermediate convergent* of x. Here, we have $p_{i,0} = p_i$, $p_{i,a_{i+1}} = p_{i+1}$, $q_{i,0} = q_i$, and $q_{i,a_{i+1}} = q_{i+1}$. Also, if x is a rational number, then its continued fraction expansion is finite. See [Hardy and Wright 08] for the continued fraction theory.

DESIGN METHOD 2. The following steps give a design method of triangular spiral multiple tilings with opposed parastichy pairs considering the continued fractions:

(1) Fix $\theta/2\pi \in \mathbb{R}\backslash\mathbb{Z}$ and an integer $v \neq 0$. Then, obtain convergents by the continued fraction expansion of $\theta/2\pi v$.

(2) Choose a pair $(m, n) = (q_i, q_{i,k})$ $(i \geq 0, 0 < k \leq a_{i+1})$ such that $(m, n) \neq (1, 1), (1, 2), (2, 1)$.

(3) For a chosen pair $(m, n) = (q_i, q_{i,k})$, $0 < r < 1$ is determined as a unique root of Equation (2.3). Thus, the family in Equation (2.1) produced by $z = re^{\sqrt{-1}\theta}$ is a triangular spiral multiple tiling of multiplicity $|v|$ with an opposed parastichy pair $(q_i, q_{i,k})$.

As a simple example, we consider triangular spiral tilings with $\theta = 2\pi(1 + \sqrt{2})$. Principal and intermediate convergents of $1 + \sqrt{2}$ are given as

$$\frac{1}{1} < \frac{2}{1} < \frac{7}{3} < \frac{12}{5} < \cdots < 1 + \sqrt{2} < \cdots < \frac{29}{12} < \frac{17}{7} < \frac{5}{2} < \frac{3}{1}.$$

Thus, we obtain $(m, n) = (3, 2), (5, 2), (5, 7), (5, 12), \ldots$ as pairs that admit spiral tilings. In fact, for each pair (m, n), $0 < r < 1$ is determined as a unique root of Equation (2.3). If we take $(m, n) = (5, 2)$, then $r = 0.9330\ldots$ is determined uniquely. Figure 3(a) shows a triangular spiral tiling with an opposed parastichy pair $(5, 2)$.

As a remark, note that triangular spiral multiple tilings of multiplicity $|v|$ with non-opposed parastichy pairs are not derived by the continued fractions of $\theta/2\pi v$.

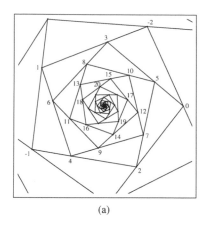 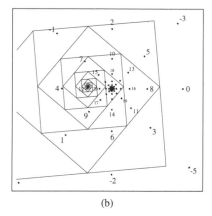

(a)   (b)

FIGURE 3. (a) A triangular spiral tiling with an opposed parastichy pair
$(5, 2)$, where $r = 0.9330\ldots$ and $\theta = 2\pi(1 + \sqrt{2})$. (b) A spiral tiling by
isosceles right triangles, with an opposed parastichy pair $(5, 3)$, where
$r = 0.9161\ldots$ and $\theta = -\frac{3\pi}{4}$.

**2.3. A design method of triangular spiral multiple tilings with opposed paras-
tichy pairs considering the shapes of triangles.** Let $m > n > 0$ be relatively prime
integers. If the three vertices z^m, z^{m+n} and z^n lie on a same line in this order of vertices,
then a quadrilateral spiral multiple tiling $\mathcal{T}$ becomes a triangular spiral multiple tiling with
an opposed parastichy pair (m, n). Suppose that $\mathrm{Arg}(z^n) < 0 < \mathrm{Arg}(z^m)$. As an important
property, the four points 0, z^m, 1, and z^n lie on a same circle in this order of vertices. Thus,
the Inscribed Angle Theorem implies that

$$\mathrm{Arg}(z^m) = \angle(1, z^m, z^n), \quad -\mathrm{Arg}(z^n) = \angle(z^m, z^n, 1),$$

where

$$\angle(z_1, z_2, z_3) := \mathrm{Arg}\left(\frac{z_1 - z_2}{z_3 - z_2}\right).$$

DESIGN METHOD 3. The following steps give a design method of triangular spiral multiple tilings with opposed parastichy pairs considering the shapes of triangles:

(1) Fix the shape of the triangle $\triangle(1, z^m, z^n)$. That is, we give the following:

$$\angle(1, z^m, z^n) = \alpha, \quad \angle(z^m, z^n, 1) = \beta.$$

(2) Fix a multiplicity v, where $v \neq 0$ is an integer.
(3) By Equation (2.2), we obtain the equation

$$n\alpha + m\beta = 2\pi v.$$

So, we obtain one or more pairs (m, n), where $(m, n) \neq (1, 2), (2, 1)$.
(4) Take a pair (m, n). Then, θ is determined. If there exists $0 < r < 1$ such that
Equation (2.3) holds, then the family in Equation (2.1) produced by $z = re^{\sqrt{-1}\theta}$
is a spiral multiple tiling by a fixed triangle of multiplicity $|v|$ with an opposed
parastichy pair (m, n).

Here, we consider whether the isosceles right triangle admits a spiral tiling of the
plane $\mathbb{C}^*$. Since the shape of a triangular tile is given as the isosceles right triangle, $\alpha = \pi/4$
and $\beta = \pi/4$ in Design Method 3. Since we consider a tiling of the plane $\mathbb{C}^*$, we suppose

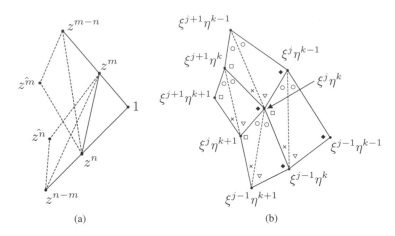

FIGURE 4. (a) A graph of the two quadrilaterals $\square(1, z^{m-n}, \hat{z^m}, z^n)$ and $\square(1, z^m, \hat{z^n}, z^{n-m})$. (b) A graph of a part of the origami sheet at the point $\xi^j \eta^k$. Angles marked with the same symbol have the same angle, and so this pattern is flat-foldable.

$v = 1$. Thus, $m + n = 8$ holds. So, we obtain the pairs $(m, n) = (1, 7), (3, 5), (5, 3), (7, 1)$, and hence $z = (0.9161\ldots)e^{-3\pi\sqrt{-1}/4}$, $z = (0.9074\ldots)e^{\pi\sqrt{-1}/4}$, $z = (0.9074\ldots)e^{-\pi\sqrt{-1}/4}$, and $z = (0.9161\ldots)e^{3\pi\sqrt{-1}/4}$ produce the respective triangular spiral tiling by isosceles right triangles. Figure 3(b) shows a spiral tiling by isosceles right triangles with an opposed parastichy pair $(5, 3)$.

3. Origami Tessellations for Triangular Spiral Multiple Tilings

In this section, we show a design method of origami sheets for origami tessellations of triangular spiral multiple tilings with opposed parastichy pairs. By representing a folding motion of an origami sheet as a one-parameter family of discrete surfaces, we show that this method allows at least one-DOF folding motion.

3.1. A design method of origami sheets for origami tessellations of triangular spiral multiple tilings with opposed parastichy pairs. Let $m, n > 0$ be relatively prime integers, and suppose that the family in Equation (2.1) produced by $z = re^{\sqrt{-1}\theta}$ is a triangular spiral multiple tiling with an opposed parastichy pair (m, n). Then, the three vertices z^m, z^{m+n}, and z^n lie on a same line in this order of vertices. Thus, we obtain the two quadrilaterals $\square(1, z^{m-n}, \hat{z^m}, z^n)$ and $\square(1, z^m, \hat{z^n}, z^{n-m})$, such as in Figure 4(a), where $\hat{z^m}$ indicates a symmetric point of z^m for the line segment $\ell(z^{m-n}, z^n)$ and $\hat{z^n}$ indicates a symmetric point of z^n for the line segment $\ell(z^m, z^{n-m})$.

DESIGN METHOD 4. The following steps give a design method of origami sheets for origami tessellations focused on the quadrilateral $\square(1, z^{m-n}, \hat{z^m}, z^n)$:

(1) The symmetric point $\hat{z^m}$ is written as

$$\hat{z^m} = z^{m-n} + (z^n - z^{m-n})\overline{\left(\frac{z^m - z^{m-n}}{z^n - z^{m-n}}\right)},$$

where $\bar{z}$ indicates the conjugate complex number of $z \in \mathbb{C}$.

(2) Consider two linear fractional transformations $f_1 : \mathbb{C} \to \mathbb{C}$ and $f_2 : \mathbb{C} \to \mathbb{C}$ with the conditions $f_1(1) = z^{m-n}$, $f_1(z^n) = \hat{z}^m$, $f_2(1) = z^n$, and $f_2(z^{m-n}) = \hat{z}^m$. By the conditions, $f_1 = f_1(w)$ and $f_2 = f_2(w)$ are written as

$$f_1(w) = \frac{(\hat{z}^m - z^{m-n})w - \hat{z}^m + z^m}{z^n - 1}, \quad f_2(w) = \frac{(\hat{z}^m - z^n)w - \hat{z}^m + z^m}{z^{m-n} - 1}.$$

(3) Let f_1^* and f_2^* be fixed points of f_1 and f_2, respectively. By solving the equations $f_1(w) = w$ and $f_2(w) = w$, f_1^* and f_2^* are written as follows:

$$f^* := f_1^* = f_2^* = \frac{\hat{z}^m - z^m}{\hat{z}^m + 1 - z^{m-n} - z^n}.$$

(4) Let

$$\xi := \frac{z^{m-n} - f^*}{1 - f^*}, \quad \eta := \frac{z^n - f^*}{1 - f^*}.$$

Then, the following holds:

$$|\xi^n| = |\xi|^n = |z^{m-n}|^n = |z^m| = |z^n|^{m-n} = |\eta|^{m-n} = |\eta^{m-n}|.$$

(5) Thus, the following families of quadrilaterals produce origami sheets for origami tessellations of triangular spiral (multiple) tilings:

$$O_1 := \{O_{j,k} : j \in \mathbb{Z}, \ k \in \mathbb{Z} \text{ with } 0 \leq k \leq |m - n| - 1\},$$
$$O_2 := \{O_{j,k} : j \in \mathbb{Z} \text{ with } 0 \leq j \leq |n| - 1, \ k \in \mathbb{Z}\},$$

where

$$O_{j,k} := \square(\xi^j \eta^k, \xi^{j+1} \eta^k, \xi^{j+1} \eta^{k+1}, \xi^j \eta^{k+1}).$$

The boundaries of $O_{j,k}$ and the line segments $\ell(\xi^{j+1}\eta^k, \xi^j\eta^{k+1})$ are crease lines. The former are mountain folds and the latter are valley folds. In particular, O_1 and O_2 are flat-foldable. (See Figure 4(b).)

In Design Method 4, by replacing (m, n) with (n, m), we can obtain origami sheets based on the quadrilateral $\square(1, z^m, \hat{z}^n, z^{n-m})$. Figure 5 shows origami sheets for a spiral tiling by isosceles right triangles shown in Figure 3(b).

3.2. A design method of one-DOF folding motion.
We show a design method of one-DOF folding motion represented as a one-parameter family of discrete surfaces described by two affine transformations of $\mathbb{R}^3$.

DESIGN METHOD 5. The following steps give a design method of one-DOF folding motion of origami sheets O_1 and O_2 obtained by Design Method 4:

(1) Suppose that

$$a = \begin{pmatrix} 1 \\ 0 \\ 0 \end{pmatrix}, \quad b = \begin{pmatrix} \mathrm{Re}(\xi) \\ \mathrm{Im}(\xi) \\ 0 \end{pmatrix}, \quad c = \begin{pmatrix} \mathrm{Re}(\xi\eta) \\ \mathrm{Im}(\xi\eta) \\ 0 \end{pmatrix}, \quad d = \begin{pmatrix} \mathrm{Re}(\eta) \\ \mathrm{Im}(\eta) \\ 0 \end{pmatrix}.$$

(2) Recall the Rodrigues rotation formula. It is a rotation matrix with rotation axis $v = (v_x, v_y, v_z) \neq (0, 0, 0)$ and rotation angle $t \in \mathbb{R}$, which is given as follows:

$$U(t; v) = I + V \sin t + V^2(1 - \cos t),$$

$$I = \begin{pmatrix} 1 & 0 & 0 \\ 0 & 1 & 0 \\ 0 & 0 & 1 \end{pmatrix}, \quad V = \begin{pmatrix} 0 & -v_z & v_y \\ v_z & 0 & -v_x \\ -v_y & v_x & 0 \end{pmatrix}.$$

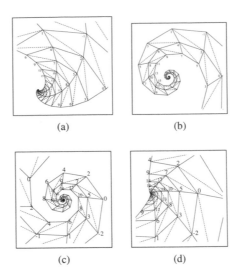

(a)   (b)

(c)   (d)

FIGURE 5. Origami sheets for a spiral tiling by isosceles right triangles shown in Figure 3(b). In each origami sheet, the solid lines indicate mountain folds and the dashed lines valley folds. When an origami sheet is folded flat, each label corresponds to the label of a triangular spiral tiling of Figure 3(b).

For $0 \leq t \leq \pi$, let

$$c(t) = U(t; v)(c - b) + b = U(t; v)(c - d) + d,$$

where

$$v = \frac{b - d}{|b - d|}.$$

(3) Consider two affine transformations

$$\psi_1 : \mathbb{R}^3 \to \mathbb{R}^3, \ \psi_1(x) := \lambda_1 U_1(x - a) + b = \lambda_1 U_1(x - d) + c(t),$$

$$\psi_2 : \mathbb{R}^3 \to \mathbb{R}^3, \ \psi_2(x) := \lambda_2 U_2(x - a) + d = \lambda_2 U_2(x - b) + c(t),$$

with conditions $\psi_1(a) = b$, $\psi_1(d) = c(t)$, $\psi_2(a) = d$, and $\psi_2(b) = c(t)$, where $\lambda_1, \lambda_2 > 0$ are scalars and U_1, U_2 are rotation matrices (3×3 orthogonal matrices).

(4) By the above conditions, we have

$$\lambda_1 = \frac{|b - c(t)|}{|a - d|}, \ \ \lambda_2 = \frac{|d - c(t)|}{|a - b|}.$$

(5) We assume that ψ_1 and ψ_2 have one fixed point each. Let x_1 and x_2 be the fixed points of ψ_1 and ψ_2, respectively. Then, fixed points x_1 and x_2 are written as

$$x_1 := (I - \lambda_1 U_1)^{-1}(b - \lambda_1 U_1 a), \ \ x_2 := (I - \lambda_2 U_2)^{-1}(d - \lambda_2 U_2 a).$$

Since two fixed points of two similarity transformations in O_1 and O_2 are the same point, we assume that $x_1 = x_2$. Here, $x_1 = x_2$ if and only if U_1 and U_2 are commutative, i.e., $U_1 U_2 = U_2 U_1$. Let v_1 and v_2 be unit vectors such that $U_1 v_1 = v_1$ and $U_2 v_2 = v_2$. Assume that $U_1, U_2 \neq I$. Then, we obtain

$$v_1 = v_2 = \frac{v}{|v|},$$

where

$$v := \left(\frac{a - d}{|a - d|} - \frac{b - c(t)}{|b - c(t)|} \right) \times \left(\frac{a - b}{|a - b|} - \frac{d - c(t)}{|d - c(t)|} \right).$$

Thus, U_1 and U_2 are determined by solving the following equations:

$$\begin{cases} U_1 v_1 & = v_1, \\ U_1 \dfrac{a - d}{|a - d|} & = \dfrac{b - c(t)}{|b - c(t)|}, \\ U_1 \left(\dfrac{a - d}{|a - d|} \times v_1 \right) & = \dfrac{b - c(t)}{|b - c(t)|} \times v_1, \end{cases} \qquad \begin{cases} U_2 v_2 & = v_2, \\ U_2 \dfrac{a - b}{|a - b|} & = \dfrac{d - c(t)}{|d - c(t)|}, \\ U_2 \left(\dfrac{a - b}{|a - b|} \times v_2 \right) & = \dfrac{d - c(t)}{|d - c(t)|} \times v_2. \end{cases}$$

Hence, ψ_1 and ψ_2 are determined for each $0 \le t \le \pi$.

(6) For each $j, k \in \mathbb{Z}$, let

$$S_{j,k}(t) := \triangle \left(\psi_1^j(\psi_2^k(a)), \psi_1^{j+1}(\psi_2^k(a)), \psi_1^j(\psi_2^{k+1}(a)) \right)$$
$$\cup \triangle \left(\psi_1^{j+1}(\psi_2^k(a)), \psi_1^{j+1}(\psi_2^{k+1}(a)), \psi_1^j(\psi_2^{k+1}(a)) \right)$$

be a facet that consists of two triangles. Then, for each $0 \le t \le \pi$, the families

$$S_1(t) := \{ S_{j,k}(t) : j \in \mathbb{Z}, \ k \in \mathbb{Z} \text{ with } 0 \le k \le |m - n| - 1 \},$$
$$S_2(t) := \{ S_{j,k}(t) : j \in \mathbb{Z} \text{ with } 0 \le j \le |n| - 1, \ k \in \mathbb{Z} \}$$

are discrete surfaces, and one-parameter families $\{ S_1(t) : 0 \le t \le \pi \}$ and $\{ S_2(t) : 0 \le t \le \pi \}$ give a one-DOF folding motion for origami sheets O_1 and O_2, respectively.

As remarks, note that ψ_i^s $(i = 1, 2)$ indicates a composition function of ψ_i iterated s times (s is a positive integer) and ψ_i^{-s} indicates a composition function of the inverse function ψ_i^{-1} of ψ_i iterated s times.

Figure 6 shows examples of the one-DOF folding motion described in Design Method 5. As a numerical result, for any $0 < t < 1$, there exists a conical surface $C(t)$ such that all vertices $\psi_1^j(\psi_2^k(a))$ $(j, k \in \mathbb{Z})$ lie on $C(t)$. Moreover, an orbit of each vertex $\psi_1^j(\psi_2^k(a))$ $(j, k \in \mathbb{Z})$ in this folding motion is an arc. Also, since the three points a, b, and d are fixed, we can observe that an orbit of the fixed points x_1 and x_2 of the affine transformations ψ_1 and ψ_2 is a half-circle.

4. Conclusion

In this work, we reviewed three design methods of triangular spiral multiple tilings and showed a design method of origami sheets for origami tessellations of triangular spiral multiple tilings with opposed parastichy pairs. Moreover, we showed that their origami sheets allow at least one-DOF folding motion. We can apply these design methods to whirlpool spirals and triangular spiral multiple tilings with non-opposed parastichy pairs such as those in Figures 1 and 7. However, an origami sheet of Figure 7(b) has intersections of facets. That is, it cannot be folded as a single sheet of paper. About origami sheets for triangular spiral multiple tilings, the following still remains as an open problem: *Which triangular spiral multiple tilings give origami sheets without intersections of facets?*

In our folding motion of origami sheets for origami tessellations of triangular spiral multiple tilings, we admitted intersections of facets. However, we want to avoid these intersections. Thus, we have the following problem: *Which triangular spiral multiple tilings give origami sheets folded by this folding motion without intersections of facets?* Also, we

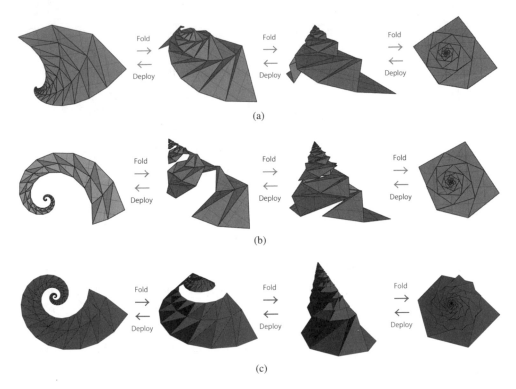

(a)

(b)

(c)

FIGURE 6. Three examples of the one-DOF folding motion of Design Method 5. (a) An origami sheet of Figure 5(a). In this case, there are no intersections of facets. (b) An origami sheet for a triangular spiral tiling of Figure 2(c). In this case, there are no intersections of facets. (c) An origami sheet of a spiral multiple tiling by right triangles with the angles 30°, 60°, and 90°. In this case, we can observe intersections of facets.

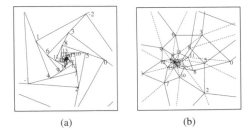

(a)   (b)

FIGURE 7. (a) A triangular spiral tiling with non-opposed parastichy pair $(3, 5)$, where $r = 0.8835$ and $\theta = 2\pi \cdot 0.41$. (b) An origami sheet of (a). This origami sheet has intersections of facets.

cannot show whether they allow two-DOF, or more, folding motions. Thus, the following still remains as an open problem: *What is a maximum DOF for folding motions of these origami sheets?*

However, we represented one-DOF folding motion as a one-parameter family of discrete surfaces described by two affine transformations of $\mathbb{R}^3$. Thus, we want to derive a mathematical relation between this folding motion and discrete differential geometry.

Acknowledgments

The authors would like to thank the anonymous referees for their helpful comments and suggestions. This work is partially supported by JSPS Kakenhi Grant No. 24654029, Ryukoku University Science and Technology Fund, and the Joint Research Center for Science and Technology of Ryukoku University.

References

[Azukawa 85] Kazuo Azukawa. "Seeds of Sunflower." *Sugaku Seminar* 7 (1985), 34–42. (In Japanese.)

[Fuse 02] Tomoko Fuse. "Twisted Multiple Towers." *MANIFOLD* 5 (2002), 8–11. (In Japanese.)

[Fuse 12] Tomoko Fuse. *Spiral: Origami | Art | Design.* Freising, Germany: Viereck Verlag, 2012.

[Grünbaum and Shephard 87] Branko Grünbaum and Geoffrey C. Shephard. *Tilings and Patterns.* San Francisco: W. H. Freeman, 1987. MR857454 (88k:52018)

[Hardy and Wright 08] Godfrey H. Hardy and Edward M. Wright. *An Introduction to the Theory of Numbers,* Sixth Edition. Oxford, UK: Oxford University Press, 2008. MR2445243 (2009i:11001)

[Hizume 05] Akio Hizume. "Fibonacci Tornado." *MANIFOLD* 11 (2005), 6–10. (In Japanese.)

[Hizume 06] Akio Hizume. *Inter-native Architecture of Music.* Tokyo: Star Cage, 2006.

[Hizume 08] Akio Hizume. "Real Tornado." *MANIFOLD* 17 (2008), 8–11. (In Japanese.)

[Hizume and Yamagishi 09] Akio Hizume and Yoshikazu Yamagishi. "Real Tornado." In *Proceedings of Bridges 2009: Mathematics, Music, Art, Architecture, Culture,* pp. 239–242. St. Albans, UK: Tarquin Books, 2009.

[Jean 94] Roger V. Jean. *Phyllotaxis: A Systemic Study in Plant Morphogenesis.* Cambridge, UK: Cambridge University Press, 1994.

[Lang and Bateman 11] Robert J. Lang and Alex Bateman. "Every Spider Web Has a Simple Flat Twist Tessellation." In *Origami⁵: Fifth International Meeting of Origami Science, Mathematics, and Education,* edited by Patsy Wang-Iverson, Robert J. Lang, and Mark Yim, pp. 455–473. Boca Raton, FL: A K Peters/CRC Press, 2011. MR2866909 (2012h:00044)

[Sushida et al. 12] Takamichi Sushida, Akio Hizume, and Yoshikazu Yamagishi. "Triangular Spiral Tilings." *Journal of Physics A: Mathematical and Theoretical* 45:23 (2012), 235203. MR2929517

[Tachi 13] Tomohiro Tachi. "Freeform Origami Tessellations by Generalizing Resch's Patterns." *Journal of Mechanical Design* 135:11 (2013), 111006.

MEIJI INSTITUTE FOR ADVANCED STUDY OF MATHEMATICAL SCIENCE, MEIJI UNIVERSITY, TOKYO, JAPAN
E-mail address: tz14024@meiji.ac.jp

DEPARTMENT OF APPLIED MATHEMATICS AND INFORMATICS, RYUKOKU UNIVERSITY, SHIGA, JAPAN
E-mail address: akio@starcage.org

DEPARTMENT OF APPLIED MATHEMATICS AND INFORMATICS, RYUKOKU UNIVERSITY, SHIGA, JAPAN
E-mail address: yg@rins.ryukoku.ac.jp

A New Scheme to Describe Twist-Fold Tessellations

Thomas R. Crain

1. Introduction

While researching a problem concerning twist-fold tessellations, it became apparent that terminology to describe and think about the problem either did not exist or was vague and imprecise. For example, a term like *square twist* might be used when there is really an infinite variety of square twists. Crease patterns can be used to show twist-fold units and their interactions [Gjerde 09]. However, having to always draw pictures is unsatisfactory and crease patterns don't readily avail themselves to numerical analyses. Language to describe twist-fold units and their interactions is needed.

With twist-fold tessellations, pattern variations may be produced depending on whether the twist folds are all placed on one side of the paper or both sides. The twist-fold units themselves can vary depending on the combination of mountain and valley folds used to produce the polygon at the core of the twist fold. The scope of the scheme to be described herein is limited to twist-fold tessellations where the twist-fold units are all placed on the same side of the paper and the sides of the twist-fold polygons are all mountain folds.

This paper will first present a nomenclature devised to precisely describe twist-fold units and the interactions among these units. Because twist-fold tessellations are usually folded on a grid, the nomenclature uses size and spacing terms that reference grid units. After the introduction of the nomenclature, two examples of its use are discussed.

2. Twist-Fold Units

Twist-fold designs are usually folded using paper that has been prepared by first folding a square or triangular grid. Using gridded paper, polygons are folded such that the vertices of the polygons coincide with intersections of grid lines. The sides of the polygon generally do not lie on grid lines. Once the sides of the polygon are pinched into place, the polygon is twisted so that it lies flat. A result of the twist is that pleats are formed that run from each vertex of the polygon to the edge of the paper or to the vertex of another polygon. How wide the pleats are depends on the particular unit being folded.

2.1. Unit parameters. There are four parameters to consider with twist-fold units: unit type, unit size, pleat width, and twist direction. An alpha-numeric symbol may be constructed to signify the first three parameters: $U_P N$; where U = unit type, P = pleat width, and N = unit number (also called unit size). When the subscript P is omitted, a pleat width of one is assumed.

Twist direction, clockwise or counterclockwise, is largely an irrelevant parameter because once the first unit is twisted into place, the direction of all subsequent twists is predetermined. This is because each twist-fold unit twists in a direction that is opposite of the units to which it is connected. Twist direction for the first polygon is usually determined by how the polygon is laid out on the grid. Some polygons are able to twist in either direction. Twist direction can, however, have a major impact on the overall design of a project in that chiral versions of a pattern can be constructed. If it is desired to indicate twist direction, a counterclockwise twist is denoted by a plus sign (+) and a clockwise twist by a minus sign (−).

2.2. Triangular-grid units. The most common polygons used with a triangular grid are regular hexagons (H), equilateral triangles (T), and rhombi (R). The upper panel of Figure 1 shows crease patterns for these unit types in various sizes, all with P = 1. Unit number (size) is determined as follows. Draw the crease pattern for the smallest possible instance of the polygon on a triangular grid where the vertices of the polygon coincide with the intersection of grid lines. It doesn't matter if the unit will fold flat. This smallest instance has a unit number of 0. H0 will fold flat, while T0 and R0 will not. To get unit number 1, draw the crease pattern for the next smallest instance of the polygon and consider the following while referring to Figure 1: On a triangular grid, any two contiguous unit triangles will form a rhombus. Notice that for each number-1 unit, each side of the polygonal unit traverses one grid rhombus along its long axis. All of these number-1 units fold flat, with T1 and R1 being closed on the opposite side while H1 is open on the opposite side. The lower panel of Figure 1 shows how to determine the unit number of any particular unit on a triangular grid using hexagons as examples. To determine the unit number, simply count the number of contiguous grid unit rhombi (along their long axes) the polygons sides traverse. Notice that both polygons in the lower panel of Figure 1 are H2 units and that they differ in their respective pleat widths. The reader should realize now that unit number is analogous with side length and that twist-fold units with identical unit numbers and identical subscripts (pleat width) have side lengths that are identical.

2.3. Square-grid units. The most common polygons used with a square grid are the square (S) and rectangle (oblong; O). Samples of these are shown in the upper panel of Figure 2. Rectangles are best thought of as adjoined squares when determining unit number. Unit number is determined as follows for square grid polygons. To get a unit of number 0, draw the crease pattern for the smallest possible instance of the polygon on a square grid where the vertices of the polygon coincide with the intersection of grid lines. Again, it doesn't matter if the polygon will fold flat. Neither S0 nor O0 folds flat. Draw the crease pattern for the next smallest instance of a square to get unit S1. Adjoin two of these squares to get rectangle O1. S1 will fold flat; O1 will not. Refer to the middle panel of Figure 2 for the following discussion of how to determine the unit number of any square or rectangular unit. To get the unit number for squares or rectangles, a right triangle is constructed such that its hypotenuse is a side of the square or a short side of the rectangle. The length of the longest leg of the right triangle measured in grid units is the unit number for the polygon. If the triangle constructed is an isosceles triangle, the unit number is the length of either leg. Notice that the length of the short leg measured in grid units will give the pleat width. For a unit whose constructed right triangle is isosceles, the unit number and pleat width are the same. As for units on a triangular grid, the subscript (P) is only included if P > 1.

The pleat width for the long side of a rectangle requires further discussion. Twist-fold rectangles need to be thought of as being composed of adjoined squares (Figure 2,

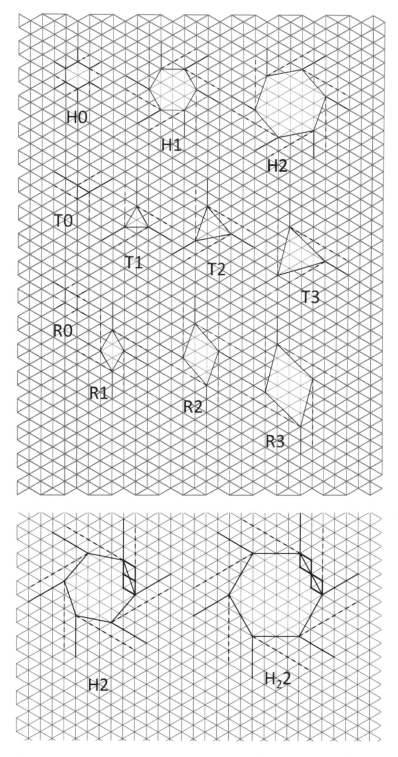

FIGURE 1. Triangular-grid twist-fold units: basic units (upper); demonstration of how to determine unit number (lower).

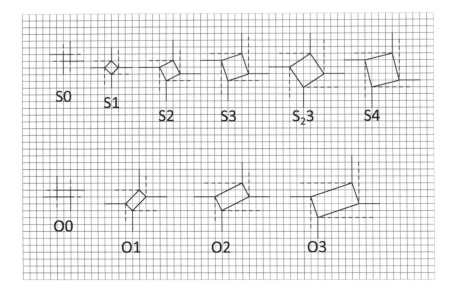

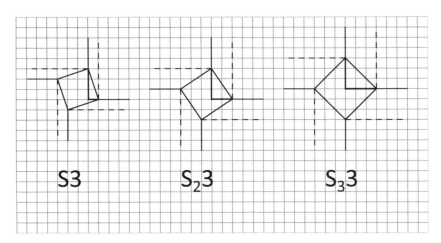

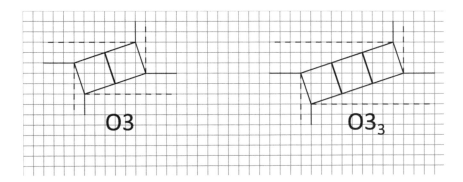

FIGURE 2. Square-grid twist-fold units: basic units (upper); demonstration of how to determine unit number (middle); calculating long-side pleat width (lower).

Pleat Width	P
Inter-unit Interval	I
Unit Type	H, T, R, S, O, etc.
Unit Number	N
Twist Direction	+, −

TABLE 1. Twist-fold tessellation parameters.

lower panel). The unit number of the rectangle indicates the maximum number of adjoined squares the rectangle may contain before the rectangle is no longer flat-foldable. The standard rectangle comprises two adjoined squares. To indicate that a rectangle is nonstandard, a numerical subscript is appended indicating the number of adjoined squares (e.g., $O3_3$). To find the long-side pleat width (P_L), determine the number of adjoined squares (A) and the short-side pleat width (P_S), then calculate $P_L = AP_S$.

2.4. Unit interactions. When the first unit of a twist-fold design is twisted into place, there will be pleats running from each vertex of the polygonal unit to the edge of the paper. When the next polygon is folded into place, one of the pleats from the original polygon will terminate at a vertex of the new polygon and the pleat becomes a flap (as seen later in Figure 8). The distance between vertices of connecting polygons is the inter-unit-interval (I) and is measured in grid units. If $I \geq 1$ then a trapezoidal flap is formed, and if $I = 0$ then a triangular flap is formed. A flap is formed every time a polygon connects to another polygon.

2.5. Summary. Thus far, basic twist-fold units have been introduced and methods to determine unit size and pleat width have been discussed. Inter-unit interval was added to the four unit parameters to make a total of five parameters that define the twist-fold tessellations that are the subject of this paper. These parameters are listed in Table 1.

3. Analyzing Patterns

The impetus for the development of the new nomenclature was a desire to analyze a twist-fold tessellation pattern to discover a specific variation of that pattern. The pattern in question was a 3.6.3.6 tessellation variation introduced by Fujimoto [Fujimoto 76] that produces a beautiful basket-weave pattern. See the top panel of Figure 3 for the author's rendition of that pattern. The 3.6.3.6 tessellation pattern comprises triangles and hexagons. Using twist-fold units of varying sizes, different effects can be achieved. It was desired to produce a basket-weave pattern similar to Fujimoto's except the weave would be more open and the triangles would be discernible in the pattern. After trying various combinations without success, it was decided to chart the combinations attempted to search for combinations not yet attempted. That is where the problem arose in that there was no terminology available with which to refer to the various sizes of the units. The nomenclature was developed, previous attempts were charted, and the desired combination was discovered, with the result shown in the lower panel of Figure 3.

It was then wondered if other combinations existed that would produce the basket-weave pattern. Various combinations were tried—some successful, some not. When enough successful combinations were discovered, a pattern emerged. The pattern revealed that an infinite number of combinations will produce the basket-weave design. Of course, only a small number of these combinations are practicably foldable. Table 2 lists the relationship rules for various combinations of hexagons (H), triangles (T), pleat width (P), and

FIGURE 3. Basket-weave patterns: original (upper); desired (lower).

		P: Positive Integer I: (multiple of P) > 0 H: (multiple of P) ≥ I T: H − I + P			
P1,I1:	H1,T1 H2,T2 H3,T3 ...,...	P2,I2:	H2,T2 H4,T4 H6,T6 ...,...	P3,I3:	H3,T3 H6,T6 H9,T9 ...,...	→ → →
P1,I2:	H2,T1 H3,T2 H4,T3 ...,...	P2,I4:	H4,T2 H6,T4 H8,T6 ...,...	P3,I6:	H6,T3 H9,T6 H12,T9 ...,...	→ → →
P1,I3:	H3,T1 H4,T2 H5,T3 ...,...	P2,I6:	H6,T2 H8,T4 H10,T6 ...,...	P3,I9:	H9,T3 H12,T6 H15,T9 ...,...	→ → →
	↓ ↓ ↓		↓ ↓ ↓		↓ ↓ ↓	→ → ↓↓

TABLE 2. Relationship rules for folding basket-weave patterns. The table can be extended indefinitely within each cell, to the right, and down.

inter-unit-interval (I) that will produce the basket-weave pattern. The results of Table 2 are just one example of the utility of the new nomenclature to analyze twist-fold tessellation patterns.

4. Structural Formulae

In twist-fold tessellations there is a basic design element that is folded in a repetitive and interlinked manner to produce the desired design. The basic design element is often referred to as a *molecule*. Considering how molecules are represented by structural formulae in chemistry, it was wondered if such a structural formula could be devised for twist-fold tessellations. If the structural formula contained all parametric information and if basic knowledge of how twist-fold tessellations are folded is understood, then it should be possible to recreate twist-fold tessellation designs without the use of a crease pattern or any accompanying text.

4.1. Reading structural formulae. Figures 4 through 7 show some sample structural formulae along with the crease patterns they represent. Three of the parameters (unit type, unit size, and pleat width) are represented in the basic symbol as discussed in Section b1. A structural formula just adds bars that represent the inter-unit interval (i.e., how many grid units apart the units are). Notice that there are as many positions for bars as there are vertices for each particular polygonal unit. A single bar means that there is a space of one grid unit between vertices of adjacent polygons (I = 1), and double bars signify a spacing of two grid units (I = 2). You should notice that some bars are accompanied by letters. For the rhombus (R) units, the letters differentiate the connections to acute-angle vertices (a) and to obtuse-angle vertices (o). The oblong units (O) use a letter to differentiate short-side (s) and long-side vertex connections (i.e., connections in which the short side or long side

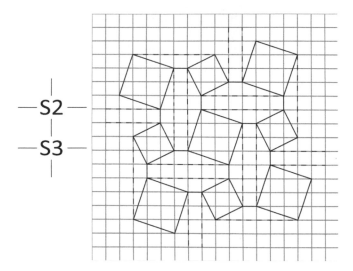

FIGURE 4. Structural formula and crease pattern it represents for a simple square-grid pattern.

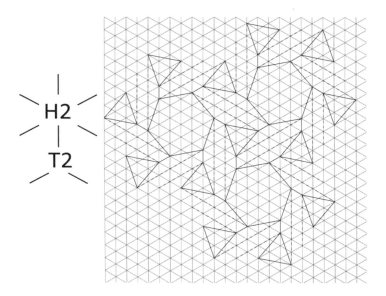

FIGURE 5. Structural formula and crease pattern it represents for a simple triangular-grid pattern.

are involved in forming the trapezoidal flap). For $I > 2$, more bars may be used or a number may be appended to a bar to indicate the value of I. If $I = 0$, a zero may be appended to the bar.

Figure 4 represents a pattern that uses two different sized square twists. In this structural formula, as in all others, if there only one connection to a particular type of vertex is shown, it means the same thing happens at all other vertices of the same type. This pattern uses S2 and S3 square twists. Each vertex of an S2 square twist connects with a vertex of

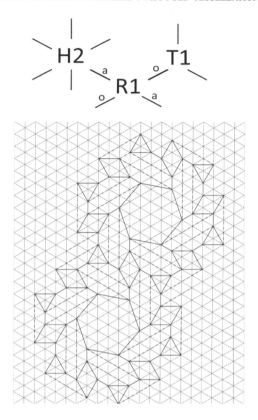

FIGURE 6. Structural formula and crease pattern it represents for a more complex triangular-grid pattern.

an S3 square twist with an inter-unit interval of one grid unit (I = 1), and every S3 vertex connects to an S2 vertex.

Figure 5 represents a 3.6.3.6 tessellation variation that produces the basket-weave design. This particular pattern uses H2 hexagon and T2 triangle twists. Each of the six vertices of the hexagon unit connects with a vertex of a triangle. Likewise, each vertex of a triangle unit connects with a vertex of a hexagon unit.

In Figure 6 things are a bit more complicated. This pattern uses three different polygons: H2 hexagons, R1 rhombi, and T1 triangles. In this pattern, every acute-angle vertex of a rhombus connects with a vertex of a hexagon, and every obtuse-angle vertex of a rhombus connects with a triangle. All vertices of hexagons connect with acute-angle vertices of rhombi, and all vertices of triangles connect with obtuse-angle vertices of rhombi.

Figure 7 adds more complexity. This pattern uses O3 rectangles with P = 1 and S_23 squares with P = 2. Recall that for standard rectangles, if the short side has P = 1, then for the long side P = 2. In the pattern, connections made horizontally have I = 1 while those made vertically have I = 2. In this pattern, short-side vertices of rectangles connect with short-side vertices of other rectangles. One long-side vertex of a rectangle connects with a square and the other long-side vertex connects with the long-side vertex of another-rectangle. With the squares, one pair of opposite vertices connects to long-side vertices of rectangles, and the orthogonal pair of opposite vertices connects with other squares.

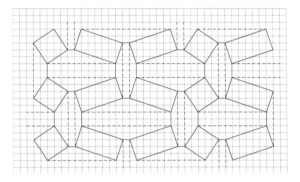

FIGURE 7. Structural formula and crease pattern it represents for a more complex square-grid pattern.

It should be seen that deciphering structural formulae is not too difficult. With this ability and knowledge of twist-fold tessellation basics, it should be relatively easy to fold a pattern given a structural formula.

5. Twist-Fold Tessellation Basics

When folding a pattern, it is usually easiest to start with the polygonal unit that has the most vertices. Pinch the paper to make creases that will form the sides of your first polygon. Twist-fold the first polygon into place. This is usually near the center of the paper depending on your design. Upon completion of the first twist-fold unit, there will be pleats running from each vertex of the polygon to the edges of the paper.

When the next polygon is folded into place, one of the pleats from the original polygon will terminate at a vertex of the new polygon and becomes a trapezoidal flap. (It will be assumed that $I \geq 1$ for this discussion.) This trapezoidal flap is an important landmark as it will guide you in determining the proper orientation of subsequent folds. As can be seen in Figure 8, the trapezoidal flap comprises four creases: three mountain and one valley. Two of the mountain creases are one side each of the adjoining polygons, and the third is the inter-unit interval (I). The two obtuse angles of the trapezoidal flap are defined by the three mountain folds. The valley crease can be considered to be the long base of the trapezoidal flap. At either end of the valley crease, the acute angles of the trapezoidal flap are formed. As mentioned earlier, every time polygons connect, flaps are formed. Looking at each vertex of the polygons in Figure 8, it should now be easy to visualize trapezoidal flaps.

To fold the next twist-fold, count over the requisite number of grid spaces (as determined by your design) from one vertex of the existing polygon to begin the next polygon.

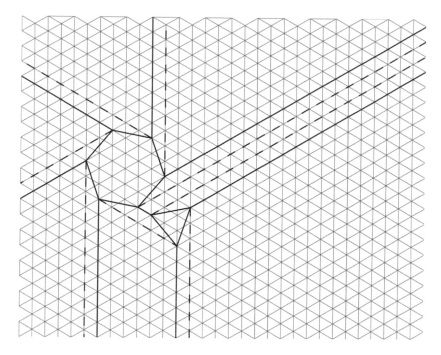

FIGURE 8. Twist-fold pleats and a trapezoidal flap.

Complete a trapezoid when you pinch in the first crease of the new polygon. This will ensure that the polygon is properly oriented. Pinch the creases to form the remaining sides of the new polygon. Twist the new polygon into place, remembering that each twist fold twists in the direction opposite of that of its neighbors. When the new polygon is twisted into place, new pleats are formed that run from the vertices of the polygon to the edges of the paper.

Work around the paper pinching, creasing, and twist-folding. Eventually a pleat formed from executing a twist fold will intersect a pleat from a previous fold. Make sure that the existing pleat is folded flat, and fold the new pleat through it as if it didn't exist. The crossed pleats will be unfolded when needed.

Using this basic information as a guide, it is possible to convert a structural formula into a folded tessellation pattern.

6. Conclusion

Only the most common twist-fold units were discussed in this paper. A vast array of designs may be developed from this small set of twist folds [Crain 15]. Using the conventions set forth in the nomenclature, symbols and names may be developed for other twist-fold units.

It was quite surprising and delightful to discover that among the infinite variations of the 3.6.3.6 tessellation pattern, there exist an infinite number of combinations that all produce a basket-weave pattern. That is just one example of the numerical analyses made possible by the nomenclature. Other uses include determining the finished size of a pattern, the amount of paper consumed in a pattern, and relationship rules for other pattern variations.

Although just doodling with paper or drawing crease patterns is probably the best way to design new patterns, once a pattern is developed the structural formula seems like the most efficient way to share the pattern with others. At the least, there now exists language with which to discuss the class of patterns and twist-fold units that were the focus of this paper. With a little more work, it should be possible to expand the scope of the current scheme to include pattern variations that have twist-fold units on both sides of the paper and twist-fold unit types whose central polygon's sides comprise combinations of mountain and valley folds.

References

[Crain 15] Thomas R. Crain. "Album: Tessellation Patterns." *Flickr.com*. Available at www.flickr.com/photos/tomcrainorigami/sets/, 2015.

[Fujimoto 76] Shuzo Fujimoto. *Nejiri Origami (Twist Origami)*. Self published, 1976.

[Gjerde 09] Eric Gjerde. *Origami Tessellation: Awe-Inspiring Geometric Designs*. Wellesley, MA: A K Peters, 2009. MR2474884 (2009m:52001)

ORIGAMI ARTIST
E-mail address: twistfold@gmail.com

Weaving a Uniformly Thick Sheet from Rectangles

Eli Davis, Erik D. Demaine, Martin L. Demaine, and Jennifer Ramseyer

1. Introduction

Many children know how to weave a few strips of paper into a sheet, which will have uniform thickness. However, the size of the sheet in this simple weaving is limited by the length of the original strips. This sheet will also require some sort of locking mechanism to hold it together: without tape or a nonuniform edge, the strips can slide apart.

By contrast, we show how to weave together finite-length strips into an infinite sheet of uniform thickness. In addition, our sheet is locked, so the strips will not slip, assuming the creases stay folded. Formally, the folded components cannot simultaneously separate via rigid motions (i.e., treating each component as a rigid object). However, our weaving requires more layers than the child's model.

Table 1 summarizes the number of layers required by our various sheet-weaving algorithms. For a long rectangular strip (aspect ratio > 2), our infinite sheet is eight layers thick. For a nearly square rectangular strip (aspect ratio ≤ 2), our infinite sheet is sixteen layers thick. In the special case of 1×5 rectangles, we can achieve a thickness of just five layers. More broadly, we study when the "strip" is a shape other than a rectangle. For any polygon that tiles the plane, where tiles appear in only finitely many orientations, we give a method for weaving an infinite sheet 18 layers thick. We also design a special concave polygon that can be woven into a sheet just four layers thick.

A more challenging goal is to create a locked *finite* sheet of uniform thickness, where boundary conditions come into play. If we just apply a portion of our infinite constructions, the edges of the sheet will be ragged, and locking the sheet while keeping the thickness constant proves difficult. We devise solutions to these problems that generate locked, uniform-thickness, finite woven sheets—but at the price of double the thickness, and only for certain tessellations. See Table 1, right column.

2. General Rectangles

Given a rectangle of dimensions 1 by > 2, we can create a locked infinite weave of eight layers. Refer to Figure 1. First, fold the two narrower edges of the rectangle to the middle. Next, weave rectangles together to form an infinite strip, interlacing the folded flaps with each other. The interlacing of the flaps forces the rectangles into a locked one-dimensional configuration. Because each unit is effectively two layers thick and we

Supported in part by NSF ODISSEI grant EFRI-1240383 and NSF Expedition grant CCF-1138967.

Polygon Type	Number of Layers		Section
	Infinite Sheet	Finite Sheet	
Rectangle, $1 \times > 2$	8	16	2
Rectangle, $1 \times \leq 2$	16	32	2
Parallelo-hexagon	16 or 32	32 or 64	2
Rectangle, 1×5	5	10	3
Tileable polygon	18*	36*	4
Special polygon	4	8	5

* Applies only to certain tilings.

TABLE 1. Our results for locked sheets: paper shapes and the resulting number of layers for infinite and finite weaves.

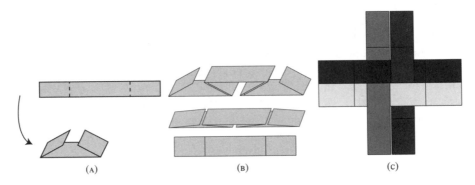

FIGURE 1. Constructing the general rectangle weave: (a) forming an individual unit, (b) lacing units into a strip and flattening, and (c) weaving strips together.

interlace each unit with another unit, we so far have four layers. Finally, weave these four-layer infinite strips into a standard cross-weave, giving us eight layers in total. Because each unit is at least as long as it is wide, the cross-weave will prevent the strips from separating, locking the construction in two dimensions.

This method can be extended to other shapes as well.

For rectangles of dimensions 1 by ≤ 2, we can fold the shape in half along the narrower edge. This operation doubles the thickness of the weave but reduces to the long-rectangle case. The result is 16 layers thick. (If we tried to apply the previous construction directly to, e.g., a square, then we could still make an infinite one-dimensional strip, but the cross-weave would not prevent the strips from coming apart by sliding the units in a perpendicular direction.)

Define a *parallelo-hexagon* to be a hexagon where each side is the same length as and parallel to the opposite side, and two pairs of opposite sides are of the same length. See [de Villiers 12] for a strict definition. We can fold such a parallelo-hexagon into a rectangle, as in Figure 2. The resulting weave is twice as thick as the rectangle weave: 16 layers if the generated rectangle is of dimensions 1 by > 2, and 32 layers otherwise.

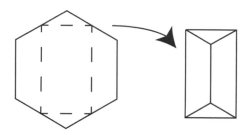

FIGURE 2. Folding a parallelo-hexagon into a rectangle.

3. 1 × 5 Rectangle

For rectangles of specific dimensions, we have found special methods that result in thinner weaves. Take the 1 × 5 rectangle. As shown in Figure 3, we can achieve a locked infinite weave of only five layers.

First, instead of folding the edges of the strip to the middle, we divide the strip into fifths and fold the flaps along the one-fifth and four-fifths marks. These folds result in the extreme thirds being two layers thick and the center third being one layer thick.

As before, we interlace these units into infinite locked one-dimensional strips. These strips alternate with squares of thickness 1 and 4.

Finally, we weave the strips together, locking them both horizontally and vertically into a weave. When weaving the strips together, we align the strips so that the four-layer-thick sections of one strip overlap with the one-layer-thick sections of the orthogonal strip. This matching is possible by arranging the horizontal strips to form a checkerboard pattern of 1 and 4 layers and arranging the vertical strips in a complementary overlapping checkerboard. Thus, our weave becomes uniformly five layers thick.

4. Tileable Shapes

For any polygonal shape (convex or nonconvex) that tiles the plane, we can generate a weaving of no more than 18 layers, as shown in Figure 4. This method also works for a finite set of polygonal shapes that jointly tile the plane. However, we must make one assumption about the tiling: Each tile can appear in only finitely many orientations. Some aperiodic tilings do not have this property [Radin 94, Sadun 98], and our construction does not apply to them.

First, starting from the given tiling, we duplicate it, stack the two tilings, and then translate one relative to the other so that no tiling edges overlap for positive length. (Tiling edges may overlap at points.) We can find such a translation for any tiling as follows. For each shape in the tiling, define the *minimum feature size* to be the shortest distance between an edge and a nonincident edge; and define the minimum feature size of the whole tiling to be the minimum over all tile shapes. (Here, the tiling has finitely many tile shapes.) Then, we translate by half this minimum feature size, in a direction not parallel to any edge. (Such a direction exists because there are finitely many tile shapes and finitely many edges per tile.)

Now we argue that, for any two edges e and f, the translation e' of e does not overlap f. Because we translate a positive amount not parallel to e, e cannot intersect its own translation e'. Because we translate by less than the minimum feature size, if e and f

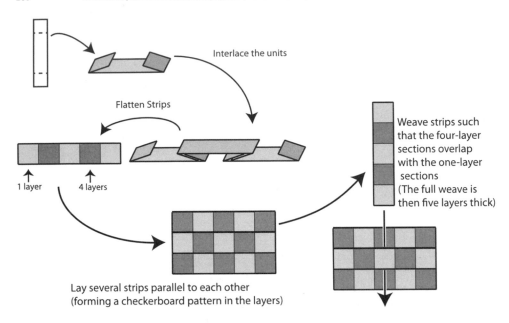

Interlace the units

Flatten Strips

Weave strips such
that the four-layer
sections overlap
with the one-layer
sections
(The full weave is
then five layers thick)

1 layer

4 layers

Lay several strips parallel to each other
(forming a checkerboard pattern in the layers)

FIGURE 3. A locked infinite weave from a 1×5 rectangle.

are not incident, then e' and f cannot intersect, let alone overlap. Finally, if e and f are incident, then they cannot be parallel, so the translation e' can intersect f only at a point.

Next, we pleat the composite sheet with many parallel creases in order to lock together all the tiles. For any two overlapping tiles, say untranslated tile s and translated tile t', compute their intersection $s \cap t'$. Because we translated by less than the minimum feature size, the untranslated tiles s and t must be incident or equal. Because there are finitely many tile types, orientations of those tiles, and vertex pairs that could be incident, there are finitely many such tile intersections. For each tile intersection, we measure the projected length in the direction of the pleat and compute the minimum such length. We uniformly pleat the sheet with two pleats (four creases) per this length so that, independent of shifting, a full pleat hits every tile intersection. The pleating triples the number of layers, for $6 = 2 \cdot 3$ layers thick so far.

Now we prove that these pleats prevent all but a one-dimensional motion, in the direction of the pleat. We have restricted the motion in this way for any pair of overlapping tiles, which forms an infinite bipartite graph of "locking" relations on the tiles; we need to prove that this graph is connected. Consider a vertex v in the original tiling and its translation v', and let T and T' be the set of untranslated and translated tiles incident to v and v', respectively. Because we translate by less than the feature size, some translated tile $t' \in T'$ overlaps v, and thus the pleats lock t' together with all tiles $s \in T$. Similarly, some untranslated tile $q \in T$ overlaps v', and thus the pleats lock q together with all $r' \in T'$. In particular, t and t' are locked together, as are q and q', so by transitivity, all tiles in $T \cup T'$ are locked together. Again by transitivity, all tiles in both tilings are locked together.

Finally, we pleat the sheet again, using the same construction as above, but in the orthogonal direction. As a result, all tiles are fully locked together, being unable to move simultaneously in two orthogonal directions. Our completed weave is $18 = 6 \cdot 3$ layers thick.

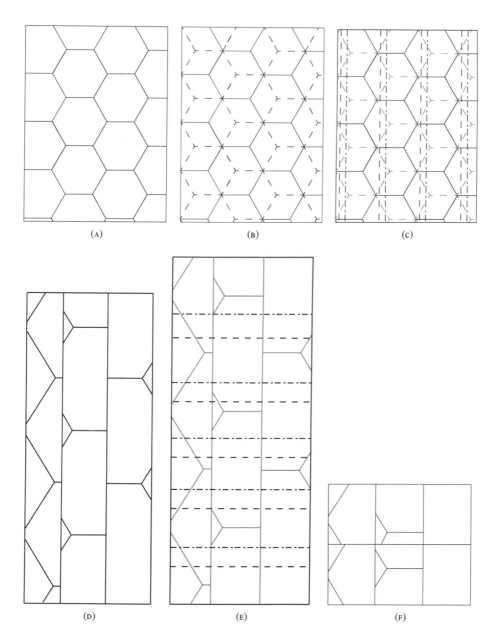

FIGURE 4. Weaving an infinite plane of hexagons: (a) A tiled plane of hexagons, (b) the two stacked planes of hexagons (dashes indicate shapes beneath), (c) creases for the vertical pleats, (d) appearance after folding the vertical pleats, (e) creases for the horizontal pleats, and (f) the finished weave after folding the horizontal pleats.

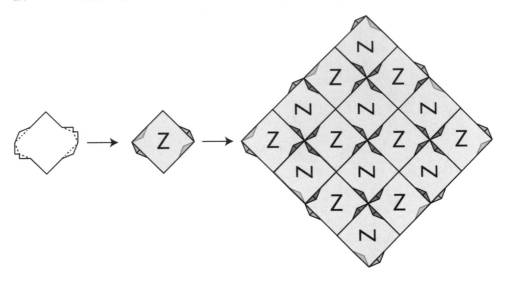

FIGURE 5. The two-layer unit and resulting woven sheet of irregular thickness (light areas are one layer thick, dark areas are two layers thick). We denote how each piece is rotated with the letter "Z" (which is 180° rotationally symmetric, like the pieces).

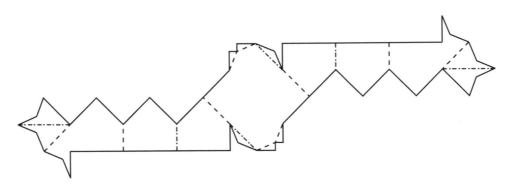

FIGURE 6. The final unit, with extra paper extensions to create a uniformly four-layer-thick weave.

5. Special Polygon

Using a carefully designed polygon, we can achieve an even smaller number of layers. Specifically, we demonstrate a shape that weaves with only four layers. We start with the folding shown in Figure 5 (left), which has two layers in some places and one in the rest. Locking together that unit with copies of itself produces the weave in Figure 5 (right). However, this weave is not uniformly thick, so we must add additional paper. We add paper until the entire folding is four layers thick, ending up with the crease pattern (and outer polygon) shown in Figure 6. Once we have folded this shape, we lock its corners together with the corners of other identical units to make a four-layer-thick weave.

6. Finite Locked Sheets

Our method for making a finite locked sheet from an infinite locked sheet is to treat the tiling as a tube with closed off ends, rather than a sheet. For this approach to work, it must be possible to carve the tiling along tile boundaries into a (roughly rectangular) supertile whose boundary satisfies the topological/metric mating conditions shown in Figure 7(a). Matching letters must meet complementarily so that they can be woven together with a uniform number of layers. The idea is that, if we fold the supertile in half vertically to bring the (equally oriented) C's together, then the C boundaries match up as if the tiling continued, and the oppositely oriented A boundaries match up with each other (one reflected by folding), as do the B's. The supertile does not need to tile the plane in a rectangular brick tiling.

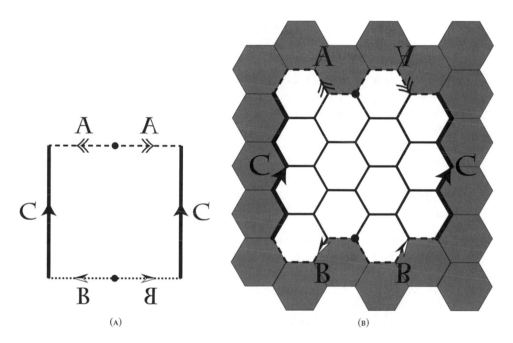

FIGURE 7. Making finite weaves out of infinite weaves: (a) Topological disc with boundary labeling of compatibility relations required of the supertile. (b) An example of finding supertiles in a tiling.

Figure 7(b) illustrates the hexagon tiling as an example. The indicated bumpy rectangle is a valid supertile, as is any bumpy rectangle with the same parity. To fold the supertile into a finite woven sheet, first glue together the equal-letter boundaries. Now treat the result as a single (double-covered) tiling with the original tile shapes, and apply the tiling method of Section 4: Offset the tiling (on the topological sphere) to form an inner and outer copy, and pleat the two copies together to lock them together. By choosing the pleat widths to evenly divide the supertile, the infinite pleat set becomes a finite pleat set.

Overall, we double the number of layers in the weaving. If we start with rectangles, parallelo-hexagons, or the special polygon, we can use the special weavings from Sections 2, 3, and 5 instead of the general tiling weaving.

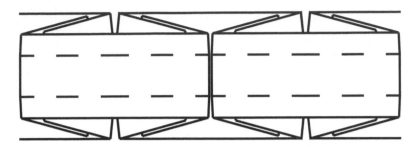

FIGURE 8. Creating the dollar bill strip, as seen from the top (mountain fold along dashed lines to lock).

7. Dollar Bill Folding

One application of this sheet weaving—and the original reason we explored this project—is to create a woven locked sheet of dollar bills. Glass blowers use sheets of newsprint folded into a "hot pad" to effectively touch hot glass without burning themselves. As part of an art project, we thought that it would be interesting to use a sheet of woven dollar bills instead of newsprint to shape the glass. The burnt dollar bills would then be displayed alongside the glass as a single sculpture, entitled *Money to Burn*.

It is important for glass-blowing hot pads to be uniformly and appropriately thick: a too-thin pad will burn the user, while a too-thick pad will mask too much feeling from the user. We based our original design off of Jed Ela's Moneywallet [Ela 04]. However, his wallet is not uniformly thick, so we created our own design.

The conventional children's weave is too thin to use as a pad and slips apart easily, so we developed the precursor to the eight-layer weave of Section 2. Because we needed the pad to be thick enough to handle the heat of the glass, we created a sixteen-layer locked weave, as follows: Fold the two narrower edges of the rectangle to the middle, as in Figure 8. Then, fold the longer edges to the middle, over the other edges. Unfold the longer edges, and interlace units together into a long strip. Fold all the longer edges together into the middle along the strip, creating a long locked strip. Create several of these strips, and weave them together into a sheet, as in Figure 9. This whole method is the same as that of the general rectangle weave in Figure 1, except with strips that are twice as thick. Each strip is eight layers thick, which, when woven, makes 16 layers. Using the tube method of Section 6, we created a finite locked sheet of 32 layers.

However, any weave has small gaps between strips. In the mathematical model, these gaps are dismissed as "infinitesimally small" points, but in physical models, the thickness of the paper may cause tiny but noticeable gaps. For glass blowing, these holes let hot steam pass through, burning the user. We therefore lined the inside of the final weave with eight additional layers of dollar bills (roughly 24 to 30 dollars' worth).

Our final dollar bill pad, shown in Figure 10, is forty layers thick and contains 140 to 146 dollar bills.

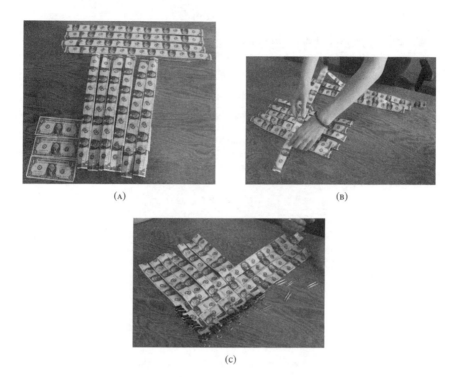

FIGURE 9. Weaving strips of dollar bills together: (a) creating a strip of dollar bills, (b) weaving the first strip, and (c) the partially completed sheet.

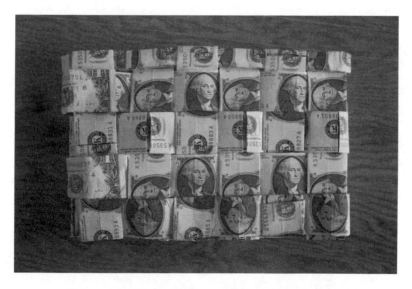

FIGURE 10. The finished woven sheet of dollar bills.

8. Conclusion

An intriguing open question is whether there is a general method for creating a locked infinite (or even finite) sheet from any possible shape.

In a forthcoming paper with Barry Hayes, we prove that a two-layer weave is possible, for an appropriate shape of paper.

Acknowledgments

We thank Barry Hayes for helpful discussions.

This research was supported in part by NSF ODISSEI grant EFRI-1240383 and NSF Expedition grant CCF-1138967.

References

[de Villiers 12] Michael de Villiers. "Relations between the Sides and Diagonals of a Set of Hexagons." *The Mathematical Gazette* 96 (July 2012), 309–315.

[Ela 04] Jed Ela. "Moneywallet." http://www.moneywallet.org/, 2004. (Accessed June 12, 2012.)

[Radin 94] Charles Radin. "The Pinwheel Tilings of the Plane." *Annals of Mathematics* 139:3 (1994), 661–702. MR1283873 (95d:52021)

[Sadun 98] Lorenzo Sadun. "Some Generalizations of the Pinwheel Tiling." *Discrete & Computational Geometry* 20:1 (1998), 79–110. MR1626703 (99e:52029)

MIT Computer Science and Artificial Intelligence Lab., Cambridge, Massachusetts
E-mail address: ebdavis@mit.edu

MIT Computer Science and Artificial Intelligence Lab., Cambridge, Massachusetts
E-mail address: edemaine@mit.edu

MIT Computer Science and Artificial Intelligence Lab., Cambridge, Massachusetts
E-mail address: mdemaine@mit.edu

MIT Computer Science and Artificial Intelligence Lab., Cambridge, Massachusetts
E-mail address: ramseyer@mit.edu

Extruding Towers by Serially Grafting Prismoids

Herng Yi Cheng

1. Introduction

Origami design has developed extensively using mathematical techniques. Many recent algorithms have aimed at designing origami polyhedral surfaces. The *Origamizer* algorithm [Tachi 10] designs general polyhedral surfaces, while a previous method by the author [Cheng 11] designs origami in the shape of *biplanars*, the convex hull of two disjoint polygons in $\mathbb{R}^3$.[1] Different methods are used in [Cheng and Cheong 12] and [Mitani 09] to design approximations to surfaces of revolution. An algorithm for folding *polycubes*, complexes of unit cubes, is detailed in [Benbernou et al. 11]. The origami in [Cheng 11, Cheng and Cheong 12, Benbernou et al. 11] and some special cases in [Mitani 09] are called *extrusion origami*, in which the folded form rises from the middle of the paper while the surrounding paper remains flat.

Among all of these algorithms, only those in [Cheng and Cheong 12] and [Benbernou et al. 11] have modular designs and folding algorithms that can, in general, be broken into a series of simpler steps by *grafting*, an important origami design technique. The other algorithms suffer from a disadvantage common to much of contemporary origami design—especially algorithmic design—that too many creases must be folded simultaneously, "collapsing" the initial piece of paper into (nearly) the end product in one complicated, indivisible maneuver. Besides the challenge for novices, industrial applications of such algorithms may be impeded by unfeasibly complex robot control that becomes necessary to automate such maneuvers.

1.1. Grafting. Grafting is a collection of origami techniques that augment an existing origami model with additional features, such as a head for a dragon, toes for a bird, or scales for a fish [Lang 03, Chapters 6–7]. Essentially, one

(i) folds a flat origami (e.g., a pattern of scales),
(ii) treats the product as a fresh sheet of paper,
(iii) folds another origami (e.g., a fish) to combine the two models.

A mathematical understanding of grafting begins with the definition of origami as a path isometry $f : P \to \mathbb{R}^3$ from a piece of paper P to three-dimensional (3D) space [belcastro and Hull 02, Demaine and O'Rourke 07]. Origami models $f : P \to \mathbb{R}^3$ and $g : Q \to \mathbb{R}^3$ are combined by treating $f(P) \subseteq Q$ as a new sheet of paper on which to fold g, producing a composite model that is the composite function $g \circ f : P \to \mathbb{R}^3$.[2]

---

[1] The polygons do not have to lie on parallel planes, thus biplanars generalize prismatoids.
[2] This interpretation reflects pattern grafting exactly and is a close analogy for other types of grafting.

Algorithm	Cheng and Cheong	Benbernou et al.
End product	Tower of n right frusta	Polycube of n cubes
Subproblem	Topmost $n - 1$ right frusta	Polycube of $n - 1$ cubes
Base case ("residue")	Right frustum	Cube
Combination step	Grafting	Grafting

TABLE 1.   Comparing the divide-and-conquer folding algorithms in [Cheng and Cheong 12] and [Benbernou et al. 11].

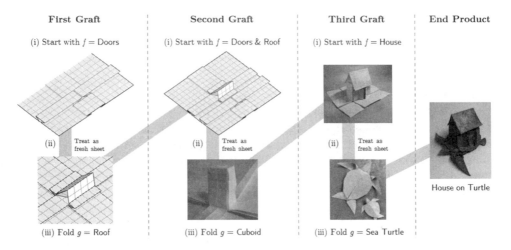

FIGURE 1.   Serial grafting can yield complex one-sheet origami by combining many simpler origami "components." (*Sea Turtle* image courtesy of its designer, Michael G. LaFosse.)

However, in the context of 3D origami, $f(P)$ does not lie within the flat Q in general. If positioned well, the origami g will fold $f(P) \cap Q$ as usual but also drag the connected components of $f(P) \setminus Q$ along with it. Extrusion origami fits this scheme particularly well, since the flat surrounding paper plays the role of $f(P) \cap Q$. This suggests a divide-and-conquer algorithm for *one-sheet* extrusion origami design, in which a target 3D shape is folded by accumulating the connected components ("residues") of $f(P) \setminus Q$ via successive origamis. Table 1 details how this was exploited in [Cheng and Cheong 12] to sequentially fold n *right frusta* (a right frustum is a section of a right pyramid between two parallel cutting planes) and combine them into polyhedral approximations of surfaces of revolution and in [Benbernou et al. 11] to sequentially fold n cubes and combine them into a polycube.

Even nonpolyhedral origami can benefit from such generalized grafting. Figure 1 shows the *House* model designed by the author via grafting, which has been further grafted onto Michael G. LaFosse's *Sea Turtle* [LaFosse 05] to produce a *House on Turtle*. Nonflat analogues of the earlier steps (i)–(iii) are used.

1.2. Tower of prismoids. This article generalizes the work of [Cheng and Cheong 12] to extrude a tower of *prismoids* (the convex hull of two parallel and angularly similar polygons in $\mathbb{R}^3$ [Demaine and O'Rourke 07, Section 22.5.1]), as opposed to the right frusta involved in [Cheng and Cheong 12]. The folding is done by grafting prismoids together, as will be presented in Algorithm 1, but Algorithms 3 and 4 find the crease pattern of the tower that results from the grafting. Some algorithms can be adapted from [Cheng 11] and [Cheng and Cheong 12], in particular algorithms to design individual prismoids.

However, the helpful symmetry of the framework in [Cheng and Cheong 12] is absent in this generalization, calling for a modification of certain procedures in [Cheng and Cheong 12]. A more efficient approach is also proposed to resolve internal overlapping in prismoids: While [Cheng and Cheong 12] subdivided problematic prismoids into smaller prismoids of the same height, the new method is proven to be optimal in the sense that the subdivision yields smaller prismoids that have unequal heights but are fewest in number.

2. Folding Prismoids by Tucking

The methods to fold individual prismoids are based on the principle of *tucking*, as applied in [Tachi 10]. The faces of the prismoid are distributed on the paper, using the volcano unfolding [Pinciu 07].[3] The paper between the faces is then folded up and hidden "underneath" the model, so that the "outer appearance" of the final model is the desired prismoid. The following definition formalizes this notion of "outer appearance" in terms of what parts of the model can be seen if an observer were able to move around the model but not pass through it.

DEFINITION 2.1 (Visible surface). The *visible surface* of some point set $A \subseteq \mathbb{R}^3$ from a given *initial vantage point* $x \in \mathbb{R}^3$ is the boundary of the connected component of $\mathbb{R}^3 - A$ that contains x.

Let π_h denote the plane with equation $z = h$ for some $h \in \mathbb{R}$. For simplicity, the paper is assumed to be π_0, as in [Cheng 11] and [Cheng and Cheong 12]. To illustrate the above definition, the general origami $f : \pi_0 \to \mathbb{R}^3$ considered here has a final model $f(\pi_0)$ that partitions $\mathbb{R}^3$ into connected components. Two components of $\mathbb{R}^3 \setminus f(\pi_0)$ are unbounded—one above the model and one below—and the boundary of the upper one constitutes the visible surface. Here, we assume that the observer sees the model from above (i.e., arbitrarily high initial vantage point), which is why folding prismoids must tuck paper only underneath.

A crease pattern is said to *fold into* a shape V if the visible surface of its folded product is the union of V with some subset of π_0. This is consistent with what the appearance of an origami model is usually considered to be, since flat paper surrounding a 3D model is immediately recognizable as a backdrop that is secondary to the 3D part.

2.1. Prismoid crease patterns.

DEFINITION 2.2 (Prismoid). A *prismoid* is a triplet $F = (R, \mathcal{H}, B)$ containing open convex polygons[4] R and B parallel to π_0, such that R is above B, as well as $\mathcal{H}$, the closure of the convex hull of $R \cup B$. Define $\partial F = \partial \mathcal{H} \setminus (R \cup B)$ as the part of the surface of $\mathcal{H}$ lying outside R and B; the faces of ∂F are required to be trapezoids.

As in [Cheng 11], R and B are respectively called the *roof* and *base* of F (Figure 2). Note that $\mathcal{H}$ is a closed set and that ∂F is topologically equivalent to a closed annulus. R and B must have the same number of vertices n, which is called the *order* of F.

---

[3]The existence of a volcano unfolding that does not overlap depends on the convexity of the prismoid.
[4]Topologically equivalent to open disks.

FIGURE 2. A prismoid $F = (R, \mathcal{H}, B)$. The top and bottom translucent faces are R and B, respectively. The shaded faces together form ∂F.

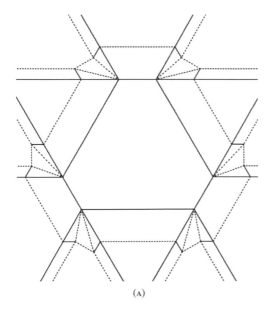

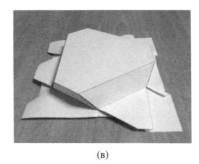

(A)   (B)

FIGURE 3. (a) Crease pattern of a prismoid. (b) The folded product.

Each prismoid $F = (R, \mathcal{H}, B)$ has R lying in some plane with equation $z = z_R$ and B lying in some plane with equation $z = z_B$; to prevent degeneracy we require that R and B lie on different planes—that is, $z_R > z_B$. Extruding a degenerate prismoid ($z_R = z_B$) would take no folding at all!

Noting that a prismoid is a special case of a biplanar, the biplanar crease pattern algorithm presented in [Cheng 11] can generate crease patterns of prismoids. The *positive right frustum* algorithm in [Cheng and Cheong 12], when applied to general prismoids, produces results identical to those of the biplanar algorithm (see Figure 3). Mountain creases will be indicated by solid lines, and dashed lines will represent valley creases.

Figure 4 illustrates how prismoid crease patterns consist of a "central body" of creases C, surrounded by pleats radiating out from C, which are labeled $p_1^{\pm}, \ldots, p_n^{\pm}$ using the notation from [Cheng and Cheong 12]. Each pair (p_j^-, p_j^+) is called a *pleat pair*. The central body comprises the part of the crease pattern that rises above π_0 to form $\mathcal{H}$ upon folding. The rest of the crease pattern comes from pleats, which preserve the flatness of the paper that eventually surrounds B. This results in the following lemma:

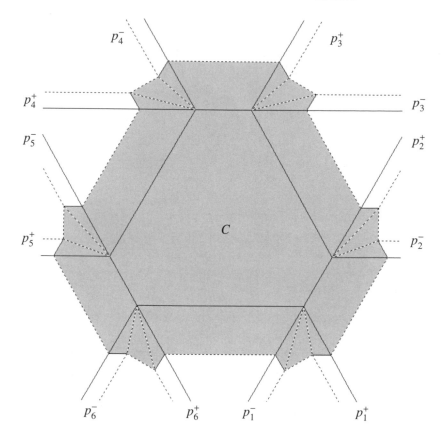

FIGURE 4. A prismoid crease pattern partitioned into a shaded central body C and pleats $p_1^\pm, \ldots p_n^\pm$.

LEMMA 2.3. *When a prismoid $(R, \mathcal{H}, B)$ satisfying $z_B = 0$ is folded, it occupies the point set A, where $\pi_0 \setminus B \subseteq A \subseteq \pi_0 \cup \mathcal{H}$.*

Let $\mathsf{CP}(F) = (C, p_1^\pm, \ldots, p_n^\pm)$ be a tuple of the central body crease pattern C of F and its $2n$ pleats; C comes from the volcano unfolding of F, centered at its roof R. We may assume that this volcano unfolding vertically translates R down to some $R' \subseteq \pi_0$, where $R' = R - z_R \hat{k} = \{r \in R \mid r - z_R \hat{k}\}$ and $\hat{k}$ is the unit z-axis vector. Hence, $\mathsf{CP}(F)$ is associated with an origami $f : \pi_0 \to \mathbb{R}$ that folds it, such that $f(R') = R$.

3. Grafting Prismoids

The desired folded product is a tower of prismoids, which is formally defined as follows:

DEFINITION 3.1 (Prismoid Tower). A *prismoid tower* is a sequence $F_1, \ldots, F_m$ of prismoids $F_i = (R_i, \mathcal{H}_i, B_i)$ such that $z_{B_m} = 0$ and $B_i = R_{i+1}$ for all $1 \le i \le m - 1$.

The following result allows the *order* of a prismoid tower to be defined; without loss of generality, it will also be denoted as n.

LEMMA 3.2. *All prismoids in a prismoid tower must have the same order.*

Given a prismoid tower $F_1, \ldots, F_m$, the objective is to generate a crease pattern that folds into $R_1 \cup \bigcup_{i=1}^{m} \partial F_i$. The intuition for accomplishing that is embodied in Algorithm 1, based on folding individual prismoids. However, the crease pattern generation algorithm for a single prismoid only handles prismoids whose bases lie in π_0, so each F_i must be translated to

$$F_i - z_{B_i}\hat{k} = (R_i - z_{B_i}\hat{k}, \mathcal{H}_i - z_{B_i}\hat{k}, B_i - z_{B_i}\hat{k}).$$

Algorithm 1: Composing prismoids.

input : Prismoid tower $F_1, \ldots, F_m$
output: Crease pattern that folds into $R_1 \cup \bigcup_{i=1}^{m} \partial F_i$
for $i \leftarrow 1$ **to** m **do**
    treat the current model as a new sheet of paper;
    fold all of the creases from $\mathsf{CP}(F_i - z_{B_i}\hat{k})$ to extrude $F_i - z_{B_i}\hat{k}$;
end
for $i \leftarrow m$ **to** 1 **do**
    unfold $F_i - z_{B_i}\hat{k}$;
end
return resultant crease pattern

Algorithm 1 exemplifies the advantages of algorithms built on grafting explained in Section 1: Lines 1–1 show the modularized *folding* algorithm, while Line 1, which reveals more of the crease pattern at each iteration, shows the modularized *design* algorithm.

3.1. Validity of Algorithm 1. Two crucial questions about Algorithm 1 concern Line 1: Is it always possible to fold the next prismoid by treating the current model as a fresh sheet of paper, and does the outcome from folding all of the prismoids produce the desired visible surface of a prismoid tower? Propositions 3.3 and 3.4 address these concerns, respectively.

PROPOSITION 3.3. *After iteration i of Line 1 in Algorithm 1, the model occupies a point set A, where*

$$\pi_0 \setminus (B_i - z_{B_i}\hat{k}) \subseteq A \subseteq \pi_0 \cup \left(\bigcup_{k=1}^{i} \mathcal{H}_k - z_{B_i}\hat{k} \right).$$

PROOF. Prove by induction on i. Lemma 2.3 yields the case $i = 1$. For any $i \in \{2, \ldots, m\}$, suppose that the proposition holds for $i - 1$; the following will demonstrate that it also holds for i.

After iteration $i-1$ of Line 1, $R' = R_i - z_{R_i}\hat{k}$ is a face of the crease pattern $\mathsf{CP}(F_i - z_{B_i}\hat{k})$, and thus the creases of $\mathsf{CP}(F_i - z_{B_i}\hat{k})$ all lie within $\pi_0 \setminus R'$. Note, however, that for all $k \in \{1, \ldots, i-2\}$, $\mathcal{H}_k - z_{B_{i-1}}\hat{k}$ lies above $B_k - z_{B_{i-1}}\hat{k}$, while $z_{B_k} > z_{B_{i-1}} = z_{R_i}$. Therefore,

$$\pi_0 \cap \left(\bigcup_{k=1}^{i-1} \mathcal{H}_k - z_{B_{i-1}}\hat{k} \right) = \pi_0 \cap (\mathcal{H}_{i-1} - z_{B_{i-1}}\hat{k}) = \overline{B_{i-1}} - z_{B_{i-1}}\hat{k} = \overline{R_i} - z_{R_i}\hat{k} = \overline{R'},$$

where $\overline{R'}$ denotes the closure of R'.

This means that the creases in $\mathsf{CP}(F_i - z_{B_i}\hat{k})$ only lie on the flat paper surrounding the 3D part of the folded model. Hence, to carry out iteration i of Line 1, we may fold the flat surrounding paper by restricting the origami $f : \pi_0 \to \mathbb{R}^3$ (corresponding to $\mathsf{CP}(F_i - z_{B_i}\hat{k})$)

to $\pi_0 \setminus R'$ and transforming the 3D part using the upwards translation of $+(z_{R_i} - z_{B_i})\hat{k}$. After folding, the model now occupies a subset of

$$\overbrace{\pi_0 \cup (\mathcal{H}_i - z_{B_i}\hat{k})}^{\text{folded CP}(F_i - z_{B_i}\hat{k})} \cup \left(\overbrace{\left(\bigcup_{k=1}^{i-1} \mathcal{H}_k - z_{R_i}\hat{k}\right) + (z_{R_i} - z_{B_i})\hat{k}}^{\text{translated 3D part}}\right) = \pi_0 \cup \left(\bigcup_{k=1}^{i} \mathcal{H}_k - z_{B_i}\hat{k}\right).$$

The new flat surrounding paper occupies the same point set as that resulting from folding $F_i - z_{B_i}\hat{k}$, which by Lemma 2.3 contains $\pi_0 \setminus (B_i - z_{B_i}\hat{k})$.

Therefore, the proposition holds for i, which completes the induction proof. $\square$

PROPOSITION 3.4. *After iteration i of Line 1 in Algorithm 1, the paper has been folded to $(R_1 \cup \bigcup_{k=1}^{i} \partial F_k) - z_{B_i}\hat{k}$.*

PROOF. Prove by induction on i. When $i = 1$, a single prismoid has been folded, and the proposition holds because of the algorithm used to fold a single prismoid.

For any $i \in \{2, \ldots, m\}$, suppose that after iteration $i - 1$ of Line 1, the paper has been folded to $(R_1 \cup \bigcup_{k=1}^{i-1} \partial F_k) - z_{B_{i-1}}\hat{k}$. That is, the model occupies the point set $A \subseteq \mathbb{R}^3$, and the upper unbounded connected component of $\mathbb{R}^3 \setminus A$, denoted by C, has boundary

$$P \cup \left(\left(R_1 \cup \bigcup_{k=1}^{i-1} \partial F_k\right) - z_{B_{i-1}}\hat{k}\right)$$

for some $P \subseteq \pi_0$. In fact, Proposition 3.3 guarantees that $\pi_0 \setminus (B_{i-1} - z_{B_{i-1}}\hat{k}) \subseteq A$, so we may assume that $P = \pi_0 \setminus (B_{i-1} - z_{B_{i-1}}\hat{k})$. This indicates that $C = U \setminus (\bigcup_{k=1}^{i-1} \mathcal{H}_k - z_{B_{i-1}}\hat{k})$, where $U = \mathbb{R}^2 \times (0, \infty)$ is the upper half-space.

Now, consider what could be the upper unbounded connected component C' of $\mathbb{R}^3 \setminus A'$, where A' is occupied by the model after carrying out iteration i of Line 1. The part of C' above the plane $\pi_{z_{R_i} - z_{B_i}}$ is simply $C + (z_{R_i} - z_{B_i})\hat{k}$, from the vertical translation argument in the proof of Proposition 3.3. A_0, the part of the model below $\pi_{z_{R_i} - z_{B_i}}$, is simply what would result from folding F_i by itself; the upper unbounded connected component of $\mathbb{R}^3 \setminus A_0$ would then be $C_0 = U \setminus (\mathcal{H}_i - z_{B_i}\hat{k})$.

Note that since

$$\mathcal{H}_i - z_{B_i}\hat{\boldsymbol{k}} \subseteq \mathbb{R}^2 \times (0, z_{R_i} - z_{B_i}]$$

$$\bigcup_{k=1}^{i-1} \mathcal{H}_k - z_{R_i}\hat{\boldsymbol{k}} + (z_{R_i} - z_{B_i})\hat{\boldsymbol{k}} = \bigcup_{k=1}^{i-1} \mathcal{H}_k - z_{B_i}\hat{\boldsymbol{k}}$$

$$\subseteq \mathbb{R}^2 \times (z_{R_i} - z_{B_i}, \infty)$$

$$\implies C_0 = (\mathbb{R}^2 \times (0, z_{R_i} - z_{B_i}]) \setminus (\mathcal{H}_i - z_{B_i}\hat{\boldsymbol{k}})$$

$$= \left((\mathbb{R}^2 \times (0, \infty)) \setminus \left(\bigcup_{k=1}^{i} \mathcal{H}_k - z_{B_i}\hat{\boldsymbol{k}} \right) \right) \cap (\mathbb{R}^2 \times (0, z_{R_i} - z_{B_i}])$$

$$C + (z_{R_i} - z_{B_i})\hat{\boldsymbol{k}} = (\mathbb{R}^2 \times (z_{R_i} - z_{B_i}, \infty)) \setminus \left(\bigcup_{k=1}^{i-1} \mathcal{H}_k - z_{B_i}\hat{\boldsymbol{k}} \right)$$

$$= \left((\mathbb{R}^2 \times (0, \infty)) \setminus \left(\bigcup_{k=1}^{i} \mathcal{H}_k - z_{B_i}\hat{\boldsymbol{k}} \right) \right) \cap (\mathbb{R}^2 \times (z_{R_i} - z_{B_i}, \infty])$$

$$\implies C' = C_0 \cup (C + (z_{R_i} - z_{B_i})\hat{\boldsymbol{k}})$$

$$= (\mathbb{R}^2 \times (0, \infty)) \setminus \left(\bigcup_{k=1}^{i} \mathcal{H}_k - z_{B_i}\hat{\boldsymbol{k}} \right).$$

Therefore, the boundary of C', outside of π_0, is the "outward boundary" of $\bigcup_{k=1}^{i} \mathcal{H}_k - z_{B_i}\hat{\boldsymbol{k}}$, namely $(R_1 \cup \bigcup_{k=1}^{i} \partial F_k) - z_{B_i}\hat{\boldsymbol{k}}$. The proposition holds for i, which completes the induction proof. $\qquad\square$

The above results establish the validity of Algorithm 1; in particular, since $z_{B_m} = 0$, Proposition 3.4 guarantees that after iteration m of Line 1, the paper has been folded to $R_1 \cup \bigcup_{k=1}^{m} \partial F_k$. However, it does not explicitly show how to compute the crease pattern. Algorithms for explicit computation will be the focus of subsequent sections.

3.2. Pleat splitting. The complexity of the crease pattern for a prismoid tower arises largely from the mutual interference of pleats between different prismoids. Figure 5 shows the outcome of folding a pleat p (consisting of parallel creases c_m and c_v), then folding a crease c on it and unfolding everything. The overall effect is that each of the three regions bounded by c_m and c_v receives a truncated copy of c; c_2 was truncated after reflecting c around c_m, while c_3 was truncated after reflecting c around c_m and then c_v. Each reflection reverses the mountain-valley assignment of the crease. This process is termed the *pleat splitting* of a crease.

The resulting set of creases $\{c_1, c_2, c_3\}$ is denoted by $\mathsf{Split}(p, c)$, in accordance with notation from [Cheng and Cheong 12], which details the computation and further properties concerning the Split operator. At Line 1 of Algorithm 1, before unfolding prismoid F_i, the paper already has some crease pattern C on it.[5] The process of unfolding F_i can roughly be decomposed into the unfolding of each individual pleat, each of which splits every crease in C within its reach.

However, pleats from the same prismoid must also split one another when they meet, as illustrated in Figure 6. The splitting of intersecting pleats is inevitable because one of the pleats must be folded before the other.

---

[5]Indeed, C is the crease pattern of the prismoid tower $F_{i+1}, \ldots, F_m$.

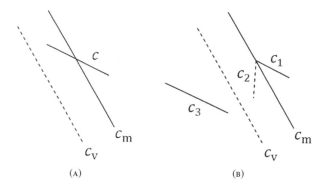

FIGURE 5. (a) A pleat with creases c_m and c_v splitting a crease c. (b) The resultant creases c_1, c_2, and c_3.

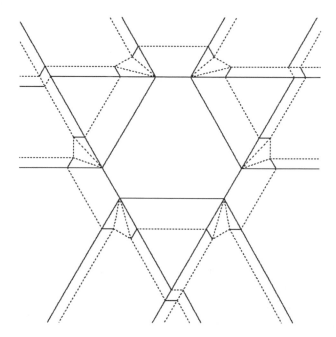

FIGURE 6. Pleats from this prismoid have split each other.

The resulting crease pattern shows a common zigzag pattern at pleat intersections, which actually coincides with the "crossover gadget" introduced by Bern and Hayes [Bern and Hayes 96].

Unfolding F_i is not exactly the successive unfolding of its pleats, because no pleat can be unfolded without distorting the origami model and consequently unfolding other pleats near it. The pleats are "coupled" with one another due to the isometry of origami, which prevents the paper from stretching or tearing. The authors of [Cheng and Cheong 12] dealt with this problem by partitioning the flat surrounding paper into *sectors*.

3.3. Modified sectors. The rationale behind the sectorial approach in [Cheng and Cheong 12] is a conceptual simplification of Line 1 of Algorithm 1. The paper

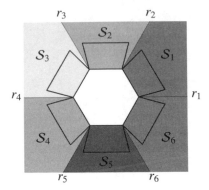

FIGURE 7. Right frusta [Cheng and Cheong 12] give rise to rotationally symmetric, disjoint sectors $S_1, \ldots, S_6$ (colored) bounded by rays $r_1, \ldots, r_6$. Thick lines outline the net (volcano unfolding) of the frustum.

is partitioned into n sectors by rays $r_1, \ldots, r_n$; each r_j is the angle bisector of the pleat pair (p_j^-, p_j^+). Before unfolding, the paper surrounding the extruded model is "cut" at the rays r_j bounding the sectors before opening it up. The cutting "decouples" the sectors to allow each sector to unfold in isolation from the others. Unfolding all of them sequentially gives the same result as not cutting the paper and unfolding everything at once. The "cutting" is done by partitioning the crease pattern into portions that lie in individual sectors (Figure 7), after which most of the "unfolding" is done with the Split operator from [Cheng and Cheong 12].

The n-fold rotational symmetry of the system was exploited in [Cheng and Cheong 12], because it led to each sector being unfolded back into itself, allowing the sector to be reused when unfolding the next F_i. More importantly, the symmetry forces the sectors to be mutually disjoint. Both of these properties no longer hold in the case of general prismoids, so the sectors at each prismoid must be recomputed. The (modified) sectors are still bounded by the angle bisector rays $r_1, \ldots, r_n$, but now sectors can overlap. The common region is simply assigned to the earliest sector it belongs to, while removing it from the other sectors, because it suffices to partition the crease pattern into regions that can be independently unfolded (Figure 8).

Algorithm 2 performs the partitioning.

The unfolding process is adapted from [Cheng and Cheong 12], and it involves one more step before performing the pleat splitting: Unfolding sector S_j moves it outward by some translation vector $t_j(F)$, which can be easily computed, as shown in Figure 9.

Algorithm 3 performs the entire process of unfolding, completed by the Split operator, resulting in a crease pattern denoted by $F \circledast (S_1, \ldots, S_n)$.

This leads to Algorithm 4, a *provisional* algorithm that generates crease patterns for prismoid towers. Let $r_j(F)$ denote the ray that bisects the angle between the pleat pair (p_j^-, p_j^+) in F.

4. Subdividing Prismoids

Unfortunately, Algorithm 4 is insufficient because successfully folding the resultant crease pattern may require the paper to penetrate itself. This *overlapping* phenomenon was highlighted in [Cheng 11] and [Cheng and Cheong 12], and the root of the problem

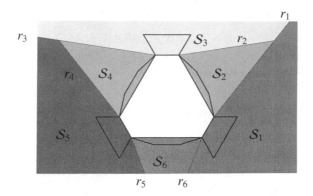

FIGURE 8. Without n-fold rotational symmetry, mutually intersecting sectors must be modified to constitute a partition. Some rays r_j are truncated into line segments as a result of overlapping sectors.

Algorithm 2: Partitioning a crease pattern into modified sectors.

input : Crease pattern C and angle bisector rays $r_1, \ldots, r_n$
output: $\text{Sect}(C, r_1, \ldots, r_n) = n$-tuple of crease patterns that partition C
for $j \leftarrow 1$ **to** n **do**
    $S_j \leftarrow \emptyset$;
    $S_j \leftarrow$ region bounded by r_j, r_{j+1} and the line segment $b_j b_{j+1}$;
    for *each crease c in C* **do**
        include into S_j the part of c lying inside S_j;
        replace the crease c in C by the part of c lying outside S_j;
    end
end
return $(S_1, \ldots, S_n)$

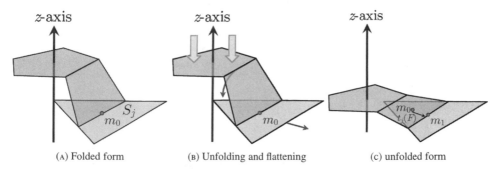

FIGURE 9. S_j, the part of the crease pattern lying inside S_j, is translated by vector $t_j(F)$ upon unfolding.

is overlapping within prismoids caused by some segments in the crease pattern that, when folded, take up space along the base edges. Given a prismoid $F = (R, \mathcal{H}, B)$, number its roof vertices $r_1, r_2, \ldots, r_n$ and base vertices $b_1, b_2, \ldots, b_n$ so that r_j and b_j are connected

Algorithm 3: Composing a prismoid with a partitioned crease pattern.

input : Prismoid F and partitioned crease pattern $(S_1, \ldots, S_n)$
output: $F \circledast (S_1, \ldots, S_n)$ = Crease pattern from extruding F, folding $\bigcup_{j=1}^{n} S_j$ then
        unfolding everything
$(C, p_1^{\pm}, \ldots, p_n^{\pm}) \leftarrow \mathsf{CP}(F)$;
for $j \leftarrow 1$ **to** n **do**
    $S_j \leftarrow S_j + t_j(F)$;
    for $j' \leftarrow 1$ **to** n **do**
        $S_j \leftarrow \bigcup_{c \in S_j} \mathsf{Split}(p_{j'}^{-}, c)$;
        include into S_j the part of the creases of $p_{j'}^{-}$ lying inside S_j;
        $S_j \leftarrow \bigcup_{c \in S_j} \mathsf{Split}(p_{j'}^{+}, c)$;
        include into S_j the part of the creases of $p_{j'}^{+}$ lying inside S_j;
    end
end
return $C \cup S_1 \cup \cdots \cup S_n$

Algorithm 4: Composing a tower of prismoids.

input : A prismoid tower $F_1, \ldots, F_m$
output: Crease pattern that folds into $R_1 \cup \bigcup_{i=1}^{m} \partial F_i$
$C \leftarrow \emptyset$;
for $i \leftarrow m$ **to** 1 **do**
    $C \leftarrow F \circledast \mathsf{Sect}(C, r_1(F_i), \ldots, r_n(F_i))$;   /* Algorithms 2 & 3 */
end
return C

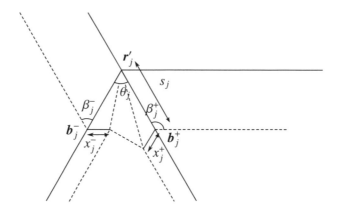

FIGURE 10. At vertex j, segments x_j^- and x_j^+ take up space along their respective base edges when folded, which can lead to overlapping.

by an edge of F. Figure 10 labels those segments by x_j^- and x_j^+, using the notation from [Cheng 11].

    Upon folding, the point r_j' moves to r_j, and both points $b_j^{\pm}$ move to b_j. This means that $s_j = \|r_j - b_j\|$ (see Figure 10). Segments x_j^+ and x_{j+1}^- take up space along base edge $b_j b_{j+1}$,

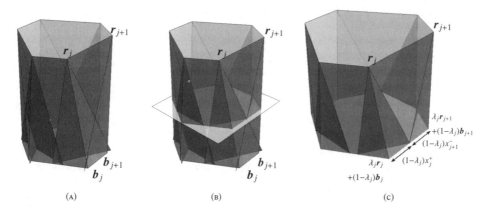

FIGURE 11. (a) A prismoid with dark triangles that show the paper to be hidden inside the prismoid upon folding. The interpenetrating triangles cause overlapping at the base edges. (b) A subdivision plane corrsponding to the ratio λ_j. (c) The smaller prismoid above the subdivision plane.

so when those segments have a greater combined length than the base edge, the prismoid cannot be folded without paper self-intersection. The lengths x_j^+ and x_{j+1}^- are calculated as follows.

Denote the angular defect of F at $\mathbf{r}_j$ by the *inner angle* θ_j, and define the *outer angle* as

$$\phi_j = \angle \mathbf{r}_j \mathbf{b}_j \mathbf{b}_{j+1} + \angle \mathbf{r}_j \mathbf{b}_j \mathbf{b}_{j-1} - \angle \mathbf{b}_{j-1} \mathbf{b}_j \mathbf{b}_{j+1} = \beta_j^+ + \beta_j^- - \angle \mathbf{b}_{j-1} \mathbf{b}_j \mathbf{b}_{j+1}.$$

Recalling that prismoids are convex prismatoids, the proof of Theorem 2 in [Cheng 11] demonstrates that $\theta_j = \phi_j$ for each $1 \le j \le n$. This simplifies the formula for the length of the line segments that take up space along the edges of B:

$$x_j^\pm = \frac{s_j \sin \frac{\theta_j}{2}}{2 \cos \frac{\theta_j + \phi_j}{4} \sin(\beta_j^\pm + \frac{\theta_j - \phi_j}{4})} = \frac{\|\mathbf{r}_j - \mathbf{b}_j\| \tan \frac{\theta_j}{2}}{2 \sin \beta_j^\pm}.$$

In [Cheng and Cheong 12], any overlapping in F is solved by subdividing it with planes, parallel to π_0, that lie between R and B; a new mathematical formulation of this process is now given for the case of general prismoids. A subdivision plane divides F into two smaller prismoids on either side, such that the top and bottom prismoids have heights in the ratio $1 - \lambda : \lambda$, where $0 < \lambda < 1$. The $x_j^\pm$ of the top and bottom prismoids have been scaled by factors $1 - \lambda$ and λ, respectively, reducing the extent of overlap in each prismoid. The objective is to divide F with enough planes into smaller prismoids so that each resulting prismoid experiences no overlap.

Figure 11 shows the paper to be hidden inside F upon folding as dark triangles. When overlapping occurs on the base edge $\mathbf{b}_j \mathbf{b}_{j+1}$, the triangles whose apexes are $\mathbf{r}_j$ and $\mathbf{r}_{j+1}$ must penetrate each other. Figure 11(a) shows that those two triangles have an "earliest" point of interpenetration, at the highest point of their intersection. If a subdivision plane π passes through that point, the corresponding base edge of the smaller prismoid above π will not experience overlap. As explained earlier, π corresponds to a subdivision ratio λ_j, which can be calculated by considering the part of the face $\mathbf{r}_j \mathbf{b}_j \mathbf{b}_{j+1} \mathbf{r}_{j+1}$ in Figure 11(c):

$$\|(\lambda_j \mathbf{r}_j + (1 - \lambda_j)\mathbf{b}_j) - (\lambda_j \mathbf{r}_{j+1} + (1 - \lambda_j)\mathbf{b}_{j+1})\| = (1 - \lambda_j)x_j^+ + (1 - \lambda_j)x_{j+1}^-.$$

Observing that $r_j - r_{j+1}$ and $b_j - b_{j+1}$ are parallel gives

$$\lambda_j \|r_j - r_{j+1}\| + (1 - \lambda_j)\|b_j - b_{j+1}\| = (1 - \lambda_j)(x_j^+ + x_{j+1}^-)$$

$$\implies \lambda_j = \frac{x_j^+ + x_{j+1}^- - \|b_j - b_{j+1}\|}{\|r_j - r_{j+1}\| + x_j^+ + x_{j+1}^- - \|b_j - b_{j+1}\|}$$

$$= 1 - \frac{\|r_j - r_{j+1}\|}{\|r_j - r_{j+1}\| + x_j^+ + x_{j+1}^- - \|b_j - b_{j+1}\|}.$$

Overlapping only occurs when $0 < \lambda_j < 1$, which corresponds to a subdivision plane that lies between R and B. F needs a subdivision plane so that the top prismoid is as large as possible, yet contains no overlapping. (This greedy heuristic leads to the most efficient subdivision, as proven later in Theorem 4.4.) The plane $\pi_{z_B + \lambda_F(z_R - z_B)}$ is the best choice, where $\lambda_F = \max\{\lambda_j : 1 \le j \le n, 0 < \lambda_j < 1\}$ exists only when overlapping occurs on some edge of B. If it exists, the prismoid is split into two by $\pi_{z_B + \lambda_F(z_R - z_B)}$, and the bottom half is tested for overlapping and handled recursively. In this manner the prismoid tower can be preprocessed so that each prismoid that has overlapping is replaced by a sequence of smaller prismoids that result from the splitting described above. Each smaller prismoid will be shallow enough to avoid overlapping when being folded, as shown in Figure 11(c). After that preprocessing, Algorithm 4 will suffice to generate the crease pattern.

4.1. Termination.

THEOREM 4.1. *The prismoid subdivision preprocessing must terminate.*

PROOF. Assume that subdivision of a prismoid $F^0 = (R^0, \mathcal{H}^0, B)$ does not terminate. The bottom half of F^0 after the first subdivision is another prismoid $F^1 = (R^1, \mathcal{H}^1, B)$. The next subdivision yields another prismoid $F^2 = (R^2, \mathcal{H}^2, B)$ as the bottom half of F^1; in this manner define an infinite sequence of prismoids $F^k = (R^k, \mathcal{H}^k, B)$ for integers $k \ge 0$, where F^k has roof vertices $r_1(F^k), r_2(F^k), \ldots, r_n(F^k)$ numbered corresponding to the base vertices $b_1, \ldots, b_n$. Similarly, define the variables $\theta_j(F^k), \beta_j^\pm(F^k), x_j^\pm(F^k)$, and $\lambda_j(F^k)$ for F^k.

However, due to the parallel subdividing planes, the corresponding angles of every F^k are unchanged, so $\theta_j(F^k) = \theta_j(F^0)$ and $\beta_j^\pm(F^k) = \beta_j^\pm(F^0)$ for all $k \ge 0$. For each $k \ge 0$, choose some $1 \le j_k \le n$ for which $\lambda_{j_k}(F^k)$ attains λ_{F^k}. The key observation from Figure 11 that

$$r_j(F^{k+1}) - b_j = \lambda_{j_k}(F^k)(r_j(F^k) - b_j) \text{ for all } k \ge 0$$

leads to the following lemma:

LEMMA 4.2. $x_j^\pm(F^{k+1}) = \lambda_{j_k}(F^k)x_j^\pm(F^k)$ *for all* $k \ge 0$ *and* $1 \le j \le n$.

PROOF.

$$x_j^\pm(F^{k+1}) = \frac{\|r_j(F^{k+1}) - b_j\| \tan\frac{\theta_j}{2}}{2 \sin\beta_j^\pm}$$

$$= \lambda_{j_k}(F^k)\frac{\|r_j(F^k) - b_j\| \tan\frac{\theta_j}{2}}{2 \sin\beta_j^\pm}$$

$$= \lambda_{j_k}(F^k)x_j^\pm(F^k).$$

$\square$

Since overlapping must occur before every subdivision, $0 < \lambda_{j_k}(F^k) < 1$ for all $k \geq 0$. It is easy to deduce from Lemma 4.2 that for all $1 \leq j \leq n$, $x_j^{\pm}(F^k) = x_j^{\pm}(F^0) \prod_{i=0}^{k-1} \lambda_{j_i}(F^i)$ and thus $x_j^{\pm}(F^0) > x_j^{\pm}(F^1) > \cdots. x_j^{\pm}(F^k)$ evolves with successive subdivisions; the key idea is to bound that evolution.

Define X as the maximum among all of the $x_j^{\pm}(F^0)$. Let L be the minimum among the roof and base edge lengths of F^0.

LEMMA 4.3. $\|r_j(F^k) - r_{j+1}(F^k)\| \geq L$ for all $k \geq 0$ and $1 \leq j \leq n$.

PROOF. Induct on k; the base case $k = 0$ follows immediately from the definition of L. For any $1 \leq j \leq n$, assume that $\|r_j(F^k) - r_{j+1}(F^k)\| \geq L$ for some $k \geq 0$. Then,

$$\|r_j(F^{k+1}) - r_{j+1}(F^{k+1})\|$$
$$= \lambda_{j_k}(F^k)\|r_j(F^k) - r_{j+1}(F^k)\| + (1 - \lambda_{j_k}(F^k))\|b_j - b_{j+1}\|$$
$$\geq \lambda_{j_k}(F^k)L + (1 - \lambda_{j_k}(F^k))L = L.$$

$\square$

This yields a bound on $\lambda_{j_k}(F^k)$:

$$0 < \lambda_{j_k}(F^k) = \frac{x_j^+(F^k) + x_{j+1}^-(F^k) - \|b_j - b_{j+1}\|}{\|r_j(F^k) - r_{j+1}(F^k)\| + x_j^+(F^k) + x_{j+1}^-(F^k) - \|b_j - b_{j+1}\|}$$

$$\leq \frac{x_j^+(F^k) + x_{j+1}^-(F^k) - \|b_j - b_{j+1}\|}{L + x_j^+(F^k) + x_{j+1}^-(F^k) - \|b_j - b_{j+1}\|}$$

$$= 1 - \frac{L}{L + x_j^+(F^k) + x_{j+1}^-(F^k) - \|b_j - b_{j+1}\|}$$

$$\leq 1 - \frac{L}{L + 2X - L} = 1 - \frac{L}{2X} < 1.$$

Returning to $x_j^{\pm}(F^k)$,

$$x_j^{\pm}(F^k) = x_j^{\pm}(F^0) \prod_{i=0}^{k-1} \lambda_{j_i}(F^i) \leq x_j^{\pm}(F^0)\left(1 - \frac{L}{2X}\right)^k.$$

This means that $x_j^+(F^k) + x_{j+1}^-(F^k)$ must decay to zero as k increases and fall below $\|b_j - b_{j+1}\|$ after some k_jth subdivision. Then, after the $(\max_{1 \leq j \leq n} k_j)$th subdivision, no overlap can occur on any edge of B, which contradicts our initial assumption that the subdivision process does not terminate.

To conclude, prismoid subdivision *must* terminate. $\square$

4.2. Optimality.

THEOREM 4.4. *The subdivision preprocessing on each prismoid uses the fewest possible subdivisions.*

PROOF. Given a prismoid $F = (R, \mathcal{H}, B)$ and any distinct *heights* $0 \leq h, h' \geq z_R - z_B$, let $F(h, h')$ denote the prismoid bounded by F and the planes $z = h + z_B$ and $z = h' + z_B$; with the notation from Theorem 4.1, define $x_j^{\pm}(F(h, h'))$ and $\lambda_j(F(h, h'))$. Subdivide F using the procedure described; Theorem 4.1 guarantees that a finite number s of planes will suffice. Let the resultant subdivision planes have equations $z = h_1 + z_B, z = h_2 + z_B, \ldots, z = h_s + z_B$, where $h_1 > \cdots > h_s > 0$.

Assume that there is a more efficient subdivision of F that resolves overlapping using t planes with equations $z = h^1 + z_B, z = h^2 + z_B, \ldots, z = h^t + z_B$, where $h^1 > \cdots > h^t > 0$. Similarly, no overlapping can occur in $F(h^i, h^{i+1})$ for $0 \leq i \leq t$, where $h^0 = z_R - z_B$ and $h^{t+1} = 0$. Greater efficiency means fewer subdivisions, so $t < s$. The key lemma is as follows:

PROPOSITION 4.5. $h_i \leq h^i$ for all $1 \leq i \leq t$.

PROOF. Prove by induction on i. Referring back to Figure 11, the plane $z = h_1 + z_B$ corresponds to the subdivision ratio λ_F, at the highest point of overlap in F. F is only free of overlap in the space above (and including) the plane $z = h_1 + z_B$, which means that $h^1 \geq h_1$—the base case $i = 1$.

Assume the induction hypothesis for some $1 \leq k \leq t - 1$, that is, that $h_k \leq h^k$. Imagine that $F^k = F(h^k, h_B)$ is subdivided by the plane $z = h_k + z_B$ into $F(h^k, h_k)$ and $F_k = F(h_k, h_B)$. Let the base vertices of F (and F^k and F_k) be $b_1, \ldots, b_n$. Similar to Equation (4.2), for every $1 \leq j \leq n$,

$$\|r_j(F_k) - r_{j+1}(F_k)\| = \frac{h_k}{h^k}\|r_j(F^k) - r_{j+1}(F^k)\| + \left(1 - \frac{h_k}{h^k}\right)\|b_j - b_{j+1}\|.$$

As in Theorem 4.1, for each $k \geq 0$, choose some $1 \leq j_k \leq n$ for which $\lambda_{j_k}(F_k)$ attains λ_{F_k}:

$$\lambda_{j_k}(F_k) = \frac{x^+_{j_k}(F_k) + x^-_{j_k+1}(F_k) - \|b_{j_k} - b_{j_k+1}\|}{\|r_{j_k}(F_k) - r_{j_k+1}(F_k)\| + x^+_{j_k}(F_k) + x^-_{j_k+1}(F_k) - \|b_{j_k} - b_{j_k+1}\|}$$

$$= \frac{\frac{h_k}{h^k}(x^+_{j_k}(F^k) + x^-_{j_k+1}(F^k)) - \|b_{j_k} - b_{j_k+1}\|}{\frac{h_k}{h^k}\|r_{j_k}(F^k) - r_{j_k+1}(F^k)\| + \left(1 - \frac{h_k}{h^k}\right)\|b_{j_k} - b_{j_k+1}\|}$$
$$+ \frac{h_k}{h^k}(x^+_{j_k}(F^k) + x^-_{j_k+1}(F^k)) - \|b_{j_k} - b_{j_k+1}\|$$

$$= \frac{x^+_{j_k}(F^k) + x^-_{j_k+1}(F^k) - \frac{h^k}{h_k}\|b_{j_k} - b_{j_k+1}\|}{\|r_{j_k}(F^k) - r_{j_k+1}(F^k)\| + x^+_{j_k}(F^k) + x^-_{j_k+1}(F^k) - \|b_{j_k} - b_{j_k+1}\|}$$

$$\leq \frac{x^+_{j_k}(F^k) + x^-_{j_k+1}(F^k) - \|b_{j_k} - b_{j_k+1}\|}{\|r_{j_k}(F^k) - r_{j_k+1}(F^k)\| + x^+_{j_k}(F^k) + x^-_{j_k+1}(F^k) - \|b_{j_k} - b_{j_k+1}\|}$$

$$= \lambda_{j_k}(F^k).$$

The inequality holds because the denominator is positive: Since $k < s$, the subdivision could not have terminated yet, so overlapping must occur on the j_kth face. That is,

$$x^+_{j_k}(F_k) + x^-_{j_k+1}(F_k) > \|b_{j_k} - b_{j_k+1}\|$$
$$\implies \|r_{j_k}(F_k) - r_{j_k+1}(F_k)\| + x^+_{j_k}(F_k) + x^-_{j_k+1}(F_k) - \|b_{j_k} - b_{j_k+1}\|$$
$$> \|r_{j_k}(F_k) - r_{j_k+1}(F_k)\| \geq 0.$$

Now consider the next subdivision planes for both algorithms (neither of them have terminated yet since $k < t < s$). The subdivision procedure dictates that F_k is to be subdivided by the plane $z = z_{k+1}$ that corresponds to the ratio $\lambda_{F_k} = h_{k+1}/h_k$. Returning to the reasoning for the base case, some plane π corresponds to the ratio $\lambda_i(F^k)$, and F^k is only free of overlapping above π. Since $F(h^k, h^{k+1})$ must be free of overlap, it follows that the plane $z = h^{k+1} + z_B$ cannot lie below π. Therefore,

$$\frac{h^{k+1}}{h^k} \geq \lambda_{F^k} \geq \lambda_{j_k}(F^k) \geq \lambda_{j_k}(F_k) = \lambda_{F_k} = \frac{h_{k+1}}{h_k} \implies \frac{h^{k+1}}{h_{k+1}} \geq \frac{h^k}{h_k} \geq 1$$

$$\implies h_{k+1} \leq h^{k+1}.$$

$\square$

However, note that $F(h^t, h^{t+1})$ also experiences no overlap, so the induction step used in Proposition 4.5 can be applied to show that $h^{t+1} \geq h_{t+1} > 0$, contradicting the fact that $h^{t+1} = 0$.

$\square$

5. Conclusion

The algorithms in [Cheng and Cheong 12] have been generalized and have undergone original modifications to generate crease patterns for extruded towers of prismoids. Crease patterns of individual prismoids in a prismoid tower can be generated by algorithms from [Cheng 11] and [Cheng and Cheong 12], and those crease patterns can be composed by grafting; the intuition has been presented in Algorithm 1. The sectorial approach in [Cheng and Cheong 12] has been modified to cope with the loss of n-fold rotational symmetry and enhanced into Algorithm 2. Algorithm 3 composes crease patterns together using the conceptual simplification afforded by the modified sectors, as long as prismoid towers are preprocessed by subdividing prismoids to mitigate overlapping.

Prismoid towers as defined here have convex cross sections when sliced parallel to π_0; future investigations could consider folding generalized prismoid towers that can have concave cross sections, or even towers of prismatoids. Algorithms may also potentially fold several prismoid towers from a single sheet of paper. The idea of grafting may give rise to more novel modularized algorithms to push the boundaries of algorithmic origami design.

Acknowledgments

We thank the reviewers for their valuable suggestions that have helped to improve this article.

References

[belcastro and Hull 02] sarah-marie belcastro and Thomas C. Hull. "Modelling the Folding of Paper into Three Dimensions Using Affine Transformations." *Linear Algebra and Its Applications* 348 (2002), 273–282. MR1902132 (2003b:15003)

[Benbernou et al. 11] Nadia M. Benbernou, Erik D. Demaine, Martin L. Demaine, and Aviv Ovadya. "Universal Hinge Patterns for Folding Orthogonal Shapes." In *Origami⁵: Fifth International Meeting of Origami Science, Mathematics, and Education*, edited by Patsy Wang-Iverson, Robert J. Lang, and Mark Yim, pp. 405–420. Boca Raton, FL: A K Peters/CRC Press, 2011. MR2866899 (2012k:00004)

[Bern and Hayes 96] Marshall Bern and Barry Hayes. "The Complexity of Flat Origami." In *Proceedings of the Seventh Annual ACM-SIAM Symposium on Discrete Algorithms*, pp. 175–183. Philadelphia: SIAM, 1996. MR1381938 (97c:52016)

[Cheng and Cheong 12] Herng Yi Cheng and Kang Hao Cheong. "Designing Crease Patterns for Polyhedra by Composing Right Frusta." *Computer-Aided Design* 44:4 (2012), 331–342.

[Cheng 11] Herng Yi Cheng. "A General Method of Drawing Biplanar Crease Patterns." In *Origami⁵: Fifth International Meeting of Origami Science, Mathematics, and Education*, edited by Patsy Wang-Iverson, Robert J. Lang, and Mark Yim, pp. 405–420. Boca Raton, FL: A K Peters/CRC Press, 2011. MR2866909 (2012h:00044)

[Demaine and O'Rourke 07] Erik D. Demaine and Joseph O'Rourke. *Geometric Folding Algorithms: Linkages, Origami, Polyhedra*. Cambridge, UK: Cambridge University Press, 2007. MR2354878 (2008g:52001)

[LaFosse 05] Michael G. LaFosse. *Advanced Origami*. Singapore: Tuttle Publishing, 2005.

[Lang 03] Robert J. Lang. *Origami Design Secrets: Mathematical Methods for an Ancient Art*. Natick, MA: A K Peters, 2003. MR2013930 (2004g:52001)

[Mitani 09] Jun Mitani. "A Design Method for 3D Origami Based on Rotational Sweep." *Computer-Aided Design and Applications* 6 (2009), 69–79.

[Pinciu 07] Val Pinciu. "On the Fewest Nets Problem for Convex Polyhedra." In *Proceedings of the 19th Annual Canadian Conference on Computational Geometry (CCCG)*, pp. 21–24. Ottawa, Canada: Carelton University, 2007.

[Tachi 10] Tomohiro Tachi. "Origamizing Polyhedral Surfaces." *IEEE Transactions on Visualization and Computer Graphics* 16 (2010), 298–311.

MASSACHUSETTS INSTITUTE OF TECHNOLOGY, CAMBRIDGE, MASSACHUSETTS
E-mail address: herngyi@mit.edu

On Pleat Rearrangements in Pureland Tessellations

Goran Konjevod

1. Introduction

Since 2005 I have folded hundreds of pureland tessellation models based on alternating of simple horizontal and vertical pleats. The simplest of these patterns was originally introduced by Paul Jackson [Jackson 91]. Most of these foldings are constructed on a uniform square grid and the pleats all follow gridlines. Despite this basic simplicity, variations in the pleating order lead to different tension forces in the folded sheet, which in turn cause curvature in the folded sheet. Thus, a simple repetitive process of folding straight lines leads naturally to a broad range of three-dimensional folded shapes.

In 2008, Andrew Hudson posted on Flickr examples of a more general approach that, in addition to simple pleating, includes the step of rearranging some pleats after the folding [Hudson 08]. No new creases are created in this process, but some change their type. This technique provides an easy way to produce some interesting visual effects. The simplest is a cyclic sequence of pleats p_1, p_2, p_3, p_4 in which p_1 apparently must be folded before p_2, p_2 before p_3, p_3 before p_4, and p_4 before p_1. (Clearly, one way to do this is to fold them in order $p_1, \ldots, p_4$ and then rearrange the intersection of p_1 and p_4 so that p_4 appears to have been folded before p_1.) For example, fields of apparently twisting squares can be folded without making a single twist fold.

Over the past few years, I have used this pleat rearrangement approach on several occasions and soon realized that there is a natural optimization problem associated with it. The number (and nature) of pleats is determined by the goal design, but the order in which the pleats are folded may change the number of rearrangements that must be performed. Because folding the rearrangements can be tricky, especially in the middle of a large sheet, minimizing the number of rearrangements will reduce the amount of work in folding the model. This observation motivates a discrete optimization problem: Find the order of pleating that minimizes the number of necessary pleat rearrangements. This problem turns out to be equivalent to an optimization problem that has been studied in the computer science literature, namely the *feedback arc set problem in bipartite tournaments*. The results in the literature show this problem to be NP-complete and also give a 4-approximation algorithm, that is, a heuristic with the guarantee that the solution it produces requires no more than four times the optimal number of rearrangements. In contrast, I will argue that a large class of designs exhibiting repetitive behavior (and thus of interest in folding tessellations) is easier to solve.

©2015 American Mathematical Society

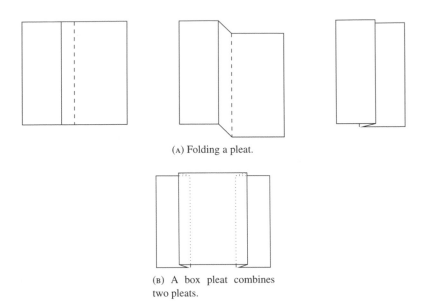

(A) Folding a pleat.

(B) A box pleat combines two pleats.

FIGURE 1. Pleats: the basic ingredients of pleat tessellations.

2. Pleat Tessellations and Rearrangements

Many origami tessellations are based on pleats, but I use the term *pleat tessellation* to mean specifically a fold consisting only of a series of pleats. Each pleat consists of a mountain fold and a parallel valley fold and runs from one edge of the sheet to the opposite edge. Furthermore, adjacent pleats do not overlap: the width of each pleat is at most a third of the distance between two adjacent pleats' mountain folds to avoid too much paper accumulation. (See Figure 1.) These pleats are the only steps used in the folding, except for possibly a few extra valley folds at the end (see Figure 2(b)). Additionally, all my examples are based on rectangular grids where every pleat is parallel to one pair of sides of the paper sheet. It is possible to use pleats that intersect at angles other than the right angle, but such intersections quickly cause problems. Indeed, with pleats intersecting at a right angle, the number of layers at any point of the folded model is either one, three, or nine. Intersections at other angles result in pleats that do not align cleanly, and the accumulation of paper layers quickly becomes unmanageable.

I have previously described a number of examples and offered a concise notation for some of the simpler ones [Konjevod and Kuprešanin 09].

Figure 2 explains the *lock* and its effect on the final shape taken by a pleat tessellation. This is the only folding step other than the usual axis-aligned pleats used in any of the pleat tessellations I folded before pleat rearrangement was discovered by Andrew Hudson.

In August 2008, Andrew Hudson posted a photograph on Flickr showing a pleat tessellation in which he had rearranged some pleats to form a new pattern that would have been impossible to fold as a simple sequence of through-pleats.

To understand the pleat rearrangement step, consider two pleats that intersect at a right angle, as in Figure 3. Folding the horizontal pleat first results in a crease pattern different from the case where the vertical pleat is folded first. The pleat rearrangement step consists of switching the relative order in which these two pleats are folded without

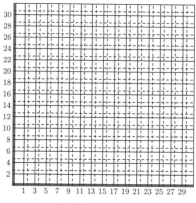

(A) Crease pattern.

(B) Folded model with and without the lock.

FIGURE 2. The basic form with and without the lock. (a) The basic crease pattern with pleat order specified. The mountain folds very close to the bottom and left edges are the optional locking folds. (b) The basic form folded with (left) and without (right) the lock. The locking folds keep the pleat ends in a fixed location. The freedom of the central sections of pleats to unfold much further contributes to the curved shape.

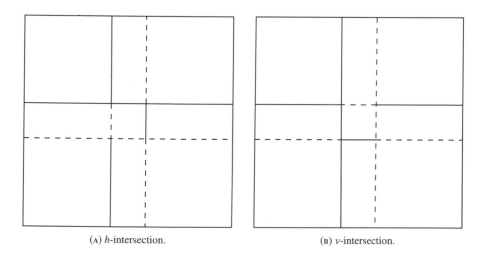

(A) *h*-intersection.　　　　　　　(B) *v*-intersection.

FIGURE 3. Two pleat-intersection crease patterns.

changing anything else. Without other pleats around, this is easy to accomplish: Just unfold everything and refold the two pleats in the opposite order. However, this step is of interest exactly when there are other pleats that have been folded already. Figure 4(c) shows a "cycle" of four pleats that requires at least one pleat rearrangement step.

There may be many such cycles in a single folded model. Figure 5 shows both sides of a folded model that uses box pleats and pleat rearrangement to generate such "impossible" cycles in every square of four adjacent pleat intersections. This pattern of cycles is visible on the box pleat side of the folded sheet, but the other side presents an even more interesting

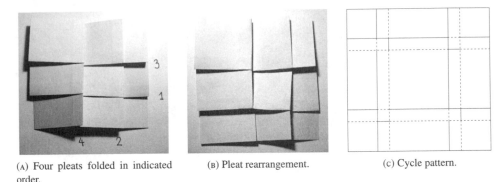

(A) Four pleats folded in indicated order.   (B) Pleat rearrangement.   (c) Cycle pattern.

FIGURE 4. The effect of one pleat rearrangement is a cycle of four pleats. The resulting model cannot be folded as a sequence of pleats without additional steps. Note the twisting of the paper's center.

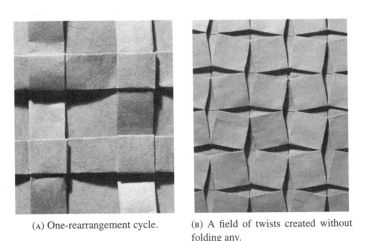

(A) One-rearrangement cycle.   (B) A field of twists created without folding any.

FIGURE 5. The fold I call *no twist* appears to be very similar to any of a family of square twist tessellations, but it requires no twist folding and is flexible: Pulling on opposite corners/sides expands the fold, twisting the squares further.

phenomenon. Because of the natural tendency of each folded crease to unfold and the regular alternation in the pleat intersections, the square faces visible on the opposite side of the folded sheet rotate slightly. This at first glance looks like a tessellation of square twists. However, no twists were folded for this model and, perhaps more interestingly, the angle of the twists is variable and may be changed by simply pulling apart the corners of the folded model (if pressed flat, the model becomes less interesting because the twist angle practically vanishes).

A completely different pattern is shown in Figure 6(a). Here, the relative order remains fixed across squares several pleats to a side, but then these larger squares form cycles that require pleat rearrangement. Within each square, the consistent preference for either

(A) Rearranged box pleats: *Multiweave*.   (B) *Rearranged Pleats* cast in iron.

FIGURE 6. My first two folds using the pleat rearrangement technique have identical structure—the only differences are in the number and type of pleats.

vertical or horizontal pleats generates enough tension to bulge the square outward like a small pillow. I find the combination of the repeated bulging effect and the alternation between dominant directions interesting and have not only folded both the simple pleat and box pleat versions of the piece, but have also used this model as a pattern for iron and bronze castings (see Figure 6(b)).

My most recent works using pleat rearrangement were done for a commission by Alameda County in California and were based on the notion of change (see Figure 7). They were folded from kozo paper that had been dyed to show color transition, and the change in the visible pattern relates to the change in the paper color.

3. Optimizing Rearrangements

The folding procedure for a pleat tessellation without pleat rearrangement is fixed: Except for potential shaping steps, the model is uniquely determined by the sequence of pleats. The presence of rearrangement steps leads to a problem of optimization: Since by rearranging pleats we can simulate any ordering of pleats, there are many different ways to fold a given model. To analyze this, note first that the number of pleats folded and, in fact, the collection of pleats still remain fixed. On the other hand, the order in which the pleats are folded and the rearrangement steps necessary to achieve the desired folded state depend on each other.

For example, suppose that we fold a pleat tessellation based on a grid of 7×7 pleats. That is, we fold seven horizontal and seven vertical pleats according to some arbitrary sequence S_1. Take any other sequence S_2 in which the same set of pleats may be folded. Now compare the 49 pleat intersections resulting from S_1 and S_2. At each intersection, S_1 and S_2 may see either the horizontal or the vertical pleat folded first. In any case, a difference between the relative order in S_1 and S_2 at this intersection may be corrected by performing a single pleat rearrangement. Thus, with at most 49 pleat rearrangements, we can transform any ordering of a set of pleats into any other ordering of the same set of pleats.

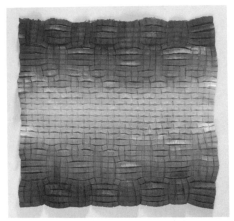

(A) Change study no. 5.

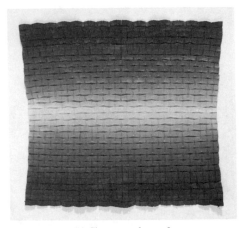

(B) Change study no. 6.

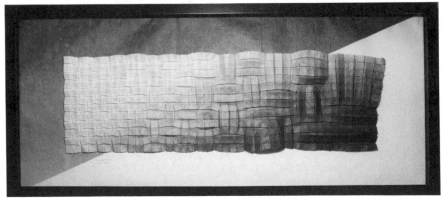

(c) Change study no. 3 (Escher).

FIGURE 7. Three from a series of pieces I folded on the theme of change. Change studies no. 5 and no. 6 were commissioned by Alameda County and are on display at the Highland Hospital in Oakland, California.

By analogy with this example, it is clear that, given a model, the set of pleats folded is the same in each case, and their ordering determines the set of rearrangement steps necessary to fold the model. The multiplicity of available choices thus motivates the optimization problem: Find the ordering of the pleat collection that minimizes the number of rearrangement steps.

3.1. Pleats and their rearrangements. In the context of this chapter, a *pleat* is a folding unit consisting of a mountain fold and a parallel valley fold. These folds are parallel to an edge of the paper sheet and run its full length, from edge to edge. The *width* of a pleat is the distance between its two fold lines.

A *pleat rearrangement* is a folding step performed at the intersection of two pleats (since we assume pleats are parallel to paper edges, if two pleats intersect, they do so at a right angle). In the crease pattern, the intersection of the two pleats forms a rectangle. The rearrangement step changes the sense of the four creases that form the edges of this rectangle (from mountain to valley, from valley to mountain). In other words, the rearrangement step reverses the relative order in which the two pleats appear to have been folded.

3.2. Pleat tessellations. In order to state the problem more formally, I make a few assumptions on the class of folded models considered. Doing so will simplify the discussion and focus it on the relevant combinatorial properties of pleat tessellations.

A *rectangular $n \times m$ pleat tessellation* is an origami model that can be folded by (1) making, in any order, a sequence of n horizontal and m vertical pleats and then (2) rearranging some of the nm intersections of these $n + m$ pleats.

Here, we consider only the case where each pleat has the same width w and its mountain fold is to the left of (for a vertical pleat) or above (for a horizontal pleat) its valley fold. Further, assume the mountain folds of each pair of adjacent parallel pleats are distance $d > 3w$ apart. This ensures that no points of two parallel pleats are mapped on top of each other in the folded state. It also reduces the set of all pleat tessellations to a set of equivalence classes. Two tessellations in the same equivalence class may differ in the width of some pleats, but they share the combinatorial arrangement of layers in the folded state.

3.3. Pleat tessellation matrix. Next, observe that the tessellation itself is completely determined by a binary $n \times m$ matrix. More formally, let a *pleat tessellation matrix* be any matrix $M \in \{h, v\}^{n \times m}$ (any matrix of size $n \times m$ whose elements belong to $\{h, v\}$). Let $\mathcal{P}_{n,m} = \{h, v\}^{n \times m}$ be the set of all such matrices of fixed size $n \times m$.

To establish the idea behind the correspondence, consider just a pair of intersecting pleats. Suppose that the horizontal pleat was folded first, then the vertical one. The resulting crease pattern is shown in Figure 3(a). Note that both the mountain fold and the valley fold of the horizontal pleat (the one folded first) are continuous in the crease pattern. In contrast, the vertical pleat's mountain fold changes to a valley at the pleat intersection, and its valley fold changes to a mountain. Denote such an intersection by the letter h and the complementary intersection, where the vertical pleat is folded first, shown in Figure 3(b), by the letter v.

Now, for an arbitrary matrix $P \in \mathcal{P}_{n,m}$, build a crease pattern by taking the crease pattern of Figure 3(a) for each h in the matrix and the crease pattern of Figure 3(b) for each v. Lay out these "unit" crease patterns in the same arrangement formed by the letters h and v of the matrix P, and "stitch" them together to form a single large crease pattern. This pattern consists of n horizontal and m vertical pleats, and at each intersection of a horizontal and vertical pleat, the local crease pattern matches the symbol at the corresponding position in the matrix. P thus corresponds to a rectangular $n \times m$ pleat tessellation.

Conversely, note that every rectangular $n \times m$ pleat tessellation corresponds to an element of $\mathcal{P}_{n,m}$. Indeed, consider the order $\sigma = (p_1, \ldots, p_{n+m})$ in which the tessellation's n horizontal and m vertical pleats were folded. For each $1 \leq i \leq n$ and each $1 \leq j \leq m$, let ℓ_i^h be the index in σ of the ith horizontal pleat and ℓ_j^v that of the jth vertical pleat. Assume without loss of generality that no pleat intersection was rearranged more than once. Define the matrix P as follows:

$$P_{i,j} = \begin{cases} h & \text{either } \ell_i^h < \ell_j^v \text{ or } (i, j) \text{ was rearranged but not both,} \\ v & \text{otherwise (either } \ell_j^v < \ell_i^h \text{ or } (i, j) \text{ was rearranged but not both).} \end{cases}$$

To complete the argument, note that the "unit" crease pattern induced by the symbol in row i and column j of P matches exactly the local crease pattern at the corresponding location of the folded pleat tessellation.

3.4. Pleat rearrangement minimization.
Note that an $n \times m$ rectangular pleat tessellation may be folded in many different ways, but in every single case, the process will require the folding of $n+m$ pleats. Thus, if we were interested in minimizing the necessary amount of work, we might ask for the folding sequence that minimizes the number of pleat rearrangements. We call this optimization problem *pleat rearrangement minimization*. As it turns out, this problem has been studied before in computer science, though not in the context of origami.

3.5. Feedback arc set problem.
We need some definitions from graph theory. A *directed graph* is a pair of finite sets $G = (V, A)$, where $A \subseteq V \times V$. We call the elements of V *vertices* and the elements of A *(directed) edges*. A *bipartite tournament* is a directed graph where

(1) V can be written as a union of two disjoint sets *(parts)*, $V = U \cup W$;
(2) $A \subseteq U \times W \cup W \times U$ (every edge of G goes between U and W);
(3) for every $u \in U$ and $w \in W$, $|\{(u, w), (w, u)\} \cap A| = 1$ (exactly one of the two pairs (u, w) and (w, u) is an edge).

A *cycle* in a directed graph $G = (V, A)$ is a sequence of edges $e_1 = (u_1, w_1), e_2 = (u_2, w_2), \ldots e_k = (u_k, w_k)$ such that $w_i = u_{i+1}$ for all $1 \le i \le k - 1$ and $w_k = u_1$. Finally, given a directed graph $G = (V, A)$, a *feedback arc set of G* is any set $A' \subseteq A$ such that in the graph $G' = (V, A \setminus A')$ there exist no cycles. The *feedback arc set problem* is to find, given a directed graph G, a feedback arc set of G whose cardinality is minimum.

3.6. Pleat rearrangement minimization equivalent to feedback arc set in bipartite tournaments.
Now we can prove that pleat rearrangement minimization is equivalent to the feedback arc set problem in bipartite tournaments.

Consider first a rectangular pleat tessellation with matrix $P \in \mathcal{P}_{n,m}$. Build a directed graph $G = (U \cup W, A)$ as follows. Let $U = \{u_1, \ldots u_n\}$ and $W = \{w_1, \ldots w_m\}$. For every $1 \le i \le n$ and $1 \le j \le m$, if $P_{i,j} = h$, include in A the edge (u_i, w_j); otherwise, include in A the edge (w_j, u_i). Since for every pair (u_i, w_j) exactly one of the possible edges is present, G is a bipartite tournament.

Let F be a feedback arc set of G. We show that $|F|$ pleat rearrangements suffice to fold the pleat tessellation that corresponds to P. When we remove the edges of F from G, we get a new graph $G' = (U \cup W, A \setminus F)$, which by definition of F contains no cycles. Let $\sigma : U \cup W \to \{1, \ldots, n + m\}$ be an ordering of the vertices of G' such that for every edge (a, b) of G', $\sigma(a) < \sigma(b)$. Let $F_P = \{(i_1, j_1), \ldots, (i_k, j_k)\}$ be the set of all row–column pairs in the matrix P consisting of endpoints of the edges in F. Fold a pleat tessellation by folding pleats in the order given by σ and then by rearranging every pair of pleats given by F_P. We claim that the matrix of the pleat tessellation folded by this process is exactly P.

Consider an entry $P_{i,j}$ of P. If $(i, j) \notin F_P$, then the edge of G with endpoints u_i and w_j is also an edge of G'. This means that if $(u_i, w_j) \in A$, then the ith horizontal pleat was folded before the jth vertical one and the pleat tessellation matrix has h as its (i, j)th entry. Conversely, if $(w_j, u_i) \in A$, the (i, j)th matrix entry should be v. In both cases, the (i, j)th entry equals that of P. If $(i, j) \in F_P$, then the order in which the ith horizontal pleat and the jth vertical pleat are folded is the opposite of that indicated by the removed edge. But, since in this case a pleat rearrangement is performed later at this intersection, the same argument can be made as in the previous case to show that the (i, j)th entry of the matrix corresponding to the folded pleat tessellation is equal to $P_{i,j}$. Thus, we find that the required number of pleat rearrangements is at most the size of the minimum feedback arc set of G.

To prove the opposite inequality, consider a process for folding the pleat tessellation and let k be the number of rearrangements. Remove from G every edge whose endpoints are the coordinates of a pleat rearrangement site, thus creating a new graph G'. Let σ : $U \cup W \to \{1, \ldots, n + m\}$ be the ordering of the vertices derived from the order in which pleats were folded by aligning each vertex with its corresponding pleat. Consider an edge of G' and let its endpoints be u_i and w_j. If the edge is (u_i, w_j), then $P_{i,j} = h$ because no rearrangements were folded at site (i, j). This implies that the ith horizontal pleat was folded before the jth vertical pleat and thus that $\sigma(u_i) < \sigma(w_j)$. Similarly, if the edge is (w_j, u_i), we find that $\sigma(w_j) < \sigma(u_i)$. In any case we have that every edge remaining in G' proceeds from an earlier to a later vertex in the ordering σ. Clearly then, G' contains no cycles and therefore G has a feedback arc set with no more than k vertices.

This completes the proof of the equivalence between pleat rearrangement minimization and feedback arc set for bipartite tournaments.

4. Complexity of Rearrangement Optimization

Since feedback arc set in bipartite tournaments has been studied before, the equivalence we have shown implies that all complexity results about it apply to pleat rearrangement optimization. Guo et al. showed that the problem is NP-complete [Guo et al. 07]. Van Zuylen gave a 4-approximation algorithm based on linear programming [van Zuylen 11]. Misra et al. studied its parameterized complexity and constructed a polynomial kernel [Misra et al. 13]. Dom et al. proved the interesting fact that a bipartite tournament has a cycle if and only if it has a 4-cycle and further that a vertex in a bipartite tournament belongs to a cycle if and only if it belongs to a 4-cycle [Dom et al. 10]. This is intriguing because, at first glance, it seems to reduce the problem to an instance of a set cover (see the appendix) with cardinality 4. However, the statement about 4-cycles refers to vertices and not edges, and so we do not get a 4-approximation algorithm via this route.

5. Special Patterns

The structure of most models that I have folded using pleat rearrangement is in fact simpler due to repetition and symmetry. The notion of *modular partition* [Misra et al. 13] is useful here.

Consider a directed graph $G = (V, A)$. For a vertex $v \in V$, denote by $N^+(v)$ the set of all *out-neighbors* of v: $N^+(v) = \{w \in V \mid vw \in A\}$. Similarly, let $N^-(v)$ be the set of all *in-neighbors*: $N^-(v) = \{w \in V \mid wv \in A\}$. A *module* of G is a set $S \subseteq V$ such that for every pair $u, v \in S$, $N^+(u) \setminus S = N^+(v) \setminus S$ and $N^-(u) \setminus S = N^-(v) \setminus S$; in other words, for any two vertices in S, their out-neighborhoods restricted to non-S vertices are equal, and the same is true of their in-neighborhoods restricted to non-S vertices.

For example, in every graph, the empty set and the set of all vertices are both modules (these are known as *trivial modules*). Furthermore, any single vertex forms a module as well. A *maximal module* is a module that cannot be enlarged by adding another vertex. A *modular partition* $\mathcal{P}$ of a directed graph (V, A) is a partition of the vertex set into $(V_1, \ldots, V_\ell)$ such that every V_i is a maximal module.

Misra et al. showed that, in a bipartite tournament, every nontrivial module is an *independent set*; that is, there are no edges between any of its vertices [Misra et al. 13].

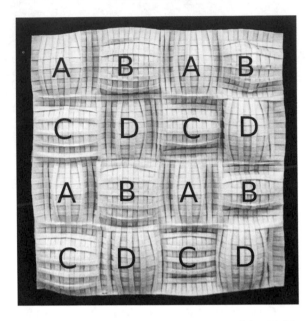

FIGURE 8. The letters placed over the photograph of the *Multiweave* tessellation indicate the edges of the quotient graph. Any of the four letters may be picked to indicate the set of pleat rearrangements; no other rearrangements are necessary. At the same time, at least that many pleat rearrangements must be made in the folding process.

Consider the modular partition $\mathcal{P} = \mathcal{A} \cup \mathcal{B}$ of a bipartite tournament $(U \cup W, A)$, where $\mathcal{A} = (A_1, \ldots)$ is a partition of U and $\mathcal{B} = (B_1, \ldots)$ is a partition of W. Take two modules $A \in \mathcal{A}$ and $B \in \mathcal{B}$. Because A and B are modules, either all edges between them are directed from A to B or all are directed from B to A.

Given a bipartite graph (V, A) and its modular partition $\mathcal{P}$, we form a new graph whose vertices correspond to the modules of the partition and edges between them are induced by the existence of edges between the corresponding modules in the original graph. We refer to such a graph as the *quotient graph* of (V, A).

Tedder et al. showed that any bipartite tournament has a unique modular partition that can be computed in linear time [Tedder et al. 08].

The several versions of my folded pleat tessellations titled *Rearranged Pleats* and *Multiweave* have particularly simple modular partitions. Indeed, for all of them, the quotient graph is C_4, the 4-cycle, and so it suffices to restrict pleat rearrangements to only one of the four edges of the quotient graph, that is, to one of the four subsets of pleat intersections (Figure 8).

6. Appendix: Feedback Arc Set as Set Covering

Finding a set cover is a classical problem in combinatorial optimization [Vazirani 01]. A *set cover* is given by a finite set $X = \{x_1, \ldots, x_n\}$ referred to as the *ground set* and a family of subsets $\mathcal{A} = \{A_1, \ldots, A_m\} \subseteq 2^X$. The goal is to find a minimum-cardinality subfamily $C \subseteq \mathcal{A}$ such that every element of X is contained in at least one set in C. To see that feedback arc set is a special case of set cover, take an instance of feedback arc set defined on the (directed) graph $G = (V, E)$. Let $X = \{C \subseteq E \mid C$ is a cycle$\}$. For each edge $e \in E$, define the set $A_e = \{C \in X \mid e \in C\}$ as the set of all cycles that contain e.

Now, it is clear that feedback arc sets of G directly correspond to set covers of X. Certain restrictions on the form of the set system in an instance of a set cover result in problems that are easier to approximate. For example, the *bounded-frequency set cover*, where each element appears in at most k sets for a constant k, is a well-known special case that allows both a simple LP-rounding algorithm as well as a primal-dual algorithm with approximation guarantee equal to the maximum frequency [Vazirani 01].

For example, if instead of vertices, we could guarantee that in a bipartite tournament every edge that was a part of a cycle was a part of a 4-cycle, we would have a reduction to set cover with maximum frequency 4 and thus a simple 4-approximation algorithm as well.

7. Conclusion

In this work, I described a class of paper-folded models that can be used to create interesting visual patterns similar to those formed by woven strips, as well as some twist-based tessellations. I formulated an optimization problem whose solution would provide the most efficient folding sequence and showed that its equivalence to the previously studied feedback arc set problem in bipartite tournaments implies that it is NP-hard. Finally, I showed that, in the case of some simple patterns (which I have actually folded in the past), the optimization problem may be solved exactly. It is left to see if a better approximation guarantee can be obtained than the previously known factor 4, as well as to characterize a larger class of instances for which optimal solutions can be easily obtained.

References

[Dom et al. 10] Michael Dom, Jiong Guo, Falk Hüffner, Rolf Niedermeier, and Anke Truß. "Fixed-Parameter Tractability Results for Feedback Set Problems in Tournaments." *J. Discrete Algorithms* 8:1 (2010), 76–86. MR2558881 (2011k:68058)

[Guo et al. 07] Jiong Guo, Falk Hüffner, and Hannes Moser. "Feedback Arc Set in Bipartite Tournaments is NP-complete." *Inf. Process. Lett.* 102:2–3 (2007), 62–65. MR2292959 (2008a:05110)

[Hudson 08] Andrew Hudson. "W(e)ave." *Flickr*, https://www.flickr.com/photos/ahudson/2726539348/, 2008.

[Jackson 91] Paul Jackson. "Bulge." In *The Encyclopedia of Origami & Papercraft*, p. 131. London: Quarto Publishing/Running Press, 1991.

[Konjevod and Kuprešanin 09] Goran Konjevod and Ana Maria Kuprešanin. "Notation for a Class of Paperfolded Models." In *Proceedings of the 12th Annual Bridges Conference, Banff*, pp. 47–54. St. Albans, UK: Tarquin Books, 2009.

[Misra et al. 13] Pranabendu Misra, Venkatesh Raman, M. S. Ramanujan, and Saket Saurabh. "A Polynomial Kernel for Feedback Arc Set on Bipartite Tournaments." *Theory Comput. Syst.* 53:4 (2013), 609–620. MR3084355

[Tedder et al. 08] Marc Tedder, Derek G. Corneil, Michel Habib, and Christophe Paul. "Simpler Linear-Time Modular Decomposition via Recursive Factorizing Permutations." In *Automata, Languages and Programming: 35th International Colloquium, ICALP 2008, Reykjavik, Iceland, July 7–11, 2008, Proceedings, Part I: Tack A: Algorithms, Automata, Complexity, and Games*, Lecture Notes in Computer Science 5125, pp. 634–645. Berlin: Springer, 2008. MR2500307 (2010j:05331)

[van Zuylen 11] Anke van Zuylen. "Linear Programming Based Approximation Algorithms for Feedback Set Problems in Bipartite Tournaments." *Theor. Comput. Sci.* 412:23 (2011), 2556–2561. MR2815797 (2012c:90079)

[Vazirani 01] Vijay V. Vazirani. *Approximation Algorithms*. Berlin: Springer, 2001. MR1851303 (2002h:68001)

ORGANICORIGAMI.COM
E-mail address: goran.konjevod@gmail.com

Graph Paper for Polygon-Packed Origami Design

Robert J. Lang and Roger C. Alperin

1. Introduction

Origami underwent a renaissance in the mid-twentieth century that led to the blossoming of new techniques for the design of origami figures, including the *circle-river* method of design, described by Lang and Meguro in the early 1990s [Meguro 92, Lang 94] and formalized over subsequent years [Lang 96, Lang 97]. The circle-river method is suitable for folding *uniaxial bases*, origami shapes whose projections are specified edge-weighted tree graphs.

The circle-river method is powerful, but it has a drawback: in general, the only way of locating the positions of many fold lines on the paper is to laboriously measure and mark according to the computed crease pattern. In addition, the angles between pairs of creases can turn out to be quite small, resulting in "sliver" facets that are aesthetically unappealing and difficult to fold precisely. For these (and perhaps other) reasons, pure circle-river design with arbitrarily chosen circle radii and river widths is relatively uncommon in the origami world.

One solution to this problem is the class of design known as *box pleating*, in which the design is carried out on a square grid. Box pleating in origami predates the development of uniaxial base theory and circle packing—work by Mooser, Elias, and Hulme, among others, in the 1950s and 1960s demonstrated many of the techniques of box pleating (and is when the term originated in the origami context). A formal link between box pleating and uniaxial base theory was drawn by Lang [Lang 11] in the development of the family of design techniques called *polygon packing*; instead of packing circles and curved rivers, one packs polygons and polygonal rivers, and by restricting the corner angles and side lengths of the polygons and rivers to fixed values, one can ensure well-behavedness of the resulting crease pattern.

Polygon-packed uniaxial base designs contain three families of creases: First, there are the *hinge* creases, which delineate the regions that become individual flaps within the origami base. In the folded form, hinge creases are perpendicular to the axis of the base. Second, there are the *axial* and *axis-parallel* creases (collectively, *axial-like* creases), which run along the axis of the base (or in the latter case, run parallel to the axis). And third, there are the *ridge* creases, which connect hinge and axial-like creases. In polygon-packed origami designs, the ridge creases are constructed as the *straight skeleton* of the hinge creases.

The authors were supported in part by NSF Grant #1332249.

The straight skeleton [Aicholzer and Aurenhammer 96] is a structure that shows up in several other contexts in the field of computational geometry and, notably, appears in a related folding problem: the *one-straight-cut* problem (osc) [Demaine et al. 98]. There are multiple connections between uniaxial base design and osc, for which there are two published solution algorithms. One, by Bern, Demaine, and Hayes [Bern et al. 98], which we will refer to as osc-DP, solved the problem via a disk packing, similar to the circle-river design method (in fact, a later version of this algorithm [Bern et al. 02] made use of a pattern, the *gusset molecule*, from uniaxial origami design [Lang 96]). The other method, by Demaine, Demaine, and Lubiw [Demaine et al. 98], used the straight skeleton as the first step in the crease construction algorithm; we will call this osc-ss. Though osc-DP typically resulted in more complex crease patterns than osc-ss, making the latter aesthetically preferable, there are patterns for which a pathological condition arises in the osc-ss construction: so-called *infinite bouncing*, in which one family of creases becomes mathematically dense in the constructed pattern, as was noted by Demaine, Demaine, and Lubiw [Demaine and O'Rourke 07].

The possibility of infinite bouncing also arises in polygon-packed origami designs (though not in circle-river designs). For certain polygon packings, it is possible that the network of axial creases becomes dense. However, there is a simple strategy to avoid this situation, which is to place all of the hinge creases upon a regular grid at the outset, for example, a square grid (as in box pleating). If we require all hinge creases of the original packing to lie on a square grid, then it is guaranteed that the construction of ridge and axial-like creases remains finite for every possible polygon packing and every possible tree graph (albeit a tree graph whose edge lengths must be quantized to integer multiples defined by the square grid).

The design algorithm for uniaxial bases using polygon packing where the hinge creases are confined to a square grid is *uniaxial box pleating* (UBP). If we quantize all polygons and polygonal rivers so that the hinge creases lie upon a square grid, the crease pattern is guaranteed to be finite. In addition, because of the regularity of the underlying grid, it becomes possible to design the origami base using nothing more complicated than a pencil and graph paper—little or no computation is required. And with all key points lying on the underlying grid, it is also possible to fold such a base by precreasing the paper along lines of the underlying grid or a subset thereof.

For these reasons, many modern origami artists have turned to uniaxial box pleating (or variations thereof) for their designs of highly complex works. However, UBP is not without its own limitations. Because squares do not pack as efficiently as circles, UBP-based designs can be significantly less efficient than their theoretical limit. In addition, the crease patterns are, to some, less interesting than those with a broader mix of angles.

In [Lang 11], author Lang introduced the concept of *uniaxial hex pleating* (UHP), wherein one could design a uniaxial base by working on an equilateral triangular, rather than square, grid. Hex pleating offers the potential for more efficient designs (because hexagons pack more efficiently than squares), and the mix of three different major angle directions for hinge lines leads to crease patterns with (potentially) more variety than those of ordinary box pleating. Like box pleating, hex pleating can be carried out with little or no computation by drawing one's design on graph paper—in this case, a graph paper composed of equilateral triangles in the familiar hexagonal lattice.

The existence of box pleating and hex pleating and the graph papers that enable them leads to a natural question: are there other graph papers that work for uniaxial base design? This question provides the motivation of this paper. In this work, we look for *origami graph paper*: a pattern of lines that can be used for a wide range of polygon-packed designs where the hinge lines are restricted to the lines of the graph paper and where every possible crease pattern for a uniaxial base drawn on this graph paper results in a finite metrically flat-foldable[1] crease pattern.

In this work, we formally define the notion of origami graph paper and consider a broad set: graph papers composed of periodic arrays of parallel lines. We show that the condition of axial finiteness leads naturally to a Diophantine equation for the parameters that define the families of origami graph papers. We solve these equations and show how all such papers may be described and indexed. For any origami graph paper, we may define a natural figure of merit that quantifies the minimum feature size that arises with the graph paper; we show that there is, in fact, another previously unrecognized origami graph paper whose figure of merit lies close to those of box pleating and hex pleating. We point out several other interesting and potentially useful origami graph papers and demonstrate an origami design using one of these new graph papers. We close with some comments and thoughts on potential directions for future exploration.

2. Polygon Packing

The general algorithm for polygon-packed origami design is described in detail in [Lang 11]; we briefly recapitulate it here. The design begins from an edge-weighted tree graph that describes the desired shape. First, the square paper (or other shape) is partitioned into polygons and polygonal "rivers" whose dimensions are given by their corresponding graph edge weights; the boundaries of the polygons and rivers then become the hinge creases of the associated design. In the folded unaxial base, the hinge creases are perpendicular to the axis of the base.

Second, a set of ridge creases are constructed. They are, as noted above, the straight skeleton of each packed polygon, with the ridge creases in rivers being constructed as a generalization of the straight skeleton.

Third, a set of axial contours are created by choosing points that (in the folded form) lie at a specified distance from the axis of the base and then propagating them within the crease pattern along directions parallel to the axis of the folded form (which is locally specified within each facet of the crease pattern). A subset of the axial *contours* become axial *folds*: folds that lie upon, or parallel to, the axis of the base in the folded form.

Last, all creases are assigned as mountain or valley folds in a way that is consistent with flat-foldability and that avoids self-intersection. (For the purposes of this paper, we will stop at the third step.)

When constructing the axial contours, as one propagates them within the crease pattern, it is possible to encounter the situation where the fold lines never close or terminate, but instead continue forever, forming a set that is dense, in the mathematical sense. In the physical sense, dense folds would imply that the paper is infinitely crumpled, and so from a practical point of view, such a design should be considered unsuccessful.

The possibility of such infinite propagation was first identified by Demaine et al. in their solution of the fold-and-cut problem, whose algorithm is similar to the polygon packing algorithm and for good reason: both focus on collapsing a polygon so that its boundary folds onto a single line (the cut line in the former case, hinge lines in the latter), and both use the straight skeleton to reflect a family of propagating creases.

---

[1]A pattern is *metrically* flat-foldable if it satisfies all of the metric conditions of flat-foldability (e.g., the Kawasaki-Justin Condition), but we do not require injectivity (non–self-intersection). Equivalently, we are finding the positions of the creases but not requiring a non–self-intersecting mountain-valley assignment.

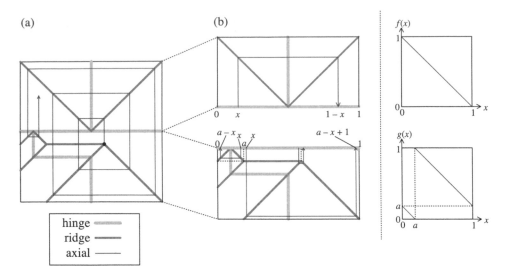

FIGURE 1. (a) A polygon packing in which the axial contours are dense. (b) Analysis of the pattern: $f(x)$ is the transfer function for the top half of the crease pattern; $g(x)$ is the transfer function for the bottom half.

A simple example of such infinite propagation is shown in Figure 1 (from [Lang 11], which is a simplified version of Demaine et al.'s pathological example [Demaine and O'Rourke 07]). Consider the axial contour emanating from the black dot on the left, and let us consider its propagation back and forth between the top half and bottom half of the crease pattern, as shown on the right. We map the dividing line between the two halves to the unit interval $(0, 1)$. For each half, we denote by x the point along this line where a contour enters the region, $f(x)$ the point where the contour exits the top half, and $g(x)$ where it exits the bottom half. By inspection, we see that

$$f(x) = 1 - x, \quad g(x) = (a - x) \mod 1,$$

and thus the position after n passes through both top and bottom halves is

$$h^{(n)}(x) = (x - na) \mod 1.$$

For all $x \in (0, 1)$, we have that $h^{(n)}(x) \in (0, 1)$, so either the line closes on itself (eventually getting back to position x), or it does not, in which case it becomes mathematically dense. The line closes on itself if and only if $(x - na)$ differs from x by some integer m, i.e., if and only if $a = m/n$ for some integers m, n. So, for this particular packing, the axial contours are non-dense if and only if the distance a is rational.

Furthermore, if $a = m/n$ and $\{m, n\}$ are relatively prime (i.e., the fraction is in lowest terms), then the spacing between the closest pair of adjacent contour lines is $1/n$. There must always be at least one folded off-axis axial-like contour halfway between two axial contours, and the separation between the axial and off-axis contours determines the minimum flap width. So, for rational $a = m/n$, the minimum flap width is $1/(2m)$.

Suppose we chose the value of a at random. The irrational numbers are more numerous than the rationals, so if we were to choose the value of a randomly along the unit interval $(0, 1)$, the probability of getting a rational value and non-infinite propagation has measure zero. So, for this particular packing, having dense axial contours is the norm: only special cases have non-dense axial contours.

Now, it was relatively straightforward to determine a condition that, for this packing, guarantees non-dense axial contours. But Figure 1 is a very simple packing. The two halves of the pattern can be thought of as "reflectors" that have an irrational spacing; any time there are two such reflectors with irrational spacing, there could be dense axial contours. In a large, complex packing, however, two or more reflectors could be widely separated within the crease pattern, and even the ridge folds that make up each individual reflector could be dispersed across the crease pattern. It is, in general, not obvious for a given polygon packing whether the straight skeleton will give rise to infinite propagation; as even this simple example showed, the odds of it happening are, in the absence of further restrictions, high.

Uniaxial box pleating and hex pleating guarantee finiteness of the crease pattern by confining the hinge creases to grid lines, and it is instructive to examine more closely why this strategy works.

3. Non-dense Contour Condition

Consider the vertices of the straight skeleton and the axial-like contour lines that emanate from them (like the axial contour shown in Figure 1). We will refer to these lines collectively as the *straight skeleton vertex contours* (SSVCs). If any one of these contours is dense in some region of the plane, then there must be dense folds in the pattern. So, a *necessary* condition for non-dense folds is that the SSVCs are themselves non-dense.

In fact, this condition is *sufficient* as well to establish that *all* contour lines—axial, off-axis, and anywhere in between—are non-dense.

To see this, pick any contour line between two parallel SSVCs that are assumed to be non-dense. Since the contour line propagates parallel to the SSVCS, it maintains a constant distance from the SSVCs to both left and right. When the contour crosses a straight skeleton fold, because the straight skeleton folds are piecewise linear between vertices of the straight skeleton, the constant spacing between the contour and the SSVCs on either side is preserved. Thus, at every point along this contour, there are SSVCs to either side at a fixed spacing. If the contour propagates aperiodically, then so, too, must the SSVCs, which would result in one or both of the adjacent SSVCs also being dense—which violates our initial assumption.

So, we have a general condition that guarantees non-denseness of every contour set in a polygon-packed crease pattern:

THEOREM 3.1 (Non-dense Contour Condition). *The contours in a polygon-packed origami crease pattern are non-dense if and only if the straight skeleton vertex contours are non-dense.*

So, all we have to do to ensure non-denseness of the axial contours is to ensure non-denseness of the SSVCs. In polygon packing, however, the construction of SSVCs happens late in the design process: first we choose the hinge creases, then we construct the straight skeleton, and only then can we construct the SSVCs, which emanate from the vertices of the straight skeleton. Ideally, we would like to impose some condition on the hinge creases that would guarantee that two steps later in the construction process, we had finite SSVCs.

The strategies of uniaxial box pleating and hex pleating have such a condition. If we force all of the hinge creases to lie on an underlying grid, then we can identify every possible line of the straight skeleton and, from that set, identify every possible straight skeleton vertex and, from *that* set, identify every possible SSVC. If this last set of all *possible* SSVCs is non-dense, then this guarantees that any *particular* set of SSVCs is non-dense.

We now formally define a grid that would have this desirable property:

DEFINITION 3.2 (Origami Graph Paper). An *origami graph paper* is a set of lines for which every possible set of hinge polygons and rivers on those lines has non-dense SSVCs.

Thus, one may use origami graph paper to design uniaxial bases whose crease patterns are guaranteed to be finite.

Of course, one can easily create a specific polygon packing that satisfies the definition of origami graph paper. What would be interesting would be *versatile* origami graph paper that would support a wide range of packings of elements of varying sizes, dimensions, and mixtures of closed polygons and rivers. The square and triangular grids of box pleating and hex pleating, respectively, have this property. The only condition that these grids impose on the tree graph is that the lengths of all graph edges are quantized to the grid size (specifically, to the spacing between parallel adjacent grid lines). These grids are periodic; if the spacing between line pairs is d, then they can be used to design tree graphs whose edge weights are integer multiples of d. In this work, we will focus our attention upon origami graph paper consisting of grids composed of two or more sets of periodically spaced parallel lines.

DEFINITION 3.3 (Doubly Periodic Origami Graph Paper). A *doubly periodic origami graph paper* is an origami graph paper that consists of two or more sets of parallel lines and that is doubly periodic.

Our goal is to find such grids that ensure non-dense SSVCs, and thus non-dense axial contours, for *any* polygon packing whose hinge lines are confined to the grid.

4. Periodic Origami Graph Paper

Let us consider first the simplest possible grid, composed of two sets of periodic lines defined by noncollinear direction vectors $\mathbf{a}$ and $\mathbf{b}$, as illustrated in Figure 2.

We can assume without loss of generality that $\mathbf{a}$ is the unit vector $(1, 0)$, that $\mathbf{b} = (b_x, b_y)$ is a general second vector lying in the first quadrant, and that our grid has a line intersection at the origin. Our grid is composed of two sets of parallel lines, one set with lines parallel to the x-axis (i.e., with direction vector $\mathbf{a}$), the other with lines parallel to vector $\mathbf{b}$.

In general, for any set of mutually parallel lines, a point $\mathbf{p}$ in the set has the parametric representation

$$\mathbf{p} = \mathbf{d} + k\mathbf{e} + s\mathbf{f}, \quad k \in \mathbb{Z}, \ s \in \mathbb{R}.$$

Vector $\mathbf{d}$ is some point in the line set, $\mathbf{e}$ determined the periodicity of the line set, and $\mathbf{f}$ is a vector along the direction of each line. The full line set can therefore be described by the ordered vector triple $(\mathbf{d}, \mathbf{e}, \mathbf{f})$, though of course, for a given line set, this representation is not unique.

For simplicity, define $\mathbf{o} = (0, 0)$ as the origin. Then, for a grid composed of two crossing line sets as shown in Figure 2, the two sets of lines are described by the ordered triples

$$\mathbf{A} = (\mathbf{o}, \mathbf{b}, \mathbf{a}), \quad \mathbf{B} = (\mathbf{o}, \mathbf{a}, \mathbf{b}),$$

where $\mathbf{A}$ is the line set with direction vector $\mathbf{a}$ and $\mathbf{B}$ is the line set with direction vector $\mathbf{b}$. Each of these sets is a *hinge line set* of the origami graph paper.

Now, we must construct every possible vertex of the straight skeleton, which would be every possible crossing of three or more lines that are the *medials* (angle bisectors) between any two lines of the hinge line sets. A medial line could be the medial between

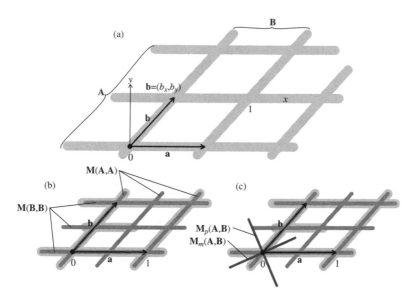

FIGURE 2. Geometry of a grid composed of two sets of periodic lines. (a) The grid of hinge-like lines. (b) Medial lines parallel to the grid lines. (c) Medial lines added between non-parallel grid lines.

two lines from the same hinge line set, in which case the medial line is the line parallel to and halfway between the two parallel hinge lines, or it could be a medial between two non-parallel hinge lines.

For medials between two lines of the same line set, there is only one line set, represented by

$$\mathbf{M(A,A)} = \left(\mathbf{o}, \frac{1}{2}\mathbf{b}, \mathbf{a}\right), \quad \mathbf{M(B,B)} = \left(\mathbf{o}, \frac{1}{2}\mathbf{a}, \mathbf{b}\right)$$

for the medials between **A**-lines and **B**-lines, respectively. These medials are shown in Figure 2(b). They consist of the original grid lines, plus grid lines parallel to and spaced halfway between the original grid lines.

For medials between lines from two different sets, i.e., between an **A**-line and a **B**-line, there are two perpendicular sets: one set of lines that pass through each intersection of an **A**-line and a **B**-line, and another set of lines passing through the same intersections but that are perpendicular to the first set. We denote these line sets by $\mathbf{M_m(A,B)}$ and $\mathbf{M_p(A,B)}$, respectively, and show the two that pass through the origin in Figure 2(c).

Let $\mathbf{t} = (t_x, t_y)$ be the direction vector for any line in the set $\mathbf{M_m(A,B)}$. In order to be the angle bisector of vectors **a** and **b**, it must satisfy

$$\frac{\mathbf{t} \cdot \mathbf{a}}{|\mathbf{a}|} = \frac{\mathbf{t} \cdot \mathbf{b}}{|\mathbf{b}|}.$$

Of course, this only defines t_x and t_y to within a common constant factor, but solving this system gives a solution

$$\mathbf{t} \equiv (t_x, t_y) = (b_y, b - b_x) \quad \text{where } b \equiv |\mathbf{b}| = \sqrt{b_x^2 + b_y^2}.$$

Now, our goal is to ensure that the straight skeleton vertex contours are non-dense, and recall that the SSVCs emanate from intersections of three or more medials. So, a necessary step on the way to ensuring that the SSVCs are non-dense is to ensure that the medials themselves are non-dense, because there are two such medial lines through each intersection of the hinge line grid.

Every line in the set $\mathbf{M}_m(\mathbf{A}, \mathbf{B})$ can be parameterized as

$$\mathbf{p}(s) = n\mathbf{a} + m\mathbf{b} + s\mathbf{t},$$

where $\mathbf{t}$ is the direction vector of the line, so we can solve for the x-intercept of the (n, m)th line, which turns out to be

$$x_{n,m} = n + m\left(b_x - b_y\frac{t_x}{t_y}\right).$$

From the above, we have

(4.1)
$$\frac{t_x}{t_y} = \frac{b_y}{b - b_x},$$

which, if we substitute in and perform some simplifications, we find that the x-intercept is simply given by

$$x_{n,m} = n - mb.$$

In order for this line family to be non-dense, b must be rational. Since we assumed $|\mathbf{a}| = 1$, this relation sets the first condition on the hinge line grid:

THEOREM 4.1 (Rationality of b/a). *The ratio of the lengths of any two basis vectors of a doubly periodic origami graph paper must be rational.*

Now, we note that every point of intersection of the hinge line grid is intersected by four distinct medials, one from each of the four families we have identified so far. Each of these points must be a (potential) vertex of the straight skeleton, and thus there is an SSVC emanating from each one that is perpendicular to the hinge lines (both $\mathbf{A}$-lines and $\mathbf{B}$-lines). If we consider first the SSVCs that are perpendicular to the $\mathbf{A}$-lines, they will be vertical, and each will have an x-intercept given by the x-coordinate of the grid point that is a crossing between lines from each of the two families of hinge lines. Those crossing vertices are given simply by

$$n\mathbf{a} + m\mathbf{b},$$

so the x-intercept of the (n, m) SSVC is simply

(4.2)
$$x_{n,m} = n + mb_x.$$

As above, in order for this set to be non-dense, the coefficient of integer m must be rational, giving our next condition that b_x be rational. More generally, for arbitrary $\mathbf{a}$ and $\mathbf{b}$, we have the following:

THEOREM 4.2 (Rationality of $\mathbf{a} \cdot \mathbf{b}$). *For any two basis vectors a and b of a doubly periodic origami graph paper, $(a \cdot b)/(|a||b|)$ must be rational.*

Theorems 4.1 and 4.2 are both necessary for the SSVCs to be non-dense. Suppose that both conditions are satisfied. Then, since

$$b_y = \sqrt{b^2 - b_x^2},$$

b_y must be the square root of some rational. From Equation (4.1), the slope of the medial lines $\mathbf{M}_m(\mathbf{A}, \mathbf{B})$ (which is t_y/t_x) must be the square root of a rational. Therefore, the slope of the medial lines $\mathbf{M}_p(\mathbf{A}, \mathbf{B})$ (which, being perpendicular to $\mathbf{M}_m(\mathbf{A}, \mathbf{B})$, is $-t_x/t_y$) must also be the square root of a rational.

From this result, it follows that every possible intersection between pairs of medial lines have rational x-intercepts, meaning that the vertical SSVCs, those perpendicular to the **A**-lines, are non-dense. The SSVCs perpendicular to the **B**-lines are just the reflections of those perpendicular to the **A**-lines, and so they, too, are non-dense. Thus, Theorems 4.1 and 4.2 are not only necessary; they are sufficient as well, to guarantee non-denseness of the SSVCs.

Because b and b_x are rational (and, by assumption, are also nonnegative), this leads to a straightforward strategy to identify all possible origami grids composed of two sets of parallel periodic lines: step through the integers for numerators and denominators of both fractions and construct grids from the resulting basis vector sets.

5. Mirror Symmetry

Choosing two basis vectors **a** and **b** such that b and b_x are rational gives rise to a grid that is origami graph paper, but the underlying grid consists of parallelograms and, in general, does not possess a line of mirror symmetry. However, most representational origami subjects do possess bilateral symmetry, and it would be desirable to have origami graph paper that exhibits the same mirror symmetry and thus could be used for mirror-symmetric crease patterns.

We can create mirror-symmetric origami graph paper by adding a line of reflection and additional hinge line basis vectors that are the reflections of the original vectors **a** and **b** and then by again looking at all possible medial lines between pairs of hinge lines and all possible intersections between pairs of medial lines.

In most origami designs of bilaterally symmetric figures, the axis is the line of mirror symmetry, and in the folded form, the hinges are perpendicular to the axis. If we restrict our search to this class of designs, then the line of mirror symmetry would be perpendicular to one of the basis vectors, meaning that that basis vector is its own reflection (to within a factor -1). We can without loss of generality assume that the line of mirror symmetry is perpendicular to **a**. Since **a** runs along the x-axis, we can choose the line of mirror symmetry to be the y-axis. Thus, we actually only need three basis vectors to describe a general grid with mirror symmetry: **a**, $\mathbf{b} = (b_x, b_y)$, and the reflection of **b** in the line of symmetry, $\mathbf{c} = (-b_x, b_y)$. This vector defines a third set of lines **C**, which are the reflections of the set **B**.

There is, however, one additional parameter needed to fully characterize all possible grids of this type. We had previously assumed that the **A** and **B** grid lines intersected at the origin, which we could do without loss of generality. If we place the line of mirror symmetry along the y-axis, then the point of intersection of the A and B families can be offset by some amount. We define b_0 as the offset of the point of intersection from the origin. Then, we can give an explicit representation of the three relevant sets of lines:

$$\mathbf{A} = (\mathbf{o}, \mathbf{b}, \mathbf{a}), \quad \mathbf{B} = ((-b_0, 0), \mathbf{a}, \mathbf{b}), \quad \mathbf{C} = ((b_0, 0), \mathbf{a}, \mathbf{c}),$$

where, as above, the first element of each triplet defines a point on one of the lines, the second describes the quantized periodicity, and the third is the direction vector of each line in the set.

We can, once again, consider whether the grid defined by the set $\{\mathbf{A}, \mathbf{B}, \mathbf{C}\}$ is origami graph paper, i.e., if the set of all SSVCs is non-dense. Certainly it is clear that any two sets taken pairwise must be origami graph paper, so by considering $\{\mathbf{A}, \mathbf{B}\}$, we must have both b and b_x be rational. This condition also gives the rationality of the grid formed by $\{\mathbf{A}, \mathbf{C}\}$.

Now we consider the grid formed by pairs $\{\mathbf{B}, \mathbf{C}\}$. It is easy to see that this grid will give rise to non-dense SSVCs if b_0 is rational. Because we have now considered all possible pairwise combinations, we have a condition that applies to the triplet of sets $\{\mathbf{A}, \mathbf{B}, \mathbf{C}\}$:

THEOREM 5.1 (Mirror-Symmetric Origami Graph Paper). *A mirror-symmetric doubly periodic origami graph paper defined by the three families of lines* $\{A, B, C\}$ *has non-dense SSVCs if and only if* b, b_x, *and* b_0 *are rational.*

As with the two-set origami graph paper, we can find all possible values of the graph paper by stepping through the rationals—now not just b and b_x but also all values of b_0 as well. For each set of rational values, there will be an origami graph paper. The resulting graph papers are not necessarily distinct, of course, since our representations of the families are also not distinct. But, if there is such a set, it will assuredly appear somewhere in our enumeration.

6. Figures of Merit

The approach of stepping through rational values for b and b_x will give a large number of grids to contemplate for origami graph paper, but some grids are going to be better than others, and it would be useful to have some way of characterizing a grid for its utility and versatility.

As already noted, the spacing between two SSVCs establishes a minimum width for the associated origami flap, which we denote by $w_{\min}$ for that grid. That minimum width is half of the minimum spacing between any two SSVCs. For 2-set grids, the x-intercepts of the SSVCs are, by Equation (4.2), integer multiples of b_x, so the minimum flap width is simply half of the reciprocal of the denominator of b_x. We call this the *characteristic width* of the grid.

For 3-set (mirror-symmetric) grids, the calculation of $w_{\min}$ is more complicated, because there are multiple denominators that could show up, depending on the values of b, b_x, and b_0, which may have different denominators. By calculating all x-intercepts for a given triple of hinge line sets and taking the least common multiple of all of their denominators, we can compute a minimum possible flap width $w_{\min}$ for the set. All flaps' widths will be integer multiples of this minimum width. As a practical matter, it is easier to make a flap narrower than to make it wider; thus, considered as a figure of merit, *larger* is better for $w_{\min}$.

The lengths of flaps are also quantized; the minimum length of any flap is half of the spacing between two consecutive parallel hinge lines. For example, for the simplest 2-set grid, the vertical spacing between **A**-lines is $b_y/2$; every flap oriented in this direction in the crease pattern has a length that is a multiple of this amount. Flaps oriented in different directions can have different quantizations, corresponding to different grid line spacings in each direction. We denote by $l_{\min,i}$ the minimum length quantization in the ith direction. If we would like to choose flap lengths arbitrarily (or as arbitrarily as possible, subject to their quantization), we would like this characteristic length to be as small as possible, no matter what the orientation of the flap is. Thus, we can define a *characteristic length* $l_{\min}$ (no second subscript) for the grid as

$$l_{\min} \equiv \max\{l_{\min,i}\}.$$

As a figure of merit, *smaller* is better for $l_{\min}$.

The merits of $w_{\min}$ and $l_{\min}$ are relative to one another. We can therefore combine the two values into a single figure of merit, the *characteristic aspect ratio* for the grid, defined

FIGURE 3. A patch of the sterling grid. Fat light gray lines are hinge lines. Medium-width medium gray are ridge lines. Thin black lines are SSVCs.

by

$$\rho \equiv l_{\min}/w_{\min}.$$

In general, $\rho \geq 1$, and smaller is better. We can use this single value to characterize the practical utility of any origami grid.

7. Good Grids

We have carried out a systematic analysis of origami graph papers by evaluating every combination of rationals with relatively small denominators for the control parameters $\{b, b_x, b_0\}$, for both 2-set and (mirror-symmetric) 3-set origami grids. We set up a Mathematica notebook to carry out the analysis. Here are the results.

A first test of the algorithm is to see if it recovers the known solutions: box pleating and hex pleating. Indeed, this is the case. Box pleating—a grid of squares—corresponds to the parameter set $(b, (b_x, b_y), b_0) = (1, (0, 1), 0)$ and has characteristic width $1/2$, characteristic length $1/2$, and characteristic aspect ratio 1.

Hex pleating also falls out of the analysis: both 2-set and 3-set versions arise, depending upon whether there is a line of mirror symmetry. Hex pleating results from the parameter set $(b, (b_x, b_y), b_0) = (1, (1/2, \sqrt{3}/2), 0)$ and has characteristic width $1/4$, characteristic length $\sqrt{3}/4$, and characteristic aspect ratio $\sqrt{3} \approx 1.732$. This is noticeably larger than the unit aspect ratio of box pleating, and it implies that the length quantization of hex pleating (for a given minimum width) is significantly coarser than that of box pleating—which is indeed the case, in practice.

The interesting open question, which motivated our original investigation, was this: are there any other grids whose aspect ratio is sufficiently small as to be of practical interest? And indeed, there is. The parameter set $(b, (b_x, b_y), b_0) = (1, (1/3, 2\sqrt{2}/3), 0)$ gives rise to the aspect ratio $\rho = 2\sqrt{2} \approx 2.828$, which, while still larger than that of hex pleating, is still small enough to be practical and useful. It is, in fact, the next smallest aspect ratio for all origami graph papers. Figure 3 displays a small patch of this pattern.

(A)   (B)

FIGURE 4. (a) A crease pattern for a frog, designed on the sterling grid.
(b) The folded frog.

We have dubbed this pattern the *sterling grid* due to its connection with the silver rectangle (which may be found within the grid, for example, the rectangle inscribed within the obvious hexagon). Some of the angles appear to be close to the origami-significant values of 22.5°, but they are not those values; in fact, none of the acute angles are integral divisions of the unit circle. Nevertheless, the grid can be used for origami design; Figure 4 shows the crease pattern and folded form of a tree frog designed using this grid.

For all other periodic mirror-symmetric origami graph papers, the aspect ratios continue to climb, making them harder, but still not impossible, to use as the basis of design. We note a few further sets offer intriguing possibilities, such as those shown in Figure 5. We will leave these for future exploration.

8. Discussion

We have developed formal conditions for the existence of doubly periodic origami graph paper, defined as periodic graph paper on which any uniaxial base can be designed with guaranteed non-dense axial contours. Using the formalism, we have found a new origami grid, the sterling grid, which is of practical utility for the design of origami uniaxial bases.

We note that the well-known 22.5° origami symmetry does not appear anywhere within this system. This can be seen from the observation that the normalized slope of all medials is a pure square root of a rational, a condition that the slopes of 22.5° lines do not satisfy (they are all of the form $n + m \sqrt{2}$ with $n \neq 0$). This omission is a bit surprising, since this angle regularly appears in highly mathematical origami crease patterns, such as those introduced by Maekawa [Kasahara and Maekawa 83]; in addition, Tachi and Demaine have shown that sets of lines based on multiples of these angles show a high degree of point-coincidence [Tachi and Demaine 11]. In origami graph paper, when one chooses basis vectors, one can choose both the angle and spacing independently. With the 22.5° system, one can choose particular spacings that force some bouncing contours

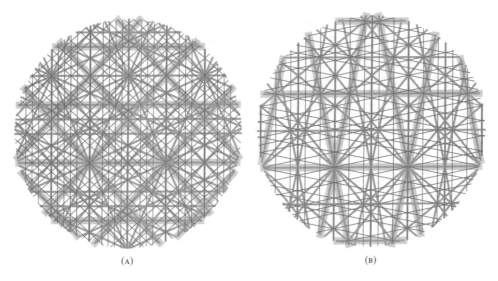

(A) (B)

FIGURE 5. (a) $(b, (b_x, b_y), b_0) = (1, (2/3, \sqrt{5}/3), 0)$ with $\rho = 2\sqrt{5} \approx 4.47214$. (b) $(b, (b_x, b_y), b_0) = (1, (1/5, 2\sqrt{6}/5), 0)$ with $\rho = 2\sqrt{6} \approx 4.89898$.

into periodicity, but there will always be some set that raises an aperiodic, and thus dense, specter.

Condition 3.1 was both necessary and sufficient for non-dense contours, but the specific approach of using periodic origami graph paper is not the only possible solution to the broader problem of finding universal design rules that guarantee finiteness. We speculate that some 22.5° grids may well play a role in some other general-purpose polygon-packed design algorithm for uniaxial bases. The design rules for such an algorithm, however, will await future work in the field.

References

[Aicholzer and Aurenhammer 96] O. Aicholzer and F. Aurenhammer. "Straight Skeletons for General Polygonal Figures in the Plane." In *Proceedings of the Second Annual International Conference on Computing and Combinatorics (COCOON)*, pp. 117–126. London: Springer-Verlag, 1996. MR1455657

[Bern et al. 98] Marshall Bern, Erik Demaine, David Eppstein, and Barry Hayes. "A Disk-Packing Algorithm for an Origami Magic Trick." In *Proceedings of the International Conference on Fun with Algorithms*, pp. 32–42. Waterloo, Canada: Carleton Scientific, 1998.

[Bern et al. 02] Marshall Bern, Erik Demaine, David Eppstein, and Barry Hayes. "A Disk-Packing Algorithm for an Origami Magic Trick." In *Origami³: Proceedings of the Third International Meeting of Origami Science, Mathematics, and Education*, edited by Thomas Hull, pp. 17–28. Natick, MA: A K Peters, 2002. MR1955756 (2004b:52030)

[Demaine and O'Rourke 07] Erik D. Demaine and Joseph O'Rourke. *Geometric Folding Algorithms: Linkages, Origami, Polyhedra.* Cambridge, UK: Cambridge University Press, 2007. MR2354878 (2008g:52001)

[Demaine et al. 98] Erik D. Demaine, Martin L. Demaine, and Anna Lubiw. "Folding and Cutting Paper." In *Discrete and Computational Geometry: Japanese Conference, JCDCG'98 Tokyo, Japan, December 9–12, 1998. Revised Papers*, Lecture Notes in Computer Science 1763, pp. 104–117. Berlin: Springer-Verlag, 1998. MR1787519

[Kasahara and Maekawa 83] Kunihiko Kasahara and Jun Maekawa. *Viva Origami.* Tokyo: Sanrio, 1983.

[Lang 94] Robert J. Lang. "Mathematical Algorithms for Origami Design." *Symmetry: Culture and Science* 5:2 (1994), 115–152. MR1309899 (95j:00008)

[Lang 96] Robert J. Lang. "A Computational Algorithm for Origami Design." In *Proceedings of the Twelfth Annual Symposium on Computational Geometry*, pp. 98–105. New York: ACM, 1996.

[Lang 97] Robert J. Lang. "The Tree Method of Origami Design." In *Origami Science and Art: Proceedings of the Second International Meeting of Origami Science and Scientific Origami*, edited by Koryo Miura, pp. 73–82. Shiga, Japan: Seian University of Art and Design, 1997.

[Lang 11] Robert J. Lang. *Origami Design Secrets: Mathematical Methods for an Ancient Art*, Second Edition. Boca Raton, FL: A K Peters/CRC Press, 2011. MR2841394

[Meguro 92] Toshiyuki Meguro. "Jitsuyou origami sekkeihou [Practical methods of origami designs]." *Origami Tanteidan Shinbun* 2 (1992), 7–14.

[Tachi and Demaine 11] Tomohiro Tachi and Erik D. Demaine. "Degenerative Coordinates in 22.5° Grid System." In *Origami^5: Fifth International Meeting of Origami Science, Mathematics, and Education*, edited by Patsy Wang-Iverson, Robert J. Lang, and Mark Yim, pp. 489–498. Boca Raton, FL: A K Peters/CRC Press, 2011. MR2866901 (2012k:00011)

LANG ORIGAMI, ALAMO, CALIFORNIA
E-mail address: robert@langorigami.com

SAN JOSE STATE UNIVERSITY, SAN JOSE, CALIFORNIA
E-mail address: roger.alperin@sjsu.edu

A Method to Fold Generalized Bird Bases from a Given Quadrilateral Containing an Inscribed Circle

Toshikazu Kawasaki

1. Introduction

Orizuru (the traditional origami crane) is one of the most famous origami models and is usually folded from a square piece of paper. Figure 1 shows the basic step of orizuru, which is known as the *bird base*. In the crease pattern, solid lines and broken lines show the mountain folds and the valley folds, respectively. This geometry has been studied in great detail. Husimi found a method to fold the bird base from a kite shape (Figure 2) [Husimi and Husimi 79]. Justin extended the Husimi bird base to apply to a *quadrilateral containing an inscribed circle* (QIC) and obtained his *perfect bird base* (PBB), Justin-zuru, shown in Figure 3 [Justin 94]. It has neck-wing interchangeability, as shown in Figure 4. Maekawa found yet another type of bird base, Maekawa-zuru (Figure 5) [Maekawa and Kasahara 89]. We perfected the *orizuru deformation theory*, including Justin's and Maekawa's work, and extended it for unbounded quadrilaterals (Figure 6) [Kawasaki 98, Kawasaki 02, Kawasaki 09, Kawasaki and Kawasaki 09]. Thus, the final bird base, the *generalized bird base* (GBB), was achieved (Figure 7).

Orizuru deformation theory is complete in terms of mathematics but not in terms of origami. It does not always give an actual folding sequence of GBB. In fact, Justin did not provide an explicit folding sequence. Excluding the rhombus bird base, we could not fold any generalized bird base before the Husimi bird base. In this work, we provide an actual folding sequence, based on generalized fish bases, to fold GBBs from an arbitrary QIC.

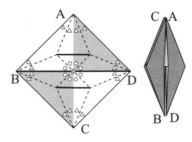

FIGURE 1. Traditional bird base.

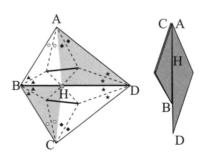

FIGURE 2. Husimi bird base.

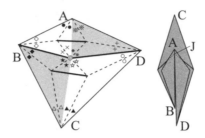

FIGURE 3. Perfect bird base.

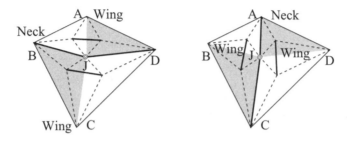

FIGURE 4. Neck-wing interchangeability.

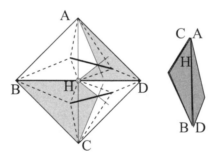

FIGURE 5. Maekawa bird base.

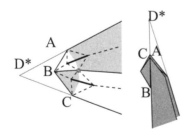

FIGURE 6. Unbounded generalized bird base.

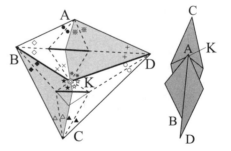

FIGURE 7. Generalized bird base.

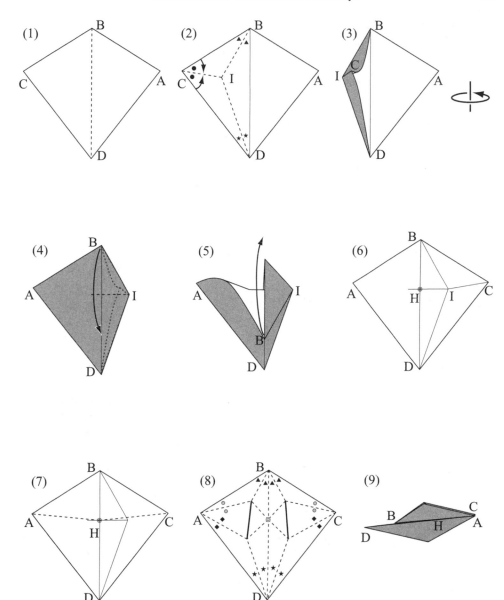

FIGURE 8. Folding sequence of Husimi bird base.

2. Folding Sequence for Husimi Bird Base

We review a method to fold the Husimi bird base (HBB), shown in Figure 8 [Husimi and Husimi 79].

(1) Make a crease along the diagonal BD.
(2) Fold along the three angle bisectors of the triangle BCD.
(3) Turn it over.
(4) Fold the right half along a line passing through the point I such that point B lands on the diagonal BD.

(5) Unfold and turn it over.

(6) Let H be the point where the fold from Step (4) intersects BD.

(7) Make two creases AH and CH.

(8) For each triangle ABH, BCH, ADH, and CDH, fold it flat along its three angle bisectors and one line segment that is perpendicular to either segment AH or CH.

(9) The Husimi bird base is completed.

3. QIC, PBB, and GBB

Justin defined the perfect bird base having neck-wing interchangeability (Justin-zuru, shown in Figure 4), where the four sides of the paper end up on a common line. He proved the following [Justin 94]:

(1) The perfect bird base can be folded from a quadrilateral if and only if the quadrilateral contains an inscribed circle.

(2) The point J in Figure 9 (left) is determined uniquely as the intersection of two hyperbolas: The first passes through points A and C with foci B and D. The second passes through points B and D with foci A and C. See Figure 9 (right).

Although Justin named point J the *center* of the PBB, we refer to it as the *perfect center* in order to distinguish it from the other centers, such as K in Figure 9 (right), that can be arbitrarily taken on the two hyperbolas. The perfect center is uniquely determined as the intersection of the two curves.

Figure 10 shows a crease pattern of a generalized bird base that does not have neck-wing interchangeability. A center K lies on the hyperbolas and passes through points A and C with foci B and D in Figure 9 [Kawasaki 98, Kawasaki 02]. Folding it flat, we have a generalized bird base where the four sides of the paper and K are on a common line.

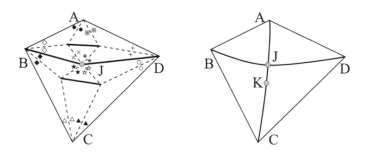

FIGURE 9. Crease pattern of a perfect bird base (left). Its perfect center J and a center K (right).

4. Generalized Fish Base

Figure 11 shows a basic step of origami known as a *fish base*. We refer to it as the *traditional fish base*; we call the origami shape in Figure 12 a *fish base* in this work. Fish bases can be generalized in the same way as bird bases by changing creases or the shape of the paper.

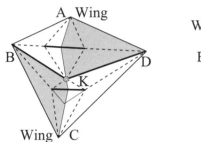
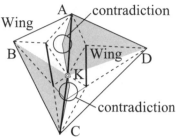

FIGURE 10. GBBs do not have neck-wing interchangeability.

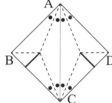

FIGURE 11. Traditional fish base.

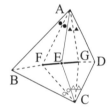

FIGURE 12. Fish base defined here.

FIGURE 13. Generalized fish base.

DEFINITION 4.1. An origami shape flat-folded from a quadrilateral is called a *generalized fish base* (GFB) if the four sides AB, BC, CD, and DA overlap on a straight line as in Figure 13 (left).

As in Figure 13 (left), the four edges AB, BC, CD, and DA and the segment AE overlap on the straight line CE. Therefore, the four creases AF, BF, CF, and EF are angle bisectors of the quadrilateral ABCE, and also the four creases CG, DG, AG, and EG are bisectors of the quadrilateral ADCE. Thus, quadrilaterals ABCE and ADCE are QICs. If two QICs, ABCE and CDAE, share two edges AE and CE, as shown in Figure 14 (left), then their union is also a QIC, as shown in Figure 14 (right). [Kawasaki 98, Kawasaki 02]. Furthermore, we can find two GFBs in the GBB shown in Figure 7. Hence, we obtain the following:

THEOREM 4.2. *A generalized fish base is folded from a quadrilateral shape of paper if and only if the quadrilateral is a QIC.*

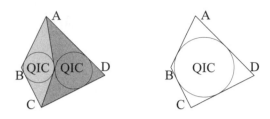

FIGURE 14. QIC + QIC = QIC.

THEOREM 4.3. *Any generalized bird base with a center K can be divided into two generalized fish bases that share two edges BK and DK.*

The two theorems satisfy an unbounded GFB, as shown in Figure 15.

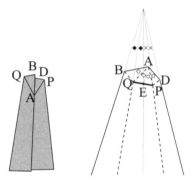

FIGURE 15. Unbounded GFB.

5. Folding Sequence for Generalized Bird Bases from a QIC

Theorems 4.2 and 4.3 give the following folding sequence of a generalized bird base from an arbitrary sheet of QIC paper, shown in Figure 16.

(1) Bisect the angles at points A and C.
(2) Take an arbitrary line b starting from B, and then fold along two lines starting from B such that edges AB and CB are on line b.
(3) Unfold.
(4) Make two valley creases PD and QD.
(5) Fold a GFB.
(6) A GFB is completed.
(7) Make the crease CD and open it.
(8) We have two QICs, BKDA and BKDC.
        Rotate the figure 90 degrees.
(9) Make valley creases as in Steps (2)–(3) from points A and C.
(10) Make four valley creases KR, KS, KT, and KU.
(11) Fold two GFBs from QICs DABK and DCBK.
(12) A GBB is completed.

Theorems 4.2 and 4.3 hold for unbounded QICs [Kawasaki 98, Kawasaki 02], [Kawasaki 09, Kawasaki and Kawasaki 09]. Therefore, we have the following folding sequence, shown in Figure 17:

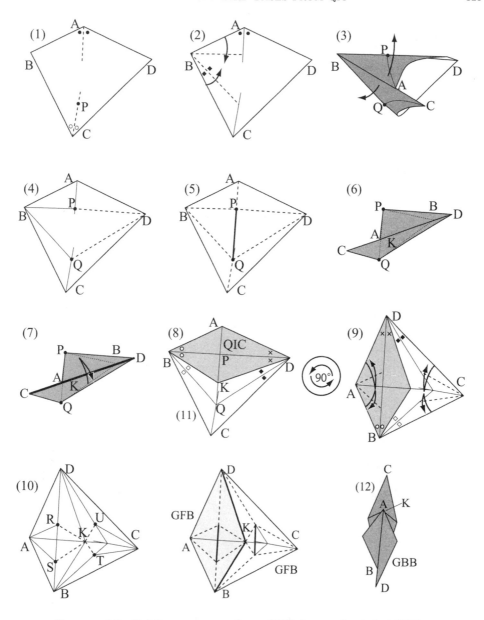

FIGURE 16. Folding sequence for a GBB from a bounded QIC.

(1) Fold along the bisectors of angles A and C.
(2) Take an arbitrary line *a* starting from A, and then fold along two lines starting from A such that edges DA and BC are on the line *a*. Do the same at corner C.
(3) Unfold.
(4) Make the mountain crease PQ.
(5) Fold along two rays (broken lines) starting from P or from Q such that the unbounded edges are on a common straight line *b* passing through B.
(6) An unbounded GFB is completed. Make a crease along the slit *b*.

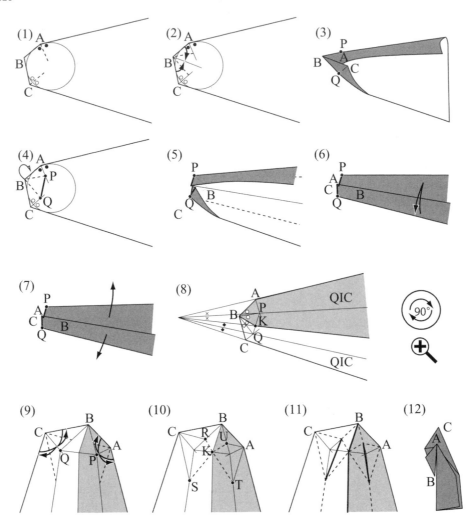

FIGURE 17. Folding sequence for a GBB from a given unbounded QIC.

(7) Unfold.
(8) We have two unbounded QICs.
    Rotate the figure 90 degrees and enlarge.
(9) Make valley creases as in Steps (2)–(3) from points A and C.
(10) Make four valley creases KR, KS, KT, and KU.
(11) Make two GFBs from each QIC.
(12) An unbounded GBB is completed.

6. Conclusion

We succeeded in obtaining an actual folding sequence to fold GBBs from a given QIC. However, the process reveals centers but does not reveal the perfect center. The challenging problem of finding the perfect center is a focus of future research.

References

[Husimi and Husimi 79] K. Husimi and M. Husimi. *Geometry of Origami.* Tokyo: Nippon-hyouronsha, 1979. (In Japanese.)

[Justin 94] J. Justin. "Mathematical Remarks about Origami Bases." *Symmetry: Culture and Science* 5:2 (1994), 153–165. MR1309900 (95j:51029)

[Kawasaki 98] T. Kawasaki. *Roses, Origami and Mathematics.* Tokyo: Morikital Publishing, 1998. (In Japanese.)

[Kawasaki 02] T. Kawasaki. "The Geometry of Orizuru." In *Origami^3: Proceedings of the Third International Meeting of Origami Science, Mathematics, and Education,* edited by Thomas Hull, pp. 61–73. Natick, MA: A K Peters, 2002. MR1955760 (2004a:52010)

[Kawasaki 09] T. Kawasaki. "A Crystal Map of the Orizuru World." In *Origami^4: Fourth International Meeting of Origami Science, Mathematics, and Education,* edited by Robert J. Lang, pp. 439–448. Wellesley, MA: A K Peters, 2009. MR2590567 (2010h:00025)

[Kawasaki and Kawasaki 09] T. Kawasaki and H. Kawasaki. "Orizuru Deformation Theory for Unbounded Quadrilaterals." In *Origami^4: Fourth International Meeting of Origami Science, Mathematics, and Education,* edited by Robert J. Lang, pp. 427–438. Wellesley, MA: A K Peters, 2009. MR2590567 (2010h:00025)

[Maekawa and Kasahara 89] J. Maekawa and K. Kasahara (editors). *Viva Origami.* Tokyo: Sanrio, 1989. (In Japanese.)

NATIONAL INSTITUTE OF TECHNOLOGY, ANAN COLLEGE, JAPAN
E-mail address: kawasaki@anan-nct.ac.jp

Pentasia: An Aperiodic Origami Surface

Robert J. Lang and Barry Hayes

1. Introduction

Modular origami is commonly used to construct origami polyhedra. While there exists a vast literature of modular origami forms, the great majority of these are based on a relatively small number of basic forms: typically the Platonic or Archimedian solids, with variations in surface decoration and/or in the structural relationship of the origami unit.

In a recent work [Lang and Hayes 13], we suggested that aperiodic patterns, such as the well-known Penrose tilings, showed great promise as a subject for modular origami development. In particular, we introduced the aperiodic surface in $\mathbb{R}^3$ by John H. Conway that he titled *Pentasia*, and we showed how it could be realized as a modular origami structure.

The same features that make aperiodic surfaces interesting for modular origami also make them suitable for single-sheet folding. In this work, we present the Pentasia surface and explain its relationship to the Penrose tiling, giving inflation and deflation rules for its generation to arbitrary size. We then turn to the problem of rendering such surfaces using single-sheet origami and show how the three-dimensional surface can be decomposed into a crease pattern tiling whose unit cells are the dual graph of the underlying Penrose tiling. Using this technique, a single-sheet crease pattern can be realized to fold an arbitrarily large section of the Pentasian surface. The decomposition technique has connections to other computational origami algorithms, ranging from the tucking molecules of Origamizer [Tachi 09, Tachi 14] to the universal molecules of tree theory [Lang 94].

2. Penrose Tiles and Pentasia

The Penrose tiles were invented by Roger Penrose [Penrose 78, Penrose 79] and popularized to a wide audience by Martin Gardner [Gardner 88]. They consist of two tiles, the *kite* and the *dart*, which, when certain matching rules on their edges are obeyed, result in a tiling that fills the plane but is aperiodic. There is extensive literature on the kite-dart tiling and related aperiodic tilings (see, e.g., [Grünbaum and Shephard 87] and references therein).

In 2002, John H. Conway[1] pointed out that one could create a surface in $\mathbb{R}^3$ composed of equilateral triangles from a kite-dart Penrose tiling, in which each of the kite and dart quadrilaterals in the plane is replaced by a pair of equilateral triangles that are joined along one edge into a folded quadrilateral. The Conway surface, which he dubbed

---

[1] In an impromptu lecture given at the conference Gathering for Gardner 5, Atlanta, GA, April 5–7, 2002.

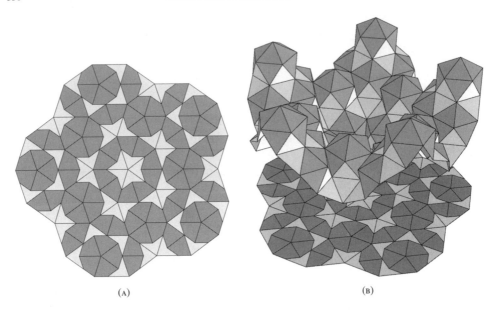

(A)   (B)

FIGURE 1. (a) A kite-dart Penrose tiling. (b) An image of a portion of
Pentasia, superimposed over its corresponding Penrose kite-dart tiling.

Pentasia, has the same symmetry and aperiodicity as the underlying kite-dart tiling. In
[Lang and Hayes 13], we described a mathematical technique for constructing the surface
and presented an implementation in modular origami.

Though one can build up regions of a Penrose tiling and/or Pentasia by assembling
tiles according to their matching rules, it is possible when adding tiles sequentially to create a region that permits no further tiling. One can, however, construct arbitrarily large
regions of either tiling by a process called, variously, *deflation* or *decomposition*, wherein
a small patch of tiles is transformed into a larger number of tiles by successively replacing patches of tiles with multiple smaller copies. Our work [Lang and Hayes 13] gives
production rules for constructing both tilings and Pentasia; a Mathematica package called
PenroseTiles3D [Lang 10] is available that contains functions for construction and rendering of both. The concept is simple. Each tile is replaced by a rhombus consisting of a
folded pair of equilateral triangles, rotated and positioned in three dimensions so that the
vertical projection of the outline of the rhombus is precisely the outline of the underlying
kite or dart tile. By suitable choice of the *z*-position of each rhombus, the resulting rhombi
can be joined edge-to-edge to form a surface composed entirely of equilateral triangles.
An example of a kite-dart tiling and its corresponding Pentasia equivalent are shown in
Figure 1.

3. Single-Sheet Construction

In [Lang and Hayes 13] we showed how to construct this surface from modular origami. We now turn our attention to the construction of a single-sheet rendition of the
Pentasia surface.

There is a general but powerful approach for constructing polyhedral surfaces from a
single sheet:

- Decompose the surface into its constituent polygons.

- Lay out the polygons in the plane.
- Find creases that hide all of the paper between the polygons.

This approach has a long history of use within the world of origami, particularly for polyhedra, and can be applied in pencil-and-paper designing (see, for example, "Stellated Cubocta" in [Lang 88, 58–63] and also [Montroll 02, Montroll 09]). A complete and formal algorithm was developed by Tachi [Tachi 09] and implemented in his program Origamizer [Tachi 14]. Origamizer takes a general surface, finds a optimal layout of the polygons numerically, and constructs the creases, which are a family Tachi called *tucking molecules*.

Whether the creases are found by hand or via computation, there are two important considerations:

- *Efficiency:* It is aesthetically and practically desirable to minimize the amount of extra paper that should be hidden. In general, the polygons of the pattern should be as large as possible for a given sheet of paper, and ideally, neighboring polygons will touch at vertices and/or along edges to reduce the amount of paper between them.
- *Geodesic distance:* The distance between any two polygon points on the paper must equal or exceed the geodesic distance between the corresponding two points on the polyhedral surface.

These two considerations are common to a wide range of origami design algorithms (e.g., tree theory [Lang 96]) and result in a general formulation of such problems as constrained optimizations: the first consideration provides the figure of merit and the second provides the constraints.

Numerical solution with a program such as Origamizer would suffice to find a single-sheet implementation of any finite piece of the Pentasia surface, but, of course, the numerical problem gets harder as the size of the problem grows (and origami packing optimizations tend to be NP-hard [Demaine et al. 11]). But, just as an arbitrarily large section of a Penrose tiling can be assembled from only two distinct tiles, we can, in principle, create an arbitrarily large section of a Pentasia surface by assembling it from a small number of distinct molecules.

3.1. Packing and layout. The first question is: how many distinct molecules do we need? It is tempting to hope for just two, corresponding to the kite and dart tile. It turns out that more are needed. If we take our cue from Tachi's tucking molecules, we note that there were *edge molecules* and *vertex molecules*. Taking a similar approach, we might seek both edge and vertex molecules. However, depending on the edge molecules' creases, we can conceivably absorb incipient edge molecules into their incident vertex molecules so that the latter entirely fill the plane and give rise to the Pentasia surface. The question, then, becomes: how many distinct vertex molecules do we need?

The count comes from the kite-dart Penrose tiling. By examining the tiling, we see that there are seven distinct types of vertex within the full tiling. Figure 2 shows a patch of a Penrose tiling that displays all seven types (each indicated by a black dot). The number of kites and darts around the vertex is unique for each type; thus, we can name each vertex type simply by the number of darts and kites around it: $nDmK$ indicates a vertex with n darts and m kites around it. Figure 3 shows the seven distinct types of vertex.

It should suffice to find the creases in the neighborhood of each vertex that produce the polygons (equilateral triangle pairs) of the surface and that hide the paper between the

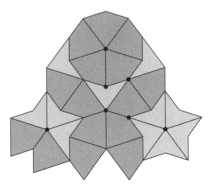

FIGURE 2. A patch of a Penrose tiling containing the seven distinct types of vertex in the pattern.

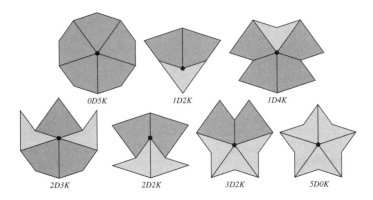

FIGURE 3. The seven distinct types of vertex in a Penrose tiling.

polygon pairs. We could then tile the Penrose tiling with copies of these vertex molecules, and this tiling should give the full crease pattern.

Because the creases of the pattern must outline the triangles and hide the paper between them, we should begin by finding a suitable mapping of the triangles to the underlying Penrose tiling, which will serve as the "scaffolding" for the crease pattern of the desired surface. In principle, this is easy; there is a one-to-one correspondence between the Penrose tiles and the corresponding triangle-pair rhombi of Pentasia. So, we must find a mapping of rhombi—the largest possible mapping, to satisfy efficiency–in which the position of each Pentasia rhombus relative to its corresponding kite or dart is the same.

The rhombi must not overlap, of course. If we take that constraint and fit the largest possible rhombi into the pattern, we achieve the arrangement shown in Figure 4, in which the kite-rhombus (crossed by a mountain fold) runs from corner to corner of the kite and the dart-rhombus (crossed by a valley fold) extends outside of its associated dart.

This arrangement is definitely efficient. It fails the geodesic distance criterion, unfortunately. With respect to Figure 4, points A and D must be brought into coincidence (same for points B and C). That means that in the folded form, points A and C must be separated by one unit (the edge length of the triangle), which they clearly are not in the crease pattern. So, this arrangement of rhombi cannot possibly give rise to a valid folded state.

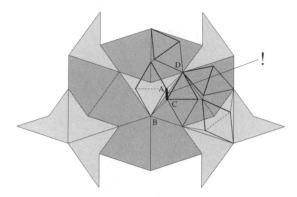

FIGURE 4. An arrangement of rhombi on a Penrose patch. Faint dashed lines connect point pairs that come together in the folded form. Path A–C violates the geodesic distance constraint.

FIGURE 5. An arrangement of rhombi on a Penrose patch that satisfy all geodesic distance constraints.

Thus, we must reduce the size of the rhombi until the separation distance between points A and C becomes equal to (or greater than) the triangle edge length. Figure 5 shows such a solution, in which path A–C is precisely equal to the edge length. To use the language of tree theory (and constrained optimization), path A–C has become *active*, along with its equivalent elsewhere in the pattern. The active paths are indicated by solid gray lines in Figure 5.

Active paths in mapped surfaces, like their counterparts in uniaxial bases, become folded creases (mountain folds, in this case). So, we can already identify some of the important creases in the crease pattern. The rhombi are themselves outlined by mountain folds (because the paper between them is tucked behind). The diagonals of the rhombi are mountains (for kite-rhombi) and valleys (for dart-rhombi). And, the active paths must also be mountain folds (again, because the paper to either side is tucked behind).

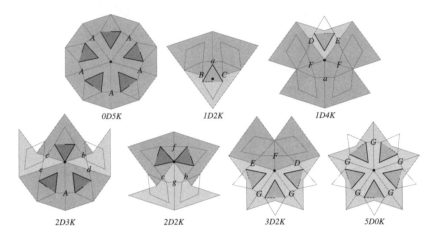

FIGURE 6. Assignment of equilateral triangles and half-creases to vertex molecules, creating dual tiles. Kite-like triangles are medium gray; dart-like triangles are lighter. Faint gray lines complete the dual tiles.

The active paths are creases, but they serve a more important purpose: active paths are crossed by no other folds, and so they serve as "isolating barriers" between different regions of the crease pattern. We can solve for crease patterns on one side of an active path while ignoring what happens on the other side. This allows a "divide-and-conquer" approach to finding crease patterns for the vertex molecules. Rather than having to look at how all molecules interact with each other, but identifying lines of isolation, we can reduce the number of possible interactions between molecules to a manageable few, occurring at well-defined interfaces.

3.2. Vertex molecules. We now return our attention to the seven types of vertex. We know the arrangement of rhombi around each vertex; we need to find crease patterns that hide the paper between the rhombi. The new creases go between the creases that surround each polygon and the mountain folds of the active paths. This confines their potential location to corridors that run along each edge. Vertex molecules will interact with one another along the edges of a Penrose tiling—but they do so in only a small number of ways.

We will build up a full crease pattern by creating vertex molecules for each of the seven types of vertex. We start this process by assigning the creases we know about—the two triangles in each rhombus—to a particular vertex tile. We divide each rhombus in half and assign one of the two triangles (and half of the crease between each triangle pair) to a vertex molecule. We adopt the rule that if a kite or dart tile is incident to the vertex at one of the two vertices on its line of mirror symmetry, then the vertex receives a triangle and half-crease from the rhombus corresponding to that tile. In this way, each vertex molecule receives between one and five triangle-and-half-crease sets. This assignment is shown in Figure 6.

We then connect corresponding triangle corners around each vertex to create tiles that together form a tiling that is a dual of the original kite-dart tiling. These dual tiles also tile the plane, and like kite-dart tiles, they must obey matching rules. The matching rules for the dual tiles are the following:

- A kite triangle can only mate with another kite triangle.

- A dart triangle can only mate with another dart triangle.
- A lettered line (upper- or lowercase) can only mate with the same letter of opposite case.

We note that there are multiple tiles that mate along the lettered lines; for example, the $0D5K$ molecule (all A's) can mate with either the $1D2K$ or $1D4K$ molecules along their a lines. We would like to find creases within each molecule that bring all of the triangle edges together and that allow all possible matings allowed by the upper- and lowercase letter combinations.

Our task is made somewhat easier by the observation that the creases we add, and the boundaries of the vertex molecules, are not fixed at the positions of the dashed lines. We can, for example, add an extrusion to the a boundaries as long as we add appropriate mating dents to all of the A's, and so forth.

When the excess paper is gathered together, it will form "flanges" that stand out from the surface (ideally, all on the underside of the surface). An open question is what angle the flanges make with the surface: do we lay them down to lie flush against the surface, stand them out at right angles, or something else? Rather than choosing a fixed angle, we will allow the angle to vary from flange to flange. In fact, we will go further; we will allow the flanges to form smooth curves (which is possible while retaining a polyhedral surface as long as the ruling lines of the curved flanges don't intersect the straight-line creases). This design choice has two nice benefits:

- It keeps the crease pattern simpler (because we don't need to include crimps where flanges come together at the polyhedral vertices).
- It allows flanges that might otherwise intersect to curve around each other and avoids self-intersection of the paper.

With those choices made, it is now a straightforward process to construct the creases for the vertex molecule. When we assemble vertex molecules, the folds of the triangles form closed polygons, all of whose edges get brought together pairwise. We can thus use the straight skeleton [Aicholzer and Aurenhammer 96] as a first approximation of the crease pattern for each region to be collapsed and then partition the creases among the participating vertex molecules.

The straight skeleton brings all of the polygon edges together to form flanges and can be designed on an edge-by-edge basis, but when we start to assemble molecules into larger groupings around vertices of the polyhedral surface, the situation can arise that flanges must pass through one another. While this is a general problem to be addressed, with this surface, it turns out to be possible to orient and curve the flanges so that they avoid intersection while maintaining isometry.

A more serious issue arises at vertices that are concave; with the flanges on the underside, the unaltered straight skeleton may not allow enough paper for the flanges to connect from one side of the vertex to the other and remain hidden. The $1D2K$ vertex, in particular, is problematic in this way. We augmented this molecule by adding a sink fold, which has the effect of splitting three connected flanges, and this gives enough paper for the surface to assume its desired three-dimensional shape.

The complete set of vertex molecules is shown in Figure 7. Note that we have added mating dents and extrusions to the A and a edges and to the G and g edges. The molecules still tile to fill the plane, and all creases are confined within (or on the edge of) each tile. Note, too, that when a crease runs along an edge of a tile, we have divided the crease into halves so that each tile contributes a half-crease.

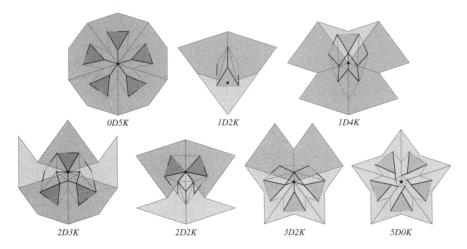

FIGURE 7. Completed vertex molecules with with mountain (solid black) and valley (dashed gray) assignments.

3.3. Single-sheet Pentasia. We now have the means to construct a crease pattern for a single-sheet rendition of Pentasia of arbitrary size. We construct the desired kite-dart tiling and then place vertex molecules on each vertex, matching the orientation of the molecule to the underlying tiling. The molecules align (by design) to create a full crease pattern, which can then be folded up (a step that contains its own challenges).

Figure 8 shows a completed crease pattern for the section of Pentasia shown in Figure 1. Figure 9 shows a photograph of the folded result. In the crease pattern, we have left the coloring of the tiles (as background) and the vertex dots to aid in identifying the individual vertex molecules.

The starting sheet was 58 cm across (bottom to top, in the orientation of Figure 8); the finished figure is approximately $22 \times 24 \times 12$ cm.

4. Conclusions

In conclusion, we have presented a construction method for an aperiodic surface, Pentasia, from a single sheet. Notably, the construction technique can be carried out "by hand," i.e., without numerical computation. As a proof of the design, we have folded a patch of Pentasia. The approach generalizes readily to arbitrarily large portions of the pattern.

In [Lang and Hayes 13], we derived a surface analogous to Pentasia that was based on the Penrose rhombus tiling, which we dubbed *Rhombonia*. Like Pentasia, Rhombonia is composed of two types of rhombus, although only one of which is folded. We recently learned[2] that a similar surface already existed, called the *Wieringa Roof* [de Bruijn 81, p. 49], [Polyakov 08, Goucher 14]. Unlike Rhombonia, neither rhombus unit in the latter needs a fold. The Wieringa Roof/Rhombonia surface did not lend itself as easily as Pentasia to a modular origami implementation, but we speculate that it may be well suited for a single-sheet implementation and that the techniques outlined here could be applied to its creation. We leave the design and folding of such a surface to future workers in the field.

---

[2]We are indebted to Jeannine Mosely for pointing us to the Wieringa Roof.

FIGURE 8. Crease pattern for a portion of Pentasia. Background shading is the original kite-dart tiling.

FIGURE 9. The folded single-sheet Pentasia: top side (left) and underside (right), showing the curved flanges.

References

[Aicholzer and Aurenhammer 96] O. Aicholzer and F. Aurenhammer. "Straight Skeletons for General Polygonal Figures in the Plane." In *Proceedings of the Second Annual International Conference on Computing and Combinatorics (COCOON)*, pp. 117–126. London: Springer-Verlag, 1996. MR1455657

[de Bruijn 81] N. G. de Bruijn. "Algebraic Theory of Penrose's Non-periodic Tilings of the Plane I." *Proceedings of the Koninklijke Nederlandse Akademie van Wetenschappen Series A* 84:1 (1981), 39–52.

[Demaine et al. 11] Erik D. Demaine, Sándor P. Fekete, and Robert J. Lang. "Circle Packing for Origami Design Is Hard." In *Origami⁵: Fifth International Meeting of Origami Science, Mathematics, and Education*, edited by Patsy Wang-Iverson, Robert J. Lang, and Mark Yim, pp. 609–626. Boca Raton, FL: A K Peters/CRC Press, 2011. MR2866908

[Gardner 88] Martin Gardner. *Penrose Tiles to Trapdoor Ciphers: And the Return of Dr. Matix*. New York: W. H. Freeman & Co., 1988. MR968892 (89m:00006)

[Goucher 14] Adam P. Goucher. "Penrose Tilings and Wieringa Roofs." *Wolfram Demonstration Project*, http://demonstrations.wolfram.com/PenroseTilingsAndWieringaRoofs/, retrieved July 10, 2014.

[Grünbaum and Shephard 87] Branko Grünbaum and G. C. Shephard. *Tilings and Patterns*. New York: W. H. Freeman & Co., 1987. MR857454 (88k:52018)

[Lang and Hayes 13] Robert J. Lang and Barry Hayes. "Paper Pentasia: An Aperiodic Surface in Modular Origami." *The Mathematical Intelligencer* 35 (2013), 61–74. MR3133766

[Lang 88] Robert J. Lang. *The Complete Book of Origami: Step-by-Step Instructions in over 1000 Diagrams*. New York: Dover Publications, 1988.

[Lang 94] Robert J. Lang. "The Tree Method of Origami Design." In *Origami Science and Art: Proceedings of the Second International Meeting of Origami Science and Scientific Origami*, edited by Koryo Miura, pp. 73–82. Shiga, Japan: Seian University of Art and Design, 1997.

[Lang 96] Robert J. Lang. "A Computational Algorithm for Origami Design." In *Proceedings of the Twelfth Annual Symposium on Computational Geometry*, pp. 98–105. New York: ACM, 1996.

[Lang 10] Robert J. Lang. "Penrose Tiles 3D." http://www.langorigami.com/science/computational/pentasia/PenroseTiles3D.nb, 2010.

[Montroll 02] John Montroll. *A Plethora of Polyhedra in Origami*. New York: Dover Publications, 2002. MR1893874 (2002m:00004)

[Montroll 09] John Montroll. *Origami Polyhedra Design*. Natick, MA: A K Peters, 2009. MR2567429 (2010i:52001)

[Penrose 78] Roger Penrose. "Pentaplexity." *Eureka* 39 (1978), 16–22.

[Penrose 79] Roger Penrose. "Pentaplexity." *The Mathematical Intelligencer* 2 (1979), 32–37. MR558670 (81d:52012)

[Polyakov 08] A A Polyakov. "Presentation of Penrose Tiling as Set of Overlapping Pentagonal Stars." *Journal of Physics: Conference Series* 98 (2008), 1–4.

[Tachi 14] Tomohiro Tachi. "Software: Freeform Origami, Origamizer, Rigid Origami Simulator." http://www.tsg.ne.jp/TT/software/, accessed July 11, 2014.

[Tachi 09] Tomohiro Tachi. "3D Origami Design Based on Tucking Molecules." In *⁴: Fourth International Meeting of Origami Science, Mathematics, and Education*, edited by Robert J. Lang, pp. 259–272. Wellesley, MA: A K Peters, 2009. MR2590567 (2010h:00025)

Lang Origami, Alamo, CA
E-mail address: robert@langorigami.com

Palo Alto, CA
E-mail address: bhayes@cs.stanford.edu

Base Design of a Snowflake Curve Model and Its Difficulties

Ushio Ikegami

1. Introduction

The possibility of folding a sheet of paper into a fractal figure is an interesting subject in origami design. A fractal figure is characterized by its noninteger dimension, often possesses self-similarity, and usually results in infinite perimeter in the two-dimensional plane. The author has previously presented a trial model of the well-known fractal figure Koch's snowflake curve (Figure 1) at 4OSME [Ikegami 09]. The goal of the model was to construct a sequence of origami works that can approximate the snowflake curve arbitrarily closely. However, because the snowflake curve has infinite perimeter, the perimeter of this origami sequence necessarily diverges to infinity. While it has been proven that origami can approach infinite perimeter, such an origami typically decreases its size to be infinitesimally small as its perimeter diverges to infinity (for example, [Lang 03]). Our model is interesting in this regard because it is designed not to change its size with each incremental step in the construction.

This paper describes the basic vertex arrangement design of the snowflake curve model, some difficulties that arise with infinite iteration, and two alternative simplified models, one of which has a perimeter that diverges to infinity without decreasing its size.

2. Vertex Arrangement Design and Crease Patterns

The first concept for the snowflake model comes from the simple hexagonal star illustrated in Figure 2(a). These two stars correspond to the initial pattern and the first iteration of the sequence constructing the snowflake curve. Figure 2(b) shows a hypothetical vertex arrangement (VA) for the second iteration of the star as a natural inference from the initial configuration and first iteration. However, this design does not produce a flat-foldable crease pattern (CP) becuase it does not satisfy the *distance condition* (DC): the distance between any two points in the CP must be at least the same distance measured along the

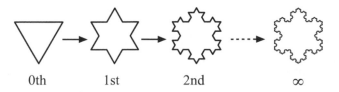

Oth   1st   2nd   ∞

FIGURE 1. Koch's snowflake curve.

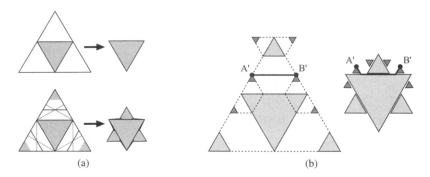

FIGURE 2. (a) The first concept and (b) its natural expansion for a second
iteration.

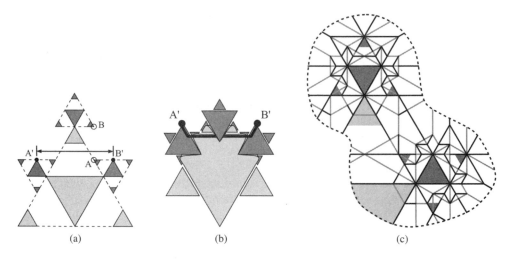

FIGURE 3. (a–b) Valid VA for second iteration and (c) its CP.

folded shape. In Figure 2(b), the distance between vertices A′ and B′ is shorter than their
distance measured on the folded shape. Thus, we use the VA of the first iteration only as
the smallest element for the entire VA design.

Construction of the second iteration with the element is shown in Figure 3(a) and (b).
The design rule of this VA is to replace all the branching parts with new vertices (darker
gray), while the middle pattern is left as originally laid out. This VA for the second iteration
satisfies the DC and gives rise to a flat-foldable CP (see [Ikegami 11] for folding diagrams).
Figure 3(c) shows the main part of the CP, and we can see the basic connection between
the elements in the CP. Note that this design does not change the size of resulting work.

Subsequent iterations of the pattern are also constructed by this rule, but they need
some asymmetric alteration on the points indicated A and B in Figure 3(a). Figure 4(a)
shows the alteration. Black dots in the figure indicate the accumulation points of the vertices. The original rule places elements on the line from A to a dotted circle (the original accumulation point). The dotted circle, however, lies within an area where only box-pleating
is allowed because the width of the area must be preserved to keep the width of the triangle

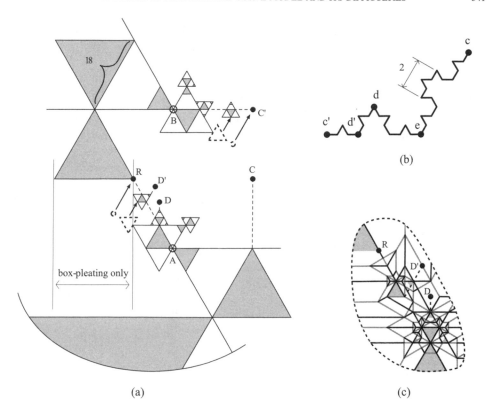

FIGURE 4. (a) Alteration of the VA, (b) points on the folded shape, and (c) CP of the alteration.

FIGURE 5. The VA with threefold rotational symmetry is asymmetric (lacks mirror symmetry).

above constant. To avoid this situation, we slide the accumulation point onto the vertex of the triangle above and shift the pattern elements onto the line AR. By this means, the complicated folds are kept outside of the box-pleating area. Point B does not have such a restricted area nearby, but we apply the same alteration to it to make the arrangement even.

Next, we must check if the VA with this alteration satisfies the DC. Given that the length of the triangle indicated in the top of Figure 4(a) is 18, we have that

$$CC' = 9\sqrt{3} > 12 = ce + ec',$$
$$DD' = \sqrt{13} > 2 = dd'.$$

This is just a small portion of the VA, but since these points are particularly close to each other, it suggests that the full VA satisfies the DC. The CP in Figure 4(c) shows the connection of the vertices around the altered area. Notice that the neighborhood of point R has the same pattern as the first iteration. Therefore, this area can contain all the vertices on the line AR and is flat-foldable at any iteration order n.

Based on these designs (Figures 2(a), 3, and 4), we can construct the entire VA and flat-foldable CPs for fourth and fifth iterations (see Figure 5, 6, and 7). We consider this VA to be an asymmetric design because the CP in Figure 6 does not have mirror symmetry. Bold lines in the CP for the fourth iteration correspond to the bold lines of its folded shape. Thus, this partial CP and its mirror images form the complete snowflake curve. The existence of the entire flat-foldable CP for the fifth iteration, however, remains in question.

3. Irregularity of the Crease Pattern

We now seek to find a set of finite constructors and their relative arrangement from the CP of the fourth and fifth iterations that would allow construction of a CP with an arbitrary iteration order n. This would provide the proof for the possibility of this origami work sequence approaching the snowflake curve. However, these patterns are irregular individually and do not have enough similarity to extract a recurring pattern. What makes the CP so irregular?

Asymmetry of the VA is, of course, a major reason. In particular, handling box-pleating in an asymmetric structure is very difficult. Although a sixfold symmetric VA might resolve this problem because the target figure has sixfold symmetry, we stay on this threefold asymmetric VA for now, since the first asymmetric step from the initial pattern to the first iteration was natural.

Another reason for the irregularity is that some of the accumulation points of the vertices in the CP do not have fixed locations on the folded form. The locations on the folded form approach points of the snowflake curve as the iteration order n becomes larger. (See Figure 8(b).)

Because of this, the back side of the folded shape cannot stay fixed; the CP of the back part changes with each iteration. To avoid this difficulty, we put extra folds around vertices that, on the folded form, will fix the locations of the accumulation points onto the snowflake curve. (See Figure 8(c).) This change simplifies the CP considerably, but a third iteration with these extra folds has not been successful. Figure 9 shows the best result thereby obtained.

4. Simplified Snowflake Curves

In this section, we examine two simplified versions of the snowflake curve—the *tree curve* and the *concave tree curve*, both shown in Figure 10. These are no longer fractal because a confined self-similarity does not produce noninteger dimension. Nevertheless, their perimeters still diverge to infinity.

As shown in Figure 10, in one iteration, an element in each curve adds one third of its length and produces three new elements to be iterated at the next iteration with the element

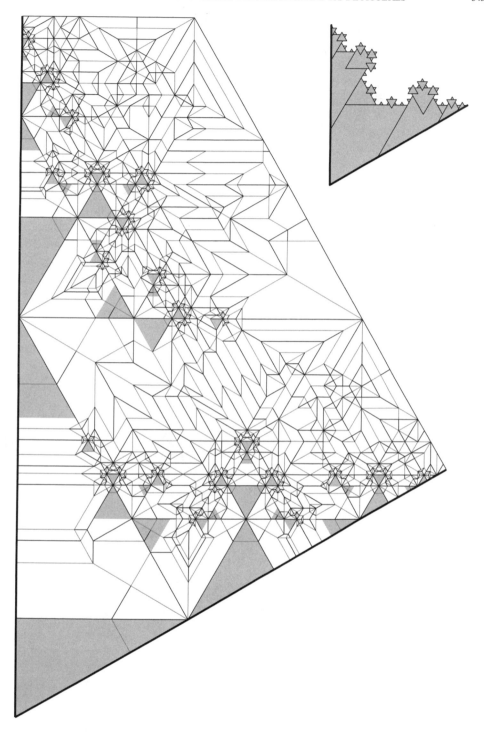

FIGURE 6. The CP of the fourth iteration.

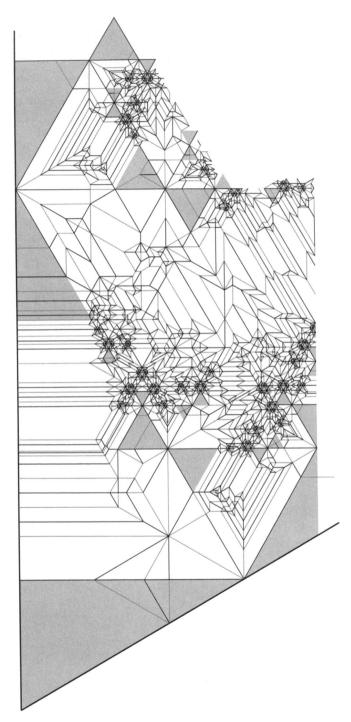

FIGURE 7. Partial CP of the fifth iteration.

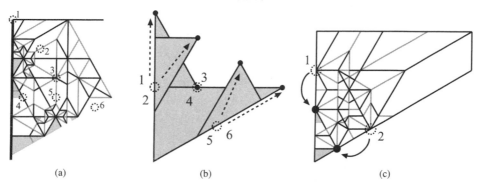

○ Accumulation points on the CP

● Points on the Koch curve

(a)   (b)   (c)

FIGURE 8. (a) The CP, (b) slide of accumulation points, and (c) its modification.

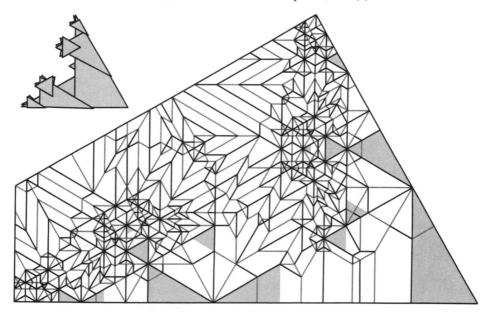

FIGURE 9. Third iteration with the extra folds.

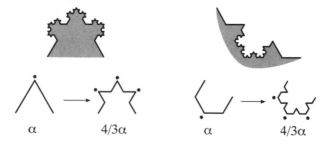

FIGURE 10. The tree curve (left) and the concave tree curve (right).

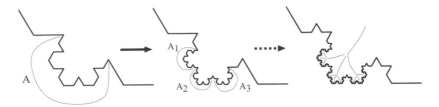

FIGURE 11. Construction of the concave tree curve.

size reduced to one third. Therefore, defining P_n as the perimeter of both curves after the nth iteration, with $P_0 \equiv \alpha$, the growth of P_n with each iteration is given by

$$P_{n+1} - P_n = (\text{length of each element of } P_n) \times \frac{1}{3} \times (\text{number of elements of } P_n)$$

$$= \left(\frac{1}{3}\right)^n \alpha \times \frac{1}{3} \times 3^n = \frac{1}{3}\alpha.$$

Hence, P_n diverges to infinity with linear growth.

4.1. The concave tree curve. Figure 8(b) shows that accumulation points of the "valley" part of the curve lie in a desirable location and do not produce the sliding problem seen earlier. The concave tree curve is made by eliminating the other accumulation points from the VA, which is an advantage of the concave tree curve over the original curve. This construction is also described in Figure 11 by similarity transformations f_1, f_2, and f_3 such that

$$f_1(A) = A_1, \qquad f_2(A) = A_2, \qquad f_3(A) = A_3.$$

The concave tree curve is obtained as the limit of these transformations. Accumulation points remaining on this curve correspond to the tips of the 3-branching tree in Figure 11 (right). The *spiral* and the *valley* patterns in the Figures 12 and 13, respectively, show approximations of the limits of f_1, f_3, and f_2 by origami. Figure 14 shows the eighth iteration that presents all of the recursive patterns.

The next task is to form the concave tree curve using both the spiral and the valley as constructors. Although we must check at least the eighth iteration to see the full possibility, only the fifth iteration has been confirmed to be flat-foldable (Figure 15). Removal of the vertices with the slide problem make the model considerably easier than the original. Nevertheless, box-pleating remains a problem. The valley pattern successfully controls box-pleated structure around its two accumulation points, but the condition of the neighborhood can change when it is applied to other locations. Currently, a general method that handles box-pleating has not been found yet.

4.2. The tree curve. The tree curve seems harder than the concave tree curve because its accumulation points have the sliding problem seen earlier and the bottom of the branch must preserve a large blank area while the top of the pattern gets ever more complex. However, Figure 9 shows the extra folds that can be applied to the tree curve at the third iteration, and using the spiral pattern ensures that the bottom area can be kept blank. These are the advantages of the tree curve over the original snowflake curve.

By combining the spiral with the extra folds, we can realize a flat-foldable CP of the tree curve and its finite set of constructors (Figures 16 and 17). Figures 18–22 show the tiling pattern of the constructors in detail. The key of this system is the box-pleating absorber shown in Figure 22. A one-sided box-pleating river, which could make the CP

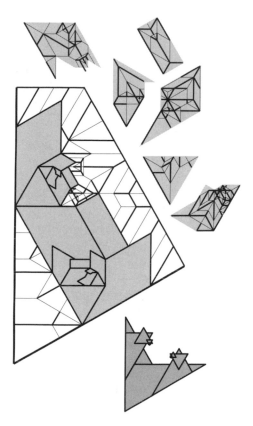

FIGURE 12. The spiral: an approximation of the limit of f_1 and f_3 (bottom) and its CP.

chaotic, is offset by an absorber with complementary box-pleating that is created by simple open-sink folds. Figure 23 shows two boundaries of the sheet of paper for the complete shape. The minimum size (left) has two accumulation points of vertices on the boundary. We can use a larger piece of paper to contain all accumulation points interior of it (center). However, the neighborhood of an accumulation point is symmetric only within a certain realm. Therefore, flat-foldability of the tree curve with the entire $\mathbb{R}^2$ sheet of paper is still not confirmed.

5. Conclusion

We have investigated the design and flat-foldability of the snowflake curve model and its two simplified models. We examined CPs up to a fifth iteration of the original snowflake model and the concave tree curve, and we found them to exhibit irregular growth, which was caused by box-pleated structure in asymmetric design. This suggests that even if these models are possible, they may require an infinite number of constructors or a large, ever-changing irregular area. However, we found the tree curve flat-foldable and capable of handling box-pleated structure with a finite set of constructors.

Since the snowflake curve is composed of the combination of the tree curve and the concave tree curve, a future task would be to address the flat-foldability of the concave tree curve: Is the absorbing system of the tree curve applicable to the concave tree curve?

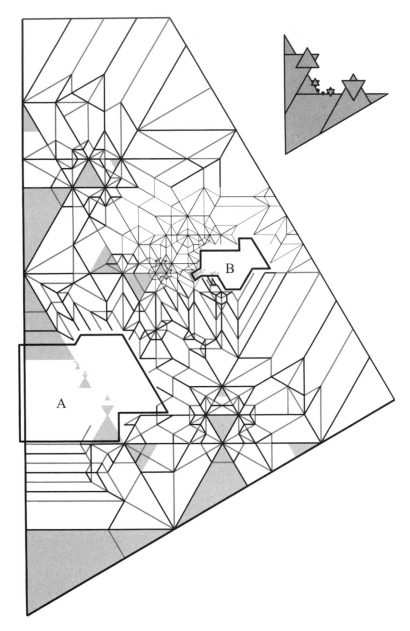

FIGURE 13. The valley: an approximation of the limit of f_2 (top right) and its CP.

Moreover, when it come to the question of combining the two simplified curves into the snowflake curve, global flat-foldability of both curves in an $\mathbb{R}^2$ sheet of paper will also be important considerations, because their relative scales to the entire VA become infinitesimally small.

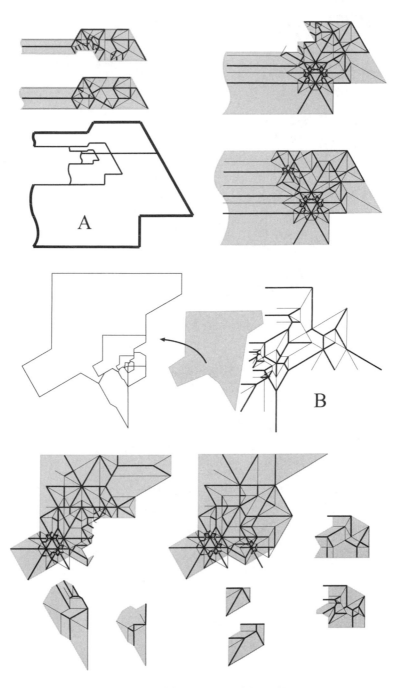

FIGURE 14. Tiling pattern of the valley.

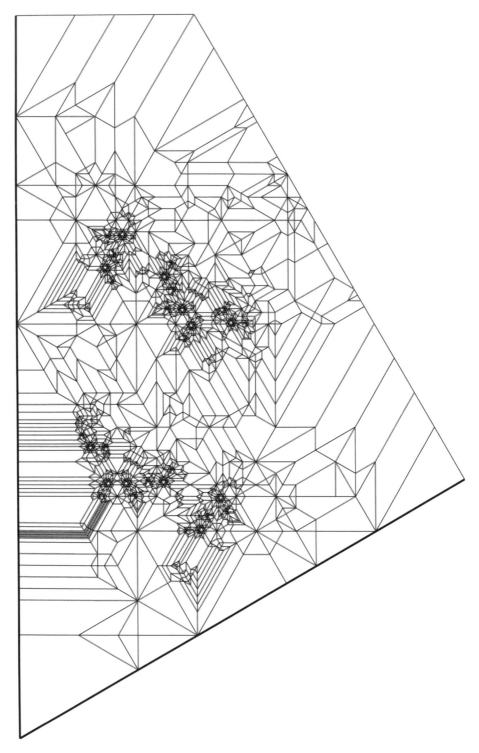

FIGURE 15. Fifth iteration of the concave tree curve: application of the spiral and the valley.

Adjuster

Builder

Starting pint of box-pleats flow

Filler

FIGURE 16. Constructors for CP of the tree curve: The builder forms the shape of the curve, the adjuster is the extra folds in Section 3, and the filler fills up the blank spaces among builders and adjusters to form a convex sheet of paper. The waving end of the starting parts of box-pleats flow changes its shape depending on its counterparts. The gray areas have more detailed patterns described in Figures 19–22.

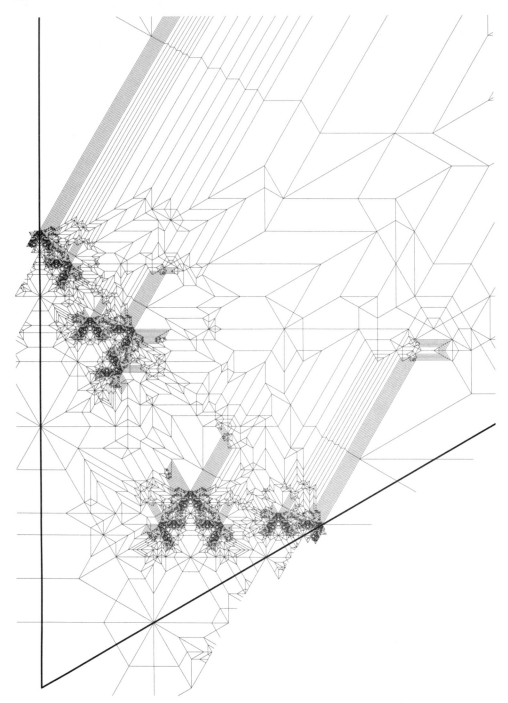

FIGURE 17. CP of the tree curve.

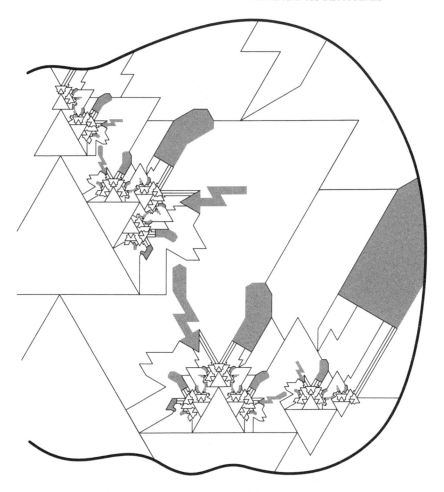

FIGURE 18. Tiling pattern of the constructors.

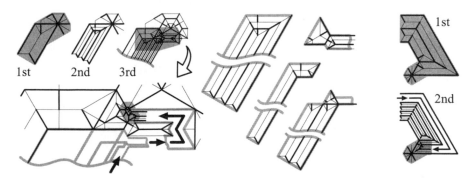

FIGURE 19. Detail of gray areas: The constructor on the bottom right has the same pattern as one on the top left, the arrow indicates the box-pleats flow, and the hexagonal gray area at the end of the arrow is box-pleating absorber-1 described in Figure 22.

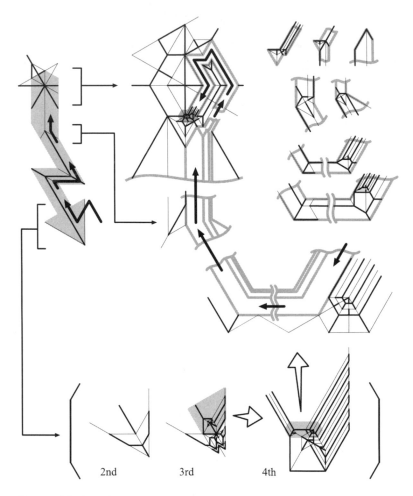

FIGURE 20. Detail of the arrow-shaped gray area and flow of box-pleats: It has the box-pleating absorber-1 at the end point of the arrow.

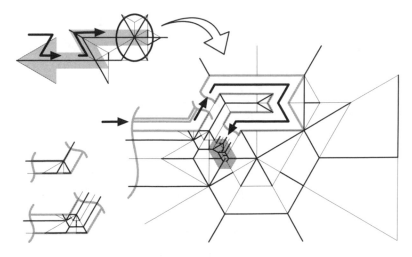

FIGURE 21. Detail of another arrow-shaped gray area: It has the box-pleating absorber-2.

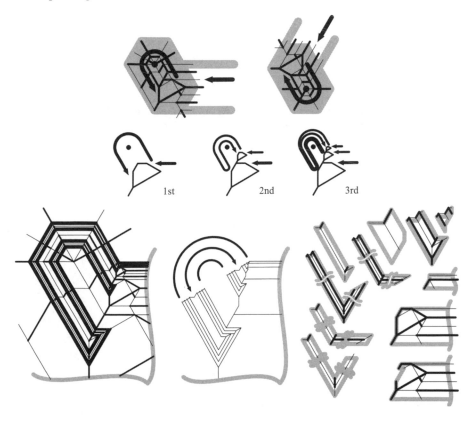

FIGURE 22. The box-pleating absorber-1 (top left) and -2 (top right): They absorb box-pleats flow by open-sinking the mountain ridge indicated by the curved arrow, and the only difference between the two is the folding state at the vertex indicated by a black dot, which is not essential to this system.

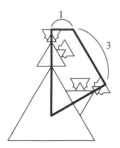  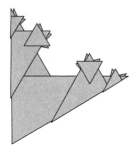

FIGURE 23. Boundaries of the sheet of paper (left and center) and their folded state (right), which complete the work with their mirror images.

References

[Ikegami 01] Ushio Ikegami. "Crease Pattern Challenge, Koch's Snow flake Curve." *Origami Tanteidan Magazine* 67 (2001), 34.

[Ikegami 02] Ushio Ikegami. "Folding Fractal Images." *Origami Tanteidan Magazine* 74 (2002), 11–13.

[Ikegami 04] Ushio Ikegami. "New Infinite Folding Patterns." *Origami Tanteidan Magazine* 88 (2004), 11–13

[Ikegami 09] Ushio Ikegami. "Fractal Crease Patterns." In *Origami⁴: Fourth International Meeting of Origami Science, Mathematics, and Education*, edited by Robert J. Lang, pp. 31–40. Wellesley, MA: A K Peters, 2009. MR2590567 (2010h:00025)

[Ikegami 11] Ushio Ikegami. "Koch's Snowflake (Iteration 2)." *Origami Tanteidan Convention Book 17*, edited by Japan Origami Academic Society, pp. 14–17. Tokyo: Japan Origami Academic Society, 2011.

[Lang 03] Robert J. Lang. "The Mrgulis Napkin Problem." In *Origami Design Sercrets: Mathematical Method for an Ancient Art*, Section 9.1.1. Natick, MA: A K Peters, 2003. MR2013930 (2004g:52001)

[Maekawa 97] Jun Maekawa. "Similarity in Origami." In *Origami Science and Art: Proceedings of the Second International Meeting of Origami Science and Scientific Origami*, edited by K. Miura, pp. 109–118. Shiga, Japan: Seian University of Art and Design, 1997.

ORIGAMI CREATOR
E-mail address: `foldable-at-its-lirnit@o.email.ne.jp`

Two Calculations for Geodesic Modular Works

Miyuki Kawamura

1. Introduction

Geodesic spheres are beautiful and interesting shapes. Here, we try to make a geodesic sphere using modular origami techniques. In this case, it's necessary to calculate the numbers of modules. We give the equation that calculates this number. Some useful tables are also given for making a geodesic sphere with some color combinations.

2. Cosmosphere

Geodesic spheres are made of great circles inscribed on the surface of a sphere whereby the intersections of the great circles become a spherical polygonal network [Wenninger 79]. I began experimenting in the 1990s with modular origami techniques to create pieces based on these shapes. In 1996 I designed "Cosmosphere" (Figures 1 and 2), a geodesic sphere-based shape built on the symmetry of a semiregular polyhedron, the snub dodecahedron [Kawamura 04].

The snub dodecahedron has 12 regular pentagonal faces and 80 regular triangular faces; for the Cosmosphere, each edge of these pentagons and triangles is further divided into three (Figure 1, lower right). The surface thus becomes a triangular mesh. There are

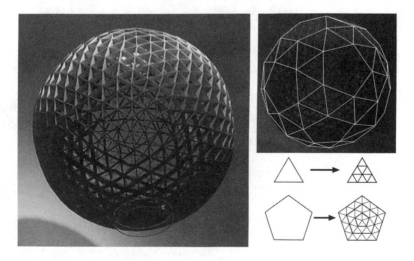

FIGURE 1. Cosmosphere.

1260 triangles and 1890 edges on the surface: 1350 "long" edges and 540 "short" edges. I designed Cosmosphere to have each edge be an individual origami module made from one piece of paper. Each type of module must connect to its neighbors with a specific angle and have a specific length to create this particular shape.

In theory, we should need modules of only two different lengths for this shape. But, due to issues arising from the paper (primarily due to paper thickness) and folding conditions (even small folding errors become significant), I found I needed to use three different lengths of modules to construct the Cosmosphere. Of the long modules, 120 needed to have their length shortened slightly. These middle-length modules successfully ease the excess tensions in the model.

The completed piece is about 56 cm in diameter when made with 7.5 cm square sheets of paper. The connections between the modules are not quite strong enough to enable the piece to stand by itself, so I needed glue to make the piece stable. It took nearly half a year to make this piece.

3. Geosphere

Ten years after Cosmosphere, in 2006, I designed another modular piece called "Geosphere" (Figure 3) [Kawamura 07a]. Like Cosmosphere, Geosphere is also made with 1890 modules, and it is based on the same symmetry as Cosmosphere. But, the Geosphere module is simpler, and all of them are identical; as a result, the final shape is not spherical, but icosahedral. Due to internal tensions, the effective length of each Geosphere module changes automatically, by bending, and the resulting surface is icosahedral. These changed module lengths correspond to the two or three different edge lengths of the Cosmosphere construction. The size change is small, however, so the triangular mesh of Geosphere remains close to regular triangles. It takes only three to seven days to make a complete Geosphere with 1890 modules, and it holds together and supports itself without using glue. Furthermore, the Geosphere module itself is very flexible, so that we can make other geodesic spheres from the same module. The final shape has "soft" edges and joints, so we can bend the "sphere" into strange shapes like the one shown at the bottom left in Figure 3.

4. Calculation for the Total Number of Edges on a Geodesic Sphere

To make a complete model of a geodesic sphere, we need to know how many modules to use to represent the shape [Kawamura 07b, Kawamura 10]. Table 1 lists the total number of edges or faces of several reference geodesic spheres, which is useful to help count the possible number of modules. Very often, the number of modules is equal to the number of edges.

Here, we will calculate the number of edges on Geosphere based on a general geodesic sphere by using a two-dimensional oblique coordinate system with an angle of 60 degrees (Figure 4).

The shape of Geosphere is approximately that of a regular icosahedron, so the total surface area and the number of edges of the model's triangular mesh can be calculated easily. With the origin point $O = (0, 0)$ of this coordinate system at one of the five-fold symmetry vertices on the surface, a point $V(m, n)$ is a position of the next five-fold symmetry vertex (Figure 5). This shape has twelve five-fold vertexes, and their coordinate-system distance is (m, n) from each other.

[Cosmosphere]
Miyuki Kawamura
Design July 5,1996

All kinds of modules are made from same size square of paper. 1890 sheets are need.

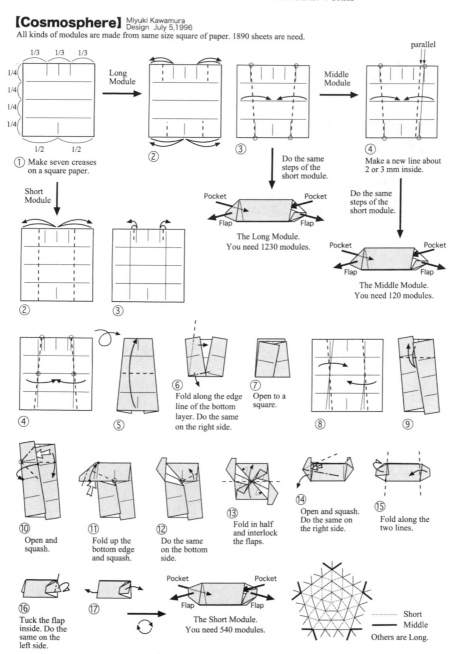

FIGURE 2. Diagrams of Cosmosphere.

Using the law of cosines, the straight-line distance L between the points O and V is

$$L^2 = m^2 + n^2 - 2mn \cdot \cos 120°$$
$$= m^2 + n^2 + mn.$$

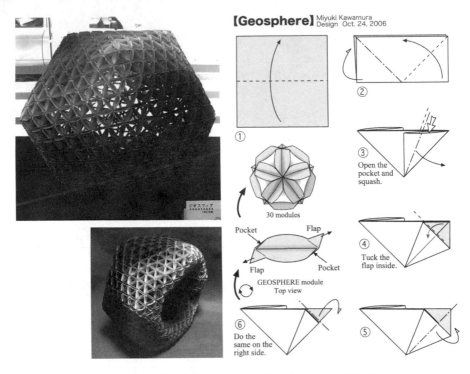

FIGURE 3. Geosphere (left) and its diagrams (right).

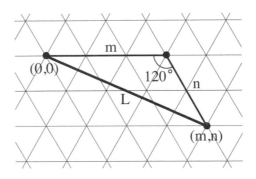

FIGURE 4. Two-dimensional oblique coordinate system.

Note that L is the length of one edge of the icosahedron, so the total area A of this icosahedron is

$$A = 20 \cdot \frac{1}{2} \cdot L \cdot \frac{L}{2} \cdot \sqrt{3} = 5 \sqrt{3} \cdot L^2.$$

On the other hand, the area of one triangle of the surface mesh is

$$B = \frac{1}{2} \cdot 1 \cdot \frac{\sqrt{3}}{2} = \frac{\sqrt{3}}{4}.$$

Therefore, the number of the triangles on the surface of the Geosphere model is

$$S = \frac{A}{B} = 20 \cdot L^2,$$

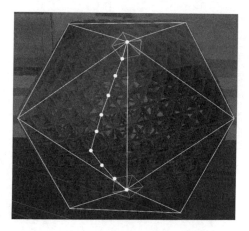

FIGURE 5. Five-fold vertices on Geosphere.

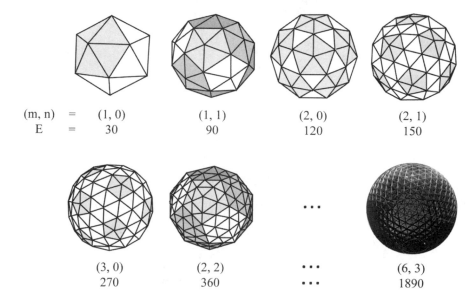

(m, n)	=	(1, 0)	(1, 1)	(2, 0)	(2, 1)
E	=	30	90	120	150

(3, 0)	(2, 2)	⋯ ⋯	(6, 3)
270	360		1890

FIGURE 6. Examples of geodesic spheres with various values of m and n.

and the number of edges, E, on the surface is

$$E = \frac{3}{2} \cdot S = 30 \cdot L^2 \qquad = 30(m^2 + n^2 + mn).$$

This gives us the general number of modules we need to construct such a geodesic sphere with varying values of m and n. The numbers m and n can be any natural numbers or 0 for an origami piece. It is remarkable that this formula holds not only for the icosahedron itself but also for any geodesic sphere based on icosahedral symmetry. When n is equal to 0, some edges of the piece lie along the edges of the regular icosahedron. There are several examples of spheres with various values of m and n, along with the resulting number of edges E, in Figure 6.

Table 1 shows more examples of the numbers of edges for various geodesic spheres, with m up to 12 and n up to 8. For example, the number of edges E for $(m, n) = (6, 3)$

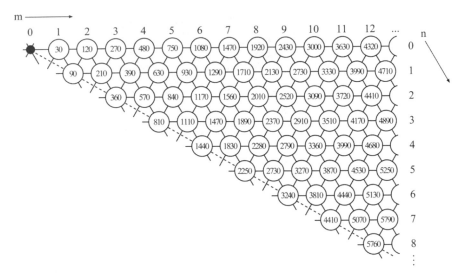

TABLE 1. Numbers of edges.

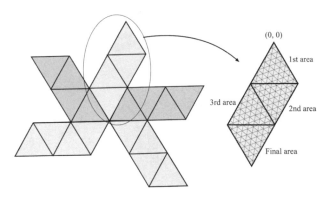

FIGURE 7. A 1/5 net of an icosahedron.

is 1890; it corresponds to the number of modules for Cosmosphere and Geosphere. The lower-left half of Table 1 is not displayed, because points (m, n) and (n, m) have the same number of edges. The two geodesic spheres of the positions (m, n) and (n, m) are mirror images of each other. When n is not equal to m, a mirror image of (m, n) certainly exists, i.e., (n, m).

5. Calculations for Color Combinations

Now we calculate other values useful for construction of a piece. First, we present some terminology. Let us divide the icosahedral-based geodesic sphere into a five strips of four triangular faces each, and call each strip a *1/5 net*. Each net consists of four areas: first, second, third, and final. (See Figure 7.)

Suppose that we first make one five-fold vertex of a geodesic sphere that contains the $(0, 0)$ point of the 1/5 nets. Then, we make a "band" on the outside of this first assembly;

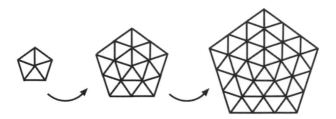

FIGURE 8. Making a geodesic sphere by adding bands.

the width of this band is the same width as that of the triangular mesh. Then, we make the next band on the outside of the existing assembly, and so on, one band at a time (Figure 8).

How many modules will be needed to make each band? Writing the number of modules in the xth band as $B[x]$, the first band that directly surrounds the five-fold vertex will be made up of ten modules. That is,

$$B[1] = 10.$$

Splitting this up to represent the contribution of each 1/5 net, $B[1]$ can be written as

$$B[1] = 5 \cdot 2.$$

That is, each 1/5 net's first area contributes two modules to the band.

Next, $B[2]$ needs 15 more modules than $B[1]$ because three modules must be added to each of the five corners of the first band (Figure 8, center). For $B[3]$, 15 more modules than $B[2]$ are needed. Continuing outward for every band until $x = m + n$, the end of the first area of the 1/5 net, the number of modules in the xth band can be written as

$$B[x] = B[1] + 5 \cdot 3(x - 1) = 5(3x - 1) \qquad (0 < x \le m + n).$$

So, the number of modules in the $(m + n)$th band is

$$B[m + n] = B[1] + 5 \cdot 3(m + n - 1) = 5 \cdot 3(m + n) - 5 \qquad (x = m + n).$$

The perimeter of the $(m + n)$th band, however, includes five five-fold vertices. In $B[m + n + 1]$, not 15 but 5 more modules will be added to $B[m + n]$, so the number of modules in $B[m + n + 1]$ is

$$B[m + n + 1] = B[m + n] + 5 \cdot 1 = 5 \cdot 3(m + n) - 5 + 5$$
$$= 5 \cdot 3(m + n) \qquad (x = m + n + 1).$$

The next band will be in the second and third areas of the 1/5 net, and it will be made up of six-fold vertices only—namely, the region of the piece that is locally cylindrical in structure—so the number of modules $B[m + n + 2]$ will be same number as $B[m + n + 1]$. For each band up to $x = m + n + m$, the end of the second and third areas, each band will have the same number of modules as $B[m + n + 1]$, i.e.,

$$B[m + n + 1] = B[m + n + 2] = B[m + n + 3] = \ldots = B[m + n + m]$$
$$= 5 \cdot 3(m + n) \qquad (m + n + 1 \le x \le 2m + n).$$

When $x = m + n + m$, the perimeter of the band includes five five-fold vertices again. So, in the next step, $x = m + n + m + 1$, the band is in the final area, and the number of modules will decrease from band to band in the reverse of what happened in bands 1 to

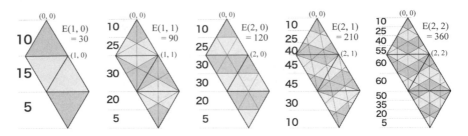

TABLE 2. Numbers of edges of each band, $E(1, n)$ and $E(2, n)$.

$x = m + n$. Two modules are decreased from each five-fold vertex of the last band, i.e., 10 modules are decreased from $B[m + n + m]$. Namely,

$$B[m + n + m + 1] = B[m + n + m] - 5 \cdot 2 = B[m + n + 1] - 5 \cdot 2$$
$$= 5 \cdot 3(m + n) - 5 \cdot 2 \qquad (x = 2m + n + 1).$$

In the next bands down from $x = m + n + m + 2$, all the vertices are six-fold, so the number of modules in one band will be 15 less than the number of the last band:

$$B[x] = B[x - 1] - 5 \cdot 3 \qquad (2m + n + 1 < x).$$

The next five-fold vertex is at the end point of the final area, so you would expect that this decrease rule would be applicable to the entire final area. However, the required numbers of modules does not actually satisfy this rule. It seems that this inconvenient situation arises from the asymmetrical design of the color pattern on the surface—that is, up-and-down symmetry is broken. So, we need to count the number of modules in the final area by hand, using the diagram of the net.

6. Conclusion

The 1/5 nets for some geodesic spheres are listed in Tables 2–6. In general, such a table can be used to make models of geodesic spheres. It will be useful not only for origami but also for other fields. In these tables, there is an imperfection of the counting rule in the final area of each net because the pattern is not symmetric around all axes. The counting rule will be changed if we use different color patterns. There are many possibilities for the color design of geodesic spheres, requiring many such tables for such geodesic spherical pieces.

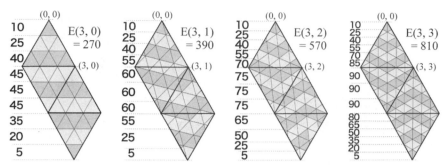

TABLE 3. Numbers of edges of each band, $E(3, n)$.

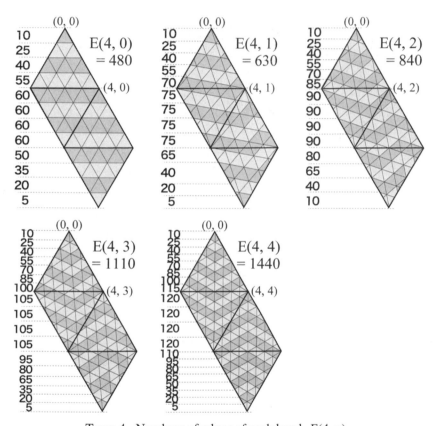

TABLE 4. Numbers of edges of each band, $E(4, n)$.

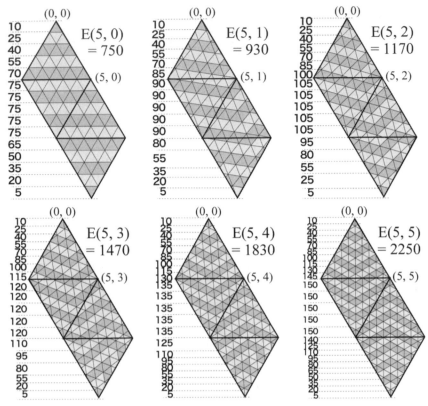

TABLE 5. Numbers of edges of each band, $E(5, n)$.

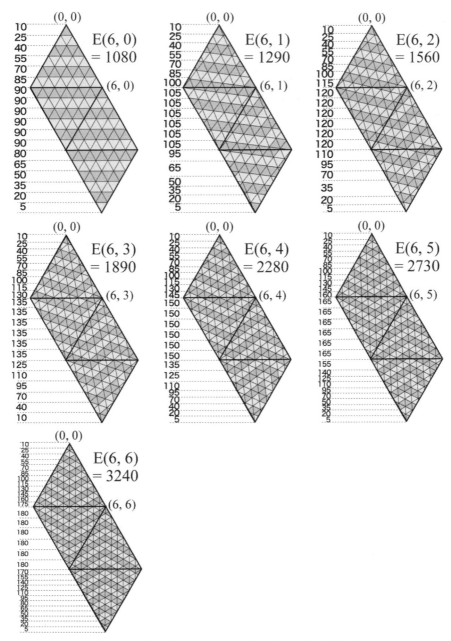

TABLE 6. Numbers of edges of each band, $E(6, n)$.

References

[Kawamura 04] Miyuki Kawamura. "Cosmosphere." In *Origami Tanteidan Convention Book*, Vol. 10, edited by Japan Origami Academic Society, pp. 148–150. Tokyo: Japan Origami Academic Society, 2004.

[Kawamura 07a] Miyuki Kawamura. "Geosphere." *Origami Tanteidan Magazine* 101 (2007), 4–7.

[Kawamura 07b] Miyuki Kawamura. "The Geodesic Dome with Geosphere Modules." *Origami Tanteidan Magazine* 105 (2007), 11–13.

[Kawamura 10] Miyuki Kawamura. "Calculation of Surface Mesh on a Geodesic Sphere." Talk given at the 9th Science of Origami Meeting, Bunkyo-ku, Tokyo, Japan, December 19, 2010.

[Wenninger 79] Magnus J. Wenninger. *Spherical Models*. Cambridge, UK: Cambridge University Press, 1979. MR552023 (81c:51020)

ORIGAMI ARTIST
E-mail address: myu3@beige.plala.or.jp

Index